A History of Ancient Egypt,
Volume 2

ALSO BY JOHN ROMER

A History of Ancient Egypt:
From the First Farmers to the Great Pyramid

JOHN ROMER

A History of Ancient Egypt, Volume 2

*From the Great Pyramid to the
Fall of the Middle Kingdom*

Thomas Dunne Books
St. Martin's Press
New York

THOMAS DUNNE BOOKS.
An imprint of St. Martin's Press.

A HISTORY OF ANCIENT EGYPT, VOLUME 2. Copyright © 2016 by John Romer. All rights reserved. Printed in the United States of America. For information, address St. Martin's Press, 175 Fifth Avenue, New York, N.Y. 10010.

www.thomasdunnebooks.com
www.stmartins.com

The Library of Congress has cataloged the first volume as follows:

Romer, John.
    A history of ancient Egypt : from the first farmers to the Great Pyramid / John Romer.—1st U.S. edition.
        p. cm.
    Includes bibliographical references and index.
    ISBN 978-1-250-03011-5 (hardcover)
    ISBN 978-1-250-03010-8 (e-book)
    1. Egypt—History—To 332 B.C. I. Title.
    DT83.R66 2013
    932—dc23

                                                                    2013012485

ISBN 978-1-250-03013-9 (hardcover)
ISBN 978-1-4668-4959-4 (e-book)

Our books may be purchased in bulk for promotional, educational, or business use. Please contact your local bookseller or the Macmillan Corporate and Premium Sales Department at 1-800-221-7945, extension 5442, or by e-mail at MacmillanSpecial Markets@macmillan.com.

First published in the United Kingdom by Allen Lane, an imprint of Penguin Books, a Penguin Random House company

First U.S. Edition: March 2017

10 9 8 7 6 5 4 3 2 1

Contents

CONTENTS

PART THREE

Old Kingdom – *The Giza Kings, 2625–2500 BC*

PART FOUR

Old Kingdom – *Abusir and After, 2500–2200 BC*

vi

PART FIVE

Old Kingdom – *Ancient Records, Ancient Lives*

PART SIX

Interregnum – *2200–2140 BC*

PART EIGHT

Middle Kingdom – *The Re-made State, 2000–1660 BC*

CONTENTS

Preface

The first volume of this history described the creation of the pharaonic state and ended at around 2550 BC with the building of the Great Pyramid of Giza. For the most part it was a silent history, since hardly any writings have survived which illuminate that millennial process. This second volume, alternatively, moves into an altogether noisier era for it begins as the archaic silence of those early pyramids is slowly broken by a growing chatter of hieroglyphic texts and it ends at around 1770 BC, with the pharaonic state in full bloom and with its scribes having created an elegant courtly literature.

The timelines of the two volumes do not meet at a single point but are spliced together at an angle across the century in which the Great Pyramid was built and at the time when the use of texts and inscriptions had started to increase. The history in this second volume, therefore, is different from that of Volume 1, for the growing presence of those texts allows the possibility of ancient thought as expressed in written language to become part of the main narrative.

History, it is commonly observed, is a dialogue between past and present worlds. As far as the modern history of ancient Egypt is concerned, where ancient texts have always been the key, it is essentially a dialogue between those ancient texts and the two centuries of Western scholarship that have followed their decipherment. A dialogue so commanding that the attitudes and opinions of a handful of leading Western academics are as much a part of modern 'ancient Egypt' as are the pyramids of Giza.

It seems to me, therefore, that to avoid confusion, the author of any new history of pharaonic culture should outline how and why their vision differs from that which underlies that standard modern version of 'ancient Egypt'.

Given that the roots of the modern humanities lie in the study of the classics it is hardly surprising that the first Western histories of that freshly deciphered ancient culture were based on the narratives of classical historians, and thus they were concerned with political, ethnic and dynastic struggle. At the same time, however, those histories were created at the beginning of the modern age in Europe, in times of social and industrial revolution, when the concepts of the nation state and of imperialism were burning fierce and fresh. So the protagonists in those pharaonic histories were fired with the spirit of that age, with themes of wealth and war, class, ethnicity and overweening power. And given contemporary Egypt's place within that nineteenth-century world, they were acted out against an oriental backdrop.

In reality, however, the hundred and fifty generations that built and maintained pharaonic culture have long gone, and precious little of them or of their history remains. And the yawning gaps in the fundamental information required to build the usual narratives of Western history books are still bridged by the attitudes and assumptions of nineteenth-century historians. And there's the rub, for although their traditional tales lend pharaoh's alien relics an illusion of familiarity, they have deeply sinister undertones.

For modern-day 'ancient Egypt' is a direct offspring of the nineteenth century's intense study of race and ancient language; those same studies whose terms and concepts later served to ratify the underlying character of Hitler's Third Reich. This is not, of course, to assert that the academics of several different nationalities who laid down the foundations of modern-day 'ancient Egypt' were particularly sadistic, or especially racist or, indeed, imperialist, but simply that they shared a tenor of their times. Georg Steindorff, for example, a one-time rector of Leipzig University and the most renowned egyptological victim of Nazi persecution, regarded himself as a full member of the nation whose high conservative values he had upheld all his life. In the years before the First World War, Steindorff had written a popular and influential history, *Die Blütezeit des Pharaonenreichs* – literally, 'the heyday – the flowering – of the pharaonic empire', which describes ancient Egypt admiringly as an imperial power. A decade earlier, Adolf Erman, the founder of modern egyptology and Steindorff's professor at Berlin, had observed that the ancient Egyptians had 'never experienced the invigorating influence of a great national war'. Though differing in expression, their phantasmagorical preoccupation with empire building as a moral force is the same and was a product of their times. Along with several other academic colleagues, however, Walter Grapow, Erman's co-editor of the standard dictionary of the ancient Egyptian language was, indeed, an ardent Nazi, a person for whom great histories were forged by mighty individuals, and such dictionary entries as 'kingdom', 'blood' and 'soil' – 'Reich,' 'Blut' and 'Boden' – held immediate contemporary resonance. And in the following generation those ideas were enlarged to contain the notion that pharaoh had been a god-like personality, the embodiment of the principles of blood and soil which, they considered, had run deep within that ancient race. Down to this day, indeed, alongside other equally unproven assumptions, many specialists would still assert that the ancient Egyptian kingdom had been born in blood and battle and that the living pharaoh had been held to be a god.

In my first years in Egypt, in the 1960s, I met and worked with several kindly scholars who had been students of some of the founders of the so-called Berlin School and they introduced me to ancient Egypt and its modern academic literature in long and generous conversations. Many now-retired professors were taught by that same generation; modern-day egyptology, indeed, is largely composed of generations who are the direct inheritors of that complex tradition. Several current university course books, also, were written by egyptologists who had enthusiastically greeted Hitler's rise to power or who were later banned outright from teaching in post-war Germany because of their disreputable activities during the 1930s.

Such works are widely used, it would appear, in the belief that at its root egyptology is a science and thus above all earthly politics, and that our knowledge of pharaonic culture and its history is a continually unfolding revelation of truth with each generation of scholars standing unquestioningly upon the shoulders of its predecessors.

Yet egyptology is not a science and neither, certainly, is the writing of history. Scientists inquire into precisely defined aspects of universal order. Most egyptological researchers, alternatively, spend their time retrieving and collating the random relics of complex and varied human activities. Nor is there a universal narrative of history, as many in the nineteenth century West believed, no world order involving race, or greed or power or growing human intelligence into which the products of egyptological research can be scientifically slotted, no clues, no breakthroughs that will represent the final pieces of a jigsaw to encompass and explain a hundred and fifty generations of an ancient culture. Yet to this day, many academic writings on the history of ancient Egypt are based upon the assumptions and beliefs of a century and more ago when egyptology and history itself, indeed, was thought to be a science. And certainly, the same discredited visions underpin the novellas, the movies and the popular 'ancient Egypt' of today.

Commentators were complaining about the inadequacies of such narrow visions of ancient history even as they were being created. Nietzsche was probably the most prescient and certainly the most vituperative; such histories, such visions of the past, he held, had nothing of the grace, the ecstatic joy of life, the ruthless precisions and perfections, the creative engagement with words and materials that he detected in so many ancient things. A decade later, he had been joined by Ibsen's Hedda Gabler complaining that contemporary historians were 'not amusing travelling companions. Not for long, at any rate . . . Just you try it! Nothing but the history of civilization morning, noon, and night'. In Hedda's day, of course, in the Belle Époque, her contemporaries deemed the culture of contemporary Europe to be the highest form of world civilization. No wonder, then, that after the Great War, Joyce would have Stephen Dedalus famously remark that history was a nightmare from which he was trying to awake.

Today as well, several leading egyptologists have little time for such traditional views of history. But they do not write books for the wider public and tend to avoid such controversies which, at their root, are expressions of political ideologies and concern the order of such human institutions as governments and universities and, ultimately, the nature of humankind itself. Now and again, however, they quietly comment on the way that things have gone. John Baines, for example, in a learned essay on the origins of pharaonic writing, finds it necessary to remind his readers that the people who created the ancient Egyptian language were surely more intelligent than most of their modern interpreters, whilst Barry Kemp, remarking about a contemporary version of the 'Blut und Boden' myth as applied to ancient Egyptian history, gently notes that 'A. Hitler' had already given the idea 'a crude airing'. At the same time too, there is a growing interest in the internal history of academic egyptology; Thomas Schneider, notably, carefully documenting the impact of the rise of Nazidom upon the Berlin School. This, then, is the heavily mottled backdrop against which this history has been written.

I originally anticipated that the opening sections of this second volume of my history – the period, that is, from the Old to the Middle Kingdom – would be fairly brief. The surviving data, after all, is relatively thin, so traditional histories devote less than a third of their texts to those eight centuries and they are generally padded out with information gleaned from later ages, a method based upon notions of the unchanging nature of so-called 'primitive' societies that I had long planned to discard.

Even as I began my researches, however, a cascade of fresh information was starting to appear. The product of various excavations undertaken within Egypt in the deserts and along the Red Sea coasts, it extended beyond all previous imaginings, the scope and scale of travel undertaken by the pharaonic court during those two long periods. At the same time too, innovative studies of long-known texts coupled with the discovery of some astonishing documents from recent excavations had further expanded our knowledge of those times. In short, excavation and research had revised all previous conceptions of Old and Middle Kingdom history. And this eventually necessitated an extension of my original scheme of this history from two volumes to three, this second volume finishing at the ending of the Middle Kingdom, a third with the ending of pharaonic culture.

As with Volume 1, my ambition has been to make a history without boundaries, without any previous theories about the composition or character of the pharaonic state beyond those evidenced or documented in the contemporary relics. I also aim to shed a common hubris of historians that pretends to explain all things, for there are huge amounts of fundamental data concerning pharaonic culture that we do not presently possess and probably never will. After two centuries of detailed and dedicated investigation academics have, however, recovered notices of most of ancient Egypt's rulers and some of their subjects and carefully placed them all together, in sequence, on a single timeline. Yet there is still insufficient information to provide a fact-based profile of any ancient individual. And such events as are recorded are hardly ever elements of continuing narratives like those of our traditional history books; those tales that Auden dubbed 'the usual squalid mess of history'.

So rather than setting the remaining information into the traditional divisions of classical dynasties or individual reigns and constructing what are, essentially, a series of fake mini-biographies of courtiers and kings, I have made a history built up from facts upon the ground. A history in which the texts and images, the stones, bricks and papyri that have survived are brought together with the scanty traces of the people who created them and are all set again within the ancient countryside, on the surrounding seas and deserts and all along the River Nile. So the surviving data – essentially, a series of random snapshots, an angry letter, a broken pot, a hair caught in a comb, a splendid jewel with pharaoh's name – are set against the *longue durée*, the underlying currents, the monuments, the harbours, mines and quarries, the ageless desert roads, the traces of abundance and disaster.

There is as well a special hazard in the telling of this history. As Wittgenstein had long ago observed, entire mythologies are held within our language. And the translation of the ancient texts has veiled our modern 'ancient Egypt' in such common Western terms as 'king' and 'nation', 'soldier', 'courtier' and 'priest'; words that by themselves alone threaten to set the surviving fragments of that lost society back into the fairy tales, the dreams and nightmares, of the recent past.

So in order to exorcize such ghosts, to expand the possibilities that are held within that quasi-academic kingdom and enable my history to move into wider realms of ancient possibility, I have added, as need arose, a second thread within my text that describes the ambience in which some of the major discoveries of our modern 'ancient Egypt' were made and, crucially, how they were first reported and translated, selected and explained; how, in short, those isolated, enigmatic ancient texts and artefacts were fitted into the standard narratives of Western history books.

I trust that the usual signposts of dates, dynasties and maps that I have set within my text will enable the reader to keep their place in ancient time and space. Accounting for the distant past in years BC/AD, however, sets up a tension all of its own, a conflict between present and past ideas of time and history. So it is good, always, to bear in mind that the first modern timetable of Egypt's ancient history was laid out by a Frenchman named Jean François Champollion in a baroque palace in the City of Turin in 1824.

My history is divided into eight parts.

Part One describes the dramatic transformation at the pharaonic court which followed its adoption of written language, a transformation that gave voice and distance to previous generations and a greater depth, therefore, to that ancient courtly culture.

Part Two shows how, following the decipherment of that ancient written language in the early nineteenth century, the foundations of our present 'ancient Egypt' were laid down.

The following three parts describe the history of the Old Kingdom, a difficult period for traditional historians, for there is hardly any evidence on which to base their usual narratives. This, however, was the age in which the core identity of the pharaonic state matured and which later pharaonic courts took as their fundamental model. It is, therefore, a key period of pharaonic history.

Part Three begins in the time of the construction of the Giza pyramids and describes the royal and courtly households and the intelligence and sensibilities that were at work within them.

Part Four describes the age of the successors of the Giza kings and the ways and means by which their courts embellished and enlarged the unique pharaonic system of nourishment and survival, both before and after death.

Part Five, alternatively, describes the astonishing literature and lively monuments which that way of life inspired and thus offers explanation of those celebrated relics.

Part Six describes the dissolution of that four-century-long kingdom and finds reasons for its violent conclusion based upon hard evidence rather than political theory. And then, and most remarkably, we find that the Old Kingdom's visions of life and death and government were taken up by farmers and administrators all along the lower Nile. And the pharaonic state was carefully and consciously revived.

The following two sections deal with the history of the Middle Kingdom; firstly with the revival of a unified pharaonic state, then with its elaboration and embellishment.

Part Seven describes the enormous efforts that were made at the beginning of the Middle Kingdom to restore the activity, the architectures and the rituals of the earlier court. The relics of this age, therefore, show us precisely what the pharaonic court of that time regarded as the essential elements of their courtly culture; of living ancient Egypt. And we witness the state literally rebuilding itself, opening old quarries, making new temples and tombs, sending expeditions across seas and deserts to obtain the essential elements of the apparatus and the materials, the rites and rituals, that were conducted in the living court and in the temples and tomb chapels. For this was not a kingdom based upon theology or social or political theory but on the daily actions of a court. Upon a sanctity of action.

Part Eight, the climax of the volume, re-creates something of the reality of the Middle Kingdom court and something also of the quality of daily life of the people in their kingdom. Hard and tough, practical and clever, this close-knit community of farmers, kings and courtiers, both the living and the dead, were bound together in a unique vision of the universe.

An Epilogue to this second volume discusses the extraordinary products of the Middle Kingdom court which are, arguably, the most perfect artefacts and writings to have survived from the three millennia of the pharaonic court's existence. These powerful and familiar images were not introduced into the body of my history. At this point, however, they may be seen afresh.

A NOTE ON THE TEXT

The majority of the translations in my text are a synthesis of those of Lichtheim, Simpson, Parkinson and Wente, and I have tried to render

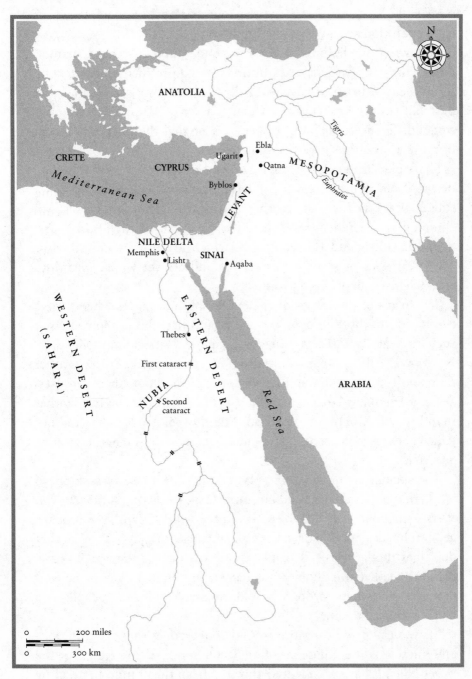

Ancient Egypt and adjacent regions during the mid second millennium BC.

those splendid works of scholarship in a uniform style that I hope is clear and consistent. Details of the sources that I have employed for each quotation are given in the Bibliography.

Following the dictums of Gardiner and Faulkner – that the ambiguities in many ancient texts ultimately require their translators to intuit their meaning – I have naturally preferred those renderings that best illustrate the narratives which I describe. Despite their occasional differences, however, it seems to me that the essential content of most translations varies very little.

I have placed an ellipsis (. . .) where a translated text is either broken or has been abbreviated and I have occasionally added words in square brackets for their further elucidation. Translations of such common translated phrases as 'Life, Prosperity and Health!' and 'King of Upper and Lower Egypt', which are usually described as royal titularies or standard modes of address yet whose meanings remain elusive, have been avoided.

The forms of the names of ancient people and places which I have employed are those in common usage and have been adopted from such works as the recent catalogues of the Metropolitan Museum, New York. All royal names are given in a single form: Sneferu rather than Snofru; Khufu and not Cheops; Khafre and not Chephren; Isesi and not Djedkare-Izozi or the like; Wenis and not Unas; Intef rather than Inyotef; Montuhotep and not Menthotpe; Amenemhet and not Amenemes; Senwosret and not Senusret, nor Senwosre nor, certainly, Sesostris!

The spelling of most Arabic place names are those of a standard work, that of John Baines and Jaromir Malek's *Atlas of Ancient Egypt*.

As with Volume 1, I have employed the word 'Egypt' as a modern geographic designation or in the case of 'ancient Egypt' as a term that describes modern visions of pharaonic culture – the term 'culture' defining a collection of objects sharing common manufacturing techniques and aesthetic properties and, by association, the people who made and used them.

I have designated the variously inhabited zones that are traditionally known as the 'kingdom of ancient Egypt', as 'the region of the lower Nile'. It had extended northwards from the granite cataract by modern-day Aswan up into the river's delta.

The term 'Memphis' does not refer to the ancient city of that name, which did not exist during the period of history covered in this volume, but to the region that was the centre of the Old Kingdom state. It is defined today by the thirty-mile-long line of monuments that extend along the west bank of the Nile opposite modern Cairo from Abu Roash in the north to Maidum in the south, and it includes the great cemeteries known loosely by the names of Saqqara, Abusir and Giza. For simplicity's sake, I have placed the site known as Abu Ghurab under the heading of Abusir, since the monuments in those two adjacent locations were part of the same working establishment, and in a similar manner I have absorbed the site now known as Mazghuna into the plain of Dahshur, which lies a little to its north. On the other hand, I have divided Saqqara with its myriad of monuments into the two separate locations of central and south Saqqara.

I have also employed the term Memphite as an adjective, this usually in opposition to the term 'provincial' or 'Theban', the former referring to all the other ancient sites in the pharaonic purview, the latter to the southern settlement of Thebes. As in Volume 1, the term 'settlement' describes all conglomerations of buildings that are not cemeteries; no ancient Egyptian towns or cities in the modern sense of those two words are known to have existed.

The central institution of the ancient state, so the texts insistently inform us, was the royal residence, a large enclosure whose name was also employed to describe the state itself. Besides housing the apartments of the royal household and audience halls, the royal residences appear to have contained craftsmen's studios along with numerous facilities that until quite recently were essential to the operation of any large domestic establishment.

The royal household appears to have contained pharaoh's large extended family, though its members' biological affiliations, let alone their emotional attachments, remain unclear. I have, accordingly, employed the term 'queen' to refer to the numerous women of the royal household and 'princes' to its somewhat less well-represented male occupants. Nothing is known of rights of succession to the throne, if such formulae had existed: precious little, indeed, is known about the role of pharaoh itself.

I have preferred the general term of 'courtier' rather than 'minister'

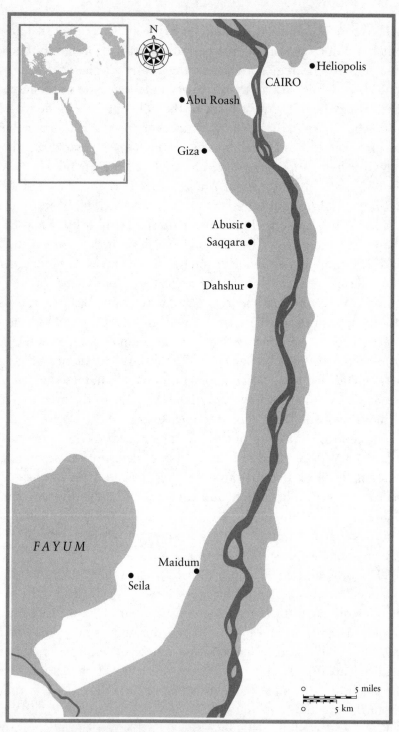

*The ancient region of Memphis, with the modern names
of the sites of the Old Kingdom Pyramids.*

to denominate those people whom contemporary texts describe as controlling some of the widespread activities of the pharaonic court, for the latter term easily suggests the existence of a highly structured bureaucracy whilst pharaoh's kingdom appears to have operated as a top-down face-to-face enterprise. The texts further suggest that the pharaohs often met with the same small group of courtiers, some of whom I have loosely designated as 'viziers', 'treasurers' and the like, after modern translations of some of the epithets and titles that are listed upon their monuments. It is not clear, however, which, if any, of those titles described specific functions and, certainly, the texts inform us that individual courtiers had performed a wide diversity of tasks.

Like pharaoh and his household, many courtiers were connected with so-called governors and officials who lived in settlements along the region of the lower Nile and who headed households that appear to have operated smaller local versions of the courts within the royal residences.

On occasion, I have employed the term 'noble' to describe both courtiers and the heads of the families of local governors and estate owners with connections to the royal household, some of whom were buried in the splendidly decorated tombs that are now fixtures on the tourist trail and form a vivid part of the sustaining imagery of modern ancient Egypt.

The culture of both the Old and Middle Kingdoms, however, was centred on the royal residence. Not only is the residue of its activities the major source of modern information about the history of those times but those same activities were the contemporary definition of the pharaonic state itself. The use of the term 'courtier', therefore, should be extended beyond the usual modern connotations of governance to include all those people connected to the royal residence whose translated titles appear to award them such professions as 'sculptors', 'jewellers' and 'priests'.

The term 'priest', indeed, is used to describe a number of ancient titles that today we would categorize as 'religious' but whose functions revolved around the collection and dispersal of the goods that were the beating heart of state activity. In similar fashion, the terms 'state cults', 'temples' and 'tomb chapels' refer to activities and establishments in which priests made offerings to the kings, to the gods and to the dead, actions that were a microcosm of the mechanisms that sustained the apparatus of the living state.

I have not employed the word 'tax', which the *Oxford English Dictionary* defines as 'an assessed money payment', to describe how the various offices and activities of state were sustained, for it is not applicable to a system that operated without that relatively modern concept. The word 'tithe' which I have used in its place should not, however, be taken in its literal sense as a tenth part of an agricultural crop, but as a portmanteau term to contain the diversity of methods that were employed to supply state institutions.

In similar fashion, I have used the term 'levee' to describe the methods employed by the pharaonic court to raise the mass labour that it required for the colossal projects that it continually undertook. The term should not suggest the horrors undergone by Egyptian villagers in the course of the last two centuries when they were conscripted *levée en masse* but simply the raising of mass labour in a non-monetary economy. For obvious reasons, I have preferred the terms 'farmer' and 'farm worker' to '*fellah*' or 'peasant'.

Finally, please note that the ancient people such as Hardjedef, Antefoker and Heqanakht who are named within my text are simply examples of those rare occurrences where a number of ancient texts that apparently refer to a single person have survived along with descriptions of some of their activities. Although I have employed their names in the hope that some idea of those lives and times may build up in the reader's mind, it should not be imagined that those individuals were necessarily outstanding historical personalities. For the most part their continued presence within the high formalities of the majority of ancient texts is but an accident of time. The vizier Antefoker, for example, was one of at least twenty Middle Kingdom so-called viziers whose names are mostly known from the inscriptions on their funerary arrangements, but of whom little other information appears to have survived.

PART ONE

After the Great Pyramids
History and Hieroglyphs

I

The Story up to Now

A History in Pyramids

After the Great Pyramid everything changed. The largest and most accurate stone block building ever made, it had been one of four similarly vast monuments that were erected in a hundred-year period at the middle of the third millennium BC. The first two of those gigantic structures were built during the lengthy reign of Sneferu; the third, the Great Pyramid with its extraordinary architectural refinement, in the reign of Khufu, his successor; the last, and the Great Pyramid's majestic partner on the Cairo skyline, for Khafre, probably one of Khufu's grandsons, who had ruled the region of the lower Nile from about 2540 BC. Apart from several other enormous building projects that were undertaken in the same span of time, those four great funerary monuments alone had consumed more than seventeen million tons of limestone. That is to say, for their completion within that single century, around 240 building blocks, each one weighing two and a half tons, would have had to have been set into their positions on one of those four great pyramids in the course of each and every working day.

Those four colossal monuments are the iconic products of the world's first-known state; a Bronze Age kingdom which had consisted of a royal residence with satellites and suppliers and myriad farming settlements set all along the flood plain of the lower Nile. With a combined population, so best estimates would currently suggest, of around a million people the logistics of provisioning the construction of those pyramids – a state-wide system of supply which had transported enormous tonnages of stone and copper, food and timber all up and down the great wide river – would have required the active participation of a large part of the population and put a strain upon

3

the rest. When it was over, the enterprise had transformed the culture of the pharaonic state giving it a unique self confidence, a powerful and mature identity.

After those four great pyramids, a 300-year-long line of smaller royal pyramids was set along the ending of the river's valley one following the other. Together, they span the era that is now known as the Old Kingdom. Each of these lesser later pyramids was built for a different king and all of them were set within a fifteen-mile line stretching southwards from the latitude of modern Cairo down along the high western horizon of the Nile Valley into the sandy desert cemeteries of Saqqara. With their dimensions standardized at around one third of the Great Pyramid's enormous bulk and with their exterior angles and their internal architecture derived from those of the older and much larger pyramids, these later monuments are relatively similar. So Western histories, which are based on narratives of incident and progress, might well conclude that after the construction of those earlier, grander and more innovative monuments, ancient Egypt's history had slowed. What, in reality, had happened was that the focus of the pharaonic court had shifted.

After the four great pyramids, and for the first time in the history of pharaonic culture, all those earlier enterprises were reassessed: the courtly offices and the organizations responsible for their construction, classified, developed and described in a mass of texts and images. The age of continuous cultural innovation had passed forever: from now on that would no longer be the pharaonic way. Over the following two millennia, pharaonic history would take the form of a series of successive periods of dissolution, stasis and renewal accompanied by bouts of deliberation and elaboration, both literary and visual, on life and death within the state that the great pyramid makers had constructed. Along with a few remarkable adventures that would shake the court from top to bottom, the story of those reflections and renaissances comprises a most exotic history, one quite foreign to the modern world.

2

Writing Changes Everything

After 2540 BC, from about the same time that the court masons had started to build royal pyramids far smaller than before, the chapels of the courtiers' tombs which previously had been little more than decorated corridors set into rectangles of stone were expanded and embellished, a metamorphosis of architecture and decoration that grew till it comprised a series of impressive rooms. Several of these celebrated monuments – the tomb chapels of Tiy, Mereruka and Ptah-hotep, for example, their shadowed walls covered with scenes of so-called 'daily life' – are now icons of pharaonic culture and firm fixtures on the tourist trail. Freestanding sculptures were also placed within these sumptuous chapels, many of considerable quality. And monumental written texts, which previously had been but sparely used, became a commonplace: texts describing the activities pictured in the reliefs covering the tomb chapels' walls; texts outlining schemes of offerings for the dead and describing lands and titles held or granted by the king; texts telling of a tomb's commissioning or recording an encounter or a correspondence with pharaoh.

About half way through those considerable processes of change, at around 2380 BC, the interior passages and chambers of the royal pyramids, which previously had not had a single image drawn upon their walls, were also engraved with hieroglyphic texts, a practice that continued down to the Old Kingdom's ending. These are the so-called 'Pyramid Texts' and they are the oldest-known body of texts to have survived from ancient Egypt.

Of themselves, the hieroglyphs that were engraved within the tomb chapels and pyramids were neither rare nor innovatory, having been employed for a wide variety of tasks for many centuries. Yet the

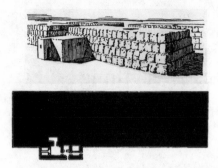
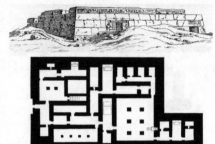

The family tomb of a courtier of Khufu, c. 2575 BC, and that of another noble family c. 2315 BC. Apart from holding deep vertical shafts leading to subterranean burial vaults, the earlier tombs are largely solid blocks of stone and rubble.

hieroglyphs engraved within the pyramids were employed in a different manner from anything that had gone before, when for the most part those same signs had been used to record names and titles and simple lists of goods. If such a usage may be considered to have had a grammar, it was a grammar like that held by labelled goods upon a supermarket shelf; that is, the signs and words had mainly served as elements of identification and numeration in a system of stocking and supply which in the case of pharaonic Egypt had provisioned the families and dependents of the kings and the officials of the royal court. Seldom had such usage required the composition of whole sentences and only very seldom had one sentence followed another. By the mid point of the third millennium BC, however, in that turning world as the size of the royal pyramids diminished, the use of hieroglyphic was extended so that it could hold a self-contained writing system with a grammar that seems to have reproduced some elements of spoken language.

Though a few surviving earlier texts anticipate this remarkable development, traditional historians have long regarded this sudden eruption of words and writing within the monuments of the later Old Kingdom as the time when the curtains of the prehistoric past had parted to reveal the living world of ancient Egypt. The contemporary scribes and courtiers, upon the other hand, had not. They considered the previous and now largely silent era when the four colossal pyramids had been built as the age in which their courtly culture gained maturity. And so in later ages, prayers were composed to Sneferu that addressed him as a god and building blocks from the temples that had stood beside the four great pyramids were placed like seeds inside the bulk of smaller, later pyramids. Texts too, that were considered to have been composed in that epic age were regarded with a kind of awe. Ruefully addressing a blank sheet of papyrus, a tongue-tied scribe of later times writes that he hopes to find different words from those used by his ancestors, whilst a passage in another text tells how a king ordered some old scrolls to be spread out before him so that he could see how things should be done 'in a proper manner'. Even the so-called 'Instruction Texts' – compilations of saws and etiquette which list some of the manners of Old Kingdom court society in excruciating detail – defer to the near silent age of the colossal pyramids: the age, so it has recently been suggested, that had been anciently identified as the epitome of the pharaonic state within a century or so of its conclusion.

Given the prestige of the early pyramid-building kings, it is hardly surprising that the first lines of one of those Instruction Texts identifies its author as a prince named Hardjedef, a man whom other texts describe as a son of the Pharaoh Khufu, for whom the Great Pyramid of Giza had been built.

> The beginning of the instruction which the hereditary prince and count, the king's son Hardjedef made for his son, named Au-ire. He says:
>
> Reprove yourself in your own eyes in order that another man does not reprove you.
>
> When you prosper, found your household and acquire for yourself a woman who is mistress of her heart, that a son will be born to you . . .

In somewhat similar fashion, a passage from a Book of the Dead – from texts written to accompany the dead a thousand years and more after King Khufu's time – describes Prince Hardjedef as having rediscovered the text of a funerary rite that had previously been 'a great secret, unseen and unperceived'.

Such assertions need not be taken at face value. Before the age of printing and modern notions of authorship and copyright, literary attributions had different purposes and meanings from those that we assume today. In claiming ancient authorship, the authors of those later texts – whose literary styles alone show that they were writing many centuries after Khufu's time – may simply have been providing the words they were about to write with the gravitas of deep antiquity.

Yet once there really was a prince of Khufu's time named Hardjedef. His tomb still stands upon the Giza Plateau in the evening shadow of that pharaoh's pyramid. And as a few rare graffiti of 'the work gang [named] Khufu-is-drunk' that are painted on some of its building blocks attest, the prince's massive stone block tomb had been built by some of that king's pyramid makers.

Copies of graffiti painted on the stone blocks of Hardjedef's mastaba, which name three contemporary stone-working gangs.

In the manner of his times, Prince Hardjedef was interred underneath the centre of his tomb in a granite sarcophagus which had been lowered down a deep vertical shaft and set into a tiny rock-hewn chamber at the bottom. 'The body', so his excavators found in 1925, 'was intact and in position. Head east, lying on left side, contracted, hands straight out in front of pelvis. Tall old man. Backbone intact but carefully severed between 8th and 9th vertebra . . . Skull had toppled over from neck and lay almost in position near south wall opposite the door.'

Hardjedef's tomb is but one of some 200 similarly enormous monuments – the so-called Giza mastabas – which in Khufu's day had been set across that windy plateau in sullen sandy grids. Many other members of the royal household were interred within those same vast cemeteries and in the same manner as Prince Hardjedef, yet most of them today are little more than the names that are inscribed upon their monuments. That single prince alone seems to have gained an aura of celebrity, and that within a century or so of his interment.

For when the archaeologists were clearing drifted sand from the area around his tomb they came across the inscribed remnants of several modest monuments set up in later ages. And one of those memorials, after asking passers-by to recite a prayer so that a courtier named Kha could receive more offerings at his tomb, continues by describing Kha as 'one who adores Hardjedef'.

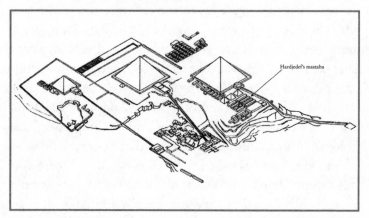

The Giza Plateau in the time of the pyramid builders, showing the position of Hardjedef's tomb.

Writing had changed everything. A single prince who present records seem to show had lived and died in a pre-literary age had been transformed into an ageless literary personality. Nor was the potential of this new-found lease of life, this extra presence amongst the living, which previously would have depended on the continuous ration of offerings placed within his tomb chapel, lost on succeeding generations. For in the following millennium court scribes would proudly claim that, rather than colossal tombs, written words were by far the best memorials.

> A man is dead; his corpse is in the ground. When all his family are laid in the earth, it is writing that lets him be remembered . . . scrolls are more useful than a house or chapels on the west, they are more perfect than palace towers and longer-lasting than a monument within a temple.
>
> Is there anyone here like Hardjedef? Is there another like Imhotep? [another literary personality] . . . They are gone, their names might be forgotten but writings cause them to be remembered.

Prince Hardjedef makes several more appearances in later texts, most famously in the elegant calligraphic script of a papyrus – known now as the Papyrus Westcar, and written some five centuries after the prince's lifetime – that tells a series of tales which are all set in the fabled courts of the great pyramid-building kings. These literary courts are a far cry from the hard reality, the dust and haste that must have filled the offices of the overseers of the construction of the four great pyramids. These texts describe tranquil, even hedonistic, palaces, where furniture is made of gold and ebony, where boatloads of scantily clad virgins are set to row across a lake to tickle the royal fancy, and Prince Hardjedef plies the Nile upon a royal barge to bring soothsayers such as the learned Djedi to entertain the king. And after Djedi had performed prodigious acts of magic for his majesty and looked deep into his kingdom's future, Khufu commanded that he was to be sent to 'the house of the king's son Hardjedef, that he may dwell there with him, where his rations should be fixed at one thousand loaves of bread, one hundred jugs of beer, an ox, and one hundred bundles of vegetables. And they did all that His Majesty had commanded'.

Such stories are not as straightforward as they might first appear. Just as it has been observed of Flaubert's *Egyptian Diaries* that rather than simply recording a visit to nineteenth-century Egypt they are also an elaboration of the accounts of earlier European travellers to the Orient, so, too, the texts that mention Hardjedef are part of a pharaonic literary tradition.

And more than that. For just as Hardjedef, a prince of Khufu's court, lived on in ancient literary memory, so today his name appears in histories of ancient Egypt where, for the lack of any other information, the simple tales of the Papyrus Westcar are taken as a prime source of the history of the period. Hardly a single modern history book, indeed, describes the historical changes that followed the building of the four colossal pyramids without reference to the tales of the Papyrus Westcar. So this slimmest of novellas, written in a different age, has become a part of ancient Egypt's modern history, part of the history of that vital period in which the largest and most complex structures the ancient world would ever make were being erected and the fundamental structures of pharaonic culture were in the process of their definition.

So whilst Hardjedef the man is represented only by his bones and by a tomb upon the Giza Plateau that bears his name, Hardjedef the literary prince appears in both ancient Egyptian literature and also in modern histories as a great sage, as the pious author of religious texts and as a character in tales fit for the Brothers Grimm, in which it is assumed genuine dynastic politics are described. And every fresh-found occurrence of that prince's name, each new-found hieroglyphic epithet, adds weight and substance to this literary figure, whilst that enormous tomb upon the Giza Plateau underlines the fact that this complex, composite, largely literary figure is based, somehow, on cold hard fact.

To that extent, Prince Hardjedef is a perfect metaphor for modern histories of pharaonic culture. Just as the Old Testament, with its descriptions of camels and coinage, of slavery and international war-fare, invests its descriptions of Bronze Age Palestine with the ills and angsts of Hellenistic Alexandria where it was compiled and edited, just as Shakespeare's kings are viewed through the politics and pre-occupations of his own times, so too our modern histories of ancient Egypt are filled with sentiments and narratives of later times and other cultures. And by far the largest of these influences are from the ages in which egyptology itself was born, which, as with Flaubert's *Diaries*, was nineteenth-century Europe.

In large part this unusual situation is a product of the lack of any other information to contradict such parochial histories. None of the texts that have survived from ancient Egypt are written histories. All which has survived from that colossal wreck is a myriad of names, epithets and titles, letters, dockets and accounts and some tracts con-cerning ritual and the afterlife. That, and a few royal records and decrees and some fragments such as the Papyrus Westcar, form a so-called literary corpus that is so ill-preserved that its remnants are presently contained in one stout paperback.

Nor is there reason to imagine that an ancient Gibbon or Macaulay lies buried in the sand. Neither, in the event that such unlikely treas-ures were to be uncovered, could it be assumed that they had performed the same roles in their society as do histories today. Unlike ancient Greece and Rome or, indeed, the modern world, the histories, theologies and legal codes of the pharaonic kingdom were not laid out in written words. It was not that kind of culture. It inhabited a different time, a different space. And at its ending, a wise Egyptian living in Hellenistic Alexandria had understood that difference, warning that the ostentatious chatter of the Greeks whose philosophy, he says, is but 'an empty noise of argument' would threaten the very core of the venerable pharaonic culture which 'uses no arguments . . .', and if that should happen, the melancholy sage continues, then the ancient and most holy valley of the Nile, 'this copy of heaven . . . the abode of shrines and temples, will be most full of graves and of dead men'.

That canny Alexandrian describes a dilemma faced by the historians of all cultures in which literature was not the main means of expression. To some extent, it is the same problem that is faced today by visitors to exhibitions of old master paintings. Like ancient Egypt, those venerable Western images have long been the focus of an academic industry whose primary means of expression is the written word. And though it is difficult to precisely detail the effects of that continuing blizzard of written information – the pictures' titles, their identification and their various explanations, the writings of historians and theologians, of Vasari, Shelley and Madame Sesostris – it inevitably alters our appreciation of those silent images. For, in the modern world, writing changes everything.

What hope, therefore, that traditional histories of ancient Egypt, which are largely based on translations of randomly surviving fragments of non-historical texts, can begin to encompass the true history of such a vastly visual culture as that of pharaonic Egypt? Nonetheless, the powerful drug of two centuries of academic research has persuaded a large part of the modern world that it can and that the yawning gap between the modern world and the most ancient of all kingdoms has been securely bridged.

Yet as you stand today amidst the graceful relics of the ancient culture of the lower Nile, in a tomb or temple or even a museum, a sense of dislocation hangs all around, like incense in the air. In earlier times the mystery of another world that seems just out of reach was explained with the aid of alchemical texts and Gnostic tracts; today, the popular media pretends that 'scientific breakthroughs' will serve for its elucidation. In reality, after two centuries of study and excavation, the non-stop flood of written data has simply heightened that age-old sense of separation.

This is the mystery of ancient Egypt. This is what keeps us peering into Tutankhamun's inlaid eyes wondering what had lain behind them. As the eminent egyptologist James Allen recently observed, we are 'like paleontologists, able to assemble impressive reconstructions of long-dead species, but still with only a vague notion of what they looked like in the flesh'.

3

Reviving Hardjedef?

Ironically enough, only the first half of the ancient culture of the lower Nile – its pre-literary phase – holds the narratives of a truly modern history within it, for its relics contain clear evidence of material and political development. The second more familiar half of Egypt's ancient history, alternatively, the age of written texts, shows no evidence of such developments. In strictly material terms, indeed, the literary pharaonic state may be said to have been a period of overall decline. Yet in that second phase a marvellous architecture was developed, the pharaohs went adventuring, Hardjedef, some bones in a sarcophagus, obtained a literary afterlife and almost every element of that courtly culture was elaborated and refined. Such opulent millennia, therefore, must surely hold great histories of their own.

That at least is the belief which has inspired a 200-year-old academic industry to continue to scrutinize the writings that survive and generate the papers, catalogues and theses that are the raw materials of traditional historians. Naturally, such text-based histories may only be revised or enlarged by the reconsideration of previously studied texts or by the incorporation of new-found documents into the previously established body of information, a process that has become an ongoing international academic project that, with its specializations and its particular vocabularies, provides the impression of a scientific progress; the illusion of 'the unfolding excellence of fact'.

There are three fundamental flaws in this approach. Firstly, the overwhelming emphasis on literary-based evidence has served to cut the seamless history of pharaonic culture into two separate halves, pre-literary and literary.

Secondly, as writing of itself was an activity restricted to relatively small circles of people inside the pharaonic state, ancient Egyptian history changes from that of a history of an entire population in its pre-literary phases to that of the history of the careers of some individual courtiers and hardly ever of the court they served. Here, however, the surviving texts sometimes provide fragments of a history that hold within them the vividness of living language, real events.

The third objection to this approach is that the spare data that the surviving texts supply are entirely insufficient to support most of the narratives of modern histories. Just one papyrus, for example, the so-called Papyrus Westcar, records the tale of Hardjedef at Khufu's court. No one knows its origin. It lacks both a beginning and an end and there is no certainty as to the date of its composition. Yet, for want of any other information, historians frequently employ that story and others in that same papyrus as prime sources for the history of the period known nowadays as the Old Kingdom.

Traditional histories of the Old Kingdom, indeed, are especially slight because, unlike the mass of extraordinary visual evidence from those times, the surviving written data is extremely scanty and the era of itself is very long. Before the 1840s, European historians had hardly noticed it at all and the four colossal pyramids were portrayed as the products of a primitive and savage age of unfathomable antiquity. In 1879, in Professor Brugsch's great history of the pharaohs, the Old Kingdom's 400 years still only occupied twenty pages in comparison with the 450 that describe the later periods. And in 1961, in the similarly sized history of Sir Alan Gardiner – arguably the greatest egyptologist to have worked in the English language – the history of the Old Kingdom only occupies twice that amount.

So slight, indeed, is surviving written information from all periods of pharaonic history that it can only serve as the solid basis for an outline of a text-based political history for a few centuries during the second millennium BC. Thus traditional histories of ancient Egypt have to be glued together from an incredible mishmash of materials; from tales like those in Papyrus Westcar, from calendar dates written on loaves of bread and jars of wine, from speculations based on everything from reconstructed family quarrels, the political use of magic, and the operation of the Roman *damnatio memoriae*, and from those rare contemporary texts that record single, usually unrelated, incidents.

This fundamental lack of data makes it impossible to construct a conventional history of pharaonic culture without the broad assumption that, allowing for some environmental differences, life in the ancient courtly culture of the lower Nile had been similar to life within the states of early modern European courts. Only then can traditional historical narratives be constructed.

The common illusion that the ways and means of European courtly culture were also operating in the ancient culture of the lower Nile is greatly aided by the terms usually employed to describe the inhabitants of pharaoh's court. Simple English words like 'dynasty' and 'kings', 'palaces' and 'fortresses', 'queens', 'priests' and 'generals' along with myriad other translated epithets and titles, encourage would-be historians to lapse into the narratives of nineteenth-century European Romanticism.

So it is hardly surprising that traditional histories of ancient Egypt tell bourgeois tales of kings and princes, of harems and fine artists, of noble courtiers, great generals with mighty armies guarding a nation state of nuclear families, with customs posts and a quasi-cash economy. At first glance, this twilight world seems able to account for almost everything in pharaohland whilst any awkward discrepancies are explained away as evidence of residual savagery or nascent orientalism. What in reality this weird scenario has produced is a mid-Victorian ancient Egypt filled up with the prejudices – racial, ethnic and social – of that era. An ancient Egypt in which pharaohs live in sensible domesticity, undertake imperial diplomacy through the usual channels, whose soldiers are adept at bivouac and manoeuvre, whose priests are envious and jealous, whose scholar-scribes are industrious and profound and whose labourers in the usual way are loyal, comical and devious. And all the while the beauteous mass of ancient things which the craftsmen of the pharaonic culture made with such an extraordinary care flap like butterflies at the window of the seminar room, unnoticed and abandoned.

The supreme irony in this is that though written texts were never at the heart of pharaonic culture, those that have survived have played a major role in the construction of modern ancient Egypt. Such a fundamental role, in fact, that ever since Jean François Champollion deciphered Egyptian hieroglyphs in the early nineteenth century, the study and translation of pharaonic texts has continuously distorted a broader understanding of that ancient culture.

This is not to pretend that hieroglyphic texts have no place in histories of pharaonic culture. Nor, certainly, that the thin corpus of historical fact derived from pharaonic texts which underpins our modern 'ancient Egypt' should be abandoned. Over the past two centuries the advances that followed Champollion's decipherment have brought us to a brand new understanding of that lost and distant past, one that the modern world, if not Egypt's ancient scribes, can readily comprehend. A reliable chronology, an essential element of any modern history, has been established. Most known texts have been analysed, translated and shrewdly judged. So along with the vocabulary of prince, priest, pyramid and the rest, which has become the language of this past's description, the information held in that research now frames all modern orderings and explanations of the ancient culture of the lower Nile.

This, then, is the stage on which all new histories of this 'ancient Egypt' are acted out. And it was made in Europe in two separate stages. The first of these, when Egyptian hieroglyphs were deciphered, when the fundamental vocabulary that yet describes the offices of pharaoh's kingdom was laid down and the broad chronology of the later literate phases of pharaonic culture was established, took place in the decades that followed the French Revolution and reflects the spirit of that age. The second stage, when that earlier vision of pharaonic culture was brought to its first maturity, when 'what had been made readable by the decipherment of hieroglyphs, was understood', took place in German universities in the decades before the First World War. This was the age in which egyptology's traditional vocabulary was endorsed in the name of science, when the structures of hieroglyphic grammar were set within the framework of classical philology and a standard hieroglyphic dictionary was compiled. And those researches are filled with the spirit, the disturbing rhetoric, of those times. And those narratives and attitudes, their sense of social order and of time and place, are an integral part of modern 'ancient Egypt'.

To make new histories of old Egypt, therefore, both elements of this strange confection – both the relics of old Egypt and their interpretation throughout the last two centuries – must be brought into play.

PART TWO

Making 'Ancient Egypt'
Champollion and his Successors

4

In the Beginning

I have only tried to indicate the many important consequences of my discovery which arose naturally from my main subject; the alphabet of the phonetic hieroglyphs ... This may perhaps add something to the record of ... the Egyptians, whose fame still echoes round the world.

Jean François Champollion, 1822

A great number of books and articles have been written describing the decipherment of pharaonic hieroglyphs by Jean François Champollion in the early 1820s, and most of them are concerned with arguments of academic precedence. Was it a Briton or a Dane, a Frenchman or a Swede who had first understood how hieroglyphs should be read? They miss the point. By the 1820s, the decipherment of ancient Eastern scripts had become a polymath's parlour game for European scholars and one that eventually resulted in what an assyriologist has called a 'cascade of decipherment'. Amongst all of the would-be decipherers of hieroglyphic, however, Champollion alone had a lifelong commitment to the study of pharaonic culture, such dedication that even his enemies had dubbed him '*l'Égyptien*'. So after he had solved a great part of the scholarly riddle of the hieroglyphs – a process in which he was aided, doubtless, by the observations of several of his contemporaries – Champollion devoted the remainder of his life to ordering, cataloguing and explaining the relics of pharaonic Egypt. And the methods and terminologies that he and his immediate successors developed remain the bedrock of the study of that culture down till today.

First news of Champollion's decipherment had stirred considerable excitement amongst fellow scholars, many of whom were occupied in the exploration of the roots of language and of European nation-hood. Further readings of his later papers, however, which appeared throughout the 1820s and were concerned with the order and history of pharaonic society, had seemed to strip the magic from a fabled kingdom that the West had considered to be a fount of wisdom and enlightenment since classical times.

Born of the Bible and the literature of ancient Greece and Rome, the antique vision of pharaonic Egypt had been spectacularly reviving in Champollion's own lifetime, cultivated by a variety of nationalists, revolutionaries and Freemasons, from Mozart's librettists to Dr Guil-lotin and General Lafayette. So in August 1793, in a commemoration of the storming of the Bastille, a giant statue of the Egyptian goddess Isis flanked by two sitting lions – a token of the power of enlightened nature and an antidote to Christianity – was placed upon its fallen stones as part of a *Fontaine de la Régénération*. And five years later, Napoleon's battalions had invaded Egypt attended by a regiment of scholars, many of whom were set to measure that country's ancient monuments, to make copies of their decorations and plans of their architecture and publish the results of those investigations in a series of enormous folios. Just as Napoleon's scholars had culled the classic arts of Rome for exhibition at the Louvre, so now the antique wisdom of the East would be gathered up, in books, in France.

Later generations have usually portrayed Napoleon's Grand Tour of Egypt as a heroic enterprise. Facing war, hunger and Mamluk guerrillas, sketching, on occasion, with musket balls pounded to a pencil point, the visible remains of the mysterious kingdom that ancient sages had described as 'the temple of the world' had intoxi-cated Napoleon's scholar-*savants*. Chief amongst those mysteries, both for the French *savants* and for the ancient Greeks and Romans who in a similar quest for ageless wisdom had interviewed Egyptian temple priests, were the ancient hieroglyphs, the 'sacred signs' that were engraved upon the tombs and temples, on statues and stone stelae, and briskly inked on everything from shrouds and coffins to

rolls of brown papyrus. After Napoleon's adventure in the east, therefore, a variety of Europeans had dabbled in decipherment.

LETTRE

A M. DACIER,

SECRÉTAIRE PERPÉTUEL DE L'ACADÉMIE ROYALE
DES INSCRIPTIONS ET BELLES-LETTRES,

RELATIVE A L'ALPHABET

DES HIEROGLYPHES PHONÉTIQUES

EMPLOYÉS PAR LES ÉGYPTIENS POUR INSCRIRE SUR LEURS MONUMENTS
LES TITRES, LES NOMS ET LES SURNOMS DES SOUVERAINS GRECS ET
ROMAINS;

PAR M. CHAMPOLLION LE JEUNE.

Champollion published the first paper describing his decipherment of
hieroglyphs – the *Lettre a M. Dacier* – in Paris, at the age of thirty-two
and just two decades after Napoleon's Egyptian escapade.

A linguistic prodigy, Champollion had taught at the University of
Grenoble from the age of nineteen. Even as a boy, people had recognized his extraordinary abilities: Joseph Fourier, the renowned
mathematician who had accompanied Napoleon to Egypt and had
shown the child, the younger brother of his secretary, some of the
savants' drawings, remarked that the precocious youth was a 'voracious chicken demanding triple rations'. Brave Fourier had stayed
with the French occupation forces in Egypt until their expulsion in

August 1801 at the hands of a British expeditionary force. As secretary to the assassinated General Kléber, who had commanded the French army after Napoleon's brisk departure, he had compiled an inventory of the antiquities that the defeated French had handed to the British, a list which had included, as Item Number 8, the celebrated bilingual stela known as the Rosetta Stone, whose texts had already aided the would-be decipherers of hieroglyphs.

After the return, Napoleon had appointed Fourier as Governor of the newly formed Department of Isère in south-eastern France, with its administrative centre at Grenoble. At the same time, the mathematician was also a leading member of a government committee charged to publish the *savants'* work in the volumes of the Napoleonic *Description de l'Égypte*, for which he would compose a powerful introduction. With a number of his fellow adventurers in Egypt, this committee controlled not only the contents of the *Description* but also the continued study of ancient Egypt within France.

The *savants* did not take kindly to Champollion's *Lettre*. Brief, simply written, and followed in good order by the lengthier and heavily illustrated *Précis du Système Hiéroglyphique*, it showed that most of the signs that they had laboriously copied in Egypt and which, in common with most other scholars of the day, they had imagined to have been philosophical symbols, actually represented the sounds and words of an ancient language that was echoed in dialects of Coptic, the language of medieval Egyptian Christians. Nor had Champollion's further observation that the ancient kingdom 'would only be known through the interpretation of the hieroglyphs' pleased them either, for they had long believed on the basis of a few bilingual inscriptions that the surviving writings of the ancient Greeks and Romans were sufficient to supply such mundane information. The *savants*, on the other hand, were after larger things; nothing less, in that electrifying age when feudalism was swept away and modern Europe was in the processes of invention, than the foundations for a brand new philosophic history for that brave new world.

It is hardly surprising, therefore, that Edme François Jomard, the *savant* secretary of the Napoleonic publishing committee, dubbed Champollion's descriptions of some religious texts as the superfluous records of long dead superstition. Jomard after all, had excavated the baselines of the Great Pyramid at Giza and discovered to his satisfaction that its measurements held, in absolute perfection, all the known units of measurement which man had ever used around the world. In other words the pyramid was that Enlightenment delight, a universal measure. In similar fashion and along with most other *savants*, Jomard also gave great credence to a theory promulgated by the Parisian scientist and anti-clerical revolutionary Charles François Dupuis, who maintained that all religions, ancient and modern, had their origins in the circuits of the heavenly bodies which had first been observed and mapped in ancient Egypt and whose movements along with their supposed accompanying influences upon life on earth had been plotted and described by ancient priests and set into the twelve signs of the zodiac. Chiming both with Freemasonry and popular anti-clericalism, Dupuis' book *Origine de tous les Cultes, ou la Religion Universelle* (*The Origin of All Religions*) had been a sensation when it had first appeared in 1781, a sensation eerily repeated a century later in the underlying narratives of Frazer's *Golden Bough*, which also enjoyed a considerable longevity. 'The wisest and oldest priests of Egypt,' Dupuis had observed, 'believed with Pliny, that ... the only gods were the Sun, the Moon, the Planets, the Stars composing the Zodiac.' Dupuis, so his translator wrote, had 'planted the torchlight of reason and history into the midst of the Dome of St Peter'.

To their great delight, Napoleon's *savants* had discovered that the ancient Egyptians had placed large and splendid zodiacs and star charts in several of their tombs and temples. Even while he was still in Egypt, Fourier had realized that, if Dupuis' theory was true, modern astronomic calculations based upon those ancient star charts could enable the year that they were made to be fixed in modern time. Given that the ancient Egyptian calendar appeared to have existed unchanged till the arrival of the Romans, the ancient star charts offered the further possibility of constructing an accurate concordance, a day-by-day connection, between the modern calendar and that of pharaoh's Egypt.

So the *savants* had made careful copies of the several zodiacs and star charts that they had found within the tombs and temples, a labour that they believed would not only serve to prove Dupuis' theories on religion but also to enable human history to penetrate a

previously unfathomable past. 'So far,' Fourier had excitedly written
to a friend on the day of his arrival back in France,

> the history of mankind and his arts and sciences had not been certain,
> Diogenes Laertes [a classical historian] traces 4,000 years before the
> Augustan age, and Newton to 1,000 years BC ... Now that astronomical
> monuments have been discovered ... we know that the current div-
> ision of the zodiac, has been established in Egypt about 15,000 years
> before the Christian era ... This perfectly confirms the conjecture
> of C. Dupuis ... and determines the age of the monuments ... the
> beautiful temple of Dendera, the latest perhaps, was probably built
> over 1,000 years before the siege of Troy.

By the time that Champollion's *Lettre a M. Dacier* had appeared in
print, Fourier along with several other of the *savants* had already published elaborate commentaries on ancient Egyptian astronomy and
zodiacs for the *Description de l'Égypte* and was working on three
further papers on the subject and an elaborate chronology of pharaonic
Egyptian history based on the same material. Jomard meanwhile, and
at huge expense, had persuaded the French government to purchase
from Mohammed Ali Pasha, Egypt's ruler, the two massive roofing
blocks of the celebrated temple of Dendera in Upper Egypt whose
decoration held one of the finest of Egyptian zodiacs. Two heroic engineers had brought the Dendera Zodiac to France, where it was
displayed within the Louvre and thousands queued for hours to see it.
To many of those visitors, the reliefs offered hard and public proof of
Dupuis' theories which claimed that the zodiac was 'three times as old
as Moses'. So the zodiac became a major topic of the Parisian salons,
whilst at that same time Dupuis' publishers were working with Jomard
on a second edition of the *Description*, and Jomard was anticipating
a promotion to the post of curator of the museums of the Louvre.

Unfortunately for all that, the first signs that Champollion and several other would-be decipherers had successfully translated were
some of the little groups of hieroglyphs which were a common feature of pharaonic inscriptions and were enclosed within so-called
'rings' or 'cartouches' – the latter term, apparently, deriving military
fashion from similarly shaped munitions used by the French army in
Egypt. Just as several would-be decipherers had previously guessed,

these cartouches usually held groups of phonetic hieroglyphs spelling out the names of kings and queens. Working from a drawing made by one of Napoleon's *savants* when the Dendera Zodiac was still *in situ*, Champollion had deciphered the contents of a cartouche from an inscription which framed the circle of the zodiac which he transliterated as the word 'autokrator', or emperor, a classical term of Hellenistic and Roman times. Underlining that most awkward of translations, other hieroglyphs in the *savants'* drawings of the temple's decorations next to the zodiac proved to spell out the names of several Roman emperors whose images were also depicted as pharaohs in the temple's other decorations. None of those scenes, therefore, nor the temple itself, was anything like as old as Moses, a fact that Champollion gleefully announced to an assembly of the Parisian Academy of Science.

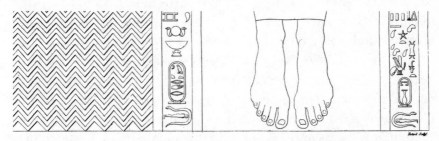

A detail of the frame of the Dendera Zodiac, as presented in the Napoleonic Description. *The cartouche to the right of the feet of a sky goddess contains the hieroglyphs that Champollion read as 'autokrator' rather than a pharaoh's name.*

Bigger souls like Fourier soon saw the light, bore Champollion no grudge and went on to more rewarding things. Many, though, including Jomard and several other Parisians, did not. Not only had the decipherment rendered null and void decades of their researches but it had also challenged their fundamental view of ancient Egypt. Hence the grand reaction. Some of the *savants* now argued that the hieroglyphs were of little consequence, merely a late adaptation of the Greek and Latin alphabets, and that Champollion's decipherment was of but small importance. Had not the celebrated *Lettre a M. Dacier*, they argued, the very paper whose publication had announced the decipherment of hieroglyphs, only managed to translate the names of Roman and Hellenistic pharaohs which, as Champollion himself had noted, were but clumsy hieroglyphic transcriptions of Greek and Latin names? Was not the celebrated Rosetta Stone, which held the same text both in Greek and hieroglyphic, composed in Hellenistic times? So began a series of lengthy arguments concerning zodiacs and hiero-glyphs that were joined by some of the other would-be decipherers who squabbled about Champollion's role in the decipherment, an argument in which bad-tempered nationalisms often played a part.

Possessed of a native wit and clear-sighted confidence, Champol-lion could easily rebuff his enemies. Yet Napoleon's *savants* controlled the study of ancient Egypt in France, whereas Champollion, a man of modest means, had already lost his post at the University of Grenoble as a result of his political activities. Despite his many supporters and admirers there was little hope of him securing government patronage in Paris to continue his researches. From that time on, he later said, his homeland would be ancient Egypt.

This, then, is the background against which hieroglyphs had been deciphered, the age in which national wealth in Europe had increased beyond all previous imaginings, and patriots were transforming from Dr Johnson's definition as 'fractious disturbers of governments' to the gallant soldiers of the world's first national armies. Champollion had been three years old when Louis XVI was guillotined, fifteen when Napoleon was defeated at Waterloo. Throughout his life, there were continuing dialogues, sometimes lethal dialogues, concerning such novel abstractions as society and economics, race and national culture. As George Steiner describes:

> immense transmutations of value and perception took place in Europe over a time-span more crowded, more sharply registered by individual and social sensibility, than any other of which we have reliable record. Hegel could argue, with rigorous logic of feeling, that history itself was passing into a new state of being, that ancient time was at an end.

All of this at the same time that the most ancient of all earthly kingdoms was being mapped, translated and catalogued for the first time in modern history.

Tableau des Signes Phonétiques

des Écritures hiéroglyphique et Démotique des anciens Égyptiens

Lettres Grecques	Signes Démotiques	Signes hiéroglyphiques
A		
B		
Γ		
Δ		
E		
Z		
H		
Θ		
I		
K		
Λ		
M		
N		
Ξ		
O		
Π		
P		
Σ		
T		
Υ		
Φ		
Ψ		
X		
Ω		
TO. TΛ.		

Champollion's list of the hieroglyphic alphabet from his Lettre a M. Dacier: *he has spelled out his own name in hieroglyphs in the cartouche at the bottom of the page.*

5

The Road to Memphis

CHAMPOLLION IN TURIN

*One of the characteristics of the French is to stare and get
excited at everything new.*

Rifa'a el-Tahtawi
(written after his stay in Paris, 1826–31)

As is well known, Napoleon's expedition to Egypt precipitated a
Europe-wide epidemic of Egyptomania and, consequently, the pillaging of that country's ancient monuments by a rag-tag mix of crooks
and consuls, soldiers and adventurers. Even as Champollion worked
on the decipherment, boats stuffed with crates of antiquities were
already sailing from Alexandria to the ports of Europe, where there
was a steadily growing market for such things.

The first and finest of these cargoes had been gathered by one
Bernardino Drovetti, who had served with Napoleon in Egypt and who
originally offered his collection to France. Stung by the debacle of the
Dendera Zodiac, however, for which they had paid a fortune, the
Parisian government had refused to buy Drovetti's antiquities, and
they were purchased by His Royal Highness Charles Felix, King of
Sardinia and Duke of Savoy, who planned to exhibit his grand new
treasures in a baroque palace in Turin.

Even as the negotiations for the purchase of Drovetti's 3,000-odd
antiquities were being finalized, ministers of the Turin court were
arranging for Champollion, the only man in all the world with a
command of hieroglyphs, to catalogue the vast collection, which

was being hauled in crates on ox-drawn gun carriages from the port of Genoa through the Ligurian Alps to Charles Felix's capital. So on 7 June 1824 Champollion also crossed the Alps to Italy, where he spent the best part of the next two years. 'The road to Memphis,' he later wrote, 'passes through Turin.' And that was true. For that city had become the proud possessor of the first museum of Egyptian antiquities in the world, and to this day its collections are among the finest of them all.

So there it was, under Champollion's scrutiny, that the methods of modern egyptology were born. Unlike other decipherers of those times, he was interested in far more than linguistics. Since childhood, indeed, when Champollion had first seen the *savants'* drawings, he had been obsessed with ancient Egypt. By his early twenties and a decade before the *Lettre a M. Dacier*, he had already published three volumes on the geography and history of the ancient kingdom culled from nuggets of information from ancient Greek and Roman sources and the works and recollections of more modern travellers, with many of whom he had directly corresponded.

This then was the considerable data bank on which he could always draw – an extensive source of written information for such central egyptological subjects as astronomy and mummification, which still frames all modern understanding of such things. At Turin, as he catalogued and ordered the grand collection of antiquities for a European king, Champollion was building on that ancient fund of knowledge, enlarging the classical and traditional vision of ancient Egypt, its history and its religious and social life.

That Champollion chose to catalogue a collection of portable antiquities rather than to sail straight to the land of his childhood dreams underlines the care with which he set about establishing the ancient Egypt he was in the process of creating. At the same time, however, it warns us that the ancient Egypt which Champollion was busily constructing was made in Europe, amongst the royal collections of the world's first museum of pharaonic treasures, and was laid out in the manner of a traditional European sculpture gallery.

A POINT OF VIEW

My method, though imperfect, I consider psychologically natural.

Konstantin Stanislavsky

The first thing that had struck Champollion on his arrival at Turin was the beauty of Egyptian sculpture. Its excellence, he wrote to his brother, bears comparison to the classical arts, a subject that had found its own Champollion some fifty years before in the figure of Johann Joachim Winckelmann. And as he set about ordering Egyptian history and the collections in Turin, Champollion was guided by many of the principles and historical narratives that Winckelmann had already developed.

A north German scholar who had spent the best part of his life in the service of Roman cardinals, Winckelmann was a fervent admirer of Greek sculpture and painting of the fifth century BC or, at least, how he had imagined the sculpture and painting of that period to have been, for he had never visited the Arcadian landscapes which he so enthusiastically describes in his writings, just as he had never seen any original works of the period he so admired, his observations being based on the evidence of classical literature and Roman copies.

Winckelmann's seminal *History of the Art of Antiquity*, an epitome of two decades of study, had first appeared in 1763, and its novel mix of clever scholarship and ardent prose had elevated the traditional European admiration for the classic arts above all others. Five years later, his murder in Trieste had given the scholar the gloss of a romantic hero, whilst his works had such wide effect on European culture that Goethe declared that age to have been the 'century of Winckelmann'.

Naturally, those writings influenced Champollion in a variety of ways. Winckelmann's use of the term 'art', for example, had transmuted a word long used to describe the skills of craftsmen and musicians into something closer to its modern meaning. For Winckelmann, the 'fine arts' were a highly specific group of artefacts that were defined by the heightened emotional response they prompted in their viewers; a response that he vividly experienced when imagining the sheer beauty of Greek sculpture. This, he considered, was an instinctive response and one common to or at least latent in all educated Europeans.

Of all the arts, so Winckelmann maintained, Greek figure sculpture was by far the finest, because he had detected in its smooth white forms what he famously described as '*edle Einfalt und stille Größe*' – 'a noble simplicity and quiet grandeur'. Such qualities, he opined, were far more than the products of fine craftsmanship. Classical artists had not copied appearances, but ennobled and transformed reality. Their works, therefore, were embodiments of the ambitions of the society in which they had been made, a society which, as its literature showed, had freely debated issues of morality and liberty and which had sought and discovered the route to human perfection. In short, it was an Enlightenment delight. After Winckelmann, therefore, the study of classical literature was no longer viewed as it had mostly been in earlier ages as an adjunct of Bible study and theology, but as a search for abstract moral value and a guide to individual self-perfection. Such was Winckelmann's effect that in the nineteenth century the disciplines of philology and the critical analysis of classical literature had become a principle component of European education. And that in turn had a profound effect upon the nature and the growth of egyptology.

As Winckelmann described it, classical culture had a tragic history that, in a subtle stylistic analysis, his *History* divided into a rakish four-staged progress that is still used today. Within this scheme, the earlier Greek arts had been finer and more elevated than those of Imperial Rome because the latter had been created in times of lower morality and less personal freedom. Such moral qualities, Winckelmann believed, could be absorbed directly from his designated works of art as part of the reaction to their beauty, a novel notion that in Champollion's lifetime had prompted a Europe-wide fashion for classical and neo-classical art and for Napoleon's plundering of the 'fine arts' of Europe for public exhibition in the royal palace of the Louvre and the education of the French.

Winckelmann's enthusiasm for art's moral value, however, had not extended to the relics of ancient Egypt; he had seen much Egyptian sculpture in Rome but was not greatly moved by it, and his writings had portrayed the pharaonic kingdom as a static and largely lifeless place. Champollion, alternatively, had gazed into the faces of the Turin sculptures and sensed the same noble qualities that Winckelmann had discovered in his Greek arts. These, he now considered, were not images of tyrants but the relics of noble kings and a gallant courtly history.

On his arrival at Turin, however, Champollion could not dignify those relics with any kind of written history beyond that held in the writings of the Greeks and Romans. Certainly, the folios of Napoleon's *Description* along with the Turin collections offered splendid illustrations for such narratives, yet the names and histories of those handsome monarchs were barely known.

WAYS AND MEANS — *THE INNOCENCE OF KNOWLEDGE*

After the museum's sun-filled courtyards and the shaded ground-floor rooms where a hundred of Drovetti's finest sculptures had been put upon display, what most interested Champollion at Turin were not the mummies and their coffins, of which the collection had a similar profusion, but the rolls of papyrus – 170 had been listed – most of which Drovetti had brought from ancient Thebes in Upper Egypt. Light and highly portable, considerable quantities of these ancient documents were entering European collections at that time; in fact, it was the greatest harvest of these fragile documents that the world would ever see. Don't buy the ones with pictures, Champollion had written to his elder brother in Grenoble, their texts describe funerary rituals; the best papyri, he continued, are those which just have writing on them, for they hold real history.

At Turin, the papyrus collection was held within a single room in which the rolls lay side by side on tables. What is remarkable in Champollion's accounts of his first examination of them is how, almost instinctively, he understood the gist of their texts, for they were not written in the formal hieroglyphs employed upon the monuments, but in a calligraphic script, an elegant and convenient abbreviation of the picture signs which the pharaonic scribes had used since the first days of hieroglyphic writing. Following an early Christian bishop, Champollion had christened this cursive writing 'hieratic'. One by one, he took up scrolls that had been rolled up at Thebes by ancient scribes and opened them again in the Turin sunlight; the famous so-called Turin Map of gold workings, the Satirical Papyrus with its images of animals playing flutes and crows on ladders climbing trees and its erotic fantasies which Champollion thought had probably been censored in its own times, but was none the less interesting for all that.

One papyrus that especially moved Champollion was but a fragment of its original size. Just three feet long today, it holds the plan of a tomb, its lines, as Champollion describes, 'very thin and nicely traced, with beautiful pale colours, as with a kind of pencil lead'. The tomb's design, he notes, is similar to one in the Valley of the Kings that was mapped by the Napoleonic expedition and published in the *Description de l'Égypte*. That the papyrus plan had a drawing of a sarcophagus at its centre, 'painted in pink granite, and very finely done', further reminded him of a description of a granite sarcophagus which had been taken from the Valley of the Kings some years before and was exhibited at Cambridge, from where an English scholar had sent Champollion a copy of its plan and texts. So the papyrus, he decided, held a plan of a royal tomb at Thebes, an identification that, after further study over the following century in some considerable detail by the egyptologists Sir Alan Gardiner and Howard Carter, has proved correct. With considerable clarity and the judicious use of comparisons gleaned from a variety of papers, books and letters, Champollion had initiated the fundamental methods of academic egyptology.

COUNTING KINGS – *THE TURIN CANON*

One evening early in November 1824, as he was finishing his first examination in the room of the papyrus rolls, Champollion learnt of another smaller room within the great *palazzo*, an abandoned monk's cell on the floor above, where the wreckage of many more papyrus rolls which had disintegrated during their trip to Europe were being stored for a final appraisal – this, essentially, the extraction of their occasional illustrations before the broken texts were thrown away.

Despite the embarrassed protestations of the museum's staff, who were never kind to the foreign scholar, a few days later Champollion entered what he would later call the 'Columbarium of History', for the tiny cell had held a dining table at its centre heaped with a dusty mass of papyrus fragments, some of which were so small and light that if the door were opened quickly they would have scattered in the resulting updraft.

'At first,' he wrote, 'I was seized with a mortal chill . . . *Quis talia fando temperet a lacrymis!* [Virgil's 'who could ever keep from tears!'],' for here, he saw, were the remains of several hundred different texts. Then, as he 'gathered the courage to glance at some of the larger fragments . . . I recognized that I had in my hand a broken piece dated to the year 24 of Pharaoh Amenophis-Memnon'.

Despite his jumbling of a royal name, prescient Champollion had realized that he held in his hand part of an ancient list of pharaohs, an ordered list in which the name of every king had been accompanied by a tally of the years that he had ruled. A chronology of kings, therefore, a skeleton for a history of those unknown ages before the records of the classical historians. So he immediately resolved to examine all the scraps upon that 'desolate table . . . and work, though with less speed and gaiety, like the farmers of our country sorting nuts in autumn evenings'.

That first-found piece of papyrus, he later told his brother, had held the fundamental order of the list, and in his usual methodical manner he had started to search for similar fragments amidst the broken documents.

How can I describe the sensations I experienced in studying the shreds of this great body of history . . . The philosophers cannot – no chapter of Aristotle or Plato is as eloquent as that pile of papyrus . . . I have seen in my hands the names and years of those whose history is completely lost, the names of gods that had offering tables for more than fifteen centuries. Barely breathing, for fear of reducing it to powder,

> I collected a small piece of papyrus that is the last and only refuge of
> the memory of a king who, in his lifetime had, perhaps, outgrown the
> immense Palace of Karnak! [sic].

Such are the beginnings of a fascination that grew throughout the
nineteenth century: the passion on which the modern academic discipline is founded.

One week later, on 15 November 1824, Champollion told his
brother that he had 'finished picking out the walnuts . . . [and had
been] fortunate enough to find a number of other fragments . . . Only
the lower part remains, however, which underlines the original extent
of this papyrus and the large amount of historical documentation that
it would have held, had barbarians not torn it to shreds . . .' Then,
almost as an afterthought, he adds that he had 'found some royal
names written in red ink in the midst of others that were written in
black; I assume those were the names of the heads of dynasties.'

In fact, they marked changes in the location of the pharaohs' residence. The dynasties to which Champollion alludes, alternatively,
were the thirty divisions of the kings of Egypt that had been listed by
the scholar priest Manetho, who had compiled a history of the pharaohs in the third century BC. Even before he had left Paris for Turin,
by comparing the surviving fragments of classical descriptions of
ancient Egyptian history and a few short lists of hieroglyphic royal
names which travellers had copied from the walls of the Egyptian
monuments, Champollion had already established an approximate
correspondence between some of the hieroglyphic names of kings
and those recorded in Manetho's thirty royal dynasties. That list,
however, had only covered the latter half of Manetho's history, from
the Thirtieth down to the Eighteenth Egyptian Dynasty. Now, a hundred or so of the larger fragments of the new papyrus in Turin had
provided Champollion with a unique register of much earlier kings.

A hasty copy of a carefully prepared original, the precious king list
whose fragments Champollion recovered and part-restored, had been
written on the back of a register of tithes which, it is now generally
agreed, had been compiled in Manetho's Nineteenth Dynasty of
pharaohs; that is, during the thirteenth century BC. Given that the
fragmented roll had originally been around one foot four inches high

and some five and a half feet long, it could easily have accommodated and listed the names of well over 300 kings, each one followed by the years that they had ruled, and all those kings set into columns in the order of their reigns and further subdivided into groups of monarchs who had ruled from one location. That sections of the papyrus' list closely corresponded to some of the sections of the classical chronology provided by Manetho served to link them and to underline their accuracy. 'To be clear,' Champollion wrote to his brother,

> I have collected the debris of a royal canon that was a genuine Manetho in hieratic ... The most striking result of this exhumation is that, without doubt, it shows that the Egyptians acquired this information at a very remote time ... for in all these fragments there is not one cartouche similar to those of Kings of the XVII, XVIII or the following dynasties.

Though he had previously known but a few of the royal names held in the new-found broken list, Champollion nonetheless considered it to have been a list of real ancient kings. And if that were true, he further understood, then Manetho's history, which described dynasties and ages so lost in human time that it had previously been disbelieved, was in fact a unique account of the succession of a long line of ancient pharaohs. Champollion had glimpsed previously unknown millennia of human history, right back to the beginning of pharaonic history.

In its present broken state, the Turin Canon, as the fragmentary papyrus is now known, still raises many questions as to its ancient point and purpose. As Champollion had already observed, given the papyrus' considerable antiquity and the similarity of its lists to those compiled almost a millennium later in Manetho's history, both of those ancient records must have drawn upon far older archives that have since been lost. All the other ancient king lists that are known to have survived, moreover, are but partial registers of honoured royal ancestors and omit many monarchs, presumably those considered to have been irrelevant or unsuitable for inclusion. Only the fragments of the Turin Canon include virtually all of the known *de facto* rulers of pharaonic Egypt, including some to whom it does not even award a royal cartouche. And, quite exceptionally, the list had once recorded the number of the years of each ruler's reign. It was, in fact, much like a modern chronology of kings, holding information that, though never a primary concern of ancient chroniclers, was of considerable importance in reconstructing Egypt's ancient history. And still today, despite its damage, the surviving fragments of the Turin Canon hold a unique ancient list of the first fifteen centuries of Egypt's pharaohs, and is a primary source of reference for many modern egyptologists:

> ... the length and order of the reigns of kings, the figures in the Turin Canon are generally accepted without comment, as this document forms the basis of the overall chronological structure of Egyptian History before the New Kingdom [i.e. before the Eighteenth Dynasty]. (Nigel Strudwick, 1985)

COUNTING TIME – *INTO AN UNKNOWN PAST*

> *I propose, Monsieur le Duc, to have the honour to speak to you in my next Letter about several other monuments relating either to Pharaohs, or to kings ... which seem so near the origin of the human race and the beginning of time.*
> Jean François Champollion, 1824

Champollion's first published accounts of the chronology of Egypt's pharaohs took the form of a series of letters written, on this occasion, to the Duc de Blacas d'Aulps, *Premier Gentilhomme de la Chambre du Roi*, an antiquarian and archaeologist and one of Champollion's faithful supporters.

In comparison with the farrago of opinion and erroneous erudition that characterizes much of the work of his opponents, the modernity of these *Lettres* is surprising; Champollion sails into the unknown kingdom of the ancient pharaohs with clear-sighted confidence. Perhaps the form of a published *Lettre* to a patron meant that, as a courtesy to its intended readers, he had to use plain language. At all events, short, clear and simply written, Champollion's *Lettres a M. le Duc de Blacas d'Aulps* are in the best traditions of the French Enlightenment, a mixture of elegance and precision.

Of course, he frequently misreads the ancient texts and employs now out-dated ways of spelling ancient names – 'Name-Atari' for example, for 'Nefertari'. The wonder, however, is that Champollion had understood those texts at all. And just as he had done in his earlier explanation of the hieroglyphs, so too, in the *Lettres a M. le Duc*, he sets out in good order, step by step, to construct a chronology for the earlier parts of the history of Egypt's ancient kings and thus to prove, just as he had previously surmised in his *Lettre a M. Dacier*, that 'phonetic writing existed in Egypt at a far distant time' and so put pay to Jomard's continued carping about the age of the Egyptian hieroglyphs.

Champollion prefaces his account with his list of source material. In comparison with what is available today, it is extraordinarily scanty, consisting of the texts that formed a part of Drovetti's Turin collection, some travellers' copies of a few short king lists taken from the standing monuments, the weighty records of the *Description de l'Égypte* and a handful of other materials from copies of the texts upon the obelisks of Rome to those odd fragments of antiquity that he and his various correspondents had copied and circulated amongst themselves.

Champollion begins his exploration of pharaonic history by proving, just as many would-be decipherers had previously assumed, that cartouches generally held the names of kings and queens. He then observes that many kings had two cartouches that frequently appear in pairs and are distinguished not only by their unchanging order, but also by some specific groups of hieroglyphs that often precede each cartouche. The first of these two cartouches, which Champollion describes as the '*prénom*', English-speaking egyptologists will later call a 'prenomen' or the 'throne name'; the second, which he calls the '*nom propre*', is usually described in English as the pharaoh's 'nomen'. Unlike the ancient scribes, however, who commonly referred to individual monarchs by their prenomens, Champollion employed the nomen to identify the individual kings and then, in order to distinguish kings with similar nomens, he set roman numerals after their translated names – Amenhotep I, II and III, for example – a system that he adopted from that of European royalty and one that is still used today.

At this time too, Champollion was already identifying some of the groups of hieroglyphs that commonly accompany the royal names as 'titles' and translating them into phrases that were subsequently rendered into English as 'Son of the Sun' and 'Beloved of [the god] Amun' – the latter having been derived from Champollion's *chéri d'Amon*'. Though those translated epithets still identify those groups of hieroglyphs today, for the most part and along with many other common hieroglyphic words and phrases their ancient purposes and meanings remain ambiguous and largely unexplored.

Next, Champollion set out to establish a firm chronology with fixed dates for the pharaohs whose names most frequently appeared in the collection at Turin; those, that is, whose names were engraved upon the beauteous sculptures that Drovetti had mostly brought from ancient Thebes. First, he tackled the relatively plentiful numbers of texts in the collection that were written in so-called Demotic script, a late form of hieroglyphic writing that had originally been used for unofficial purposes but later, as on such lapidary records as the Rosetta Stone, for formal courtly documents. When dealing with such late-period inscriptions, Champollion could occasionally cross-reference his translation of their texts with contemporary classical writings and so verify not only his decipherment but also his identification of the hieroglyphic names of kings.

As he moved further back in time, however, into those ages before Demotic had been used, the historical sources were far more fragmentary. Many of the cartouches on the Turin sculptures named monarchs of Manetho's Eighteenth and Nineteenth royal dynasties – names that Greek historians had long since given classical forms such as Amenhotep, Tuthmosis and Ramesses, along with typically classical histories. In many of those statues, too, Champollion detected strong physical and even familial resemblances. Using Manetho's list and the fragments of the Turin Canon as his guide, he set these royal names and images into a somewhat jumbled order and added up the joint years of their rule as listed in the Turin Canon and the classical sources. Thus he produced a date for the beginning of the dynasties of Amenhotep and Ramesses at a point before 1822 BC, a figure that differs from present estimates by just three centuries.

More important than that single date, however, was that for the first time in modern history Champollion had constructed a roughly continuous chronology of the later dynasties of Egyptian kings. By joining the chronologies of the classical pharaohs of the Greek and Roman periods to some of the older Egyptian dynasties he had also proved beyond all reasonable doubt, and over and above the continuing objections of the *savants*, that the hieroglyphs themselves were of considerable antiquity.

Though incorrect, Champollion's list of dated kings had also demonstrated that the latter half of Manetho's list of kings, those sections from the Eighteenth to the Thirtieth Dynasty of kings, were more than myth. What he could well have added to this leap into the distant past, but did not, was that his data had underlined the veracity of both Manetho's list and of the Turin Canon. And that, in turn, could have provided dates for the earlier dynasties of kings to push pharaonic chronology and history back into the third millennium BC.

In the 1820s, however, such a claim, which would have doubled the span of recorded human history, would have been injudicious, for it called into question Europe's traditional guide to early history, the so-called Biblical Chronology, which clerical scholars had long-since divided – like Winckelmann's later division of classical culture – into four separate ages. Beginning with the Creation as described in the Book of Genesis, which is called the Adamic Age, this first age is followed by a second initiated by Noah's Flood, which in turn is succeeded by a third age which starts with the travels of the Prophet Abraham and terminates with the coming of Christ, who ushers in the final, fourth and present epoch. Though many well-known figures of the Enlightenment had long since questioned the validity of this scheme of history, the only people who would publicly discard the Biblical Chronology for a different scheme of things – for even in the 1820s, there was no firmly established historical data to directly contradict it – were revolutionaries and anti-clericals like Dupuis who were pleased to offer insults to royalty and to the Church. But by the 1820s, with Napoleonic laws forbidding insult to the clergy and the subsequent restoration of the monarchy in France, such old-fashioned anti-clericals had to bite their collective tongue.

Neither could Champollion afford to alienate his pious patrons. Nonetheless, it was clear to those who were reading the numerous printed papers issuing from Turin that he was engaged in building a chronology for pharaohs far older than any of the Bible's characters. One of his critics, accordingly, claimed that hieroglyphics had been invented by the Devil to defend the fiction of Manetho's history; another simply dubbed Champollion the Antichrist, the 'Robespierre of Grenoble'. Hardly bothering to publicly respond to such criticisms or, indeed, to Jomard's continuing jibes, he entered his new-made list of kings – the only one in all the world – into a pocket book, and in the spring of 1826 he took a tour of the Italian peninsula.

A printer's flower from the title page of Champollion's Lettre a m. le duc de Blacas d'Aulps – monuments historiques.

CHAMPOLLION *TRIUMPHANS*

The miracle of Champollion's achievement lay less in the initial discovery than in the amazing use he was able to make of it.
                                        Sir Alan Gardiner, 1961

Back in France, the tide was turning for Champollion. Government ministers had realized that with their expenditure of considerable amounts of money on Jomard's recommendation to purchase the now 'accursed Zodiac of Dendera' they had lost the opportunity of acquiring for the Louvre the Turin collection, which as Champollion had demonstrated held previously unknown histories within it and thus considerable national prestige. The *savants* had had their day. Now Champollion was commissioned to buy some of the other antiquities that were still flooding out of Egypt.

As he visited several of the numerous courts of the Italian principalities, Champollion was surprised to find that news of his decipherment preceded him. At Florence he had met the family of Leopold II, the amiable Duke of Tuscany who was already employing Ippolito Rosellini, a professor of oriental languages at the ducal university of Pisa, to teach Champollion's system of decipherment at his court. And so the two scholars had travelled together to Livorno, the Tuscan free port, to inspect the Egyptian cargoes stored in the antiquities merchants' warehouses and buy the best of them for exhibition at the Louvre.

At Rome, where to general amazement Champollion had read out aloud for the first time in two millennia the inscriptions on the city's Egyptian obelisks, he again found that 'hieroglyphs are in great honour'. And so was he, being persuaded to give short courses on his decipherment to groups of ambassadors and noblemen and even to attend a private audience with the secretary of the Pope.

Unlike the court of Tuscany, the invitation had not signalled a papal interest in hieroglyphics. Just as Galileo's investigations two centuries before, Dupuis' unholy theories which challenged the Biblical account of history had greatly disturbed the Holy See: perhaps, Champollion had privately surmised, Egyptian zodiacs had been especially created 'to give bishops sleepless nights'. At Rome, however, he was solemnly informed that his earlier somewhat ill-judged remarks on the correct age of the Dendera Zodiac had 'done the church a beautiful and good service' and that the French ambassador had been asked to canvass his king to grant him an honour for being 'the saviour of the biblical chronology'. A son of the Enlightenment, Champollion privately regarded clerics as guardians of superstition, and must surely have been bemused. Nonetheless, in May of that same year, a decree of '*le bien-aimé*' Charles X, the brother of the guillotined King Louis, established a Museum of Egyptian Antiquities at the Louvre and Champollion was named as its curator.

Two years on, in November 1828, Champollion and Rosellini were in Egypt, the joint leaders of a Franco-Tuscan Expedition. In that interval of time, Rosellini had studied with Champollion at the Louvre as egyptology's first student. A charming and somewhat self-effacing man, Rosellini was a long-time protégée of the Grand Duke, who had subsidized his traditional theological education at Pisa in which the young man had taken to the study of Biblical languages with such zeal that the Duke had sent him to Bologna to study under the extraordinary polyglot Cardinal Mezzofanti. It was there that he first read Champollion's papers on the decipherment and had been enchanted. Thus these two friends were the first representatives of the main streams of egyptology's subsequent recruitment and research: those who come to the study of ancient Egypt through a fascination with the subject of itself, and those who come to ancient Egypt through their study of the Bible.

In Egypt and through the good offices of the Duc de Blacas d'Aulps, the two egyptologists, master and pupil, were co-directors of a team of two architects and seven draughtsmen. Remarkably enough, although the project had been jointly funded by a Grand Duke and the government of France, the collection of antiquities took second place, its primary purpose being the study of the standing monuments and to investigate in the light of Champollion's decipherment the history, society and religion of pharaonic Egypt. So their joint expedition sailed the length of the lower Nile making fresh copies of the monuments' images and inscriptions, drawings that would later be published in the manner of Napoleon's *Description de l'Égypte*, in a series of fine folios.

So it was that Champollion finally saw the temple of Dendera for himself. Their boat, he wrote to his brother, had moored late in the evening on the river's bend and everyone had set out to walk to that fabled monument across moonlit fields. An hour later they had passed through the temple's majestic gateway, and were amazed. 'The temple', he wrote, 'is a unity of grace and majesty . . . a building easy to survey in the manner of the *savants*, but impossible to describe . . . For two hours, we were in ecstasy, running down the great halls with our poor torches, trying to read the external inscriptions in the moonlight.' And when they returned at sunrise the next day, what had appeared spectacular 'in the brightness of the moon was even more so as the rays of the sunlight chiselled out the details . . .'

Dendera temple in Champollion's time, from a drawing by Vivant Denon.

'The most ancient part,' Champollion observes, 'is the external wall of the temple's extremity, where the colossal sculptures of Cleopatra and her son Ptolemaeus-Caesar are found. The upper bas-reliefs are from the time of Emperor Augustus.' His excited yet precise description continues unabated until the voyagers arrived at the hole in the roof created by the removal of the famous zodiac. And what he found there raised an ironic smile, for the Parisian engineers had left sections of the zodiac's framing inscriptions behind, including the part in which, some eight years earlier, Champollion had deciphered the word 'autocrator/emperor' from a *savant*'s drawing. In reality, though, at Dendera in the hard Egyptian sunlight, there was but an empty space where that tell-tale term had appeared within the drawing; a blank cartouche whose interior, as Champollion described it, had never been 'touched by the tapping of a chisel'. The draughts-man *savant*, it appeared, had simply filled it up with hieroglyphs copied from another cartouche! Champollion had been tricked by poor copying.

'Yet,' he continued, 'my enemies should not begin to crow again,' for his examination of the other cartouches in the temple had proved that all its interior decorations, including those of the missing zodiac, were no older than the Roman emperors Trajan and Antonius Pius. And with a last swipe at the *savants* who had described the temple's reliefs as very ancient and quite beautiful, Champollion observes that though the temple's architecture is, indeed, a masterpiece: 'its reliefs are hideous and neither do they decorate a temple dedicated to the goddess Isis [as Jomard's captions in the Napoleonic *Description* state], but to the goddess Hathor as the thousand and one dedications with which it is powdered clearly tell'.

This was the meeting of Western egyptology and the ancient monuments. For the first time in two millennia the standing monuments of old Egypt had been put under informed scrutiny in everything from a reading of their texts to Champollion's aesthetic judgement.

On his return from Egypt and despite continued opposition from the usual quarters, a chair was created for Champollion at the Collège de France; suitably enough, he was the first professor of Egyptian history in the world. In the following year, however, at the age of just 42, he died of a stroke and the chair fell into abeyance. A posthumous likeness shows the man sporting a modest Byronic collar and a white cravat, his dark hair cut short in the Parisian manner; slight of build, sallow and round faced, with the sharp brown eyes of a southern Frenchman. At the time of his death he had been working on texts gathered on his Egyptian journey, material that both Rosellini and Champollion's devoted brother along with several other scholars would continue to publish in the course of the following half century, as the man himself took on the legendary role of scientific hero:

Champollion, Jean François (1790–1832). The Founder and 'Father' of Egyptology and the decipherer of hieroglyphs; commonly called 'Le Jeune' to distinguish him from his brother . . . his statue was placed in the vestibule of the College de France after his death . . . (*Who Was Who in Egyptology*, 2012)

6

Aftermath

THREE KINGDOMS – *THE CHEVALIER BUNSEN*

One man, especially, had been intrigued by the sight of Champollion striding white-stockinged round the streets of Rome, pausing only to scribble down the hieroglyphic texts engraved upon the city's Egyptian obelisks. Baron Christian Karl Josias von Bunsen, a learned and most pious Protestant and secretary to the Prussian ambassador at Rome, had read the papers on the decipherment and written excitedly to his ambassador, the great classical scholar Carsten Niebuhr: 'What is your opinion of the *Précis du Système Hiéroglyphique* by Champollion? . . . I have a kind of shrinking from it, because the knowledge of Coptic is probably indispensable to its comprehension: and the system of signs would seem arbitrary and farfetched.'

Despite his preliminary misgivings, the Baron was completely hooked. And so began a study that engrossed him for the remainder of his life, a labour that in 1844 resulted in a five-volume work entitled *Egypt's Place in Universal History*. Bunsen writes in the Preface,

> Twenty years have now elapsed since I became convinced by Champollion's lectures and writings, as well as by my own examination of the Egyptian monuments at Rome, and particularly the obelisks, that the great discovery of the Hieroglyphical System would prove to be of the highest importance for the ancient history of Mankind . . . three questions presented themselves. Is the Chronology of Egypt, as embodied in the Dynasties of Manetho, capable of restoration . . . ? . . . may we hope . . . to obtain for the History of Mankind a more sure

and unfailing foundation than we at present possess . . . ? Will the Egyptian language enable us to establish the position of the Egyptians, as a nation, in primeval history, and especially their connection with the tribes of the Aramaic and Indo-Germanic stock?

Writing before Darwin, yet in the spirit of the age, Bunsen had sensed that an underlying evolution, a set of processes, had guided the progress of the human race since the days of its beginnings. And to discover what those primary principles had been, his five volumes attempted to fit the writings of ancient Greece and Rome, of India and China, of Russia, Japan and Tibet and Champollion's new chronology of ancient Egypt into the four ages of the Biblical Chronology: Adamic, Post-Diluvial, Abrahamic and the final, Christian Era.

The notion that recent human history is not a product of human intellect and endeavour but part of a natural evolution of race, ethnicity and language is now properly regarded as a relic of Western nineteenth-century thought. And a dangerous one at that. Along with those of others of his times some of Bunsen's theories are innocent precursors of the calamities of twentieth-century Europe. The main protagonists of his Universal History, for example, are groups of languages that he and many other scholars of the time had transformed into imaginary tribes and nations, amongst which were the Aryans, whose history he traces from the Himalayas to Winckelmann's idealized ancient Greece and from there to modern Germany, and the Semites, who were widely considered to have been the Aryans' historic foil and the antecedents of European Jewry.

Nonetheless, Bunsen's eccentric volumes have had a fundamental impact upon egyptology. However faulty his racial theories, the Baron had detected in the surviving record of ancient Egypt a pattern that encouraged him to divide Champollion's lengthy chronology of kings into three separate ages, which he labelled the Old, Middle and New Empires. Following the replacement of the term 'Empire', a relic from the days when French had been the scholarly language of Europe, these are the Old, Middle and New Kingdoms that are still used today.

Such generalities have advantages and disadvantages. For the most part, Bunsen's scheme had followed the dynastic divisions of Manetho and has found broad archaeological confirmation on the ground: the

New Kingdom, notably, still runs from Dynasty Eighteen to Dynasty Twenty. Bunsen's Middle Kingdom, however, which was limited to Manetho's Twelfth Dynasty, has subsequently been expanded to encompass not one but two and a half of Manetho's dynasties; that is, from mid Dynasty Eleven to the end of Dynasty Thirteen, and to contain two different seats of government, Thebes and Memphis. Thus this modern Middle Kingdom departs both from Bunsen's definition and from the fundamental structure of the Turin Canon, which is based upon the location of the seat of government.

What Bunsen had clearly seen, however, was that many of Manetho's thirty dynasties were little more than literary devices; several of them, for example, are symmetrically divided into groups of nine rulers each and his Seventh Dynasty consists of 'seventy kings of Memphis who ruled for 70 days'. The construction of such picaresque dynasties, Bunsen considered, had masked times when court record-keeping had failed; disordered periods, therefore, and times of invasion even, just as the Greek and Roman historians briefly describe.

Naturally enough, most traditional historians have directed the best part of their studies to the periods of Bunsen's three great kingdoms – the well-documented periods represented by mighty monuments and famous rulers – and have tended to describe the confusions of the intervening periods as times of governmental collapse. In the 1920s, however, as further evidence began to come to light, the two vague periods between Bunsen's three well-studied kingdoms were awarded the titles of the First and Second Intermediate Periods. And in the 1960s, the equally fragmented period between the ending of Bunsen's New Kingdom and the sixth century BC – a period with which Champollion had many chronological difficulties – was awarded the title of the Third Intermediate Period.

Nowadays, as further evidence accumulates, livelier histories have been discerned for pharaoh's Egypt than those contained within the three mighty kingdoms of the Baron Bunsen. Just as Champollion well knew from personal experience – for as a young man he had been personally involved in the fiery contemporary politics of France – periods in which civic order is disturbed are often times in which the government and culture of the state is scrutinized and redefined. And so today, the histories of the centuries that divide the Baron's kingdoms offer fascinating and vivid alternatives to the popular versions of ancient Egypt as a thrice-recurring monolithic power.

DENKMÄLER – *PROFESSOR LEPSIUS*

For acquiring of philosophy, some sensible monuments are
necessary, by which our past thoughts may be not only
reduced, but also registered every one in its own order.

Thomas Hobbes, 1656

That Bunsen's tripartite scheme was taken up so quickly and has lasted for so long was due to two main factors. First was the fact that ambiguities and omissions in both Manetho's history and the Turin Canon allowed no absolute agreement upon the dates that the first pharaohs had ruled or even those of the reigns and monuments of some of the most celebrated pharaohs. So Bunsen's terminology handily defined common areas of historical interest without the necessity to continually engage in ongoing debates about the accuracy of various alternative chronologies.

The second reason for its swift adoption was that Bunsen's scheme was taken up by Professor Richard Lepsius of Berlin University. A one-time protégé of Bunsen, Lepsius was the originator and editor of another series of folios illustrating the Egyptian monuments, a publication which on this occasion contained the records of a Prussian expedition to the Nile during the winter of 1842–5, which Lepsius himself directed.

Subsidized by the Berlin government and *Seiner Majestät dem Koenige von Preussen Friedrich Wilhelm IV*, Lepsius' great volumes – *Denkmäler aus Aegypten und Aethiopien* (Berlin, 1849–59) – exceeded the physical size and weight of both the Napoleonic and the Franco-Tuscan publications, and its drawings were of a far higher level of accuracy. To this day, the *Denkmäler* are some of the world's largest printed books. In their own time, they were the apotheosis of an intense half century of study by bands of adventurous and eccentric European scholar-travellers who were copying directly from the monuments so as to satisfy, as Sir Alan Gardiner put it, an 'urgent need for more material and better copies'. Most of these scholars' marvellous folios of original drawings, however, had not been reproduced. Only after the publication of the lithographs and steel plate engravings of Lepsius' *Denkmäler* in 1859 could the best part of the inscriptions on the standing monuments of Egypt be studied and translated in the libraries of Europe. For the first time, also, the *Denkmäler* provided a detailed account of the inscriptions of ancient Memphis, especially those in the cemeteries of Giza and Saqqara which Champollion and Rosellini had largely circumvented during their Egyptian expedition, in order, it would appear, not to compromise the Biblical Chronology which the family of the Dukes of Tuscany firmly upheld.

Now, though, Lepsius' splendid folios reproduced drawings of King Khufu's name as it appears in graffiti within the Great Pyramid's interior; genuine contemporary evidence that the prodigious monument had been built for that most ancient king who, though listed both in the Turin Canon and in Manetho's Fourth Dynasty of monarchs, had previously been but little documented outside the tales of ancient Greek and Roman travellers. Along with dozens of architectural plans of paintings and reliefs in tomb chapels of similar age, Lepsius listed all those monuments as memorials of the '*Altes Reich*' – Bunsen's Old Kingdom: this, as opposed to the later monuments that his expedition also measured up and drew which were labelled as having been made in the times of the '*Neues Reich*' – or the New Kingdom. Thus, Bunsen's terms have lasted till today.

Lepsius had first met Bunsen in the 1830s, when he was studying exotic languages in Paris, which at that time was the European centre for linguistics. A few years later, Bunsen invited the young man to serve as his secretary in the offices of the nascent Prussian Archaeological Institute at Rome. Doubtless Lepsius' considerable linguistic abilities would have been of great help to the Baron in the compilation of his 'Universal History'. At the same time and on Bunsen's recommendation, Lepsius had taken up the study of hieroglyphs with Rosellini, who was teaching Champollion's system of decipherment at the University of Pisa. As Lepsius later told his biographer, by that time he had wanted to become the 'German Champollion'.

It was an astute ambition. Following Champollion's death in 1832, lawsuits and a clamour of bitter gossip had broken out around his papers and there had been a brief lull in the study of hieroglyphic. Then in 1837 Lepsius used the posthumous publication of Champollion's *Egyptian Grammar* as the basis of a scholarly re-examination of the various criticisms and theories which yet surrounded the decipherment and published his results in his *Lettre à M. le Professeur Rosellini ... sur l'alphabet hiéroglyphique*. This essay forcefully confirmed the fundamental accuracy of Champollion's system whilst at the same time making some corrections to it, for neither the Frenchman nor his Italian friend had seen that most of the hieroglyphs which they had assumed to have been single alphabetic letters – signs, that is, denoting 'uniliteral' consonants – had actually represented entire syllables of sound, that is, sounds that were 'multiliteral'.

After Lepsius' *Lettre*, all but a handful of eccentrics had accepted that Champollion's system of translation was the only sound tool for the further study of hieroglyphic, and for the first time work undertaken by a small number of English, French and German enthusiasts – lawyers, preachers, school inspectors, wine merchants and museum curators – started to come to grips with the grammar of the hieroglyphs and to translate entire sentences and texts.

Like Champollion before him, Lepsius also constructed a chronology of Egypt's ancient kings. Based as ever on classical and a few Egyptian texts and augmented by his own discoveries in Egypt, it refined all earlier versions and remains the basis of modern chronologies of Egypt's pharaohs to this day. Yet for a century and more considerable differences remained between the absolute dates attributed to many dynasties and kings, various schools of egyptologists employing one of two separate versions – one German and one ancient Egyptian, as an embattled contemporary described them.

Nowadays, the combined products of two centuries of epigraphy and excavation plus Carbon-14 measurement and other techniques of scientific dating have produced a broad chronological agreement and thus have provided relatively fixed dates for Bunsen's kingdoms and the better part of Manetho's dynasties. Now, it seems, that Bunsen's Old Kingdom had lasted some 450 years and finished with the ending of Manetho's Sixth Dynasty of pharaohs at around 2200 BC, and that the Middle Kingdom of more modern histories had started after an interval of 200 years and finished some three and a half centuries later, at around 1650 BC.

It is often said that Lepsius' *Lettre à M. le Professeur Rosellini* was the final act in the decipherment of hieroglyphic. With the aid of Bunsen and other luminaries of the Prussian court, the same publication had also led to Lepsius' commission to head the state expedition to Egypt from which he did, indeed, return as the German Champollion, compiling the main volumes of the *Denkmäler*, holding the first chair in egyptology at Berlin University and being appointed as Director of the Egyptian collections in that city's great museums, as a Privy Councillor, as a Keeper of the Royal Library and as an advisor to the establishment of Prussian – later German – archaeological institutes in several foreign lands. In those same decades, between the 1840s and the 1880s, the term 'Egyptology' and the profession of 'Egyptologist' were both born. Champollion had laid the foundations of all that. By an act of imagination, by confronting earlier visions of a long lost age with the order and rationality of his time, he had created the basis of the now-traditional European image of 'Ancient Egypt'.

THE LEGACY – *CHAMPOLLION'S ANCIENT EGYPT*

The Pasha is due to return from his pleasure trip upon the water. I will introduce you to him as a clever architect.
    from the first act of Mozart's Abduction from the Seraglio *(1792)*

From a survey of his surviving papers, it appears that Champollion had considered the lives of pharaoh and his courtiers to have been similar to those of the rulers of the Ottoman Empire, with whose Egyptian viceroy, Muhammad Ali Pasha, he had enjoyed a lively correspondence whilst travelling throughout that province. Fortunately for egyptology, this vision of the ancient East was closer to that of

Mozart than that of Verdi. So Champollion's ancient Egyptians are not draped in heavy velvets nor even the neo-classical togas that decorate the images of temple priests in the *Description de l'Égypte's* reconstructions of ancient life. Champollion's Orient, alternatively, is delightfully rococo; *The Abduction from the Seraglio*, after all, had been commissioned by an uncle of Rosellini's patron, the Duke of Tuscany.

This was a world in which the primary divisions in human society were not those of ethnicity or nationhood, but those that 'naturally' exist between various grades of nobility and an underlying peasantry. So a group portrait of the Franco-Tuscan expedition at their work in Egypt shows most of the expedition's members wearing the silk and cotton robes of middle-ranking Ottoman officials, the ranks they also held at European courts. After the expeditions of Champollion and Lepsius, however, after the 1860s, as Western attitudes to non-Western cultures shifted and the word 'Egyptologist' came into use, travelling scholars wore European clothes.

Before those silk-clad adventurers had begun their work, the greatest source of information upon 'ancient Egypt' had been the writings of the classical historians. And naturally, when Champollion started to establish his chronology of ancient Egypt, he too had used Manetho's king list as his general guide and employed the Hellenistic historian's device of subdividing the great long list of monarchs into thirty separate dynasties.

Now 'dynasty' is a term widely used in classical literature and also in translations of the Bible. In its earliest manifestations, in the works of Hesiod and Homer, the term denotes a group of able men, and though in later centuries it gathered connotations of lordship and domination, only in Roman times did it attain its modern meaning of a familial succession of kings or princes. So unsurprisingly, and like so many other terms in the common egyptological vocabulary, 'dynasty' has no equivalent in the hieroglyphic dictionary. In Champollion's day, however, when European culture and education was saturated in classical imagery, dynasties of kings were a familiar fact of schoolroom histories. So, naturally enough, in following decades, as more lengthy hieroglyphic texts were translated, the history of ancient Egypt was assumed to have consisted of a succession of ruling families, an assumption which is a part of the same easy vision which assumes that the pharaohs had ruled quasi-European courts in the manner of Shakespeare's Cleopatra.

Yet it is far from proven that the ancient pharaohs had ruled in the manner of those later dynasties of kings or, indeed, that they had obeyed the same rules of succession or, certainly, that they had held the ominous notion of the blood line – either in the sense of *sangre azul* of Castilian aristocrats or the Germanic notion of *Blut und Boden* – that would order the dynasties of the European kingdoms and disorder so many of their subjects.

Nonetheless, the attitudes of Champollion and his successors to the ancient Egypt they were engaged in building was greatly bolstered by the fact that they enjoyed personal and practical familiarity with many aspects of that most ancient culture. For though Europe has no deserts and no Nile, Champollion and Ramesses both lived in small-scale wheat-based economies founded on the technologies of the Middle Eastern Bronze Age. Broadly speaking, the material elements of those two economies – stone-cutting and metal-smelting, animal husbandry and farming and the everyday technologies of house and home – weaving, potting, baking, brewing, cheese-making and the rest – were much the same. So, as a man of his own time, as a French bourgeois from a small, well-watered farming community in central southern France, when Champollion viewed images of Ramesses in his battle chariot, he shared the ancient charioteers' eye for horses and had a practical understanding of their harnesses and tackle, just as the pretty images of so-called 'scenes of daily life' that decorate the walls of many a pharaonic tomb chapel were also common scenes in Champollion's day. He walked in stables and over threshing floors like those of pharaoh. He too lived in houses with hierarchies of servants working at many of the same tasks as those undertaken in the households pictured in the monuments of pharaoh's courtiers. And Champollion also lived within the orbit of the courts and governments of Europe as a kind of courtier; his life's work, indeed, depended upon their patronage, and he had circumscribed his personal beliefs to sustain that patronage.

So it is not surprising that Champollion and his successors had assumed that ancient Egyptian society had a similar composition to traditional Western European society; that it too had consisted of peasants, land-owning aristocrats, soldiers, sailors and the clergy. And that, in turn, led to the use of such terms as 'king' and 'prince', 'peasant', 'soldier' and 'priest', which, though there is scant contemporary evidence for such structures, gives the easy impression of early European governmental institutions.

Yet even as Champollion and his successors were employing such terms to describe the elements of pharaonic society, the traditional way of life that they imply was coming to its end. The various revolutions that had accompanied the demise of feudalism and the rise of the industrial state served to redefine most aspects of European society down to the very names of the months of the year. And at the same time, terms like 'nation', 'art', 'economy' and 'slave' were undergoing their modern re-invention. Today, of course, the traditional structures of the pharaonic state described by the early egyptologists are found only in the world of children's books and historical reconstructions. That, indeed, is the reason why the traditional image of 'ancient Egypt' seems so familiar. Though loaded with more modern terminologies, at root its traditional vocabulary reaches deep within the European past and casts the ancient world as its exotic mirror image.

Should new and different words, therefore, be substituted for traditional terms such as 'king', 'courtier' and 'priest'? Would they be less contaminated by alien worlds and thus provide less-weighted visions of that lost society; replace 'noble', say, with 'a sector of an elite'? Experience, however, shows that the trick of replacing one jargon with another from a different discipline serves to implant yet another set of alien concepts into the unique pharaonic enterprise. Better then to nod to egyptology's own history and to translate and describe the ancient relics in a selective handful of the old familiar terms – but with the understanding that they carry two centuries of European baggage and that a 'king' in the pharaonic context is an archaic chess piece extracted from a game whose rules are scarcely known and hardly understood and whose relics, therefore, hold yet untold possibilities.

Though Hardjedef is called a prince today, he was not a Prince of Denmark nor of Wales. For Hardjedef was not a *European* prince and life at pharaoh's court need not have been a hotbed of dynastic struggle or political ambition. If, alternatively, this pharaonic 'prince' is seen by virtue of his tomb and titles to have been a favoured member of King Khufu's household – then the friction of the mismatch between the ancient and modern meaning of the word may help to stimulate alternative visions of how that ancient, so-called 'court' had functioned.

Neither should it be assumed, however familiar Ramesses' sculpted battle horses may appear, that images of fighting pharaohs represent a quasi-European monarch leading a national army to protect or extend the boundaries of a nation state. The sense of space and state and nationhood held within the ancient populations of the region of the lower Nile was quite different from that of nineteenth-century Europeans. Rather than possessing boundaries defined by cartographic dotted lines, the pharaonic state was conceived from the centre out, that is, from the brick walls of the royal residence – the *per'a*, which is also the origin of the word 'pharaoh' – rather than from the ill-defined extremities which in various locations and at different phases in pharaonic history appear to traditional historians to indicate the edges of an empire.

Nor are such constricted re-interpretations limited to the spheres of geography and politics. As the curator of several grand collections, one of Champollion's first tasks had been to bring order and identity to the innumerable images of gods they held, for which he made a prettily illustrated catalogue, *Le Panthéon Égyptien*, in which the attributes and iconographies of ancient gods are pictured and described as if they were the attributes of Christian saints. Pinned onto their pages like butterflies in boxes, Champollion's Egyptian gods are presented, *sui generis*, in the same manner in which Champollion had quietly viewed religions of his own time, as a mass of signs and superstition, his explanatory commentaries outlining the classical myths in which the pharaonic deities appear. This was an attitude to faith from the age in which Goethe famously described Christianity as 'a mishmash of fallacy and violence', and it denied the ancient culture of the lower Nile all sense of piety and purpose and, indeed, its own particular intelligence. Ironically enough, the same view would be commonly held by many Christian egyptologists of later generations who came to ancient Egypt through their study of the Bible and held their faith to be the only true religion.

To this extent, Jomard's misgivings about Champollion were well founded. For he had replaced the traditional European image of ancient Egypt as a culture of unfathomable wisdom, which is an inherently respectful attitude, with one that reduced the profound metaphors of the pharaonic scribes and craftsmen – their 'symbolism' as Champollion's successors call it – with what W. H. Auden would describe as 'false and boring allegory'. And when such explanations fail, as fail they must, the ancient mysteries are explained away as products of oriental inscrutability or archaic primitivism.

Nonetheless, Champollion's work laid the foundations of a framework by which a previously unintelligible heap of relics and ruins of unknown age has been transformed into the memorials of a millennial ancient culture. This framework, though, is not of itself pharaonic. Not the contents of the library, but its shelves, its pressmarks and its catalogues: in short, the alien apparatus that has set that surviving mass of millennial pharaonic relics into an order that modern people may readily understand. So though the system is frequently presented as an authentic outline of ancient sensibility and history along the valley of the lower Nile, it certainly is not. There is a wealth of ancient life, good news yet to hear, and fine things to be seen, beyond the confines of that library.

How then, to begin? A particular advantage of this history is that it opens in the times of Hardjedef and the Giza kings, in an age that, despite all the scholars' catalogues, chronologies and plans, traditional historians still consider to be largely enigmatic; as mysterious, indeed, as the great stone Sphinx that crouches on the Giza Plateau beside those three colossal pyramids. Here, then, we face a choice. Either to adopt the historians' traditional assumptions about the nature of all nations and primitive and oriental government and construct another history of that lost society based upon those limited parameters, or to start again, to gratefully accept the data that Champollion and his successors have so patiently collected and, thus equipped, walk out again onto the Giza Plateau wondering the while, what on earth it was those ancient people had imagined they were doing?

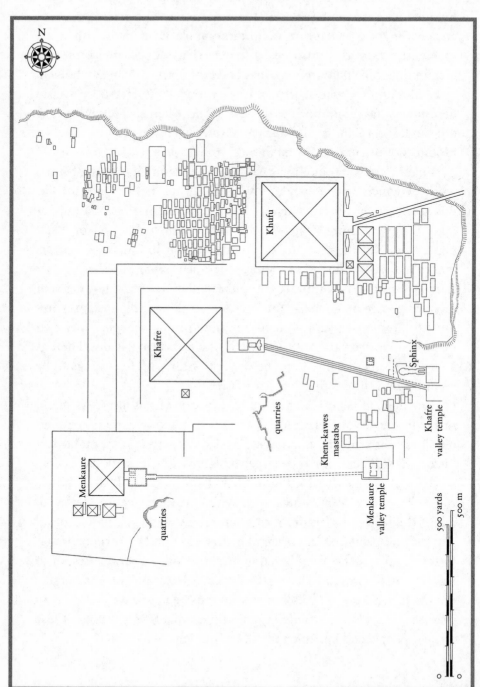

N

Khufu

Khafre

Menkaure

quarries

quarries

Khent-kawes
mastaba

Sphinx

Menkaure
valley temple

Khafre
valley temple

500 yards

500 m

The major monuments on the Giza Plateau.

PART THREE

Old Kingdom
The Giza Kings,
2625–2500 BC

7

The Eloquence of Statues

THE GIZA SPHINX – *STONE AND HISTORY*

What that before-time was, I think scarcely Sphinx can tell . . .

Sir Philip Sidney, 1581

The Sphinx holds many mysteries. Tourists trudging through the Giza sand are frequently perplexed by it. Why so much fuss, they ask, about this dusty knoll of rock? And so, indeed, are many egyptologists, for, unlike the three huge pyramids that stand upon the plateau up above and were the tombs of pharaohs, the Giza Sphinx has no known purpose.

Yet in its day this image of a recumbent lion with the head of a man had been a mighty presence. Prayers were offered to the Giza Sphinx and temples set beside it. Its pose, its workmanship, the shape of its eyes and ears, the broad proportions of its face, the drawing of its headdress, all served as millennial models for later, smaller sphinxes. At the command of pharaohs, emperors and kings, its considerable bulk was freed from drifting sands and its eroding stone restored. Its outline too – a rare occurrence this – was drawn onto offering stelae, where it was placed within a sort of hieroglyphic landscape: a 240-foot-long cat, the largest of all ancient sculptures, sitting at the desert's edge framed by the pyramids of Khufu and Khafre and tended by phalanxes of priests. Then, after several more millennia, the monstrous feline changed its size and sex, grew wings, and flew

Four of the hundreds of small stelae dedicated by princes, courtiers and scribes and their families in temples set near the Great Giza Sphinx. Carved in fine white limestone, the largest is some two feet high.

onto the Hampstead desk of Dr Freud via neo-classical Vienna and Winckelmann's ancient Greece.

All that traditional historians can truly say about this sphinx is that it is an image of a pharaoh and that the shape and proportions of its jawline, ears and cheeks set its manufacture squarely within the Fourth Egyptian Dynasty; that is, at some time around 2550 BC, when Giza's three great pyramids were being built. An eroded granite stela set up in later times between its two enormous paws appears to describe it as a work of Khafre's reign. Yet it does not seem to have been a part of the architecture built to accompany his pyramid, for when Khafre's masons built a splendid granite temple close to the Sphinx and laid a causeway from that temple to the royal pyramid above, both the temple and its causeway had to be especially angled to accommodate the Sphinx which, it may therefore be assumed, is older than either of those monuments. It is likely, therefore, that work upon the Giza Sphinx had started in the decades before Khafre came to the throne; that is, in the times of Khufu or those of his little-known successor, Djedefre. As for the point and purpose of that monument, however, all modern theories from those of crackpots to professors are based on little more than speculation and the literatures of later ages.

So the Great Sphinx is a nameless product of the Fourth Dynasty of pharaohs, that archetypal and non-literary age whose pyramids token, like the Sphinx itself, an extraordinary obsession with worked stone; the Sphinx, indeed, is carved from an isolated knoll of rock that stood in one of the pyramid builders' quarries. Certainly, the sculpture is a synthesis of works made in earlier millennia at far smaller sizes when Nile-side craftsmen had most beautifully modelled the languor and vitality of the lions that roared in the darkness of the desert night. In the Fourth Dynasty of kings, however, beside the dusty quay-sides of the Giza harbour and with the greatest labours of the Bronze Age under way on the plateau up above, sculptors had enlarged those earlier forms and set the head of pharaoh on a colossal image of a lion.

When the Sphinx was freshly finished, the great blocks of building stone that were destined for the pyramids on the plateau up above were being towed in lighters to the Giza harbour down a long canal running through the Nile-side marshes and the silty fields beyond. As you sailed into that harbour, with its busy mass of barges and stone-hauling gangs, the Sphinx's perfect human head would have stood high and calm above the noisy dusty dock, a gentle presence in the bright blue sky lit from the surrounding pavements as if by some faint light from beneath a sea.

From the beginning, the ancient people of the lower Nile always ordered and described their courtly culture in splendid images. The Giza Sphinx, we may be sure, was part of that complex visual system whose images and architectures were already very ancient and so elaborately layered that we today who set our explanations into words can hardly grasp at their complexity. That is why this golden Sphinx, with bullet-riddled eyes and half-eroded smile, is a perfect metaphor for ancient Egypt.

KHAFRE AND THE GOLDEN HAWK

To the southeast side of the Great Sphinx of Giza, there is a building made of granite and alabaster ... In one of the rooms of this temple is a well ... From the bottom of this pit, where it had been bundled at an unknown time, we removed the statue of Khafre and the hawk.

Auguste Mariette, 1869

The hawk is a steadfast bird. Hour on hour, day by day, perched high on posts and trees, it stands watching for predators that would invade the nest. Chest puffed, claws clenched, hawk hieroglyphs had similarly guarded the names of the Egyptian kings since their beginnings. Set on a variety of perches, the same silhouetted image came to signify both the horizon in the west and several pharaonic gods, most particularly Horus, who in the last decades before the age of the colossal

Horus makes his first known appearance in human form in this commanding image, where he is called 'Horus of the royal residence', and embraces an otherwise unrecorded king named Qahedjet, who is usually identified as Sneferu's predecessor, Huni. The limestone stela is just twenty inches tall.

pyramids seems to have been the first of the pharaonic deities to be drawn in human form; a hawk's head set on a human body.

The same fierce protective bird stands behind the head of the Pharaoh Khafre as part of the long-celebrated statue which, in the early 1850s, one of the work gangs of *archéologue extraordinaire* Auguste Mariette dug out of a pit in the floor of a granite temple by the Sphinx. Perched on the highest point of the royal throne, the stone hawk protects the sculpted image of a king who ruled the region of the lower Nile for around a quarter of a century, from about 2540 BC.

It is a masterpiece of three-dimensional design. Seen from above, the hemisphere of the royal head is gently held inside the soft enclosing angles of its wings. Seen from the side, the double angle of those same two wings echo the forms of the statue's face, so that together they make a series of sharply radiating lines that strike out in lively angles from the lappets of the royal headdress – the so-called *nemes*, which in life was made of striped and pleated linen. Seen from the front, however, the powerful bird and all its sculptural subtleties are entirely hidden by the royal face and headdress, its qualities absorbed into the seated figure of the king.

And the statue seems to quiver, as if the gently smiling monarch is about to rise up from his lion-headed throne and swing a stony fist. In two short columns inscribed upon the statue's shining base, his name appears in hieroglyphics: 'Khafre, the golden Horus'.

Though seemingly far larger, Khafre's dark stone statue is in reality life-sized, an illusion created by the relative proportions of its parts; the feet, head and limbs are huge and heavy, the torso flat and narrow-waisted, the face enormous. In that sense and in common with others of its time, the statue may be said to be grotesque. Here though the impact of those curious proportions is softened by some gratuitous injuries to the stone, two missing parts of the throne back and a damaged royal arm and leg, that when completed by a modern imagination, tend to thin down the statue's missing limbs and project its shoulders forward from the throne, as if Khafre were about to rise.

From the first days of its rediscovery, this single image had seemed to encapsulate the power and order of that ancient state. So too, throughout pharaonic history, the making of such regal images continued to define the head of the pharaonic state with similar unspoken clarity.

It had taken the sculptors of the lower Nile millennia to attain the skills required to make such complex and enduring works as Khafre and the hawk. Like the Giza Sphinx, it was made during that period of transition which occurs in many sculptural traditions, when craftsmen begin to overlay the formalism of archaic and more abstract sculptures with a greater realism, when they begin to model details of human skin and muscle upon the surfaces of a version of the human frame whose poses, forms and proportions had long since been established.

Made in an age-old way, by slowly bashing out the sculpture's forms with rocks then rubbing down those rough-made forms with stone and abrasive powders, the texture of the surface of King Khafre's sculpture is similar to that of human skin. Such processes give the work a quality not easily reproduced by modern tools, the dramatic exceptions being the small sharp lines such as those cut around its eyes and mouth, where, at a considerable cost to the crafts-men's copper tools, a fine sharp edge has been produced with smart blows from a succession of small flat chisels. Here too – and this is a great rarity amongst such ancient sculptures – the royal face is perfectly preserved. So you may clearly see that the angle of its cheek-bones and the proportions of its heavy thrusting jaw are similar to those of the Giza Sphinx. Here, though, unlike the Sphinx's damaged and eroded limestone, the statue's remarkable perfection serves to animate its dully shining stone.

The dark green mottled gneiss from which Khafre's statue was extracted is only found in a small part of the Saharan desert, which is named now after the Greek version of Khafre's name as the quarry of 'Chephren diorite'. In desert sunlight, this stone emits a low blue glow, an effect that, though lost in the artificial lights of a museum, was surely seen by the sharp eyes of ancient prospectors and quarry men when they had first stood amongst the custard-yellow sand and sized up the ragged outcrops of the near-black rock. These, then, the rocks and boulders of this unearthly metamorphic stone, were dragged along a specially constructed roadway to the Nile and shipped 600 miles north to Giza to be transformed into a wealth of works including King Khafre's matchless statue.

Procuring and working such hard exotic stone as Chephren diorite required resources similar to those employed in pyramid building and thus was probably undertaken by a workforce from the royal court. Huge amounts of time and effort must have been taken up by the slow progress of cutting down the block of Khafre's statue; by pounding it and cutting it and polishing its surfaces with abrasives. For people with such fine clear judgement, those slow processes would have offered so much precision in the making of the statue that one might regard its creation as a kind of meditation.

HARD HISTORIES – *A LINEAGE OF STATUARY*

The reader must not expect too much from the short sketch of Egyptian history which follows: to a great degree our knowledge consists merely of the names of the kings and their order of succession, and in several periods even these are not certainly determined. As a rule but few facts can be gleaned from the inscriptions, which mostly contain foolish exaggerations of the glory of the monarch; a hundred texts will tell us that the Pharaoh was the 'friend of the gods', and that he 'overthrew all the barbarians' . . .

Adolph Erman, c. 1895

To this day, traditional histories have little to say about the kings for whom the four colossal pyramids were made. Though their monuments yet dominate the Memphis skyline and a handful of the people such as Hardjedef were celebrated in later literature, they ruled, it now appears, in a pre-literary age. So the only known contemporary records of those kings' lives and times are their pyramids and statues, their written names and some accompanying hieroglyphic phrases.

Yet sculpted images like the Great Sphinx and Khafre and the hawk offer genuine glimpses of the tenor of that court. And the changing architectures of the contemporary pyramids, tombs and temples show that lively processes of experiment and change were under way.

Unfortunately, the record is very partial. The surviving statues of Sneferu, for example, the king for whom the first colossal pyramids were made, are heavily eroded and would appear to be late examples of earlier archaic traditions. Nor can a single court statue be definitively assigned to the decades of his successor Khufu, for whom the Great Pyramid was built. Some nameless heads might represent that monarch, and a few fine fragments found at Giza, some of them deriving from a life-sized alabaster statue of a king with a hawk behind his head, may also have been sculpted in his lifetime, but only a tiny ivory statuette is known today that bears King Khufu's name.

The loss is considerable. This was the age in which the millennial image of pharaonic kings was brought to its maturity and the court sculptors were superb craftsmen: the rare fragments of their relief sculpture that have survived are of the finest quality. Fortunately, the same soft limestone used for those reliefs was also employed for a series of anonymous heads and busts that were placed in some of the tomb shafts of the tombs of Khufu's courtiers. And though they are not images of pharaoh, they are as fine a group of sculptures as any that have survived from pharaoh's Egypt.

Most of these sculptures were made at the same scale as King Khafre's splendid statue with the hawk, which was made in the following generation. Like that work, these limestone heads and busts show something of the move from archaism towards a greater realism. Several also show the use of fine-ground plaster as a micro-medium, which was laid over the finished surfaces of the sculptures as a heavy wash and then gently re-worked with fine abrasives to render the smallest subtleties of the surfaces of a human face. First, the craftsmen sculpted the soft white limestone in an older and more formal mode and then, as if by magic, they added an extra layer of reality to bring the heads alive.

Many of these heads and busts, indeed, appear to share a remarkable concern for replicating the features of specific individuals – presumably a few of Khufu's courtiers – to the extent that some of the features of these carefully sculpted faces have been brusquely re-adjusted with a few swift chisel cuts after their final finish had been applied. These, then, show the skills within King Khufu's court, the sensitivities, the precisions of workmanship and observation inherited by a following generation that enabled its craftsmen to sculpt the statue of Khafre and the hawk.

Some missing links between those limestone heads and Khafre's hard-stone image were uncovered by French archaeologists in the 1920s when excavating the ruins of the pyramid of Djedefre, the pharaoh who had ruled in the decade between King Khufu and King Khafre. Though Djedefre could well have been the original subject of the Giza Sphinx, his modestly made pyramid was not built at Giza but on a lone hilltop some seven miles to the north. There it was, beside his pyramid in the mud-brick ruin of a miserable temple, that pieces of no less than twenty exquisitely sculpted statues of the king were excavated.

One of the best preserved of these smashed sculptures showed Djedefre enthroned. Though only the head and neck survive and the nose is broken, it is a very splendid piece. Set inside the angles of the *nemes* headdress, the chisel-sharpened forms of the eyes, ears and mouth of the life-sized face owe much to the techniques of the earlier limestone sculptures of King Khufu's nobles. Here, though, the craftsmen have worked in red quartzite, a hard crystalline material from the quarries on the rocky outcrop of the Gebel Ahmar just a few miles to the east of Djedefre's pyramid on the far bank of the Nile. And that glistening pinkish stone has been polished to a skin-like finish, which serves to embellish and expand the simple limestone forms of the earlier sculptor's so that, to the modern eye, they seem monumental. Like the Giza Sphinx, a cobra was set at the centre of this sculpture's forehead, its rearing head and hood steadied by the languorous curves of its body as it runs back over the royal cranium. This is the so-called uraeus, the fire-spitting snake that will become a traditional identifying attribute of images of pharaoh.

King Khafre, who succeeded Djedefre, may have been King Khufu's grandson: the right of succession, if such a thing existed in those distant times, is yet unknown and the spare terms in the surviving funerary texts describing familial relationships are, by modern lights, ambiguous. What the monuments show, however, is that after the reign of Djedefre the stoneworkers of the royal court returned to Giza and supervised the building of King Khafre's colossal pyramid, with its near 700-yard-long causeway and its two accompanying temples.

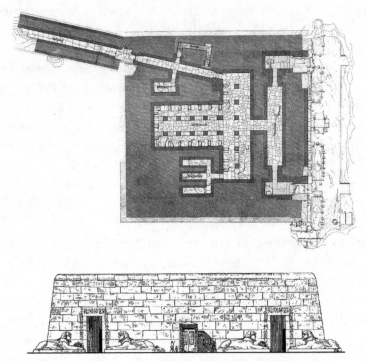

Hölscher's restoration of the plan and façade of Khafre's valley temple. The building was 150 feet square and lined and encolumned with blocks of Aswan granite. Four huge sphinxes flanked its doorways.

There it was, at Giza, inside the lower of those two great temples, that Mariette's men found the splendid statue of King Khafre and the hawk. Not that it had stood alone. In the winter of 1909–10, when the German architect Uvo Hölscher undertook the re-excavation and planning of that temple, he recovered hundreds of small fragments of other royal statues, all of which appear to have been made in Khafre's time.

The temple had been packed with statues. Four huge hard-stone sphinxes had sat at its two great entrance doorways and dozens of others had been set up inside, including some twenty statues similar to the statue of Khafre and the hawk that Mariette's workmen had pulled out of a pit. These, it would appear, had been placed in rows around the four sides of a central open court, the diorite statues standing in semi-darkness on plinths of shining cream-coloured alabaster and framed by huge square-sectioned beams and pillars cut from dull red granite.

Some small choice pieces of Khafre's statues, heads and faces mostly, in a variety of stones and sizes, seem to have escaped Hölscher's workmen or were extracted from the sanded temple before his excavations had begun. Most of these strays were sold upon the international market, though for many years the lower half of a splendid seated life-sized Khafre statue in Chephren diorite had stood in an alleyway in old Cairo, at the back of Hatoun's Bazaar. Nonetheless, at the ending of the work, Hölscher sent fragments of half a dozen statues of the same fine type as Khafre and the hawk to the museum in the Tahrir Square; beauteous torsos and headless figures that curators with fewer wonders at their disposal would happily set in pride of place within their public galleries.

PLACING PHARAOH – *THE FIGURE AT THE CENTRE*

Though the sculpture of Khafre and the hawk has come to exemplify the age in which the four colossal pyramids were built, beyond such great grand monuments we know nothing of the man who sat upon that throne and little of his role within the state. Perhaps it was a combination of those colossal pyramids and judgements such as that which describe the royal statuary as possessing a 'remote and divine perfection' that first prompted the now-common notion that, like Hernán Cortés and Captain Cook, pharaohs such as Khafre had been regarded as living gods. Yet the notion of pharaonic divinity is as unsubstantiated as the modern myths that have come to surround Cortés and Cook, and all are products of their proponents regarding alien cultures with a patronizing eye.

Superficially, of course, some things are similar. Just as many European monarchs piously believed, as did their citizens, in their divine right of rule, so pharaohs also sat on thrones and, certainly, the officers of the kingdom had operated in the royal name. Just as the role of pharaoh in that state may have been entirely different from those of European kings, so too may have been the key concept of divinity.

Modern distinctions between natural and supernatural, mortal and divine, simply may not have existed: 'In some religions,' as the egyptologist Ragnhild Finnestad remarks, ' . . . *ultimate reality*, concurs within the terrestrial world'.

In such circumstances, all the world but only the world would have existence. And in that world, the modern line between divine and earthly power, between gods and mortals, the seen and unseen, the living and the dead, would simply demarcate a change of state within a single living system. If that were true within the ancient valley of the Nile, then pharaoh's Egypt would have been conceived as completely self-contained. A universe in which all life, from the rising of the Nile to the movements of the sun and stars, from a seated king to a sprouting seed, from a wheeling hawk to a couchant lion, shares a common invigorating unseen energy; the same energy that is held within the wings that touch the sides of Khafre's head. In such a lively universe, the mystery of the Sphinx is no longer a Christmas cracker riddle: its solution, that the grandiose combination of lion and snake and a portrait of the living king had manifested some previously unseen aspects of the royal office.

This conception of the world would explain why some of the names in the oldest surviving king lists are those of gods, for both the gods and humankind would have been conceived as different entities, seen and unseen, inhabiting the same living world. It would also explain why such care had been lavished upon the dead of the lower Nile since the age of the first farmers. Though their spirit and body could be seen to have divided, their ultimate reality, seen and unseen, remained within the living valley.

In concrete terms, some of the first-known images of pharaoh show him clutching a mace and in the act of taking life. The same archaic pharaohs are also shown sitting at the centre of open courts overseeing the presentation and offering of tithes that will supply the royal households and those of their courtiers with food and all their other needs. And in those open courts, both animals and people are dispatched. Whether brandishing a mace or seated at the centre of an offering court, the images of the early pharaohs consistently show them as the active and sustaining link between the seen and unseen aspects of the courtly state.

*The pharaoh Den, who ruled two centuries before King Khafre, pictured
in two contemporary ivory plaques. One shows him in the classic pose
of smiting an enemy, the other, ceremonially enthroned within an open
court. Both are less than two inches high.*

Coupled with efficient systems of tithing and supply conducted in
the name of pharaoh, the valley's prodigious fertility had promoted
such colossal surpluses within the state that, after some four centuries,
the government was able to conceive and undertake the construction
of four colossal pyramids and their attendant temples. And the
temples of those pyramids were centred around facilities for offering
where those same archaic rites of presentation were yet undertaken.
And the small rooms in these temples held some of the physical trap-
pings of archaic kingship.

Surviving fragments of relief from the walls of those same temples –
temples where statues such as those of Sneferu and Khafre were set
up – show rows of bearers bringing produce from the royal estates as
offerings to the royal cult of the dead kings whose carefully preserved
corpses lay within the pyramids beyond. Such images are miniature
versions of the state's system of supply, the system that had enabled
the creation of those tomb chapels and temples, supplied offerings to
the dead kings and provisioned the living court. Such offerings had
once been presented to the kings in the archaic courts, whilst links
between previous and present generations were also maintained
within the pyramids' attendant cemeteries where, in the royal name,
the dead courtiers were also presented with regular offerings by
specially appointed officiants. Along with making tombs and temples,

these well-regulated year-round activities were the living definition of the state.

And pharaoh was the focus of this state, the fulcrum of that system which served and supplied the households of the court in life and death. So the essential office of the man sitting at the centre of this system – King Khafre and his hawk, his antecedents and successors – is best described in modern terms as that of a sacerdotal priest, the single figure whose offices in life and death penetrated and synchronized the energies contained within the ancient valley of the lower Nile and placed them at the service of his people.

8

Finding Menkaure

*The Excavations of George Andrew
Reisner, 1906–10*

PYRAMID TEMPLE

*There they lay, rosy and solemn in the distance – those old,
majestical, mystical, familiar edifices.*

William Thackeray, Giza, October 1844

Three great pyramids comprise the celebrated line of monuments at
Giza. Excavations at the third and smallest of them began on Christmas Day 1906, when George Andrew Reisner's workmen laid down
a small iron railway line to transport carriageloads of surface sand
and rubble to a nearby dump. Then the great Harvard archaeologist
ordered his team of sixty excavators to dig down into the ruin of the
temple that lay upon the pyramid's east side.

The pyramid and its adjacent temple had been built to house the
burial and the funeral cult of King Menkaure, who had succeeded
Khafre to the throne. Menkaure was later celebrated in the tales of
Greek travellers as the king who, on being told that he would live for
but a few short years, outwitted the prophecy by doubling his time on
earth with the night-time use of flaming torches, a process perhaps
describing a pharaonic siesta that turned one day into two.

In Menkaure's own time, his craftsmen had taken a similarly
unusual route, setting his pyramid immediately behind his father's
monument, which was more than twice its height, and striping a
large part of its exterior with blocks of rough red granite. And so
today, though its size would not be matched again in all of Egypt's
history, Menkaure's pyramid appears as a delicate and compact

monument, the smallest of that famous line of three, set back from the great cemeteries, alone within the silent desert.

As if in compensation for its diminutive size, parts of the temple wall that Reisner's men first freed from the surrounding sand and rubble were found to hold some of the largest blocks of stone that pharaonic masons would ever use. Weighing more than 200 tons, they had been dragged up the escarpment and into their positions at the pyramid's east face from the limestone quarries down below. Reisner's men found plentiful evidence of these extraordinary labours; some of those colossal blocks are still sitting on the granite rollers with which they had been manoeuvred into position, whilst red-brushed survey marks within the temple and some small neat stones set up and down the causeway record the various levels that Menkaure's masons and builders had established as they worked.

By mid March, as excavation continued, Reisner could see that the pyramid's temple had never been completed. Many of its walls were but half built, and some of its rooms were yet filled with building rubble. Texts on the surviving fragments of a small stone stela told the story. In Reisner's translation:

> Under the Majesty of the King of Upper and Lower Egypt, Shepseskaf, the Horus, in the year of the first census of the large and small cattle, he made it, as his monument for his father, the King of Upper and Lower Egypt [Menkaure].

In the manner of the times, the dead king's successor to the throne had completed the arrangements for his predecessor's burial and funerary cult, the royal builders finishing Menkaure's monuments in mud brick rather than in limestone; so as Reisner's men dug ever deeper into the windblown sand that filled the temple's corridors and rooms they found it darkened with silt from mud bricks that had part-dissolved in desert downpours.

In one of the narrow columned halls still part-protected by the temple's roofing blocks, the workmen found a little Roman cemetery, some twenty bodies all carefully interred and decorated with charms and amulets made in the first century AD. Medieval Arab coins were also scattered through the building, dropped, so Reisner assumed, by treasure seekers or by masons quarrying some of the temple's stone.

Beneath all that, several of the temple's magazines still held the original paraphernalia of royal offering: fragments of some very ancient
hard-stone bowls, some domestic pottery, and caches of flint slaughtering knives, dull from wear, such as had been made and used within
the royal court since its beginning. There, too, were mud sealings
from long-lost boxes and papyrus rolls, many of them bearing the
impressions of the names of a variety of kings from the reign of
Shepseskaf to the last monarchs of the Old Kingdom – for the temple
had been used to offer to the cult of Menkaure for several centuries.
In those same times, so Reisner found, the later generations of officiating priests had rebuilt and reshaped parts of the great old temple
and made burial chambers and tomb chapels for their families and
themselves within a nearby quarry.

As Reisner's men dug down onto the temple's flagstone floor, they
found scattered fragments of alabaster statues, large and small, and
what later proved to be, after several of its fragments had been set
back together, a majestic over life-sized alabaster statue of King Menkaure seated on a throne. This statue, Reisner thought, was set up in
a small room which had overlooked the temple's open court and had
been the focus of the produce and provisions that the priests had
offered to the dead king down through the generations.

The statue stands today in a museum in Boston, Massachusetts,
the town in which Reisner lived and worked. Unlike the statue of
Khafre and the hawk, it is little celebrated but it is nonetheless extraordinary for all that. Flanked by the two striped triangles of the
nemes headdress, the king's wide-eyed almost friendly face is beautifully sculpted, the brisk marks of copper chisels showing its sculptor
cutting directly into the creamy stone in an almost modern way,
leaving only some quick black brushstrokes to delineate the royal
eyebrows and moustache. This friendly face, however, was set upon a
torso and a pair of shoulders so improbably wide as to give the king
the appearance of an American football player: another attempt, perhaps, following Khafre's statues and the Sphinx, to express the special
qualities of the man who sat upon the throne. Yet, just as that statue
appears a little odd to us today, so too this experiment in altering the
scale of those parts of the standard pharaonic figure would seldom be
repeated.

VALLEY TEMPLE

In 1906–07, assisted by Mr. C. M. Firth, I cleared the temple against the eastern face of the Third Pyramid . . . In the summer of 1908, with Mr. Oric Bates as field director, the excavation of the valley temple was begun, and in 1909–10 it was completed by myself and Mr. C. S. Fisher.

George Andrew Reisner, 1931

The next season's excavations, Reisner single-mindedly decided, would begin in June 1908, in the roaring heat of summer. With the excavation of Menkaure's pyramid temple completed, he was looking for the second temple which, precedent affirmed, should lie at the other end of the causeway whose traces could still be seem running westwards from the portal of the pyramid temple down towards the Nile Valley. The lower section of this causeway, however, had simply vanished into the sand. So the hunt began with the expedition's surveyors setting a series of iron rods into the limestone plateau at a hundred yards apart, running down from the pyramid temple in a line which followed the scars in the rock that echoed the lines of the largely vanished causeway. A week later, after six such rods had been set down, deep in the sandy valley which lies to the east of the three great pyramids, they came across the upper sections of mud-brick walls. Some 300 yards from Khafre's splendid valley temple and the Giza Sphinx, close to the quays of the pharaonic harbour, they had uncovered part of the ruins of Menkaure's long-lost valley temple, buried deep in placid horizontal strata that had been deposited by flash floods running off the desert at the ending of the Old Kingdom.

From the beginning of the work Reisner saw that, like the pyramid temple high above, this temple had also been left unfinished, presumably at the death of Menkaure. Unlike the temple by the pyramid, however, building at the valley temple had barely started, and once again Shepseskaf's builders had finished the monument, erecting a considerable structure for the reception of his father's mortuary cult, with thick mud-brick walls and wooden columns and doorways set on flagstone floors.

Reisner's excavators had begun their clearance where the first mud-brick walls had come to light and these, so it transpired, had been built behind the temple's open courtyard. Ten feet high and well preserved, these corridor-like rooms were entirely filled with soft windblown sand stained with the gentle dust of decayed mud brick. And there it was, deep in that fine dust, just ten days after the excavation had begun and close to the Nile's water table, that statues started to appear within those dank interiors. Tilted and askew, stacked one behind the other and carved from grey-green siltstone, each sculpted block held two or three exquisitely carved figures some four and five feet high.

On 10 July 1908, Reisner records, at 3.30 in the afternoon in the narrow room that they had numbered three, the first of the triads was uncovered; half an hour later, another had been located, and in the following half hour two more. During the months that followed, as they excavated the entire temple, more fine sculpture and thousands of sculptured fragments were found, some of which, as their inscriptions showed, had been made in times both earlier and later than the reign of Menkaure. In one area, they found twelve unfinished sculptures in various stages of completion. And here, the craftsmen had stored their tools along with those uncompleted works; stone pounders for roughing out the hard-stone blocks and tiny copper chisels to finish and outline the smallest forms. All together, it was the largest and most complete group of Old Kingdom royal sculptures ever found, the soft sand and dissolving mud-brick storerooms having preserved many of those works in a state of near perfection.

As soon as the statues were freed from the sand and silt, groups of Reisner's workmen, singing as they walked, carried the finest pieces in padded wooden slings to his nearby camp. In the division at the ending of the dig, and after considerable negotiations between the various colonial agencies who were controlling Egypt at that time, the great cache of sculptures was divided between the Cairo Museum and the Boston Museum of Fine Arts.

Reisner subsequently devoted a second five-month season to the further clearance of the temple, working through the winter of

1909 and into the spring of the following year. In the other narrow storerooms, buried once again in the compacted silt, they found quantities of objects that had been used by the temple priests and lain largely untouched since the last days of the royal cult. And they found masses of stone vases too, splendid specimens, many of them centuries old in the time of Menkaure and Shepseskaf, and some of them, indeed, bearing the names of the first pharaohs.

Wonders of a different order had come to light as Reisner's workmen had dug further into this desert time capsule. At the upper temple beside Menkaure's pyramid, they had excavated a central open court whose paving stones were smoothed by centuries of ritual, as generations of priests had presented the offerings of the royal cult. In the lower temple, however, those same priestly generations had built a dozen houses in its central open courtyard; tiny high-walled dwellings set higgledy-piggledy upon its splendid limestone floor amongst a maze of alleys, so that the entire courtyard, a paved rectangle of twenty by forty-seven yards, had been packed with various domestic necessities – with bedrooms and reception rooms, with ovens, animal pens, pottery workshops and clusters of rounded grain bins standing side by side like gatherings of mud cocoons. Just as a little stone stela found in the excavations proclaimed, this had been the 'pyramid settlement of Menkaure' and had thrived for centuries.

The presence of this small community within the open court provided an explanation for the splendid statues that had been stacked up nearby in the temple's so-called storerooms. Statues which, as Hölscher's excavations in the nearby temple of King Khafre suggest, had once stood around the four sides of a central court. So as the open court of Menkaure's valley temple had been transformed into a priestly settlement, its statuary had been carefully gathered up and stored in the temple's little rooms behind the open court.

These substantial modifications to the royal architecture of offering had not signalled the ending of court involvement with this temple. Reisner found that in the Old Kingdom's final decades, some three centuries after its foundation, the temple had been changed again. Though the little settlement within its courtyard was left untouched, a massive rectangle of brand new mud brick had been set right around the temple, complete with a grand new entrance. And a new small offering hall was built behind the houses of the settlement, with a row of four great wooden columns and two pairs of life-sized alabaster seated statues of King Menkaure. Though badly damaged, Reisner found large parts of those four statues still standing where the ancient builders set them. Antique when they were placed in their new setting, for they were surely taken from the nearby sculpture storerooms, they yet held a considerable beauty.

9

Royal Households

KINGS AND QUEENS

The bulk of the evidence preserved to us of the arts, the crafts, and the culture of Dynasty IV, one of the great creative periods of Egyptian civilization, was contained in the royal cemetery at Giza.

George Andrew Reisner, 1931

'In the temples of Mycerinus,' Reisner calculated, 'the Harvard-Boston Expedition found seventeen statues equal in preservation to the thirteen already known of Dynasty IV and in addition fifteen statuettes ... Five of the seventeen statues were practically perfect, and two were nearly complete, giving us seven portraits of Mycerinus, one of the queen, and eight faces of Hathor and the nome-deities.' This was the largest haul of royal Old Kingdom statues ever to be found.

The 'queen' to which Reisner refers is one of two slightly under life-sized figures of a perfectly preserved, though entirely uninscribed, dyad in which a woman stands beside the figure of a *nemes*-wearing king who has the features of a man identified on the bases of several of the other sculptures as Menkaure. Reisner's 'nome-deities', alternatively, are sculpted images of both men and women wearing elaborate headdresses whose forms are those of the hieroglyphic names of some of the geographic regions – the so-called 'nomes' – of ancient Egypt. In each of those fine sculptures, the figure of the king is named as Menkaure upon its base and is flanked on one side by a nome deity and on the other by the goddess Hathor, the mother of Horus and thus a goddess with very close connection to the ruling monarch.

Four of these triads were recovered in near-perfect condition along with fragments of several others, whilst other similar pieces had already appeared on the antiquities market before Reisner had begun his excavation. Originally, so it has been suggested, there had been eight of these fine groups, one for each region that later in pharaonic history would have especial connection with Hathor. An alternative suggestion is that there had once been more than forty of them, one for each pharaonic nome. At all events, those that have survived are remarkable and rare sculptures and the first-known examples of their type.

Reisner found pieces of several other types of statue at the temple, most of which were images of the king. Some had been made of ivory, red granite and alabaster, others of diorite and porphyry, whilst several inlaid crystal eyes and a single wooden arm found loose within the temple's filling hint at lost works that had been made of more fragile materials. The better part of Menkaure's surviving statues, however, were sculpted in a placid and finely textured siltstone brought from a quarry in the Eastern Desert which had been quarried by craftsmen 3,000 years before the time of Menkaure and was yet used in Roman times.

If it is firmly struck and the chisels are frequently re-sharpened, this siltstone can be worked with copper tools. It can also be cut with copper saws provided their teeth are fed with a stream of powdered carbide or corundum dust; Reisner found tell-tale traces of a bright green copper oxide from those saw blades still lying in saw cuts on the sculptures' bases. With the aid of just such abrasives, siltstone can also be brought to a high and even polish, a quality subtly employed by Menkaure's craftsmen to emphasize the faces and upper torsos of their sculptures, so that their detail sparkles and the eye is drawn towards them.

The surviving fragments show that hundreds of working craftsmen had been making sculptures for all the kings for whom great pyramids were made. Like the labour forces that built pyramids, the royal sculpture workshops must have been a considerable enterprise in

which the state supplied everything from provisions for the craftsmen's households to the smelted copper of their tools and the blocks
of desert stone on which they worked.

It is not yet known where these sculpture workshops or the dwellings of the craftsmen's households had been situated. Though Reisner
recovered some fifteen unfinished hard-stone sculptures in various
states of completion he found no dust or chippings from their manufacture, which would suggest that they had been brought to the valley
temple from the royal workshops, presumably after the king had died
and work upon his projects halted. In all likelihood, those studios had
been situated in the general vicinity of the Giza harbour, along with
the royal residence and the large and various settlements built to house
and provision the pyramid builders and which are presently in the
processes of excavation. Presumably the sculptor craftsmen and their
households had followed the pyramid builders and the royal residence,
generation after generation, as they had moved up and down the west
bank of the Nile from the site of one great pyramid to the next.

This scenario is supported by the consistency and quality of the
surviving royal sculptures which, though the contemporary pyramids
are some twenty miles apart, are all products of a century-long sculptural tradition that held within it a characteristic range of techniques
and of drawing, along with a developing royal iconography and a
standard set of royal poses. In no way, however, was this a sculptural
tradition in a Western sense; not a part of an improving journey
towards the imitation of a kind of 'naturalism' in which successive
generations endeavoured to make works of art that 'look more real'
than before.

Nonetheless, some changes were made within those generations
that appear to have been based upon aesthetic choice. Earlier archaic
craftsmen, for example, had generally sculpted the heads of their
human subjects at a larger size in relation to the rest of the human
body than that of later times. To that extent, at least, Sneferu's sculptures and those of some of his successors represent a relatively new
and more 'realistic' canon for the human figure. Yet the giant alabaster statue of Menkaure has a far smaller head upon its shoulders than
those of the earlier kings. In similar fashion, the heads of some of the
sculptures of King Menkaure also appear less abstract, less formal to

the modern eye than the earlier head of Khafre with his hawk; they are so realistic, even, that they appear to represent the king in youth and middle age. Some of the fine limestone heads of Khufu's time, however, are yet more subtle in their detail and they had been made a half-century earlier. This apparent 'realism', therefore, speaks not of progress in a Western sense, but of choice and, ultimately, of the pharaonic sculptors' enduring fascination with their ability to endow hard stone with life. These, then, are the relics of a school of sculpture that enlarged, explored and re-made a set of archaic forms to create the beginnings of a sophisticated millennial tradition that flourished till the times of the last pharaohs.

QUEENS AND GODDESSES

... it is in vain that we say what we see; what we see never resides in what we say.

Michel Foucault, 2002

In the dark world of Menkaure's siltstone sculptures the females in those statue groups – the goddesses, the nome deities and the unnamed woman of the perfect dyad – show off their archaic inheritance more insistently than the male figures, every one of them displaying the prominent geometric pubic triangle that is a direct inheritance from first-known female figurines of prehistoric times. With their high rounded breasts and their filmy skin-tight dresses, such formal elements set within the otherwise subtle modelling impart a curiously hypnagogic quality to these smoothly sculpted women.

As Reisner noted, Menkaure's craftsmen placed his images in the company of a variety of goddesses who, though their faces have different features from those of the sculpted king, are all similar to one another. And like the images of Menkaure who stands beside them, each one of them seems to be alone. For most of the figures in these sculptured groups have been made at different sizes; half life-sized to almost full life-sized figures appearing side by side giving a curious impression of their isolation that is further emphasized by the slight turn of many of the figure's heads, which makes them appear as if they are moving away from each other. So although their sculptors set them side by side within the same block of stone, to the modern eye each figure seems to inhabit its own space. Adding further to this sense of separation, every one of these sculpted figures is set upon an individual axis that runs right through its centre, a technique of stone working which provides most ancient Egyptian images with a profound sense of symmetry and stillness.

That is why, when the arms of one of those isolate stone women are sculpted so that they reach out so to embrace the king, the gesture seems electric. In the middle of the rock, these remote out-of-scale figures are joined by human gesture. Like the feathered wings of Khafre's little hawk, the care, the warm touch in the cold stone, is palpable. In a craftsman's act of super-realism, an instinctive gesture reaches out through time, through vagueness and confusion, as those women seem to present the figure of the king as might a proud mother set down her child before a family gathering.

MORTAL AND IMMORTAL

His family were himself and his wife and daughters, two mayds, and a man.

Star Chamber sessions, 1631–2

Inscriptions in the cemeteries beside the Giza pyramids tell that those most splendid monuments were not only made for male courtiers such as Hardjedef but also for women, for so-called queens, princesses and queen mothers. Confusingly, some of these women's names were employed for generation after generation, whilst the translations of their epithets and titles are not nearly as precise as some of their translations would suggest. So names alone cannot pinpoint a specific individual, whilst translated affiliations such as 'king's wife' or 'king's mother' should not be automatically employed as they often are, in ways that would horrify the genealogists of *Burke's Peerage* or the *Almanach de Gotha*.

Rather than representing physical interrelationship or, certainly, the relationships in modern marriage, such epithets appear to have been used as they often are in other societies, including our own, where terms like 'mother' and 'son' might stand for mother-in-law or friend or a picturesque variety of other designations. At the same time, however, the accumulation of those epithets within the cemeteries, their constant naming of the king and the placing of the tombs, suggests that they had housed the burials and cults of a group of men and women who appear to have been members of a single household, the household of the king.

Royal households were durable institutions. From the time of Sneferu and the first colossal pyramids down to the ending of the Old Kingdom, throughout that four-century span, the surviving records appear to indicate that the throne had moved between diverse branches of a single household.

Nothing is known of this household's domestic arrangements. Traditionally, historians have graded the royal women, who are more numerous than men, according to the size and number of their monuments and the translations of their inscriptions as a 'king's wife and/or mother', or as a 'minor wife' who might also be termed as fancy takes, a 'concubine', a member of the harem and, even, a 'sub-wife'. At all events, the numbers and interrelationships of those named and buried within royal cemeteries shows that the royal household was not a family unit in the manner of the households built in the courtyard of Menkaure's valley temple. Nor, indeed, does it appear to have been the same as those within the households of contemporary courtiers.

Given that the numerous monuments of the royal women hold none of the titles which appear in the tombs of male members of the royal household or those, indeed, of male courtiers, it appears that they had no stated role in court affairs or government administration. Nonetheless, within the Giza cemeteries of Khufu's time their names are more frequently recorded than those of the male princes; the so-called 'queen's tombs' taking up the best part of the space beside the royal pyramid. Traditionally described as 'great queens', three of these women appear to have been buried in the row of three small pyramids, each one with its own diminutive temple, that stand beside King Khufu's great monument, a pattern that is repeated alongside the pyramid of Menkaure. At Giza, then, the continuing power and presence of some of the women of the royal household was marked by mighty tombs and nourished in ritual offerings in their temples. Perhaps the powerful presence of women in the royal cemeteries not only stemmed from a personal association with the living king but also from the awareness that the force of life, the force of society itself, which the works of the court craftsmen so insistently celebrate, is the vital product of both sexes.

At all events, the traditional assumption that the pharaohs had ruled like European kings and kept closed harems is based on those traditional translations, on nineteenth-century courtly manners and, ultimately, Champollion's secular vision. Better to drop such Eurocentric notions along with the quaint assumption that the 'family' of the king held genius in its generations and was stuffed with princely craftsmen, architects and engineers endowed with the abilities to raise vast pyramids and make some of the world's great sculptures. Better to conceive the Old Kingdom court as an environment where such talents had been cultivated within a series of courtly households grouped around that of the ruling house.

And the single central office in that rare society was that of pharaoh. It sustained the living and the dead. It alone bestrode the households of the gods and those of humankind. No wonder, then, that unlike the households of the courtiers there is no evidence of an established order of direct familial succession for the throne.

10

After Giza

MARKING TIME

By the ending of the Old Kingdom, a twenty-mile-long line of pyramids stood on the western horizon at the end of the Nile Valley. From the stepped silhouettes of the earliest pyramids to the smooth-shining magnificence of the colossal monuments of Sneferu, Khufu and Khafre and the smaller pyramids of later kings, each one of those royal tombs had been a separate enterprise for a different king and was the product of a series of events in passing time. These pyramids, therefore, mark the arrival of a different kind of time within the ancient valley of the lower Nile, a fresh representation of its passing from that held within the prehistoric settlements where time had been measured by the movements of the sun and moon and stars, the annual processes of flood and drought, sowing, growth and harvest.

The royal sculptures of the pyramid-building kings share this same new sense of time. Whereas generations of prehistoric craftsmen had made generic images whose forms had hardly changed down through millennia, the craftsmen of the Old Kingdom court made different images for every king. Yet the ancient scribes do not appear to have written individual histories for them. Nor did they bother to record their lineal descent, such records as survive serving only to record the years of individual reigns. To that extent at least, the pharaonic state, its kings and queens, its gods and goddesses, maintained the rhythms of prehistoric life within the region of the lower Nile; continuity, after all, was fundamental to the concept and identity of the offices of pharaoh, and its fundamental expression was the form of the royal pyramid.

At the same time and with considerable care, scribal chronologers compiled lists of the names of successive pharaohs. A later example of just such a list is the so-called Canon that Champollion discovered in Turin. Similar records had been compiled since the days of the first pharaohs. And in the centuries after the four colossal pyramids were built, some of the information held in those early records, along with brief accountings of some of the court's activities, were set into lengthy lists engraved on slabs of stone.

THE PALERMO STONE AND OTHER ANNALS

The most celebrated fragment of the ancient king lists – the so-called royal annals – is an irregular piece of diorite known as the Palermo

The Palermo Stone, the largest surviving fragment of the Old Kingdom's royal annals. The basalt slab is 17 inches high, 2.5 inches thick and has texts on both sides.

Stone after the Sicilian town in whose museum it somewhat mysteriously resides. Just seventeen inches high and a foot wide, the relic came from the collections of Antonio Salinas, a classicist, who took part in several excavations on that perfumed island in the last decades of the nineteenth century. How he had acquired his greatest treasure is unrecorded. Where originally had that stone stood? Did Salinas find it during an excavation or had it been part of the ballast of an ancient boat brought up in a fisherman's nets and sold to the local *professore*?

Other smaller fragments engraved with similar texts to those on the Palermo Stone appeared on the Cairo antiquities market in the first decades of the twentieth century. They could be fragments of the same set of annals or morsels of other king lists that are otherwise unknown. That some of them were rumoured to have been built into the walls of medieval Cairo suggests that they had been taken from the region of ancient Memphis, which is but a few miles south of the modern capital on the west bank of the Nile.

Another, different set of Old Kingdom annals came to light in the 1990s and is known as the South Saqqara Stone. Found in Memphis' southern cemeteries, its inscriptions had been haphazardly engraved upon an antique eight-foot-long rectangular slab of basalt that had been re-polished and re-used as a coffin lid for the burial of a late Old Kingdom queen. Though excavated in the 1930s, its ill-cut texts had been mostly rubbed away during the stone's re-polishing and they were only recognized as another set of royal annals decades after the slab's discovery.

If, as is most likely, all of these variously fragmented inscriptions had been engraved at some time late in the Old Kingdom, they would be the world's oldest compilations of historical records. For though each separate entry in these annals has been compiled in the same distinctive format as the terse accounts of individual events from the times of the first pharaohs which had been engraved on small rectangular plaques of ebony and ivory, these later annals appear to have gathered all that information together and placed it into gridded rectangles in the manner in which contemporary accounting scribes entered lists of goods and people on papyri.

First, the name of every individual king was set at the top of a section of the grid, each king's name having been placed within the grid in the order in which he had reigned. Underneath those royal names further sets of horizontal lines were subdivided into equally sized rectangles, each one of which represented a year of an individual's rule. These held spare descriptions of court events that had taken place during that time. Underneath those lines of yearly records, further short texts set into another narrow register listed the height of each year's inundation, the single essential forecast in that rainless land of the coming harvest and thus of the resources that the court would have at its disposal.

Given that translations of such archaic texts differ widely in interpretation, and that what survives is very fragmented, a rare near intact example of an entry on the Palermo Stone, a record of a year of Sneferu's reign holds something resembling the following information:

[King] Sneferu [year 14?]

Setting up 35 estates with people and 122 cattle-farms.

Construction of one ship of cedar/pine wood [named] 'Adoring the Two Lands', of 100 cubits [c.170 feet], and two ships of 100 cubits of meru wood.

Seventh occasion of the count [a cattle census].

[Nile height] 5 cubits, 1 palm, 1 finger [8 feet 10 4/5 inches].

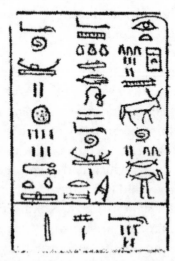

The record of a single year on the Palermo Stone – probably that of year 14 of the reign of Sneferu. A tentative translation is given above.

If the annals of the Palermo Stone had held the names of all the kings of the first five dynasties, then the size of the gently quavering grid lines that yet survive on both its front and back suggest that those annals had originally extended for some seven feet and more. In similar fashion, the South Saqqara Stone seems to have provided an equivalent record for the kings of the Sixth Dynasty, its listings finishing, it would appear, around 2150 BC, about half way through the lengthy reign of Pepi II, who is considered to have been the Old Kingdom's last major monarch.

Happily, the few surviving year dates on the stone annals share broad agreement with the fragments of the Turin Canon that was compiled more than a millennium later. Their data also tallies with some other shorter king lists that were engraved and painted in some of the later standing monuments and they tally too, though less precisely, with most of the surviving fragments of Manetho's history. In their present highly damaged state, however, their somewhat inscrutable texts provide little more than keyhole histories of the individual years of largely anonymous reigns.

What these broken annals do clearly show is the type of information that the Old Kingdom court wanted to preserve, that is, a year-by-year account of some of its activities: a statue of a god was made, land colonized, a chapel built, a census undertaken. The vast work of constructing pyramids and other courtly tombs is never mentioned, only the lesser activities of the living court: that, and the all-commanding fact of the height of the annual flood.

None of these records, however, not the annals nor all the other ancient king lists put together, contain sufficient data to enable the construction of an unbroken timeline for pharaonic history. Even the fragments of the Turin Canon, the yardstick against which all other records are yet judged, preserve the names of less than half the Old Kingdom monarchs that are recorded on the monuments. Since the times of Champollion and Lepsius, therefore, one of the great prizes of traditional egyptological research has been the retrieval of texts and inscriptions that augment the data of those broken king lists; these, for the most part being builders' graffiti left on the blocks of tombs and pyramids and similar short texts which for a variety of purposes record the year of rule, the season, month and day, in the reign of a specific king.

Some 200 of those useful documents are now known from Old Kingdom times alone, from hieratic notations scribbled on pots and papyrus to quarryman's dockets sloppily painted in red ochre on the limestone of a pyramid block. In 1999, one such graffito found on a rock in the Sahara, provided a unique record of a 'year 24' of the reign of Khufu and served, therefore, as a correction to his previously recorded reign length of 23 years as is recorded in the Turin Canon.

TIME PRESENT AND TIME PAST

Thomasin's hair ... was braided according to a calendric system: the more important the day the more numerous the braids.

Thomas Hardy, 1878

As generations of scholars worked to build a precise chronology for ancient Egypt they had to struggle with a knotty puzzle bequeathed by Fourier and Dupuis. Like those two eighteenth-century academicians, the ancient Egyptians had been inveterate stargazers and from the earliest of times had recorded the specific year and season, month and day in the reign of a specific king in which certain celestial events had taken place. Many pharaonic monuments, too, were precisely orientated to specific celestial events and many of them held the names of the kings in whose reigns they had been constructed. All of which, it seemed to the chronologers, held out the possibility of retrieving a scientifically determined chronology of the pharaohs based on a modern mathematical re-calculation of the dates of those ancient celestial events.

The ancient fascination with stargazing was an unfathomable inheritance. Since the times of the hunter gatherers, humankind had recorded observations that had tracked celestial events that marked intervals of human time. With the coming of the kings, these observations were employed to set the monuments and the rhythms of court life and temple ritual in concert with the movements of the sun, moon and stars. Just as the passage of the sun marked day and night, just as the waxing and waning of the moon marked out months of time, just as the rising of a star could mark the duration of a year, so too, a variety of solar and stellar events were used to orientate the baselines of pyramids to high degrees of accuracy and to set the axes of many tombs and temples.

Rather than straightforwardly employing a lunar calendar like most other ancient peoples, by the times of the great pyramids the principal pharaonic calendar was fixed by the so-called tropical year, that is, by the year that is measured out in solar solstices, which in the strange environment of the valley of the lower Nile with its north–south axis had immediate and tangible concordance. The tropical year was then subdivided into twelve months of thirty days with five extra days added at the beginning of each year – the 'five outside the year', as they were sometimes called – which were intended to keep that 360-day calendar attached to the rhythms of the farming year. This is the calendar, so it appears, that was later adopted by the Romans, who added an additional day every fourth year to further slow its progress around the farming year. As one authority has remarked, it is 'the only intelligent calendar which has ever existed in human history', and with a few further tweaks it is the calendar of the modern world.

In that rainless kingdom where the annual flooding of the Nile heralded a season of cultivation and harvest, which in turn was succeeded by months of fiery heat, the agricultural year was divided into just three seasons – *Akhet*, *Peret* and *Shemu* – the translations of which have been variously disputed since Champollion's day, but which represent, respectively, such terms as '[Nile] Flood' or 'Autumn'; 'Growing' or 'Winter'; and 'Summer' or 'Harvest'. Lacking the Roman leap year, however, the 365-day calendar moved inexorably round the farming year, and though the rate of this disjunction would hardly have been apparent in the course of a few decades, for a great deal of the time the two would not have coincided and farmers would have found themselves sowing in the season named as 'Harvest'. But then, of course, all farmers are well aware of the times of planting and of harvest and would hardly be confused by the names of a man-made calendar. Nor is the simultaneous use of two different calendars, one for the court and another for the farm, particularly confusing. Christmas, for example, is a solar festival, and so it travels around the modern week; Easter, on the other hand, a traditional time for planting in the Christian world, is determined by the phases of the moon and fixed to a three-day period at the end-ing of a week.

The farming year along the lower Nile was also marked by other celestial events. The rising of Sirius, for example, the brightest of all stars, is but briefly seen in the early morning of one day in every year before it fades away as the sun lightens the dawn sky. This remark-able event occurred around the same time as the beginning of the Nile's annual inundation – a connection that was recognized when Sirius was dubbed 'the opener of the year'. So the heliacal rising of Sirius, as it is now called, was described in texts inscribed upon the walls of pyramids where the rising of that star and the annual inun-dation of the Nile are both identified as aspects of the endless transformations, from death to life, of the dead kings. And the spe-cific day and month of Sirius' rising within the tropical calendar was frequently recorded, in temple calendars and in graffiti and on water clocks and papyri, beside the name of the living king and the number of years that he had ruled when the observation had been made.

Yet Sirius' heliacal rising was never an infallible herald of the Nile flood. At Aswan in the south, the flood waters rose ten days before their arrival in the region of Memphis close to modern Cairo and then again, the flood might be weeks early or weeks late in its long journey north. The day of Sirius' annual rising, moreover, changes according to the latitude at which it is observed, there being a two or three day difference between Aswan and ancient Memphis, which are some 500 miles apart. So like the festival of Easter, the observation of such cosmic events set the Egyptians gently, rather than scientifically, in tune with the universe's rhythms. Not Newton but the Nile.

There is as well a considerable element of imprecision when observ-ations of stellar events are made with the naked eye. The visibility and positioning of stars, especially those low down on the horizon, are subject to a range of climatic variations that can bend their light and make precise observation of a recurrent event well-nigh impos-sible. Even the phases of the moon can appear to vary in the eyes of different observers from between 28 to 30 days.

Many of these imprecisions and ambiguities seem relatively small. Yet the spans of time with which modern chronologers of ancient Egypt have to contend are so vast that entire generations can disappear within such small divergences. Lacking the additional day that a leap year provides, for example, the 365 days of the ancient Egyptian year had spun around the true annual calendar in a 1,460 year cycle – a fact that, until the 1940s, had led some chronologers to build an extra cycle into their dates and thus to place the construction of the first pyramids a millennium and half earlier than their present, well-established, dates.

Given such a host of variables, the accurate placement of anciently recorded cosmic events in modern time still requires the ancient astronomical data to be checked against the king lists of conventional chronologies. And that, of course, defeats the purposes of Fourier's original exercise.

Nonetheless, two centuries of stargazing and calendar counting has provided remarkable evidence of how time was measured in the ancient communities of the lower Nile and how, eventually, the state moved to control it. For the yearly records of the earliest kings whose reigns are recorded on the Palermo Stone are not counted in tropical years but from the rising of the Nile, and the months that follow are measured by lunar observations. In archaic times, therefore, the beginning of each year could have been counted differently at separate locations and might well have been divided at those different locations into eleven, twelve or even thirteen lunar months, depending upon individual observations of the moon on the day that the Nile had been seen to start to rise in flood, or even the day that Sirius had been observed to rise.

Such straightforward arrangements would have provided a well-measured life for a community of farmers. At the same time, every separate settlement up and down the river could have had a slightly different calendar, an arrangement that was hardly satisfactory for co-ordinating the operations of a court drawing supplies and sustenance from settlements all along the valley of the lower Nile. Unfortunately, the fragmentary record of the Palermo Stone does not show when the 360 days plus five days of the solar calendar was introduced, only that it was in operation in the reign of Menkaure. In all probability it had been implemented when the colossal pyramids were under construction, and a single operating calendar for the entire kingdom would have been of huge advantage. A further pointer to the time of its adoption may well be held in the alignments of several small non-funerary pyramids that were built along the lower Nile in the ages before and during the reign of Sneferu. For recent measurements suggest that these little monuments may have been orientated to form parts of a single solar sighting system that had enabled the establishment of the same solar calendar throughout the kingdom.

At all events, in later history both those calendars, solar and stellar, were specifically identified with the offices of pharaoh, part of the rites of accession including a royal vow to leave the order of the year unchanged. At accession, therefore, pharaoh took control not only of the land and all of its resources – the very space of ancient Egypt – but also of its time; facts that had been majestically announced long since in the near perfect cosmic orientation of the four great pyramids and the very materials of their construction, drawn as they were from all along the valley of the lower Nile.

TIME AND HISTORY

Where are the Jesters, the Buffoons, the Scarramuccioes?
Will not these afford a more pleasing entertainment?
                                        Vincent Alsop, 1696

Chronologies and calendars are not histories, of course, merely the scaffoldings on which histories are set. A scaffolding that two centuries of study has largely established. As far as pharaonic history is concerned, however, there is a crippling lack of data, so that traditional historians have had to shift as best they can, frequently constructing their narratives from accidental and quite random sources: odd scribbles on a rock, an inscribed axe head from a foreign river bed, a building sequence in a line of monuments, extrapolations from texts that for the most part are formal, formulaic and repetitive. In consequence, the resulting histories are reminiscent of the party game in which different people write single lines of text each ending with the words 'and then' onto a folded sheet of paper, which is then unfolded and read out as if it were a genuine continuous narrative.

Most historians, of course, tell stories based on cause and effect, on progressions and declines – the narrative of 'and then'. Thus constructed, traditional histories of ancient Egypt provide the impression that its history had been similarly driven. Setting pharaonic history in numbered years BC/AD simply adds to this seductive illusion of an underlying narrative of progress; it even seems to confirm a direct link to more modern histories. This, then, many yet believe, is real history; a bird's eye view, an evolutionary overview. As far as pharaoh's Egypt is concerned, however, the resulting histories do not reflect the unfolding story of that courtly culture as it is held in its surviving relics but, by treating the scanty fragments of the remaining evidence as if they were items in a single story, descend into simple cliché and compress whole generations.

They are the products of a narrow vision. Just as Western easel painting has traditionally represented three-dimensional objects in two dimensions and we easily assume that such images are 'true' and even 'scientific' – the latter claim supported by the impression that those old canvases bear resemblance to the monocular images of photographs – so traditional Western histories of ancient Egypt provide similar illusions. Yet even the most skilled draughtsmen of non-Western cultures may find such images curious and contradictory and require re-training before they can be taught to draw in the traditional Western manner. Certainly, neither Hardjedef nor the craftsmen of his day would have readily understood such images as photographs nor, indeed, the bird's eye views of archaeological reconstructions. They and the things they made inhabited a different space, another time, another universe.

When the ancient scribes and craftsmen drew out scenes of procession or of temple ritual as they often did, those happenings were not portrayed as an event that was taking place in time. This was not a Newtonian world, where time equates with a progress through space. Pharaonic narratives, alternatively, show different aspects of an event with images of its various protagonists set side by side. Nor are those images framed in narrative sequence as in a strip cartoon. There are

no befores and afters, no causes and effects, no narratives of progress. Like the texts that describe the destinies of the dead, those
images are not set in the past or in the future but in the present, in the
here and now.

Alongside the shared experiences of all humanity, hearth and
home, birth, death and procreation, the courtly culture of the lower
Nile inhabited a space in which the kings and gods, the seen and the
unseen, the living and the dead were all present in the living world.
Founded within the bounteous regular landscapes of the lower Nile,
this vision has the potential to provide a genuine narrative for ancient
Egypt. If its surviving relics are regarded in a manner that George
Kubler once described as embracing 'the whole range of man-made
things, including all tools and writing in addition to the . . . beautiful,
and poetic things of the world', it offers the promise of a direct contact
with the ancient people through the things they made. And as it traces
the history of those products through periods of plenty and impover-
ishment it provides a history of ancient Egypt as a series of spectacular
adventures in which succeeding generations heroically maintain a
single vision of an eternal present.

PART FOUR

Old Kingdom
Abusir and After,
2500–2200 BC

II

Abusir and Saqqara

BORCHARDT AT ABUSIR

On a fine day, standing on the breezy ridge of Memphis' desert cemeteries, the better part of Egypt's pyramids are in clear view, from Sneferu's colossal pyramids on the plain of Dahshur in the south to Giza's famous line of three dark triangles. Built for the most part in the twenty-sixth century BC, those mighty pyramids stand as bookends to a line of smaller ones that over the course of the next 300 years were set down between them: eleven royal monuments at least and maybe more yet to be discovered, along with their attendant temples and an uncounted mass of accompanying tombs.

Though these later pyramids were far smaller than their predecessors, their architecture less accurate, their masonry relatively rough and ill-assembled, they were nonetheless considerable monuments in their own right so that, although their temples and their causeways were abandoned and smothered in deep sand within centuries of their construction, most of the pyramids were never lost to view. So in the first half of the nineteenth century, the better part of them were picked and prodded by the work gangs of European adventurers and architects, most of whom were interested in the royal burial chambers and the treasures that they might contain. But hardly anyone had touched the buried temples that had stood beside them.

Large sand-choked monuments require archaeology on a heroic scale for their excavation, long-term well-funded enterprises that, in the majority of cases, it was these temples' good fortune to host: a succession of French archaeologists and the Egyptian *Service des Antiquités* working in the Saqqara cemeteries throughout the best part of the last century, a project that continues to this day. The heroic age of pyramid excavation, however, which set the pace for all later work, was undertaken in the decades before the First World War by George Reisner at Giza and by the Berlin archaeologist Ludwig Borchardt, who excavated a cluster of pyramids and temples on the Saqqara ridge some seven miles south of the Giza Plateau.

In Borchardt's time, the desert landscape in which those pyramids and temples had lain was different from that of today. Nowadays, you walk up to them past the farmhouses and villas of the village of Abusir from which these pyramids derive their modern name, past mud-plastered walls and shadowed groves of silvered palms, before stepping out onto the steep bright slopes of the desert beyond and, up above it all, the blunted tops of groups of sanded pyramids. In Borchardt's day, however, as in the distant past, those same pyramids had stood open to the Nile's valley and its wide green fields, a lonely landscape far smaller in its scale than Giza's high plateau. And the desert had been fringed with a spiky line of camel grass that marked the edges of the water table and framed the crops below.

After the scorching summer season in which the fields had cracked and nothing grew, after Sirius had risen with the Nile, the pyramids and temples of Abusir had stood close to the reflecting waters of the inundation, the flood covering the fields on both sides of the river. Then as it receded, so Borchardt's photographs show, it had left oxbow lakes and lines of water shining in the mud; these, perhaps, the distant echoes of ancient harbours and canals. After the 1960s, however, when the High Dam was built and filled and the annual flood had stopped, and tractors, pumps and irrigation schemes were introduced, the fields grew larger in their sizes and the deserts by the pyramids were inundated by a concrete flood of cemeteries and villas. The ancient ways of life beside the pyramids began to disappear, along with the landscapes in which those monuments had long been the commanding element. So the records of those early excavators – Reisner at Giza and Borchardt at Abusir, who were amongst the first to use photography to document their excavations – show the

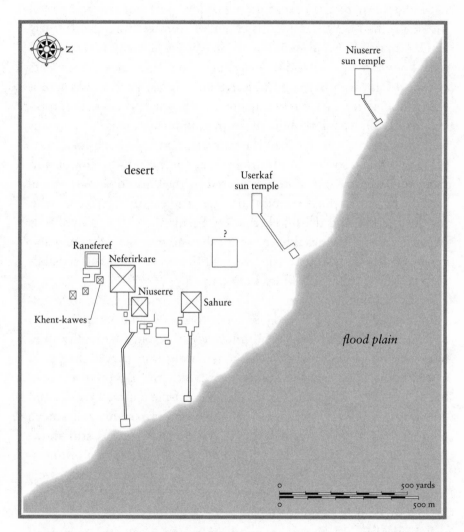

The major pyramids and temples of Abusir.

pyramids much as they had appeared during the previous 4,000 years, with billows of windblown sand covering their temples and their causeways, and the pyramids' peaks framing the edges of a broad green plain.

Unlike Reisner's Giza excavations, which apart from the temples of Menkaure had concentrated on courtiers' tombs, Borchardt largely worked upon the regal monuments at Abusir, clearing several of its eight known pyramids and temples, including the largest monuments at the site, those of Sahure, Niuserre and Neferirkare. And there it was, amongst the major monuments, that he made the most remarkable of his finds, for though those pyramids were smaller and less well built than those at Giza, the tumbled temples which lay beside those pyramids, so Borchardt discovered, had been more complex in their architecture and more variegated in their use of desert stone. And the beauty of those temples' architectural elements, the columns, the door jambs and the lintels that lay beside their ruined pyramids like necklaces half-buried in the sand, showed that the craftsmen and masons of the kings of Abusir had held the same skills and sensibilities as those of the Giza kings before them.

Borchardt uncovered wonders in those ruined temples. Granite columns carved in the perfected geometric forms of tight-bound bundles of papyrus stalks. Smooth round columns emblazoned with the names of kings with capitals like palm fronds so beautifully carved that, even in museums, their granite seems to wave in the Egyptian evening breeze. Even the huge monolithic elements of the temples' rooms and doorways, ramps and staircases that had been cut from massive blocks of stone had a light, fresh elegance. As his photographs still show, Borchardt's previous career as a *Königlicher Regierungsbauführer* – as a master builder of the King of Prussia – came to the fore as his work gangs struggled to manipulate and re-erect by hand and rope those dangerously tumbled ruins.

Published in a series of splendid folios and essays that extended from 1905 into the following decades, Borchardt's descriptions of the major monuments of Abusir and his architectural reconstructions of how they had appeared just after they were built – especially his distinctive graphics showing sharp blank buildings drawn in black and white and seen either from a bird's eye view or with a vanishing point

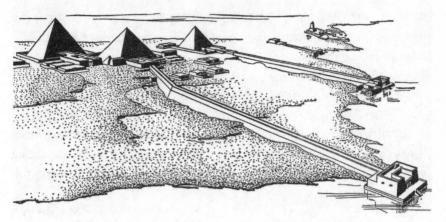

A bird's eye view of Abusir, after Ludwig Borchardt.

close to the ground – have influenced all subsequent visions of Egyptian pyramids.

A HISTORY IN PYRAMIDS

The kings whose pyramids stand at Abusir were the successors of the monarchs for whom the Giza pyramids were built. Like those of Giza, the royal pyramids at Abusir are also clustered in a group with some set one behind the other. And as at Giza, after some sixty years of pyramid building at Abusir, the kings' construction teams moved southwards once again, down along the desert's ridge back into the ancient cemeteries of Saqqara, where they made more tombs and pyramids over the next two centuries, down to the Old Kingdom's ending.

Little is known of the beginnings of the long-lived royal house for whom those pyramids had been constructed. In all probability, the pharaoh Sneferu, in whose reign the first two of the four colossal pyramids were built, was of the household of a little known predecessor called Huni, who is listed as the last ruler of Manetho's Third Dynasty of kings but whose funerary enclosure is yet undiscovered and whose memorials are small and brief. Certainly, from Sneferu down to Menkaure, the last of the Giza kings, the surviving evidence shows the throne passing down through generations of that same household and that the smaller pyramids and tombs built beside those three colossi in those same times were made for members of that royal household and for some leading members of the households of the courtiers.

In the decade following the death of Menkaure around 2515 BC, no pyramids were built at all; just two oblong monuments, long low bench-like rectangles of stone, architectural variants on the archaic so-called mastaba tomb, marking two colossal granite-lined burial vaults cut deep into the underlying desert. These show, at least, that pharaoh's craftsmen built pyramids by choice rather than blindly following tradition.

One of these unusual monuments had been built for Shepseskaf, Menkaure's successor to the throne, and was set in the desert of Saqqara some ten miles to the south of Menkaure's pyramid. The other smaller more elaborate monument was built within a Giza quarry. Its inscriptions tell that it had been made for a woman named Khent-kawes, who appears to have borne the epithet 'mother of two kings' but who, to the consternation of chronologers, appears to have been shown upon a granite doorway of that monument wearing a false beard, which is part of the regalia worn by the images of kings.

Traditional histories of the decade that followed the building of the Giza pyramids have been greatly enlivened by the prophecies of the elderly magician who appears alongside Hardjedef in the tales of the Papyrus Westcar, the last of whose stories relate how Djedi the soothsayer foretold that a certain Redjedet, the wife of a provincial priest, would give birth to triplets each one of whom would be a king of Egypt. As two of her triplet's names resemble those of two kings of Abusir, the Lady Redjedet was identified as Queen Khent-kawes the bearded matriarch and described as acting as co-regent with two of those named kings.

The monuments, however, also show that a pyramid was built at Abusir for a woman of the court whose name was also Khent-kawes. And a generation later, yet another tomb was made for a further – or perhaps the same? – queen called Khent-kawes. As ever, there is entirely insufficient data to accurately reconstruct a family tree. Yet the recurrence of that name at Giza and Abusir, along with other names like Hetep-heres and Meres-ankh, who are similarly designated in traditional translations as mothers, daughters and the consorts of the kings of those same times, suggests a strong continuity between the kings at Abusir and Giza; that there had been a carefully cultivated monarchic succession within a single household. As for the prophecies of the Papyrus Westcar, best to resist the temptation to set selected snippets from its magic tales to dance upon the points of pyramids.

Amongst the host of tombs that surround the pyramid of King Teti at Saqqara, a monarch who reigned a century after the kings of Abusir, stands one built for a certain Khent-kawes who is often designated as Queen Khent-kawes III, and another for a queen named Iput. And once again, translations of the texts that accompany these royal women variously designate them as the consorts, mothers and the children of the kings. That Iput's tomb was originally built as a mastaba and then converted into a pyramid during the lengthy later reign of Pepi I certainly suggests that she had been a long-lived presence in the royal household, though the theory that the king himself demanded a change in the design of his mother's tomb to improve her status is a product, surely, of the consumer age.

Remarkably enough, Iput's burial was found relatively undisturbed. A middle-aged woman with long brown hair, she had been laid within a cedar coffin set inside a stone sarcophagus and was surrounded by a scattering of broken jewellery and other fragments of the paraphernalia of courtly burial. Like so much of what remains from ancient Egypt, they are the intimate relics of an entirely enigmatic figure.

By Iput's day, that royal house had attained a remarkable and apparently benign longevity. At its ending, two kings, Pepi I and Pepi II, appear to have reigned over the best part of a century and a half, a period well attested in good hard stone by the continuous elaboration of those kings' funerary complexes and by the continuing accretion of smaller pyramids and tombs and temples at the royal burial grounds and in such profusion that they are in the processes of excavation to this day. Suddenly, though, at around 2200 BC the building stops. And in the following generation, for lack of monuments and inscriptions, the long-lived household which had ruled throughout the period that Baron Bunsen christened the 'Old Kingdom' quite disappears from view.

DISSOLUTION

Build the limekiln ten feet across, twenty feet from top to bottom, sloping the sides in to a width of three feet at the top . . . Be careful to keep the fire burning constantly, and do not let it die down at night or at any other time.

Marcus Cato, second century BC

Unlike Reisner's Giza excavations, Borchardt recovered huge quantities of limestone fragments at Abusir, scraps of the walls of the largely vanished royal temples and the detritus of an industry that had mined the monuments of pharaoh for stone and for the raw material of builder's mortar. Hellenistic architects and engineers had introduced lime mortar into Egypt in the last centuries BC, and it quickly replaced the softer and less tenacious gypsum plaster used in pharaonic times. At Abusir, the kilns that had rendered the temple's stone into slaked lime appear to have operated over several centuries, for Borchardt found graffiti on some of the temples' fragments that had been made between the fourth and sixth centuries AD when, judging from the angle that they were drawn, the temples' walls had still been vertical and, therefore, in their original positions.

Hungry limekilns devoured a great part of ancient and classical architecture and sculpture, a slow-burning tragedy that was yet under way in the fifteenth century AD when the letters of the travelling merchant Cyriaco d'Ancona sorrowfully described classical marbles being fed to the kilns in various locations throughout the eastern Mediterranean. These same processes were also responsible for the destruction of much of ancient Memphis and its cemeteries; long before the arrival of the European collectors, a great deal of its monuments' decorated limestone blocks having been taken down and burnt.

The especial attraction that Abusir and the other Memphite cemeteries held for lime-makers was the fine quality of the blocks of imported limestone with which many of the tomb chapels and temples had been faced. A soft, white, even stone, it had provided a

perfect medium for pharaonic craftsmen, who had used it for everything from facing the great pyramids to the doorjambs of modest
tomb chapels. Quarried, for the most part, in small-sized blocks from
the cliffs of Tura across the river from Saqqara, the stone was easily
rendered into slaked lime by splitting the blocks with chisels and
firing the resulting fragments to red heat in a simple updraft kiln.

At Saqqara, some of the main actors in this terrific drama were the
monks of the desert Monastery of Apa Jeremiah, a considerable settlement of mud-brick buildings which had been built in the sand of the
Saqqara cemeteries and was surrounded by several splendid churches,
whose fallen Roman columns cluster still, like log-jams in the windblown sand. Founded in the fifth century by the saint himself on the
footings of some pharaonic tomb chapels, his monks ranged far and
wide throughout the Memphite cemeteries during the three centuries
of the monastery's existence, demolishing monuments, making slaked
limes and taking many fine white limestone blocks for use within their
monastery. So a bishop's sarcophagus was cut from a great limestone
lintel engraved with superb Late Period hieroglyphs, whilst another
re-used lintel elegantly carved with King Sahure's name was transformed into a door sill at the monastery's olive presses; the latter,
presumably, having been brought from one of the king's monuments
at Abusir, where monks had converted a temple storeroom into a little
chapel. Other similarly procured limestone blocks were swiftly
re-carved with the passionate tendrils and acanthus of Byzantine capitals or transformed into stumpy columns decorated with the zigzag
geometries and spirals typical of local Christian stone work of the
times. In those days, many monastic communities throughout Egypt
were attacking and re-using the materials of ancient monuments with
a similar enthusiasm, not a little venom and even, perhaps, some fear,
for many of the early fathers believed that spiteful spirits inhabited the
ancient tombs and temples.

At Abusir, Borchardt quickly discovered that lime-burners and
quarrymen had demolished entire temples along with their connecting
causeways. Yet as his excavators cleared the drifted sand from their
foundations, they gathered up some 10,000 fragments of decorated
wall reliefs along with odd blocks that still held disembodied portions
of most beautiful relief, parts of large scenes that had extended all

across the temples' high white walls. Strewn out of context by the lime burners, many of these fragments were of the finest quality and of nicely portable size; just the sort of antiquity that dealers and collectors are eager to obtain. Broken images of kings and gods and their earthly retinues, dislocated fragments of hunting, sailing and offering scenes, a shattered picture of the pharaonic universe, scraps of an ancient *Description de l'Égypte* of which, Borchardt estimated, just one per cent of the original remained.

RESTORATION

There was but limited evidence of the original locations of most of the fragments of relief that Borchardt found at Abusir – which walls, which courts, which temple, even, they had once decorated. Such was the conservatism of the reliefs' designers, however, that most pieces could be identified and placed as elements in one of a small group of scenes – butchering and hunting, fishing and boating, festival, offering and the like – which had been engraved and painted on the walls of other temples and tomb chapels for a century and more before the times of the kings of Abusir and had continued to be employed in the decorations of monuments throughout the following millennia. So as Borchardt's team started to put those enormous broken jigsaws back together they were able to compare the Abusir fragments with a huge corpus of similar images and scenes, many of which were still complete. In this way, the original positions of many fragments from those vanished walls were identified and entire scenes were reconstructed. It was a major step forward in modern understanding of pharaonic culture, not the least because some of those scenes had served as exemplars of their genre over the following millennia: a few broken blocks from a wall of the pyramid temple of Sahure, for example, yet bear the lines of copying grids drawn some eighteen centuries later by the craftsmen of another pharaonic court.

Laid out in elegant folios, Borchardt's masterly drawings reconstructing several of the reliefs from the temple of King Sahure – of which more remained than those from other temples – show that the master craftsmen of the court of Abusir had designed some of the most

Three fecund deities bring life, sovereignty and satisfaction in the shape of the ankh, user *and* hetep *hieroglyphs to the offering tables of the royal cult, one of several similar reliefs which Borchardt found at Abusir. The grids running over these fine figures appear to have been drawn many centuries later as an aid to their being copied by the craftsmen of another pharaonic court.*

elaborate examples of pharaonic wall decoration ever made, their compositions extending, on occasion, for fifty feet and more. At the same time, the fragments also showed that the execution of those great scenes had been every bit as fine as the work of earlier generations. There too, amongst the many splendid images of courts and kings, were many tiny details – those 'Oh! Look at that' moments – that are popular today as illustrations of ancient Egyptian art: a monkey plays with a little boy, a mongoose climbs the bending stem of a papyrus plant, a wounded hyena attempts to paw a hunter's arrow from his eye. Lively details that have the appearance of being the products of direct observation from life yet would also be repeated time and time again with similar vivacity throughout the following millennia alongside the standard repertoire of gods, courtiers and kings.

Given this sparkling combination of formal magnificence and their lively account of some of the minutiae of daily life, it is tempting to claim the Abusir reliefs as the prototypes of many of the standard scenes of later pharaonic wall decoration, especially as the limekilns have consumed most earlier reliefs leaving but tiny fragments. Yet there is no firm indication of how or when many of those standard scenes had been invented, nor even if they had been created for the royal monuments or the courtiers' tomb chapels.

Certainly, some of the typical themes of pharaonic temple and tomb-chapel decoration that appear at Abusir – such as hunting, fishing and bird-snaring, dancing, boating and offering – already had extensive pedigrees. Scenes of hippopotamus-hunting, for example, an activity in which Egyptian monarchs from Sahure to Roman pharaohs are pictured taking part, had been drawn on prehistoric pots and scratched into some of the slate cosmetic grinding palettes of those far off days. In Sahure's temple, however, the scene had been set within the context of court ritual.

Other Abusir reliefs, alternatively, show exclusive royal activities and images and had appeared in various forms since the beginning of that office; scenes such as those showing the king marking out the foundations of great buildings, the so-called 'Heb Sed festival' and the iconic image of pharaoh smiting captives with a mace. Other scenes, however, some lavish and complex compositions of court ceremonial and some of those that show Sahure in the company of court deities, have scant pedigree. With or without precedent, many of these royal images would be reproduced throughout the following millennia and became the subject matter of the colossal reliefs on the walls of the greatest Egyptian temples.

What, then, had been the point and purposes in placing these elaborate visual presentations within the temples of Abusir? Their continued repetition, temple after temple, age after age, underlines the fact that they are not the biographical memorials of individual rulers. Whatever fragments of personal information the Abusir reliefs might once have held about an individual monarch's love of hunting, boating and the rest was subsumed into scenes that display the proper order of the offices of state. For whatever other purposes they served, all those great grand compositions of parades, of ritual and the royal hunt had laid out the structure and high etiquette of the pharaonic court as it undertook those various activities: an order that is reduced to its essentials in the scenes of indoor ceremonial and temple rite. In similar fashion, the short texts that had accompanied those visual

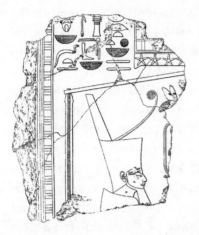

Some of the fragmentary scenes that were reassembled by Borchardt's expedition. Six pieces (left) form a small part of a large scene of jubilee which had shown King Sahure enthroned; three others (right) are part of a large processional of offerings being brought to the pharaonic cult. The circular cut in one of the fragments shows that its destroyers had intended to use its limestone for utilitarian purposes, but that it had broken before the masons had finished that work.

pageants provide more lessons, more instruction, in the way that things should be done.

In comparison with the rare earlier examples of those same scenes that have survived, their elaboration in the temples of Abusir suggests a genuine historical development. For here the subject matter of the earlier reliefs was transformed into a series of complex diagrams displaying the precedence of the king, his household and his court; diagrams in which the state's officials, some of whom are identified by name, are shown in serried ranks performing their various appointed tasks. At Abusir, therefore, these scenes appear as part of the continuing processes of state definition; a formalization of the offices of a court which appears to have increased in complexity and size since the times of the construction of the Giza pyramids, when governance appears to have been based on face-to-face contact within a group of people from related households. At Abusir, however, as row upon row of courtiers and servants, sailors and farmers had bowed to praise the king, the scenes had underlined a trend in the contemporary tomb chapels in which the titles of the courtiers became more numerous and complex in the generations after Sahure than they had ever been before.

In similar fashion, some of the later royal reliefs in the Saqqara temples show that the scenes in the Abusir temples were increasingly formalized. In the pyramid temple of Pepi II, for example, the previously lively scene of a royal hunt has been transformed into one showing the ritual slaughter of a desert antelope. Such elaborations, however, did not stop later generations of craftsmen returning such activities to their original settings. Following their appearance in the royal temples, even such apparently simple tomb-chapel scenes as a noble hunting in the desert or fishing in the Nile's marshes would have held meaning and resonance beyond the images of daily life that they so faithfully portray.

With care and acumen, Borchardt was able to place many of these reconstructed reliefs back in the architecture of the broken temples. Their entrances, he found, had often been decorated with scenes in which the kings were embraced and sometimes suckled by the gods, which speaks of those buildings serving as the climax of a route to the temple's ritual heart, where sustaining offerings were regularly made to the royal spirit. Beyond those doorways, the temples' corridors and rooms had contained the huge reliefs with their vivid and exquisite detail. And at their centres, close to the offering tables, were smaller simpler scenes of ritual and offering, images of the activities that were undertaken in that same area within the temple on each and every day.

There is no evidence of the intended audience of these reliefs. Large parts of them were set so high upon the walls that in the darkness of those enclosed spaces they would have required a lamp and ladder for their viewing. This implies that they were not intended to advertise the messages of power and propaganda that have been traditionally attributed to them, even if those areas within the temples had been open to those literate in courtly texts and imagery. Judging by their quality and subject matter, the point and purposes of the reliefs was the continuing definition, the dialogues involved in the creation of such complex scenes, the further realization of the aura and activities of the pharaonic court.

12

Meat, Bread and Stone

An Economy of Offering

HELIOPOLIS

In one respect the site of Heliopolis is very unusual. Nearly all great and celebrated cities were abundantly occupied in the Roman age, and have a great mass of Greco-Roman material over the older strata. At Heliopolis, on the contrary, not a scrap of Roman pottery is found.

W. M. Flinders Petrie, 1915

Not far from the pyramids of Abusir but on the east bank of the river lies a fabled district that bears the ancient classical name of Heliopolis – the 'City of the Sun' – where once had stood the obelisks that are now in London and New York. Trapped today beneath a mesh of tarmac roads and Cairo's northern suburbs, Heliopolis has become a largely literary location, its monuments having perished to the point where a single standing obelisk, some reconstructed columns and a few stone blocks now mark the site. Even the enormous mud-brick enclosure walls mapped by Napoleon's *savants* have largely disappeared, along with an avenue of sphinxes which had so impressed their early European visitors.

Like Memphis on the river's other bank, two centuries of desultory and often rapacious digging uncovered a millennial diversity of relics at Heliopolis. Still today, foundations dug for new villas and apartments in the area bring to light the tombs of priests, the mud-brick walls of ancient houses or a confusing scattering of smaller relics, everything from prehistoric pottery to that of the times of the last

*Heliopolis in the 1840s; the eroded mud-brick walls of the temple's
ancient enclosure stand in an empty plain.*

native pharaohs. Not a trace, however, has been found of Heliopolis'
most famous monument and the font of its millennial celebrity. For
many ancient texts describe ancient *Iunu*, as it was known, as holding one of the greatest of pharaonic shrines. And at its heart, they tell,
had stood a mysterious monument that marked the centre of the cult
of the sun god Re. Known as the Benben, it is pictured in a hieroglyph as a somewhat stumpy obelisk; an obelisk said to have been
capped with sheets of gold.

It is as difficult today to uncover the origins of the god Re as it is
to trace the architecture of his shrine at Heliopolis. Re's role in
the pharaonic kingdom was enormously elaborated in later periods,
and traditional historians tend to cast that later grand complexity
back into the ages of the god's beginnings. Real evidence, however, is
extremely thin.

Like several pharaonic deities, some of the hieroglyphs that are associated with Re had prehistoric origins. The god first makes his
appearance in human form, however, as a hawk-headed man in the
company of several other gods, a member of a household of deities centred on the living king. In the times of the four great pyramids, that
common kinship, Re and pharaoh, god and man, was described by the
royal epithet which, following Champollion's translators, is usually rendered as the 'Son of Re'. In the following centuries – in the decorations

of the pyramid temples both at Abusir and Saqqara – the circle of the sun, the simple hieroglyph that denominates Re's name, was joined to the wings of a hawk, that high-flying bird whose graphic image was a royal emblem older than the sun disk. So the image of Re the sun god, the father of the king, was joined to the image of Horakhty, Horus of the horizon, and the great state deity Re-Horakhty was born.

As a sun god, Re would be described by later scribes as a life creator and sustainer, whilst the daily progress of his disk through the sky made him a measurer of time. So as sons of Re, the living kings were similarly identified as the creators and sustainers of the state and, like the sun god, they too ordered human time. Without Re and his earthly son, therefore, the order and the very time in which the royal court existed would cease, and thus the valley of the lower Nile would no longer sustain the order of pharaonic culture. It is not surprising, therefore, that one of the titles of senior Old Kingdom courtiers was that of the chief official of Re's shrine at Heliopolis. Often translated as 'chief of seers', the epithet has been literally interpreted as evidence that this great enclosure with the mysterious Benben at its centre had been the point from which the court observed the solstices and thus was the place from where the kingdom's yearly calendar was regulated. A great mud mound, which later scribes described as the primeval mound, the first landfall to emerge as the waters of creation had receded, was said to stand at the centre of Heliopolis and has been tentatively identified as the archaic platform from which those solar observations were first made.

All of those descriptions, however, are derived from the texts of later ages. Nor, it would appear, were great stone monuments erected at Heliopolis in the times of the early pyramid builders. A few broken fragments of a modest limestone shrine made in the time of Djoser, the pharaoh for whom the first pyramid had been built, were found in the rubbish of a refuse pit at Heliopolis, which shows that royal monuments may have been set up there at that time, though not necessarily for the sun god Re, who makes his first-known appearance in human form only in the following century. Some priestly tombs, however, the fragments of another shrine and the tip of a modest limestone obelisk, the oldest-known example of that archetypal pharaonic monument, show further evidence of state building works at Heliopolis in Old Kingdom times. And though none of those fragments have the name of Re upon them, the broken obelisks hint strongly of his presence at the site, for like the Benben, obelisks were associated with that solar deity.

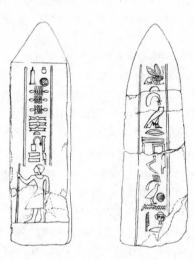

Two Old Kingdom obelisks from Heliopolis. Their inscriptions name the 'royal scribe of Heliopolis, Sheshi' (left) and the 'overseer of the estate, Neheri' (right). They are respectively 30 and 23 inches high, and both are cut from limestone.

The mirage of Old Kingdom Heliopolis, City of the Sun God, has recently been enlivened with the observation that some of the pyramids on the west bank of the Nile may have been orientated to the shrine of Re at Heliopolis. The famous line of pyramids at Giza, for example, is said to have been aligned to the mysterious Benben that stood some fifteen miles away across the marshy valley. The pyramids of Abusir, alternatively, and all the pyramids of Saqqara were screened from a direct line of sight with Heliopolis by the high cliffs of the Gebel Muqattam that stands behind Old Cairo. A few hundred yards to the north of the Abusir pyramids, however, exactly at the point at which the direct line of sight to Heliopolis had disappeared behind the cliffs of the Muqattam, texts tell that several of the Abusir kings had temples erected in their name, each one with a stumpy obelisk set at their centre. These were the so-called 'sun temples', whose names are listed as 'the Field of Re', 'the Birthplace of Re', 'the Horizon of Re', 'the Offering Table of Re' and 'the Place of the Heart of Re'.

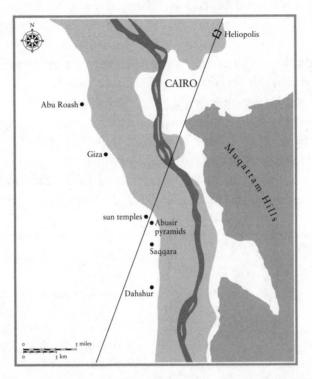

Map showing the particular relationship of the sun temples to Heliopolis. Before the limestone ridges of the Muqattam Hills were quarried away, Heliopolis was not visible from Abusir, Saqqara or Dahshur.

Just two of these sun temples have been located and excavated. Both were originally built of mud brick and subsequently elaborated and rebuilt in more permanent materials. The focus of their architecture resembled the hieroglyph that represents the Benben of Heliopolis, and in comparison with the nearby pyramids their stocky obelisks are of relatively modest size. In their final phases, however, after considerable elaboration and enlargement, those structures had been enlarged and elaborated and stood within architectural complexes similar to those of the nearby pyramids, each one with two attendant temples, the upper joined by a lengthy causeway to a lower temple. At least one of the upper temples had a splendid series of reliefs engraved upon its limestone walls which, so the remaining fragments show, had been of equal size and quality to those within the nearby royal temples at Abusir. Great offering tables had stood at the centre of the courtyards of the upper temples in front of their Heliopolitan-style obelisks and were open to the sky. Standing by those altars, looking out across the yellow desert over the fields, the shining river and the bright green marsh, the temple priests could see the Benben at Heliopolis, its gold cap glinting in the sun.

As to the purposes of those most innovative temples: rare fragmentary papyri found at Abusir show that they had played a vital role within the system of tithing, offering and distribution in those times; the processes which defined and sustained that state, its gods, its priestly households and the generations of its kings and courtiers.

The left-hand sign is a contemporary hieroglyph for 'pyramid'; the central sign, the earliest-known hieroglyph for 'sun temple', would appear to show a mound topped by a perch for hawks. The right-hand image is Borchardt's reconstruction of the silhouette of a new-built sun temple.

THE ABUSIR PAPYRI

A large part of Egypt's economic activity amounted to nothing more than the management and distribution of commodities . . .

Hratch Papazian, 2005

Tithes or offringes beyng in Spirituelx mens handes . . .
English Rolls of Parliament, 1451

Few papyri have survived from Old Kingdom times. Made from the sticky pithy strips of the stalks of papyrus, a flowering sedge that grew in profusion along the Nile's marshlands, papyri were stored in rolls and, though tougher than paper when they were new, their sheets are now extremely brittle and easily fragmented. So precious little remains of the considerable accounting systems that surely had accompanied the construction of the royal pyramids, let alone the written communications between the various support networks whose offices had run throughout the state. Remarkably, however, the tattered fragments of three different temple archives have been found in the sands of Abusir. The first of these was discovered in illicit excavations during the decade before Borchardt's arrival and may well have encouraged his interest in the site. Broken, divided and sold piecemeal to museums in Cairo, London, Berlin and Paris, its contents were resurrected in the course of a lifetime's research by the French egyptologist Paule Posener-Kriéger. The other two archives were recovered by Czech archaeologists who in the 1970s followed Borchardt in the excavation of Abusir and are still working at the site.

These archives were found in the pyramid temples of two kings, Neferirkare and Raneferef, and that of a Queen Khent-kawes. The better part of them describe some of the activities that took place within those temples long after the times of those for whom these monuments

Part of a papyrus from King Raneferef's pyramid temple at Abusir, whose archives had recorded the activities of the temple's staff throughout several later reigns.

were made. Between them, they allow glimpses of the daily routines, the pulse, of the pharaonic state in the times of the Abusir kings and yet beyond – a span from around 2500 BC of well over a century.

The archives' contents fall into four main categories. First, they hold inventories of the temples and their various furnishings, and document their wear and tear. Secondly, they contain the rosters and the lists of names of people involved in the ceremonies and other activities that took place within those temples. Thirdly, they record some of the produce and materials that were sent between the pyramid temples, the sun temples and the storerooms of the royal household. And lastly, they record a number of royal decrees regulating those temples' activities. As one would expect from a culture that had organized huge labour forces and erected colossal and astonishingly precise pyramids over considerable periods of time, these records are carefully laid out and highly detailed.

Set in vertical columns and with two, three and even four sub-headings, the inventories resemble the tabulation of the near-contemporary Palermo Stone. A single knife, for example, listed under a sub-category of materials as being made of flint, is described in another column as being the only one of its kind, and further, in another column detailing its condition, it is described as being chipped and its handle as having been repaired. Two other flint knives, alternatively, are described as 'chipped from having been dropped', whilst a bowl identified in the sub-category of materials as being of Egyptian alabaster is further categorized as 'white', and its condition, in the appropriate column, as having had repairs to its rim, sides and base.

As well as showing that those pieces of temple equipment, examples of which are exhibited today as ancient treasures, were similarly prized in ancient times, these objects' well-worn condition underlines the fact that those inventories were compiled decades after the temples which had housed them had first come into use. In similar fashion, another equally detailed inventory of the architecture of one of those temples describes a mud-brick doorway as being damaged, whilst an accounting of deliveries of wood and mud brick to that same temple apparently records the quantities of the materials required for a doorway's restoration.

As their archaeology confirms, these temples were well used and for considerable periods of time, the rites and ceremonies that the papyri list as having taken place within them describing in some detail what their 300-odd personnel had undertaken on a daily, monthly and yearly basis. Two different types of personnel were engaged in these activities. One was a permanent staff of priests, scribes and servants, the other, a group of ten overseers. Remarkably, the latter group had functioned in a rotating system resembling the routines of the present-day guards of the remains of those same temples.

In the times of the Abusir kings, the papyri record that the temples' permanent staff had undertaken rites in which the numerous statues in the temples' open courts, some of which are listed as wearing golden jewellery and other precious accoutrements, were censed and purified. The rotating staff, alternatively, had performed the intricate rituals in which the statues of the king that were enshrined in the dark rooms behind the temple's offering tables were brought into the light at sunrise and then purified and dressed and presented with offerings before they were shut up again and sealed into their shrines at sunset. Thus the statues of the reigning king and those of his predecessors had joined the living world each day in royal dignity.

SUN TEMPLES AND SLAUGHTERHOUSES

Month 4 of Flood, day 6

king's mother, Khent-kawes	*hind leg*
inspector of priests, Merneter-nesut	*hind leg*
supervisor of priests, Werka	*foreleg*
palace hairdresser, Userkaef-ankh	*foreleg femur*
palace officials	*foreleg femur*
overseer of provisioning, Niankh-ra	*[. . .]*
palace surgeon, Nishepses-nesut	*hind leg*
lector, Washka	*pancreas [?]*
canal-cutter, Tiy	*top of foreleg*
inspector of accountants, Sopedhotep	*ditto*
palace official for oils, Ptahhotep	*ditto*

supervisor of the library, Kakai-ankh	*ditto*
courtier, Bebib	*ditto*
director[?], Menheteput-kakai	*ditto*
canal officials	*ditto*

*A list of meat offerings to the cult and thus to members of
the community of the living court. From the temple archives
of King Neferirkare*

The sections of the Abusir Papyri which have attracted the most attention are those that deal in daily life within the temples, listing the delivery of supplies of cloth and building materials and, most particularly, the provisions which were distributed to the temple's staff and the households of their communities, along with those of numerous other priests and officials and, indeed, the household of the royal residence.

Those ancient records further show that in the times of the Abusir kings, the sun temples had been centres for the processing and distribution of provisions gathered from across the regions of the lower Nile. It also appears that the sun-temple staff had processed some of those supplies and operated breweries and bakeries, for some of the surviving papyri describe how cooked food was sent to the nearby pyramid temples on a daily basis. In partial confirmation, archaeology has shown that the two sun temples that have been excavated had held considerable numbers of magazines and storerooms, and also that they had undergone considerable enlargements in reigns later than those in which they had been built. The sun temples, therefore, had been major and enlarging elements in the system of supply of food and provisions to the core offices of state.

One of the papyri also contains an edict stipulating the amount of provisions that were to be sent from the Abusir temples to the offering cults of some of the courtiers' tomb chapels; offerings that would have supported the priestly communities who were serving the cults within the growing numbers of such chapels in the Giza and Saqqara cemeteries. In life, as their inscriptions tell, the court officials for whom those tomb chapels were made had worked within the state machine, producing the materials that it required and controlling its storage and processing facilities; many of their tomb chapels, indeed, contain reliefs that show them overseeing such activities. This, then, had been a highly structured system of supply that had operated within the court and had served both the living and the dead.

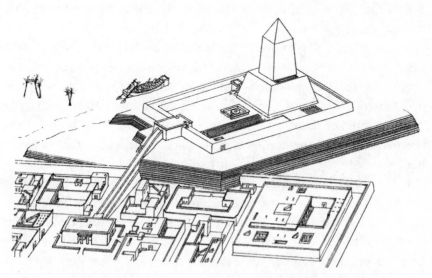

Borchardt's reconstruction of the sun temple of King Niuserre. The side of the temple courtyard nearest to the viewer was filled with workshops, magazines and slaughterhouses; the opposing side had held an offering temple decorated with reliefs showing the activities of the farming and hunting year and the presentation of their products to the royal cult. The unique full-sized mud-brick model of a boat that Borchardt uncovered outside the temple compound appears to have served the same purposes as the genuine river craft that were buried beside many royal pyramids. The dwellings beneath the platform of the valley temple were, presumably, those of the temple's staff.

Though sharing the same layout as the royal pyramid complexes, with two temples, an upper and a lower joined by a causeway, the sun temples were smaller constructions. However, the enclosures of both their lower temples and their causeways were far larger in size than their equivalents at the royal pyramids, as were the open courts within their upper temples that held a Benben at their centre. The accounts in the papyri suggest that these modifications represent practical arrangements for herding, slaughtering and butchering the large quantities of cattle which, the records show, had passed through those facilities. Both known sun temples, indeed, still hold some of the amenities required for work on such a scale; the remains of elaborate drainage systems and rows of elegant and substantial alabaster basins that, though they stand bone white today within the yellow desert, would once have held the gore of slaughter.

Hardly anything remains of the standing architecture of those two excavated temples; Borchardt and his successors performed remarkable feats of archaeological detection simply to determine their original forms. In the 1970s, however, Miroslav Verner excavated another, smaller, contemporary abattoir that had been built beside the pyramid of Raneferef, which he had also excavated. Anciently named 'the house of the knife', it had been a robust, large, rectangular mud-brick building containing a slaughtering chamber measuring some 30 by 20 feet with three tethering stones set into its floor and a chopping block raised at its centre. This room had been open to the sky. Some of the fifteen smaller enclosed chambers in the building had been used for smaller-scale meat preparation, others, as their red burnt brick suggested, had served as kitchens. One small room had held a staircase that must have led up to the roof where, so tomb-chapel representations of such slaughterhouses suggest, strips and joints of meat may have been strung up in the sun to dry. Traces of both blood and cooking fires yet remained within the ruin of this slaughterhouse, as did the marks of its washing out with water on its whitewashed walls. A papyrus fragment from one of the temple archives tells that it had handled thirteen beasts a day.

At one of the nearby sun temples – whose upper courtyard was more than ten times larger than 'the house of the knife' – a central offering table yet consists of five huge alabaster blocks, all of them precisely cut and beautifully matched in the translucent veining of their stones and set together in a sophisticated geometry. The circular hieroglyph of the sun's disk stands at its centre and is represented by a perfect cylinder of honeyed alabaster some three feet high, which is framed by a quadrangle of four colossal so-called *hetep* hieroglyphs of similarly fine materials and dimensions: four images of a loaf upon a mat, each one some twelve feet long. This massive and near-abstract image is presently unique: Re's sun disk surrounded by four massive hieroglyphs, signifying 'offering' or 'satisfaction' standing quite alone, upon an ancient limestone pavement.

Meat offerings were important elements of the funeral rites of both kings and courtiers and also, so the papyrus archives tell, of the daily rituals of offering that were conducted in the royal name within the temples. Thus scenes of slaughtering and butchery are common in tomb chapels and temples of all periods of pharaonic history. Slaughtering, indeed, appears to have been considered an activity similar to hunting and both were bound in ritual, though the kings themselves are seldom shown as temple slaughterers; in the Abusir reliefs, monarchs are pictured killing desert animals trapped inside man-made enclosures with a bow and arrow, whilst a later rare relief in a Saqqara temple shows the king slitting the throat of a wild desert antelope in an act of sacrifice.

Such vast facilities for slaughter – surviving data suggests that the two known sun temples alone could have supplied more than 200 carcasses a day to the various offices of state – raises important questions of supply. Like the activities of quarrying and mining and the erection of stone monuments, the rearing of large herds of cattle required more resources than those available in simple farming settlements, where village households usually reared pigs and fowl. Effectively, therefore, livestock breeding on such a scale was an enterprise conducted under the auspices of the state. So it is hardly surprising that, in common with many other ancient societies, the mass slaughtering of cattle appears to have taken place within a context of the courtly rituals that defined such ancient states.

It would appear, therefore, that tokens of the enormous quantities of animals that, the records show, were slaughtered and butchered in the courtyards of the sun temples – traditionally the animal's forelegs, head and heart – were laid out as offerings on the alabaster tables in front of the Benben monument. And then, as the papyri archives tell, there had followed a carefully structured and recorded distribution of diverse cuts of meat and offal, rank by rank, to the various households of the royal court and other groups, such as the households of the funerary priests. Later texts describe meat-eating as an especial delight – it was, after all, both a rare, rich food and the product of a ritual performed under the aegis of the king. One famous text, indeed, describes the acts of killing, cooking and eating a bull by a king and various gods with such literary gusto that until quite recently those cosmic gourmets had been construed as cannibals!

Ever since the days of the first pharaohs, and probably in earlier times as well, quantities of cattle and meat products had been shipped to the settlements of the first pharaonic courts, which had assembled on the narrow silt plains of Memphis where there was insufficient land for their support. Great herds had been kept on scrub land along the Nile's valley, some of which were sent downstream to the river's delta during the dry season for fattening on its plains and marshlands. Those same broad delta wetlands had also supported large and well-established colonial estates that since the times of the archaic kings had specialized in meat production, and, as recent archaeology and the Palermo Stone both inform us, the kings of Abusir had also held estates.

Like the settlements of Maadi and Merimda, which in previous millennia had served as conduits between the communities of the river's valley and its delta, Heliopolis with its shrine of Re was also situated at that juncture in the Nile's progress where the valley's limestone cliffs slowly begin to disappear and the silt plains of its delta start to fan out towards the Mediterranean. And it is this, the fact of its location along with the relationship of its Benben and its related sight lines, that underlines the links between the shrine of Re at Heliopolis and the sun temples at Abusir.

For though considerable quantities of meat were shipped to the sun temples in the times of the Abusir kings, and their facilities for slaughtering were substantial, there is not a trace of the corrals that would have been required to hold the living herds of cattle on their arrival from the great estates. Here, then, the enclosures at Heliopolis, which were far larger than those at the sun temples, may well have served as depots in the manner of similarly enormous mud-brick enclosures that had been built in the times of the first kings. The same state systems of transportation and supply, indeed, had been in use in those archaic times, when boats had been buried beside some of those mud-brick enclosures, a process echoed at one of the excavated Abusir sun temples which had a mud-brick replica of a boat beside it.

Continuing this same underlying theme, near-contemporary royal texts naming Heliopolis as the site where the gods reside commonly describe them as bulls from the grasslands or cows who, in the forms of queenly goddesses, suckle and nourish the king, whilst a common royal epithet describes the king himself as a great bull. In such a vivid landscape, the sight lines between Heliopolis in the east and the sun temples in the west, the continuous traffic on the silver river, the bloody rituals in those temples, all mapped the power and majesty, the daily drama, of the journey of the pharaoh and the sun from sunrise at the Benben to sunset at the line of pyramids.

THE VALUE AND THE WORTH OF THINGS

Divine offerings established for the spirits of Heliopolis on the first festival, and on the occasion of every subsequent festival for all eternity.

4,252 measures of bread and beer
40 oxen 4 [?] ibex
132 geese 1[?] duck
>   The first entry for the reign of Userkaf on the
>   Palermo Stone, c. 2450 BC

As the surviving texts from tombs and temples had long suggested, and the detail of the Abusir Papyri has further underlined, the state's resources were controlled in pharaoh's name. Its warrant oversaw the construction of the pyramids; it authorized the provisioning of the royal palaces and the workshops of the state; it administered estates both in the Nile's delta and its valley; it maintained the state's considerable transportation network; and it controlled the manufacture, processing and storage of its provisions and supplies.

Yet the living kings, the archaeological record suggests, had lived in modest mud-brick settlements whilst the officials of the state appear to have operated a simple system of direct and personal control. A modern mind might sense a contradiction. Had not the offices of this ancient kingdom cut and moved millions of tons of stone with an unmatched speed and built pyramids of phenomenal accuracy? Had not its workshops produced considerable quantities of beauteous objects for centuries? And does not all of that, in turn, speak of elaborate governmental structures?

Essentially, there were two groups of people in Old Kingdom Egypt. The first consisted of the farmers and the workers in allied trades who between them comprised the bulk of the population of the lower Nile, which at that time, so best estimates suggest, was close to a million people. The second group comprised those people who were not directly employed in food production: the households of the officers of state, those of the priests and scribes and palace servants, the masons, sculptors, jewellers and storekeepers, the boat captains, the master builders and the staff of offices throughout the kingdom that oversaw the transportation of supplies to the royal household and all its various activities. In the days of the Giza kings this courtly community, the combined households that contained the living reality of ancient Egyptian courtly culture, may have held as little as 10,000 adults, though when labour-intensive activities such as mining and quarrying and the construction of pyramids and temples were under way, they could pull farm workers and the other tradespeople into that rare orbit as required. In the times of the Abusir kings, although the numbers of tomb chapels and named court officials was certainly enlarging, the kernel of that enterprise still seems to have been controlled by a small body of men, perhaps 150 in number. In all probability, those people were known directly to the king. As well as administering the regions of the lower Nile in pharaoh's name, they may also have managed agricultural estates.

Ultimately, as the paintings and reliefs in the temples and tomb chapels tacitly acknowledge, everything depended on the labour of the farmers. Before the modern age, when human societies were more delicately balanced between prosperity and oblivion, few rulers or courtiers had been foolish enough to kill the farmers or even to remove them from the land. For farmers, as one text observes, 'made everything'.

By definition, subsistence farmers do not produce large surpluses, so if the offices of the pyramid-building courts had simply tithed communities of subsistence farmers they could hardly have collected supplies sufficient to their needs. Traditionally, egyptologists have assumed that the ancient situation had been similar to the cruel regimes of nineteenth-century Egypt, and much is made of tomb chapel images of wily peasants being beaten so that they will give up part of their harvest. More balanced analyses, however, suggest that the real secret of the phenomenal prosperity of pharaoh's court is that from its beginnings it had provided the farmers of the lower Nile with sufficient resources – everything from standardized agricultural equipment to the organization of the labour systems that cut and maintained canals and irrigation basins – to enable the production of far larger amounts of food than the farmers and their households could ever have required.

The Old Kingdom court also continued the colonization of unused flood plains in the regions of the lower Nile, a policy which appears to have begun in the time of the first pharaohs, when many newly established settlements and royal estates had supplied the offering tables of the tomb chapels and the courtly settlements of early Memphis.

This was part of a millennial process. From its beginnings to its end, the history of pharaonic agriculture is one of internal colonization, of further exploitation and enlargement of the cultivable regions of the lower Nile under the aegis of the king and court. And right from its beginning, that process had been so successful, the produce of the world's most fertile flood plain so superabundant, that in the first centuries after the state's establishment the archaic kings were being buried in massive tombs filled with vast amounts of courtly objects, the products of the courts' considerable workshops. And this continuing pattern of ever-growing farming surpluses had enabled the construction of the colossal pyramids of Sneferu, Khufu and Khafre and, in later centuries, the monuments of Abusir and Saqqara.

In the first years of their construction, when their bases were wide and access to them had been easy, the great royal pyramids would have required workforces of 40,000 or 50,000 people. Those pyramids alone, therefore, are unequivocal evidence of the remarkable success of the state's farming system. And grain had been the basis of that enterprise, as the archaeology of Old Kingdom courtly settlements and the abundant images of grain stores in the tomb chapels both serve to underscore. Even though the focus of the state had changed after the age of the Giza kings and considerable herds of cattle were being slaughtered on the altars of Abusir, grain rather than the relatively profligate activity of rearing cattle had yet remained the lynchpin of the state economy.

Whilst the pharaonic court held sufficient supplies of grain and manpower to maintain its various offices and build stone monuments, that situation did not change until the coming of the Greeks, when active irrigation systems and new strains of wheat were imported into Egypt. Until that time, everything had depended on the government's efficiency and the size and regularity of the river's annual inundation. There was no economic progress in a modern sense, no 'storm blowing from paradise' that is so essential to the economies of the modern world. And that fact alone opens a yawning gap between present-day experience and that of the pharaonic kingdom, most immediately in the use of the word 'economy', whose modern meaning is less than a century old. For it is not a term that the pharaonic government would have understood, nor do any ancient texts encompass similar abstractions.

Best then to employ a different vocabulary for modern descriptions of the order of this ancient state. One that blurs distinctions between sacred and profane – between rites of offering and the order and supply of the agencies of state. One that describes, for example, the pharaonic government's extraction of its resources from the lands of the lower Nile as 'tithing' rather than the more usual 'taxing'. For the old-fashioned English term 'tithing' has the advantage of isolating the ancient processes of supply from imaginary parallels with today, and the use of the term 'taxes' – which are monies paid towards the upkeep of government – simply monetizes pharaoh. And money, which is an abstract measure of labour, goods and services, was not employed within the valley of the Nile until the final phases of ancient Egypt's history, when Hellenism was sweeping through the cultures of the ancient East.

Just as it is difficult today to imagine how the order of a successful state, its history, its theologies, its legal codes were not laid down in written words, so it is equally difficult to imagine how such an opulent court could have operated without a form of money – without an abstract and precise measure by which everything, land and property values, commodity prices, salaries, slaves and servants, could have been evaluated and controlled. So traditional historians imagine that such societies had invented faux monetary systems of their own; hence the common assumption that the pharaonic economy was based on measures of grain or on gold or on copper rings of standard sizes.

Such assumptions lead to a variety of confusions. The notion of ancient Egyptian slavery, for example, a pure product of monetizing pharaoh, assumes the existence of modern concepts of personal ownership, of individual freedom and abstract independent wealth. Those ideas arrived in the territories of the lower Nile with the introduction of stamped metal coinage in the first millennium BC. In pharaonic Egypt, as in the rest of the eastern Mediterranean, the advent of Hellenism changed human perception within the ancient Middle Eastern world. So the philosopher Heraclitus, who had flourished at the time when money had first entered circulation, conceived his pre-atomic theory of matter as consisting of units of abstract energy that, like money, were interchangeable 'like goods for gold and gold for goods' – 'goods' that Aristotle would later define as 'things whose value is measured in money'.

Just as a character in one of the plays of Aristophanes declares that he is longing for his village, 'which never said, "Buy charcoal!", "Buy wine!", "Buy oil!" For my village did not know the word "buy" but produced everything itself, with no buying', so, too, there are no separate words in ancient Egyptian for buying and selling. Nor were there goods in Aristotle's abstract sense, just cows and bricks, boats and thrones, people both alive and dead, grain, pyramids and offering tables, pharaoh and the gods.

This is but one of the reasons why it is so difficult today to enter the world laid out in the fragments of relief from the temples of Abusir and, indeed, most other products of that ancient court. Just as there was no 'art' in Winckelmann's definition of the term within that world, so neither were there any of Aristotle's goods. Notice, for example, that despite the seemingly endless repetitions of pose and subject matter in most ancient reliefs there is a sensuousness in virtually every image:

the ancient craftsmen show us neither goods nor crowds, but the individuality of every element in his universe. From a plant to a cow, a king or god, the great majority of the craftsmen's images, including hieroglyphic signs, which are mostly based on the forms of living things, carefully delineate the various qualities of life within the things that are portrayed. Yet modern awareness of the originality of those things is easily blunted by our largely mass-produced environment, so that when we look at the surviving fragments of those things we easily imagine that they are but curious works of art.

Those same qualities of individual life are found in the omnipresent images of offering bearers who carry pots and baskets along the long walls of the royal temples and the nobles' tomb chapels. In their seemingly endless duplication these scenes appear to be going nowhere, and to a modern eye there is a curious contradiction between their repetitive forms and the endless variety in the representation of their various elements: a peasant, another peasant, three nobles, a herd of cows, two boats, a king, a god, a plant. And all of them are different.

In the same way, the obsessive detail of the inventories on the Abusir Papyri describes *individual* things rather than merely providing an account of a temple's assets. Just as the information recorded on the Palermo Stone that the Pharaoh Sneferu took more captives from the southlands than that region with its meagre lands could ever have supported, so too the lists of the Abusir Papyri do not itemize components of an abstract 'national economy'. The cloth and beer, the bread, bricks and onions and all the good things of daily offering that they carefully record, document the fulfilment of the state's obligation to provide life to the offices of pharaoh and the gods, and to the households of the court both alive and dead, in the prescribed and proper manner.

This is what concerned the scribes and craftsmen as they carefully and fondly drew and sculpted those familiar images, scenes and offering lists within the tomb chapels and temples, as they loaded almost every one of their images with a flashing eye, a pulsing limb. As they recorded the exact qualities of a catfish's skin or a butterfly's wing, as they carefully distinguished the different species of birds and fish within the lower Nile, as they showed wild and domestic animals engaged in hunting, killing and copulating, and, rather more sedately, men and women working, talking, eating and engaging in ceremonial: every element was alive and in its proper place within the rich universe of the lower Nile. So the ancient craftsmen were not dominated by a rigid system of design or a demand for the endless duplication of set forms; not torpor nor conservatism but, rather, the closed format of the courtly style allowed every craftsman world enough and time to concentrate upon the one essential: that every image, every hieroglyph they drew was imbued with the visual attributes of life.

There is, of course, an endless fascination in enlivening images made of stone, paint and wood, a process that in pharaoh's Egypt was also fundamental to the ancient rite of funeral and offering in which the dead themselves were re-enlivened. And all such acts were based in the belief that care, craftsmanship and repeated acts of offering served to situate that courtly culture at the very centre of the lively rhythms of the year as manifested in the kingdom's bounteous landscapes.

By modern lights, a courtly culture with such preoccupations may well appear obtuse. Yet the continuously dynamic processes of offering and craftsmanship served both to confirm the powerful office of pharaoh and, through rites of offering and tithing, to physically sustain the royal household and the court. And though that court, its scribes and craftsmen grew ever more sophisticated throughout the following millennia, essentially it never changed.

13

The Living Court

PER'A – THE PALACE

Beyond the temples, pyramids and tomb chapels, there is precious little evidence upon the ground that holds firm traces of the world in which the Abusir Papyri had been written. Some clipped and scrappy texts on the Palermo Stone, along with a few rare papyrus notes and letters, suggest that the royal residence, the centre of that state, was set close to the pyramid and temples of the living king. Yet though several documents record a number of these residences by name, archaeologists have found no trace of them.

At Abusir, the pyramids had been placed closer to the desert's edge than their predecessors, so it is likely that, in common with most ancient settlements along the lower Nile, the royal residences had been built upon the river's silt, and lie today some fifteen feet beneath the fields and well below the present water table. Some of their ghosts, perhaps, may be detected by the positioning of some of the pyramids' lower temples, which appear to have been angled to accommodate long-vanished buildings that may have stood beside them.

Pyramid building required a state-wide administration that in turn would have necessitated the construction of settlements, storerooms and enclosures to sustain that substantial industry. And many of these facilities, as both archaeology and the scanty written record show, were built within the desert cemeteries and close by the pyramids. Between those storehouses, workers settlements and palaces there were considerable gatherings of buildings in the shadow of the rising pyramids.

The earliest-known evidence of contemporary settlements beside the pyramids are the modest ruins of some kilns and their attendant workshops that stand near Sneferu's two great pyramids on the high desert plain at Dahshur. In all probability, the residence of Sneferu himself, the construction of which is part described on the Palermo Stone, had stood nearby. Down by the fields, indeed by the village of Dahshur, parts of the pyramid's ancient harbour are presently under investigation, so the remains of Sneferu's palace may well be located in coming years. Presently, however, the desert plain at the foot of the Giza Plateau, to the south of the site of Giza's ancient harbour, holds the oldest-known examples of pharaonic pyramid-building settlements.

Built of enormous blocks of stone dragged from nearby quarries, a great long wall runs westwards up the low slope of the Giza Plateau and separates this mass of ancient mud-brick buildings from the area of the harbour, the pyramids, their valley temples and the Sphinx. Spanned by two great lintels, a single monolithic gateway some twenty-two feet high gave access from the harbour to these settlements, which are built hard up against that massive wall. It is likely, therefore, that the residences of the Giza kings had stood on the same side of the wall and that those huge building blocks are the 'northern settlement' that some tomb-chapel texts describe as being attached to Khufu's palace.

Hemmed in today by modern cemeteries and village houses, an area of some 300 by 400 yards, part of that considerable ancient settlement is presently under excavation. Working since 1988, teams of Egyptian and US archaeologists led by Mark Lehner have revealed a close-set group of rectangular and regularly planned enclosures, with two somewhat randomly built additions set against their sides. Built and rebuilt over a period of some fifty years, these are the remains of settlements that had housed and provisioned considerable numbers of people in the times of King Khafre and King Menkaure. Parts of these enclosures had held substantial structures of mud brick that appear to have contained some thirty dormitories, each one of which had its own small guardhouse and could have provided spare accommodation for some twenty people. Close by, other regularly planned settlements enclosed within stout walls of field stone and mud mortar had housed storerooms, potteries and bakeries.

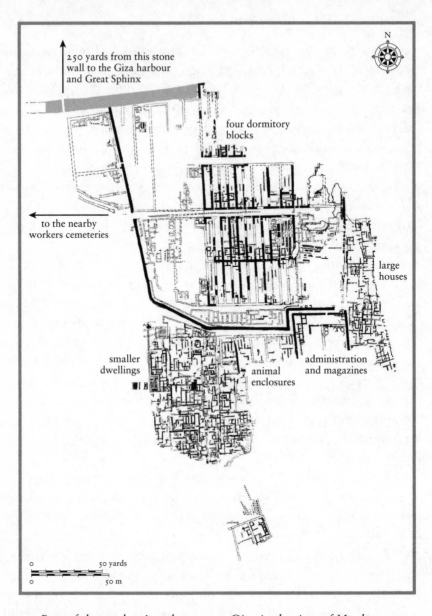

250 yards from this stone
wall to the Giza harbour
and Great Sphinx

N

four dormitory
blocks

to the nearby
workers cemeteries

large
houses

smaller
dwellings

animal
enclosures

administration
and magazines

0   50 yards

0   50 m

Part of the workers' settlements at Giza in the time of Menkaure.
The four blocks with gate houses and kitchens that had stood at the centre
of the large walled compound appear to have served as dormitories, the
adjacent units housing facilities for the pyramid builders' upkeep and
operations: potteries, bakeries, breweries, copper smelters and the like.
The contents and character of the sprawling vernacular architecture that
lay outside the central state-planned zone neatly divides into two different
types: the large units in the eastern group containing the households of
scribes and administrators, those to the west, the families of the
settlement's own workforce. The stone wall to the north of the settlement
also appears in the figure on p. 9.

The amounts of animal bones recovered from these excavations, along with the tiny flakes of flint that are the products of re-sharpening the blades of traditional slaughtering knives, show that large quantities of pigs, sheep and cattle had been butchered in these settlements. The lack of pollen in the ruins, however, or any other vegetable remains suggests that, as in the later sun temples, those animals had been brought into the compounds for slaughtering rather than for husbandry.

Both the surviving fragments of mud sealings from now-lost papyri and the quantities of cattle bones that were found in some of the larger house-like elements of the central settlement suggest that court officials had worked within the complex and may have lived in family households. There are, as well, precise divisions inside the settlement, the various elements of their storehouses and living quarters de-marcated by guardhouses, strong high walls and long surrounding corridors. Whilst the barrack-like dormitories suggest temporary ac-commodations, the east of the settlement appears to have held the large houses of officials and their families, whilst the smaller dwell-ings in the western sections, which yielded evidence of its occupants' more modest diets, may well have contained the households of the families of the artisans who had worked within the potteries and bakeries.

In the desert to the west of those settlements, set into the side of a rocky ridge, is a considerable cemetery that has been excavated by teams led by the Egyptian archaeologist Zahi Hawass. The biggest tombs, so the texts and reliefs of its tomb chapels tell, were those of bakers and officials. The skeletons in the smaller tombs, which are some 600 in number and consist of simple shafts and superstruc-tures, show that their occupants had endured much hard labour and sustained a range of injuries, suggesting that these are the burial places of pyramid builders. Many of these small tombs are topped by eccentric structures made of mud. Some are shaped like beehives, others tiny pyramids. Several are studded with fragments of red gran-ite, the workshop detritus of the huge blocks of stone that had been shipped to Giza from Aswan as building material for the royal funer-ary architecture.

These relatively recent excavations in the plain at Giza afford a unique glimpse of the world of the pyramid makers and also the lives of some of the officials of the state administration. The scanty written evidence in the tomb chapels of that age – which largely consists of the titles and epithets of courtly nobles – suggests that the royal administration of the period in the times of the Giza kings may have been controlled by members of the royal household, a conclusion underlined by the recent discovery of a boat captain's papyrus that records the delivery of stone blocks to the Great Pyramid's construction site.

Here, then, amidst these gentle ruins is the day-by-day reality of that lost world. Part of the physical structures of an administration that with the state's adoption of colossal pyramid building had been inflated out of all proportion from those of earlier times. Further investigations of these settlements, especially their eastwards extensions, which presently lie under the houses of a modern village and southwards under some desert stables and a football pitch, could well provide fresh wonders – even, perhaps, some royal palaces.

Where, then, in this mix of text and ruin is Memphis, the legendary City of the White Walls celebrated by classical histories, and long-since regarded by traditional historians as the capital city of ancient Egypt? Obviously, there was no place in pharaoh's Egypt for a city in the modern sense of that word; such cities, just as Aristophanes' character bemoans, were dependent on their survival for monetary exchanges in the market place. To that extent, at least, there were no 'urban populations' in pharaoh's Egypt. Nothing beyond the pyramid builders' settlements and a network of institutions up and down the river involved in their supply. Old Kingdom Memphis, therefore, was composed of various gatherings of courtly settlements, of warehouses, studios and shipyards that shifted over the twenty-mile region on the west bank of the river in concert with the various locations chosen for the pyramid of the living king. The Memphis of today, the ruins visited by tourists, was a product of later ages. Early Memphis was not a city, but a region.

Nor would the temporary nature of these settlements have presented many problems to the communities of pyramid builders. Mud bricks are swiftly made from Nile silt, and field stone is easily obtained from the little deserts and the cliffs beyond the river's silt plains. So courtly settlements were quickly made. From its beginnings, pharaonic rule had been a peripatetic phenomenon, the royal household sailing in flotilla through the landscapes of the lower Nile establishing temporary courts of residence. In similar fashion, the settlements at Giza appear to have been rapidly constructed, easily adapted and enlarged, and swiftly denuded of their wood and cut stone when the pyramid builders moved on to other sites. Seen in this light, the pyramids, those great stone tents pitched high on the horizon, were the antithesis of the living state.

CONSTANCY AND CHANGE

The first signs of the profound changes that occurred within the order of the state following the abandonment of building colossal pyramids can be dated to around 2500 BC and are found at the pyramid of the Pharaoh Userkaf, who succeeded Shepseskaf, the king who had abandoned the traditional form of the royal tomb in favour of a massive mastaba of stone.

As if to emphasize the return to orthodoxy, Userkaf's pyramid was sited at the centre of the old Saqqara cemeteries, close to the enclosure wall of Djoser's Step Pyramid, the first-built pyramid of them all. A dangerous and shapeless ruin, Userkaf's half-excavated funerary complex had once consisted of a rectangular wall that had enclosed both the royal pyramid and a compact and innovatory gathering of

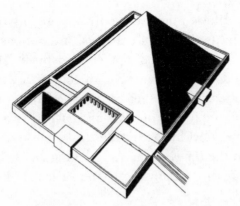

A reconstruction of Userkaf's pyramid complex; an architecture that had held a thoughtful mix of innovation and tradition.

temples and subsidiary, so-called 'queens', pyramids. Built at around a third of the size of the colossal pyramids, this royal pyramid signalled the dramatic change of scale in royal building that, with some slight variations, was adopted by all the later Memphite pharaohs.

The change was both dramatic and historic. When the baselines of Userkaf's pyramid were laid out, the construction of the four colossal pyramids had been completed just thirty years before. Yet the extensive supply systems which were built up in that heroic century had already been diminished. The best part of the fleets of boats and barges, the huge regiments of copper miners and quarrymen, the armies of stone haulers, the settlements of the largest labour force the world had ever known, were no longer in operation.

The court's utter concentration on royal pyramid construction had run its course, and as its architectural emphasis had changed so did the nature of the court itself. By the time of Userkaf's successors, when the pyramid builders of Abusir were making pyramids of similar size to that of Userkaf's, the change within the court is apparent both in the enlarging number and diversity of courtiers' tombs and in the ever-lengthening lists of names and titles which are recorded in them. And that in turn suggests that the pharaonic administration was supporting more households than before and thus ever increasing numbers of the courtly dead, whose cults, as the surviving records demonstrate, were served by growing numbers of priestly households who operated much the same rota systems as those employed within the royal temples.

In these same times, priests not only appear to have increased in number but also, as their tomb chapels' inscriptions suggest, their roles within the court were more precisely defined. The loose translation 'priest', indeed, covers a group of courtly titles which include in more literal translations the terms 'god's servant', 'pure one', 'god's father' and even, simply, 'old one'. As distinct offices held by different people within the court hierarchy, these different terms started to be differentiated in the times of the Abusir kings; previously, they had been sprinkled amongst many vague and varied epithets recorded in the tomb chapels.

Having diverted a great part of its activities away from the act of building colossal pyramids, the resources of the state had turned towards elaborating and monumentalizing in stone architecture the offices of the largely anonymous and undocumented government machine that it had inherited from the Giza kings. To this extent, the sun temples of Abusir, those innovatory and somewhat temporary structures, mark the beginning of a process by which the vast systems of supply and offering that had built the four great pyramids were formalized and elaborated. And as the complexity of the royal administration enlarged, so had the numbers of state officials outside the circle of the royal household.

Though the households of these new officials may also have been subsidized from private estates, this seemingly rapid increase in the size of the formal administration and in the offering cults of its dead officials could easily have been accommodated by the surplus state resources which had resulted from the abandonment of building colossal pyramids. These swift changes in the distribution of state resources may also account for the sudden appearance of the sun temples at Abusir, those major, novel distribution conduits, the first of which was built in the reign of Userkaf. That the two excavated sun temples show evidence of considerable and continuous enlargement throughout their working lives may further reflect these changing patterns in the distribution of state resources.

Within this changing state, court life was ordered in cycles of rite and celebration. In the times of the Abusir kings, so the remaining offering facilities and the surviving archives both suggest, the daily rituals of the court were still derived from those celebrated in the times of the archaic kings, when monarchs had been ceremonially dressed for the rites of presentation and offering that had been celebrated in royal courts throughout the region of the lower Nile. At Abusir, the living kings were represented by statues that were variously enshrined within the pyramid temples and the sun temples, whilst at the royal palace, so texts of the following century inform us, a similar round of daily ritual, timed to coincide with the passage of the sun, revolved around the person of the living king himself. And all those daily rites were punctuated by the regular celebration of festivals accompanying events within the farming and calendric years, and others that are traditionally termed 'jubilees' marked special years in the reigns of individual pharaohs.

Sections of the Abusir Papyri list rotas in which the same named personnel are described as moving between the royal temples, the sun temples and the royal residences, where, presumably, they performed the same ritual duties, which suggests that the daily rites undertaken in those three courtly settings were fundamentally one and the same. That those same papyri name individuals who are described as working at the sun temples yet who are also known from inscriptions in their tomb chapels to have been close to the living king and to have held offices in the administration shows that this rota of ritual and offering was integrated with what the modern world would term the secular arm of government.

Some of these people, so their titles tell, were members of groups that were denominated in hieroglyphic as *z'a* and which today are more usually described as 'phyles', an ancient Greek term for a clan or a quasi-tribal group. Once more, the origins of these groups appear to lie in the days of the first kings, when some of the names of those same phyles were inscribed on the pots and vases of the first royal funerary cults. Deriving from compass points and parts of boats, several of these phyles' names also appear in the graffiti of the work gangs who were engaged in building the colossal pyramids. And at Abusir as well, one of the temple phyles appears to have been involved in quarrying and hauling stone for the royal pyramid.

Though evidence is slight, it would appear that these phyles were a broad-based system of allegiances whose memberships could include both courtiers and workmen from the same household or even, perhaps, people who had shared a common place of birth. At all events, within the offering cults of the kings of Abusir these traditional groupings had operated a ten-month system of rotation; a system that is reflected in the architecture of both the pyramids and the sun temples of Abusir, where, as their archaeologists discovered, each phyle had its own designated storeroom.

MODELLING THE UNIVERSE

Just as the phyles had a long-established place within the order of the living state and set locations in the architecture of its temples, so, too, from their papyrus-shaped columns to the stars painted on their ceilings, the temples were designed in the image and the order of the kingdom. The very limestone of their walls had been quarried from the Nile cliffs, whilst the glistening hard stones of the temples' pavements, columns and doorways and the copper of the masons' chisels had been shipped from the far ends of the kingdom. And if the meat on the sun temples' altars had come mostly from the delta, then the river's valley had supplied the better part of the grain, from which the copious offerings of bread and beer were made.

These continuous acts of gathering and ordering of the physical substance of the kingdom in the form of the temples' architecture and rites of offerings was further reflected in the division of the temples' staff into northern and southern sections, which, like the order of the phyles, reflected their roles both in terms of the daily ritual and, as the tomb chapels' inscriptions also show, in the governance of the king-dom's regions. Just as the temples' reliefs laid out the order and activity of the court, so the fundamental elements and order of its kingdom were reflected in the temples' architecture. This it would appear is the underlying reason why, although the royal palaces and settlements were made of friable mud brick, its courtly tombs and temples were fashioned from enduring stone: the form and order of the state required endurance.

In the beginning, the cemeteries of the prehistoric settlements of the lower Nile had been set close to the mud houses of the living, and the dead had been buried with the finest goods their culture could pro-vide, and offerings of food were left beside the grave. It was a simple system in which the living and the dead participated in maintaining the settlement's identity and order. And that same system would underlie the order of the later state. Just as the early farmers had vis-ited the graveyards beside their settlements and slaughtered animals and feasted amongst the graves, so phalanxes of pharaoh's priests and slaughterers and various officials cooked foods, brewed beer and presented daily offerings to the dead kings in the great temples that had been built beside the royal tombs for that especial purpose. Just as today a person might declare that, without faith, life would have no form or purpose, so without the continuing operation of those obligations and activities, without the daily work of tomb and temple building and of provisioning the ancestors, the gods and the living communities of the court, the ancient culture would have dissolved.

Manifested in its networks of tithing, collection and supply, the efficacy of this unique culture was reaffirmed at the beginning of every reign when the state machine began to build another pyramid. So the architecture of the pyramid complexes manifests the living systems of that state in good hard stone, and the structures of tithing and supply which had enabled their construction continued to be acted out in dramatic continuation after pharaoh's death in rites of offering. Like the inhabitants of the early farming settlements, at Abusir, the state system operated within the archaic theatres of life and death.

These are the fundamental principles that explain all of the surviving manifestations of the pharaonic kingdom of the lower Nile. It was not a complex system. Though to modern minds its splendidly sophisticated and often enigmatic relics might first suggest the operation of a near-modern state with an elaborate theology, in reality they are a millennial duplication, elegant, consistent and concise, of a single set of rites – the rites of presentation and of offering, on which the state was founded.

14
The Living Kingdom

COPPER AND THE KINGS

After Giza, the huge reduction in the quality and size of royal pyramid construction had transformed pharaonic culture. One practical example of this great change was a product of the increased availability of copper, the raw material that in the form of saws and chisels had shaped the four great pyramids and the timbers of the enormous barges that shipped much of their stone.

Before the construction of the four great pyramids, the craftsmen's studios and the building works of even the longest reigns had required, at most, some seventy tons of the red metal. Just the first year of working on the Great Pyramid, however, had consumed a similar amount and that monument had taken some fourteen years to build. All in all, during the century in which the four colossal pyramids were built, some 950 tons of the metal would have been mined, smelted and sent to Memphis to make the tools used by the masons and the shipwrights of the court. Such extraordinary levels of production represented a tenfold increase in the size of personnel, provisions and supplies required – the food and water, tools and fuel – to support the copper miners in such hostile deserts as those of the peninsula of Sinai.

These sudden, burgeoning needs impelled, in turn, a considerable upgrading of the kingdom's transport networks. In the case of copper, as recent archaeology and some recently discovered papyri have shown, this prompted the establishment of new routes to the Sinai copper mines. These crossed Egypt's eastern deserts to give access to newly made ports on the Red Sea coast and the sea lanes which ran up the stormy northern reaches of that narrow waterway to harbours and transit stations close to the Sinai copper mines.

Pyramids of the size of Userkaf's and those of later kings, alternatively, required but a thirtieth of the materials needed for the construction of those four great pyramids. So even if the best part of the pharaonic mining camps and shipyards established in earlier times had been speedily closed down, within a state machine that was not driven by money but on a continuity of activity and a regularity of supply there would have been a considerable build up of such materials as copper, plaster, timber and hard desert stone. It is hardly surprising, therefore, that as well as the royal architecture containing considerable quantities of beautiful granites, quartzites, and basalts, the first temple to be built at Abusir had a remarkable solid copper drainpipe some 330 yards long running down through the desert to the cultivated land and, as Borchardt would report, huge wooden doors secured with massive bolts and chains and catches, all beautifully and ingeniously wrought from large quantities of copper.

At the same time, there was also a greatly increased use of copper outside the orbit of the court. When the colossal pyramids had been under construction, the use of such materials had been largely confined to the pyramids and their adjacent cemeteries, and there were few monuments of cut stone outside the region of Memphis. After the age of the four great pyramids, however, increasing numbers of tomb chapels were quarried, finished and engraved throughout the valley of the lower Nile, every element of which – their architecture, inscriptions and relief – was cut with copper tools. The growing numbers of these monuments, therefore, witness the slow diffusion of that courtly metal, along with the culture of the Memphite court, throughout the valley of the lower Nile.

NEKI-ANKH AT TIHNA

The first-known example of the use of copper tools on a large scale outside the region of Memphis is a large rock-cut tomb that was made a generation before the reign of Userkaf, in the time of Menkaure, when one Neki-ankh, a 'steward of the royal residence, governor of new settlements', set his monument high in the Nile-side cliffs 100 miles to the south of Saqqara and close today to the village of Tihna, in the region that is now called Middle Egypt. Neki-ankh's tomb was the first of a line of similar monuments to be cut into that dramatic cliff for succeeding generations of his household. Though badly damaged now, sufficient of their inscriptions survive to show that Neki-ankh had bequeathed to his successors parcels of land that had been granted to him by the king, as recorded in one of his tomb-chapel inscriptions, which was also duplicated in the adjacent tomb of his successor, his namesake and, probably, his eldest son.

Similar texts of the same period describe other examples of what appear to have been royal gifts of land, but most of them are very damaged. A few rare, rather ambiguous inscriptions in earlier Memphite tomb chapels suggest that royal grants of land had also been awarded to courtiers for their development as farms. Unlike Neki-ankh's land grant, however, those of the earlier colonizers seem not to have been hereditary and appear to have undergone further exchanges in stewardship. At all events, it is hardly likely that any of those royal grants had awarded courtiers 'ownership' of land in the modern sense of that word.

Ultimately, the names of the Old Kingdom pharaohs commanded the flood plain, the quarries and mines in the surrounding deserts and the organization of the various labour forces that made the products of that courtly culture. A host of tomb-chapel inscriptions, for example, describe how the kings of Abusir and their successors provided their courtiers with fine stone for their tomb chapels and desert stone for their sarcophagi and even, on occasion, supplied the court's workshops with exotic woods and other materials for the manufacture of their courtiers' burial equipment.

It would appear, therefore, that the lands of the lower Nile were at the disposal of pharaoh, who, through the offices of the royal court, encouraged their further development for both cattle raising and for cultivation. Several inscriptions from the times of the Abusir kings record pharaoh's personal interest in schemes of canal making and water conservation, whilst texts in several provincial tomb chapels describe the founding and controlling of new settlements and large tracts of land. The role of the offices of the king in such enterprises is further underlined by the incorporation of the royal name within many of these so-called 'new settlements', whilst the fact that, in reality, some of those lands had long since held communities bearing other names, simply endorses pharaoh's continuing drive for renewal and increased agricultural production.

Based on the assumption that ancient states were similar to modern ones, traditional historians usually describe the relocation of the households of some of the Memphite courtiers into the provinces as the beginning of a catastrophic dissipation of centralized pharaonic power that led, eventually, to the ending of the Old Kingdom. What the surviving monuments show, however, is another aspect of the changes that occurred when the court, having diverted a great part of its resources away from the single-minded act of building colossal pyramids, had turned its attentions to consolidating and perpetuating the systems of supply that it had previously created and extended. And that, in turn, prompted the physical extension of the culture of the Abusir courts, its monuments and rituals, throughout the region of the lower Nile.

VISITING THE TOMBS

For the majority of Westerners, the grand tour of Egypt had started in the 1870s when Thomas Cook & Sons obtained a concession from the Khedive Ismail to run Nile steamboats and dahabiyyas – luxurious sailing boats – from Cairo up to Aswan and into northern Nubia. Isolated on the quiet wide river, Cook's tourists were afforded intimate views into the very heart of rural Upper Egypt. And as the boats moved gently on the stream, these privileged travellers could also spot the doors of ancient rock-cut tomb chapels, lines of shadowed rectangles standing over screes of bright white limestone chip set high up in the gilded cliffs that framed the riverside's fields.

For Cook's tourists, the cliff-cut tombs promised exciting and bumpy rides on carriages and donkeys along the muddy edges of the fields and out onto the little hot deserts that lay beneath the limestone cliffs, before scrambling up pathways in the loose scree and entering the cool gloom of tomb chapels whose stained and broken walls were covered in scenes showing agricultural activities similar to those they had observed in life, from the promenades of their floating hotels. For archaeologists, those same tomb chapels indicated that there had been a substantial ancient settlement in the area; one with craftsmen and copper enough to support the making of such courtly monuments and to equip the ancient burials, which might still lay undisturbed beneath the tomb chapels, at the bottom of rock-cut shafts.

More than a thousand decorated tomb chapels are known to have survived from the age of the Old Kingdom, of which some 600 are still standing. Almost a third of that number are provincial tombs and were excavated in the limestone of the Nile-side cliffs. Even as the craftsmen of the court were decorating the temples of Abusir with elegant scenes of country life, some contemporary courtiers were casting their eyes over rural landscapes that their forefathers had long since abandoned for Memphis and a life at court.

Hardly any funerary monuments had been made outside of the central Memphis cemeteries in the times of Khufu and Khafre, and most of those had been set close to the archaic royal burying grounds at Abydos in Upper Egypt. In the times of the Abusir kings, however, at least ten large rock-cut tombs are known to have been excavated in the Nile's valley south of Memphis, whilst in the following 150 years, over a hundred more such monuments were made. Most of these rock-cut tombs are clustered in twenty-odd sites between Memphis and Aswan and are known today by the musical Arabic names of nearby towns and villages: Dishasha, Hagarsa, Naga el-Deir, Qaw el-Kebir, Sidmant, Meir, Edfu, Girga and the like. In their own day, it must have seemed as if a courtly colonization of the lower Nile was under way. For in those times, large tracts of land both in the river's valley and its delta were uncultivated.

These provincial monuments are different from those of their Memphite predecessors. In the delta, where the evidence is comparatively thin, mastaba tombs were still made in the traditional way, and blocks of limestone were sometimes shipped from quarries in the river's valley to aid in their construction. Most of the provincial tombs within the Nile Valley, however, did not continue that archaic tradition, and were excavated in the cliffs along the valley's edge, a method that appears to have been invented in the cemeteries of Giza,

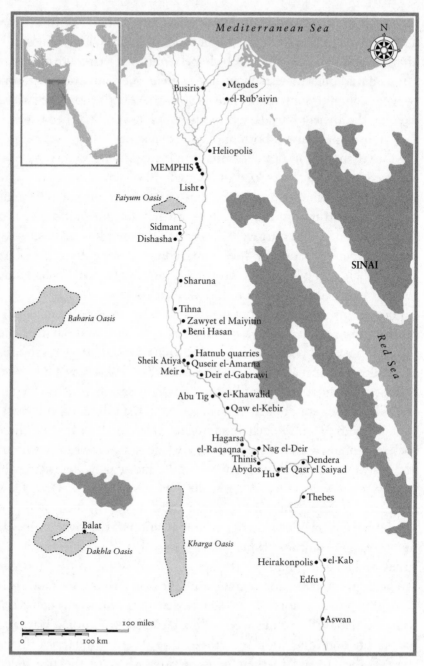

Map showing the locations of Old Kingdom tomb chapels, more
than 90 per cent of which were made in the last century of that era.
Set close to settlements with, presumably, strong links to central
Memphite culture, the map effectively plots the courtly colonization
of the regions of the lower Nile.

where the ranks of the older, earlier stone-block mastabas had been set so close together that there was little room for the facilities of offering or to make space for the burials of later generations of the courtly households.

An early and influential solution to the growing shortage of space within the Giza cemeteries had been to excavate the bedrock underneath one of the great stone mastabas of Khufu's queens, and then to fashion an entrance doorway that led to two rock-cut rooms beyond: one holding an offering chapel, the other a burial shaft. In the following decades, this simple scheme was extended so that other doorways resembling that of a mastaba's offering chapel were cut into the walls of the nearby stone quarries, and the same two-room plan was excavated in the rock beyond. These are the first-known rock-cut tombs in Egypt, and their design was adopted by the provincial courtiers so that the lines of their doorways – rectangles of shadow marked with white screes of chippings beneath them from the tombs' excavation – came to punctuate whole sections of that narrow landscape. At first, those provincial tombs consisted of the two-room scheme of the Giza tombs: the first room, an offering chapel with decorations similar to those in the earlier mastaba tombs, the second room holding a deep shaft with a sarcophagus at its bottom. Ever inventive, however, the craftsmen swiftly rang a peal of variations on those basic units and the later provincial rock tombs took on many different forms.

ALL ALONG THE VALLEY

Set high up in the cliffs and far removed from human settlement, most of the provincial rock-cut tomb chapels of the Old Kingdom had been of little practical use to the later farmers of the Nile Valley, and so until quite recently most of them lay open and abandoned. Stained by wasp nests and bat droppings, their wall scenes were difficult to see, many of their ceilings had collapsed in ancient earthquakes, half burying the chambers' decorations, and most of the darkest chambers held dangerously deep burial-chamber shafts cut straight into their floors. Yet more discouraging was the fact that the tomb chapels' surviving decorations were often scarred by the chisellings of antiquities merchants, who would remove odd chunks of museum-worthy decoration by cutting a rectangular frame deep into the wall around the section that they wanted to remove, then slicing off the isolated portion of relief with frayed wire cable, which cuts the soft white limestone with horrifying efficiency. Many of these tomb chapels are now beautifully restored and are well-known fixtures on the tourist trail. Some of the more desolate and isolated examples, however, have yet to be examined, and doubtless there are many more, whole cemeteries perhaps, still buried in the screes of debris that lie along the valley's cliffs.

These provincial tomb chapels represent a new strand in the pharaonic courtly culture that quickly developed a vigorous character of its own. At the beginning, there is firm evidence of individual Memphite craftsmen working up and down the Nile Valley, for some of the scenes within the provincial tomb chapels were derived from the reliefs within the temples of the kings. Others, however, were copied from the reliefs in the tomb chapels of Memphis, where there were two different schools of craftsmanship and design working side by side.

In the times of the Abusir kings the bulk of the contemporary courtiers had built their funerary monuments of stone blocks set in the form of archaic mastabas and built either in the traditional burying grounds of the Giza Plateau, beside the three great pyramids, or in the desert burying grounds of Saqqara, where they were dominated by the ancient pyramid enclosure of King Djoser, which in those days appears to have housed the administrative offices of those ancient cemeteries.

Following the clearance of their protecting sand drifts in the last decades of the nineteenth century, many of the Saqqara tomb chapels have been eroded by the raw desert winds. Others have simply disappeared, having been taken away, block by block, by antiquities merchants who were following in the footsteps of the early archaeologists and supplying the museums of Europe and America with whole walls and sometimes entire tomb chapels covered in fine relief. What survives, however – the vividly decorated so-called 'Tomb of the Two Brothers', for example, along with such famous monuments as the mastabas of Ptahhotep, Tiy and Mereruka – shows that a highly inventive school of craftsmen was working at Saqqara in the latter half of the Old Kingdom, craftsmen who were greatly elaborating and extending earlier tomb-chapel decoration and even, on occasion, employing painting rather than engraving, which gives their scenes a livelier and freer air.

At Giza, on the other hand, there was a separate school of craftsmen working in a manner more in keeping with the great grand monuments on that high plateau, which had retained a style of tomb-chapel decoration that is more formal, more reserved, than the sprightlier Saqqara scenes.

Both of those two Memphite schools can be detected in the provincial cemeteries along the valley of the lower Nile. The tomb chapels at Tihna, for example, bear direct relationship to earlier work within the Giza cemeteries, whilst the scenes from several Saqqara tombs were directly copied onto the walls of a variety of rock-cut tomb chapels in other sites in Middle Egypt. Here, one might imagine, the craftsmen had used a medium such as a sheet of linen or papyrus on which to copy the Memphite originals and had then transported their copies to the provincial tomb chapels, where they had been redrawn and re-carved. At that same time there was a lively traffic in statues made in the Memphite workshops, excavations at sites all over Upper Egypt yielding works of high court style as well as many local imitations.

Along with the occasional idiosyncrasy of style or draftsmanship, the high quality of some of the reliefs in these provincial rock-cut tombs suggests that they were engraved by travelling craftsmen from the Saqqara cemeteries. Other later tombs, alternatively, show very different hands at work: provincial craftsmen working in several different cemeteries busily engaged in translating some of those traditional Memphite scenes in fresh and vivid ways. Some of these tomb chapels show an uncommon delight in strong patterning and provide highly original observations of provincial life which, over time, through reign after reign, served to transform the relatively staid composure of the older decorations into vigorous, if somewhat folksy, renderings of the same iconic scenes but drawn now with an eye for local detail and wry caricature: a quail watches a reaper at his work, a monkey imitates the gestures of a dancer, dogs sitting beneath their master's chair scoff a good fat goose.

A traditional explanation of such scenes and their accompanying texts in all these tomb chapels is that they are the product of a simple-minded concern with the preservation of the tomb owner's spirit; that such scenes were a magical means of supplying him with a perpetual source of stony foodstuffs. What they ultimately describe, however, and this holds true for both the Memphite and provincial tomb chapels, is the role of the tomb chapel's proprietor within the structures of the state.

Typically, at Giza, at Saqqara and the provinces, images of the tomb chapel's owner were placed on either side of its entrance doorway accompanied by texts listing the courtier's epithets and titles. Sometimes seated, but more usually standing, further images of him will appear throughout his monument. Like the figures of the kings within their temples, the tomb owners are shown beside offering tables and on full-sized reproductions of a wooden house door – the so-called 'false doors' – that were carved in relief so that the noble dead may pass each day into the living world. These false doors are the targets towards which, line on line, figure after figure, the decorations in these chapels guide the eye. And offerings were laid on low altars set at their foot.

The tomb owner's figures, always the principal subjects of these graphic compositions, are shown viewing the activities portrayed in the manner of a supervisor. Line on line, the figures – the tomb owner, his wife and children, his household officers and servants – are ranked in size, the largest being the monument's proprietor. His accompanying household and family are drawn at smaller sizes, while smaller still are the estate personnel, who are shown in various workshops, on the river, and in the fields and granaries. Though more complex in their detail and their composition than earlier examples of such scenes, the subject matter hardly ever changes nor, even, the poses of the participants, hunting in the marshes and the desert, servants making and preparing the goods and provisions that define courtly life and, finally, workers undertaking a variety of activities which supported that way of life: building boats, cultivating fields, herding livestock and making pots, statues, vases and jewellery. Throughout it all a rigorous hierarchy is observed. And neither kings nor gods are ever shown within the private tomb chapels, nor, of course, are scenes of royal ritual. In the nobles' tomb chapels, the courtiers themselves are shown in the manner of the kings, as lords of everything in their domain.

SCENES FROM LIFE

A common scene in the provincial tomb chapels, and one appropriate to their time and place, shows cows and bulls of different colours, plain and spotted, black and white; bulls in herds, bulls fighting, cows giving birth, cattle at the plough and cattle being expertly butchered by their slaughterers. It would appear, therefore, that as well as the long-established delta farms that were breeding and fattening bulls for the Abusir temples, some of the estates of the provincial courtiers within the Nile's valley were also supplying those protein-rich cargoes to the courts of Abusir and Saqqara. And the texts alongside many of those images show that the tomb-chapel owners had been proud to cultivate those splendid beasts.

Such enormous animals were not usually a part of a subsistence farmer's holdings. Yet their pre-eminence as offerings and as a preferred food of the living court had given them an important role in its agricultural undertakings since the state's beginning. The annals of the early kings, indeed, list the numbers of cattle counts that had taken place in individual reigns and frequently employ those numbered cattle counts, rather than a monarch's years of rule, to mark the lengths of individual reigns.

So those painted cows upon the wall of the provincial tomb chapels are evidence of the continuing role of the tomb chapel's owners within the culture of the court. That some of those cattle-breeding nobles had established households in provinces far from Memphis underlines the fact that by the times of the Abusir kings even the most far-flung courtiers were provisioning the royal court.

The great wide river, the essential artery of that traffic and the medium by which, for centuries past, vast tonnages of provisions, men and building stone had moved with ease throughout the kingdom, bound all the settlements along the lower Nile, large and small alike, directly to Memphis and the offices of state. And travel on that most beauteous of metros was swift and easy: Senedjemib Inti's sarcophagus, so his son records in his tomb-chapel texts, had been barged to Memphis from quarries at the southernmost point of the kingdom in less than a week; other courtiers, moreover, had held estates throughout the kingdom and sent their children off to Memphis for education at the royal residence. In short, the river's state-wide span, its steady flow and countervailing winds, had enabled and defined that most fortunate of kingdoms from its beginnings.

There was, therefore, no need, no place, for towns or cities in this realm, nothing larger than the settlements of pharaoh close by the pyramids. As Donald Redford puts it, 'the metropolitan states of Western Asia and the Mediterranean, with an elite separated from the agricultural basis of their existence by many social strata, does not find a parallel on the banks of the Nile River.'

Most earlier egyptologists, however, had assumed that such celebrated sites as Aswan, Edfu and Hierakonpolis, Memphis, Buto and Bubastis had once been ancient cities. Yet Memphis of the 'White Walls' – the Memphis of the Greek and Roman travellers and of nineteenth-century imagination – was sustained by markets and a monetary economy, and the Old Kingdom had been very far removed from such classical or modern concepts of urban life. The fundamental nature of that most ancient state was agricultural. The gulf between Memphis and its provinces was not nearly as great as one might at first imagine. Even the royal residence was set beside canals and at the edge of farmland. And, certainly, the life style of the court as it is depicted in its courtiers' myriad tomb chapels is always shown as country life and never as taking place within the confines of some kind of city.

Like the majority of inhabitants of this planet before quite recent times, pharaoh's people had lived rural lives. In the delta where the broad silt plains stretched to the horizon, the settlements and farms were spaced amongst the river's ever-changing branches. In the narrow valley, from Memphis to Aswan, the farms and settlements, which in Old Kingdom times are usually estimated to have numbered fewer than 2,000, were set within the silty ribbons that lay on each side of the great wide river.

Almost nothing is known about the realities of those farming settlements within the Nile Valley. Beyond a few excavations of some unusual communities – a carefully planned complex beside the Giza Plateau built to house the pyramid makers, an island settlement at Aswan provisioned by the government, some desert mansions and a few odd houses set on ancient mounds – nothing else is known.

In a similarly disappointing fashion, although archaeologists have indeed uncovered Old Kingdom farming settlements within the Nile Delta, most of their plans conform to the typical patterns of state planning: large orthogonally planned complexes somewhat similar to the settlements beside the Giza pyramids. Rather than indigenous farms or villages, these appear to have been purpose-built state colonies and are probably the ruins of estates like those that are named in the offering processions within the tombs and temples, and thus are hardly typical of life down on the farm.

In prehistoric times, the people of the region of the lower Nile had lived in settlements that at most comprised the dwellings of a few hundred people and were built on the river's silt plain, amidst the fields that they cultivated. Within the river valley, the most densely populated regions were where the silt plains were at their narrowest and irrigation easily controlled; that is, in the region between Aswan and Abydos in the south and in the final hundred miles of the river's progress before the Memphite region, where the silt slowly starts to widen into the delta. As the season cooled and the time of the annual flood drew near, those farmers had retreated with their grain stocks and their animals to higher ground. In the Nile Delta these elevated refuges were the so-called turtlebacks or levees that had been thrown up by sandstorms and the river's sluggish flow. In the valley, they were mostly situated at the edges of the little deserts that lay beyond the silt plain and the valley's fringing cliffs.

Modern analysis of farming settlements along the valley of the Nile in those millennia shows that those early farmers had moved ever closer to the marshes on the river's banks, a trend that may well have continued in the times of the Memphite pharaohs, when large sections of the lower Nile were still not under cultivation. And this is an especial disadvantage for archaeologists, for the course of the Nile has moved back and forth across its black silt plain over the last few thousand years virtually obliterating all evidence of ancient life within that area not made of stone. At all events, not a single Old

Kingdom farm or hamlet has yet been excavated within the Nile Valley.

That lost life, however, is reflected in scenes within the courtiers' tomb chapels and is implied in the farming implements, their wooden handles still shiny from use, that have been found in some contemporary tombs. Both those sources show that the techniques of farming had hardly changed until relatively recently; that though the silt plain of the river valley had been entirely colonized in the following millennia, the beautiful environment that the early farmers had started to create would remain virtually unchanged until modern times. Napoleon's cartographers, indeed, had mapped it during their invasion of Egypt.

Not surprisingly, the surviving tools and utensils of the Old Kingdom show that the vast ongoing movements of people and supplies, which the pyramid-building kings had accelerated, had also consolidated the processes of state-wide standardization. So when the potter's kick wheel, a device that offered both an increased speed of production and a saving of worked raw clay, was introduced in the times of the Abusir kings it had been quickly taken up throughout the kingdom. From the weights and measures used to quantify the harvests to the style and shapes of workaday objects used in carpentry and weaving, in brewing and baking, cloth making and pottery, there was a state-wide conformity of culture beyond that of most other ancient societies. Many of the forms and techniques of this ancient way of life, indeed, had hardly changed until quite recently; some of the loaves of bread that have been found in ancient tombs, for example, are similar in size and manufacture to some of those made in Upper Egyptian villages to this day.

Wheat, too, the single staple crop that provided bread and beer throughout the land, was largely standardized. Unlike today, however, the eyes and taste buds of the ancient scribes made a firm distinction between the grain of the river's valley and its delta. Both in the valley and the delta households, however, bread and beer were made side by side and, as brewing and baking both required ceramic jars and moulds, a potter's studio and kiln were generally to be found close to the grinding stones, the kilns and ovens. Captioned and labelled, images of all those essential activities of daily life are shown side by side in many a courtier's tomb chapel, alongside other images of daily life in courtly households.

Many of these scenes are accompanied by short exclamatory texts as lively as the images beside them. So workers tying down a cow for slaughter might tell their partners to 'Pull hard, my friend!' – an exhortation that is often followed by an ominous 'Do it, make it happen, hurry!' – and reapers gathering stooks of wheat destined for the household's threshing floors tell their comrades 'Look, the donkeys are coming!', 'Tie the sack!', 'Steady the pannier!', whilst a herdsman in a tiny boat transporting cows and calves across a crocodile-infested stream urges his companion to 'Row, comrade! Go slowly!', and a sailor on a Nile boat exclaims 'Pay attention to the ropes!' or 'Turn to starboard right away, so that we may fare well!'

Down by the riverside, the Nile's silt descended into lush marsh lands with rippling stands of sedge, reed and papyrus. Quiet, closed areas of considerable beauty, these water meads were inhabited by a variety of small mammals, by frogs and water snakes, by the occasional crocodile and hippopotamus and, in their proper seasons, by huge flocks of migrating birds, from pelicans to pintails, thirsty for the riverine oasis and hungry for the food that it sustained. Here fishermen cast their nets as their boats slid slowly between the reeded islands that shifted shape and rose and fell according to the height and season of the flood. And here as well, amongst those closed and narrow waterways, huntsmen and courtiers alike caught fish and water fowl, the latter being taken with the aid of an ingenious array of decoys and throw sticks, traps and clap nets. And all this is shown with great delight within the courtiers' tomb chapels.

Flat and incredibly fertile, the farmed sections of two alluvial plains that lay behind the marshes were divided, in the usual way of hand-worked farms, into small-sized strips. Traversed by narrow, dusty and slightly elevated pathways tufted with supporting grasses, these little fields were watered from small channels which ran alongside the pathways and carried carefully measured parcels of the river water which had been trapped and conserved in wide and shallow water basins when the annual flood waters had retreated. The farmers were expert at maintaining water levels in their fields, and there was virtually no rain. No crops grew anywhere within the regions of the lower Nile unless they were constantly watered by human hands or unless their roots reached down into the underlying water table. But the crops grew large and luscious under that deep blue sky and were beautifully celebrated in the tombs and temples in images of bounteous offerings.

Stands of trees stood beside the little pathways that ran alongside the irrigation channels. Apart from high-curving date palms, these were mostly low and straggling tamarisks and acacias, native shallow-rooted hardwood trees with gnarled and twisted branches whose hard brown wood was used in boat building and in mud-brick architecture. Cultivated in copses, such trees also provided the farmers with firewood. And as rain hardly ever fell, a fine film of silt and sand lay thick upon their leaves, giving them a celadon-dry glaze that turned their vivid foliage into the vaguest shades of green, their small bright flowers shining like stars against the copses' shadowed interiors.

Tamarisks and acacias thrive in all but the most arid deserts, yet they easily survived the Nile's annual flood, and as their small leaves are often encrusted with salt they also provided, along with several species of tough low bushes, tasty pasturage for sheep and goats, who managed to avoid the considerable spikes that were hidden in their vegetation. All vegetation growing in the narrow valley was well used and much appreciated. Court jewellers mimicked their small bright flowers in shining desert stones of red and yellow and copied the colours and forms of the fruits and flowers, the grapes, the pomegranates, carob pods, sycamore figs and jasmine that the farmers cultivated in walled orchards and vegetable gardens.

Rare surviving images show that traditional farmhouses were usually two-storeyed mud-brick buildings surrounded by high mud-brick walls and shaded by courtyard trees. Inside the enclosure walls, as well as the living quarters, which were usually composed of a series of straggling rooms built and enlarged according to the household's needs, there might be cattle pens and pig sties, fowl coops and threshing floors, grain stores, vine arbours and gardens; all of those rural paradises gifts of the sweet waters of the river and the antithesis of the dazzling desert vastness of the pyramids and their attending temples.

Wheat, alternatively, was cultivated in the narrow open fields, within the simple archaic systems of low dykes designed to trap the receding waters of the annual flood on the flat silt fields. Both these low dykes and the channels that ran away from them were parts of a fundamental irrigation system that necessitated group labour and flexible notions of land ownership. Just such a system, indeed, was still in operation in the Nile Valley in Champollion's day when, under the control of local potentates and village worthies, entire communities saw to the upkeep of the dykes, the irrigation channels and the digging and the cleaning of canals.

A detail of the atlas of Egypt prepared during the Napoleonic invasion, showing the ageless patterns of villages and fields within the Nile's flood plain. The area shown is just a few miles south of modern-day Asyut in Middle Egypt.

This, then, had been an ancient state like no other. A kingdom of lush riverine landscapes, an intimate environment in which agriculture and human habitation, courtier and peasant, lived close together. And though the greater part of this population has left no trace whatever on this earth, rare and poignant papyri from a settlement at Gebelein in Upper Egypt provide a partial list of the names and occupations of a handful of the members of the provincial population in the times of the Abusir kings: bakers and brewers, potters, metal workers and herdsmen and some farm workers who are named as 'kings-people', a title that a tomb text describes as one held by a group of people who were working lands that had been granted to a courtier by the king. Along with boat builders and sailors and, inevitably, the scribes and clerks who counted and tithed the harvests, such occupations made up the bulk of ancient Egypt's population; men and women who, the same papyri show, were liable for enlistment by the officials of the court for works of state.

Scenes such as those shown inside the nobles' tomb chapels would be repeated with an extraordinary fidelity over the following millennia in the tomb chapels of later generations. Like modern wedding photographs, the aim of those tomb-chapel designers was to present harmony and continuity working within society – the operation of a social compact that some of the texts of later ages would extol as a pillar of society. In similar fashion, the assertion in the texts of some of those later tomb chapels, which proudly announce that their owners had provided for the welfare of local populations in time of hardship, is a declaration that stems from an awareness of the benefits of promoting a benevolent and prospering society, just as is shown in operation, time and again, within the tomb chapels of the Old Kingdom courtiers.

15

Cult and Kingdom

OF COURTLY CULTS

At the same time that many courtiers were establishing households outside Memphis, so too temples dedicated to the royal cult were being established in the provinces.

This, of itself, was not a new phenomenon. In the times of Sneferu, so the Palermo Stone records, six statues of the king had been made for variously located shrines, whilst the line of little pyramids that had been erected all along the lower valley of the Nile during that same reign had simple accommodation for the cult of royal offering, at least one of those provincial monuments having a royal statue and an offering table set beside it, whilst another had stood next to a scribal office whose officials dealt in state supply.

Such modest arrangements would suggest that, in the times of the colossal pyramids, those provincial cults had served as foci and collection points for the supply of provisions and materials destined for the pyramid makers and the living court at Memphis, just as some of the rare surviving reliefs of those same times show that large numbers of provincial estates had similarly maintained the royal cults within the Memphite temples.

The provincial shrines and temples established in the times of the kings of Abusir and Saqqara, however, were of a different order. Dedicated both to the royal cult and to some of the state gods, these shrines and temples were elaborately sustained *in situ* by royal decree, so that the full operation of the royal cult was continuously observed in shrines and temples throughout the kingdom:

A royal decree . . .

[Regarding] the overseer and inspector of the priests of the god Min in Coptos [the modern town of Qift, in Upper Egypt] . . . [and] all the dependents and the possessions of the estate of Min, the functionaries and the entourage and daily service of Min and the workmen and builders of his temple who are employed there.

My majesty does not permit that they be sent to the royal works, or to cattle or donkey pastures, or with other animals, or with the administration of the guards, or [suffer] any [other] duty or tithing of the royal estate, for all eternity.

Their exemption [from such work] is renewed today by the command of the King Neferkare [Pepi II] . . . With regard to any chief or great one . . . [who shall] set them to any work; it is a conspiracy akin to rebellion!

The king of the Valley and the Delta, Neferkare, may he live for ever, has commanded that this document be put into the form of this decree and set up in hard stone at the gate of the temple of Min in Coptos of the Coptite region, so that the functionaries of that region should see [it] and that they do not take away these priests for any work . . .

. . . Sealed in the presence of the king himself.

Many of these new provincial foundations were built at the sites of archaic and pre-pharaonic shrines. At Coptos, for example, where several royal decrees had been preserved in stone inscriptions, there was a very ancient shrine of the God Min. In similar fashion, various excavations that have been undertaken at sites as far apart as the islands of the First Cataract and the northern delta have revealed how other archaic sanctuaries that had previously accommodated but a few ceramic offering tables, flint knives and some small images of animals and humans had been rebuilt and enlarged so that they came to house some of the grand high-shining products of Memphite courtly culture: sophisticated pieces of ritual paraphernalia embellished with royal names; wands, sceptres and fine vases of translucent alabasters, royal statues made from hard stone, and objects, on occasion, that recorded the celebration of individual royal festivals.

Measuring on average some fifteen by eighteen yards and enclosed by straight thick rectangular walls made of well-laid mud bricks, the interiors of these newly founded shrines echoed the forms of the central areas of the pyramid temples at Abusir and Saqqara and were divided into a series of narrow oblong chambers. In comparison with the skimpy informality of the older shrines, these buildings and their impressive contents speak of the opulence of central government and the imposed regularity of state control.

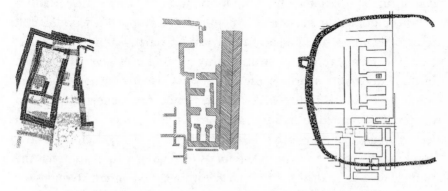

Plans of three late Old Kingdom provincial temples plotted by their various excavators. Left to right, that at Tell Ibrahim Awad in the eastern Nile Delta, and Abydos and Hierakonpolis in Upper Egypt, the latter two having three same-sized shrines set side by side. All three shrines were made of mud brick and were built over prehistoric shrines – the 'C' drawn around the shrine of Hierakonpolis representing an archaic revetment on which the later temple had been set. Although the delta shrine was somewhat smaller than the others, the area around all three yielded impressive quantities of well-made artefacts, the shrine of Hierakonpolis holding amongst its many other treasures a splendid golden hawk within its central shrine.

In all probability, the number of these new shrines was greater than their surviving remains suggest. Evidence is sparse, partly because many of these structures were elaborated and overbuilt during the following millennia so that today their locations are marked by some of the most celebrated of the Egyptian temples, whose inscriptions occasionally describe their humble origins in a near-mythic pre-pharaonic past.

Hierakonpolis, on the other hand, one of the earliest centres of settlement in the lower Nile Valley was not greatly favoured by the builders of the later kings, and the considerable clutter of archaic objects that had accumulated in its clustered shrines, fine objects such as Narmer's celebrated palette, had been carefully reburied when the later Old Kingdom monarchs had built and furnished a provincial shrine within the prehistoric compound, thus preserving a unique treasury of archaic artefacts which was recovered in the late 1890s. The archaeologists also revealed the ruin of a fine four-square provincial shrine of the later Old Kingdom and at its centre they found a life-sized golden hawk's head which had once topped a wooden cult image. Set in its original position within a narrow mud-brick sanctum, the carnelian of the bird's darkly shining eyes gives the golden bird an unearthly spark of life. Close by this shrine the excavators found two exquisite life-sized statues made from sheets of beaten copper, one named in its inscription as King Pepi I, the other nameless, though identifiable by its iconography as a royal child. Those regal images must have been the focus of regular rituals in much the same way as were their counterparts within the Memphite temples, or indeed the figure of the living king within the confines of his palace. The oldest-known life-sized metal statues in the world, the two sculptures are now ranked as masterpieces of pharaonic art. And they yet hold something of the living presence of the pharaohs of that age.

Just as their early excavators had seen, such splendid objects shine out from the dust of ruined mud-brick buildings. In consequence, during the following decades, dealers dug out many more such treasures in illicit excavations undertaken at several remote locations, which were then sold into the international antiquities market. So the original find spots of many of those remarkable objects are now lost along with any understanding of their ancient context and, thus, their roles within the daily rituals of the royal rites. And that is an especial shame, for similarly splendid objects of the royal cult are hardly ever found within the Memphite temples. Nevertheless, in their new roles as glittering treasures in museum cases, their crisp inscriptions and fine craftsmanship still testify that, in the later Old Kingdom, there was a powerful royal presence throughout the provinces of the ancient kingdom of the lower Nile.

A HISTORY OF GODS

Just as the state-wide diffusion of the royal cult along the lower Nile could be described as a monumentalization of the pulse of tithing and offering that had sustained the Memphite court from its beginnings so too, as the mix of kings and gods in the triads of Menkaure had shown, the roles of the kings and gods within the royal cult had long been intertwined. From their first appearances, indeed, the familiar gods of ancient Egypt are shown as members of the pharaonic household, and like the other members of that extended family they were included in the essential round of tithe, offering and sustenance.

The origins of these state deities are presently unknown. Certainly, many of their hieroglyphic attributes, the signs and iconographies by which they are identified, were created in prehistoric times, yet that fact alone does not prove that those same gods were already in existence in those distant ages. As with many other faiths, those ancient icons could well have been awarded to new-made gods as suitable attributes of deity.

The hawk, for example, is a truly archaic sign of royalty, as many images testify. The name of the first pharaoh, indeed, was set inside an image of the royal residence beneath the same archaic image of a hawk, whilst a later variant of the royal name, invented in the time of the colossal pyramids, the so-called 'name of gold', was similarly set beneath that sign. The god Horus, on the other hand, whose name is also determined in formal hieroglyphs by the image of a hawk, is presently recorded as making his debut as a god in the reign of Huni, Sneferu's predecessor, when a court craftsman drew a hawk's head upon the body of a man – a process that was cleverly reversed in the following century when court sculptors set a human head upon an animal's body and made the sphinx.

In his first-known appearance in human form, Horus is identified in the accompanying inscription as 'Horus of the royal residence', thus underlining his close relationship to pharaoh and his house. And that new-made deity stands shoulder to shoulder with King Huni, their eyes, the human's and the raptor's, caught in common if unearthly gaze whilst Horus' hands and arms wrap tenderly around the royal torso, just as the sculpted hawk's wings embrace the back of Khafre's head in that most celebrated statue.

Whenever the state gods were first conceived, they were without exception brought into sharp focus and given human form within the Memphite workshops. Along with the rest of pharaonic culture – the offering tables, the nobles' tomb chapels, the pyramids, the regalia and throne of pharaoh, the architectures that contained the offices of royal ritual – those anthropomorphic deities were literally the products of the studios of Memphite craftsmen. Certainly, there is no evidence of the existence in those times of an abstract theology – of 'a science of things divine', as Dean Hooker has described it – which had prompted their creation. Nothing but those elegant synthetic images. Nor, indeed, is there evidence to suggest that those new-made deities had been worshipped in Old Kingdom times by the various populations of the lower Nile.

One of the peculiarly modern difficulties in appreciating the nature of such ancient gods is the common tendency to assume that they had similar literary personalities to those that we associate with gods today: that they were like the frisky deities on Winckelmann's Mount Olympus or that they had been elements of one of those so-called 'primitive' religions catalogued by Victorian anthropologists. Yet the pharaonic deities cannot be explained by labelling them as figures in a myth or gods of this or that, or as symbols of life or death, the rising wheat, the sun, the moon. And though later in pharaonic history many of them came to embody complex contradictions of living human beings, and thus appear as personalities, they were neither sub-Freudian personifications of aspects of human consciousness nor elements in a kind of anthropomorphic science that had been invented to explain the order of the universe.

In short, these early courtly deities do not appear to have been parts of a coherent religion such as Champollion or the modern world would recognize. Not Western gods at all. All that the surviving relics show is that the rites that were conducted in their shrines and temples were modelled on those that ordered the life of pharaoh and the royal household and the ritual within the royal mortuary temples; that they, too, were sustained by the day-to-day processes of provisioning and offering. Later texts, therefore, describe these 'gods' in the present tense, just as they describe the courtly dead as living in the living world. They rise up with the sun *today*, they move *now* upon the wind, with the swaying of the palms and sycamores, with the rhythms of sun and moon and stars, with the round of the royal festivals and the daily cult. Unlike the earthly members of the court, however, if these unseen members of the royal household were granted offerings they too would live throughout the generations along with the populations of the dead and the offices of state.

SEEN AND UNSEEN

God; in which is contained Father, King, and Lord.
                                        Thomas Hobbes, 1651

That two complementary worlds, seen and unseen, existed side by side in pharaoh's kingdom was a prehistoric inheritance. The excavated graves of those distant periods confirm that the early farming communities along the lower Nile had similarly assumed that not all of the person had died when life was seen to have left their bodies; that although those intangible, unseen aspects of living beings had separated from the physical body at the time of death their vitality had not left the living world and could yet form a vital and continuing part of community identity. So the living had catered for the survival of those unseen aspects of their group by making elaborate arrangements for individual burials and by nourishing the continuing presence of the dead through acts of offering and feasting at the grave. Just as modern archaeologists describe and define those early cultures from material which for the most part has been recovered from their cemeteries, so too in prehistoric times, without the energies that the early farmers had continued to lavish on their dead, those living settlements would have lost touch with their ancestors and thus lost the continuity of group identity.

Along with the elaborate rites of burial, such continued acts of offering were also the defining activities of the pharaonic state and engaged the best part of its resources, prompting the building of its monuments and the maintenance of both the living court and of the noble dead; the past and present state. And the cult of offering, the ceremonial conducted daily in the royal palace, the rituals of royal burial and enthronement, the rites that were performed in a myriad shadowed shrines throughout the regions of the lower Nile, continuously maintained those vital links between the mundane and the mysterious, between the seen and unseen.

Such activities as pyramid building and temple ritual provide a peculiarly modern difficulty of understanding, for they are not readily pigeon-holed in such terms as 'art', 'religion' or 'economics'. And that in turn affects our understanding of the role of pharaoh and the narratives of pharaonic history.

If those kings had ruled, as many historians have assumed, by divine right in the manner of early modern European monarchs, or if they are imagined to have governed in the brutal manner of Old Testament kings or of Roman emperors, or even as modern dictators, then the ages that followed the building of the four colossal pyramids, the age of the kings of Abusir and Saqqara, can only be portrayed as a time of crisis and deterioration, for such a huge decline in pyramid building must have inevitably signalled a weakening of pharaonic power and a rise of superstitious provincialism.

What the surviving relics show, alternatively, is that the nature of the state had changed. That as the courtly systems which had overseen the building of the colossal pyramids were elaborated and monumentalized, so too the unseen aspects of that ancient courtly world were similarly systemized, and gods like Horus, Hathor and Re, who previously had been but vague presences, were brought into clear view whilst others, like the god Osiris, made their first appearance.

At the temples of Abusir, the kings were shown suckling at the breasts of huge lion-headed goddesses. Carved in beautiful low relief on the massive stone posts of the temples' entrance doors, those images were given a majestic intimacy by the court craftsmen, with the added frisson of placing the king's head close to that of a cold impassive feline. Like the Hathor figures in the statue groups of Menkaure, such powerful images set pharaoh clearly within a group of deities.

In similar fashion, the texts in Tihna's tomb chapels describe the provincial nobles both as estate administrators and as priests of a now-vanished temple named as the 'house of Hathor' – Hathor, a mother goddess who was so close to the living king that her very name means 'House of Horus'. Other texts within those chapels record that a royal donation of some forty acres had been specifically provided to support the activities of Hathor's cult down through the generations. Here too, as in the Memphite temples, offerings would have been made in the royal name and priests would have dressed the figure of the goddess every day and made offerings to her in the same manner in which the rituals of the royal cult were celebrated.

In modern terms, translated epithets in those tomb chapels designate those courtiers as 'overseers of priests' and as 'provincial lords', apparently distinguishing their civil and religious roles. In reality, of course, they were aspects of a single social order. To that extent, the gods of ancient Egypt were more practical and less given to easy explanation than Champollion and many of his successors have imagined. Pharaoh had sat at the centre of an intricate net of rituals and relationships that had encompassed every aspect of courtly life and death within the region of the lower Nile. And that it was which gave the role of pharaoh a numinosity that, in some small part, surrounds the offices of heads of state down to this day.

PART FIVE

Old Kingdom
Ancient Records,
Ancient Lives

16

Papyrus to Stone

LETTERS FROM A KING

On arriving at the foot of the Giza Plateau, most visitors walk up the tarmac road towards the Great Pyramid. And as they walk along that windy, shimmering strip towards the majestic space between the three vast pyramids, they often notice a pair of small encolumned doorways standing on a rocky ridge above the Great Pyramid's north-western corner. Built within the mastaba cemetery of Khufu's nobles some two centuries after those ponderous ranks were first laid out and marked today by a smoothly modern restoration, they are the porticoes of two tomb chapels, part of the small cemetery of a noble household that had flourished after the age of the kings of Abusir.

Those two restored doorways lead to the largest and oldest chapels within this little group of tombs, those of their founder, the courtier Senedjemib Inti, and the man who in the tomb chapels' inscriptions is named as his son and successor, Senedjemib Mehi. Apart from the poor quality of the stone, which renders the weathered reliefs somewhat difficult to see, visiting the tomb chapels of Inti and Mehi is much like visiting the remains of dozens of other monuments of average quality in the cemeteries of Giza and Saqqara. What makes these two tomb chapels remarkable, however, is a collage of texts that provide a brief biography of Inti and describe something of his work at court. Compiled, the texts inform us, by Inti and Mehi themselves, they include three passages whose opening words are literally translated as 'royal decrees', but in modern translation they may also be described as letters; three royal letters concerning the construction of some buildings at the royal residence that were sent to Inti from the offices of the long-lived King Isesi who ruled around 2400 BC.

> Royal decree to the chief justice and vizier, the overseer of all works of the king and overseer of scribes of royal documents, Senedjemib: My Majesty has reviewed this ground plan which you sent to be considered by the court for the precinct of the broad court belonging to the jubilee palace of Isesi: 'Now you say to My Majesty that you have made it a 1,000 cubits [573 yards] by more than 440 cubits [252 yards] . . .

> Royal decree to the chief justice and vizier, the overseer of scribes of royal documents and overseer of all works of the king, Senedjemib: My Majesty has read this letter of yours which you wrote in order to inform My Majesty of everything that you have done in drafting the decoration for the Hathor Chapel of Isesi, which is in the grounds of the palace . . .

Once more, writing changes everything. Here, it would appear, is the authentic voice of pharaoh, a voice that in the first half of the letters appears detached, but concludes with flourishes of encouragement.

> My Majesty knows that you are more skilful than any overseer of works has ever been in this entire land . . . You have indeed achieved distinction [?] innumerable times and you shall serve as overseer of all works of the king . . . You are one who says what Isesi likes better than any functionary who has ever been in this land.
> . . . You have performed innumerable deeds so that [your king] should love you, and you know full well that I love you . . .

King Isesi appears to have been a man of letters, for another of Inti's texts describes him as writing 'with his two fingers, in order to praise me for everything that I had done'. Isesi, indeed, seems to have promoted a literary trend in contemporary court society, for another of his letters written to another courtier – who also carved its words into the walls of the courtyard of his tomb – is entirely concerned with the quality of the courtier's prose:

> Royal decree to the chief justice and vizier, the overseer of scribes of royal documents, Ra-shepses: My Majesty has read at court this

very fine letter that you sent on this fine day . . . It was more desirable
to My Majesty than anything else to read your letter, for you surely
know how to express what My Majesty likes above all else, and your
diction is more pleasing to me than anything else . . . As truly as Isesi
lives forever, you should immediately express any wish of yours in a
letter from you today, so that My Majesty might have it immediately
fulfilled.

Both memorialized on the stone of a tomb-chapel wall or yet surviving on their original papyrus sheets, such letters are very rare, and
they are now mostly damaged. Less than fifty such are presently
known from the four-century-long period of the Old Kingdom, and
the best part of them are fragments of private correspondences, thirty
having been recently discovered in a remote oasis and more in a seaside harbour. Other letters, alternatively, were written to the dead
and concern domestic problems that the departed had bequeathed the
living. Can those scanty fragments offer a keyhole though which to
view the living state? Or must the tone of their translation and present understanding of the situations of their authors and recipients,
inevitably misrepresent their tone and content?

Year 11, first month of the third season, day 23

It is the overseer of work gangs who says: The vizier's letter has been
delivered to me, your humble servant, to the effect that the gang of
crewmen of the Tura quarries should be brought to the Western
Enclosure to be fitted with clothes in his presence. However, I, your
humble servant, protest against going to such out-of-the-way locations
since you are going to come anyway to Tura with the barge, whereas,
I, your humble servant, have to spend six days at the Residence with
this work gang before it gets its clothing. This is what obstructs the
work in your humble servant's charge, since only one day needs be
wasted for this work gang to get its clothing. I, your humble servant,
speak that you may be informed.

Found in the 1920s during the excavation of the Step Pyramid's
enclosure, this unique Old Kingdom letter seems very blunt in comparison with other surviving pharaonic correspondence and lacks the
usual mode of address. Possibly, its tone reflects the urgency with

which the state's stone-working gangs had long addressed their tasks; a graffito of another work gang, for example, prays for a good wind to speed the stone barges. When it was found, the unique letter had been torn in half – the product, so one of its translators has suggested, of the anger of its recipient!

WORDS AND WRITING

The thing which heer I report in vnpolisht proez, waz thear pronounced in good meeter and matter.

The Laneham Letter, c. 1575

Though modern translations of these archaic letters appear to mirror forms of speech, it cannot be assumed that they represent the spoken language of their time. Different parts of the pharaonic state, different communities even, may have communicated in different tongues and certainly, as later scribes remark, in a variety of accents, whilst writing of itself occupied a very different place in pharaonic society from that which it does today. Only a tiny percentage of the population of the lower Nile would have understood the literary syntax that the scribes were still in the processes of creating, a syntax that is likely to have been based upon the formal spoken language of the court. This new-made written language, therefore, was synthetic, a product of a lengthy process in which the archaic repertoire of a thousand hieroglyphs that had previously been employed to list the constituents of court life – names and titles, epithets, year dates and the quantities and categories of supplies and artefacts – was fined down to around 300 signs whilst the functions of those remaining signs were expanded so that they could impart information in linear sequence – that is, in written sentences – rather than the stand-alone data of lists and labels.

Best estimates presently suggest that some ten scribes were at the disposal of every Old Kingdom courtier for whom a tomb chapel was made and that, at any one time, some ten such tomb chapels were in the process of completion. Such figures would imply that there had been thousands upon thousands of written documents circulating throughout the Old Kingdom court administration and that the tiny quantities that survive are relics of a vanished mountain of such writings – a mountain whose ghosts appear today in sculptures, paintings and reliefs as images of scrolls held in the hands of scribes, priests and courtiers. This period, therefore, must have been one of extraordinary creativity for the scribes who were still engaged in the centuries-long process of representing sentences or, more accurately perhaps, of patterns of speech in groups of hieroglyphic signs.

As to the tone and texture of those rare surviving texts, those from king to courtier appear to show a genuine warmth, a relationship conducted with candour and a kind of homeliness, but held within the bounds of a precise propriety. They are the literary equivalents of the relationship between king and subject shown in the Abusir reliefs; a formal yet surprisingly forthright bond contained within a particular relationship that the egyptologist John Baines has characterized as that of 'decorum' and which will permeate the courtly air of products of that society down to its ending.

Beyond those rare literary expressions there is little evidence of the day-to-day realities of pharaonic government. One can, of course – and this indeed is a popular enough image of that ancient state today – imagine that the officers of the pharaonic court administered the valley of the lower Nile in the manner of a modern despotic state; that the court had controlled the population by fear and propaganda whilst it enriched itself by brutality and force of arms. That would give pharaoh's seeming literary warmth something of a crocodile smile. Yet neither the Old Kingdom's spare archaeology nor later literary tales bear out any such assumptions. One might, alternatively, imagine pharaoh's subjects to have lived in Champollion's Mozartian Orient or a feudal empire ruled by the will of God under a succession of Habsburg-style dynasties. Given our present state of knowledge, however, such speculations are unwise, for there is no firm evidence that pharaoh's Egypt had laboured under any of those highly developed forms of government.

Better, then, to take the ancient words and nothing but those words at their face value, but with the understanding that modern translations cannot hope to match contemporary moods. Nor can we even sense the resonances that individual hieroglyphs, those archaic images of living fragments of that courtly world, had added to ancient readings of those same texts. And yet despite all this, some of the surviving texts seem to provide brief glimpses of courtly life in the centuries after the four colossal pyramids were built.

BRIEF LIVES – *THE SAVOUR OF A COURTLY PAST*

To write His own Memoirs, and leave His Heirs
High Schemes of Government ...

Matthew Prior, 1700

Set half way up the Giza Plateau and deep within the tumbledown quarries that lie in drifts of sand behind the Sphinx, the rock-cut tomb and tomb chapel of the courtier Debehni was made in the brief transitional period between the completion of the Giza pyramids and those of the kings of Abusir; that is, between the reigns of Menkaure and Sahure, at around 2500 BC. It is an unusually interesting monument, for Debehni's sculptors filled its chambers with a series of innovatory inscriptions and reliefs, not the least of which depicts in lively and quite unexpected detail Debehni's funeral procession. And that, in turn, inspired a procession of scholars from Lepsius down till today to visit this now dark and sooty cave, which until quite recently had been used for the performance of *zikrs* – hypnotic Sufi prayers performed in unison by groups of men – in honour of a local saint, Sidi Hammed es-Semman, who is said to have once lived within Debehni's pillared halls.

In the history of hieroglyphic writing, this tomb holds two great novelties. The first is a list of offerings that was inscribed alongside the images of Debehni's funeral on the west wall of his funerary chapel. This is one of the earliest-known examples of a list of the ninety or so provisions and accoutrements that would become the

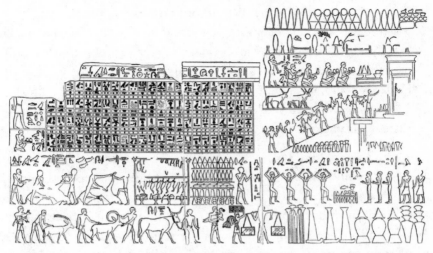

Part of the funerary scenes carved in relief on the walls of Debehni's tomb chapel at Giza. The left side holds a list of offerings. Underneath, images of animals and birds, wild and cultivated, are being led towards the tomb chapel, whilst meats raw and air-dried are also being prepared for presentation at the cult. The right side of the scene shows some of those products along with others that are stored in pots being presented at the tomb chapel to a standing statue of Debehni, which is now mostly destroyed. And women clap and sing.

physical components of a ritual that was celebrated at the funerals of kings and courtiers alike down to ancient Egypt's ending.

The second literary novelty in Debehni's tomb chapel is a somewhat broken wall text that was carved above a dozen rock-cut sculptures of the man himself. Composed in the time of Menkaure, for whom the last and smallest of the three great Giza pyramids was built, it is one of the earliest surviving examples of a type of text which are collectively known as 'biographies'. 'As for this tomb,' Debehni's damaged writings tell,

> it is the king . . . who assigned this spot to me while he was on the road toward the pyramid plateau in order to inspect the work upon the pyramid named 'Menkaure is Divine' . . . fifty artisans [were assigned] to do the work on it every day . . . His Majesty ordered, moreover, that the site should be cleared of rubbish . . . and decreed

the bringing of stone from Tura in order to encase the chapel . . . together with two doors for this tomb, the master of the crew and the two directors of artisans, and the king's carpenter and mason, who brought me a statue which is done after life . . . and the stone workers made the tomb one hundred cubits in its length [86 yards], and fifty cubits in its width [29 yards], and . . . cubits [high] . . . [The text continues by listing a range of other royal gifts to Debehni.]

The originality and liveliness of both the words and images in Debehni's tomb chapel show a distinct change of tone within the monuments of Giza, a shift away from the spare formalities of the earlier tombs and the massive stone-block monuments of the age of Khufu and Prince Hardjedef. As for Debehni's so-called biographic text, similarly lively descriptions of royal donations and the kings' various encounters with their courtiers would continue to be composed throughout the following centuries.

So, around a decade after Debehni's death, an inscription in the tomb chapel of the courtier Niankhsekhmet, whose titles suggest that he performed a role of healer in the royal court, record how his small Saqqara mastaba made of rough blocks of local stone had been provided with a false door at the command of the pharaoh Sahure. A single stone of the finest limestone shipped across the river from the Tura quarries and standing ten and a half feet high, Niankhsekhmet's false door is one of the largest to have survived from the times of the Old Kingdom and out of all proportion to the rest of his somewhat humble monument. Beautifully engraved with columns of fine hieroglyphs and images of the healer and his wife and children, parts of its lengthy texts tell how such a remarkable object came to be set in such an ordinary tomb.

> . . . Niankhsekhmet spoke before his majesty: 'beloved of Re, would you command that there be given to me a false door of stone for this, my tomb within the cemetery'. And his majesty ordered that two false doors of stone be brought for him from Tura and that they be laid in the audience hall of the palace 'Sahure-Shines-with-Crowns', and that the two high priests of Memphis and the artisans of the . . . be assigned to them, and that the work upon them be done in the presence of the king himself. The stone work went on every day; there was a daily

inspection of that which was done on them and His Majesty had blue colour painted onto them.

And his majesty said to the chief healer Niankhsekhmet: 'As these my nostrils [i.e. 'as I'] enjoy health, as the gods love me, may you depart into the cemetery at an advanced old age as one revered . . .' When anything goes forth from the mouth of his majesty it immediately comes to pass . . . he is more august than any god.

Once again, the text describes the king's personal interest in the central activities of state, that is, in the construction and decoration of stone monuments and, on this occasion, how a courtier's false door had been carved in the royal palace under the daily supervision of the king. Under such circumstances, it is hardly surprising that the text was not voiced, as was Debehni's memoir, as coming from the owner of the tomb, but by a royal scribe – and despite that scribe's description of the making of two false doors, there is only space for one within the tomb!

The near-contemporary tomb of the courtier Washptah had stood close to the mastaba of the court healer, two amongst dozens of such monuments uncovered during the exploration of that great wide sand plain by Mariette in the 1850s, when Niankhsekhmet's splendid false door had been uncovered, dug out and sent off to Cairo and the Khedival museum. The fate of Washptah's mastaba, however, and one shared by several other tomb chapels in that vicinity, was that its limestone walls were dismantled following Mariette's excavations and its blocks collected by antiquities dealers supplying the museums of Europe and America with examples of Old Kingdom craftsmanship, a period that previously had excited scant interest amongst antiquarians.

Presently residing in Aberdeen, Cairo, Copenhagen and London, the blocks of Washptah's tomb chapel hold a similarly vivid inscription to those of his one-time neighbour, in this instance a now heavily damaged text describing the dramatic last days of Washptah's life. Like some of the texts in Inti's tomb at Giza, this inscription, so its opening lines still tell, had been compiled on the orders of his successor as head of household: 'it was his eldest son who acted for him when he was in his tomb . . .'

King Sahure's successor, Neferirkare, so the broken narrative continues, had been inspecting progress on his pyramid at Abusir in the company of Washptah, when the elderly courtier had suddenly collapsed. Washptah was bandaged up and taken to the royal palace, where the king had anxiously sought a cure for his now-comatose companion. 'His Majesty caused a chest of writings to be taken to him ... concerning the spasms ... then they told His Majesty that he was unconscious. And His Majesty praised Re ...' But all to no avail it appears, for snatches of the broken text go on to record how the king ordered a splendid burial for Washptah, 'that eight alabaster vessels be filled for him and put into a box of ebony', and never the like has been done for anyone since the beginning of time, so the inscription then avers, 'and His Majesty placed a life-giving amulet onto his nose', and ordered that his body be anointed and prepared for its entombment.

Once again, pharaoh is portrayed as showing care and sympathy towards his close associates – a care that is apparent in several other fragmentary inscriptions, one of which describes how a king ordered a carrying chair to be taken to a sick courtier. At the same time, the straightforward description of royal distress in Washptah's inscription injects a firm note of reality into the West's traditional notions of pharaoh's alleged 'divinity'. For though the king does many things to aid his dying courtier, and despite his direct appeal to 'his father Re', the scribe carefully records pharaoh's helplessness and grief in the face of Washptah's approaching death.

Further intimations of how the pharaohs of these times were regarded by their contemporaries are contained in another memoir of a courtier's encounter with the same king, Neferirkare, who had taken such care with Washptah. This time, an inscription reports the adventures of a certain Ra-wer, a courtier intimately involved in royal ritual, whose tomb lies in the Giza quarries close to that of Debehni. The occasion of Ra-wer's brush with the royal presence is that of a procession at a water festival:

> The King of the Valley and the Delta, Neferirkare, was appearing as King of the Delta on the day of drawing the prow rope of the god's boat. Whilst Ra-wer was following the steps of his majesty in his office of sem priest and keeper of accoutrements, a royal staff which

was in his majesty's hand blocked the foot of the sem priest Ra-wer.
And his majesty said: 'Be sound! He [Ra-wer] is beloved of me; he is
very well, no beating will be done to him. Behold, he is more precious
to his majesty than any [other] man.' His majesty ordered this to be
put in writing on his tomb that is in the necropolis . . . in accordance
with what is said.

Ra-wer's inscription has often been employed to demonstrate the
alleged sacredness of pharaoh's person. Even the royal staff, so it has
been affirmed, held such sacred presence that only the prompt intervention of the king had saved the courtier from a beating after it had
touched his foot. More likely, however, is that, just as the author of
Washptah's texts had not invested pharaoh with the ability to stave
off his courtier's approaching death, so Ra-wer is not described as
having kicked the sacred staff of a divinity but as simply having
impeded the earthly progress of a state procession.

Ra-wer's mastaba is a large and straggling monument surrounded,
like so many of the courtiers' tomb chapels, by the simple graves of
the members of his household. Most remarkably, buried in its stony
bulk, it had no less than twenty-five closed rooms of a type especially
designed for storing statues. Known today as serdabs, these sculpture

rooms have no doors, just narrow slits within their walls so that the eyes of the statues that were entombed within them could stare outwards and Ra-wer's mortuary priests could make offerings directly to them. Most of the courtiers' mastabas of Ra-wer's time usually held one or two serdabs in them, each one of which would have held but a few statues. Ra-wer's tomb chapel, however, had more than a hundred statues walled up in those serdabs, most of which were set around a central pillared hall. Though lime burners had destroyed the best part of the mastaba, when the archaeologist Selim Hassan excavated its remains in the 1930s he found many splendid fragments of alabaster, limestone and granite statues and some beautiful wall reliefs in its remains. Here, then, would appear to be a personal preference at work; another individual aspect of a courtier other than written texts preserved within the architecture of his tomb. That several of Ra-wer's serdabs had had steps before them and slits high up in their walls to light their dark interiors suggests a practical desire on behalf of the tomb's designers – and, presumably, Ra-wer as well – to enable his multitude of images to be viewed by living people.

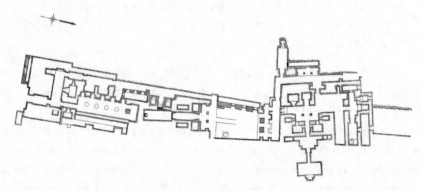

The plan of Ra-wer's remarkable tomb chapel cum sculpture gallery which, over the course of several reigns, was extended some 300 feet from its initial form of an orthodox oblong mastaba by utilising the irregular spaces between some nearby mastabas. Each of the myriad niches within its structure indicates the presence of a slotted peep-hole from which the eyes of Ra-wer's sculptures placed in the rooms behind could regard their visitors. The courtier and his family appear to have been buried in a number of nearby burial shafts.

Unlike Ra-wer's splendid images, however, the so-called biographic texts seldom provide rounded portraits of the owners of the tombs in which they were engraved. Even in such tombs as Ra-wer's and Debehni's, where the biographic texts were placed close to statues of the tombs' owners – the block holding Ra-wer's inscription having been found lying in one of his serdabs – they appear to have served as captions to the tomb-chapel images in the same way that many of the activities shown in their reliefs are described in written titles. Like the contemporary scenes of court life that were engraved within the temples at Abusir, what essentially these and later 'biographic' texts describe is an event or a sequence of events which epitomise aspects of the relationship of the tomb owner to the living monarch, their personal relationship to the man upon the throne.

Our great good fortune is that these lively documents survive from a world that is otherwise entirely lost and that they suggest alternatives to those traditional explanations of life and belief at the court of the Abusir kings, which describe the manners and modes of being at that court to have been credulous and brutal. What, in reality, their surviving texts, their relics and their architecture show is that pharaoh's courtiers and subjects had remarkable sensitivities and an impressive measure of those qualities that the anthropologist Gananath Obeyesekere has described as 'practical rationality' – the ability to make reflective reasoned judgements. Like all the peoples of the world, those of the Memphite kingdom were constrained by our common biological inheritance, yet at the same time their culture was self-contained and self-constructed and the product of a unique environment. The difference, therefore, is one of understanding, for this was a culture whose rationale and mode of being was different from any in the modern world.

17

Writing in the Pyramids

AFTER ABUSIR – *A HISTORY IN PYRAMIDS*

At around 2400 BC, the royal workforce moved south again from Abusir into the ancient burial grounds of Saqqara. And there they made pyramids and temples for several kings within that desert and, presumably, set new palaces and settlements upon the plains below.

Isesi, the letter-writing pharaoh, had been the first to move. Known locally today as the Haram el-Shawwaf – the Pyramid of the Watchman – his ruined tomb stands on a spur of desert limestone some three miles to the south of Abusir and close to Shepseskaf's colossal mastaba, at the site generally known as 'south Saqqara'. Wenis and Teti, alternatively, the two succeeding kings, set their pyramids a little to the north, in the centre of the old Saqqara cemeteries near the pyramid of Userkaf and close to the ancient rectangle of the Step Pyramid's enclosure walls.

Despite these relocations, the external architecture and dimensions of these later pyramids stayed much the same as those of Abusir. Now, though, the pyramids' interior apartments were further standardized, and those of Isesi were adopted as the single architectural design of the interiors of all of the following major pyramids of the late Old Kingdom. After Isesi, therefore, the dead kings' journey to the darkness of their burial chambers began on the sunlit pavements of their pyramids' northern face, where a square-sectioned doorway angled sharply down through the living rock towards a point beneath the apex of the pyramid. Just a yard in height and, in Isesi's pyramid,

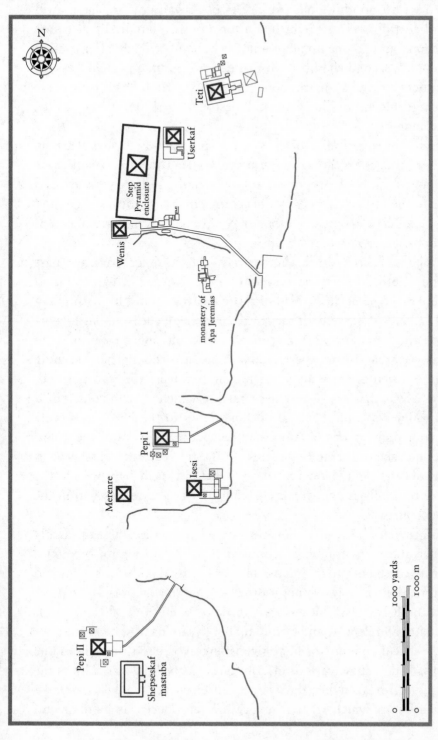

The major pyramids of central and south Saqqara. Many buried structures and sanded monuments in the area are yet unmapped and unexplored.

lined with smoothly polished blocks of Aswan granite, these awkward corridors ran straight down for almost a hundred feet before levelling out and opening into a narrow chamber. Then after passing through a second chamber with three great granite portcullises, the corridors entered a square room with a gabled roof. Beautifully made of large blocks of the whitest limestone, these are the so-called 'antechambers'.

Here, the straight line of the entrance passageway divides. Turning at right angles to the east, the corridors lead to three small stone chambers similar in proportion to others in the earlier pyramids, and also to the little chambers by the central shrines of royal shrines and temples. These rooms, therefore, may have held statues, ritual equipment or served as stores for offerings.

Angling to the west, alternatively, the entrance passages pass through other low stone doorways that give access to the burial chambers. And at the far end of those narrow rooms, beneath splendid gabled roofs, were set the royal sarcophagi; cut from hard desert stone and of impressive dimensions, these could only have been set in their positions before the chambers' massive roofing blocks, more than a dozen of them above each chamber, were slid into position. Here it was that the royal burial parties, which in such constrained environments could have hardly amounted to the baroque processions of popular imagination, had concluded the rites of the kings' interment before scrambling back up the tiny entrance passageways towards the light, blocking the way behind them by lowering the three portcullises and, finally, paving over the entrances within the open courts.

Constricted, pressured, hot and muffled in acoustic, these unearthly subterranean environments would serve as inspiration for the architecture of all later royal tombs. This of itself would be of but limited historical interest were it not for the fact that the interiors of the pyramids built by Isesi's successors – those of Wenis and of Teti, Pepi I, Merenre and Pepi II, and of the smaller pyramids of several queens – had vertical columns of hieroglyphs engraved upon their limestone walls. Today, these various inscriptions are known generically as the 'Pyramid Texts'. In their day, they had been part of that historic transformation in which written texts were reproduced as monumental

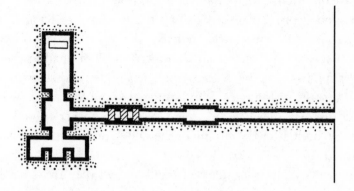

The underlying plan of the interiors of all the royal pyramids of the later Old Kingdom: a constricted entrance corridor passes through two antechambers before turning east into three small shrine-like chambers, and west towards the royal burial crypt and its sarcophagus.

inscriptions – the reproduction, for example, in courtly hieroglyphs of letters such as those of King Isesi's on the walls of tomb chapels or of the so-called biographic texts of nobles such as Debehni and Washptah. The texts within the pyramids, however, are of a different order from those within the courtiers' monuments, and their influence both inside and outside the pharaonic state has been long-lasting and profound.

Presently, the earliest-known examples of these Pyramid Texts are those cut into the walls of the burial chamber and antechamber of the pyramid of Wenis in central Saqqara. Later pyramids, however, have far more texts engraved within them and their contents are often different from earlier examples. Their locations too within the pyramids were gradually extended, until they came to cover the best part of the interior rooms and corridors. As a corpus of inscriptions, the Pyramid Texts comprise more than 900 separate verses, at least 330 of which continued to be used in funerary settings all along the lower Nile down to the ending of pharaonic culture. Carved in a clear and workmanlike manner, though cast in archaic and frequently impenetrable prose, they are the foundations of all later pharaonic texts that describe the rites of funeral and the destinies of death.

Ten pyramids are presently known to have held Pyramid Texts

within them. Eight, including those in the pyramids of Pepi I, Merenre and Pepi II, are set close by the pyramid of King Isesi at south Saqqara and are ruined, many of the pyramids so robbed of stone that several of their burial chambers had lain open to the sky. Though similarly despoiled, four smaller, simpler and steeper-sided structures, some of the queen's pyramids at south Saqqara, also had Pyramid Tests engraved within them, as does another ruined pyramid nearby, built after the ending of the Old Kingdom for an obscure king named Ibi.

Set on bedrock on either side of a small sandy valley above a rolling sea of silver palms, the considerable cluster of the south Saqqara pyramids was set apart from the rest of the Saqqara cemeteries. As well as the curious mastaba of King Shepseskaf (p. 110), south Saqqara also holds the royal pyramids' accompanying temples, whose architectures and wall reliefs were but modest variations of the same arrangements as those at Abusir. Unknown numbers of courtiers' tombs also lie amidst the south Saqqara pyramids, along with the smaller graves of members of their households, though, like the monuments of Abusir, the greater part of this enormous congregation lost much of its stone to the limekilns of the Monastery of Apa Jeremiah and other later builders. Nonetheless, the present mass of wind-blown sand and ruined monuments is one of ancient Egypt's greatest burying grounds, its future promise held in the scattered lines of half-buried walls and heaps of fine white limestone that lie within its yellow drifts. In the year 2000, a previously unknown queen's pyramid was brought to light at south Saqqara with another set of Pyramid Texts inscribed upon its burial chamber walls.

Although the best part of the limestone blocks on which the south Saqqara Pyramid Texts had been inscribed are shattered, the fragments that survive are usually in good condition, having been preserved within the sand and rubble of their ruined pyramids. From the first days of their discovery, therefore, their fragmentary condition, the different versions of their verses that are found in various pyramids, and their sheer literary ambiguity presented a perfect academic puzzle.

1. To the delight of Wisdom and the Arts and the accompaniment of Fame sounding her timeless trumpet, the world's first great collection of Egyptian antiquities is borne into the City of Turin in 1824 under the seal of Charles Felix, Duke of Savoy, King of Sardinia. Unfortunately, the pioneering lithographer Francesco Gonin had no knowledge of the newly purchased treasures, so all he shows us as the procession moves slowly towards the Palazzo Accademia delle Scienze is a single sphinx and a classical sarcophagus.

2. Khufu and the hawk, one of many such sculptures set up within his Giza temples.

THE VALLEY TEMPLE OF KING MYCERINUS

Offering Hall

crude brick First Temple: SHEPSESKAF.
" " : additions to First Temple.
" " : Second Temple: PEPI II (?)
" " : intrusions on floor of court.
" " : walls on floor debris of court.
" " : " " over walls of First Temple.
" " : indeterminable.

Scales

3. George Andrew Reisner's plan of Menkaure's valley temple; a
careful record of its excavation in the years before the First World War.

4. One of the four so-called Menkaure Triads, that Reisner uncovered during his excavation of the king's valley temple. It shows Menkaure supported on his right by the goddess Hathor, who, the inscription tells us, loves him, and on his left by a provincial deity who grants him all the offerings of the southlands forever. Carved from grey schist, the sculpture is just three feet high.

5. The pyramid and causeway of King Sahure at Abusir.

6. Ludwig Borchardt's workmen reassembling some of the fallen blocks of Sahure's valley temple in December 1907.

7. Sahure's valley temple during its excavation and in the months following the annual inundation of the Nile. The pools left by the retreating flood waters may well echo the path of the canals that gave access to the valley temple at the bottom of the causeway.

8. The head of the so-called 'Louvre scribe', a nameless life-sized sculpture of a man sitting cross-legged holding a pen and an open papyrus. The whites of his eyes are made from polished magnesite with a fine red veining, their pupils of rock crystal.

INTO THE CRYPT

This thy cavern, is the broad hall of Osiris, o King Pepi,
which brings the wind and [guides] the north wind. It raises
thee as Osiris, o King Pepi ... Those who behold the Nile
tossing in waves tremble. The marshes laugh, the shores are
overflowed, the divine offerings descend, men give praise
and the heart of the gods rejoices.

Pyramid Texts 1551–4, translated by James
Henry Breasted before 1912

The first fragments of the Pyramid Texts to be uncovered in modern times were found amidst the ruins of some of the south Saqqara pyramids that were so devastated that Mariette had taken them to be fragments of relief from plundered mastabas. In the following year, however, in 1881, the opening of Wenis' pyramid, some of whose pristine interior walls were covered in 900 lengthy columns of fine-made hieroglyphs, had confirmed the dawning recognition that, after Abusir, the Old Kingdom pyramids had texts engraved within them.

In their perfection, the texts in Wenis' modest pyramid appeared to come from nowhere, for there is not the slightest trace of any writing on the interior walls of any earlier pyramid. And yet there had been precedents. For the craftsmen who had made the burial apartments for several of the courtiers of kings before the reign of Wenis had already broken with all previous custom and set short texts upon their walls. An antechamber to the burial chamber of Senedjemib Inti, for example – the recipient of some of King Isesi's letters – holds a list of offerings drawn in a watery black wash with a wide soft brush upon a specially prepared panel of white plaster. Like the other early examples in such tomb texts, these lists are similar to those in the tomb chapels above. In the darkness of those burial apartments, however, the draughtsmen's technique is freer and far livelier.

When Reisner's excavators had first entered the plundered burial chamber of Senedjemib Inti in November 1913, they found the courtier himself still lying in a heavy grey granite sarcophagus emblazoned with his name. Though robbed, it had never been a rich interment but rather one of grand simplicity; the carefully mummified corpse of an aged man lying on its back accompanied by jars of imported ointments and a single splendid staff, a visible sign, perhaps, of Senedjemib Inti's role at court.

Little more than roughly quarried caverns, the poor and usually fractured desert rock in which such funerary crypts were cut had to be especially prepared before any texts could have been set within them, and it became common practice during the following reigns to either smooth those rough rock surfaces entirely or to erect whole walls of stone or mud brick within them so that some form of decoration could be applied. The texts placed in the interior of Wenis' pyramid, therefore, were quite in keeping with these courtly trends, though with the resources of the entire state machine behind them they were on a grander scale and more complex than any earlier examples.

Like the entrance to King Isesi's near-contemporary pyramid, the corridor leading into Senedjemib Inti's burial chamber runs straight down into the living rock, this passageway of itself being something of an innovation as the burial chambers of most earlier nobles' tombs had been set at the bottom of vertical shafts. The subterranean text, the list of offerings, had been painted on the wall of a small antechamber through which the entrance corridor passes on its way down to the burial crypt. Squared and quartered in the manner of the Abusir accounting papyri, it is a common list, parts of that same offering register having already been inscribed upon the walls of Debehni's tomb chapel, whilst yet earlier shorter examples are amongst the oldest-known forms of hieroglyphic text.

The damaged list of offerings in Inti's burial apartments held all that a member of the court would have required to keep him in the manner in which he had lived, everything from clothes and water to ointments and eye paint and a marvellous array of food: some eighteen types of seeds and flour, breads plain and toasted, a lengthy and meticulously differentiated list of domestic and wild birds, various cuts of meat both raw and cooked, and quantities of onions which, as their modern vendors in that same region rightly claim, would have been as sweet as honey. A capacious hamper for the afterlife complete with wine and fruit, and one of which various versions appear within

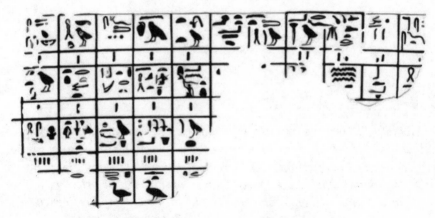

*Part of the offering list that was lightly sketched onto a wall of
Senedjemib Inti's burial apartments.*

the Pyramid Texts, from their first appearance in King Wenis' burial
chamber down to the Old Kingdom's ending.

Such offering lists had long since been inscribed in the courtiers'
tomb chapels, and fragmentary versions of those same lists had also
been inscribed on the walls of the royal temples of Abusir and later,
too, in those of south Saqqara, where they are shown as lists of offerings presented to the living king. The same offerings, therefore, were
presented to the living and the dead. In the temples, however, these lists
are often accompanied by images of officiating priests holding rolls of
papyrus. Like the letters in the courtiers' tombs, it would appear that
these monumental lists had also been copied out from scrolls. In this
instance, however, the written scrolls had not held the words of letters
or biography, but those that the priests had read out during the rites of
offering, for numerous verses of the Pyramid Texts including those of
their offering lists are topped and tailed by such introductory and concluding phrases as 'recitation' and 'end of section'.

Just as the move to decorate burial chambers had been under way
decades before its first appearance in King Wenis' pyramid so, too,
the form that the calligraphic texts of the papyrus rolls would take in
their monumental hieroglyphic versions had already been formalized. The letters inscribed in Inti's tomb chapel, for example – those
that had been sent by Wenis' predecessor, King Isesi – had been
engraved around the doorway of his tomb chapel in long vertical

Holding and reciting from papyrus rolls, priests officiate at a ceremony
that took place before mealtimes in courtly households and also in tomb
chapels before offerings were presented. This relief from the Saqqara
tomb chapel of the courtier Kagemni shows those priestly
incantations being accompanied by hand-washing and enlivened
by a rhythmic beating of the chest.

columns in a manner similar to the texts sculpted in the later pyramids. And in much the same fashion, the memoirs inscribed in the
tomb chapels of Debehni, Ra-wer and Ra-shepses were also set in vertical columns.

So when Wenis came to the throne, the sudden majestic appearance of hundreds upon hundreds of lines of columned texts inside
his pyramid had modest if practical precedent, one that in typical
pharaonic fashion also had a practical explanation. For Wenis' pyramid, which is the smallest of the Old Kingdom's royal pyramids, had
been built at the centre of a very crowded cemetery – the pavement
slabs of its pyramid temple, indeed, had overlaid the underground
apartments of the tomb of an archaic king. There was little room,
therefore, in that cramped environment for any architectural additions once the pyramid and its adjacent temple had been built. Yet
Wenis appears to have ruled for several decades, and that, as would
often be the case with other lengthy reigns, provided an ample opportunity for the court machine, with its ongoing processes of offering
and manufacture, to elaborate and enlarge their original conception
of such royal monuments.

At almost half a mile, the causeway running down from Wenis' pyramid was nearly as long as that of the Great Pyramid, and on its way
down through the cemeteries to the desert's edge a series of high well-built
embankments had bridged some ancient quarries and had overlaid many

earlier tombs, burying them in their pristine state until their excavation in the 1960s. Before the lime burners destroyed the better part of them, the causeway's walls had held a remarkable series of reliefs with an innovatory range of subject matter; one unique surviving scene, depicting celebrations following the placing of the capstone upon the royal pyramid, proves it to be a late addition to Wenis' other monuments.

In similar fashion, two long narrow pits such as had not been made for generations were cut into the rock by the sides of the causeway's embankments; pits similar in size and form to those beside the Great Pyramid of Giza, in which the disassembled planks of King Khufu's boats were placed at the time of the royal funeral. And at the far end of this great long causeway and in an equally sumptuous fashion, the architecture of a now badly ruined temple had been continually elaborated so that, in its final form, it had been as grand as any of those at Abusir. Set close to the desert's edge and an archaic canal, it is likely that this valley temple had stood near Wenis' palace and its associated settlements.

Here, then, building over decades in somewhat straitened circumstances, the architecture of the royal funerary arrangements which had been developed over centuries was brought to its maturity. Of all those elaborations and innovations, however, to modern eyes the most remarkable are the texts that were cut in columns on the walls inside Wenis' pyramid itself.

THE VOICE INSIDE THE PYRAMID

O West, where is Bati?

Bati [a god] is in the water with the fish,
He speaks with the catfish and converses with the Oxyrhyn-
chus fish

O West, where is Bati?

Bati is devoted to the West.
                    A shepherd's song, c. 2440 BC, from an inscription
                                    in the tomb chapel of Tiy

O father of Pepi, take Pepi with you
to your mother Nut!

Let the gates of sky, open for Pepi,
Let the gates to the Cool Waters, open for Pepi,

Pepi comes to you, so that you may make him live!
For you have commanded this Pepi to sit beside you,
At the shoulder of him who rises at dawn!

From Pyramid Text 573

The Pyramid Texts are generally regarded as rhetorical writings, for they are set in the present tense and their voice appears to be lively and authoritative. Nor was this mode of writing in itself an innovation. By the time of their first appearance in the pyramid of Wenis, commands and exclamations and even the words of little songs had long since been inscribed above many of the scenes on tomb chapel and temple walls.

In common with most speech patterns, the Pyramid Texts' 900-odd verses are seldom more than a few hundred words long, and most are shorter. None of them, however, offer any explanation, any doctrine or dogma. Nor are they parts of a continuous narrative.

To the modern world, this seeming lack of purpose combined with their frequently impenetrable prose may well appear deliberately obtuse, mysterious or even mystical. Yet in their contemporary context it is not surprising, for the core of the ancient culture of the lower Nile was never contained within its written texts. This, after all, was a society that in the centuries before those texts appeared had already built colossal pyramids and temples and whose courtiers and scribes had managed those vast enterprises with skill and energy but without a word of written explanation. Down to its ending, pharaonic Egypt was ordered by a visual intelligence and found its most profound and typical expressions in making and moving things.

For the modern Western world, alternatively, whose culture is founded on the written word and whose visions of ancient Egypt were based upon Champollion's literary researches, the sudden discovery of texts within the pyramids promised revelations. They held out not only the possibility of a written explanation of the beliefs of those who had planned and built the fabled pyramids of Egypt but also the promise of a literary pedigree for a culture whose origins stretched back beyond those pyramids into deep prehistory.

So it is hardly surprising that, following their abrupt rediscovery in the 1880s, the study of the Pyramid Texts became one of egyptology's largest ongoing projects. One that has provided and continues to provide a greater understanding of ancient Egyptian grammar and has given new depth and quality to the understanding and translation of the ancient texts. Yet like the work of Champollion and his successors, this second vital phase in the decipherment of ancient Egyptian history was shaped by contemporary European circumstance.

18

The Dead and the Quick

Processing the Past

As with many archaeological discoveries, the first Pyramid Texts to be seen in modern times were uncovered in excavations undertaken to fill the cases of museums; in this instance, a new Khedival Museum of Antiquities in Cairo. By 1880, when the first of those texts were found, Mariette Pasha, the museum's founder, designer and director, had excavated sites all up and down the lower Nile for a quarter of a century. Using thousands of peasant farmers working *en corvée* to free the country's greatest tombs and temples from the sands and buildings that had come to fill them, these had been the glory years of the recovery of pharaonic culture, if not for the hapless farmers who were driven to undertake those works. And in the process of those labours, Mariette had recovered many of ancient Egypt's best-known relics: by 1880, he was keen to display those treasures in the order of pharaonic history and in a new museum.

But cash was short. In an ambitious drive for modernization, the Khedive Ismael, Egypt's ruler, had built up enormous debts to European banks so that, during the decades of Mariette's excavations, their repayments had resulted in pitiless systems of taxation that had brought famine to the rural population, forced the sale in 1875 of the Suez Canal to the British government, and triggered the imposition of a so-called European Ministry, with English and French officials working in Cairo. So Mariette, who had planned to fill some of the historical gaps in his collection during the first months of 1880 by undertaking further excavations, was forced to concentrate his excavations at just two locations, forty labourers being put to work beside the temples at the Giza Sphinx where, at the beginning of his work in Egypt, he had found the famous statue of Khafre, whilst just twenty men and boys were sent to dig into the gentle hills of south Saqqara, a site that his work gangs had briefly touched in earlier years, but whose stone-studded sands had always promised further treasures.

In late February 1880, Mariette visited the south Saqqara excavations, which were proceeding under Reis – that is, 'chief' or 'headman' – Rubi Hamzawy, with whom the ebullient Frenchman had worked side by side since his first days in Egypt. Part of Reis Rubi's excavations had entailed digging into a hill of sand and loose stone blocks where, at its centre, the work gangs had uncovered slabs of fine white limestone bearing vertical columns of blue-painted hieroglyphs containing the cartouches of Pepi II. Knowing full well the rarity of lengthy Old Kingdom inscriptions, Mariette had paper 'squeezes' taken from those stones. This was a fairly disastrous process in which sheets of heavy hand-made paper soaked in water were pressed against the surface of an engraved stone whilst a stippling brush was banged against the soggy sheet so that, after it had dried, the stiffened card would hold a reproduction, in negative, of the original – a copy often decorated with traces of detached ancient pigment.

In late spring of that same year, as Cairo started to warm up to its torrid summer, Mariette, a long-time sufferer from diabetes and in increasingly poor health, had sailed for France. At Paris, he showed his south Saqqara squeezes to Gaston Maspero, his one-time protégée but by that time a brilliant young professor of Egyptian philology at the Collège de France and the author of a recent groundbreaking history of the ancient Orient. Maspero later said that he had immediately understood that the texts on Mariette's squeezes had come from the burial chamber of a royal pyramid. Mariette, alternatively, had thought that they were from the chapel of a courtier's tomb, for he had found many a king's cartouche engraved in tomb chapels but not a single hieroglyph upon the walls of royal pyramids.

After meeting Maspero in Paris, Mariette took himself to a tiny mountain spa in central France, but his health did not improve and he became increasingly depressed. In Cairo at that same time, an

International Committee of Liquidation consisting of four European bureaucrats was imposed on the Egyptian government expressly to control the nation's finances and so enable the repayment of the national debt to foreign banks. Within the month, the committee's British representative, an old India hand and a member of a prominent German banking family, one Captain Evelyn Baring, later Lord Cromer, had proposed a savage list of reforms: there would be further cuts to education, to the army and the civil service, whilst the levels of taxation that had caused famine and unrest over the past few years would not be relaxed.

By October, and after visiting his home town of Boulogne-sur-Mer, Mariette had decided to return to Egypt, for he felt that he was dying. And he wrote to his old friend, the German egyptologist Heinrich Brugsch, an extraordinary and prodigious scholar who had worked with Mariette since the beginning of his excavations, asking him to come again to Egypt. After a month-long voyage, Mariette arrived in Alexandria, haemorrhaging profusely. As soon as he reached Cairo, Émile Brugsch, the brother of Heinrich and a curator at the new museum, set up a couch for Mariette outside his family's apartment, on the museum's open porch.

Back in Paris, the word was out that Mariette was mortally ill. Who, then, would take up his central role in the cultural affairs of Egypt, a role that France had held since Napoleon's Grand Tour of the East?

> What will become of the Bulaq Museum, if Mariette dies? There would be nothing to be done, nothing to be expected. Considering that the event may be imminent we should act promptly. Do not let Turin be enriched again at our expense! . . . and if you, good patriot and Frenchman, if you had the capacity to do it, what glory for you!

The man addressed in this epistolary call to arms was Professor Maspero; the writer, one Arthur Rhone, a friend of Maspero's and an official of the French government, where the possibility of this situation arising had long since been discussed. The Baron de Ring, the French Consul-General in Egypt, had already proposed that the role which Mariette had forged for himself within the administration of Egypt's antiquities – an organization for the collection and protection of antiquities – should be formalized by the controlling European powers and that a French institute should be established in Cairo along the lines that Baron Bunsen had defined for the Prussian institutes of archaeology in Rome and Athens.

Maspero rose promptly to the challenge. On 13 November 1880 the Baron de Ring appointed him head of a mission of French archaeologists to Egypt and officially requested him to establish an Institute of Oriental Archaeology in Cairo. Even as Maspero had packed for Cairo, a French government decree had ratified the Baron's proposals and granted funds for their support.

Brugsch Bey, meanwhile, had abandoned the chair of egyptology at Göttingen University and reached Cairo before his dying friend. And as they sat together on the museum's wooden porch, Mariette asked him to inspect the south Saqqara excavations, where Reis Rubi had uncovered two more sets of texts similar to those from which Mariette had made the squeezes that he had shown to Maspero in Cairo. All those texts, Reis Rubi had since told Mariette, lay at the centres of destroyed pyramids. So Brugsch Bey and his brother took the train to Memphis and rode donkeys up into the sand hills of south Saqqara, where they found that Mariette's workforce had been augmented by the Giza teams and that they were working side by side. Here, then, the brothers found that, as Reis Rubi had described, there were the ruins of no less than three royal pyramids, which had been so denuded by stone robbers that their interiors lay exposed and part open to the sky. These, Brugsch recognized from the inscribed cartouches in their inscriptions, had been the burial chambers of Pepi I and Pepi II and that of the intermediary ruler Merenre. The texts, however, were now dangerously located: the entrance corridors had partially collapsed, whilst following the excavation of their sand and rubble filling some of the great blocks of the burial chambers' broken roofs hung unsupported. And as in many desert excavations, there was an ever-present danger of sudden burial in soft-flowing sand.

'*Il y a donc, malgré tout, des pyramides écrites, je ne l'aurais jamais cru!*' Mariette is famously reported to have said on hearing Brugsch's report that same evening – 'There are then, in spite of everything, writings in the pyramids, I would not have believed it.'

The next day, the two brothers returned to south Saqqara and scrambled through the ruined pyramids once more to check the copies of the texts that they had made the day before. The mummy of a young man, eviscerated, embalmed and wrapped in fine linen, 'the skin well preserved, the outlines of the features distinct, eyes closed, nose fallen in', quite possibly the king himself but probably a later and intrusive burial, had been dug out of Merenre's ruined burial chamber. Right away, the brothers decided to take this strange package to the bedside of Mariette so that he might gaze at last upon the face of pharaoh. And as they carried the brittle cadaver down from the pyramids to the local railway station, they met Charles Wilbour, an American student of Professor Maspero. A lively diarist on his way to view Mariette's south Saqqara excavations, Wilbour describes the brothers Brugsch as covered in dust, their trousers ripped, their knees bloodied, with one of them at the mummy's head, the other at its feet. Later in its journey up to Cairo, Brugsch Bey recalled, it had broken into two: Mariette, he tells, was not delighted with their dusty offering. It was his last coherent conversation with his friend.

Accompanied by three students, a draughtsman and a publicist, Maspero had arrived in Cairo two days later, on 7 January 1881, and the following day the international Cairo press – at that time the city long-since called 'the Klondike on the Nile' had more than 100,000 European residents and several foreign-language newspapers – announced the founding of a new French Institute in Egypt. On paying a visit to his old professor, whom Wilbour found supervising the unpacking of his library and his household goods, Maspero told him that he was astonished to be sent to Cairo and thought that Mariette might live for years. He then asked the American, somewhat nervously, about Brugsch Bey's activities. And all this whilst lines of people were yet visiting the dying Mariette; from the workmen, the sailors and the reis who had worked on his vast excavations to ministers of the Egyptian government, the Baron de Ring and hosts of consuls and ambassadors.

At that same time, Egypt was herself in agony. Two years before, a famine brought on by low Niles and high taxation had killed an estimated 700,000 of the rural population. At Dendera in Upper Egypt, it was said that a Cook's Tour boat had fed a thousand starving people with loaves baked in the steamer's kitchens. In Cairo and Alexandria, several nationalist groups were inspired by the aim of wresting Egypt's governance from foreign rulers. Backed by the regiments of Egypt's army the most prominent of these movements, the Free National Party – *el-Hizb el-Watani el Hurr* – had as its most vocal leader Colonel Ahmad Arabi, who was alternatively arrested, threatened with execution and assassination and appointed as Minister of War. Both London and Paris became increasingly alarmed at the developing situation that threatened both the servicing of Egypt's debt and control of the Suez Canal, which was the route to British India and the Far East.

On 12 January 1881, just a few days after Maspero's arrival in Egypt, the governments of Britain and France had sent a joint note to the Egyptian government backing the Khedive and threatening military intervention should the *status quo* be threatened. Thus the die was cast that, within two years, saw a devastating bombardment of Alexandria by a British fleet, the military defeat and subsequent exile of Ahmad Arabi and the establishment of the so-called 'veiled' protectorate by which Britain would rule Egypt *de facto* until the 1950s.

Mariette died at his museum six days after the delivery of the joint note to the Egyptian parliament, and his funeral was held the following day. The diary of one of Maspero's accompanying students, the 22-year-old Victor Loret, describes the scene at Bulaq which at that time was a Nile-side Cairo suburb but now lies at the centre of the modern city.

> His assistants had gathered at the Museum: the funeral procession was to be at 3 pm. The grille between the garden of Mariette and the Museum was open, armchairs and chairs in the Egyptian style and covered in red leather were scattered in the yard ... The coffin, sycamore, Egyptian in form, very simple and closed by red wax seals was exhibited in the main hall of the Museum ... the court was full of mourners, soldiers, red fezzes and Franciscans, with the addition of the pharaohs and Egyptian sphinxes, old Memphite and Roman tombs, and in the middle on its high green pedestal, impassive Khafre [and the hawk], below which, it seems, we will raise the tomb of Mr Mariette!

Ultimately, however, Mariette was placed, suitably enough, in a granite sarcophagus of pharaonic style but European manufacture in the gardens of the present Cairo Museum, which he would never see but which, essentially, his energies had stocked and founded: the first national museum of antiquities outside of Europe.

Mariette had wanted Brugsch Bey to succeed him in his post of Direct of Egyptian Antiquities and had called him to Cairo expressly for that purpose. Egypt, however, had greatly changed since the days when he and his friend had first excavated at Saqqara, and the Baron de Ring had moved swiftly amongst the international committees and the ministers of the Khedival government to ensure that Maspero would take charge of Egypt's antiquities. So at Mariette's funeral Brugsch walked behind the coffin disappointed and alone, separated from all the other foreigners. In the following days, French government funds paid for the ongoing excavations at south Saqqara, Mariette's papers and library were purchased for France, his debts were settled (for he was never rich), and his two beloved daughters, who had been left penniless in Cairo, were given passage back to Paris. So hastily were those arrangements executed that Mariette's inventory of the antiquities in the new Khedival Museum was shipped to France in error and had to be returned.

In those same days, Arabi's regiments marched on Cairo and sacked the Law Courts and some government ministries. Then, following the protests of the Khedive and at the behest of Captain Baring, the British Commissioner, the Baron de Ring, who had taken the part of Arabi's rebellious officers, was recalled to France and later sent as minister to the Ottoman court in Constantinople. Meanwhile, the Saqqara excavations, which had been re-financed with funds from France and the offices of Cook's Tours, were extended to include the ruins of the pyramids of central Saqqara where, on 28 February 1881, the interior of Wenis' pyramid with its near-perfect set of Pyramid Texts was opened for the first time in the modern era. A month later, the nearby pyramid of Wenis' successor, Teti, was also entered and that, too, was found to hold similar texts upon its walls.

Even as Mariette's old reis had been opening Teti's ruined pyramid, Maspero, along with his wife and staff and several French government agents, took a tour of inspection down the Nile in Mariette's old steam boat, the *Menchiéh*. One of his prime objectives on that triumphant voyage was the location of an unknown tomb or tombs that for a decade and more had been supplying the museums of the West

The entrance to Wenis' pyramid at the time of its opening by Maspero's workmen.

PYRAMIDE DU ROI OUNAS

A section through the interior apartments of Wenis' pyramid, from Maspero's edition of the Pyramid Texts.

with fine papyri and other splendid funerary objects. At Luxor, where, two years before, some of the children of the town had been kept alive with daily rations of fresh milk from the tourist boats, the local police arrested three brothers of a prominent local family, the Abd er-Rassul, who after months of threat and torture revealed the location of a cache of mummies that included those of many famed Egyptian pharaohs. By that time, however, Maspero had already returned to France, and so it fell to Émile Brugsch and Ahmed Kamal Bey, one of the few trained Egyptian egyptologists of the day, employed at the new museum as a secretary, to empty that most remarkable of funerary crypts. And all of those extraordinary finds, the Pyramid Texts, the royal mummies, were hailed in the European press as masterstrokes of Professor Maspero and his new administration.

With the aid of Egypt's British rulers, the affable Parisian professor would dominate the control of Egypt's antiquities with such success that in 1909 he received an honorary knighthood from the British crown. From his offices at the Museum he oversaw the government's publications of the national collections and shaped their presentation in a new national museum. At the same time, as the Director of the *Service des Antiquités*, Maspero also granted permits for all excavations within Egypt and supervised the distribution of their finds between their excavators, who were mostly foreign patrons, and the national museum. The directorate was held by Maspero and successive French scholars until the Egyptian Revolution of 1956. So for some seventy years, throughout a fundamental period of ancient Egypt's excavation and interpretation, the processes of recovering pharaonic monuments and relics were guided by the requirements, the demands and social attitudes of contemporary European academics and international museums, by foreign nationalisms and high finance, influences that cast enormous shadows over ancient Egyptian history down to this day.

STONE TO PAPER – *FROM SAQQARA TO BERLIN*

Even as Maspero was taking his first trip up the Nile in the *Menchiéh*, a young Englishman took a day off from surveying the Great Pyramid to walk across the desert to the excavations at south Saqqara, where, at the behest of Dr Birch of the British Museum, he climbed down through the broken roof of Pepi I's burial chamber and re-copied some of the texts which Brugsch Bey and his brother had copied down a week before. And so it was that William Matthew Flinders Petrie, that most gifted of contemporary archaeologists, on his first trip to Egypt enabled an 'anonymous correspondent' writing in the April edition of the *Athenaeum* magazine to release the first public news of the discovery of the Pyramid Texts.

Two months later, an article jointly written by Birch and Brugsch Bey containing transcriptions and translations of those same texts was published in the *Proceedings of the Society for Biblical Archaeology*, a leading egyptological journal of the day to which Professor Maspero had also sent many contributions. Though 'full of difficulties', as its authors readily acknowledged, it was already recognized that these most ancient texts from Egypt's pyramids could hold fresh chapters of human history and religious revelations and the prospect of establishing a relationship between the world's most ancient religious writings and those of the Old Testament.

The two British articles vexed the French establishment. In earlier times, precedence of publication had been a matter of courtesy between

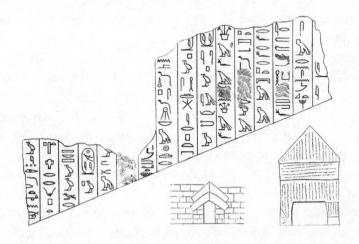

The world's first glimpse of the Pyramid Texts; two published sketches of their architectural context by Petrie, and a hand copy of part of their contents by Heinrich Brugsch.

interested gentlemen; now such issues had assumed political and professional dimensions. Though trifling and inaccurate, their appearance had stolen the public moment of the revelation of the world's most ancient religious writings, leaving Maspero to publish sections of the 4,000 then-known columns of Pyramid Texts over the following decade until, in 1894, his full edition of *Les inscriptions des pyramides de Saqqarah* finally appeared.

A copious and lively writer from the days of his youth, Maspero's celebrated history of the ancient Orient, which first appeared in 1875, had become a standard text of historians and Bible scholars alike and indeed had first brought the professor to the attention of the Baron de Ring. Though a latecomer to that celebrated Parisian circle of linguistic scholarship which had already drawn Champollion, Bunsen, Lepsius and many others to that liveliest of cities, Maspero was already a luminary of the Collège de France. Not surprisingly, therefore, after an initial six-year stint in Cairo, he left his various Egyptian projects in the hands of his students and returned to Paris and the Collège de France. And there it was, in 1895, that he first met a precocious sixteen-year-old named Alan Gardiner just out of Charterhouse, whose father, a silk merchant and City banker, had sent his young son off to Paris at the lad's request to study at the Collège de France; as Gardiner later recalled, even 'as a boy nearing the end of his schooldays . . . I was fired with the desire to become an Egyptologist'.

One fine Parisian morning, after suffering the elaborate French of one of Maspero's lectures on a single verse of the texts within the pyramids, Gardiner had asked the good professor, who had just published his full edition of those elusive documents, what, exactly, was its meaning. 'I have a lot of imagination, you know!' Maspero had replied, 'I think the explanation I gave you just now was very good, but I assure you that I could have given you twenty explanations equally good!' To young Gardiner, who would always strive for clarity and had already come to the opinion that Maspero was 'an unsound grammarian', such Gallic self-assurance seemed utterly unwarranted, and thereupon he ceased to attend the great man's lectures.

In later years, however, Sir Alan Gardiner, arguably the greatest egyptologist England has produced, reluctantly came to a similar conclusion concerning ancient Egyptian religious texts:

> The meaning of the large majority of the words employed is either already known or else can be elicited through comparison with other examples: but not the precise nuances of meaning, only the kind of meaning, its general direction and its approximative emotional quality . . . [so that with] texts of a purely moralizing character, where there is no concrete background against which the appropriateness of this or that rendering shows up unmistakably, must present extraordinary difficulties.

Which underlines the fact that, from the days of their discovery, the Pyramid Texts, the most ambiguous, the most archaic of all Egyptian literature, had presented egyptologists with especial difficulties of understanding. Even as Maspero was lecturing in Paris, however, a group of Berlin-based philologists, part of a century-old school of research whose ambition – described by one of its most illustrious students as 'the conquest of the ancient world by scholarship' – was revolutionizing the study of ancient Egypt and its hieroglyphs, its religion and its history.

So it was that in 1902, a year after graduating from Oxford University, Gardiner travelled to Berlin and stayed in that city for twelve years of study, buying a house, building a library and starting a family, and all the while contributing to the task of creating a great grand hieroglyphic dictionary whose ultimate aim was to include all known occurrences of the words of all known hieroglyphic texts.

That work brought Gardiner into daily contact with Professor Adolf Erman, the founder of the so-called Berlin School of Egyptology and also of its hieroglyphic dictionary. Of the same generation as Maspero, Erman was a son and grandson of eminent Berlin academics, who in their turn were descendants of a charmed circle of humanists and intellectuals who had founded a university in Berlin at the turn of the eighteenth century and had made that institution the most influential centre of learning in the world. And the continuing studies and researches in that university have had a greater influence upon modern views of ancient Egypt than have the works of Jean François Champollion.

'STUDIOSUS PHILOLOGIAE' – *THE CONQUEST OF THE PAST*

The fundamental revolution in the modern understanding of ancient Egypt has its origins in the pretty town of Göttingen, south of Berlin, where George II of England, Duke of Brunswick and Prince Elector of Hanover, had established a university from which, in 1777, one Friedrich August Wolf had matriculated after enrolling, so it was said, as a 'Studiosus philologiae' – as a student of philology – as a student, that is, of a university department which at that time did not exist within the Western world.

Of itself, of course, the study of exotic literature and ancient written records was hardly new. As a means for the better interpretation of both the Bible and the law, that study had run wide and deep throughout the courts and monasteries of post-renaissance Europe. Winckelmann's view of ancient Greek culture as the epitome of human society, however, had shifted the focus of that traditional scholarship and, like most educated Europeans of his time, Wolf, who was Winckelmann's biographer, was also a disciple. At Göttingen, therefore, at that most liberal of eighteenth-century universities, Wolf began employing philology's traditional tools not to further aid an understanding of the writings of the church, but in an attempt to recover something of the lost reality of pagan ancient Greece.

At the beginning of those investigations, Wolf had undertaken an analysis of the language of what was considered to be the noblest and the oldest of all Greek texts, the *Iliad* and the *Odyssey*, a study that had led him to the conclusion, revolutionary for those times, that the two venerable works had not been written by a single poet but were compilations of the works of several different authors. Until that time, such ancient texts had simply been regarded as the prime source of ancient history. Wolf's groundbreaking philological analysis, however, had shown that classical literature of itself could reveal a previously unknown history, an intellectual history, and an entirely new dimension of the past. Its retrieval, though, would clearly be a massive task, for if all of classical literature was to be subjected to such close analysis, entire schools of specially trained philologists would be required. And that in turn led Wolf to re-invent the seminar, originally a medieval form of study, in which groups of students gathered under the guidance of a professor to conduct original research.

Throughout the nineteenth century, the sciences of linguistics and textual criticism were developed in German universities, and both classical and Biblical scholarship were taken on entirely different paths from anything before, a process that had extraordinary impact in academia and caused enormous division and disruption within the European churches.

A further consequence of this revolution in the world of learning was that the University of Göttingen became a centre of the new language studies and of Biblical, Sanskrit and classical literature. In 1867, before he was called to Cairo to run a short-lived Khedival school of egyptology, Brugsch Bey had occupied a new-made chair of egyptology at that university, and by the 1870s chairs of egyptology were being established in the universities of Leipzig, Berlin and Paris, and the academic discipline itself – the study, that is, of ancient Egyptian language – had begun to find its professional academic base.

At the same time, a revision of the nature of history itself was also under way, a revision that had also been prompted by the growth in the study of philology and an accompanying re-evaluation of the role of original documents rather than the continual re-use of old and ancient historical commentaries. Concurrently, the increasing use of the seminar as a tool of learning had led to the invention of such brand new academic disciplines as sociology, anthropology, ethnography, linguistics and the history of art. That these various new-founded disciplines were developing at the same time that the physical sciences were also established within European universities encouraged the adoption of a common academic language of investigation. So the study of history, for example, had a brand new range of tools and methods and *Altertumswissenschaft* – 'the science of history' as Wolf had originally described his philological investigations – became a common project of many university departments; that same project that Ulrich von Wilamowitz-Moellendorff would later describe as the 'conquest of the past by scholarship'.

After that of Göttingen, the university at Berlin – presently, the

Humboldt University of Berlin – had been a major mover in the astonishing processes of partitioning new areas of study into different academic disciplines. The primary university first of Prussia and later of the Kingdom of Germany, Berlin's university had been established in the first decade of the nineteenth century as the pinnacle of Alexander von Humboldt's visionary notion of an education system for the entire Prussian population, a system which operated as a meritocracy and was designed to inculcate the values of that highly structured, highly autocratic state. Set amidst the wide well-ordered avenues of a city that in the 1890s had reminded Mark Twain of Chicago, Berlin's university was directly financed by the state – projects such as Erman's dictionary being funded by a specially appointed state commission. Many of its professors, too, were powerful parliamentary and courtly presences. And all of them shared the same stern work ethic, a strong sense of a fundamental order in civilized human society, a fierce belief in the logical processes and progress of science, philology and history and a powerful loyalty both to their academic disciplines and to the university in which they passed their lives. It was, in short, a unique academic culture, its hierarchies and its learning methods generating a monk-like dedication to study that even in its own time was known as *Kulturprotestantismus* – cultural Protestantism.

GRAMMARS AND DICTIONARIES

Born in 1854, Professor Adolf Erman had played only a late role in the construction of Germany's remarkable academic machine, but one in which modern perceptions of ancient Egypt would be transformed. For Erman, who had been born into that high academic culture, it was a most necessary transformation for egyptology, which though popular amongst the general public had not benefited from the rapid philological developments that had taken place in the study of other ancient languages. So, at the beginning of his career, Erman had found that his fellow academics regarded his chosen subject as lacking in full academic rigour and its translations of the ancient texts and its accounts of pharaonic history somewhat fanciful.

Erman changed all that. In the 1870s whilst yet in his twenties and working as an assistant to Lepsius – who was himself refused a teaching post at Berlin's university on the grounds that egyptology was not required – he was employing the methodologies of classical philology and the advancing science of linguistics to analyse the grammar of hieroglyphic texts and beginning to publish a brilliant stream of technical articles upon the subject. At this point, he later recalled, the relative isolation of ancient Egyptian from the study of other ancient languages had been an asset to him, for he was able to construct an individual methodology for his subject based entirely on pharaonic texts and the syntax of classical philology.

A single essential perception lay behind the process by which Erman transformed contemporary Western views of ancient Egypt, and he employed it from the beginning of his work. This was that the key to the deeper understanding of the hieroglyphic language, which had been employed over several millennia and whose ultimate expression had been written in Coptic Greek, lay in isolating, comparing and describing its various phases as they had developed through time. Erman started by dividing the history of the language into successive stages in the same way that other academics had long since divided other languages. Broadly speaking, Erman's bipartite linguistic division corresponding to Bunsen's tripartition of pharaonic history: Erman's 'Old Egyptian' being the written language of Bunsen's Old and Middle Kingdoms, with Erman's so-called 'Later Egyptian' appearing during the New Kingdom's later phases.

In 1880, Erman, a neat bespectacled young man of twenty-six, published his *Neuägyptische Grammatik*, a business-like grammar of Later Egyptian. Nine years later, his prodigious command both of the development of the ancient language and of the ancient scribes' calligraphy enabled him to produce *Die Sprache des Papyrus Westcar*, a grammatical analysis of that papyrus' 'fairy stories', as Erman called them, about Hardjedef, the magician Djedi and the priest's wife who had given birth to kings. Erman had discovered the unique document unrolled but yet unpublished amongst Lepsius' papers, for its translation had eluded all earlier scholars. Just a few years later, in 1894, Erman published a more comprehensive grammar, *Aegyptische Grammatik*, in which he employed examples of texts from various periods of pharaonic history and showed how the grammar of the written language had developed through time. And for his main source of 'Old Egyptian' he used the Pyramid Texts – his lucid translations made just a decade after Brugsch's first faltering attempts to copy and decipher them.

Erman's studies rendered all earlier grammars obsolete. In everything from his method of transcribing hieroglyphs into the Latin alphabet – which he developed from contemporary Semitic studies – to the very elements of grammar that he described, the novelty of Erman's work was such that his American translator had to invent English equivalents for some of his technical terms. Almost single-handedly, he had created the foundations of modern egyptology and made Berlin the world centre of its study.

It is said that whilst working on his *Aegyptische Grammatik* Erman had contacted Maspero, asking for a fresh copy to be made of a passage of the Pyramid Texts whose impressions were held on Mariette's paper squeezes which were kept in Paris. 'What a pity', Erman is reported to have said upon receiving the corrected text from his Parisian colleague, 'that even at this early period the Egyptians could not write correctly!' 'What a pity', Maspero is said to have remarked on hearing Erman's comments, 'that the Egyptians of the Old Kingdom had not read M. Erman's grammar!'

It was not arrogance, Gardiner later observed, that led to a split in egyptology between those trained in the methods of the Berlin School and many other egyptologists of the day – most notably those of the French and British universities and museums. It was simply the Berliners' 'habit of disregarding the work of any except those of their own persuasion', an attitude that was largely due to the rigorous methods of the Berlin School, which had replaced the individual, often haphazard, intuitions of earlier interpreters. At Berlin, egyptology was considered to be science, its study a definitive project to be undertaken by generations of researchers who would advance the subject stage by stage, so that a great text-based source of knowledge would represent in logical and documented detail all aspects of the ancient civilization.

By 1897, the core activity of this extraordinary enterprise was the compilation of Erman's hieroglyphic dictionary, which entailed the copying, translation and listing of the words and phrases on the texts upon the standing monuments of Egypt and those held in the world's museums. It was a precise and hugely time-consuming undertaking, yet one that found a willing and expert staff. For since the publication of Erman's grammar books, egyptologists such as Gardiner were travelling from all over Europe and America to study at Berlin. And as the best young talents of the day studied the newly created science of egyptology with its inventor, they were put to work upon the compilation of the 'Wörterbuch', as the Berlin hieroglyphic dictionary has come to be affectionately known.

In broad terms, a group of German and Austrian scholars were set to copying the ancient texts in Egypt and those held in Great Britain, whilst Kurt Sethe, the closest of Erman's academic colleagues and his one-time student, worked upon the Pyramid Texts, and James Henry Breasted, a talented American student who had published an English translation of Erman's *Aegyptische Grammatik* in the year of its German publication, travelled the museums of Europe copying the texts in those collections. Gardiner had joined the Wörterbuch's staff a few years after Breasted. Never one of Erman's students and classed in the strict terminology of Berlin academia as a 'junior associate', he spent much time in the museums of Leiden and Turin, where he transcribed many of the papyri that Champollion had unrolled almost a century before, rendering those calligraphic texts into lines of neatly written hieroglyphs. A pioneering labour following upon Erman's translation of Papyrus Westcar, Gardiner's work on those papyri widened the dictionary's scope so that it included a considerable body of handwritten ancient documents rather than just the monumental inscriptions on wood and stone that most of his co-workers were engaged in copying.

Aided by dozens of fellow researchers in other German universities, this enormous lexicographical enterprise eventually produced 1,200,000 individual slips of paper, each one of which held some thirty words or so in blocks of hieroglyphs, most of which had been analysed and translated under the critical eye of Erman and some other senior editors. Filed and numbered in extensive catalogues, every word on every slip was then cross-referenced so that its every known occurrence was indexed and listed. This it was that formed the basis of the Berlin dictionary; a dictionary that, in the manner of the *Oxford English Dictionary*, defines each word by quotation and thus traces its development and changes throughout three millennia. Issued in various forms from the early 1920s, though with the products of that research already present in the works of many scholars long before the First World War, it was and yet remains a remarkable accomplishment. At the same time, however, it employed philology's principle virtue of scientific accuracy to quietly set the attitudes and opinions of the Berlin School, specifically those of Professor Erman and the German academics of his day, into the modern vision of ancient Egypt. And as one might expect, these were the products of their time and place: the earlier vision of Winckelmann and Humboldt allied to the political currents of late nineteenth-century Germany, which were all perfectly encapsulated by Erman in 1886 in the Preface to his *Life in Ancient Egypt*, the widely influential work that introduced the new-made ancient Egypt of the Berlin seminars to the Western world:

> In making comparisons between the youthful joyous art of Greece and the severe sober art of Egypt we must remember that the latter sprang to life on the sad soil of the Nile valley, where hard work is required of everyone . . .
>
> The hard logic of facts teaches us that an autocratic government is always necessary in order to control and regulate irrigation. In fact, the earliest knowledge we have of the conditions of life in Egypt shows us a strict administration of political and agrarian relations; a state in which the individual was of little account . . .
>
> Their language, religion, and government developed in a similar way to those of later nations . . . those eternal laws which ruled them are still in force . . . the old kingdoms were founded by wars similar to those by which are founded the kingdoms of modern times . . .

ANCIENT RECORDS, MODERN HISTORIES

Though Gardiner came to dislike the exclusivity of the Berlin School, its powerful values and extraordinary work ethic had resonated strongly with the hard-working young American James Henry

Breasted, who hailed from the not dissimilar background of contemporary Mid-Western Congregationalism. Those stern principles, doubtless allied to the fact that the public education system in America had been largely modelled upon that of Prussia's, had given the University of Berlin, the high temple of that academic order, a special aura in the young man's eyes and indeed had led him to Professor Erman's seminar.

As a student in Berlin, Breasted had transcribed large numbers of hieroglyphic inscriptions for their inclusion in the *Wörterbuch*. Combined with extra field work in Egypt and the European museums, a decade later he employed those same materials for his *Ancient Records of Egypt*, a remarkable five-volume epic of translation covering 2,500 years of pharaonic documents which for the best part of the twentieth century served as standard English versions of most ancient Egyptian historical texts. In those same years too, following his appointment as the first professor of egyptology in America, Breasted mined those texts for his majestic *A History of Egypt* which first appeared in 1906. Along with his *Ancient Records*, this too served as a standard general history of ancient Egypt for generations of historians. Written in lively and authoritative prose, in its preoccupation with politics and economics, in its judgements and in its characterizations, consciously or unconsciously, most modern histories still follow Breasted's impressive narratives.

A decade later, Breasted published the first of two works on the development of ancient Egyptian religion, both of which took as their starting points views that had been argued over and discussed in the Berlin seminar before the First World War; indeed, the first and most influential of those volumes, *The Development of Religion and Thought in Ancient Egypt*, is dedicated with gratitude and affection to Professor Erman, who, as one of Erman's eminent contemporaries had previously remarked, had been 'the first to present the Egyptian religion in historical perspective'.

Described as a classic and a monument of scholarship, Breasted's first volume on ancient Egyptian religion has had almost as large an impact on the modern visions of ancient Egypt as his historical works. And they share the same central themes, for all of them recount the history of ancient Egypt as a narrative of ethical and material progress. His second volume on religion, for example, describes a millennial journey from savagery through barbarism to decadence and dissolution – a journey that, for both Breasted and northern Europeans such as Erman, echoed a pessimistic vision of the history of ancient religion as a progress from paganism to high-church decadence that, lacking the saving grace of Protestant Christianity, must lead inevitably to decay and dissolution.

Just as Erman's earlier popular books had introduced ancient Egypt to generations of German-speakers, so Breasted's writings, more than those of any other single individual, have transmitted Berlin's attitudes to ancient Egyptian history and culture to the English-speaking world, a connection generously acknowledged by Breasted's pious Maecenas, John D. Rockefeller, who would finance the publication of Erman's *Wörterbuch* in Berlin during that city's poverty-stricken decades after the First World War.

In similar fashion, following its first appearance in 1927, Gardiner's *Egyptian Grammar*, became the crib of successive generations of egyptological students around the world, echoing the shorter volumes of Erman's earlier grammars in both its structure and even in its typographic layout. Setting the study of hieroglyphic writing firmly, as had Erman, within the pages of a classical grammar, 'Gardiner's *Grammar*', as it is affectionately known, offered and yet still offers students the old epigraphic promise of the 'conquest of the past by scholarship'. Just as Friedrich August Wolf had laid down at Göttingen more than a century before, and as Erman and Sethe had taught at Berlin, the past and the progress of ancient history would be revealed by following the seductive discipline and methodologies of traditional classical philology, as Gardiner reaffirmed in his biographical essay of 1961:

> . . . as a boy nearing the end of his schooldays . . . I was fired with the desire to become an Egyptologist, and my budding interest lay almost as much in the course and methods of discovery as in the things to be discovered.

19
Interpreting the Pyramids

KURT SETHE AND THE PYRAMID TEXTS

An offering which the king gives! An offering which Anubis
gives! Thy thousand of young antelope from the highland,
they come to thee with bowed head. An offering which the
king gives! An offering which Anubis gives! Thy thousand of
bread! Thy thousand of beer! Thy thousand of incense, that
came forth from the palace hall! Thy thousand of everything
pleasant! Thy thousand of cattle! Thy thousand of every-
thing thou eatest, on which thy desire is set!

> *Pyramid Text 806, transcribed by Kurt Sethe*
> *and translated by James Henry Breasted, 1912*

Alongside his work on the Berlin dictionary, one of Sethe's considerable contributions to egyptology and a labour that engaged him over
the best part of his life was an edition in hand-copied hieroglyphs,
translations and commentary of all of the then-known texts that were
engraved in pyramids. From the first part of this work, which appeared
in 1908, to the last, which was posthumously published with Gardiner's help in 1962, Sethe's edition has underpinned virtually all
discussion of the pyramids' texts: it had been Sethe, indeed, who first
named those texts, collectively, 'Pyramidentexten' – Pyramid Texts.

In Maspero's *Les inscriptions des pyramides de Saqqarah*, each
separate verse of the pyramids' texts had been accompanied by a
translation and an explanation of their meaning based on Maspero's
understanding of the funerary texts of later ages, for there was

nothing else with which those earliest of such documents could be compared. Given their inscrutable nature, it was a subtle work, but one that, as Maspero himself readily acknowledged, was largely based on intuition founded upon a long immersion in modern studies of ancient Egypt and its religion.

Maspero's publication set the long columned texts of engraved hieroglyphs into the cold hard forms of a letterpress hieroglyphic font and abandoned the vertical columns of the ancient originals as Sethe's would later do, arranging them in horizontal lines, in the manner of Western writing, from left to right. In similar fashion, though the ancient texts give no indication of a fixed order in which they were intended to be read, both Maspero and Sethe began their editions of the pyramids' ancient verses with the lists of offerings inscribed on the north wall of the pyramids' burial chambers before moving outwards towards the pyramids' entrances, ordering the texts as they had been placed on successive corridors and chambers. Sethe also followed Maspero in basing his edition on the texts in Wenis' pyramid, which were and still are the oldest-known and best preserved examples of them all. Covering but limited parts of the pyramid's interior architecture, they give the impression of being the primary version, the *editio princeps*, of the longer sets of texts in later pyramids.

There, however, the similarity between the two versions stopped, for Sethe's methods of analysis and explanation were based upon the analytical methods of nineteenth-century German classical and Biblical scholarship – such borrowings being neatly underlined by his adoption of the term '*Sprüche*' – 'Proverbs'– as the name for the texts' different verses. Sethe also set the verses of the texts in a numbered order following the order of his presentation, from burial chamber to doorway, a system that had originally been devised by another of the Berlin seminar's egyptological collaborators, Count Hans Schack-Schackenburg, and one that is still widely used today. And in the manner of Göttingen's classical seminars, whose primary aim was the analysis of differing and often damaged versions of a single text in order to establish an earlier, theoretical, lost original, Sethe placed differing versions of the various verses from all of the then-known pyramids, one after another within his numerical sequence, adding new-found verses as they were discovered under

CHAMBRE DE L'OUEST (A).

(Parois a—c.)

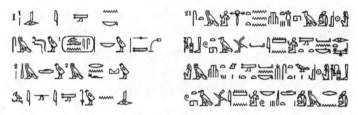

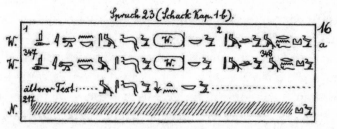

*Lines from Maspero's and Sethe's editions of the Pyramid Texts.
Maspero presents and numbers the various verses in the order they
appear to visitors to Wenis' pyramid. Sethe, alternatively, a philologist
in the classical tradition, provides five different versions of
Maspero's verse number one.*

new numbers at the ending of his list, a process that has continued to
this day as hundreds of new verses, along with variants of well-known
older ones, have been found in newly excavated pyramids.

Coupled with the leap in understanding of the ancient language
forged in the Berlin seminars, the accuracy and linguistic perception
of Sethe's studies of the Pyramid Texts gave his copies, translations
and commentaries a level of coherence beyond all previous imagining.
Such was the force of this accomplishment, indeed, that it was only in
1968 that the texts of a single pyramid – those of Wenis, once again –
were published and translated as a separate entity in their own right.

Yet the transference of those dark columns of engravings from the
walls of pyramids into the ordered processes of a European seminar had
a profound effect upon their modern understanding. Indexed and cross-
referenced, analysed and ordered line by line as they had never been
before, the effect of Sethe's 'Pyramidentexten' was that the modern
world now read those ancient verses as if they were passages in books.

One effect was to encourage a search for some joining narrative within the numbered verses. Another was the employment of the Pyramid Texts as an esoteric encyclopaedia from whose capacious indices odd lines could be extracted like plums from a pudding in explanation of everything ancient Egyptian, from the sacredness of grasshoppers to the use of coloured stone in temple architecture. Another effect was that in analysing the Pyramid Texts in the manners and method of classical and Bible scholarship they were often assumed to be filled with 'metaphors' and 'symbolisms'. Unlike true metaphors or symbols, however, whose very purposes are ambivalence and whose meanings shift and change, the images in the Pyramid Texts were considered to be sets of cyphers which had encoded simple and straightforward beliefs. Breasted's commentaries, for example, assume that selected passages could serve as guides to an understanding of the genesis of Western moral and ethical behaviour; others, alternatively, imagine that they hold myths to explain the origins and constitution of the universe, whilst others yet again, consider them to be descriptions of the rituals performed at royal funerals, somewhat in the manner of the Book of Common Prayer. After a century and more of study, all such approaches have gained considerable academic pedigree and a language of their own.

TIMELY MEDITATIONS

As a professor of classical philology at the University of Basle, Friedrich Nietzsche had understood the dangers in studying ancient texts in the manner employed by Erman and by Breasted decades before their work began. Written during the 1870s after he had resigned his post at the ending of a bitter controversy, Nietzsche's writings on this subject, a dazzling blast of insult and insight known today as 'We Philologists', are his impassioned valediction to nineteenth-century German academia.

Like countless other Europeans of his time, Nietzsche held an overwhelming vision of classical antiquity, derived from Winckelmann and Goethe, as an age of profound accomplishment. Nietzsche's conception of classical Greece, however, differed from that of his contemporaries, who considered that the social harmony and artistic accomplishments of Winckelmann's ancient Greece could be revisited with the aid of strong government and a classical education and that, thus equipped, industrial Europe, and more especially the German nation, could re-attain those antique levels of perfection. Nietzsche's view was that the urban culture of classical Greece had been the absolute antithesis of contemporary European society. 'The better the state is organized,' he declared, with an eye towards the city of Berlin, which had recently become the immaculate capital of the newly founded German Empire, 'the duller humanity will be.' Nietzsche, therefore, considered that the academic professors of philology, the gatekeepers of antiquity, had grossly misinterpreted the ancient writings and were guilty of providing false visions of the classical past and thus of providing the modern world with dangerous aspirations.

Nietzsche's classical antiquity, alternatively, was a fierce free thing that could never be encompassed by other members of his one-time profession whom, he observed, had more affection for study and academic life than for the realities of the past and whose vision of ancient history was tempered by 'shallow rationalism' and a 'timid submission' typical of state-funded professionals!

Though the historical detail of Nietzsche's arguments have been superseded, the fundamental question posed by his diatribe are valid to this day. How should the past be viewed? Does philology hold a genuine scientific key to its understanding? Are philology and history even sciences? Does the nineteenth-century division of ancient societies into epigraphic, economic, cultural, religious and political components aid or hinder our understanding of the ancient past? Can such approaches ever provide the reason why those lines of cattle waiting patiently to be slaughtered had been assembled amidst the dust at Abusir? Can they place those massive living presences, those solid shadowed animals standing amidst clouds of incense and the stench of blood and dung, as acts of offering and provision, and relate them to the making of flint slaughtering knives, to the construction of temples and fine statues, to pyramids and river barges, to the identification of the pharaoh as the bull of his own mother?

Nietzsche was especially critical of a method common amongst other academics of his century that defined and isolated certain elements in ancient societies as 'religious' within a Christian meaning of that word, a method espoused by both Champollion and the Berlin School. With no proof whatsoever, Nietzsche observed, such an attitude assumes that an awareness of the divine and an innate need to worship had been a constant factor throughout all human history. What if, he proposed, '. . . morality was not based on religion . . . that there were no priests of religion, no guild of priests, no Holy Writ in all antiquity, only priests of the individual gods'.

THE BONES OF THE HELL-HOUNDS TREMBLE — *PRIMITIVISM AND THE BERLIN SEMINARS*

Clouds darken the sky,
The stars rain down,
The Bows [a constellation] stagger,
The bones of the hell-hounds tremble,
The [porters] are silent,
When they see king Wenis dawning as a soul,
As a god living on his fathers,
Feeding on his mothers . . .

King Wenis is one who eats men and lives on gods,
Lord of messengers, who despatches his messages;
It is 'Grasper-of-Forelocks' living in Kehew
Who binds them for King Wenis.
It is 'Punisher-of-all-Evil-doers'
Who stabs them for King Wenis.
He takes out for him their entrails . . .

Shesmu cuts them up for King Wenis
And cooks for him a portion of them
In his evening kettles.
King Wenis is he who eats their charms,
And devours their glorious ones.
Their great ones are for his morning portion,
Their middle ones are for his evening portion,
Their little ones are for his night portion.

Their old men and their old women are for his incense-burning.
It is the 'Great-Ones-North-of-the-Sky'
Who set for him the fire to the kettles containing them,
With the legs of their oldest ones (as fuel).

King Wenis has dawned again in the sky,
Shining as lord of the horizon.

From Breasted's 1915 translation of
Sethe's Pyramid Texts numbers 393–414

Christened the 'Cannibal Hymn' in the early years of the last century, the Pyramid Texts that Sethe numbered 393 to 414 hold but one of the multifarious descriptions of the events that follow the death and rebirth of pharaoh. In common with many other verses, they tell of the dead king's journey to join the populations that inhabit the unseen world, which here is presented as the night sky of the lower Nile, and concludes with pharaoh's establishment as a star 'Shining as lord of the horizon' alongside the other gods.

That the progress of this cosmic transfiguration is told in terms of slaughtering, cooking and eating several of the gods marks the Cannibal Hymn as unique amongst known Pyramid Texts. Nor was it greatly favoured by the ancient scribes, for after its inscription within Wenis' pyramid it only appeared once again, in the pyramid of his successor, Teti. Breasted thought that the unusual violence of its imagery was a picture of 'grotesque cannibalism . . . The gods are hunted down, lassoed, bound, and slaughtered like wild cattle', and he explained its presence amongst the other texts that describe the same migration in more prayerful or liturgic tones as 'surviving from vastly remote prehistoric days, in which we see the savage Pharaoh ferociously preying upon the gods like a blood-thirsty hunter in the jungle'.

Modern explanations of the Cannibal Hymn, alternatively, consider its fierce imagery to have been based upon an account of the slaughtering, butchering, cooking and eating of a sacrificial bull. That one of its verses describes Wenis as 'the bull of the sky' – that is, as a dead king who has been translated to the unseen world in the form of a bull – equates the act of ritual slaughter with the death and, ultimately, the regeneration of the king. And that in turn shows those verses to be a variant of the circular narratives that are central to funerary texts of all periods of pharaonic history, which deal with the awkward physical problem posed by the recurring acts of spontaneous regeneration from life to death to life to death that took place continuously in the pharaonic universe in concert with the rhythms of the year.

Another near-contemporary version of that same theme and one that involved powerful physical contact between the unseen and the visible living world was the slaughtering of bulls and other living offerings in the temples of Abusir: acts conducted in the royal name that crossed the boundaries of the visible living world whilst at the same time serving to nourish both the living and the dead. A later variant on this same circular theme describes pharaoh regenerating by an act of masturbation, another as 'the bull of his mother', the common latter notion of incest as a means of self-procreation being present in an abbreviated form in the Pyramid Texts' account of similar acts amongst the family of state gods.

The key to this multi-layered re-interpretation of the Cannibal Hymn lies in the identification of King Wenis as 'the bull of the sky' that appears in a section of the text that Breasted did not include in his translation as he considered it to be exceptionally obscure. The problem did not lie in Breasted's command of the ancient language, for he was a considerable philologist, but rather, as Gardiner commented in a near-contemporary study of a similarly ambiguous document, in the translator's attitude to the text itself: 'The only basis we can have for preferring one rendering to another, when once the exigencies of grammar and dictionary have been satisfied and these leave a large margin for divergencies, is an intuitive appreciation of the trend of the ancient writer's mind.' Intent on cannibalism, therefore, all that Breasted could discern in that verse was that it 'contains an important statement that the king "lives on the being of every god, eating their organs who come with their belly filled with charms."'

Why cannibalism? Like his fellow members of the Berlin seminars, Breasted considered the people of the Old Kingdom to have been primitive and assumed that the ancient Egyptians of later eras had inherited their savage ways. As Erman himself wrote in 1904, in an introduction to a handbook about ancient Egyptian religion for the Berlin Imperial Museums:

> Those to whom the following explanation of Egyptian ideas may seem far too simple, should remember that for the most part they were conceived by a race of naked, half-savage peasants. These ideas were inherited by the Egyptians of historical times, the subjects of Cheops, Amenemhet and Ramses, who preserved them for us.

Erman's judgement was made on a philological basis at a time when few Old Kingdom texts other than the Pyramid Texts had been translated and its arts and architecture were still little known. In consequence, that vastly complex period was considered to have been semi-literate and hence a primitive and largely ahistoric era. Until 1890, indeed, and the publication of Erman's pioneering translation of the Papyrus Westcar with its tales of Prince Hardjedef and the regal twins, the same view of the Old Kingdom as a semi-literate and deeply primitive culture had extended to the Middle Kingdom, which is the era in which that remarkable papyrus is believed to have been composed.

New Kingdom texts, in contrast, were relatively plentiful in the nineteenth century, and many of them could be conveniently studied in Champollion's old hunting grounds of the European museums and the tombs and temples of Egyptian Thebes. So, in a brief outline of Egyptian history published in 1894, Erman deals with all the earlier periods of pharaonic history in a few pages but had sufficient New Kingdom literary material at his disposal to provide a reign-by-reign account of a succession of some New Kingdom pharaohs; narratives he largely tells in nineteenth-century terms of war and conquest. It is hardly surprising, therefore, that he characterized the New Kingdom as a prosperous and splendid age which 'had arisen out of darkness'.

The unfortunate image of Breasted's enjungled pharaoh was born of that same understanding of 'the primitive' which had been seasoned by contemporary descriptions of some of the sub-Saharan cultures that Westerners were encountering during the so-called Scramble for Africa. For the African rites and rituals that the colonizers' were witnessing seemed so removed from their previous experience that they assumed their celebrants to be irrational and ferocious and could hardly distinguish reality from magic and superstition; a primitive state, the missionaries claimed, that also resulted in the lamentable social and moral order which they perceived within those societies. To many scholars of the time, such cultures appeared to be living examples of the reality of early pharaonic culture.

By tracing the evolution of moral elements in Sethe's Pyramid Texts, Breasted's commentaries put a somewhat optimistic spin on Berlin's usual attitudes. People of Erman and Sethe's background were less malleable. The ancient Egyptians, Erman had written in 1886, lived in a hard and monotonous landscape that had produced prosaic people and pale and formless gods, quite unlike those of the Greeks, who with their snow-capped mountains, their sea-foamed winds and flower-decked meadows had set joyous youthful deities on Mount Olympus.

Winckelmann's late romantic vision had cleaved European visions of the past in half, into those cultures that had thrived before the perfections of the Classical Age, and those that had come after it. As to the cultures of those former ages, Winckelmann had long since concluded, those of the Persians, Phoenicians and the Egyptians had been lower than the Greeks, less civilized, more primitive. Even their bodies, Winckelmann observed, had been less finely made and were less noble, as were their laws, their customs and religions.

It was a vision that had drawn on earlier Western images of a primitive world, in which humanity had lived in harmony with plants and animals yet without the constraints or inhibitions of Christian civilization. Chiming well with the rise of the Enlightenment and, latterly, evolutionary theorists – Darwin himself declaring that early humans had been as promiscuous as gorillas – the idea of the primitive as a dawn-land, as mankind's childhood, as a universal stage in human development, offered a handy rationale for the European imperial ambition to lead such 'lower races' towards the light. Later it would serve as explanation for such European disasters as the First World War, which could be counted as relapses, as slides back down the evolutionary ladder into temporary primitiveness.

Throughout the nineteenth century the notion of a primitive, lower stage of human development was extended to include virtually all cultures not of European descent, and aspects of those so-called primitive cultures, ancient and modern, had been scientifically classified and analysed by a range of newly emerging academic disciplines that usually considered the subjects of their studies as sub-species in relation to European accomplishments; from their various physical attributes and languages, to their religions and their arts, their social structures, their histories and ethnicity.

Many of these studies were undertaken by renowned academics who are regarded as the fathers of the modern social sciences. Distorted and politicized during the 1920s and 1930s, caricatures of that same vision provided a scientific pedigree to the students who burnt 'un-German' books in the court of Berlin University, to those who chased Erman's Jewish students into exile, and to the newly appointed professors of egyptology, all products of the Berlin seminars, who gave lectures at Göttingen and Leipzig dressed in Nazi uniform.

As far as the creation of modern ancient Egypt is concerned, Erman's vision of primitive pharaonic society had permeated the study of other areas of the culture as early as the 1890s, when many of his colleagues and students began to branch out from pure philology and undertake a series of pioneering studies in ancient Egyptian chronology, art history and architecture. Reisner and Borchardt, for example, both studied with Erman, and they and their followers discussed the sublime architectures of Giza and Abusir and those of other ancient Egyptian sites in terms of magical and so-called primitive religion, employing as need arose terms extracted from early anthropological studies of the cultures of colonial India and Africa.

In similar fashion, the assumption that the texts within the pyramids were products of a dawn-land of primitive religion long served to isolate those dark columns of hieroglyphs from the living world that drew them. As Harold Hays, one of the Pyramid Texts' most acute commentators recently observed; 'the agent and event are erased, and without them there is no human history.'

For history's sake, therefore, better to consider the Pyramid Texts at the moment when they were being cut onto the walls of pyramids, when they were part of the contemporary courtly activities of offering, sculpting and building. For there is no material evidence that they ever were intended to be the record of a national religion or theology, nor even of a book of prayer. Those acts of sculpting in the cramped darkness of a pyramid had encompassed something else again.

READING IN THE DARK

You need a ladder and a torch today to read the columned texts within a pyramid. And as you walk from room to room, from corridor to corridor, their order is fragmented, dependent upon the placement of the verses, upon the light available and on the choice that every individual makes in their journey through those rooms and corridors. Nor were those texts set down in a predetermined order from pyramid to pyramid. No single reading, therefore, is definitive, nor is their arrangement logical, sequential or consistent. How, then, are they to be understood?

Tell-tale marks of the sculptors' chisels and the correcting guidelines of the scribes who drew them out show many corrections, changes and mistakes. And that simple fact, along with the note that the scribes have occasionally inserted into those texts indicating that the exemplar from which a verse was being copied was either damaged or incomplete, shows that those scribes and craftsmen were adapting those columns of well-made formal hieroglyphs from exemplars written in a calligraphic hand on scrolls; scrolls such as are shown in the hands of the images of priests that appear in the wall scenes of contemporary tomb chapels and temples.

Recent text analyses, moreover, show that, contrary to the earlier assumptions of Maspero and Sethe, the verses within Wenis' pyramid are not an *editio princeps* of those inscribed in later pyramids; that the oldest-known examples of the Pyramid Texts are neither simpler nor less corrupted versions of those that were engraved in later pyramids. Which, in turn, suggests that the texts in each individual pyramid have been extracted from elaborate, long-lost archives and taken to the pyramids in scrolls where they were recast into vertical columns of formal hieroglyphs.

Unlike the contemporary royal letters that were similarly re-copied onto the walls of the nobles' tomb chapels and which report specific events, the texts within the pyramids do not report or hold a single linear narrative. Nor, despite their vigorous rhetorical qualities, are they the scripts of the rites of pharaonic burial. Those noisy words are set down without a hint of guidance, direction or explanation.

Deriving from the shape and order of a distant, living world, their coherence is now largely lost.

Certainly, like many of old Egypt's relics, the texts within the pyramids are residues of the activities and actions that had bound and, indeed, defined the living state. Like the gestures of familial affection that were carefully reproduced in courtly statues, like the forms of pyramids and tombs, they encompass a variety of reactions, spontaneous and ritualized, to the act of dying, to the division of body and spirit and to the destiny of the dead on their journey from the houses of the living across the Nile and through the bankside reeds to the western desert and out into the living universe. They are intimations of realms outside the mundane, and, like music, acts of ritual slaughter and the smoke of incense, they aim to permeate and synchronize with the life-giving energies that were held within the valley of the lower Nile.

Some of the verses of the Pyramid Texts are expressions of pure grief, as are certain texts and wall reliefs within the nobles' tomb chapels. Others, specifically some of those within the later pyramids, show that, in common with the developing order in the contemporary state bureaucracy, the roles of gods such as Re and Osiris were being elaborated and enlarged. Others, alternatively, hold formal words of offering and funeral – to that extent, they chime with something that Maspero and Sethe had both assumed. Yet the span and scope of the combined texts is far larger than any such concerns: nothing less than multifaceted descriptions of the death and rebirth of kings in terms of the rhythms and energies held within the region of the ancient lower Nile, in its lunar and solar cycles, in procreation, in its bulls, its gods, its desert lions, in the rising of Sirius and its great wide river, within the fields of silt, the sprouting seed and the encroaching sand, in grasshoppers, fish and fowl.

Like the slaughterers of Abusir and the craftsmen builders of the royal court, those who drew and engraved the signs and verses upon the walls of pyramids were penetrating the boundaries between the seen and unseen that had long since been established by that courtly culture. A culture in which the living and the dead, pharaoh, his people and the gods were all sustained and vivified by acts of offering and building, statewide and transubstantiate.

20

Look at Us!

Meet the Courtiers

IMAGE AND PRESENTATION

About a thousand freestanding statues of the courtiers of the Memphite kings are known to have survived until today, along with fragments of several thousand more – three centuries of cheery bright-eyed faces that had once peered through the millennial darkness of their tomb chapels and now greet us from under the spotlights of the world's museum cases. Faces from a time when there were few mirrors, no cameras and hardly any literature. When images of the self and others were different from those of today. When people lived within bubbles of personal interaction. When there was gossip but no news and most of the population of the lower Nile had lived and worked in farming settlements beside their great wide river.

Along with the explosion of reliefs and texts within the courtiers' tomb chapels, the greater part of that glorious body of sculpture was a consequence of the increasing availability of copper in the times of the kings of Abusir and Saqqara. In those same times, as well, and unlike most of the sculptures and reliefs that were made during the era of the Giza kings, the patrons of many of these later works did not have a close relationship with pharaoh. As a commentator of the last century observed: 'there has never been middle-class sculpture of such extraordinary quality in any other time in history.' Eighty years before, Mariette, who excavated large numbers of those nobles' statues, had thought them to be as chic as contemporary Parisians.

Washed for the best part with hot ochre pigments from the desert and mostly named and titled in lines of hieroglyphs engraved upon their bases, the archetypes of this riotous regiment of scribes and dwarfs, courtiers and princes, wives and daughters, were the sculptures made in the times of the Giza kings. This, not only in their splendid sculptural qualities, but also in their presence and their very bearing.

The first known examples of the so-called 'scribe statue', for example, the famous pose of a seated crossed-legged man with a papyrus spread open on his lap, was made, as many broken fragments have confirmed, as an image of senior male members of the royal household; presently, the oldest-known examples, inscribed with a cartouche of Khufu and the name of the royal prince Kawab, were found within that prince's mastaba, which lies within the Great Pyramid's Eastern Cemetery, close to that of Hardjedef. Such works appear to tell us that these princes had mastered the arts of hieroglyphic writing, just as Hardjedef was reputed to have done. And the quality of the fragments of those early stony scribes is the equal of the sculptures of their kings, and they are clearly products of the royal workshops.

In the following generations the pose of the 'seated scribe' that had originally been sculpted in a variety of hard desert stone was reproduced in the soft white limestones that were used for the majority of courtiers' statues. Following earlier examples made in the royal workshops, the eyes of some of these scribal statues were inlaid with shining stone: white alabaster mounted in copper set deep into the dry red-painted limestone, so that the eye's orb seems to be alive and wet. Sometimes, a cornea-sized hole was drilled into the centre of these alabaster inlays and filled with a cylinder of highly polished clear rock crystal backed with a circular copper iris, with a small hole at its centre to represent the pupil. The effect is startlingly real. Heads held high in the old royal pose and with a slight smile of confidence seemingly playing on their lips, those sculptures' shining eyes appear to follow you attentively around the room as if a scribe was poised to write and waiting for you to speak, an effect cleverly augmented by the sculptor's slight offsetting of the two bright eyes, adding to the illusion that they are in constant motion.

At first glance, such tricks might seem more appropriate to waxworks than stone sculpture. Here, however, they are a logical extension of the ancient craftsmen's obsession with filling their works with life, those clear bright eyes setting the stone figure in that half-zone between death and life, past and present. And so successful were those sculptors that, when Mariette's Saqqara workmen first opened up the mud-brick mastaba of the courtier Ka-apar and revealed its now celebrated standing image of a middle-aged man, the near life-sized wooden statue with its inlaid eyes had held such presence, such immediacy, that they had recognized it there and then as the village headman – their 'Sheik el-Beled' – which is the name Ka-aper's statue bears to this day.

Blackly bewigged and clad in fine white linens, the mass of courtiers' statues are images of sturdy well-proportioned people, some sensual, some as coldly formal as a diagram of an ideal human form, but all of them posed with heads aloft looking confidently forward, and each one with a quality of life. Sometimes, as in the great cache of statues that were set in the serdabs of the tomb chapel of the courtier Ra-wer, the sculptors might carve two or even three images of the same subject side by side within the same stone block: Ra-wer seated and standing in duplicate and triplicate. Alternatively, they could show their subjects at different stages of their life, from childhood into middle age, and mostly clothed though sometimes nude, with females portrayed as uniformly young and sheathed in the sheerest linens and mostly set in pair statues, man and woman. Though males are often shown at much larger sizes than their partners in such groups, the sexes still touch each other with the same soft electricity that is held in the gestures of Menkaure's sculptural companions.

Occasionally, the sculptors rang surprising changes. The fond image of Seneb the dwarf, for example, its little legs crossed scribal-style upon the standard block that often passes for a sculptured chair in such small-scale works, has two children standing side by side in front of Seneb's image, taking the places more usually held by the subject's two stout legs. Seneb himself sits smilingly beside his wife, who holds him as proudly as any of Menkaure's siltstone goddesses had held their king. In an entirely different mode, a splendid dark wood life-sized statue thought to represent Senedjemib Mehi has something of the air of cold command that one might expect today of high officials, and this despite the fact that both its inlaid eyes have been brutally hacked out.

Whilst the grandest pieces of the nobles' funerary ensemble, such as Niankhsekhmet's huge false door and Senedjemib Inti's granite sarcophagus, were made as royal favours in the court's workshops, the majority of the nobles' statues appear to have been the products of the craftsmen who had built and decorated the courtiers' tombs. Here then, as the agreements that are recorded in some of those tomb chapels state, the households of the commissioning courtiers would have supported those of the sculptors. These independent craftsmen's studios may well account for slight differences in many of the sculptures' poses, in the diversity of their iconography and the different methods of sculpting some of the detail in the nobles' hands, heads and faces. Some of these idiosyncrasies, alternatively, may have resulted from dialogues between the craftsmen and their patrons, part of a continuing search that, if not necessarily concerned with modern notions of personality or portrait-like verisimilitude, might well reflect how nobles such as Kawab, Seneb and Senedjemib Mehi had wanted to appear.

In a grand reversal of earlier practice, the nobles' sculpture sometimes appears to influence the products of the royal workshops. The sculptures of the Giza kings, which had been the models for many of the earlier nobles' works, had been made from big blocks of hard stone, which had greatly restricted their range of poses. The nobles' sculptures, on the other hand, were sometimes made from wood or soft white limestone; the limbs of Ka-aper's wooden statue, for example, move freely and openly in space and are constructed from several separate blocks all pegged together. Such lively images, it would appear, had served to free later royal sculpture from the strict forms imposed by the hard-stone block, a change reflected in some of the later royal statues, in which, although they show the south Saqqara kings seated on a throne in the usual way, the figures' limbs and other forms stand out freely from the stone.

In those later ages the austerity of the earlier sculptures was transformed by a kind of mannerism in which the huge full forms of the Giza workshops were thinned down, the sculptures' waists nipped in, their eyes widened and enlarged. At the same time – this perhaps a tendency especially prevalent in provincial work – the surfaces of both the courtiers' and the royal sculptures were treated in a different way, those newly attenuated forms veiled in a kind of realism, within a live elastic skin. Then, too, the royal sculptors had largely abandoned working in hard desert stone in favour of softer and lighter materials such as alabaster and copper sheet, which could be easily worked to attain such silky surfaces.

And all the while, throughout the generations of that slowly developing tradition, the sculptors of both the kings and courtiers had worked with a small set of poses and the same strict rules of drawing and proportion, the craftsmen consciously and carefully maintaining such a close relationship to their way of working that the system was never garbled or modified. This was, quite simply, part of the visual language of a courtly culture concerned above all to transform images of the everyday into living aspects of an unseen world. For those great crowds of sculptures set within the darkness of the courtiers' tomb chapels had been made for people who well knew that, on their death, those sculptures would be lost from sight just as they themselves would be at death, but who had believed that their living presence would remain within the world, sight unseen.

RANKS AND TITLES

If his Highness will make you dukes and earls ... England will quake to hear that they are returning to Egypt, to the garlick and onions of a kingdom.

Sir Arthur Haselrig,
Roundhead parliamentarian, 1657

hereditary prince and true count, overseer of all the works of the king, master of secrets of every command of the king, favourite of the king wherever he is, one honoured by Wenis, King of the Valley and the Delta and a possessor of honour with the great god ... Senedjemib Mehi.

Statue-base inscription

royal companion, friend of the great house, beloved of his lord, overseer of weaving in the palace, great one of the

*carrying chair, overseer of the royal boats, bearer of the god's
seal . . . Seneb.*

Memphite tomb chapel inscription

*seal bearer of the King of the Delta, unique associate,
lector-priest, staff of the Apis Bull, controller of bird traps,
director of priests, initiate, honoured by the great god . . .
Tjetji*

Statue-base inscription

yeoman *A servant or attendant in a royal or noble household, usually of a superior grade, ranking between a sergeant
and a groom or between a squire and a page.*

Oxford English Dictionary

The last in that list of epigraphs encapsulates how the epithets and
titles that were endlessly inscribed within the courtiers' tomb chapels
and on their statues have been traditionally viewed: that they define
the elements of a highly structured bureaucracy. Ever since Champollion's day, most egyptologists have assumed that, from kings to
farmers, pharaoh's people had shared a traditional European understanding of class and had translated the courtiers' titles accordingly,
as steps upon a social ladder that had represented the order of
pharaonic society. And as the pharaonic state made mighty pyramids
and was surely, as Gardiner describes, 'one of the best organized civilizations that the world has ever seen', it is easy to assume that those
same epithets and titles had indeed described the tasks allotted to the
higher echelons of that remarkable organization.

Yet whilst numerous inscriptions identify such workaday professions as sailors and potters, farm workers, goldsmiths and the like
with straightforward simplicity, the courtiers' epithets and titles are
so plentiful in number and so ambiguous in meaning that most of
them have defied attempts to define any role they may have signified
within the pharaonic hierarchy.

That it is well-nigh impossible today to discern the practical purposes of most of the courtiers' epithets and titles is due in part to the

fact that the order of the state which they allegedly describe underwent several major changes. In the beginning, for example, in the times of the first pharaohs, the few titles that are recorded relate to pharaoh's progress through the kingdom, when his close attendants had travelled with the king and held tithing courts in various locations along the lower Nile. And those same titles would be held by members of the king's immediate entourage some three millennia later. In the times of the colossal pyramids, however, those archaic processes of collection were reversed, and the produce of the lower Nile was being shipped to Memphis, and whilst the number of recorded courtly epithets and titles had considerably enlarged most of them were still held by people close to the royal household, whose tombs still stand *en échelon* upon the Giza Plateau.

Even at this early stage of their development, just as those epithets and titles do not accurately describe physical relationship to the person of the king, so neither do they encompass occupations connected to the government's consuming task: the construction of mighty monuments. So with the possible exception of the royal prince Ankhhaf, whom a recently discovered papyrus describes as the overseer of an office controlling the delivery of building stone shipped to the Giza Plateau, the tremendous tasks of constructing one of the Giza pyramids can only be described as a project organized by unidentified officials leading a nameless workforce.

In the times of the kings of Abusir and Saqqara, when there were major ongoing changes in both court supply and governance, the number of the courtiers' epithets and titles ballooned from less than a hundred to well over 2,000. The diminution in the size of royal pyramids, the increase in the number of decorated tomb chapels, and the relocation of some of the courtiers' households away from Memphis and into the provinces might well have prompted this multiplication of epithets and titles, whilst the deployment of court officials into the provinces had distanced those courtiers from day-to-day contact with the royal residence and had probably transformed a simple face-to-face system of communication into a written chain of command.

At all events, the inscriptions show that the few spare designations held by the earlier generations of courtiers had been overlaid, reign by reign, century by century, with a mass of other epithets and titles. Some of these had originated as antique phrases that may once have denoted roles and affiliations within the pharaoh's household; others, alternatively, may have been honorific or bestowed as mortuary favours after death. Yet others still may have described a real function in pharaonic government or, perhaps, a single task successfully performed.

In the past half-century, all of those epithets and titles have been subject to several close analyses. Yet the results have been so inconclusive that it is still impossible to know what most of them actually denoted. Just as Sir Alan Gardiner had observed in the last age before computerization, 'Valiant attempts have been made to infuse life and reality into the titularies of which the tombs are so lavish, but the highly precarious nature of the results has to be admitted.'

So those grandiose *orientaliste* bureaucracies that we might well imagine had been directed by the holders of such translated titles as 'Overseers of the Royal Documents / of Works / of the Treasury / of the Granaries' are little more than mirages. Were the 'Overseers of the Royal Documents', for example, librarians and archivists, or were they involved in day-to-day affairs? Had the 'Overseers of Works' conceived and supervised the pyramids, or had they overseen the craftsmen's workshops and/or the kingdom's agriculture and canals? Had the 'Overseers of the Granaries' controlled the tithing of the harvests and/or the storage silos? Had the 'Overseers of the Treasury' managed the distribution of collected riches or simply counted up the tithes? And then, of course, the meanings of many of these apparently straightforwardly translated titles, such as 'general' and 'priest', had changed down through the millennia, just as have the tasks of the Gentleman Usher of the Black Rod of the House of Lords, a position presently occupied by a military man, a Lieutenant-General, Companion of the Order of St Michael and St George, Commander of the Most Excellent Order of the British Empire, one-time chairman of the National Children's Orchestra and Director General of the European Union Military Staff in the Council of the European Union.

In similar fashion, the texts within the courtiers' tomb chapels suggest that they too had undertaken many different tasks; that they may have served the court at various times as diplomats, as priests, as captains of militia, as mine supervisors, sailors and accountants, as builders and as controllers of quarries, royal workshops and the temples' musicians as need arose, rather than that such tasks had been allotted to specialized professionals and ministries as in more modern governments.

Some of the more permanent structures of government within the Memphite court, however, were revealed in the course of those painstaking analyses. Along with hosts of other titles and epithets, for example, more than eighty courtiers over a span of 300 years are known to have borne the title of *shee'ati*, a term that is traditionally translated as 'vizier' – a Turkish word that in the nineteenth century was attached to officials within the Ottoman Empire and at the Sublime Porte at Constantinople. Invariably, these pharaonic 'viziers' had also borne another title, that of *iry pet*, one of those few titles that appear on the relics of the first pharaoh and were held by men close to pharaoh's person down through the millennia.

The post of vizier, however, first appears in the time of the colossal pyramids, when it was held exclusively by senior members of the royal household who were also entitled 'king's sons', an epithet that of itself does not necessarily imply that they were the physical offspring of the king. In those days, the title of vizier was paired with descriptive epithets such as 'he of the curtain' or 'he of the door', implying that it had then denoted a chamberlain-like presence in royal audience. In later ages, alternatively, the title of vizier was borne by officials such as Senedjemib Inti, who were directly concerned with royal construction projects and who also appear to have been close to the king but were not members of the royal household and might well serve several monarchs in succession. And in their turn those viziers' households sometimes supplied a succession of viziers to the royal court. Adding to the general confusion, such viziers could also be entitled by terms that are traditionally translated as 'hereditary prince', 'chiropodist' and 'butler'.

So the texts within the enormous mastaba of the Vizier Ptah-shepses that stands beside the pyramids of Abusir inform us that he had held the posts of royal chiropodist, hairdresser and also provincial governor, and that he had married a king's daughter and served no less than six successive monarchs in a variety of roles, from a 'keeper of the royal diadem' to the custodian of 'the secret, sacred writings of the words of the gods'. Clearly, Vizier Ptah-shepses had long and last-ing influence at the court of the Abusir kings and was a senior courtier, just as the title of vizier would imply. Yet the epithets and titles within his tomb chapel, that sonorous and scrambled mass of ambiguity, hardly amount to a history of the man or of his times.

To pretend, for example, as some traditional historians have done, that Ptah-shepses had climbed up a ladder of success, and that he had owed his splendid vizier's monument to his physical relationship to pharaoh as hairdresser and royal nail-clipper is to fall victim to the illusion that pharaoh's Egypt was a fairy-tale version of a modern state in which Margaret the Thatcher had been appointed Prime Minister after the Queen had found her mending the roof of Bucking-ham Palace. In all likelihood, pharaonic society had been less socially aggressive and more integrated than most modern people might at first imagine.

ORDERING THE KINGDOM – *LAND AND SOCIETY*

We may today think of the French aristocracy of the ancien
*régime as a class; but surely it was imagined this way only
very late. To the question 'Who is the Comte de X?' the normal answer would have been, not 'a member of the
aristocracy', but 'the lord of X', 'the uncle of the Baronne de
Y', or 'a client of the Duc de Z'.*

Benedict Anderson, 1991

Life in the sheltered hothouse of the lower Nile was one of the easiest in the Bronze Age world. A farming culture, it was, essentially, a small-scale face-to-face society. A world in which scribes and court-iers had dealt directly with the minutiae of everyday – with erring servants, deliveries of materials and goods, and a work day lost when the arrival of a pyramid gang's clothing ration had been delayed.

Those same attitudes are equally apparent in the care with which the blocks of the four colossal pyramids were dressed and placed. Blocks whose production, as some of their graffiti show, had been the individual responsibility of small gangs of quarriers and craftsmen. Ultimately, the Great Pyramid of Giza is a vast product of the labours of large numbers of those small gangs who cut its stones with integrity and care and set them as straight and true as the irrigation ditches in the Nile-side fields.

Those small-sized gangs, however, were working in state-wide co-ordination and under a consistent and masterful direction. So whilst the rural nature of that workforce is apparent in the qualities of each and every stone they laid, so the firm and subtle manner of the pharaonic administration is equally apparent in the Great Pyramid's astonishing accuracy and consistency over long years of construction. This, then, had been a state whose culture had not been founded on brute force or notions of national boundaries, but whose identity had flowed outwards from the royal residence, the courtly rituals, its building yards and craftsmen's workshops.

And the fundamental order of the state was of its households, large and small. Just as the royal court was the nucleus around which the households of the Memphite courtiers revolved, so in their turn those courtly households were the nuclei of the households of a variety of craftsmen and scribes, servants and farmers, who were sometimes named and pictured in the courtiers' tomb chapels, where they are regarded with a fond eye.

And the households of the provincial courtiers of those times were modelled upon those of the court they served, to the extent that many of their tomb chapels had cemeteries of simpler graves – mostly shaft and pit tombs – laid out in the little deserts at the foot of the valley's cliffs in the manner of the Memphite cemeteries. These, it would appear, were the graves of the heads of smaller households, mostly farmers, some of whom appear to have performed a role like that of village headmen, a post that in the late Old Kingdom was formally recognized by the officers of the court.

Just as the essential order of the living court is preserved within its cemeteries, so too that same order is apparent in the smaller cemeteries of farmers that lie beyond their fields in the lower slopes of the little Nile-side deserts. And like the tomb chapels of the contemporary courtiers and kings, the contents of those farmers' tombs also change through time, from the era of the Giza kings to those of the kings of Abusir and Saqqara.

The sites that best show those changes under way were excavated during the first decades of the last century by George Reisner, whilst he also worked within the cemeteries and temples upon the Giza Plateau. Set some twelve miles from Abydos, close to the modern village of Naga el-Deir and on the east bank of the river, these rural cemeteries are part of a continuous band of burial grounds of differing ages that run for miles along the edges of a wide silt plain whose bounteous crops of wheat and barley, lentils, beans and millet make it still one of the most fertile regions in the Nile Valley.

In the time of the four colossal pyramids, most of the tombs at Naga el-Deir were but simple pits marked by mounds of sand and stone or rough-made mud-brick walls, their placement echoing those of the Giza courtiers, with clusters of such graves grouped around a line of small mud-brick mastabas. All these graves were anonymous and sparsely furnished, although the burial chamber of one of the brick mastabas contained a splendid diorite bowl of courtly workmanship engraved with Sneferu's name; this, Reisner suggested, was a royal gift to a village headman. The pattern here presumably reflects the settlements in which the dead had lived, where generations of a single household enjoying royal patronage had overseen a local population of farmers.

The goods buried in the cemeteries of the following generations at Naga el-Deir reflect the changes in pharaonic society that were taking place after the construction of colossal pyramids had been abandoned. Whereas the earlier graves had held few objects, mostly brought from living households, these later burials held more goods and were generally of better quality, some of them containing jewellery and stamp seals that had been made especially for burial. At that same time, inscriptions carrying the names of the dead appear within these modest graveyards; names accompanied by simple descriptions such as 'overseer of herds', which suggests that their occupants may have played a role, for example, in the supply of cattle to the sun temples.

By the times of the Saqqara kings, the names and titles of provincial governors and priests were engraved and painted on flakes of limestone that were left on graves within these little cemeteries. Though not written in courtly hieroglyphs but in forms closer to the bureaucrats' workaday calligraphy, these modest texts bear witness, as do the courtiers' contemporary tomb chapels, to the increasing definition of the order of the kingdom. And in those later times, the grave furnishings of the people of Naga el-Deir were yet more generous, Reisner cataloguing almost 500 amulets that had been placed within the burials. It would appear, therefore, that in the times of the kings of Abusir and Saqqara, the households who created the cemeteries of Naga el-Deir had herds and harvests sufficient to sustain the court and its extensive building programmes and simultaneously support an increase in the size and the prosperity of their own communities, alive and dead. The decision of the Memphite court to diminish the size of the royal pyramids, therefore, had not only changed the rhythm, scope and culture of the court itself, but had also provided better lives for the communities that sustained it.

Like the burials of the courtiers and kings, the graves at Naga el-Deir show a considerable concern for the wellbeing and continued maintenance of the dead. Along with a thread of common culture, which from the graves of the farmers to those of the kings is found at every burial site in Egypt, both pharaoh and his subjects shared the prospect of a common destiny. It would appear, therefore, that the efficacy, the sheer power, of the courtly culture had been confirmed when the resources of the entire kingdom were exploited by the court, when huge quantities of materials and provisions were sent to Memphis from all along the kingdom, and thousands upon thousands of farmers had been brought together to build the royal pyramids. Whilst setting skills amidst the general population that were neither typical nor indeed required for subsistence farming, that enterprise had shown the people of the lower Nile an order that was entirely different from those of rural households and communities.

Yet the vast cooperative labours of pyramid making were not entirely foreign to the farmers of the lower Nile. Since prehistoric times, they had worked in groups to cut canals and maintain irrigation systems, labours that must have cemented a sense of the power and value of community amongst the people of the farming settlements. To that extent at least, building pyramids had simply extended those communal activities to the furthest reaches of the kingdom and gathered them together at the court of Memphis.

Pyramid building has been traditionally described as 'corvée labour' after a medieval system of forced labour in which peasants had worked unpaid in the fields of the local lord or had been conscripted by French courts of later ages for road making, a system which had been brutally adapted in the nineteenth century by the European masters of Egypt for the construction of the Suez Canal. There is no evidence, however, of that same cruel process operating in Old Kingdom times, nor is its application suggested by the intense precision and high levels of organization that were required for the construction of such monuments. For building pyramids and temples entailed the attentions of large numbers of skilled people working over decades with considerable concentration, qualities not readily associated with conscription and bullying coercion.

Though the scenes within the courtiers' tomb chapels give glimpses of the tenor of the times, little is known of the social interaction between the court and the rest of the population. In later ages, the notion that the courtiers, at least, should conform to a closely defined code of behaviour was attributed to the times of the Memphite kings of Giza and Abusir, and many lengthy texts describe that code in detail. Although the 'Instructions of Hardjedef', which the ancient scribes regarded as one of the earliest of such documents, are largely lost, several others from the era have survived; Gardiner describes the prime virtues listed in these 'Instructions', as all such texts are called, as consisting of obedience to fathers and superiors, the ability to keep silent in all circumstances, of employing tact and good manners in social intercourse, faithfulness in delivering messages, and a humility little short of subservience. Then, as the Vizier Ptahhotep, who is credited with compiling one of the longest of these texts, informs his son, 'you will conquer like a crocodile', a sentiment that the elderly Sir Alan Gardiner had heartily endorsed!

There was as well a shared code of behaviour outside the orbit of the Memphite court, a strong set of common values within households large and small and amongst a population of around a million people. Certainly, there was a wide diversity in the size of households along the lower Nile, from the estates and farming colonies of the kings and courtiers to holdings whose modest sizes are suggested by the smaller graves at Naga el-Deir. Yet, just as little is known about the intercourse between the people of those various estates and households large and small, so nothing whatever is known about the ownership of the land holdings that are recorded nor if such concepts as 'leasehold', 'freehold', 'tenancy' and the rest were even part of the reality of the pharaonic state.

Surveying and land measurement, marking out the areas of different farms upon those flat silt plains, had been subjects of tomb and temple relief since earliest times and were under the ultimate control of pharaoh and the gods. Nor is that surprising, for field boundaries were liable to have been obscured by each successive flood. Yet in the times of the Memphite kings much of the flood plain remained uncultivated, which suggests that, rather than confirming the ownership of specific plots of land in a modern manner, pharaonic land surveys were concerned with the laying out of crops and irrigation schemes and, perhaps, in determining the projected size of individual harvests.

Ultimately, of course, and as the texts insist, everything devolved to pharaoh, although, in something of the manner of a feudal system, rights to the exploitation of various holdings passed down through generations of the same households. Rare surviving texts record agreements undertaken in front of witnesses for transactions such as the transferal of land use or the ceding of parts of a funerary estate to the cult of another dead person.

As ever, what survives is often fragmented and usually ambiguous. The texts, however, seem to show pharaonic society operating within a widely observed code of social obligation that had occasionally required a form of state arbitration and forms of punishment. This system was so broad-based, indeed, that it finds expression in some of the verses of the Pyramid Texts, which insist that the dead king does not have to undergo such processes.

> Pepi is one of that great group born aforetime in Heliopolis,
> Who are not carried off on behalf of a king,
> Who are not brought before officials,
> Who are not accused,

Who are not found guilty.
This is true of Pepi,
He will not suffer,
He will not be carried off on behalf of a king,
He will not be brought before officials,
The opponents of Pepi will not triumph.
Pepi will not hunger,
His fingernails will not grow long,
No bone in him will be broken.
[Pyramid Text 486]

Filled with the slow-burning ire of lengthy disputes, indignant letters addressed to individuals in the community of the ever-present dead display the living basis of that code of social conduct – the role of personal pledges, of household honour, precedence and possession:

It is a widow who addresses her [dead] partner . . .

This is a reminder of the fact that . . . you said . . . May the wood of the bed that bears me rot, should the son of a man be debarred from his household furniture.

Now, in fact, the woman Wabut came together with Izezi, and they have devastated your household: in order to enrich Izezi and to impoverish your son, she removed everything. Will . . . you remain calm about this? I had rather that you should fetch me to your side so that I might be there beside you than to see your son dependent upon Izezi.

Awaken your father Iy! . . . Rouse yourself against them; you, your fathers, your brothers and your relations . . .

And once again:

It is Shepsi who addresses his mother, Iy:

This is a reminder of the fact that you once said to me, your son, 'You shall bring me some quails that I may eat them' and I then brought you seven quails and you ate them . . .

If only you might decide between me and Sobekhotep, whom I brought back from another settlement to be interred among his companions after giving him his shroud. Why is he injuring me, your son, so wrongfully, when there is nothing that I said or did? Wrongdoing is disgusting to the gods!

THE COURT ABROAD

Nothing in the surviving record suggests that the era of the Memphite pharaohs was other than a time of peace; a time when the court had spent its surpluses on building pyramids and tombs and temples and there had been no enemies. Nor, certainly, is there a trace within the tomb chapels, the temples or the archaeological record of a military caste or culture at the royal court nor indeed in any other household in the kingdom.

In consequence of this seeming passivity, ancient Egypt is frequently described as an isolated culture; by modern standards, doubtless, that is true. The ancient world, however, was a relatively empty place. Apart from the city states set down along the Tigris and Euphrates, the populations of the contemporary Levantine cultures of Palestine, Syria and Anatolia were tiny in comparison with those of pharaoh's kingdom, their courts small in size and number, frequently aggressive and usually short-lived.

Nonetheless, there is considerable evidence of contact between those variously shifting cultures and the court of Memphis, interactions that were the direct successors of the ageless prehistoric traffic in such goods as lapis lazuli, amber and obsidian, which had connected such far-flung regions as the Baltic and Afghanistan, Mesopotamia and the Sudan. So it is hardly surprising that, as well as containing tiny fragments of exotica from such remote locations, some of the chambers in the nobles' mastabas of Giza and Saqqara also had quantities of Levantine pottery within them which had contained resins, wines and oils which, though they only grew in northern and more temperate zones, had been significant ingredients of the courtly culture of the lower Nile since its beginnings.

In similar fashion, many of the woods used for pharaonic furniture and boats – cedar, juniper, yew, box, cypress and hornbeam – were also imported from the north. Cedar wood especially, huge bulks cut from the ancient forests of the Lebanon, served as the major structural elements of pharaonic boats and barges, whilst cedar timbers were also used in tomb and temple construction and as the material of many architectural elements of state buildings, such as doorways and columns. Copper, the single essential material in the creation of pharaonic culture, had long since been imported from the mines and furnaces of southern Jordan, along the so-called 'Kings Highway' that ran down through those copper fields to the port of Aqaba on the north-eastern Red Sea coast, from where it was shipped or sent in caravan to Memphis. Alternatively, another ancient land bridge linking the Levant to the lower Nile – the so-called 'Way of Horus' – had followed the Lebanese coastline down along the eastern Mediterranean to the Nile's delta. This 500-mile trek was hardly suited to the transportation of heavy cargoes such as timber, so the bulk of that traffic was sent down the shipping lanes which ran parallel to that coast, from the Levantine ports into the Nile's delta, a week-long voyage which, in the best sailing season though in vessels lacking navigation aids, would have involved travelling by day and putting up each night in ports or on the seashore.

These, then, were the two fixed routes by which many traditional imports from the Levant and regions further north – exotica such as lapis lazuli, silver and amber – had long been sent down into the region of the lower Nile. In the times of the archaic kings and due in all probability to disturbances throughout those regions, there had been a cessation in that most ancient traffic. Those traditional imports begin to reappear in the archaeological record of the times of the Giza kings, and traffic grows again in the succeeding periods to the extent that some of the temple reliefs of Abusir showed foreign boats and their distinctive imports being carried into a royal audience: large oil jars whose shapes are well-designed for stowing in the curving hulls of wooden vessels, live brown bears from Syria and quantities of animal skins, along with fruits and other fragile perishable goods that appear to have been widely exchanged throughout the Caucasus and the Levant but have left scant trace today for archaeologists.

A major centre of this millennial traffic was the ancient port at Byblos, in modern-day Lebanon, where French archaeologists have found warehouses stacked with locally made olive oil jars designed for shipping. Quantities of identical containers have also been excavated from the Giza mastabas and from the glittering tomb chamber of Queen Hetep-heres, a contemporary of Sneferu and Khufu. And in later ages, as the households of the courtiers moved out into the provinces, so too, as fragments of those same exotic storage jars and a single courtly text still testify, the imported goods that they had held were shipped to the provincial courts:

> I was sent to Byblos under the majesty of Merenre, my lord. I brought back three Byblos boats ... I brought back lapis lazuli, tin [or lead?], silver, sefety-oil [a perfumed unguent?] and every good product he desired. I was praised for it in the court and gold rewards were given to me ... Never was the like done before by any expedition leader that any god [i.e. king] had sent. Honoured before the great god lord of the West, sole friend, lector priest, seal bearer of the god in the two big ships, who brings the products of the foreign lands to his god, the courtier Ini.

By 2300 BC, when that text had been inscribed within Ini's Saqqara tomb chapel, the courtly traffic between Byblos and the Memphite court that the much-travelled noble Ini obligingly describes was very well established. His text, however, is unique. Apart from this single recently recovered written record, only the far-flung physical remnants of that traffic have survived. Nor is there any evidence of the operation of a trade or bartering system. In exchange for such imports, the court of pharaoh appears to have sent courtly goods and provisions to the courts of the northlands – quantities of wheat and fine linens perhaps, now long lost, along with some of the more durable products of the Memphite workshops.

At Byblos, for example, fine stone jars and round stone offering tables, bearing the names of Khufu, Hetep-heres and several later kings, have been excavated from in and around the precinct of that port's largest temple, parts of whose architecture have a distinctly pharaonic air and were measured and laid out in Egyptian cubits. That some of those Memphite products name this temple – that of a local deity Ba'alat Gabal – as the 'Lady of Byblos' suggests that those fine-made items had been sent abroad as royal gifts to a goddess who, as a pharaonic sealing found within the temple shows, had been equated with the goddess Hathor. Similar courtly products, vessels of hard desert stone, gold and shining alabaster, have been found in excavations in settlements across the eastern Mediterranean and the Levant: from ancient Ugarit on the beautiful Syrian coastline by modern Latakia, to Crete and Palestine and Ebla, a considerable ancient city on the edge of the high Euphrates basin, and also to sites in Anatolia, where in the 1950s an illicit excavation recovered strips of gold which bore the name of the Pharaoh Sahure and appear to have been attached to a box or palanquin made in the workshops of Abusir and sent off to the ruler of an unknown court. Nothing, however, suggests that these far-flung discoveries of the products of the Memphite workshops had amounted to a pharaonic 'foreign policy', as they have been traditionally described. Rather, they appear as part of an ageless traffic in delight and esoterica that ran right throughout the courts of the ancient Middle East, as tokens of respect and obligation between two courtly households engaged in ancient systems of exchange.

DESERTS, BOATS AND DONKEYS – *THE GREAT EXPLORERS*

Besides importing copper ingots from the mines of Jordan and Palestine and places further north, the Memphite court operated large numbers of copper mines on its own account. Cut into the deep red rock of south-western Sinai, a lengthy series of inscriptions and reliefs testifies to the millennial presence of pharaoh's copper miners in that desolate region where as well as smelting huge quantities of copper ore close to their workings, they had mined the distinctive fine blue turquoise of the area.

Both the eastern and western deserts of the Nile Valley had been similarly prospected, and they were not only mined sporadically for gold and copper ores but quarried also, for rare stone. So the great statue of Khafre and the hawk had been cut from mottled gneiss shipped from the Nubian desert, and most of Menkaure's statues were made of stone quarried deep in the Eastern Desert, whilst a large part of the alabaster worked in the royal workshops was taken from the desert quarries of Hatnub, near the modern Nile-side town of Mallawi. Donkeys, boats and barges played key roles in this considerable traffic, and they are assets that are widely pictured in tomb chapels and temples in scenes of donkey herds, of sea-going ships and of huge barges with monolithic granite columns lashed to their decks.

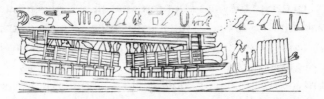

*A barge with a cargo of columns; a sketch compiled from reliefs in
the causeway of the pyramid of Wenis.*

The most remarkable surviving element of these extensive transportation networks, and perhaps the rarest of all surviving relics
from the times of the Memphite pharaohs, was discovered in 2008 on
the bleak west coast of the Red Sea, some ninety miles south of the
modern port of Suez at a site now known as the Wadi el-Jarf. Here lie
the substantial ruins of an ancient port from the times of Khufu, with
a man-made harbour and a 120-yard-long L-shaped mole built straight
out from the beach into the sea. Close by that beach, Pierre Tallet and
his team excavated and mapped two chandleries built from field
stone, whose plans were similar to those of the magazines at Giza.
Here, however, they were part filled with barnacled stone anchors
from sea-going boats. Three miles inland and cut deep into the low
limestone ridge that runs along behind that coastline, thirty long
caves which had served as the warehouses of the ancient port were
opened by the French archaeologists. Inside, within that all-preserving
desert dryness, were the remains of boat timbers and rope, along
with huge quantities of globular water pots. Though previously
denied, these discoveries proved beyond all doubt that, like those of
their northern neighbours, the ships of the ancient pharaohs had also
sailed upon the sea.

Three potteries had operated beside the warehouses, all of them
producing those distinctive water pots. They appear to have been
made to hold the waters of a solitary spring that still rises in the desert a few miles inland and beyond the warehouses, at the lonely
monastery of St Paul. On that barren arid coast, this rare water
source would surely have determined the port's location, supporting
the 300-odd men that are estimated to have lived and worked within
it. Judging by the quantities of smashed ceramics found both in the

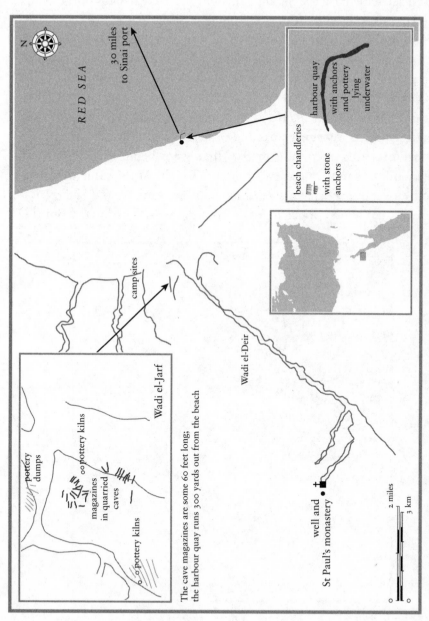

The following labels appear on the map:

N

RED SEA

30 miles to Sinai port

harbour quay with anchors and pottery lying underwater

beach chandleries with stone anchors

camp sites

Wadi el-Jarf

pottery dumps

oo pottery kilns

magazines in quarried caves

o pottery kilns

The cave magazines are some 60 feet long; the harbour quay runs 300 yards out from the beach

Wadi el-Deir

well and St Paul's monastery

2 miles

3 km

The harbour and its supporting installations at Wadi el-Jarf that were in operation during the reign of Khufu.

settlement and in the shallow waters of the harbour, that same spring water had also been shipped thirty miles across the Red Sea to another desert settlement on the Sinai peninsula. Set in clear sight of the Wadi el-Jarf, this solid 144-foot-wide circular stone enclosure, a unique structure for its time, had been set in dunes above the northern end of the beach of the el-Markha Plain, a five-mile-wide wash of sand and gravel that lies north of the oil fields of Abu Rodeis.

Chips of turquoise and small globules of copper excavated from within that robust enclosure by its American discoverers suggest that it had served as a staging post and processing station for some of the copper ores and turquoise matrix that were being extracted from the mountains in the deserts behind the beach. At the same time, the enclosure may also have served as a stopping place and shelter for caravans carrying copper ingots across the wastes of Sinai from the

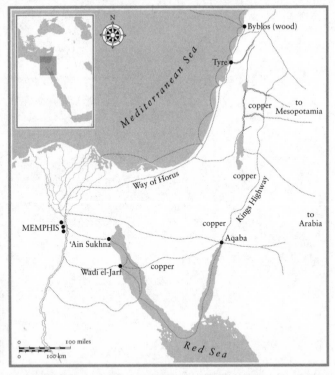

The major routes to the Levant in Old Kingdom times showing the role of the two recently discovered Red Sea ports in the acquisition of copper for the pyramids and workshops of the Memphite court.

mines of the Levant, although, as the new-found port at the Wadi el-Jarf suggests, Levantine copper could also have been shipped by sea, directly from the Gulf of Aqaba to the west coast of the Red Sea.

Tallet's discovery of sheets and fragments of inscribed papyri at the warehouses of the Wadi el-Jarf show that the port was part of the supply system which had supported and facilitated the construction of the Great Pyramid of Giza. Written in practised scribal hands and laid out in the manner of the later papyri found in the temples of Abusir, some of these documents contain lists of produce and provisions brought from the Nile Delta and destined, presumably, for Memphis. Others, astonishingly, hold the day books of one Merer, an official of King Khufu's court in charge of 200 men. Over a period of several months, he had supervised the shipment of fine white limestone blocks to the work on Great Pyramid during the final phases of its construction. Apart from listing his various loads and voyages from the Tura quarries across the Nile to the Giza harbours, Merer's day books also record the checking of his cargoes on their arrival at the dock-side offices of the Vizier Ankh-haf, a prince of the royal household who, like Hardjedef, would be buried in one of Giza's splendid mastabas. That these day books describe work and supply at Giza rather than the port of Wadi el-Jarf where they were found suggests that Merer and his contemporaries had worked right across the state supply systems of the age and that the pharaonic transportation system had been highly integrated.

The oldest-known inscribed papyri to have survived from ancient Egypt, these unique documents hold the only known evidence, beyond the presence of the monuments themselves, of the extensive supply systems that enabled the construction of the colossal pyramids. An important added bonus from Wadi el-Jarf is that the ancient gangs had sealed the port's warehouses with enormous blocks of stone – some of which yet bear the names of Khufu's work gangs – that they had slid up against the open doorways of the warehouses on ramps of muddy shale and slats of cedar wood. This is the only hard evidence of the methods used by the Great Pyramid's stone workers to move such vast stone blocks.

The implications of the remarkable discoveries at the Wadi el-Jarf will reverberate for many years. Nor is that work complete. What is

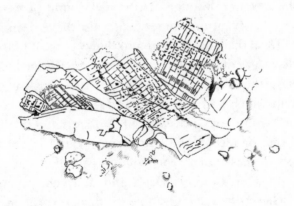

A crumpled sheet of the Wadi el-Jarf papyri lying as it was found, by the entrance to one of the port's cave magazines.

already clear, however, is that much of the copper used to make the chisels of the masons who worked on the Great Pyramid had been carried in caravan, along with the turquoise destined for the crafts-men of the royal court, from the mines in the Sinai Mountains down to the circular storehouse on the el-Markha Plain, from where it was shipped to the port at Wadi el-Jarf. From there, the copper and tur-quoise would have been taken by donkey caravans on a month-long trek through the mountains of the Eastern Desert, along the Wadi Arabah to the valley of the Nile, where, once again, it was loaded onto ships sailing downstream to Giza and the royal workshops.

That time was of the essence in building royal pyramids, both in regards to provisioning the workforce and finishing the pyramid within the lifetime of the king, is underlined by the fact that Khufu's immediate successors swiftly abandoned his port at Wadi el-Jarf for another which they established some sixty miles up the coast. Though this new location doubled the short sea voyage to the circular caravanserai on the el-Markha Plain, it halved the month-long trek to the valley of the Nile up through the eastern mountains from the Wadi el-Jarf, enabling the caravans of copper and turquoise to take a shorter route to Memphis, through the relatively flat land-scapes along the route of the modern Cairo–Suez road, and to deliver their loads directly to the royal workshops and the pyramids' con-struction sites.

Like Khufu's port, this new dock and settlement was set close to a fresh water source, in this instance the hot springs that rise today beside the seaside resort of 'Ain Sukhna. Rock inscriptions at the site dating from the times of Khafre and later show that this new port held potteries and also elaborate copper-smelting facilities of its own and that it remained a vital part of the state's support networks over the following seven centuries, supplying both turquoise and the copper used by the court's craftsmen, masons and ship builders.

Along with the finds of ancient ropes, ships timbers, oars and sail fragments lying as they were stored within another set of cave-cut warehouses, evidence from later ages at the site suggests that the Old Kingdom's Red Sea boats, which were largely made from Levantine cedar wood, had been built in dockyards by the river Nile, then disassembled and transported, piece by piece to 'Ain Sukhna, where they were reassembled on the beach. As at Wadi el-Jarf, these boats were sent to sea with cargoes of water collected from the nearby springs, along with supplies of food and the timbers of the ships themselves that had been carried from the valley of the lower Nile.

These sea-going vessels were called 'Byblos boats' by the Memphite scribes, and later examples of their unique design show that they would barely change throughout the following millennia. Unlike pharaonic stone-carrying barges, which could be huge constructions and accommodate enormous tonnages, the various representations of these Byblos boats along with their surviving timbers show that their beautifully shaped hulls had been some seventy feet in length and could have held cargoes of fifteen tons.

As their name suggests, these Byblos boats had also sailed upon the Mediterranean, voyages that are celebrated in the fragmentary reliefs of Sahure's temples that show some of those elegant vessels at the dockside of a delta port, their sails furled, their masts lowered. As well as bringing the products of the Levant to Memphis and turquoise and copper from the Sinai, Byblos boats also plied the southern Red Sea coast, embarking in late autumn to take advantage of the local winds that blow up in the winter months. Two such sailings are recorded in the Abusir temples, where they are described as voyages to the exotic 'Land of Punt', or 'God's Land' as it was sometimes called. Temple reliefs from the times of Isesi and Sahure show the presentation of

*The crew of one of Sahure's fleet of sea-going boats greet the
king on their return to port.*

some of Punt's matchless southern products at pharaoh's court: gold
and ebony, perfumed frankincense and myrrh, exotic pelts and sap-
ling incense trees for the temple gardens of the lower Nile.

Pharaoh's intrepid mariners had long since sailed the upper reaches
of the Nile. Though the cataract at Aswan had hampered their progress
to the south – especially at the time of inundation, when a whitewater
torrent tore through that granite gorge – slipways were cut to bypass
the cataract and enable the passage of river boats throughout the
year, so that those ancient voyagers sailed to regions well beyond the
Nubian quarries from which the stone of Khafre's celebrated state
had been cut.

Before the construction of the High Dam, the names and titles of
several Memphite scribes and courtiers could be seen on rocks above
the great wide river beside the Nubian villages of Tumas, Tuska and
Abu Simbel, some 200 miles south of Aswan. About 200 miles further
up river, at Buhen, where there were riverine deposits of gold and
abundant copper ores, a small mining settlement of the times of the
Giza kings had smelted copper. Yet further up stream, close to
el-Dakka and at the entrance of the Wadi Allaqi, where there were
rich gold deposits, yet more graffiti record the presence of two officials
from the south Saqqara court who appear to have been prospecting
for rare metals, whilst other graffiti in those same southern regions
tell of further expeditions ranging deep into the eastern deserts.

Pharaonic caravans also travelled in the Western Desert, on such
remarkably long journeys that their full extent has yet to be determined. Since the 1970s, desert archaeologists have been retracing

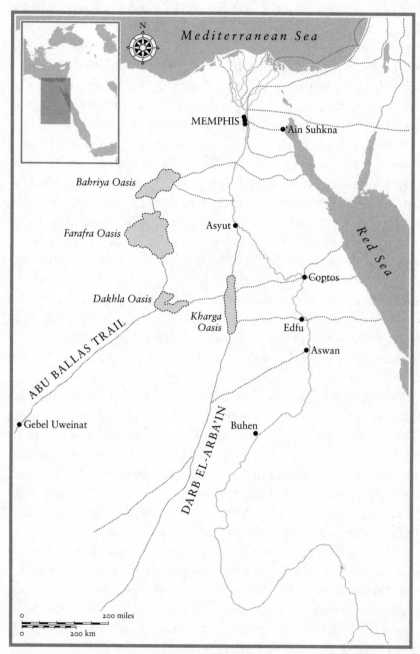

The major western caravan routes to and from the valley of the lower Nile during the Old Kingdom. The ancient destinations of the Abu Ballas Trail and the Darb el-Arba'in are unknown; their general direction suggests the regions of northern Chad and Darfur in central Sudan.

some of these ancient trails that are still marked by cairns of rocks, by heaps of discarded water pots and the distinctive concave tracks that donkey hooves produce. Here, pharaoh's caravanners would have encountered the peoples of the desert – those of the so-called Sheik Muftah Culture – the successors of the neolithic hunters who in earlier and more temperate millennia had raised herds of cattle and baked bread from the wild cereals of the Sahara.

These pharaonic trails through the Sahara strike south and west from the three oases of Bahriya, Dakhla and Kharga, which lie in parallel a hundred miles to the west of the Nile Valley and which in turn were joined both to each other and to the Nile's valley by webs of desert tracks. By the age of the south Saqqara kings, and probably in earlier times as well, Kharga Oasis, literally 'the outer' and the one furthest from the valley of the Nile, held considerable pharaonic settlements, whose leading citizens lived in substantial household enclosures and were buried in large mud-brick mastabas. The surviving records tell that the officials of those settlements had regarded the desert people – who, somewhat confusingly, have been traditionally translated as 'Libyans' – with a careful eye and kept a watch upon their movements.

Like the mining expeditions to the Sinai, journeying south from these oases into the high Sahara was a considerable undertaking requiring planning, experience and skill. Before camels were introduced into the Sahara in the first millennium BC, donkeys were the main beasts of burden in both the valley and the desert, having been domesticated in the first farming settlements within the lower Nile. Though they carry smaller loads than camels, donkeys are their equals in desert conditions, and mature animals in good condition can carry loads of up to 200 pounds and suffer only 30 per cent dehydration, so that on a desert trek those patient beasts will journey for three days without water before they die of thirst. In such extreme conditions the caravanners had to take considerable care of their animals, setting their loads precisely and with an even balance – loads that in great part consisted of soft water skins made from a single goat pelt, the contents of which could be decanted into the large ceramic jars when they were emptied of the other provisions that they had previously held.

During those expeditions, the donkeys, in their turn, had been reliant on their drivers' understanding of the desert, on their knowledge of available sources of water and forage and on their calculations of the amounts of sustenance they had to carry to ensure that man and beast came safely home. So the drivers had to ensure their donkey's hooves did not split from the heat of the sand, and in summer, when daytime temperatures were intolerable, they travelled by night, navigating by the stars and from their memories of the outlines of the landscapes through which they passed. In such a way, pharaoh's caravans could have travelled at walking speed for around twelve hours each day. Like that of the ancient sailors, the knowledge required to successfully complete such desert journeys is largely lost today: journeys undertaken by small bands of men driving large numbers of those gentle animals, just as the donkey drivers of the Sudanese and West African deserts do to this day.

Rare inscriptions on one of the great stone outcrops that rise like sentinels out of the flat Sahara plain tell that, in Khufu's time, one of these desert expeditions was undertaken in order to obtain a rare desert ochre which the court craftsmen appear to have used as pigment for their paint. And in the shade of that high rock pillar, one of those ancient caravanners had cooked a pot of locusts on a desert hearth. Many such ancient encampments were set up by those rocky outcrops and are still marked today upon the surface of the desert by the egg-shell shapes of burnt brown storage jars half buried in the sand, just as the tracks ahead are marked by cairns and standing stones, by wind shelters and watchtowers.

Named now as the Abu Ballas Trail – the trail of the 'The Father of Water Pots' – one of these tracks leads out from Dakhla Oasis some 250 miles south and west across the Sahara to the edges of the Great Sand Sea and the plateau of the Gilf Kebir, where another lengthy desert trek may well have passed through that lonely region of dunes and rock to a further oasis, from where lower Nubia and even the region of modern-day Chad would have been within striking distance.

Following in the footsteps of the desert traveller Carlo Bergmann, the discoverer of this long-lost route through the Sahara, since the 1980s German archaeologists have mapped a chain of more than twenty ancient sites along the Abu Ballas Trail, each of those staging posts set two or three days caravanning apart and all of them sprinkled with sherds and clustered groups of ancient pottery made in the Dakhla Oasis or the Nile Valley in the times of the Saqqara kings. Set by rocky outcrops that provide a minimum of shade, some of these way stations appear to have operated as miniature man-made oases. Some yet hold stores of ceramics that could have contained some seventy gallons of water and provisioned a caravan of eighty donkeys; before the recent advent of desert tourism, many of those distinctive vessels had lain intact upon the desert. Other way stations, alternatively, held facilities for baking hundreds of loaves of bread, whilst the dry sands had also preserved donkey harnesses and baskets and numerous examples of the various ropes and knots that were as essential to the ancient donkey tackle and tethers as they were to pharaoh's sea-going sailors.

Such desert trails had served a variety of purposes over the millennia. Judging from the splendid neolithic rock drawings that have been found along the Abu Ballas Trail, it was a route by which those ancient cattle herders had moved their stock north through the more temperate savannah of those times to water in the Egyptian oases. In the times of the Saqqara kings, alternatively, several tomb-chapel inscriptions describe desert journeys which appear to have struck far further south and westwards, to the ranges of the Gebel Uweinat, where the borders of Libya, Egypt and the Sudan presently meet. And from that remote oasis, pharaoh's donkey caravans may have journeyed further south again, into the region that the tomb chapels' texts call the Land of Yam, as a text in the tomb chapel of the noble Harkhuf at Aswan appears to describe:

> King Merenre, my lord, sent me together with my father ... Iry to Yam to open the road to this foreign land. I reached it in seven months ... and I returned with 300 donkeys laden with incense, ebony, oil, aromatics, leopard skins, ivory carvings, boomerangs, and all good products.

Though many of the regions named in Harkhuf's descriptions of his several southern journeys have not been identified, it seems likely that this great explorer from Aswan had travelled to the Land of Yam along a trail that runs closer to the Nile than the high desert route of the Abu Ballas Trail, a trail that is still well used today and known now as the Darb el-Arba'in, the 'Track of Forty Days'. Though the desert offers few human comforts, tracks such as the Darb el-Arba'in are more direct than the routes that pass through the settlements along the valley of the Nile, and, as they are largely free of human settlement, they hold the great advantage of discretion. So, in the 1970s, Nubian camel drivers dressed in their white desert robes and carrying great silver-handled whips still ran alongside their trotting herds up through these deserts to the Cairo markets.

In medieval times, the Darb el-Arba'in was traversed by caravans of thousands of camels and considerable numbers of slaves, along with cargoes of the same commodities as those that Yam's friendly rulers had presented to the courtier Harkhuf 3,000 years before. In his day, the Darb el-Arba'in appears to have started at Asyut in Middle Egypt and passed through the oasis of Kharga on its way down to Yam and west Sudan. Harkhuf's expedition, however, had probably joined the well-worn track via a desert wadi close to his home town of Aswan, where rock graffiti record the millennial comings and goings of just such desert travellers. The classical name of Elephantine Island at Aswan, indeed, is more likely to have derived from the term the 'road of ivory', the road, that is, that joins Aswan to the Darb el-Arba'in, than the common modern observation that the shapes of its granite boulders resemble those of elephants.

Set high in the cliffs outside Aswan, always an ancient settlement of quarrymen and travellers rather than of farmers, the shadowed doorway of Harkhuf's tomb chapel is one of several similar punctuations, a series of shadowed rectangles, cut into a sandstone outcrop. Amongst numerous prayers and offering lists, several texts within those tomb chapels describe epic journeys undertaken by some of Aswan's leading citizens, who travelled as court officials both across the desert and also upon the sea to Byblos and other Levantine ports from the ports of 'Ain Sukhna and others in the Nile Delta. Such voyages were dangerous; one tomb-chapel inscription at Aswan records how an adventurer had retrieved the body of his father, who had been killed in the course of just such a journey, for burial in the land of pharaoh. These were not military expeditions, however, simply trips undertaken with modest escorts that generally avoided hostile and ill-disposed communities and met friendly foreign rulers with gifts and courtly greetings. And in return, along with wood and copper, these travellers brought back to pharaoh's kingdom ebony and ivory, incense and the leopard skins that were worn by court priests.

So highly regarded were the narratives of these travelling courtiers that those lively texts founded a new literary form, one that describes the journey from the issuing of the royal warrant, the contact with other cultures, a description of a triumphant return laden with precious goods and the travellers' subsequent honours and rewards at the hand of pharaoh. Each text stresses the uniqueness of the journey it describes, the explorer's close relationship to his king and the gifts that they received on their return which, in Harkhuf's case, so his inscription tells, had included 'barges laden with date wine, cakes, bread, and beer', which had been sent out from the royal residence as the thirsty caravan had embarked on the voyage downstream to Memphis.

A well-known example of pharaoh's delight in these exotic outings is contained in a record of a royal letter that had been sent to Harkhuf by the young King Pepi II, in about the year 2380 BC, which was subsequently engraved on the façade of Harkhuf's tomb chapel; a letter 'sealed by the king personally in Year 2, on the 15th day of the third month of the first season.' This royal missive tells that Harkhuf had already informed His Majesty that, along with the usual southern treasures, his expedition was bringing a dancing pygmy to the royal court 'from the land of the horizon dwellers'. Now, dwarfs had lived within the royal residence since the times of the first kings, serving both as courtiers and retainers and also as providers of such entertainments as the 'god's dances'. So King Pepi's letter tells Harkhuf to 'come sailing north to the Residence at once!' Bring him to me hale and healthy, he continues, and 'when he goes with you aboard the ship, assign able men to be around about him on deck lest he fall into the water. And when he sleeps at night, assign able men to sleep around his tent and inspect him ten times over, for My Majesty wishes to see this dwarf more than the products of Sinai or of Punt.' And if the dancing pygmy arrives at court alive and well, the letter promises, the young king will give Harkhuf rewards that will be remembered down through the generations.

RICH AND RICHER – *WENI OF ABYDOS*

Despite the generally repetitive nature of the surviving texts, and though all other sources offer but fleeting glances of life within the Memphite court, its scribes and craftsmen fashioned identities for several courtiers, men like Hardjedef, Seneb and Harkhuf, that to the modern eye are more rounded than those of any of their kings.

Yet the images of Seneb the dwarf and the lively texts of expedition leaders such as Harkhuf are hardly typical of the usual run of things, and the greater part of the courtiers' texts are formulaic and repetitive, so that, like the kings they served, they are little more than names. The career of one courtier and royal confidant, however, the Vizier Weni, stands as an exception to this generality, largely because of the sheer size of an inscription placed in his tomb chapel at Abydos, which describes incidents and adventures that had taken place during a long career within the royal household and state government.

Beautifully engraved upon enormous blocks of Tura limestone that are a little under two feet thick, some ten feet long and five feet high, Breasted described Weni's fifty-one vertical columns of hieroglyphs, which are as finely cut as the contemporary Pyramid Texts, as 'the longest narrative inscription and the most important historical document from the Old Kingdom'. Even Gardiner, whose judgements were generally less sanguine than those of his old friend, considered the text to be an exception from 'the triviality, from the historical point of view, of most of the so-called autobiographical inscriptions belonging to the Old Kingdom'.

In fact, the text engraved upon those fine white stones describes Weni's sixty-odd-year career as a courtier during the reigns of Teti, Pepi I and Merenre. Though filled with the stock phrases of most other so-called autobiographies of the day, it outlines a life so filled with incident and adventure that Gardiner was left to wonder at the sheer energy of the man. Its story starts in Weni's youth when, in common with the children of other provincial governors, he was sent from his family home at Abydos to Memphis and the court of King Teti. Here, along with other young nobles, he began a lifetime's service in relatively minor roles, performing many of the functions for the living king that some of his counterparts were undertaking in the royal temples of the time, where they washed, clothed and fed the royal statues every day.

Weni grew up within the palace, in the immediate circle of pharaoh's household rather than those of the officials of the state administration. The extent to which he had risen in royal estimation, so his inscription tells, is measured by the fact that that King Teti's successor, Pepi I, charged him to undertake a discreet, not to say secret, inquiry 'alone, without any vizier or other state official', concerning an unnamed and therefore, perhaps, an erring and punished queen, the details of which are not described and which may or may not relate to other trials and tribulations within that court which egyptologists have detected and reconstructed by interpreting the obliteration of the names of courtiers in their tomb chapels as state acts of punishment.

Following this in-house inquisition, the inscription tells us, Weni had served as a kind of military commander, when towards the end of a reign that lasted for almost half a century Pepi I charged him to recruit a body of men from both the kingdom and the southlands, to undertake no less than six expeditions into the south Levant. At this point, the hieroglyphs upon the great stone stela burst into verse:

This army returned safely, having harried the land of the sand dwellers,
This army returned safely, having razed the land of the sand dwellers,
This army returned safely, having overthrown its walled settlements,
This army returned safely, having cut down its figs and its vines,
This army returned safely, having set fire to the crops of all its people,
This army returned safely, having slain its troops of many tens of
    thousands,
This army returned safely, having brought back many troops as captives,
And his Majesty praised me on account of it more than anything.

Despite the grandiloquence of the translation, this is not a description of a war. Like most ancient Egyptian accounts of expeditions to quarries, mines and regions outside the lower Nile, the poem stresses both the danger of the enterprise and also the safe return of the participants, whilst the numbers of slain and captured and the damage done are, in the usual way of such inscriptions, considerably exaggerated. In a world where human existence was more fragile than today, it was hardly practical to lay bare great tracts of farmland or to exterminate the farmers. We may imagine, therefore, that Weni had directed donkey caravans of men carrying large quantities of supplies into the deserts of north Sinai and the south Levant, where they had pursued and castigated sections of the indigenous population, who, as other adventurers describe, had probably attempted to block their further progress. Then, these caravans appear to have travelled further north, into regions with neither central control nor, certainly, standing armies. And they raided farms and took their figs and vines and destroyed some of the walled settlements that had lain along their route.

Around 2310 BC the elderly Pepi I was buried in his pyramid, and the new king, Merenre, so the inscription tells, gave Weni a role in the governance of the kingdom, sending the middle-aged courtier, along with several of his contemporaries, back to the various southern provinces in which they had been born.

One of these contemporaries, a certain Qar, appears to have been charged with the collection of grain tithes from the region of the valley of the lower Nile. Weni, alternatively, was appointed to the newly created post of governor of that same region, from Aswan to Memphis, in which capacity, he tells us, he undertook a number of tasks connected with the construction of Merenre's monuments. In Nubia he oversaw the quarrying of the desert stone from which Merenre's sarcophagus and the capstone of his pyramid would be made and the construction of cargo boats for their transportation. At Aswan he supervised the quarrying of blocks of granite for the royal temples, along with the excavation of five slipways to provide boats with a safe passage through the cataract. And at Hatnub, at the centre of the kingdom, he oversaw the extraction of blocks of alabaster from the desert quarries out of which a great offering table was to be constructed, and there, too, he attended to the construction of a 100-foot barge to transport that enormous stone.

Such tasks echo the description of a favour which, Weni's text informs us, he had earlier requested of King Teti I whilst he had served within the royal household: that at royal command – and in the same manner which many texts of the earlier courtiers describe – a sarcophagus and some choice elements of his tomb chapel's architecture should be cut from blocks of the finest limestone from the Tura quarries and designed and sculpted in the royal workshops. And following his appointment as governor of the Nile Valley, many fine white stones were indeed transported along with the unique blocks bearing Weni's long inscription, to the great plain of Abydos and installed within his enormous mud-brick mastaba which stood close to the monument of his father, on the broad desert that lies beyond the fields.

Weni appears to have built an imposing residence for his household at Abydos. As his lengthy text describes, his new position away from court appears to have been part of a late change within the order of the state in which a parallel administration composed of men drawn from the households of provincial head men yet with strong personal connections to the royal house appears to have operated alongside the vizier's administration and controlled the supply of provisions and materials to the Memphite court.

Weni, it appears, had died at a ripe old age in around 2390 BC at a time of national prosperity and increasing population, during the early years of the reign of Pepi II.

As to the man himself, his prodigious tomb text paints him in the usual manner of such documents, as the perfect courtier with a life-long and selfless devotion to the three kings that he served. Yet Weni also appears to have been a man from relatively humble origins who had ended his career controlling the resources of a great part of the lower Nile Valley and with the personal means to build a lavish tomb on the desert plain of Abydos close to the burial grounds of the first pharaohs. As to his profession, he is best described, perhaps, as a tire-less organizer of various royal labour forces, of desert caravans and labour gangs recruited from all over the kingdom and beyond to under-take expeditions, to oversee work in desert quarries and to organize the transportation and shipping of the quarried blocks both to Memphis and to his tomb at Abydos.

In truth, however, it is far from certain that Weni had accom-panied the various Levantine excursions that he had organized or, indeed, that he personally supervised any of the other enterprises which his text describes. For though that text is very long and filled with praise and place names, it is also packed with elusive and

formulaic expressions which, along with the present lack of understanding of the order and functioning of the contemporary pharaonic
court, make it difficult to assimilate the governor's long career into a
modern history. Best then, to let the man describe himself in the last
words of his great funerary text:

> I was one beloved of his father, praised of his mother and favoured by
> his brothers. The senior courtier and true overseer of the southland,
> venerated before Osiris, Weni.

PART SIX

Interregnum
2200–2140 BC

21

Suddenly it Stops

HISTORY WITHOUT PYRAMIDS

Suddenly, around 2200 BC, after half a millennium of monument making, the court stopped building. And at the same time, the royal house
in whose name those monuments were built entirely disappeared. For
the next century and a half, not one king, not one court, utilized the
kingdom's resources, the river, the copper, the wheat crop, to build a
sizable monument of stone. In southern Sinai, the long line of royal
inscriptions commemorating courtly expeditions to obtain the necessary copper comes to an abrupt halt. Traditional histories blink, stutter
and stop after the reign of Pepi II, and so final was that termination
that the length of the interregnum that followed can only be determined by the dates which have been recently established for the reigns
of the monument-making kings who ruled on either side of it.

In that same blank period, most of the Memphite pyramids were
opened, the lids of their sarcophagi smashed and slid aside, the royal
corpses taken out and stripped. The best part of the nobles' tombs
were also part destroyed, their burial shafts left open and abandoned
to owls and bats. And the statues in the temples and the nobles' tomb
chapels were attacked. Within the royal temples, the shock of those
attacks was so sudden that surprising quantities of their original contents, some of their richly decorated ritual equipment, some valuable
copper fittings and even the fragile papyrus records of their scribes
lay buried and untouched beneath the temples' rubble until the present age. In similar fashion, though his burial was sacked, Wenis'
Pyramid Texts were found perfectly preserved, for the entrance to
that pyramid had been buried deep in rubble.

The violence of those events is echoed in the very name of Memphis, the name that the classical historians gave to the living city that lay beneath the plateau of Saqqara. For that name had been derived from one of the last Memphite pyramids to have been built, which was called 'Men-nefer-Pepi', 'the beauty of Pepi abides', its continued use in later pharaonic times and its eventual transference to the nearby township reflecting the fact that it had been one of the last royal monuments to have been built at Memphis before that fierce, destructive era.

Traditionally, the heavy level of the destruction suffered by the Memphite monuments was considered to have been the joint labours of limekiln workers, of plundering stone masons and of gangs of Christians who methodically mutilated many pagan monuments during the first centuries of the present era. More recently, temple blocks have been taken down or sawn apart and statues have been smashed by thieves and collectors who, lacking the facilities to move large works in their entirety, have simply broken off their heads.

Yet archaeologists often find shattered statues, every single piece of them, still lying in the serdabs of their owners' tomb chapels, whilst many of the life-sized royal statues of the Giza kings were reduced to tiny fragments, a process which, as many had been cut from some of the hardest stones that the pharaonic craftsmen ever worked, would have required enormous and concentrated effort. Nor is there the slightest evidence at Giza that the stone of those mighty works was re-used to make smaller statues or bowls and vases. One might well imagine, therefore, that the diorite statue of Khafre and the hawk had been thrown down the temple well in desperation after the other dozen or so similarly obdurate images of the king had been laboriously smashed into little pieces.

So complete was this assault that the bulk of royal statuary which yet remains is composed of the statues which Reisner found more than a century ago in Menkaure's valley temple, a site that escaped serious damage at the ending of the Memphite kingdom. In that same king's pyramid temple, alternatively, Reisner and his workmen found the huge alabaster sculpture of Menkaure smashed to pieces, its fragments strewn throughout the building's rooms and corridors where previously it had served as a focus of the royal cult. With a few rare exceptions, this was the fate of almost all the sculptures of the later Memphite kings, most of the examples that remain having been found in unlikely corners of the kingdom, which suggests that those shrines and temples had not suffered the ferocious first wave of attacks which had taken place within the Memphite monuments.

Later ancient Egyptian references to this hiatus in the span of courtly culture reveal a great deal about how the scribes and courts of later pharaohs viewed their institutions and their history, for in all of the surviving annals the gap is hardly marked at all. There are no breaks in the lengthy lists of royal names recorded on the walls of tomb chapels and temples. Even the surviving fragments of the Turin Canon, the most accurate of all known ancient records, seems to have continued listing the successive rulers, one by one, without any indication of that lengthy period when no new large stone monuments had been made and the funerary cults of the Memphite kings were plundered and broken. The Turin Canon, indeed, appears to have set the entire first millennium of pharaonic history from around 3000 BC under a single heading.

Despite their reluctance to admit this period of disruption the gap in the ancient historic record led the ancient chronologers to change their usual ways of working. Rather than listing the names of individual kings one after the other, some classical texts simply give the total lengths of the next four dynasties in years, whereas the pharaonic scribes list rulers whose names are otherwise unrecorded and employ a term which is commonly translated as 'lacuna' and is understood to indicate a gap in the record that was being copied. A charming, somewhat poetic, reflection of the confusions caused by this historical hiatus is found in the various extant versions of Manetho's history, one of which has Pepi II ending his Sixth Dynasty of kings, followed by a Seventh Dynasty ruled by 'seventy kings in seventy years'. Another version, alternatively, describes the Seventh Dynasty as comprising five kings who ruled for seventy-five days and yet another as consisting of five kings who ruled for seventy-five years. All of this, and a brief biography of a Ninth Dynasty king called Achthoes, who, it is reported, was crueller than his predecessors, and had been smitten with madness and eaten by a crocodile.

A sure sign that the classical historians had considered this eccentric period to have been the product of a time when pharaoh's throne had wobbled and then disintegrated is that some of them declare the last pharaoh of the Memphite kingdom to have been a woman; in this instance a certain Queen Nitocris, who one of the versions of Manetho's history described as 'the most beautiful of all the women, fair-skinned with red cheeks', and who is listed as having ruled after the reign of Pepi II, though the Greek Herodotus states that Nitocris' reign had been cut short by a bizarre act of suicide after she had arranged the drowning of a dinner party of conspiratorial courtiers. In somewhat similar vein, a fragmentary pharaonic tale composed just two centuries after the reign of Pepi II tells of his secret nightly visits to the household of a male courtier, thus providing the office of the last pyramid-building Memphite pharaoh with a similar sexual ambivalence to that of Pharaoh Nitocris, whilst at the same time hinting that the roots of such folk tales of the classical historians may have reached deep into the past.

LAMENTATIONS AND ADMONITIONS

Oh but the builders of pyramids have become farmers . . .
No one sails north to Byblos today. What shall we do for
cedar for our mummies? Priests were buried with that pro-
duce, and courtiers were embalmed with that oil . . .
　　Oh but Elephantine and Thinis in the river's valley do not
render tithes because of strife . . . What is a treasury without
its revenues? The heart of the king must indeed be happy
when true tithes come to him! And the foreigners claim 'This
is our water! These are our crops!' What can we do about it?
Things have fallen into ruin!
　　　　　　From the Admonitions of an Egyptian Scribe

Later literary texts offer eloquent meditations on life and death along the lower Nile following the breakdown of the pharaonic state and the accompanying lack of civic order. Known now as Lamentations,

Admonitions and Disputes, this novel genre was created by scribes working in the courts of a re-founded and re-unified pharaonic kingdom some two centuries after the Memphite state had disappeared.

The order whose collapse those texts so vividly describe is that of the pharaonic universe. Without it there is only chaos, which the texts describe in terms of widespread criminality and foreign invasion, in the muddling of roles within society, in the pillaging of tombs and pyramids and in the unnatural behaviour of people, animals and even of the great wide river that ran through the centre of pharaonic life. The role of pharaoh and court culture that these texts insistently describe was to maintain the cosmic and civil balance within the region of the lower Nile. It appears that the interregnum had challenged the colossal certainties held within the Memphite court and changed the mindset of pharaonic society forever.

Historians have often used those novel texts to describe conditions during the interregnum. Yet at the beginning of the last century, in a preface to an *editio princeps* of one of those remarkable documents, Gardiner had already observed that it was as difficult to place the circumstances which those documents describe in historic time as it was to establish the dates of their composition. Nonetheless, as he wisely observes in the manner of his times, 'unless some support in facts had been forthcoming for his thesis, the Egyptian writer would have imagined an Egypt given over to anarchy and foreign invaders not much more easily than an English novelist could imagine an England subject to the Turks.'

So whether or not those texts are journalistic accounts of real events – which by the scale and poetry of their descriptions must seem incredible – or simply literary meditations on the collapse of good government, in the manner of similar musings from many other cultures, they certainly display, for the first time in pharaonic history, an acute awareness of the preciousness and, indeed, fragility of the courtly order that their predecessors had invented.

In the same decade that Gardiner wrote his commentary upon 'The Admonitions of an Egyptian Scribe', the term 'intermediate period' was invented to describe this remarkable hiatus in pharaonic courtly history, that jumbled age which challenges the common modern notion that 'ancient Egypt' had been a single solid entity whose attitudes and opinions had lasted like the pyramids themselves, down through the millennia. First employed by Gardiner with a lower-case 'i', the term appears to have gained capitalization, and thus a personality of its own, in an essay by the egyptologist Henri Frankfort, published in 1926 and entitled 'Egypt and Syria in the First Intermediate Period'.

Much more is known about that period today than when Frankfort wrote that pioneering paper. Its history, however, in the traditional sense of the word, even the briefest narrative of contemporary rulers and events, is still largely lost, its confusions compounded by a fundamental lack of archaeological evidence, by the contradictory king lists of the ancient historians and by the re-use of a limited group of names amongst the kings and nobles so that it is often impossible to distinguish one individual from another.

So though its relics are plentiful enough, they are the products of an untidy era. Yet in their lively eccentricity, they offer a remarkable counterpoint, a marvellous if somewhat inadvertent commentary, on the grand culture of their predecessors.

A sheet of the sole-surviving papyrus that holds the so-called
'Admonitions of an Egyptian Scribe'. The text is 7 inches high.

MEMPHIS, HERAKLEOPOLIS AND THEBES

Gleaned for the most part from the tales of classical historians and a careful selection of pharaonic texts, traditional histories tell that after the reign of Pepi II several separate states had grown up inside the old pharaonic kingdom, one following the other, with the locations of their ruling households corresponding to Manetho's division of the interregnum into the four dynasties that are numbered seven to ten. Archaeology, alternatively, suggests that some of those cultural centres had flourished concurrently and that, in reality, some of the monarchs that Manetho lists as ruling in successive dynasties may have lived as neighbours in the same period.

The modest monuments of those times that were built in the Saqqara cemeteries show straggling similarities with those of earlier ages. The beginnings of a little pyramid, for example, were built close to the earlier pyramids of south Saqqara, and an entrance corridor and burial chamber were engraved with Pyramid Texts. It was intended for a king named Ibi, of whom nothing other than that monument is known. Nearby, in central Saqqara, recent excavations have uncovered tomb chapels bearing the cartouches of little-known kings whose names are similar to those of the earlier Memphite monarchs and whose monuments, like King Ibi's pyramid, appear to claim continuance if not direct familial relationship with those of the later Memphite kings.

Another cemetery of the interregnum was built on a wide silt plain some fifty miles south of Saqqara at Herakleopolis, a huge and ruined ancient site of dusty mounds, stone blocks and camel grass that is presently surrounded by the modern town of Ihnasya el-Medina. Constructed, it appears, for the courtiers of the kings of Manetho's Ninth and Tenth Dynasties, whom he describes as ruling from Herakleopolis, many of these tomb chapels touchingly reproduce in miniature the elements of the grander earlier Saqqara monuments and even, on occasion, quote a few Pyramid Texts. That the craftsmanship and palaeography in these monuments resembles the earlier monuments of south Saqqara suggests that the craftsmen who made them had direct connection with those of the earlier court. Such

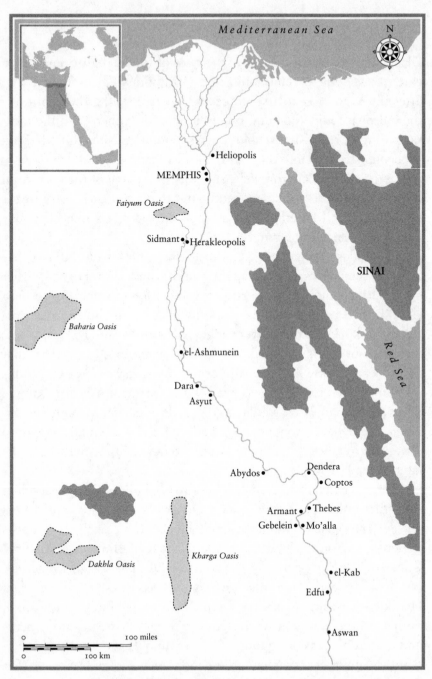

The known cemeteries and settlements of the First Intermediate Period,
several of which appear to have been new foundations.

destruction has been visited on these tomb chapels, however, and so partial is their excavation, that the history of the court for which they had been made has yet to be determined. The tombs of Manetho's Herakleopolitan kings, moreover, have yet to be discovered; perhaps they lie beneath the sand of Saqqara. Alternatively, they may have been built at the site of the modern village of Deir el-Bersha some ninety miles further upstream, where traces of the tomb chapels of the viziers of some of those same kings have recently been uncovered.

In those same times, the local governors of several regions up and down the lower Nile made tombs and tomb chapels in the manner of the provincial courtiers of the Memphite kings, some of them set in the Nile-side cliffs that stand above various modern towns and cities in the valley. Unmistakable in their styles and palaeography, and with their texts filled with idiosyncrasy, the better part of them, unfortunately, are badly damaged.

Many of these tomb-chapel texts proclaim their owners' loyalty to Herakleopolitan kings, whose fiefdom appears to have extended at least as far up river as the modern village of Mo'alla, some thirty miles south of ancient Thebes and modern Luxor. Here, the remarkable cliff tomb of Ankhtifi, which is set at the centre of a low-sloping desert hill reminiscent of a sand-bound Memphite pyramid, describes its patron as lord of the great settlements of Edfu and of Hierakonpolis and holds the cartouche of a certain Neferkare, a common name of several Herakleopolitan kings and which would appear to show that they claimed connection with the earlier Memphite monarchs, for Neferkare had been the prenomen of Pepi II.

As both their monuments and inscriptions tell, the court which brought the full span of the Memphite kingdom under a single central governance was that of the local lords of Thebes, whose influence appears to have worked its way, principality by principality, generation by generation, up the great river past Ankhtifi's Mo'alla to the granite cataract at Aswan and downstream to Herakleopolis, Memphis and the delta. Just as the court of the Memphite kings had disappeared when state building stopped, so too the full panoply of the pharaonic state – its craftsmanship, its command of the resources of the region of the lower Nile – is signalled by the resumption of stone-block building and, ultimately, by national construction projects.

WHY THE CENTRE HAD NOT HELD

Founded upon the visions of Champollion and the European nineteenth century, traditional histories describe the dynastic confusions
of the centuries that had followed the reign of Pepi II as the dissolution of a rich and powerful kingdom. Just as Gardiner had stated
that the pyramids could only have been built by a 'strong and highly
organized administration', so too the dissolution of such a state could
only have resulted from a failure within central government. As
Breasted's *History* described it in 1909, the fall of the Old Kingdom
had been brought about by lack of leadership. 'It had been a thousand
years of inexhaustible fertility,' he writes. ' . . . In every direction we
see the products of a national freshness and vigour which are never
spent; the union of the country under a single guiding hand which
had quelled internal dissensions and directed the combined energies
of a great people toward harmonious effort . . .'

How could such a thing have ever happened? Why had power slowly
slipped from pharaoh's hands? Some suggested that, as the last three of
the Memphite kings had reigned for at least 150 years, the government
had simply fossilized! Longer-term analyses observed that following
the age of the Giza kings most courtly titles were no longer borne by
members of the royal household, which implied that the royal family
were losing their grip on government. That in those same times the titles
in the nobles' tomb chapels had greatly multiplied suggested that a
broader-based, less centralized bureaucracy had taken over, especially
as some of the courtiers had moved their households out of Memphis
into the provinces. Though the ending had been swift enough, the argument ran, the final collapse was the inevitable product of a lengthy and
systemic process involving generations of weak kings and competitive,
ambitious courtiers. And then, as Breasted puts it, 'the foes of the old
regime wreaked vengeance upon those who had represented and upheld
it,' or, as another commentator observed more than a century later,
'The state had been the guarantor of prosperity and security for almost
a millennium. It was in everyone's interest to serve the state. Suddenly,
private self-interest was not only encouraged but also permitted . . .
Moral values . . . no longer served any practical purpose.'

So the ancient kingdom of the lower Nile had descended willy-nilly into a narrow ribbon of quarrelling principalities; a condition, naturally enough, that was cured by force of arms after the rulers of one of those little states had gathered sufficient military power to place the entire span of the fallen Memphite kingdom under their direct control. No wonder that Heinrich Brugsch, who had witnessed at first hand the construction of Imperial Germany from an amalgamation of smaller territories and was himself a courtier and diplomat both of Prussia and of the Khedives of Egypt, had described the obscure era which had followed the ending of the Old Kingdom as a Dark Age. Nor, indeed, that Erman and Sethe had similarly described that period in the Berlin seminars, thus colouring the background against which Gardiner and Breasted and later generations would transcribe and translate the Lamentations, Admonitions and Disputes. They had seen the worm within the rose. The mighty kingdom that had built the Memphite pyramids, so it was generally agreed, had suffered a similar fate to the Roman Empire as envisaged by the Victorians: weak government and moral decadence had occasioned a descent to anarchy.

In reality, however, there is little evidence that pharaoh had controlled a highly structured bureaucracy similar to that of a contemporary state, and modern archaeology and the standing monuments tell a very different story: that, for example, the ending of the 400-year activity of making monuments from blocks of stone had been part-provoked by changes in the environment. For that same long span of time had seen a gradual desiccation throughout the Eurasian landmass which in the Egyptian deserts had caused changes in its flora that would lead to the disappearance of elephants, rhinoceros and other grazing animals. In Sinai too, in those same times, communities that had long cultivated desert farmlands had reverted to a pastoral way of life. At Giza also, the pyramid builders' settlements had been covered in deep sand drifts shortly after their abandonment, when the kings had moved the royal residence to other sites. Similarly at Dahshur, at Abusir and Abu Roash, sand dunes had built up against the mastabas and pyramids and engulfed some of the nearby fields. And by the times of the south Saqqara kings, a great number of the older Memphite monuments were already deep in windblown sand.

Yet by themselves such slow processes of desertification would not have caused widespread famine nor, certainly, a loss of governmental control. Similar climatic changes were taking place from Anatolia to Sind and the various peoples of those regions had adapted to the new conditions without great hardship. In pharaoh's kingdom too, even as the drifts of sand had moved ever closer to the kingdom, the extensive cults of the kings and courtiers had remained in operation, more pyramids were built, and the necessary corvees had been raised along with the considerable tithes which had supported them. At that same time, however, another unrelated natural phenomenon was taking place along the lower Nile, one that was ultimately dependent upon the monsoons of the Ethiopian uplands, and this had a fundamental affect upon the Nile itself. For from the times that the first colossal pyramids had been built there had been a slight slow drop, decade upon decade, in the levels of the annual flood, a trend that, in its turn, had brought about a gradual diminution in the size of the annual harvest and the pharaonic tithe.

Sadly, there are no consistent records of the heights of annual floods from the times of the later Old Kingdom. At Aswan, however, where the annual high-flooding Nile had first roared into the domain of pharaoh through the gates of the granite cataract, the building lines of long-established settlements on two little islands in the centre of the stream show a drop of some five feet throughout the period of the Memphite kings. A drop, indeed, that served to fill the gap between those two islands with silt and thus enable the formation of the single island of Elephantine that we know today. And there, built right upon that fresh silt bank, are buildings of the First Intermediate Period. House building at Aswan, therefore, shows a drop in the levels of the annual Nile flood of around one and a third feet per century during the times of the pyramid-building kings, a drop that gently reverses at the ending of that age.

Of itself, that figure may seem small. Yet a difference of just two feet in the annual flood was the difference between a mean and insufficient harvest and a disastrous overabundance of water whose effects are graphically described in the Biblical plagues of Egypt. The impact of that gradual diminution, therefore, would have been a tiny but constant lessening of harvests and tithes over the period in which the

Memphite pyramids were being built; a situation that is graphically
borne out in the recent excavation of parts of the dried-out bed of the
ancient lake of Abusir, which served as a main port for stone delivery
to the pyramids, temples and cemeteries of Abusir and Saqqara. At
the edges of this lake, Czech archaeologists have excavated part of a
large mud-brick structure built in the times of the Giza kings, a kind
of causeway that had led to the cemeteries in the deserts above, which,
like the rest of the Saqqara monuments, had been covered first in substantial drifts of windblown sand, then by alluvial deposits of rich
black Nile silts, in thin strata typical of those deposited by artificial
irrigation, a new development in that region. As the remains of animals and insects from the area confirm, the ecology of the Memphite
cemeteries had been changing throughout the times of the pyramid-
building kings as the river's flow had decreased.

Given that the amounts of limestone that the pharaonic state could
quarry to make its monuments was ultimately dependent upon the
food it could supply to its builders and thus upon the bounty of the
annual flood, the drop in the size and quality of monuments throughout the era of the Memphite kings may simply reflect the changing
sizes of the harvests of the times. First, the royal pyramids were made
far smaller than the colossal monuments of the Giza kings. Then, following the move from Abusir to south Saqqara, the size and quality of
the temples which accompanied the royal pyramids had also been
reduced, a diminution that is also apparent in the courtiers' tomb
chapels of those times. After enjoying an extraordinary florescence,
these tombs were similarly diminished, so that, by the time of the
south Saqqara pyramids, many of the courtiers were buried in small
mud-brick mastabas and some of the queens had been interred in the
storerooms of the pyramid temples, their bodies laid in sarcophagi
made of blocks of stone re-used from older monuments. The output of
the royal sculpture studios seems to have undergone a similar im-
poverishment, for no life-sized royal statues of the later kings appear
to have been made at all, only smaller works which were mostly made
of alabaster or limestone and hardly ever fashioned from the hard
desert rock employed in earlier times.

This gradual reduction in the annual harvests might also have
prompted the relocation into the provinces of the households of some

of the Memphite courtiers and may reflect the courtiers' increasing involvement in the direct oversight of the supply of tithes and offerings; the flow of grain and meat to Memphis.

So by the times of the south Saqqara kings, several senior members of the royal household, courtiers like Qar and Weni, both children of the households of district governors, had gone back to the provinces of their birth, where, so some of the texts in their tomb chapels inform us, they set about reorganizing the systems of farming and of tithing. The courtier Qar, for example, went back to the settlement of his childhood, Edfu in southern Upper Egypt, where a number of huge circular grain silos of a later age, similar in type and size to some of those at the royal settlements at Giza, have recently been excavated.

> ... King Merenre told me to journey upstream to Edfu as overseer of southern grain and overseer of priests ... I came to my settlement as overlord of the entire south ... I caused the oxen of the province to live with the cows in the cattle yards ... [and] by virtue of my watchfulness, my management was effective for the royal residence ... I gave bread to the hungry and clothes to the naked ... and I measured out the grain of the valley of the Nile ...

In similar fashion, Weni's return to his family household at Abydos, in the province of Thinis, may well have been connected with schemes to colonize parts of the valley which had previously been largely unfarmed, for Weni was a considerable organizer of state projects and Abydos lay at the centre of a region of marsh and wide silt plains which in those days were still relatively wild.

So though the traditional pharaonic system of tithe and offering had functioned well in earlier times, it would appear that by the time of Qar and Weni, with the harvests yet diminishing, the court's direct control of food production was extended far beyond Memphis and the temples and households of the Memphite courtiers. At the same time, however, the Memphite cemeteries, with their multitudes of offering cults, with century after century of courtly ancestors each with a tomb chapel, with offering altars and their accompanying families of priests, had stretched for mile after mile along the desert's edge, from the pyramids of Abu Roash and Giza in the north to those of south Saqqara and Maidum. And so it was, in those late times, that the Memphite kingdom appears to have lost its equilibrium of harvest, tithe and offering, and reached a tipping point in the court's prosperity that stopped all pyramid building.

There is no evidence, however, that this had engendered national calamities such as war or famine. Quite the reverse, in fact. Recent excavations throughout the length and breath of Egypt have shown that, notwithstanding the Lamentations and Admonitions of later courtly scribes, in the settlements of the so-called First Intermediate Period life had been more prosperous, the graveyards more numerous, and the goods within the tombs more plentiful than ever before; and the bones of the occupants of those graves show no more signs of malnutrition, stress or mutilation than those of earlier times.

Nor should this be surprising. With the collapse of the central tithing system and the state building programme, the communities of the lower Nile would have had more resources at their disposal than before, especially as the long-term diminution of the Nile's annual flood that had occurred in the times of the Memphite kings appears to have stopped during the interregnum, and flood levels may even have begun to slowly rise in that same period.

At Elephantine, for example, where government stores and workshops had long since been established, the island settlement had continued after the reign of Pepi II, and the local offices of government had been as busy, it would appear, as ever. Here too, German excavators have uncovered traces of a novel offering cult that was established during the era of the First Intermediate Period to serve the spirits of some of the earlier courtiers of that settlement; men such as Harkhuf, who had traded south from Aswan and policed the gates of pharaoh's kingdom. At this same time, the facilities of some of the old houses of the senior local officials at Aswan had been considerably enlarged, and a great bakery with a high columned hall was built beside them which continued to serve that settlement for centuries to come.

At Abydos too, at the desert's edge, not a mile away from Weni's tomb and close to that courtier's family residence, a large-sized settlement grew up and prospered during the First Intermediate Period. Unlike the earlier Giza settlements, where the dwellings of courtiers and workers were carefully demarcated, this group of homesteads was made up of a variety of buildings, large and small, each one with its own grain bins and each one set close beside its neighbour amidst a mass of tiny twisting alleyways. Inside these houses, their archaeologists report, were objects that had been imported from other parts of the lower Nile, which shows that as at Aswan there had been a continuing consistency in trafficking and barter throughout the regions of the earlier kingdom. Here, alongside the kitchens and the bakeries, the animal pens and workshops, archaeologists uncovered the ruins of a workshop that had produced small objects made of faience, a high-fired ceramic whose brilliant blue glazes, the colour of Egypt's summer sky, were produced in considerable quantity throughout all later periods of ancient Egyptian history. That the production of this non-essential but eternally favourite material of pharaonic culture had not ceased in times of political decentralization is by itself a further indication of the quality and order of local life in those vague times.

Similar observations on life during this interregnum can be gleaned from the excavation of other settlements. Recent archaeology has shown, for example, that the households of the courtiers who had controlled the oases, who in the times of Pepi II had ruled those isolated mini-states within the Western Desert and were buried within impressive cemeteries, had not been looted in some kind of general anarchy when the Memphite state had disappeared. In Dakhla Oasis, moreover, the governors' residence had continued to flourish throughout the First Intermediate Period and into later periods as well. In the delta also, the farming settlements appear to have continued unmolested, though to what extent that region had been inhabited and controlled solely by people of pharaonic culture is an open question: the lines in the Admonitions that were traditionally translated as an account of a foreign invasion of the Nile Delta may well record an increase in the population of that region's indigenous Levantine culture during the First Intermediate Period.

In short, though the diminishing flood levels appear to have finally rendered the building of further pyramids impossible, neither war nor famine appear to have visited the regions of the lower Nile during this interregnum: just as before, the ancient farms and settlements appear to have been prosperous. Now, however, and for the first time in some 800 years, the populations of the lower Nile no longer owed allegiance to the Memphite pharaohs but to the governors of the provinces and regions in which they lived.

So the shibboleth that 'what's good for General Motors is good for the USA' is not a universal truth. For pyramids, like motorcars, are but limited indicators of prosperity. As far as pharaoh's Egypt is concerned, the cessation of the mass quarrying of stone for state building projects seems to have resulted from a lack of the necessary supplies – that is, state surpluses – that were required to feed those who made such monuments.

THE EXISTENTIAL SMASH–UP

Paradoxically, the contemporaneous understanding of ancient history which influenced Hume, Malthus, Marx and Ricardo, and Smith is still alive in the 'laws of economics'.
David Warburton, 2010

Historians of ancient Egypt have generally agreed that the term *iwn*, which is derived from the root 'to bring', was an ancient name of the pharaonic 'tithe' as I have termed it. It is perhaps not surprising that *iwn* is usually described by economic historians as a non-monetary tax. There is, however, an objection to that definition, for economics of itself is but a youthful discipline. A product of the European Enlightenment and an abstraction created by and for European scholarship and government, economics, in common with a large part of the portmanteau of academic disciplines used to describe alien and ancient worlds, had no contemporary reality in pharaonic Egypt. So as with the histories of other modern abstractions, such as art, politics and religion, to make economic histories of the tithes and rations of the pharaonic kingdom, tiny grains of evidence have to be extracted from their ancient contexts and heavily re-ordered.

The great advantage of such modern disciplines, however, is that they allow all of the world's cultures and societies to be analysed according to a single set of principles, and thus universal lessons can be drawn. The disadvantage, however, is that individual cultures such as pharaoh's Egypt lose all their freshness and originality and are slotted into a synthetic world-wide history in which ancient people move zombie-like through a series of similar situations, sharing the same ways of thought and the same goals as the people of more modern worlds. Fit the secular visions of Malthus, Adam Smith and Marx over Champollion's pharaonic court and the terms of Erman's *Wörterbuch*, and the court of pharaoh can easily be described as one of many early modern 'elite' cultures that served up awe and propaganda to a gullible citizenry in the form of magic and religion, dressed in fine clothes and imported jewels, skilled in the arts of war and, of course, in the construction of monstrous buildings.

Nowhere are the fundamental weaknesses of such narratives so obviously exposed as in such times as the First Intermediate Period, when stone block building had entirely stopped. For modern archaeology has clearly shown that the regions, the populations, of the lower Nile had not collapsed into anarchy and immorality after the last Memphite pyramid had been built. All that had happened was that monuments and offerings were no longer being made. The court's activities of tithing and of offering, the building of stone-block monuments, and all of those various activities that had defined the state, the boundaries of the material and immaterial, the living and the dead within the narrow kingdom had gone. And in consequence the Memphite court had lost its purpose.

This is the reason why the pyramid temples, the royal burials and statues and most of the monuments of the Memphite court had been physically attacked when state activity had stopped. Those monuments had not been broken down by gangs of anarchist barbarians, by thieves or envious courtiers, but by people who, as the remains of their own modest monuments still clearly show, had shared the same vision of their world, the same courtly culture as their predecessors, but who no longer wished the region of the lower Nile to be inhabited by ancestors and the images of ancestors who had belonged to a world that had ceased to function.

Nor were their attacks limited to the monuments of Memphis. At Hierakonpolis, several caches of court statues, vases and quantities of ritual implements had been carefully concealed from this widespread destruction; acts that literally saved some of the early kings from near oblivion when their courtly relics were eventually retrieved by archaeologists. At Abydos, alternatively, the enormous subterranean tombs of the first pharaohs were broken down and burnt, the fires within their huge wood-lined burial chambers raging with such ferocity that their walls, colossal bulks of dun mud brick, were transformed into a lurid ceramic redness. And in those same times, Weni's tomb was also broken down, along with most other monuments that had been built on that wide desert plain, the courtier's mummy pulled from his huge sarcophagus, his splendid burial chamber splashed with the oils that had been left there and ignited so that, millennia later, when archaeologists re-entered it, they found a blackened tomb chamber with a broken sarcophagus lying sad and empty at its centre. In modern if not ancient terms, Memphite culture had been an aesthetic enterprise, and with the smashing of its central images and objects it had suffered an aesthetic ending.

A BRAVE NEW AGE – *ANKHTIFI AT MO'ALLA*

A string of pretty villages edge the narrow valley between Luxor and Aswan. There the light is pellucid, the Nile low and wide, the crops stand luminous within the fields and the little deserts and the cliffs beyond rise like golden curtains in a faience sky. Half way through that enchanted region, opposite the ancient west-bank settlement of Gebelein, is the site of Hefat, where in the times of the First Intermediate Period a local governor, Ankhtifi, had lived and ruled.

An old colonial train line, its small half-timbered Surrey-style station still intact, runs beside the valley road and divides the desert from the fields. Cross the asphalt and the railway tracks and walk into Mo'alla, the village lying closest to the centre of Ankhtifi's ancient governorate, and you enter a world of friendly, solid mud-brick houses faced with *mouna*, an ageless mix of silt and fine-chopped straw whose enzymes impart an egg-shell hardness to their lively hand-made finish. Beyond the village, the shops, the people and their children, the fragments of ceramic lying in the mix of sand and chaff on which you walk, might just as well be trimmings from new-laid water pipes or sherds of pottery from prehistoric graves. For the people of this region have used the little deserts that lie behind their villages as graveyards throughout prehistoric and pharaonic times and later too, for Greek and Roman, Christian and Muslim burials. And there are cemeteries of ancient Nubians, the southerners whom the pharaohs had employed to police their state; and their graves, too, were made according to the customs of their people.

Ankhtifi's tomb chapel appears today as one of a line of tell-tale rectangles of shadow at the centre of a low-sloping hill, a natural pyramid. Though the other tombs in that row appear to be of similar age to Ankhtifi's, most of their texts and decorations have disappeared. Ankhtifi's tomb chapel, alternatively, is the best preserved of all known monuments of the First Intermediate Period, and since the 1920s, the time of its uncovering, its texts and images have greatly coloured modern visions of the character and qualities of that first interregnum.

When the modern valley of the Nile was still in the process of formation, the pyramid-shaped hill that would later hold Ankhtifi's tomb had loosened and slid down in primeval rains, from the peak of the high terraces of the cliffs into the bottom of the valley. That fine hard limestone from the upper terraces is of better quality than that of the lower levels, which proved an advantage for Ankhtifi's craftsmen, since that long slide down the cliffs had so stressed that great white triangle of rock that, when it came to rest, it was riddled with joints and fractures. And that, in turn, made it a convenient source for quarrymen of many different ages, the fine white limestone lying in small convenient seams that could be cut and carried off with relative ease. The scars of some of those ancient workings, indeed, can still be seen at the south end of the pyramid.

As you approach the doorway of Ankhtifi's monument, you walk through a large square open courtyard. Part-filled with baulks of ancient brickwork, this area has not been excavated. The outline of its plan, however, suggests that its designers had followed the general layout of the Memphite pyramid temples, placing a wide and sunny courtyard before the darkness of a columned hall beyond.

Walk through the doorway of Ankhtifi's tomb chapel and you enter the re-created gloom of just such an ancient temple, for it is shaded by a wooden roof that was set over the ruined chapel following its rediscovery by local quarrymen. Fortunately for us, if not for Ankhtifi's mortuary cult, the original roof of his tomb chapel had collapsed shortly after work on its decoration was completed, burying its walls and columns in a scree of hillside rubble which preserved the better part of them from the destruction that most other tombs of those times have suffered. Ankhtifi, indeed, appears to have lain untouched within his tomb for some considerable time, since the splendid fragments of contemporary funerary furniture which are known to have come from the vicinity of Mo'alla surfaced on the antiquities market in the years immediately before his tomb was first visited by egyptologists.

The texts accompanying the two reliefs carved left and right upon the tomb chapel's doorjambs announce its one-time owner in the traditional way: Ankhtifi, nobleman and governor of Hierakonpolis and Edfu, chief of priests, a manager and commander of men and farms. Pass through that straight and well-cut portal, and you stand in one of the strangest of all pharaonic tomb chapels, a forest of twisting columns sliding left and right some thirty feet and more on either side, gathered in a narrow envelope of space in which every element of architecture, both the waving walls and the cock-eyed columns, follow the angles of the joints and fractures that run right through that natural pyramid.

In the usual way of nobles' tomb chapels, a deep and dangerous burial shaft lies some eight feet into the gloom beyond the sunlight of the entrance doorway. A crude little offering stela engraved in the traditional design showing Ankhtifi and his wife, Nebi, seated at an offering table is cut onto the wall of that rough shaft. And the stumps of those thirty tilted and irregularly spaced columns, some round, some square, stand all around like stalagmites, whilst, in the gloom beyond, the images on the chamber walls shift and shimmer, a distant mirage of the Memphite kingdom.

A tiny cartouche painted in a curiously iridescent green upon the *mouna* plaster of the chapel's walls holds the name of a King Neferkare, the Herakleopolitan monarch to whom Ankhtifi paid allegiance and the king on whose behalf, so one of the tomb chapel's inscriptions tells, the god Horus had sent full and fruitful floods.

That Ankhtifi's craftsmen had followed the natural but irregular fissures in the rock rather than rendering the elements of its architecture symmetrical and true in the Memphite manner suggests that Ankhtifi had but a scant supply of copper at his disposal. Such ways of working would have made but few demands upon copper tools; in the 1970s, two men using crowbars levered out a garage for a Land Rover from similarly fissured rock in just two days. That copper, along with several of the other commodities essential for a Memphite courtier's burial, was scarce in Ankhtifi's time can also be inferred from one of several texts carved into the chapel's columns.

> . . . it is with my own copper that I acquired my coffin and all the elements of this my tomb, for in this my tomb there is no door which comes from somewhere else, no upright which comes from somewhere else . . . it is with wooden planks, from trees in the region of Coptos [some fifty miles downstream] that I built this my coffin. No other person can say as much, for I was a hero who had no equal . . .

All along the chapel's lengthy walls and wrapped round many of the columns that are not engraved with text, there are the usual scenes of Memphite tomb chapels: Ankhtifi and his family hunt in the marshes and oversee the harvest, fine bulls and cows sway to the slaughter, and the governor's family, seated on the fine furniture of their household, feast from the wealth of their estates. But all these scenes are displaced from the positions that they had previously held within the Memphite tomb chapels

Whilst seven of the columns chatter and brag in lively hieroglyphic the words and phrases of Ankhtifi's unique biography, the wall scenes illustrate some of the same themes in images of festival and conflict. Lively archers jog along in rows. There are remnants also of a broken scene of fighting in which a man has been hit by an arrow, and of a festival in celebration of a local god that is overseen by Ankhtifi, his wife and his beloved daughters, his four sons and the family dogs. Further images show the celebrations that had followed the grain harvest, which was stored in the ten great granaries that Ankhtifi tells us he controlled.

A rococo variation on earlier examples, Ankhtifi's tomb chapel re-sets the traditional versions of such scenes in joyous celebration of life lived in a different age. Such is their confusion, however – quite frequently, snippets of scenes flit from wall to column and from column back to wall again – that some of their subject matter can only be identified by comparison to earlier, more sober-sided versions of the same activities.

The tomb chapel's lengthy inscriptions, alternatively, that wobbly encolumned library, are the longest continuous texts which are known to have survived from the First Intermediate Period and are unique. And from the first days of their discovery translations of their vivid, if perhaps to modern tastes rather vainglorious, prose have been a prime source of information – and misinformation – about the times in which Ankhtifi lived and ruled.

NOMES AND NOMARCHS

What, then, to make of this merry-go-round of a monument that has become the very symbol, the most discussed, the most debated relic of its times? At first, Ankhtifi was viewed in the traditional way, as a local warlord whose tomb-chapel texts and paintings were illustrations of his battles on behalf of northern kings. And the style and manner of those texts and decorations served as an exemplar of the low state of his age.

Others came to view Ankhtifi's tomb chapel as representing a kind of liberation. Whilst acknowledging that its texts and images were ultimately derived from those of earlier times, they held that Ankhtifi's scribes and draughtsmen had injected energy and joy into old staid formulae. And certainly the manner of Ankhtifi's monument along with others of the times, both their texts and images, would have considerable influence upon courtly monuments of later ages.

Above all else, however, the interpretations of Ankhtifi's tomb chapel have been shaped by its lengthy texts and the varying translations and interpretations they have inspired. Some, for example, talk of Ankhtifi providing the planks for a simple coffin; others as providing great wooden boards for a sarcophagus. More importantly – and here it is that translation directly colours our vision of the man and of his times – some of Ankhtifi's titles have been variously translated, as royal general or as commander of a neighbourhood police force.

Similarly, the title *ha-ati*, which literally means 'foremost of position', has been variously translated as 'chief', 'baron' and 'mayor'. It has also been translated as 'nomarch', which is the classical title applied to the governor of a 'nome', or one of the regions of Egypt into which that kingdom was divided in far later times, for some of the territories of those later southern nomes reflect the names of regions which Ankhtifi claims to have fallen within his purview. Yet the settlements under Ankhtifi's control also reflect the names of far older centres of authority, so it is best, perhaps, to describe Ankhtifi simply as a governor, as the provincial overlord, of the three southernmost centres of the earlier Memphite kingdom, namely Elephantine, Edfu and, so it would appear, the otherwise little-recorded settlement of Hefat. Another indication of Ankhtifi's role within that new-made world is that some of the titles in his tomb describe him as performing priestly offices in the areas under his control, duties which had been previously undertaken by the officials of the Memphite pharaohs.

At all events, and whatever the intricacies of his titles may or may not imply, it is clear that, in modern terms, Ankhtifi was a local leader in southern Upper Egypt. He was also something of a local, self-made leader, for though his tomb displays discreet allegiance to a Herakleopolitan king its texts and scenes show that he had not called upon the craftsmen or designers of that northern court. The architecture of Ankhtifi's tomb chapel, indeed, is as different in style and quality from the earlier Memphite monuments as are Weni's tomb at Abydos or those of the caravanning governors of Aswan.

As its inscriptions insistently inform us, Ankhtifi made this tomb chapel for himself and with his own resources. In times when the northern courts no longer had the reserves to build large monuments, and the households of the families of the old provincial courtiers seemed to have disappeared along with the household of their kings, new households like that of Ankhtifi had arisen and, though their monuments had retained some of the manners and titles of the Memphite court, they describe another world.

From Aswan and Gebelein in the south, to Asyut, Meir and Qaw el-Kebir in Middle Egypt and at Memphis and beyond, the same sense of change and adaptation runs through all the other tomb chapels made during the First Intermediate Period. Though they are now badly damaged, their surviving fragments show that, following the dissolution of the Memphite state, the local governors for whom those monuments were made all claim in common with Ankhtifi that they had maintained order at a provincial level and promoted the welfare of their people, even as one would care for one's own household.

Such claims, of course, echo those made by the courtiers of earlier times, just as the images of Ankhtifi's tomb chapel hold attitudes and poses similar to those of the earlier age. To this extent, they remain part of the enduring common culture of the lower Nile: from the great grand Memphite settlements to provincial Hefat, the fundamental unit of ancient Egyptian civic order was the pharaonic household.

Yet Ankhtifi's texts also hold a novel air of pride in them, a sense of personal responsibility, and they certainly display a greater autonomy of action than those of any earlier courtier. They do not, however, tell much about the circumstances of his age. Beyond the subtle indications of the changing levels of the Nile's flood, and the scenes of festival and harvest in his tomb chapel, we have little real idea of the conditions on the ground during Ankhtifi's lifetime.

PEACE AND WAR

If, as they are traditionally interpreted, Ankhtifi and the other governors of the regions of a fragmented kingdom are envisaged as ambitious princes running petty kingdoms of their own, then, as Matthew xxiv:7 announces and nineteenth-century Europeans widely believed, war was inevitable, for 'Nation shall rise against kingdom, and kingdom against kingdom', a message that the Reverend James Mozley pondered in a sermon of 1871, which 'in view of the circumstances of the present time' was reprinted in 1915. 'War', the Reverend asserts, is a kingdom's inherent right, 'because under the division of mankind into distinct nations it becomes a necessity'.

If Ankhtifi's titles are translated in the light of such sentiments, then he naturally becomes a commander of armies with divisions of foot soldiers and elite longbowmen, of *Nahkampftruppen* and

Elite-Langbogen Männer, of whom small samples appear within his tomb. And if Ankhtifi's vivid descriptions of his policing are not seen as the actions of a governor creating and maintaining peace and security within his provinces but rather as those of a European warlord fighting battles, then large-scale military campaigns may easily be conjured up from texts like Ankhtifi's, and an internal history of the First Intermediate Period can easily be constructed as a series of extended military campaigns.

So traditional historians filled out Brugsch's earlier imaginings of the First Intermediate Period as a chaotic Dark Age, seeing it as a time of civil war like those that had afflicted early modern Europe. Drawing on the surviving fragments of contemporary documents and narratives from later periods, Ankhtifi's troops were said to have fought the rulers of Thebes, who were attempting to withdraw from a military alliance with the kings of Herakleopolis. And the combined armies of Thebes and Coptos had besieged the fortresses of Armant close to Thebes, an action broken Blücher-style on behalf of Herakleopolitan kings by Ankhtifi's troops, who then pursued the Thebans into the south. But then, the story goes, the Theban nomarchs had somehow turned the tables, gaining control first of Ankhtifi's domains and finally, as the later pharaonic monuments assert, of all the lands within the ancient Memphite kingdom.

Such narratives, however, are entirely absent from all other records, of the time, which contain virtually no references to wars nor hardly any tomb-chapel texts boasting of a pride in arms. Nor, indeed, have any military installations of the time of the First Intermediate Period been excavated at Armant or any other site in Egypt, no ash of pillage, no corpses that were slain in battle. In purely literary terms, moreover, it is hard to reconcile such notions of a sweeping military victory by a dynasty of southern princes with the texts of the Lamentations, Admonitions and Disputes, which are set in the court of the Herakleopolitan kings who appear as righteous pharaohs rather than reviled or defeated enemies. And in recent decades, as more information on the period of the interregnum have come to light, it has become clear that the various confrontations described in contemporary texts cannot be set together end to end to make a history of a campaign of war nor, indeed, can the order or sizes of those incidents be quantified.

Pitched battles or small-scale civic disturbances? Drawn in three registers upon its eastern walls, Ankhtifi's tomb holds splendid images of forty-six archers, some of whom can be identified by their weapons and their headbands as Nubians. Men, perhaps, who had lived across the river from Ankhtifi's Hefat in the settlement at Gebelein, where many tombs and stelae of that period have been excavated, some of which hold sparkling pharaonic images of Nubian households.

The small force shown in Ankhtifi's tomb chapel, indeed, might well have represented the full extent of his so-called 'army'. Similar numbers of armed men are pictured on the walls of other contemporary tombs, whilst the two famous wooden models of groups of soldiers that were found in the tomb of Mesehty, a near-contemporary governor of Asyut with allegiance to the court of Herakleopolis, each hold forty similar soldiers in four rows of ten. To modern eyes, those celebrated sculptures might well give the appearance of a regiment marching to the orders of a sergeant major; in reality, those little bands of archers and spear carriers are following the evenly spaced parallel tracks of desert caravans, just as similarly sized bands of desert caravanners do today.

Desert graffiti of the period, indeed, record that such militia were policing and maintaining the desert tracks in the names of various local governors. Rather than generals leading conquering armies up and down the valley of the Nile, therefore, these images and texts are more likely to record the exploits of little bands of local militia patrolling the various regions of the lower Nile, maintaining, in the absence of central state control, the ancient pharaonic virtue of good order for their local populace. Given the resources at his disposal, Ankhtifi might well celebrate the provisioning of such a force within his tomb chapel. So, as the desert graffiti would suggest, in reality the 'battle' texts of the traditional historians probably describe the novel situation of various regional authorities disputing adjoining areas of control.

Certainly, the fearful links between war, nationhood and sovereignty that the Reverend Mozley would later celebrate in his Oxford sermon were not yet forged; those very concepts, indeed, had no existence in that distant past. There are as many donkeys as soldiers drawn on the walls of Ankhtifi's tomb chapel, just as there were in other tomb chapels, where fine food, civic welfare and the good life are presented as their owners' ambitions and accomplishments.

FAMINE AND PLENTY

Ears up, eyes wide open, row upon row of light grey prick-eared donkeys, each one with wheat sacks tied securely to its back, still trot along the bottom registers of Ankhtifi's tomb chapel towards the scene of a funerary feast, where the great man sits with his 'beloved wife', Nebi, and his 'beloved daughter', both of whom appear to have died before him. In lively intimacy, images of little people bob around that central group, offering them food and drink. A harpist plays, a cow is slaughtered, hares, marsh ducks and luscious fat fish, their scales drawn in iridescent green, are all brought to the feast. It is a scene, in short, whose literary description could just as well describe a similar event shown in a Memphite tomb chapel.

At Mo'alla, however, these scenes are filled with sharp-eyed observations of local life within the valley of the lower Nile, and they have been composed without the usual regulating baselines so that every image inhabits its own space. The whole is held in a single wall-wide tapestry of movement by the unrelenting ochre of the figures' skin tones and the draughtsman's insistent use of the sharp, angular forms whose formal ancestry, the large eyes, the thin limbs, and a lively and attenuated manner of drawing had been developed in the later Memphite court.

As the images of Ankhtifi's funerary feast beautifully celebrate, the texts within his tomb chapel insistently describe his lands as rich in grain and livestock. Ten large round granaries are painted on his chapel walls, and beside them are scenes of harvest and perhaps of winnowing and dancing, along with a scene showing the filling of those huge grains stores in the presence of Ankhtifi and his pen-poised scribes. The chapel texts tell that measures of this grain were sent to other provinces, and that in times of need these same grain stores had fed the hungry. Those same texts, however, also tell us that in Ankhtifi's time people had hugged their fathers' killers and that he had refounded ancient Edfu after it had been abandoned! This, it would appear, is a scribal encomium composed for a provincial governor listing aspects of their lord's benevolence, and it is probably unwise to imagine, as some historians have done, that the texts document times of real famine, especially as archaeology shows that at this time the Nile's flood was on the rise.

In all likelihood, the localization of the resources of the Memphite state had brought immediate benefit to the wider population of the lower Nile. The previous centuries had seen parts of the kingdom's crops pass under the direct control of the offices of court in the form of funerary endowments and royal grants, colonies and governor's estates; a system that appears to have been designed to increase the harvest's surpluses and ensure the court's provisions which, as it had neared its ending, had led the central government to dispatch courtiers like Qar and Weni back to the provinces.

Once that centuries-old state system had dissolved, however, and people were no longer tithed to feed the making of great monuments or the offering tables of the royal temples and the tomb chapels of the courtiers, the harvests would have reverted to the people of the provinces, to the farmsteads, the settlements and the households of the local governors like Ankhtifi, who boasts of having controlled and improved the irrigation of the farmers' lands.

In contrast with the Memphite tomb chapels, which are filled with the sentiments of people living on the produce of a tithe, Ankhtifi's tomb chapel in common with those of other governors of his times have something of the down-to-earth air of farmers in them, and something also of a farmer's pride: 'I am rich, a possessor of wealth . . . a master of cows . . . a master of goats . . . a master of wheat . . . a master of clothes. I say this in truth, and not just for the necropolis.'

TOMBS OF THE TIMES

More small tombs were made during the period of the interregnum than in any earlier period of pharaonic history, and they present a new and very different aspect of that courtly culture. Set within the valley's little deserts that lie beyond the area of silt and cultivation, the disposition of these cemeteries often copies the layout of the Memphite cemeteries, in that they are grouped below the grander cliff-cut tombs of the provincial governors and their officials. For the most part, these tombs have little or no superstructure and are composed of modest shafts cut into the valley's underlying limestone, with rough-cut burial vaults containing the coffins and sarcophagi of burial along with other accoutrements, often an eclectic range of grave goods that included lively and novel adaptations of the burial arrangements of the Memphite courtiers. The relatively fine burial of Mesehty, for example, a governor of Asyut, was accompanied by painted wooden models of activities, soldiering, baking, brewing, potting and weaving, which had previously been painted and engraved upon the walls of tomb chapels. Nor was this at all remarkable. More than double the number of wooden statues has survived from this period than from earlier times – lively figures that have broken free from the thin envelope of space in which their predecessors had been held upon the chambers' walls, figures that stand in three dimensions, accompanied on occasion by stately sculptures of women bearing offerings to the tomb in the age-old way.

For the first time, too, heavily painted masks were placed over the heads of the enlinened dead, this an elaboration of practices that had flowered in the tombs of the Giza courtiers, when some of the courtiers' mummies were entirely encased in a skin of modelled plaster, giving their corpses the presence of a sculpture or a living person. Now, too, some of the texts that had previously been placed upon the walls of burial crypts were painted directly onto the coffins and sarcophagi of the burial, which lay in rough undecorated chambers. Here, then, either the ancient tombs had been revisited by copying scribes or some of the archives from which the Memphite Pyramid Texts had been copied in the days of monarchy were still in use.

Lacking the measured excellence of the Memphite craftsmen, the best part of this mass of new-fangled provincial burial goods might first appear, like Ankhtifi's tomb chapel, as rustic travesties of earlier courtly works. The comparison, however, is ill-chosen, for the sheer numbers of such grave goods show that the greater part of them had been made for the graves of people who in earlier times had hardly possessed grave goods at all. Now, though, and for the first time, grave goods were produced in quantity by local craftsmen according to what they knew of earlier courtly styles and from images of animals, plants and people observed at first hand in their local landscapes. So the successors of many of those who had provisioned and built the great memorials of Memphite culture now had the resources to construct burials of their own. And, touchingly enough, the tombs they made show that, although their forebears had worked and died without memorial, they too had harboured the kings' and courtiers' ambition to continue after death.

A VERY LOCAL FESTIVAL

Outside the households of the court, there is precious little trace of that mass of people who had lived and died in the centuries in which the Memphite pyramids were built. That workforce may indeed have suffered cruelty and privation, just as the Greek and Roman authors had imagined and many modern-day historians believe. Yet those same histories also describe the First Intermediate Period as an age of chaos and moral decay, as a time in which the neo-Darwinian forces of 'human nature' came to the fore, modern notions of personal advancement had ruled the roost and war and famine had stalked the land until a prince had risen like a lion out of the south and by force of arms had re-established the order and manners of the good old days.

More modern views, alternatively, regard the First Intermediate Period as a time of relative plenty, when harvests were kept close to home, when local governors like Ankhtifi had employed small militias to deal with local feuds and to discourage robbery and illicit incursions into the territories under their control, and when a larger section of the population than ever before had sufficient resources at their disposal to participate in some of the forms of traditional courtly burial.

The single biggest scene in Ankhtifi's tomb chapel once showed a regatta, a water festival with Ankhtifi drawn large and leaning on a staff, with his four sons darting up and down the river in diminutive five-paddled skiffs. To Ankhtifi's right, fishermen pull in full nets, which a nearby inscription implies are a product of a bountiful flood made by the god Horus for King Neferkare. Above the fishermen, slaughterers turn the neck of a black-spotted cow towards the knife; presumably its meat will serve for offering and feasting at the festival. And, to Ankhtifi's left, the climax of this tableau it appears had shown the spearing of a captured hippopotamus, an incident reduced to the faint outline of a small round animal impaled on multiple harpoons.

Long-boats with thirty oarsmen sail across the centre of this water pageant; a cowhide shield tied to the cabin of one of these vessels suggests their other purposes. With their banks of oarsmen, they would have been an effective means of delivering Ankhtifi's militia to settlements up and down the river, offering swift alternatives to marching through the Nile-side fields or caravanning on desert tracks. Here, then, the civic role of Ankhtifi's waterborne militia had been underlined in the regatta's climax, for the dispatching of a hippopotamus was an ancient image of the victory over the enemies of order.

Sadly, this unique scene was badly damaged, first in ancient rock falls and then again during a clumsy robbery in the 1960s. Without an accompanying text on a nearby column, and a few further references to the little-known deity Hemen, the god in whose name the regatta appears to have been held, it would be difficult to decipher what that confused and broken scene had represented. That a text on a nearby column refers to a procession of the god Hemen along the riverbank, however, makes it likely that the regatta had been a festival that had accompanied the excursion of Hemen's statue from his temple at Hefat.

To record such an event within a tomb chapel was a complete departure from the practices of earlier times. Hemen's festival seems closer to the peregrinations of the archaic pharaohs and a product also of the narrow environment of Upper Egypt, which was dominated by the central presence of the river. In later ages, waterborne processionals became a major ritual of the pharaonic court, whilst images of hippopotami were used to represent all forms of evil and instability, lurking in the darkness of life after death and kept like pets in pens within the delta court of foreign immigrants.

In reality, this interregnum was not 'intermediate' in any major sense but a remarkably creative period of pharaonic history, in which the roles of gods and courts within pharaonic culture were transformed and enlarged whilst a previously invisible section of the population became active and participating members of pharaonic culture. Yet whilst the air of Ankhtifi's wild and wonderful tomb chapel is one of novelty and fresh new sentiment, its texts and images still move within the universe that had been created at the Memphite court in the course of the previous eight centuries:

> It is the prince, nobleman, seal-bearer of the king of the delta regions, sole companion, lector priest, overseer of priests, commander of the Nubian militia, overseer of the desert regions, great overlord of the provinces of Edfu and Hierakonpolis, Ankhtifi the brave, who says: 'I built a door up to the sky so that it is in the air. Its ceiling is a sky strewn with stars and the uraeus frieze of its architrave is very solid. The uprights are made with cedar wood and are higher than dom palm-trees. Its [granite] threshold brought from Elephantine is like a hippopotamus . . .

PART SEVEN

Middle Kingdom
Remaking the State,
2140–1780 BC

22

Sema Towy

Binding the Kingdom

NAMES AND GRAVES – *A CHRONOLOGY OF KINGS*

Almost 115 cemeteries had been in active use in Old Kingdom times, of which a hundred are situated in the Nile Valley, the remainder in the delta. These it would appear had been the cemeteries of major pharaonic settlements, or at least the cemeteries of settlements with access to sufficient supplies of copper and other courtly materials to make fine grave goods and monuments of stone.

Almost half of those cemeteries had been established during the last centuries before the Old Kingdom had disappeared and would appear to be a product of the courtiers' move out into the provinces, which the contemporary inscriptions of men such as Qar of Edfu and Weni of Abydos describe as resulting from the decision of the Memphite court to take direct local control over the systems of state supply. In Weni's time, indeed, clusters of new cemeteries were established in his home region of Abydos.

At all events, that sudden increase in the numbers of provincial cemeteries represents a major change in the distribution of courtly commodities, an outflowing that stopped at the beginning of the First Intermediate Period when some two thirds of all Old Kingdom cemeteries were abandoned. In the following centuries, the cemeteries that remained in use had housed the graves of the courtiers of minor kings or local governors, whilst a handful of newly risen provincial rulers founded some new burial grounds at sites such as Mo'alla, which holds Ankhtifi's tomb, and Dara in Middle Egypt, where an enormous though utterly anonymous mud-brick mastaba stands at the centre of a large unexcavated cemetery. Such are the ragged out-lines of the political geography of that dislocated age for which there is no firm chronology, few links having been discovered between the diverse individuals who are buried in those various cemeteries. Nor, certainly, is there any known connection between any of those local rulers and the remarkable sequence of events that subsequently led to the establishment of the Middle Kingdom.

Contemporary inscriptions, however, tell that in the last decades of the interregnum, from around 2140 BC, the successive generations of a household of provincial governors from Thebes had taken royal titularies and slowly gained control of all the territories of the old Memphite kingdom. Then, in about 1980 BC, they had moved their court from Thebes up to the north and established a royal residence close to ancient Memphis, which they named 'Amenemhet Itj-towy' or 'King Amenemhet takes possession of the two lands'. This, then, had signalled the ending of a considerable era of consolidation and the beginning of Baron Bunsen's Middle Kingdom.

Just like its Memphite predecessors, the refounded court built grand monuments, supported artisans and craftsmen, quarrymen and copper furnaces, maintained mortuary cults for kings and courtiers, re-instated the archaic phyle system and dispatched caravans and ships to foreign lands to obtain the court's traditional imports of oils, woods and precious stones. Right from its beginnings, indeed, at Thebes, it had carefully and consciously initiated the re-establishment of the defining activities of the earlier Memphite state.

The history of the Theban beginnings of this grand new kingdom has been recovered from a mix of information gathered from contem-porary texts, a few temple reliefs that reverently record the names and images of the royal predecessors, and the fragmented records of later chronicles that tell that the first monarch in this line of aspiring phar-aohs had been named Montuhotep – 'Montu' being the name of a local Theban god, and 'hotep' implying that his god was satisfied with him. That these same texts, however, record one of his royal names as *tepi'a*, which may be translated as 'the ancestor', gives this particular Montuhotep – now numbered Montuhotep I – a somewhat literary air.

Contemporary records of this aspiring royal line, alternatively, document three successive Theban princes who were all named Intef.

With their names set in royal cartouches and their accompanying titularies and epithets composed in a style that is closer to the texts in near-contemporary tomb chapels than those of Memphite times, they are a historian's joy. For in a few short phrases, the consecutive titularies of those three Theban princes seem to describe a single joint ambition of refounding the kingdom of the lower Nile: that of Intef I being *seher tawy*, 'he who has contented the two lands' – that is, the river's valley and its delta – that of Intef II being *wah'ankh*, or 'everlasting life', and that of Intef III being the 'victorious'.

The next monarch in the line was a real live Montuhotep – numbered II in modern histories – who was buried in a fine large tomb at Thebes that stands to this day. Remarkably, some of the names of this long-lived ruler were changed three times over, whilst further elements of the Memphite royal titulary that his Intef predecessors had not employed were revived. And these phrases further reflect the progress by which the Theban court was taking control of all the regions of the Memphite kingdom. So Montuhotep II 'he who sustains the idea of the two lands' later became Montuhotep II 'he who wears the crown of the delta region', and finally 'he who unites the two lands'. A man of many monuments, Montuhotep II was followed by two similarly named though far less documented rulers, namely Montuhotep III 'he who sustains his two lands' and Montuhotep IV 'the lord of the two lands of Re'.

Around 1980 BC, the Intefs and the Montuhoteps were followed by King Amenemhet, the founder of the northern residence of 'Amenemhet Itj-towy' – whose name the ancient scribes had swiftly abbreviated to the simpler 'Itj-towy'. And in his turn Amenemhet changed his prenomen from 'the unifier' to 'the one who has repeated births' – that is, from one who has re-joined the river's valley and its delta to one who has made another beginning. And his monuments mark a genuine return to Memphite ways. For in Amenemhet's time the location of the royal tomb was moved from the royal household's ancestral home at Thebes to sites in the region south of Memphis between the valley and the delta, where the new royal residence of Itj-towy had been established and where a great royal pyramid, the first to have been erected for more than two centuries, was built to house his burial.

Amenemhet's pyramid stands today near the pretty modern village

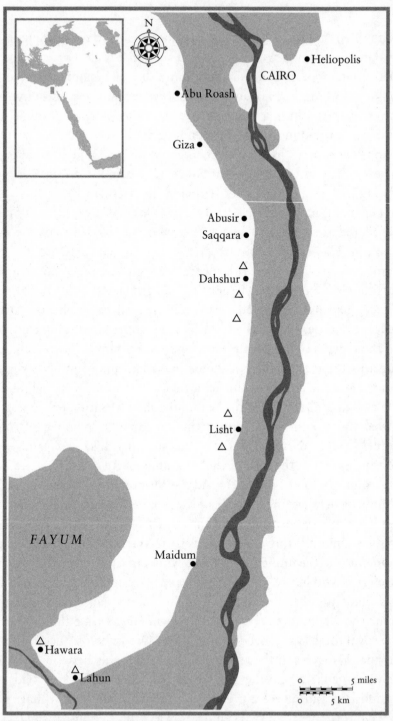

The locations of the major Middle Kingdom pyramids, as indicated by white triangles. Many other ruined pyramids lie within this area but some were never finished, others are yet unexcavated and the names of their intended owners are unknown.

of Lisht and the small white dome of the tomb of a local sheik. And the new pyramid was made a little larger than those of the last Memphite kings, which could still have been seen across the desert plain standing deep in the sands of south Saqqara, some fourteen miles to the north.

This careful re-establishment of the ways and manners of the court of Memphis continued during the reign of Amenemhet's successor, for whom another slightly larger pyramid was built a little over a mile away from that of his predecessor, on that same plain. The first of three monarchs to bear the name Senwosret, his prenomen – 'the one who has lived through the rebirth' – had similarly characterized his age as one of renaissance and revival.

Eight centuries on, the compiler of the Turin Canon acknowledged Amenemhet's founding of a new royal residence at Itj-towy as a time of decisive change in pharaonic history, for the broken list appears to describe the four Amenemhets and three Senwosrets who had ruled from that newly founded royal residence as the members of the first new royal house in a millennium of pharaohs, just as the Turin Canon (VI, 3) describes:

> TOTAL: kings of the residence of Itj-towy: eight kings, making 213 years, 1 month, 17 days.

THE KING, THE PALACE AND THE STATE – *DESIGNING A NEW KINGDOM*

> *If someone points to a chess piece and says 'This is the king'*
> *this does not tell him the use of this piece – how to move it,*
> *its importance, etcetera – unless he already knows the rules*
> *of the game . . .*
>
> Ludwig Wittgenstein. 1953

Although their names and the accompanying titularies seem to consistently portray the Intefs and Montuhoteps as holding the ambition to rule over a re-unified state, the kingdom that their successors eventually controlled was not defined as a bordered area of land. Just as the Memphite pharaohs could not have identified their kingdom upon a modern map, so neither Amenemhet I nor his courtiers would have understood the abstract idea of a nation as we understand that word today, as the term's absence from the Berlin dictionary along with many other fundamental terms of modern government neatly underlines. Not until classical times, indeed, would pharaonic scribes describe the valley of the lower Nile as the homeland of a nation, a people and a race; in earlier ages, the land beside the river was simply known as *kemet*, as the black land, the zone of silt. Only the romantic European concept of the nation state with a homeland, a compact indigenous population and a characterful ethnic entity led traditional historians to capitalize *Kemet* as 'The Black Land', as if it were the Federal Republic of Germany or the United States of America. *Kemet*, in fact, was neither the ancient name of the pharaonic state nor even a description of an abstract colour in a modern sense, but simply a description of the Nile's silt in opposition to the bright and sandy desert that lay beyond, the *djesret*, which is translated as the 'red land'. Another, similar, opposition is found in the two terms for mountain land and flat land, which contrasted the crags of the surrounding deserts with the plain of river silt.

The kingdom of the Intefs and Montuhoteps, like all other epochs of pharaonic courtly culture, was defined by the reach of their government and its various activities; by the extent of the settlements and farms, their herding and hunting lands, their mines and quarries and by the construction, maintenance and supply of a variety of cults. In this geography, the tombs, temples and residences of the kings and courtiers, the nodes of those supply lines, determined the kingdom's extent and character. And the term the ancient scribes used to describe their kingdom was the same as that which they used to describe the royal residence itself. So as you left or entered areas within the compass of that courtly culture you were said to pass through a door, the physical evidences of its extent being the numerous surviving so-called 'boundary stelae' that are engraved with the names of living kings on quarried stones and natural rocks, whose positions did not define the perimeters of a nation state but marked the extent of pharaonic control as it was exercised at different times on different desert roads and river banks.

The term *kemet* was not employed in the texts of the Old Kingdom. Only in the age of the Intefs and Montuhoteps, who, in their journey of reunification had travelled northwards up along the silty band within the Nile Valley, were the terms *kemet* and *djesret*, the black and red lands, first employed, and then only in formal texts. So, for example, a text in a tomb chapel at Dendera, close to Thebes, describes its owner as 'overseer of the black place, overseer of the red place'.

Several more novel terms for the pharaonic state came into play during the times of the re-founded kingdom. 'Sema Towy', for example – 'the joiner of the two lands' – along with the phrase that is commonly translated in the Champollionesque tradition as 'King of Upper and Lower Egypt' – king of the valley and the delta – or, more literally, reflecting the images of its elegant hieroglyphs, as 'king of the lands of the sedge and the bee'. This poetic visual opposition of a green reed – *juncus maritimus* – with a hard dry black and yellow insect – *vespa orientalis* – defines the two regions of the kingdom by opposing the rushy flatlands of the delta with the thin strip of the river's black silty valley set within the yellow desert. And here, once more, the ancient scribes are describing the physical characteristics of the region of the lower Nile as dualities, just as the valley landscape of the homeland of the new kings was itself a landscape of dualities.

After the founding of Itj-towy, the new royal residence from where the various state networks of tithing, building and offering were all controlled, the word 'residence' again became the usual term by which the kingdom was described. This was not a kingdom founded on abstract principles. Its activities alone provided both its earthly order and a kind of immortality by the creation of enduring monuments and the upkeep of cults of offering.

Nothing better demonstrates the depth of the Intefs' and Montuhoteps' particular ambitions in this respect, and nothing sets them further apart from other provincial leaders such as Ankhtifi, as their building programme. From the outset, the Theban court undertook the traditional activities of the ancient Memphite kingdom, the Intefs founding and re-establishing shrines and temples, modest buildings, mostly, of mud brick with portals made of stone, which were set up in various locations from Aswan to Abydos. Prominently engraved with their names set in royal cartouches, these small-scale works

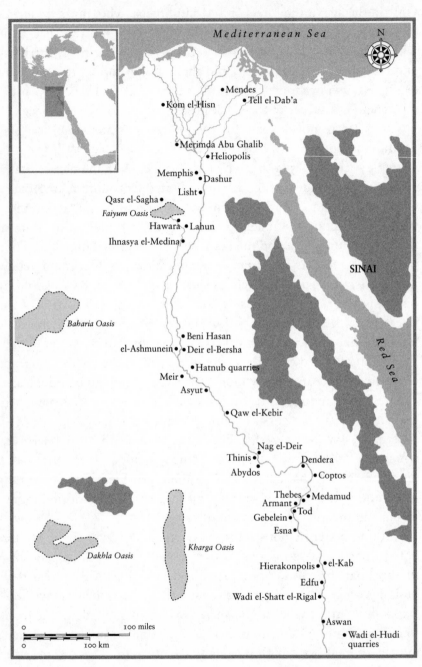

The locations of major Middle Kingdom sites.

represent the beginnings of the re-establishment of full pharaonic order throughout the region of the lower Nile. They are, as well, a fascinating archaeological record, for some of Egypt's most celebrated great temples were later set up where those little monuments were placed, so that the sandstone blocks which were quarried and decorated by the work gangs of the Intefs, typically columns, paving stones and doorways, are now mostly found as odd re-used blocks embedded in the lower sections of larger later monuments.

So on Elephantine Island, at the Nile's last cataract, a scattering of blocks show that a millennial archaic shrine had been covered over by a little temple that had been paved with sandstone slabs and whose roof had been supported by a dozen octagonal columns bearing the names of Intef II. In the following decades, the masons of Montuhotep III had erected another temple on the island; a half-century later, so its remains still tell, the craftsmen of Senwosret I had returned and elaborated and enlarged the little building that the builders of Intef II had set over the archaic shrine.

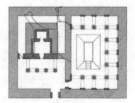

The century-long enlargement of an archaic rock shrine on Elephantine Island at Aswan, first under the three Intefs, then into the extended architecture of the temple of Mentuhotep II, which was built above the rocks and covered the earlier shrines. In its later phases, the mud brick of the central shrine was clad in stone but varied little in its size, being slightly less than six feet wide.

More of the Intefs' distinctive sandstone blocks have been found at Hierakonpolis, that huge archaic site, and also at the ancient settlements of Medamud and Tod on either side of Thebes. And at Armant, on the west bank of the river close to Tod, an old provincial temple of the times of the Memphite kings, the house of a local god, one Montu, from whom the Montuhoteps had derived their royal name, had been renewed and decorated with reliefs of their royal ancestors.

Similarly, at the ancient sites of Gebelein and Dendera the masons of Montuhotep II erected some splendid freestanding shrines, which, though they were dismantled and re-used in later times, have been reconstructed on paper from their remaining fragments. At Abydos, also, the Intefs and the Montuhoteps set stone shrines and gateways within the compound of the mud-brick temple of the local god Khentyamentiu, a programme of working that the courts of later kings consciously adopted and enlarged, as the fragments of a great granite offering altar sculpted by the craftsmen of Senwosret I and dedicated to his predecessor, Montuhotep III, attests. In those same times, the great desert plain behind the ancient Abydos temple became a burying ground and, perhaps, a place of pilgrimage, where an annual regatta in the manner of Ankhtifi's living festival at Hefat was followed by a procession of the living and the dead together, out across the low dunes of the windy desert to the subterranean graves of the archaic kings.

AT THE BEGINNING – *EASTERN THEBES*

> ... *the great island in the midst of the marsh on which the gods and the swallows alight*
>
> ... *the hill of creation; which rose up as the Benben rose within its enclosure in Heliopolis*
>
> From Pyramid Texts 519 and 600

The Nile was not always the mild slow-running river that it is today. Until the 1960s, when the High Dam checked its flow, the billowing brown torrent of the annual flood had swung violently through its valley edging the river's bed ever more towards its western side and shifting, dividing and dropping silty islands in its stream. Though hazardous to shipping, for they could enlarge or shrink or disappear in each successive flood, these new banks of silt, with their fast-growing stands of reed and rush and lush green grass, were swiftly colonized by local farmers. Animals were brought to graze upon them, small fields were laid out, crops were planted, and huts of dry reeds, mud and straw were built to shelter the farmers' families, as evening breezes carrying echelons of wild duck blew north along the river.

So pure, so verdant, were these fresh-made lands, the fine black earth, the clear water lapping at their little beaches, that they had long been a model of the world's beginnings, the first solid things which had appeared amidst a mass of formless water. Swallows, storks and hawks had rested on that virgin island and the gods of the pharaonic kingdom had come to live within the farmer's shelter, the measurements of which would be recorded on the walls of later temples built to house those self-same gods. The pattern of the reeds that grew upon those islands was reproduced within the gods' shrines at the centre of the temples and their foundations were marked out in the way that farmers laid out their fields and irrigation ditches, the river's silt measured with tightened cords and the resulting lines marked out with the farmers' traditional hoe-like tool. Then the newly dug foundation trenches were sprinkled with natron, a desert salt long used in mummification and also in the rites of purification celebrated by the priests of Memphis before they entered the temples and the tomb chapels. Thus, the land inside that fresh-drawn rectangle at the beginning of the world was suitable to house a god.

Given that the rites of establishing new temples had been pictured on temple walls since archaic times and that the fundamentals hardly changed throughout three millennia, it is inconceivable that the shrines and temples of the Intefs and the Montuhoteps had not been established according to those age-old rules. All of their monuments, however, excepting one, had been established close to older shrines or in the vicinity of cemeteries where similar rites would have already taken place. Just one of their foundations was set on virgin ground, upon an island in the river's stream that, in the course of its westward thrust, had been joined by further silt deposits to its eastern bank. And this small shrine was the beginning of the vast gathering of temples known today as Karnak, the largest of all pharaonic temple complexes and the home of ancient Egypt's great state god.

In common with the rest of the Intefs' monuments, the little temple that they built at Karnak is only represented now by some of their uninscribed yet distinctive slabs of sandstone and a single broken octagonal column of that same material which was extracted from the ruins of a later building in 1985. Standing, originally, no more than eight feet high, this slender, slightly wobbly shaft is similar to those erected by the same king within the temple at Elephantine and some of the other monuments of the Intefs and had probably formed part of a portico which had given access to a small structure with three shrines set side by side, each some ten or twelve feet long.

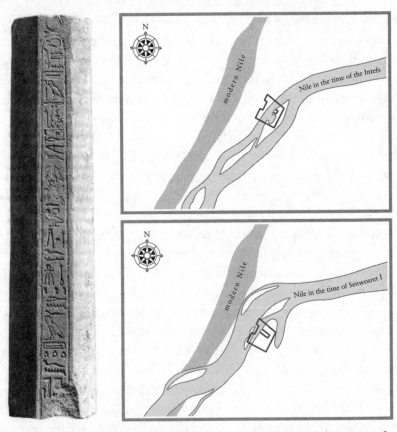

A column of Intef II from the first-known Karnak temple. It is just five feet high. The accompanying maps reconstruct the changing course of the river during the early phases of the temple's construction, as the island on which the Intefs' temple had been built was joined to the Nile's west bank by natural deposits of river silt. The black rectangle outlines the present position of the temple's walls, which are around a third of a mile long.

A broken line of sparkling hieroglyphs engraved down one face of this solitary column states the ambitions held within the generations of the Intefs and something also of how those southern princes had envisaged the re-unification and revival of the pharaonic state, a process that would be undertaken with the aid of gods quite different from the family of Memphite deities:

> [monument for] Amun-Re, lord of heaven, by the mighty of the land, pillar of victorious Thebes, the praised one, the beloved one, the protecting Horus, king of the sedge and the bee, the son of Re, Intef [II], the great one, the victorious one, born of Neferu, he made this monument on behalf of this god . . .

This remarkable inscription holds one of the first-known mentions of the composite deity Amun-Re, whose cult would dominate the pantheon of pharaonic gods throughout the following millennium and whose establishments grew to such a size that they came to play a central role within the history of the state. A scantily recorded deity in earlier times, Amun is hardly mentioned in the Pyramid Texts and had no earlier known connection with Thebes before the recent excavation of this column. Here, however, the scribes and craftsmen of Intef II had joined Amun in their lively hieroglyphs with the god Re of Heliopolis, whose very name had been incorporated into the names of many Memphite kings, their temples and their pyramids.

Joining the name of that great Memphite deity with that of Amun, whose name means 'the hidden one', was an entirely novel synthesis, as was the housing of this new god in a temple on new-made land, an island of creation in the heartland of the Intefs' kingdom. Nor was this merely an act of symbolism: it was a product of the most ancient courtly way of thinking in blocks of stone, in images and hieroglyphs. In its profoundest sense, it was the creation of a new reality. Combining the greatest god of the northern pharaohs with a previously little-known deity and housing this novel synthesis in the deep south of the country revitalised the ancient kingdom.

The cult of Amun-Re at Karnak grew along with the ambitions of the southern princes. From the beginning, there is some evidence of additions to the original little temple in the form of granite offering tables and doorframes, made by the craftsmen of both the Intefs and the Montuhoteps. Later evidence suggests that the ritual celebrated within the temple, if not perhaps the priesthood of itself, had been derived from the temples at Coptos, some twenty-five miles to the north of Thebes. These temples, whose origins had lain in deep pre-history, had been dignified by the Memphite kings and thrived during the interregnum but appear to have suffered something of an eclipse in the following generations; this perhaps because their priesthood had been removed to Thebes. At all events, by joining Re of Heliopolis, Amun, the hidden one and the rites of the temple of Min at Coptos, the court of Intef had created a composite deity that encompassed the categories of politics and theology, rite, ritual and statehood as one.

> As when a new Particle of Matter doth begin to exist ... which had before no Being; and this we call Creation.

RISING LIKE TEMPLES — *WESTERN THEBES*

> *I filled his temple with magnificent jars for offering libations. This is something that was not done by the forefathers ... I built temples [for the gods], set out their staircases and made their doorways permanent and established their offering endowments ...*
>
> *... you, you that are upon the earth, who love life and the passing of hate, you who will walk past this grave, say; a thousand bread and beer, oxen and fowl, alabaster vessels and garments, a thousand of all good things for the Horus wah'ankh, king of the sedge and the bee, son of Re: Intef the Great.*
>
> *From a grave stela of Intef II*

The tombs of the three Intefs, whose architecture was cut largely from living rock, had been astonishing affairs. Nowadays they are all but obliterated. Once, however, each of their enormous monuments had been entered from a little doorway opening onto a courtyard 1,000 feet and more in length and some 250 feet wide, with two rows of twenty-four

enormous four-square pillars standing at their ends supporting shadowed porticos. Short corridors cut into the centre of the back walls of
those porticos had opened into little pillared cult chambers and deep
burial shafts, whose dimensions suggest that their now-lost sarcophagi
were of considerable size. Dozens of smaller tombs were cut into the
long walls of these vast courtyards, the graves of courtiers attending on
those of their kings, and hundreds more tombs, miniature versions of
the three great royal monuments, lay all around them.

*The courtyard, offering chapel and tomb of Intef II, called the
Saff el-Kisasiya. Some 250 yards long, it was one of three
similar monuments set side by side.*

This architecture of great wide courtyards with lines of doughty
pillars at their endings, and an offering chapel and burial shaft cut
into the rock behind, is only found in the region around Thebes;
smaller and perhaps yet older versions of that same design, their columns built with mud brick, still stand at nearby Gebelein. Today, such
monuments are known as 'saff' or 'row' tombs, a term derived from
the pillars that are now their most distinctive remaining features.

Extending for a mile and more and set opposite their new-made
temple of Amun-Re, upon the river's eastern bank, the Intefs' vast
new burying ground was set low down on the valley's floor, its tombs

excavated in the cemented gravels of an enormous fan-shaped wash that, in earlier ages, desert floods had carried down the long and winding valley, whose head is now known as the Wadi Biban el-Moluk, the Valley of the Kings.

Once, the Intefs' splendid horizontal architectures, their columns and the open courts, had measured and manipulated the natural land-scape. Now they are not a sight for tourists. Half of the courtyards of those three great tombs have long-since vanished under cultivated fields or were sliced away in the nineteenth century by the digging of an irrigation canal, and most of what remains is buried underneath the concrete houses of the district of el-Tarif. Only a few of the columns at the head of the courtyard of the tomb of the first Intef still stand in sunlight. In the 1970s, however, a house-by-house investigation by a team of German egyptologists planned the outlines of all the tombs within the Intefs' cemetery. Small pieces of sarcophagi, cut from both limestone and sandstone, were all that remained of the royal burials. Fragments of a few well-made stelae had been set into some of the courtyards' walls alongside areas of white plaster that had been but sparsely decorated. Standing carbon-black in subterranean darkness, the better part of the great square columns of the three royal tombs are now trapped between a series of erratic cellars laced with water pipes and electric cables that serve the houses up above.

El-Tarif had been a cemetery different from all others, a space where the Intefs and their courtiers had celebrated their roles within their newly founded world. The pharaonic culture whose archaic ori-gins had lain in southern Egypt had come home again, the southern court injecting new life, new energies, new forms into those of the ancient long-lost court of Memphis.

With the passing of the Intefs, the craftsmen and designers of the next king, Montuhotep II, moved the location of the royal burial grounds some two miles from the wide white slopes of el-Tarif, up into a natural amphitheatre at the centre of the tawny massif that stands above the western bank of Thebes. And in its turn this warm and silent place became the centre of another huge necropolis, set in that unique landscape where the cliffs above reflect the sun's light and heat into the sand and rock below, drying and preserving everything that humankind has ever left within that wide arena.

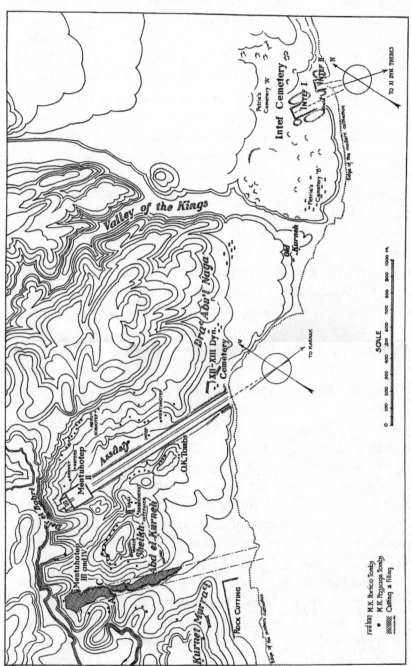

An adaptation of Winlock's map from his classic study of Middle Kingdom Thebes, showing the relationship of the Intefs' tombs to Montuhotep IIs temple at Deir el-Bahari. Nowadays, the unfinished temple labelled here as that of 'Mentuhotep III and IV' is attributed to Amenembet I.

Like the better part of the cliffs which frame the valley of the lower Nile, the Theban hills rise at their maximum extent for almost 1,000 feet and are composed of three limestone terraces, one atop the other. Beneath them lies a band of green-grey shale, a soft dense stratum with the appearance of the closed pages of a book, which when it is soaked in water turns to the oleaginous clay that the potters of the region have turned to their great advantage since prehistoric times.

It was this dark band at the bottom of the Theban cliffs that Montuhotep's workmen cut with heavy six-foot levers made from the trunks of acacia trees. Fire-hardened and employed with skill, such tools were more than a match for that soft shale. And they cut away the steeply angled band of scree and shale so that it seemed that the vertical fissures in the cliffs above ran straight ran down into the valley floor.

If the remnants of the monuments of the Intefs had something of the giddy air of Ankhtifi's tomb chapel about them, if all that southern architecture and its accompanying imagery seems brash and awkward in comparison with the quiet solemnity of the earlier work of the Memphite craftsmen, then the temple tomb that Montuhotep's craftsmen built at the foot of the Theban cliffs may be said to have returned to something of that earlier aesthetic, its long enclosure walls of stone and brick running out at angles from the bottom of those cliffs, in building lines as straight and perfect as those of a Memphite pyramid.

Those walls enclose a 200-yard-long man-made plain of fragmented shale that lies before the temple, and the corridor leading to Montuhotep's original burial runs deep into that carefully graded forecourt in the manner of the entrances to the burial chambers of the Memphite pyramids. Low and saff-like on the bright white plain, the temple's façade consists of two elegant terraces and a pillared temple standing behind them in the shadow of the cliffs. In contrast to the Memphite pyramids but like the Intefs' tombs, this novel monument does not dominate its landscape but sits within it. And the measured rhythms of its forms, its columns, ramps and terraces, give the cliffs that rise up all around it the scale and measure of a man-made thing.

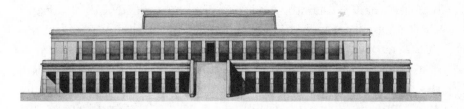

Winlock's restoration of the façade of Montuhotep's temple tomb at Deir el-Bahari. Another structure had crowned the great square podium at the centre of the upper terrace, but its form is presently unknown.

The starting point of Montuhotep's temple designers had been the open courts of the Intefs' saff tombs, with their long open courtyards and their columned rows beyond. Here, though, after you had walked up from the riverside along a straight stone causeway to the shaded temple, you would have passed through a carefully laid-out park of trees and flowerbeds. Sycamore figs, whose large green leaves provided an ample shade, and wispy acacias that provided none at all, were planted in circular pits cut into the desert rock in measured rows, each one filled with a gardener's mix of sand and silt brought from the fields below. Their roots and stumps still stand within those pits today.

Behind the measured lines of trees, the temple had risen like a half-memory of the earlier pyramid temples, a mix of Upper Egyptian sensitivities and Memphite architectural form. Echoing the three great saff tombs in the plain below, the temple's façade also consists of parallel rows of twenty-four columns. Now, though, there were two such rows set one above the other, the lower divided by a central ramp that rose up to the full height of the columns to give access to the second portico above. Behind this high façade was an ambulatory, a considerable construction consisting of 140 crystalline columns set in three lines, with at their centre a square and solid structure whose walls were decorated, like the porticoes of the façades, with royal relief.

An open court once lay beyond those lines of pillars, and from the centre of its sandstone pavement, a large passage ran straight down some 200 feet to a second burial chamber, an impressive crypt with walls of fine-cut alabaster. Set right underneath the soaring cliffs a hypostyle hall had lain beyond the open court, filled with a forest of 140 octagonal columns, each one, like the other columns of the monument, engraved with Montuhotep's names and titles. And at the rear of that great shaded hall, cut deep in the dark brown shale, there stood the temple sanctuary with offering altars and statues of the king and Amun-Re. Even in its ruin, the quiet archaic grandeur of this monument is overwhelming.

Nor was the extraordinary building ever finished. Following the ill-assorted labours of various nineteenth-century adventurers and excavators, a careful re-examination of the site by the American archaeologist Herbert Winlock detected three successive phases of construction, which he determined from both the structure of the surviving architecture and the simple fact that Montuhotep's thrice-changed name appeared in sequence on the three phases of his temple's architecture.

Later examinations have since established earlier structures at the site, though these might well reflect the presence of other older buildings that were swept away; a temple perhaps, or a cenotaph for ancestors. These vanished buildings may also be reflected in the strange asymmetry of the fine-made walls that radiate across the valley floor from Montuhotep's temple. The piles of weathered plaster that now lie along their edges, however, are not the remains of this long-lost architecture, simply the fragments of one of Cecil B. DeMille's film sets.

At all events, those strangely angled walls that demarcate the temple's forecourt, the changes in its architecture, the king's two burial chambers and the arrangements for the burials of more than thirty females of Montuhotep's household, tell of continuous creative change and innovation during the decades of its construction. Like the Step Pyramid's enclosure, like the pyramid and temples of King Wenis, like Karnak temple and all the other great grand building projects of pharaonic culture, Montuhotep's temple was always a work in progress. To that extent, the unique structure encapsulates the essence of the ancient state, which was itself an endless work in progress – a fact eerily underlined by Winlock's discovery within the temple's precincts of stone masons' mallets, copper chisels, hoes and picks and other tools, along with fifty labourers' baskets of woven palm-leaves all laid in line and filled with crumbled shale and debris from the building work. This was, indeed, a project without end.

Even in its ruin and with some of its finest panels of relief hauled off to decorate various museums and the walls of the country house of an Anglo-Irish lord, Montuhotep's temple is a synthesis of the universe in which its makers lived. Yet it is generally ignored today by the visitors walking up and down the heavily restored terraces of the adjacent temple of Queen Hatshepsut, where once had stood the early Christian monastery that provided this grandly sculpted rock bay with its modern name of Deir el-Bahari, 'the Northern Monastery'.

NORTH TO ITJ-TOWY – *MOVING CLOSE TO MEMPHIS*

The tombs of Montuhotep II's two successors are unknown. A short walk to the north of his temple tomb, however, ancient cuttings in a rock bay of similar size to that at Deir el-Bahari show that it too had been prepared to accommodate a monument like that of Montuhotep II, the grey-green shale cut back to the bottom of the limestone cliffs, and the form of a platform left standing on the valley floor the same size as the central solid square of Montuhotep's monument. And just as at Montuhotep's temple tomb, shafts for the burials of some of the women of the royal household had already been cut deep into this shaley platform, and a sloping corridor runs down through the platform's centre into an empty burial chamber most beautifully lined with blocks of fine white limestone.

A scatter of contemporary pottery and the contents of some nearby tomb chapels of courtiers show that work on this unfinished and unlettered monument was begun in the decades after the reign of Montuhotep II, and that it may well have been intended to house the burial of his eventual successor, King Amenemhet I. This, indeed, would nicely correspond with what little is known of the history of the court at those times, for Amenemhet I reigned for some thirty years and, as his thrice-changed epithets inform us, he appears to have instituted another era of revival when the royal residence was moved up to the north. It is likely, therefore, that this Theban tomb was left unfinished when the royal residence was relocated to a site south of ancient Memphis, where, in true renaissance spirit, the royal builders made Amenemhet I a pyramid.

Started late in Amenemhet's reign, around 1960 BC, the construction of his pyramid and its two associated temples was very hurried. When new, its fine limestone facing had concealed an ill-laid mix of local stone, mud brick and sand, an unstable combination which had moved and cracked under its own weight, a decline that with the aid of quarrymen and lime burners has reduced the monument to its present form of a dusty stone-studded hill. An unexpected bonus during its excavation was that Amenemhet's builders had borrowed blocks of stone from other older royal monuments. The passage to his burial chamber, for example, which lies beneath the present water table and has never been re-entered, had been closed in the traditional way of Memphite pyramids, with enormous granite plugs. Here, however, so their inscriptions tell, those hefty square-sectioned blocks had been removed from the temples of King Khafre at Giza some twenty miles to the north. And both the body of the pyramid and the fabric of its accompanying temples held more blocks of beautifully carved relief that had been brought from the tumbled monuments of Giza and Dahshur. Whether the translation of those rare and venerable relics had been made in a spirit of reverence or practicality, or in neither or in both, is impossible to say. At all events, Amenemhet's hasty pyramid had inadvertently preserved the largest and finest fragments of several long-vanished monuments.

No less than ten smaller pyramids, all of them designed in the Memphite manner to house the burials of some of the female members of the royal household, were built around the next pyramid in this new line, that of Senwosret I. Taking their cue from Amenemhet's pyramid, which stood a short distance to the north, Senwosret's masons devised another speedy system of construction, by which a series of parallel stone walls were built up inside the form of the rising pyramid, the gaps between them filled with field stone, mud brick, sand and plaster, and the whole faced once again, with blocks of fine white limestone. As the ancient cracks in its remaining casing stones still show, the system was no more successful than that employed within his predecessor's pyramid. Nonetheless, various methods of building soft-centred pyramids were adopted by no less than six successive kings. Thus, subsidence and stone robbery has transformed all the pyramids of the Itj-towy monarchs, the 200-year succession of Amenemhets and Senwosrets, into a scattered series of ruins that stand today like the buttes of Monument Valley, in the western deserts south of Memphis.

HELIOPOLIS AND ABYDOS — *RE AND OSIRIS*

Year 3, the 3rd month of the inundation, day 8, under the majesty of the Dual King: Kheperkare, Son of Re: Senwosret [I], true of voice, may he live forever.

The king appeared in the double-crown and a sitting took place in the audience hall, a consultation with his retinue, the courtiers of the palace and the officials of the private chambers . . .

'Look, I am planning works to be remembered, I shall make a monument for the future . . . I will build a temple in the precinct of [Re-] Horakhty . . .'

. . . and the [surveying] rope was let loose, the line put on the ground, and made into [the shape of] this mansion.

From the Berlin Leather Roll, c. 1970 BC

At the time that the work gangs and stone masons of the Itj-towy kings were making royal pyramids, they were also building temples which, though the best part of their fabric is now lost, their blocks either burnt in the limekilns or taken down and used as the fillings and foundations of later buildings, would leave indelible marks on all later phases of pharaonic history.

At Heliopolis, within the huge old sanctuary of Re-Horakhty, new temples were erected that are now represented only by the text on the so-called Berlin Leather Roll, by a plan scratched on a slip of stone, and by a single obelisk, the relic of a pair, standing in a Cairo park.

In the delta, where building stone had to be shipped in from the valley, all that remains of the temples of the Itj-towy kings are their building lines and some fragments of relief. In the valley also, where the Itj-towy temple-building programme had followed directly in the footsteps of that of the Intefs and the Montuhoteps, many building blocks hold parts of scenes that were engraved upon the walls of long-lost temples, one of whose pretty ruins stands within the modern town of Tod, near Thebes, where one block yet holds the names and images of their honoured predecessors, the Intefs and the Montuhoteps. And at Thebes itself, a grand temple was erected to replace the Intefs' little shrine for Amun-Re, but that, too, has all but disappeared.

Those lost temples signalled a considerable change, a revision and expansion, in the very nature of the court. For whilst some of them had simply re-housed the earlier and smaller temples built in the times of the later Memphite kingdom, one of them, at least, had given a grand new home to the new god Amun-Re at Karnak, whilst another had provided an obscure Memphite deity named Osiris with a temple such as he had never had before, within the venerable compound of the god Khentyamentiu at Abydos. Osiris' brand new home transformed Abydos into a site of national pilgrimage.

Unlike Re, a sun god who may be said to have had genuine archaic origins, who had been omnipresent throughout the Old Kingdom and whose very name had been incorporated into those of the sun temples and that of many Memphite kings, Osiris seems to have been a relative newcomer and to have sprung from nowhere. His first-known appearance is at Saqqara, in a private tomb chapel of the times of the Abusir kings, where he appears as an ill-defined deity and is described as a god of the delta town of Busiris and of Abydos, to the north of Thebes. As a powerful, rounded presence, however, Osiris makes a sudden grand appearance in the darkness of the Memphite pyramids, thus underlying the connection of the Pyramid Texts with the lost Memphite courtly archives, specifically, as some of Osiris' epithets within those texts describe, with the temples of Heliopolis. Osiris' ultimate origins, however, remain mysterious, as those of a deity should be. An authoritative dictionary of egyptology, for example, lists no less than thirteen well-argued scholarly alternatives for the origin of his name and thus, it is assumed, his root identity.

Both the new god Amun-Re and the mysterious Osiris became powerful national presences in the times of the Itj-towy kings. Like Amun-Re, Osiris is also described as having a dual geographic origin of delta and valley – a pan-state identity – in the same manner that the royal titularies describe pharaoh as king of the sedge and the bee, the delta and the valley. Nor were such identifications simple acts of piety: the sudden thrust to prominence of both Amun-Re and Osiris shows the Itj-towy court making careful, conscious choices about the nature of the state they were engaged in building.

Like Amun-Re, Osiris does not appear to have had a temple of his own in the times of the Memphite monarchy, his role within that kingdom presently defined by the Pyramid Texts' identification of the dead kings with Osiris – as 'the Osiris King so-and-so'. Outside those texts, however, outside the pyramids' interiors, the kings were always described, as were the courtiers in their tomb chapels, in terms of the roles they had fulfilled in life. The addition of the name of Osiris to that of the dead kings, therefore, appears to have identified that god as a fleeting presence, as an agent of transition from life through death to rebirth, a powerful role perhaps, but one that in Old Kingdom times seems to have not warranted the building of a separate temple for the god.

Nonetheless, both Osiris and Re were given a form and definition similar in some respects to those of the Itj-towy kings themselves. Holding the distinctive implements known as the crook and flail and wearing the high white crown of Upper Egypt, hundreds of royal statues standing in a wrapped-up mummy-like pose – the so-called 'Osiride' pose that later ages would identify as an attribute of that god – were attached to the columns of several temples, and they also line the pyramid causeways of the Itj-towy kings, where, so it appears, they stood as images of the king himself in transition, the king as Osiris on route to his tomb. And in an extension of that same condition, the masons of Senwosret I erected a temple for Osiris at Abydos, a major project that was continually restored and enlarged by the courts of the later Itj-towy kings.

From the beginning, Osiris' temple at Abydos was planned as a considerable monument; its surviving fragments show that its court-yards had once held lines of fifteen-foot-high red granite statues of

Two of the many so-called Osiride sculptures which had stood on either side of the causeway leading up to the pyramid of Senwosret I at Lisht. When complete, they were almost eight feet high.

Senwosret I standing in Osiris' pose. At the same time, the burial ground of the archaic kings, a gathering of huge brick subterranean tombs that lay in the desert a mile to the west of the new temple and had been burnt and plundered during the interregnum, were partially restored, and the tomb of one of those archaic rulers, a king named Djet who had lived almost 1,000 years before Senwosret's time, was identified as Osiris' tomb.

Later kings placed several statues in Osiris' tomb at Abydos. One such shows the god recumbent, dead, his penis and his person being restored to life by the gently flapping wings of the goddess Isis, Osiris' wife, in the guise of a hawk. Following Osiris' revivification, Isis will give birth to Horus, whose archaic image as a hawk had been the hieroglyph that had first identified the name of pharaoh. So after the interregnum, this Osiris, whose previous role had been to aid the rebirth of the Memphite kings, was promoted to a powerful sacral presence, an arbiter of the endless cycle of dying and rebirth, a god whose dark domain was emptied and refilled each day with the passage of the sun, each month with the new moon and each year with the annual flood. At Abydos, therefore, that god had been joined with the first pharaohs as a monarch in his own right, as Lord of Abydos and the ruler of the realm of death.

Osiris' continued presence at Abydos was assured in the age-old way, by rounds of offering and recitation and also by the collective ritual of an annual pilgrimage that was undertaken by both the living and the dead, a pilgrimage which, though the details of all such ancient mysteries are now little known or understood, appears to have had as their focus Osiris' archaic tomb out in the desert.

This vast millennial pilgrimage appears to have begun as the courtiers and state officials of the Itj-towy kings were laying down considerable cemeteries at Abydos, siting their tombs and funerary monuments to the north of the shallow valley that runs between the grave of Osiris and the enclosure of his temple, on sites first occupied by the graves of the time of the Montuhoteps, when the annual festival may only have had a local character. Many of the graves were marked with mud-brick superstructures holding beautifully sculpted limestone stelae that described their owners' roles within the state and named and pictured members of their families and households. At that same time, large numbers of vaulted mud-brick shrines and more simple graves were set upon the desert rise behind the temple, many of them similarly equipped with fine stone stelae, designed to stand as a presence at the annual pilgrimage for people who had been interred in other places but who, as part of their continuing existence in the kingdom after death, intended to continue making the annual pilgrimage to Abydos.

So the Itj-towy court transformed Osiris into a figure of state-wide and even, perhaps, popular devotion: 'I myself laid the bricks of this offering chapel at Abydos,' one of the small stelae informs us, and there were thousands of such monuments within those little shrines, more than half a mile of them clustered likes ants' nests along the desert track that led up to Osiris' tomb. During the past two centuries, however, most of those little shrines were broken down in a destructive search for their stelae, which are greatly prized by museums and collectors.

Beyond the archaic royal tombs, beyond Osiris' tomb, in the sands that run up to the foot of the fringing cliffs, there are no temples, tombs or cenotaphs at all, simply low dunes and a U-shaped gorge that leads up through the cliffs onto the high desert beyond. And this natural area in the cliffs became part of the powerful theatre that the Itj-towy court created at Abydos, for that lonely gorge is filled with softly singing sands whose sounds later scribes describe as the voices of the generations of the dead who have joined the annual pilgrimage to Abydos by desert caravan. Just as at Montuhotep's temple tomb at Deir el-Bahari, the Upper Egyptians' profound empathy with the landscape of their narrow valley, their desire to integrate rather than to dominate its forms, held the living and the dead in eerie equilibrium.

THE MANSIONS OF AMUN-RE – *THE FESTIVALS OF THEBES*

Of all the rebirths and innovations of the Itj-towy court, the one that had the most profound effect upon the history of pharaonic culture was the construction of a grand new temple for Amun-Re to replace the modest earlier monument of the Intefs and the Montuhoteps. Like all the other temples of those times, this building has all but disappeared, and yet its impact, its physical size, its scale and its alignments are yet held within the rectangle of open empty space that lies at the very heart of Karnak.

Built over and around the early simple shrine set up by the Intefs' stone masons, and changed, enlarged and modified over generations till it obtained its final form in the reign of Senwosret I, this great temple stood and served as the house of Amun-Re for some four centuries before the building gangs took down the better part of its limestone walls and re-used their blocks as the foundations and fillings of the walls of other buildings. Only in the early 1900s, during the restoration of those later buildings, were some of its beautifully carved exterior walls brought back into the light. Some of the prettiest of those blocks were exhibited in various museums along with the better-preserved portions of the sculptures that had once stood within the vanished temple. Less attractive pieces were placed in the magazines and storage areas built amongst Karnak's restored temples, which yet contain a treasure trove of sculpture and disembodied architectural fragments. In 1998, after studying those widely scattered fragments and combining the information they held with data from the re-excavation of the site on which Senwosret's temple had stood, the French archaeologist Luc Gabolde published a paper re-construction of the long-lost temple.

The Itj-towy designers appear to have taken a traditional Memphite plan as their basic model for the 'Mansion of Amun-Re', as Senwosret's temple was named, building a low rectangular struc-ture with a single central doorway that led first to an open courtyard and then to a series of small stone rooms arranged around a central shrine. In the age-old manner, the temple had been set inside a large, stout, rectangular mud-brick enclosure. And a settlement was built within that compound, its houses, streets and storerooms laid out in the strict orthography typical of state-constructed and state-supported communities since the age of the Giza kings.

The Mansion of Amun-Re was made of the finest limestone from the Tura quarries, which were close to Memphis. A hundred and thirty feet square and standing nearly twenty feet high, its river-facing façade had a shadowed portico supported by a row of twelve great square columns, echoing the Intefs' saff tombs. Here, however, each column had a colossal statue of King Senwosret attached to it, twelve great standing figures in Osiride pose. These, though, were images of the living pharaoh and had not held the attributes of Osiris in their hands, no crook and flail, but two so-called *ankh* signs, the hiero-glyphic sign of life.

A reconstruction of the façade of Senwosret I's temple at Karnak.
It is estimated to have been 140 feet wide.

After passing through that splendid portico and a great two-leaved cedar door framed by a high pink granite portal, one entered a bright rectangular court lined with columns similar in size to those along the portico, although without the standing figures of the king. More high doorways lay in the semi-darkness beyond that open court, each one separated by sets of wooden doors giving access to various storerooms holding the fine linens, incense, natron, bowls, dishes and cosmetics and the stores of offerings that the priests required to keep and cleanse the cult statue of Amun-Re as if it were a living king. Finally, set against the back wall of the temple amidst further rows of rooms and chambers and at the top of a flight of steps cut from a single splendid block of alabaster had stood, as Gabolde describes, the shrine of Amun-Re.

Marked now by the remnants of the alabaster shrine and some crumbling granite doorsills, the central axis of Senwosret's temple laid down the line which in later ages determined the placing of many of Karnak's grandest monuments: the orientation of its obelisks, its colossal pylons, its Hypostyle Hall. Set precisely on an azimuth of 116° 43', this axial building line was that of the rising sun at the winter solstice in the times of the Itj-towy kings, a precise concordance with one of the two moments in the year when sunrise appears to stand still – that is, when the sun rises at the same point on the horizon for two successive days – which chimes with the inscriptions that describe the Karnak temple as the 'Heliopolis of the South' – that is, as a second state observatory.

Thus Senwosret's temple appears to have served as one of the instruments by which a state-wide calendar had been re-set. That six of the twelve months of this calendar were named after Theban festivals further suggests that state time had been re-established at the centre of the newly founded state. At all events, aligning the warming light of the rising winter sun with the heart of Senwosret's temple was a powerful expression of the continuing search for cosmic harmony amidst the monuments of Thebes, for in earlier decades the temple tomb of Montuhotep II on the west bank had been similarly aligned.

Yet Montuhotep's temple tomb across the river was not the only monument in western Thebes whose central axis had been aligned to the winter solstice. The court designers of his shadowy successor, Montuhotep III, had similarly set the axis of a far more modest monument to the same azimuth and with yet greater precision. They, however, had not placed their temple in the river valley but high up on the horizon, on the very crest of the cliffs of western Thebes. A basic mud-brick structure with the usual three small chambers at its rear, the temple's façade consists of a distinctively angled pair of high walls and two so-called pylons, at that time an architectural novelty at Thebes whose forms had been adopted from the architecture of the entrances to the last of the Memphite pyramid temples. And still today, the gap between those ruined pylons notches the mountain's silhouette and marks the ancient azimuth of the winter solstice.

It is difficult today to appreciate the fundamental importance of marking the alignment of such events upon the earth. Until clocks were mounted in church towers and town halls, European life had been similarly ordered by the sun and seasons, which in their turn were precisely ordered by the observation of just such cosmic events as solstices, equinoxes and the movement of the stars.

Now, the site of pharaonic Thebes is one of the few places in the valley of the lower Nile where the river runs at ninety degrees to the azimuth of the winter equinox. Given that most pharaonic temples and tombs and, indeed, the patterns of the fields and most other spaces of pharaonic daily life had been orientated to the angle of the river's flow, Thebes was one of those rare places where cosmic and earthly geographies were as one. Unlike the astronomical precisions of the four colossal pyramids, each one of which holds its own cosmic alignments inside its tented architecture, at Thebes those same harmonies were held in the natural landscape. Thus, when you crossed the Nile at Thebes, when you journeyed from the quay of Karnak temple to the landing stage that led to Montuhotep's temple tomb at Deir el-Bahari, you undertook a perfect journey, balanced both in space and time.

Just such a cosmic excursion had been recorded in fine relief on a wall of Montuhotep's temple tomb, where the accompanying hieroglyphs had labelled it as a journey of 'Amun, lord of the two lands'. The scene had shown the king steering a little river boat, with a throne, a royal standard and a closed shrine set upon its deck – the shrine, presumably, containing the image of Amun-Re, the hidden god. Two generations later, a similar scene had been engraved upon a wall of Senwosret's Karnak temple, the king steering a small boat carrying the same group of objects. These are the first-known images of a voyage that in later centuries would become a primary event in the pharaonic calendar. Popularly known as the 'Feast of the Valley', it entailed a journey across land and water, part procession, part regatta, in which the statue of Amun-re's had left Karnak to visit the images of the gods housed in temples on the west bank of the river. From the beginning, the god's excursion had held huge significance; ledges high in the western cliffs still hold graffiti of the period of the Itj-towy kings recording the names of the priests of Karnak temple who had climbed up those cliffs to watch for the first signs, the clustered boats, the flash of the gilding on the god's shrine, that proclaimed the approach of Karnak's deity to Montuhotep II's temple tomb:

> The priest Neferabed. Giving praise to Amun, kissing the ground before the Lord of the Gods on his Festival . . . when he appears on the Day of Ferrying Over to the Valley of Nebhepetre [Montuhotep II].
>
> [written] by the priest of Amun, Neferabed

Though those first-known reliefs show the king crossing the river from Karnak to the west of Thebes on a single boat, the festival was soon elaborated and two state boats were employed. One was used to transport the royal entourage, the other to hold the statue of Amun-Re, which was enclosed within a golden shrine, set upon the deck of a model boat, that was carried between the temples on two stout poles supported by a band of a dozen priests, in the manner of a giant palanquin. Fifteen feet long, three feet wide, and in its later forms heavily draped and gilded, the model boat had an elaborately decorated prow, two long steering oars at its stern and statues and several courtly standards resting on its decks. Bobbing through the Theban landscape, shrouded in fine linens, fogged by clouds of incense and attended by a noisy, lively cortège, the passage of the golden shrine was that of the pharaonic cosmos.

Although there is no hard evidence of how this extraordinary confection had developed, an epithet of Montuhotep had described him as being 'in possession of the steering oar of the boat of Re', and a funerary stela of a priest of the time of Senwosret I had described how he had carried the Lord of the Gods 'upon my shoulders', which suggests that the festival had been developed during those intervening decades, a timespan underlined by the design of a small, stone square-columned kiosk made in Senwosret's reign that contains a central pedestal on which Amun-re's carrying bark had been rested during its travels through the Theban landscape. Two low staircases on either side of this pedestal had enabled those carrying the bark to move easily through the little kiosk; a groove deep into the centre of the stairs having been cut so it is said, by the hull of the bark as it had been dragged into its position. At all events, the gilded shrine, the hidden god, the statues, oars and hefty model bark would have been a mighty load in the Egyptian summer, and the heavily costumed carrying priests would have been pleased to take a rest.

Extracted from the foundations of later buildings, with its blocks in a near perfect state of preservation, this little kiosk, a so-called bark shrine with every surface of its harmonious architecture exquisitely engraved with hieroglyphs and images of kings and gods, is one of the greatest surviving works of pharaonic architecture. When the golden bark of Amun-Re had rested on its central pedestal, that gilded elegantly upcurving hull subtly framed by the long low rising lines of the kiosk's limestone stairways, it must have been one of the most remarkable architectural assemblies that humankind has ever made.

The kiosk's elegant inscriptions tell that a so-called Heb Sed festival had been held during Senwosret's reign. This was an elaborate set of archaic rites which, in the times of the Itj-towy kings, appears to have been celebrated when the monarch had passed some thirty years upon the throne. And that points to another purpose served by those grand processional monuments and the festivals that they had enframed, for Amun-Re's journey to Montuhotep's temple tomb rapidly multiplied to include a variety of other journeys, other festivals and other gods. Alongside the ancient daily rituals that surrounded both gods and kings, those great processionals became principal elements of pharaonic culture, and images of them were engraved upon the walls of Theban temples throughout the following millennium.

Even in the times of the Intefs and the Montuhoteps, the cosmic concordances of the Theban temples had been woven into an extended web of astronomical and topographical alliance embracing other gods in other temples.

One of these temples, a building identical in design and size to the tripartite shrine set on the crest of the western horizon, was established low down on the west bank of Thebes, a mile and a half to the south of Montuhotep II's temple tomb, at a site that is known today as Medinet Habu. It appears to have housed anther form of the god Amun, and as at Senwosret's Karnak temple and, indeed, the earlier temples at Heliopolis this temple contained the mound of primeval creation. Nor were these multiplications contradictory. Like the religious icons of today, each temple, every image of a god, each primeval mound, held its own unique validity. Elaborated and enlarged over two millennia and enclosed within the huge mud-brick walls of a royal mortuary temple, this jewel-like complex is the most perfect example of its kind in all Egypt, a miniature Karnak, with its oldest buildings at its centre and a series of courtyards, columns and pylons added over the following millennia to provide ever larger frames for the processions that gave such temples life and relevance.

Across the river, three miles to the east of Medinet Habu and directly opposite that little temple, another shrine of the same age appears to have been built on the site where Luxor temple presently stands. There are indications also that another processional way, a land route connecting the temples at Karnak and Luxor, had already been marked out in these times.

At all events, those four sites, Karnak and Deir el-Bahari, Luxor and Medinet Habu, became the nodes, the focal points, of later Theban festivals that are echoed to this day in the annual festival and procession in honour of a local Muslim saint, Sheik Abu el-Haggag, when the children of the modern City of Luxor are loaded onto three small Nile boats set on carts and lorries and taken in procession around the ancient temple.

Such water festivals appear to have been a southern phenomenon, a product of life within that narrow valley, the first-known record of such an event being that celebrated for the god Hemen, in the days of Ankhtifi at Mo'alla, another being the annual pilgrimage to Abydos. In the north the only processional boat rides that are recorded from the times of the Memphite kings are pharaoh's final journey from the residence to the royal pyramid. The early Theban kings, however, seem to have taken the notion of the water festival to the north, for a text from the time of Amenemhet II records that a river bark was carried in procession around the walls of Itj-towy.

Now, however, the Theban landscape and its temples contained the

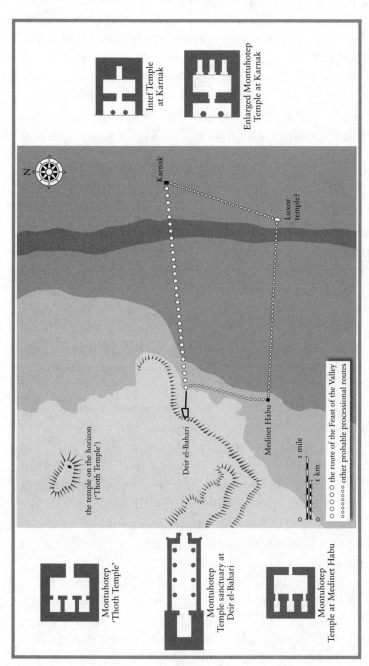

Intef Temple
at Karnak

Enlarged Montuhotep
Temple at Karnak

N

Karnak

Luxor
temple?

Deir el-Bahari

Medinet Habu

the temple on the horizon
('Thoth Temple')

1 mile

1 km

ooooo the route of the Feast of the Valley
oooooooo other probable processional routes

Montuhotep
'Thoth Temple'

Montuhotep
Temple sanctuary at
Deir el-Bahari

Montuhotep
Temple at Medinet Habu

Reconstructions of the plans of the central shrines of the early Theban temples and the routes of the processional ways by which most of them were joined. The Nile's path as shown is modern. Anciently, both Karnak and any hypothetical early temple located at modern-day Luxor had probably stood upon the river's bank (cf. the figure on p. 328). The dark grey area marks the present zone of cultivation.

mechanism of the pharaonic clock. Dozens of feasts and festivals, regattas and processions are recorded in the later Theban monuments: pharaonic jubilees, the accessions of new kings, the harvest and the coming flood, and journeys between the houses of many different gods – Min of Coptos, Sokar, Nefertem and Renenutet, Khnum and Shesmu, Re and Amun, Horus and Hathor, deities who, with their spouses and their various offspring, might change their characters and parentage from text to text, image to image, or combine and recombine to form synthetic gods like Amun-Re, an endless number of creations, an infinity of destinies.

Traditional scholars diligently reconstruct family trees within these pantheons and detect all manner of symbolisms within that dark dense forest. Yet the puzzles, inconsistencies and contradictions held in those cosmological entanglements never seem to have affected the joyous celebration of their rites, and only once in all pharaonic history was the chaos outlawed and a single dogma set up briefly in its place. For the most part, the living state was not a product of theory or theology but of the activities of rite and ritual, of offering, making and building. And in the times of the Itj-towy kings, the epicentre of those activities was the settlement anciently known as *Waset* or the 'Southern Heliopolis', which the Greeks would later describe as hundred-gated Thebes.

At the beginning, as the statues from the Giza temples make clear, the royal cult stood at the centre of the state. Although pharaoh's family of gods had also played a role, the monuments of the royal cult were made far larger and were better equipped than those of any of the gods, and the offices performed within the temples of those gods were largely based on those enacted in the royal residence and the temples of the royal cult. In the times of the Memphite kings, therefore, the kings alone bestrode the households of both humankind and the gods of state.

During the interregnum, this situation changed when local rulers took on the pharaonic role of tithing and offering. And in the process, the gods' roles had also changed, so the rise of the new kings, the Intefs, is mostly documented in the remains of the temples that they erected for a variety of gods throughout the southern settlements, whilst at Thebes, great Montuhotep is described as steering

Amun's bark, and shrines were erected beside his temple tomb for Amun and for the goddess Hathor.

These fundamental changes in the relationship of the rulers to their gods continue to be reflected in the building programmes of the later kings in whose names huge temples were erected for a range of deities, from newly promoted gods such as Amun-Re at Karnak and Osiris at Abydos, to those for older gods such as Bastet at Busiris in the delta, Min at Coptos and Satet at Aswan.

Whereas the construction of the Old Kingdom pyramids in the region between the valley and the delta had given form and substance to the pharaonic state, the scale and measure of that culture had southern prehistoric origins. And as the southern court had rebuilt that broken ancient kingdom, it had acted in a different way to its Memphite predecessors, a way attuned to life within the narrow valley. So the royal court had only travelled downstream back to Memphis after the state had been re-established, after they had re-centred the kingdom's sacral heart within the southlands, where nature itself, the river's valley rather than an abstract pyramid and its attendant temples, was the model of the perfected state.

That is why so many of the texts describe the processionals of Thebes as festivals of renewal, of jubilee, as occasions when the family of gods grant the living monarch, the living image of the state on earth, long years of rule. For those processions were now the primary occasions when the living kings joined with the gods in cosmic and geographic harmony, in that endless cycle of events in which the living and the dead, the sun, the seasons, the families of the gods and kings would all participate.

23

The Court of Thebes

THE KING'S MEN – *WADI EL-SHATT EL-RIGAL*

There exists, it is said, near Gebel Silsileh a valley in the midst of the desert, where the rocks preserve the names, cut by ancient travellers, of nearly all the kings of the XIth dynasty; in the tongue of the land that is called the Hunter's Rest . . .

Auguste Mariette, 1879

Sailing upstream from Luxor, the boat turns gently eastwards rounding the end of a ridge in the Sahara's limestone plateau before angling sharply south again, past Tod, Gebelein and Mo'alla and after forty miles or so the town of Esna with its bridge, lock and barrage. But then, as the boat glides past the ruin fields of Hierakonpolis and the dark walls of the ancient settlement of el-Kab, the landscape starts to change. The curtaining cliffs that had previously contained the valley's landscape start to pull back into a low horizon, and the river runs through a landscape of dark brown dune-covered sandstone ridges, through stripes of small green fields on narrow strips of silt, and lines of palm trees and acacias along the river's banks.

Exposed by the millennial flow of primeval Niles, the sandstone strata beyond the narrow fields are part of the formations that underlie much of the Sahara and the limestone cliffs along the edges of the river's valley that run from Esna up to Cairo. The broad blue river, which further north had irrigated fields two and three miles across, now feeds fields a fraction of that size, for sandstone is less permeable and far harder than the valley's limestone and its horizontal strata have trapped little of the river's silts.

Before the building of the High Dam at Aswan, travellers used to say that Nubia began some sixty miles north of Aswan, in this enchanted province where the river exchanged its deep limestone frame for a shallow sandstone pavement. Here, too, the spoken language in the villages began to change from Arabic to Nubian, and the homely dun mud dwellings of more northern regions gave way to elegant whitened houses that often stood amidst giant tumbled slabs of sandstone that seemed to have been strewn around like playing cards and which sometimes served as roofs for byres and houses.

Fifty miles from Aswan, just before the silt upon the west bank of the river entirely disappears and the sandstone strata folds up into the gorge of Gebel el-Silsila, which seems almost to choke the river in its course, there is a small sand-filled wadi just 150 feet wide. Unremarkable of itself – in earlier and wetter ages dozens of similar ravines had drained the edges of the Western Desert – this dry little valley, which is named Wadi el-Shatt el-Rigal, that is, the wadi of 'the lion men' or perhaps of 'the men of the embankment', snakes left and right for a mile and more on its way up into the desert. Weathered slabs of sandstone have tumbled from the wadi's sides and sit like piles of books half buried in the sand. At first, it seems to hold a small and empty space.

But there, uniquely, on its shaded northern side, a near vertical rock face revealed by an ancient collapse of stone has provided a pharaonic craftsman with a smooth dark canvas on which to advertise an image of their king. Here, then, and larger than life size – the largest indeed, of all known images of the pharaoh for whom the temple tomb of Deir el-Bahari was made – is Montuhotep II, uniter of the two lands, wearing the double crown of the valley and the delta, a pointed royal beard and a lion's tail belt. Holding a long stave in his left hand and a killing mace in his right, this fearsome image is accompanied by another, of a woman who the accompanying texts describe as his mother, I'ah. She stands behind her son in the same pose and at the same diminutive scale as do thousands of female companions in earlier pharaonic compositions. And images of two men stand in front of that of the great king, which is almost twice their size.

The drawing of this grand relief is confident and expansive, the forms carefully modelled in the manner of the day, the hieroglyphs, announcing peoples names and titles, well made and carefully designed. And the composition sits lightly on the surface of the rock, the work of its sculpting having cut through the sandstone's natural weathered surface of

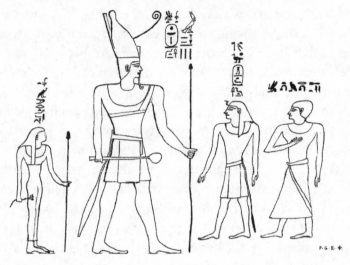

Montuhotep II in the Shatt el-Rigal. The king's image is life size and the group stands some six feet above present ground level. As its initials proclaim, the drawing is a joint work by Flinders Petrie and the eminent egyptologist Francis Llewellyn Griffiths.

rusty brown to give the images the lighter tint of more recently exposed stone. Unlike the images of the two men before the king, who stand uneasily on an ill-determined baseline, the feet of Montuhotep and his mother are placed on a horizontal fissure in the sandstone, which allied to the traditional skills of pharaonic draughtsmen bonds those images further to the surfaces on which they have been drawn. It is a powerful and controlling image and it fills the lonely little valley.

The nearest of the two images of men in front of Montuhotep appears to be another king, for he wears the royal uraeus on his forehead and his name, Intef, is enclosed in a cartouche and accompanied by royal epithets. This could well be Montuhotep's predecessor, Intef III, the husband of Queen I'ah, which would give the scene, like several others of that age, the quality of a memorial to a line of familial succession. The other figure, alternatively, wears the long kilt of a senior courtier and stands with his right arm clasped to his chest in a gesture of submission. This, the accompanying inscription tells, is Khety, who is entitled as a royal seal bearer.

Khety's figure appears once more in another smaller scene on the rocks of the Wadi el-Shatt el-Rigal. He is again shown waiting attendance on the king, who on this occasion is dressed in a costume generally associated with the celebration of a royal jubilee. Clearly, Khety was an important presence at King Montuhotep's court. A great tomb was made for him in the western cliffs of Thebes, whilst the titles that are recorded on some of his other monuments – a granite altar found at Karnak temple, a graffito at Aswan recording an expedition to the south – conjure images of Khety's presence in an exotic court: 'overseer of silver and gold, of lapis lazuli and turquoise', 'overseer of what is sealed in the entire land', 'director of the king's acquaintances', 'overseer of horn, hoof, feather and scale'.

Khety's name, in fact, was very common. It had been such a common name amongst the kings of Herakleopolis, indeed, that the Turin Canon describes their court as that of 'the house of Khety'. It is likely, therefore, that, along with several other courtiers of Montuhotep who were close to the king, Khety had northern roots. And that, in turn, gives the lie to the simple notion that Montuhotep's kingdom had been unified by conquest and brute force. It hints, rather, at some kind of joint arrangement between various local governorates to re-establish a single kingship throughout the region of the lower Nile. Nor would such a notion be absurd, for only the offices of a court operating along the length and breadth of the earlier Memphite kingdom – from the granite quarries at Aswan to the copper mines of Sinai – could have enabled the full operation of the pharaonic state and the provisioning, equipping and construction of such splendid monuments as Montuhotep's temple tomb at Deir el-Bahari.

SANDSTONE AND LIMESTONE

The priest, the controller of Hatnub, the sculptor in the royal residence and the superintendent of sculptors, User, son of Intef

Graffito 473, Wadi el-Shatt el-Rigal

Written in monumental eight-inch hieroglyphs, the lines translated in this epigraph are part of the largest of the texts inscribed upon the rocks of the Wadi el-Shatt el-Rigal. Despite the usual difficulties in understanding what such epithets and titles can tell about User, son of Intef, and his roles at court, they clearly contain references to royal sculpture and to the quarries of Hatnub in Middle Egypt, from where much of the fine veined alabaster used in the projects of almost every pharaoh over three millennia had been obtained.

Here, then, seems to be the answer to the puzzle of why such a gathering of courtly images should appear within a modest wadi that offers neither access to the ports on the Red Sea coast nor a route for desert caravans. For User was a courtier who was concerned with stone. And though the Wadi el-Shatt el-Rigal is not an obvious quarry site and none of its investigators have found the tell-tale marks of a quarryman's chisel on its rocks, their colour when freshly cut is lighter in tone than the coarser sandstones that were used in most pharaonic architecture, which were extracted for the most part from the quarries of Gebel el-Silsila, a few miles to the south of Wadi el-Shatt el-Rigal. Moreover, the sandstone blocks that have survived from the temples of both the Intefs and the Montuhoteps were cut from the same fine-grained distinctively coloured sandstone – which has been variously described as light pink or even slightly purple-tinted – as is that found in the vicinity of the Wadi el-Shatt el-Rigal. That stone, indeed, is a silent signature of the first architecture of the revived pharaonic state and was used in its various temples at Deir el-Bahari, Medinet Habu, Elephantine, Tod, Armant, Karnak and Abydos.

The builders of the Intefs and the Montuhoteps did not employ vast blocks of sandstone like those used in later monuments. Their masons, by comparison, cut relatively small neat elements of architecture, posts and beams, sills, lintels, ceiling blocks and pavements, which could be fashioned from loose rocks, such as are still lying in the Wadi el-Shatt el-Rigal, or from rock prised from the fissured cliffs in a manner akin to levering the shale from the cliffs of Thebes. In an age when the resources of the pharaonic state were yet developing, the fallen blocks lying in and around the Wadi el-Shatt el-Rigal would have provided a convenient way of acquiring building stone and at a site close to the river, whilst the full extent of the quantities of stone they shipped may well be hidden nowadays, by the meniscus of yellow windblown sand covering the wadi floor.

Coarse and fine, both varieties of southern sandstone were very well suited for building the high and heavy architecture of the pharaonic designers, and they survive extremely well in a desert climate even when the quarried blocks are set directly on damp silt. Egyptian limestone, alternatively, the other major building medium of pharaonic masons, is both lighter and softer than sandstone and thus easier for its quarrymen to extract and for its sculptors to work and to obtain a fine smooth finish. Yet, as the high cliffs cut by ancient Niles still amply demonstrate, the limestone of the lower valley of the Nile is far more susceptible to erosion than the hard bluff southern sandstone. Limestone, too, is more brittle, less elastic, and thus not as suited for use in lintels as it tends to spall and split. Its high salt content also renders it susceptible to humidity and ground water infiltration.

Sandstone's crystalline grain, however, does not permit anything like the same level of detail as fine limestone, so the finished sculpted surfaces of sandstone architecture were usually washed with plaster and the smaller details of the scenes and hieroglyphs either painted on in rich bright colours or, as at Montuhotep's temple tomb at Deir el-Bahari, the hieroglyphs which had been lightly engraved upon rows of columns were picked out in pale blue against a ground of white gypsum.

Here then is a practical intelligence at work. Southern sandstone had not been used by the stone masons of the court of Memphis. At Deir el-Bahari, however, Montuhotep's builders used Shatt el-Rigal sandstone for all 400-odd of its octagonal columns and the better part of the temple's doorways, and all of those building units were cut from slabs in which the grain runs vertically. The temple's paving stones and roofing blocks were cut from thinner sheets of lighter-bedded rock in which the grain runs horizontally. The fine reliefs upon the temple's walls, however, were engraved in the traditional medium of limestone; and not the local Theban limestone but an especially selected grey-beige stone shipped from east bank quarries twenty miles to the south of Thebes. Though relatively dull of finish, that imported stone was far easier to work with copper tools.

NAMES AND TITLES

According to its last investigators there are some 800 graffiti in the Wadi el-Shatt el-Rigal. Many of them are prehistoric images of animals, elephants, ostriches and giraffes, some of whose long necks sway just below King Montuhotep's feet. There are, as well, brief texts written in the times of kings who ruled in ages earlier and also later than that of Montuhotep II, and these are part of a continuum of such graffiti that appear throughout the region. Though most of the written graffiti were hastily scratched onto the rock, the select group of eight names that includes that of User of Hatnub are as elegantly engraved as the grand scene of Intef, Khety and the king. And all of them seem to record the names of high-ranking courtiers at Montuhotep's court, whose translated titles award them such posts as viziers and treasurers, seal bearers and stewards of 'what the sky gives and the earth creates'.

Hundreds upon hundreds of other texts provide further, wider ranges of names, titles and epithets from the time of the Montuhoteps. Offering apparently straightforward translations, they would appear to promise a detailed vision of the government that was emerging in that era. Once again, however, that promise has not been fulfilled; indeed, there is a wider range of theories about the order of this new-made state than those of earlier times.

Some things, however, are clear. Many of the 1,400 titles of Montuhotep's courtiers are quite different from those held by the courtiers of the earlier Memphite kings. Half of all the titles given in the inscriptions of the courtiers of the newly founded court appear to have been freshly invented and were only held by people who had lived in the first generations of the newly founded kingdom. These, therefore, might be more properly defined as epithets. Other titles, alternatively, appear to have been derived from those held by officials at the courts of provincial governors like Ankhtifi: yet others, including those considered to denote the highest authorities in the kingdom, appear to have been inherited from those of the regional court of Herakleopolis and echo, though often with scant regard to their original application, some of the highest titles in the earlier Memphite court.

The overall impression, therefore, is that the first kings of the remade state had ruled in the manner of provincial overlords, as father-governors, and that some of their courtiers had come from the households of provincial courts such as those of Thebes and Hierakonpolis and had performed a variety of tasks in and around the royal residence. That the venerable Memphite title commonly translated as 'vizier' only reappears in monuments of the time of Montuhotep II further suggests that the order of the state administration was itself refining, as the traditional state activities of tithing, offering and building were being revived throughout the kingdom.

As with the Memphite court, however, there remains the perennial problem of matching a title to a specific administrative post. The term that is frequently translated as 'treasurer', for example, is found in a wide variety of texts that name a range of individuals, yet those texts describe those treasurers as controlling building works at Abydos and stone and copper mining in the Sinai, as supervising the extraction of gemstones and building blocks from quarries in the high desert – tasks that one would not naturally associate with the post of treasurer. In similar fashion, the seals of people holding such venerable titles as 'vizier' and who are described as supervising activities within the largest temples in the kingdom have been excavated in meagre settlements in Nubia, whilst various 'royal stewards', 'priests' and 'overseers of the royal harem' are recorded as policing and managing royal estates or as overseeing royal building projects, whilst a courtier entitled 'overseer of the marsh dwellers', traditionally the title of the official charged with guarding the eastern and western marches of the delta, is named in a graffito at Aswan at the southern end of the kingdom, where he appears to have been involved in quarrying hard stone!

So the structure of the bureaucracy within this new, highly innovative kingdom, which oversaw and provisioned the quarrying of stone and the building and timetabling of barges, which mined and smelted the copper with which all of its splendid monuments were cut, is yet elusive. Only, perhaps, in the last half mile on the way up into the wide rock bay of Deir el-Bahari can something of the intrinsic order of that court be found, in both the contents and the positions of the

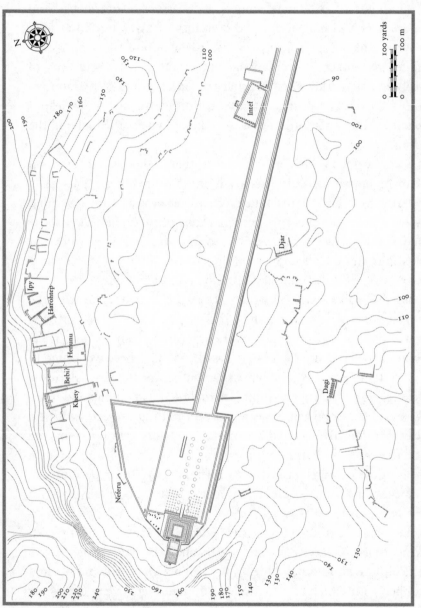

Deir el-Bahari in the early Middle Kingdom, showing the tombs of Montuhotep II's courtiers surrounding his temple's open courts and causeway. The black rectangles in and around his temple mark the tombs of female members of the royal household; the dotted circles in its main court, the beds of plants and trees.

monuments that were cut into the plain and the cliffs and hills surrounding Montuhotep's temple tomb.

THE COURT ASSEMBLED – *WESTERN THEBES*

The cemeteries of the Middle Kingdom courtiers at Deir el-Bahari
were created over some seventy years, from the time of the foundation of Montuhotep II's temple tomb to that of the court's departure
for Itj-towy and the north.

The most prominent of these tomb chapels, a line of twenty majestic monuments set side by side, was excavated in the high cliffs along
the north side of Deir el-Bahari; a row of up-ended saff-like courtyard tombs each one some thirty feet in width and a hundred yards
and more in length, all standing in attendance on Montuhotep's
temple tomb below. Half way up the bright white cliffs, the steep-sloping
courtyards of these twenty tombs end in a blank façade with a shadowed doorway at its centre. Each of those doorways opens into
spacious corridors, each with an offering chapel and the darkness of
a burial chamber beyond.

The courtyards of just three of these enormous tombs reach right
down onto the valley floor. They are largest in this line of tombs and
lie closest to the walled courtyard in front of Montuhotep's temple
tomb. As is frequently the case with pharaonic monuments, the name
of the owner of the largest of those three great tombs is lost. It is flanked
on either side, however, by the tombs of Khety and the courtier Henenu.

As his name suggests, Khety seems to have joined the Theban court
from Herakleopolis: he was, indeed, the first-known individual to
bear the venerable Memphite title of treasurer at the southern court.
As well as the image showing him attending King Montuhotep in the
Wadi el-Shatt el-Rigal, Khety appeared in the reliefs at that king's
temple tomb, which along with the size and location of his monument
underlines his close attachment to the throne.

The courtier's relationship with the royal house is further defined by
the fact that at least three of the women of Montuhotep's household,
who were buried within the precincts of his temple tomb, took linens

to their graves marked with Khety's name. For that implies that the women of Khety's household were close to those of the royal residence; though all the courtiers' households of those times had woven prodigious amounts of fine linens, including the nobles' lavish shrouds and mummy wrappings, few of their products are represented by name in royal burials.

The fringed selvage of a linen sheet, from the tomb of the Lady Henhenet at Deir el-Bahari.

Along with Khety and several other nobles, Henenu, a contemporary, was entitled a 'royal seal bearer', which, since seals were used to close storerooms, granaries and documents, was a common badge of office – some of the surviving fragments of the courtiers' tomb-chapel reliefs show these officials with simple roll seals strung around their necks. Indeed, in the 1960s, as the last of the great Deir el-Bahari tombs was excavated, a small alabaster box containing three royal roll seals slipped onto the antiquities market, all of them cast from an unusual lead and copper alloy which had allowed the molten mix to flow more freely than pure copper and thus preserve every detail of Montuhotep II's fine-drawn names.

One of three royal cylinder seals bearing the name of Montuhotep II, and the alabaster box in which they were kept. The seal is held in a golden mount.

Like Khety, Henenu was entitled an 'overseer of horn, hoof, feather and scale' and also, rather splendidly, of 'fowls that swim and fly' and of 'what is and what is not'. His chief title, however, appears to be that of steward, and he is the first-known person to have held that title in the new state. Though the literal translation of that title is 'overseer of the great house' and it appears amongst the titles of senior Itj-towy courtiers throughout their generations, what specific roles of government, if any, it may have signified is yet elusive; possibly, it was connected with the royal household and estates.

Henenu's name also appears in the inscriptions in the Wadi el-Shatt el-Rigal, in Montuhotep's temple tomb, and some linens from his household too were found in the grave of a female of the royal household at Montuhotep's temple tomb. Henenu out-lived Khety, serving at the court of Montuhotep's II's successor, the third king of that line, at which time inscriptions describe him leading caravans into the desert and undertaking sea voyages to the Land of Punt.

If, as seems most likely, a treasurer, steward and vizier had served as a triumvirate of senior courtiers both in the administration of the Montuhoteps and at the court of the later kings of Itj-towy, then the larger yet utterly anonymous tomb that lies between those of Khety and Henenu is likely to have been that of the vizier Bebi, who was their contemporary. At all events, Bebi was the second man within the new administration known to have held that ancient title; the tomb chapel of his predecessor, alternatively, is in an ancestral household cemetery near modern day Deir el-Bersha to the north of Thebes, where that vizier had also been a local governor. Bebi, therefore, would appear to have been a northern governor who had joined the southern court.

Along with Henenu and Khety, Bebi is also named in the Wadi el-Shatt el-Rigal inscriptions and also in the reliefs of Montuhotep's temple tomb, although the titles that describe him in those two locations do not include that of vizier, which suggests that, like Henenu, he too had a long career at court – an impression reinforced by the style of the surviving fragments of his tomb-chapel reliefs, which are the work of craftsmen of a later generation and display the increasing influence of the manners of the earlier Memphite studios rather then the distinctive Theban style of earlier generations.

Several other courtiers whose monuments stand in that stately line of cliff tombs at Deir el-Bahari are similarly named at Wadi el-Shatt el-Rigal, including some of those who lived and worked in later generations. Though still employing the same long sloping courtyards and the same internal architecture, these later tombs had additional chambers quarried into them. A chamber, for example, was sometimes cut into the floor of the entrance corridor, a rough-cut room to house wooden models like those introduced in the times of the interregnum to represent some of the scenes which had been engraved upon the walls of the Memphite tomb chapels. Other chambers were cut into the sides of the tombs' long courtyards. Some of these additional rooms were made to house the specialized equipment, the salt and sawdust, the funerary beds, the aromatic oils, the cloth and rags, that had been used in the processes of the courtiers' embalming. Other chambers were simply used as small subsidiary tombs, the burial places of the courtiers' factotums, the managers of their households, whose crypts were set in the manner of the subsidiary tombs that had been cut into the courtyards of the earlier tombs of the three Intefs.

So a modest crypt was cut into the causeway of the courtyard of the tomb of Henenu's successor at the court, the steward Mekhet-re, who, though he had been named in the Wadi el-Shatt el-Rigal inscriptions, had relocated generations later to the court of Itj-towy. And that small courtyard grave at Thebes had held the burial of Mekhet-re's estate manager, a man named Wah, whose mummy, wrapped in a thousand-yard cocoon of fine white linens, was decorated with jewellery. Found in the early 1920s during Winlock's excavations, Wah's exquisite treasures now decorate the Metropolitan Museum in New York.

THE ROYAL HOUSEHOLD

The architecture of the tombs that were set around the plain of Deir el-Bahari and beside the causeway of Montuhotep's temple tomb further echo the manner of older saff-style tombs, in that they have rows of square-sectioned columns at the ending of their courtyards announcing the position of the central corridor that leads to the tomb chapel and the burial chamber beyond. Quarried from the shale and the unstable rock that underlies the surrounding cliffs, the columns and corridors of these tombs were sometimes reinforced with mud brick and plaster, onto which local draughtsmen painted directly in a relatively unsophisticated style. The corridors and chambers in the tombs in the cliffs above, on the other hand, were usually lined with finest limestone and carved in the most elegant manner of the times.

The varying ages of these monuments, the growing sophistication of the reliefs and paintings made by the craftsmen of the newly founded court, show the early development of skills and sensitivities that would lead in the following centuries to the production of some of the finest examples of all pharaonic craftsmanship. And this despite the fact that, as Norman de Garis Davies, one of the greatest epigraphers, remarks, both Montuhotep's temple tomb and those of his courtiers 'are wrecks of their former beauty', and their qualities are now mostly displayed in exquisite fragments exhibited in the museums of the world.

These growing courtly skills were lavished on the offering altars and the sarcophagi of the women of the royal household, who were buried within Montuhotep's temple, many of their tomb shafts being hidden underneath the pavement of its upper platform. And their partial survival is remarkable, for scarcely any evidence of the burials of the females of the courtiers' households appears to have survived.

In many ways, the overall order of burial at Deir el-Bahari is a continuation of the royal cemeteries of earlier ages, with the monuments of the royal household set close to those of the courtiers, who stand at a respectful distance. There is a lively air of domesticity, however, in the graves of the royal household at Deir el-Bahari, one reminiscent of the earlier provincial tombs but set within the archaic elegance of the beginning of the renewal of fine court style. Here lay the monuments of Kawit, Ashayet, Henhenet, Kemsit, Sadeh, Mayet and a dozen other women of the court. Although their shrines were mostly shattered, a few of their burials were found intact. Some of the sarcophagi are engraved with beautiful reliefs of servants dressing and feeding the women in the royal residence, with images of the cows that provided those queens with milk to drink and of manservants who pour the milk into shallow bowls, as women standing behind their mistresses' chairs set curls into the elaborate wigs of the period. And all the while, beautiful, bejewelled and sheathed in the finest linen, the women of the royal household sit like archaic pompadours, their mirrors in their hands, as the palace servants go about their tasks around them.

Not all of the women of the royal household who were buried in the enclosure of Montuhotep II's temple tomb appear to have the same roles within the court. Some may have served as priests to the king, who on occasion appears to be equated with Amun, Min or other gods. Other women appear to be named as daughters or as consorts; hennaed and tattooed, one of the surviving mummies, at least, has the tattoos of a dancing girl. Models of just such figures, made of bright blue faience, their pubis and joints tattooed in the same distinctive dotted patterns, accompany some of the burials of the male members of lesser households. But all these courtly women bear the titles that are traditionally translated as 'king's wife, whom he loves', and most are graced with epithets describing them as possessing charm, as fresh, young and fragrant, as lovable 'royal ornaments'. None of these epithets were awarded to members of the households of the courtiers whose tombs lie at a respectful distance outside the royal domain.

Three contemporary dolls of blue faience showing the patterns of tattooing at Montuhotep's court, along with necklaces, amulets and waistbands of beads and cowrie shells.

Like Ankhtifi's tomb chapel and other monuments of the inter-regnum, although elegant, these female burials also have a homely air. Just as burial linens from the households of Khety, Bebi and Henenu and some other courtiers suggest close relationships between the royal residence and the households of some of the courtiers, so, once again, the impression is that the pharaonic court was based on an intense alliance between a few noble households, an alliance in which kings ruled by tacit if not formal, acclamation; by reciprocity rather than by brute force or a dictatorship. Winlock's thorough clearance of the courtiers' shattered cemeteries, moreover, brought further vivid evidence of this courtly domesticity, and also of its fundamentally rural nature, back into the light.

Following the half-century-long reign of Montuhotep II, the line of courtyard tombs had filled the northern cliffs at Deir el-Bahari, and several courtiers had set their monuments in other places. So the enormous courtyard tomb of the royal steward Mekhet-re was situated in the cliffs in the adjacent valley to that of Deir el-Bahari, high above the temple tomb that would be left unfinished by Montuhotep II's successors when the court had left for Itj-towy. And there it was in a little chamber cut into the floor of that tomb's enormous entrance corridor that Winlock's excavators uncovered a marvellous group of wooden models stacked and mostly boxed just as the burial party had left them; three-dimensional representations of the traditional scenes of so-called 'daily' life and of the carrying of offerings and grave goods to the tomb, scenes which had been painted and engraved upon the walls of pharaonic tomb chapels for many centuries.

Some of Mekhet-re's models show him at home: a finely modelled image of the man shows him seated at the portico of his house with his son beside him, watching herdsmen guiding black-, brown- and white-spotted cattle past the sharp eye of his accounting scribes; another has Mekhet-re aboard his splendid swing-hulled boats with a fleet of smaller vessels in attendance, one with musicians, another with a working kitchen, and all the boats with their sails furled and rows of oarsmen powering them upstream. With a marvellous simplicity, other models show the workshop of Mekhet-re's carpenter, his fishermen's skiffs, his household's brewery and weaving studio, its gardens, a cattle byre and butchery; the activities of a considerable country house jostling in models so realistic, so engaging, that they seem to breathe the living air of ancient Thebes. So well made, indeed, are these little tableaux that Winlock's descriptions of their detail have become standard references to such diverse subjects as the design of pharaonic houses, orchards and gardens, of weaving studios, boat rigging, brewing and baking, slaughtering and carpentry.

When Winlock had first found them, the impressions of the sweating hands that had carried Mekhet-re's model world into their small dark resting place 4,000 years before could still be seen, and the dust and flyblow that had lain on them at that time showed that they had stood in a living environment for several years before they had been entombed. Presumably they had been lodged within the household of Mekhet-re himself, tangible evidence of his place within the ancient scheme of things, which would suggest that the innumerable representations of similar scenes in pharaonic tomb chapels may well have performed similarly affirmative roles for the tombs' eventual occupants whilst they had yet lived.

The weaving studio of a courtly household.

A FARMER'S ARCHIVE – *THE HEQANAKHT PAPYRI*

Standing on Deir el-Bahari's cliffs amidst that bright white silence under that faience sky, it is hard to imagine that same spare landscape alive with priests and offering bearers, craftsmen and quarry workers. Yet as Winlock and his enormous teams of excavators worked through the remnants of its ancient cemeteries, those lost pharaonic industries were part-revived by the recovery of scanty fragments of those ancient lives: accounts, letters and prayers inscribed on bundles of papyri, slips of stone and sherds of pottery.

In 'a cranny of a little tomb' close to the courtyard of the courtier Harhotep's monument in Deir el-Bahari's northern cliffs, Winlock's workmen found three scraps of writing. The first was an incomplete papyrus holding both a list of rations that had been distributed amongst a group of men and part of a hymn or prayer destined, presumably, for recitation in a nearby tomb chapel. The second papyrus fragment held part of a calendar of accounts, listing the quantities of dates and grain issued to some court officials. The third, inscribed in charcoal on a potsherd, was a letter purporting to have been composed by the deceased Harhotep but which is probably a brief exemplar of a formal letter that had been scratched out by a scribe for a pupil's benefit:

Harhotep speaks to Udja'a . . .

How are you? Are you alive, prosperous, and healthy? . . .
You are supported by Amen-Re, everyday,

says Harhotep justified [i.e. dead]

A similarly disparate group of documents was found hidden in another hole in the sloping courtyard of the tomb of Mekhet-re. This time, parts of another papyrus held a list of loaves of bread that had been distributed amongst a team of tomb makers: the overseer Sebekhotep and the overseers of the gangs of miners and labourers, their assistant, a draughtsman, four engravers, eight quarrymen and five sculptors – the latter, perhaps, the craftsmen who had outlined and engraved the exquisite reliefs and statues that had once decorated the royal steward's tomb chapel, of which but tiny fragments have survived.

The same papyrus also held another text, listing agricultural lands in various parts of the kingdom – lands, perhaps, that had been set aside to provide the living of a funerary priest and for his offerings at a tomb chapel. Another broken papyrus from the same small cache held a few lines of a letter that had informed its recipient of a delivery of geese and other fowl, which, as it had invoked one of the local gods of Herakleopolis, hints at the origins of the poultry and serves to underline the continuing connections between the Theban burying grounds and the new court at Itj-towy. Vizier Mekhet-re, indeed, appears to have been buried in his Theban tomb after the royal court had relocated to the north.

The most celebrated of these written caches, however, is a bundle of eight papyri which had been carelessly buried in the rubble floor of a modest tomb excavated in the sides of the courtyard of one of the huge courtier's tombs on the northern slopes of Deir el-Bahari, that of a vizier named Ipy, a near contemporary of Mekhet-re.

Neatly written in vertical columns of jet black ink on sheets of papyri ten and eleven inches high, the cache held some workaday accounts and five letters concerning the household and the lands of one Heqanakht. All the documents had been made ready for dispatch: some had been tightly rolled, others folded and refolded in the manner of a miniature map so that they had looked like small hard cushions. Two of the papyri, indeed, were on discovery still ready for dispatch, still tightly closed, addressed, tied up with string and sealed with two small lumps of clay impressed with an oval seal.

Together with the other debris found in the same spread of rubble that lay across the chamber floor – the fragments of a wooden box that had once held blocks of ink, a blank papyrus and the pith of some papyrus stems, a ball of fine linen string for tying letters and a cake of fine-sieved sealing mud – it appeared that Winlock's excavators had found part of the contents of a scribal office which had been swept away and buried in the floor amidst a mass of dust and rubble when the little tomb had been readied for a burial. That such scribal offices had, indeed, existed within the Deir el-Bahari cemeteries of

Signed, sealed but never delivered, this folded letter from the Deir el-Bahari archive is addressed to one of Heqanakht's neighbours and concerns their joint dealings in oil and wheat.

that age finds confirmation in the model letter that Winlock's team uncovered at the nearby tomb of the courtier Harhotep.

All of Heqanakht's eight documents appear to have been written within a short period of time in the first decade of the reign of Senwosret I – some thirty years, that is, after the court had left Thebes for Itj-towy. That his letters describe Heqanakht as a funeral priest and the little archive was discovered in the floor of a small tomb adjacent to the tomb of the vizier Ipy, who had flourished in the first decades of the Itj-towy kings, suggests that Heqanakht may have inherited the position of Ipy's funerary priest after the previous incumbent had died. Some of the documents, indeed, describe Heqanakht managing land close to Abydos, far away from his household's farm, which further suggests that those lands may have been part of a priestly living such as had been conferred on mortuary priests by the nobles since the times of the Memphite kings.

Three different hands have been detected in the hieratic script of those eight documents. Two long letters in a stubby, somewhat old-fashioned hand were probably written by Heqanakht himself, who also appears to have compiled some of the accounts. Portions of three letters, however, two of which are addressed to estate managers, are more formal in their address than Heqanakht's missives and appear to have been written by a professional scribe working from dictation. And one more hand, at least, appears in the accounting lists.

Unlike the letters of the scribe, which employ modes of address used at the court of Itj-towy, Heqanakht writes in an older manner with usages similar to those of the earlier Memphite court. So when he urges his household to be trusting and loyal, for example, he employs such venerable tropes as, 'I gave bread to the hungry', which appear in innumerable older texts, whilst his apparently dramatic remark that 'they are eating people here' is simply another literary phrase that need not be taken at face value. The better part of Heqanakht's writing, however, is vivid and direct, with little of the extravagant epistolary manner of professional scribes.

Though Heqanakht's accounts resemble those in the papyri found in the royal temples at Abusir, the life that they describe takes place on a far smaller stage. Heqanakht's world was rural, one born within the age of the Middle Eastern Neolithic. Just two major commodities are listed in his documents that were not directly concerned with food and food production – bolts of linen produced in his household's weaving studios and quantities of copper that must have been obtained elsewhere. All the members of his immediate family and most of the other people named in these letters and accounts worked directly on the land, either with the field crops or with the cattle: 'Northern barley is what you should sow on that parcel of land,' Heqanakht tells a farm manager, in the same manner as the later Roman authors and, indeed, Piers Plowman, and he continues with the order, 'Don't sow emmer there; unless it ends up being a high Nile, then you should sow it with emmer.' So the little archive offers a remarkable, indeed unique, glimpse of a practical Nile-side farmer ordering the affairs of his estates, raising cattle, recording his harvests in sacks of barley and emmer, in bundles of flax and stacks of wood, whilst synchronizing those activities with the traditional pharaonic farming calendar based upon the date of the rising of Sirius and the inundation of the Nile.

In common with most of the pharaonic population, Heqanakht's household was dependent on the produce that it farmed for its daily bread, and, as the translations show, his letters are peppered with exhortations to 'care' and to be 'diligent' and peremptory phrases such as 'now look here' and 'don't be neglectful', for Heqanakht is nagged by the anxiety that the coming inundation may be lower than the year before and the following harvest will be insufficient to feed his household and its dependents. 'Our rations are fixed for us in measure with the inundation. Endure . . . I've managed to keep you alive up to today.' Clearly, the farmer took his responsibilities as head of household and as its provider very seriously.

Employing a rhetorical style that sometimes seems akin to sarcasm and stinginess, such comments as 'Be very assiduous, since you eat my food', or 'Why must I nag you?' or 'Make sure the housemaid is thrown out . . .' have given Heqanakht a reputation as something of a grumpy bully, though in truth there are hardly any other documents of a similar type, so that translated tone may be misleading. At all events, the little archive provides an idiosyncratic picture of an absentee farmer worrying about a looming scarcity of water and provisions, urging fortitude and simultaneously attempting to control the kitchen dramas in his household.

Though the names of Heqanakht's properties are recorded in his correspondence, there is no indication of where many of them are to be found on the map of modern Egypt. Most scholars have assumed, as the letters were found at Thebes, that the farmer-priest had been a southerner and that his major landholdings and home had been close by. That some of the letters invoke the northern gods of Memphis and Herakleopolis, they presumed, was because Heqanakht had written them at Memphis or at the newly established court of Itj-towy. James Allen, however, the papyri's latest editor, detected a northern accent in Heqanakht's writings and has suggested that his farmstead was close to Memphis and Itj-towy. The letters and accounts, he considers, were composed at Thebes whilst Heqanakht was attempting to control his family business in the north at the same time that he was undertaking his duties in the south at Ipi's tomb, ministering daily to the vizier's cult and ensuring his continued presence in the Theban temples on days of feasting and festival.

By pharaonic standards the letters in Heqanakht's own hand are very long. Whereas translations of the majority of pharaonic letters that have survived may be rendered in translation in 300 words or less, some of Heqanakht's run to 800, one to more than 1,000. The longest of all is addressed to one Merisu, his estate manager and probably a son, who was in charge of Heqanakht's household in his absence. First, the letter deals with the business of the home farm, then with household problems. When Heqanakht writes to his mother, on the other hand, he deals primarily with his household. Twelve senior members of his extended family grouping are identified by name. As well as Merisu and his mother, Ipi, there are people that modern translators conventionally describe as 'aunts' and 'sisters', as 'brothers', 'sons' and 'daughters' as well as a woman who is variously described as Heqanakht's 'new bride' or 'concubine', according to the taste of the translator.

With the exception of a cattle herder and a farm manager, the people he continually names in the correspondence appear to be members of this intimate household, and he is especially affectionate towards his mother – 'Greet my mother Ipi, a thousand times, a million times!' He also worries indulgently about a son named Sneferu – 'there is nothing more important than him' – and scolds various members of his household for the manner in which they have treated his 'new bride [?]' – 'Now, what about this evil treatment? You go too far.' Time and again, however, his concern extends beyond the circle that the modern world would describe as his immediate family; 'All the people of my household,' he writes, 'are the same as my children.' A household, we glimpse, that included sharecropping farmers who were living on his land. So, though governing with what might now seem to be a stern assurance and a harsh tongue, the letters also show the farmer-priest engaged in caring for and controlling a self-sufficient farming community in which all its various members had a place at table.

Whilst the eight papyri provide a brilliant snapshot of lives lived in the pharaonic state on a far smaller scale than that at the pharaonic residence, they also show that the structure of Heqanakht's domain is essentially the same as that of the households of pharaoh and his courtiers. Indeed, the farmer's household has the same hierarchy and its members are involved in the same daily activities as those portrayed in the scenes within the nobles' tomb chapels and in the splendid models that Winlock found within the tomb of Mekhet-re.

Yet none of Heqanakht's documents give an indication of his role or position in the pharaonic state, and there is no mention of the king or of a courtier. Was his position of funerary priest an obligatory inheritance? Was his household typical of many others? Was he buried in one of the heavy, mostly anonymous wooden coffins of the period that have been found in their hundreds along the valley of the lower Nile? Or was he, alternatively, interred in a manner similar to the owners of many of the splendid provincial tombs of those same times, men whose titles suggest that they had played but modest roles in the pharaonic administrations yet had commanded sufficient resources to make fine monuments in the pharaonic manner. For as the fragmentary accounts found beside the tomb of Mekhet-re serve to underline, the creation of such splendid monuments had required the labours of relatively small gangs of workers and for limited periods of time. Within this wider picture, therefore, Heqanakht remains a mystery.

As with letters of all ages, both the senders and their recipients took their common world for granted and never for a moment thought it to be in need of explanation, so the context of many of the people and places the farmer-priest so vigorously conjures is similarly mysterious. So there is no indication of the number of people who lived within the orbit of Heqanakht's household nor whether or not the loans and rations lists of his accounts were provided to subsidiary households or to individuals. Once again, we come up against a common truth of ancient history. With an overall population in Heqanakht's day that is estimated at less than two million souls, most of his contemporaries have left no trace and are not represented in the cemeteries or the desert settlements that have been excavated. In common with the farmer-priest Heqanakht himself, beyond those eight fragile papyri they have all completely disappeared.

What remains, however, both from Heqanakht's small archive and from all the other surviving relics of his age, is the fundamental order of pharaonic culture. Like Heqanakht's, the households of the kings and courtiers were composed of a key senior group operating under a paterfamilias, a king, a nobleman, a local landowner. Quite unrelated to that central group as kin, other members of the household might work as scribes or managers, priests and courtiers, as shepherds, farm workers or house servants, in boatyards and in craftsmen's workshops, making monuments and tombs.

Heqanakht's household, of course, was not filled with such professionals. With many of its members working directly on the land, his family might well be described as subsistence farmers. Yet his literacy and book-keeping, the means and methods of his correspondence, and his interests right across the kingdom were all enabled by the machinery of the state. His use of copper, for example, whose extraction was beyond the resources of a private household, shows how the produce of the state had circulated throughout the kingdom. And Heqanakht had travelled as widely as the courtiers. Some fourteen place names are mentioned in Heqanakht's accounts, and though the locations of many of them are unknown the span of scholarly opinion places them close to the centres of Thebes, Abydos and Memphis. So, from his dealings with the living to his work at Deir el-Bahari serving the courtly dead, the order and the culture of the pharaonic kingdom had dominated the farmer-priest's life. It had, indeed, enabled his existence.

24

The Materials of State

The Court at Work

COPPER — *THE MINES OF SINAI*

Many of the materials that sanctified and empowered the core activities of pharaonic culture were foreign to the valley of the lower Nile. From its beginnings, pharaoh's Egypt had required coniferous timber for its coffins, boats and barges, exotic oils and incense for its temples and its dead, gold and hard stone, gems and copper from the surrounding deserts and ebony, ivory and exotic pelts from the south. So to re-instate the essence of that ancient order the officers of the new-made court had to travel north and south, east and west, re-opening mines and quarries outside the region of the lower Nile and retracing the routes by which the other essential ingredients of the courtly culture could be brought into the kingdom once again.

The single essential element was copper. Copper tools had shaped the pyramids, enabled the construction of state boats and barges, and cut the fine relief within the tomb chapels and temples of Giza, Abusir and Saqqara and all the other works of Memphite craftsmen. The better part of it had been obtained from the Levant and from mines and furnaces on the peninsula of Sinai.

If the scale of importation of copper from the Levant had been considerable, the output of the Sinai mines was and would again become enormous. The remaining slag heaps in the Wadi Nasb alone, a single valley in south-western Sinai, have been estimated at 100,000 tons and stretch for miles along the valley's sides. They are the product of some 3,000 furnaces, modest freestone structures made up of rows of fire boxes, each one some three to four feet long and two feet high, sited with such subtlety that with the use of

379

imported fuel and the aid of the prevailing winds they had easily attained the necessary temperatures – 1250 °C/2300 °F – required to render that region's high-quality ores into slag and copper.

Four pharaonic furnaces. The open flues are around a foot high; the dry-stone wall construction, some four feet deep.

Dramatic evidence of the re-opening of the Sinai copper mines in the times of the Montuhoteps and their subsequent enlargement under the Itj-towy kings was discovered in the 1990s at the modern resort of 'Ain Sukhna on the Red Sea Coast, where from the time of Khafre onwards the court of the Memphite pharaohs had operated a sizeable port. From the first generations of the new kingdom, the man-made caves that had been excavated in Memphite times to serve as magazines and chandleries were re-opened and put to use again.

Numerous inscriptions and graffiti at the site record the return of these state mining expeditions, some of them led by high officials such as the treasurer Ipy, who had succeeded Mekhet-re and who would later attain the title of vizier at the court of Itj-towy. The most ancient of these texts, though given the considerable building projects of his predecessors this was certainly not the first copper-mining expedition that the Theban court had sent to the southern Sinai, bears the name of the last Montuhotep, numbered IV. Here, however, beneath the name and image of that ruler, a brief text records the vague logistics of an expedition that had been mounted shortly after his accession to the throne at a time, presumably, when the court was in need of large quantities of copper for the new king's funerary monuments, just as many desert inscriptions underline:

> Year 1, arrival of the king's men; workforce: 3,000, to bring back turquoise, copper, bronze [?] and all fine products of the desert.

Whilst serving as it had in earlier centuries as a base for expeditions into southern Sinai, the port at 'Ain Sukhna also had its own copper-mining and smelting industry, an undertaking that the numerous expeditions of the Itj-towy kings would enlarge and improve, for the lines of copper furnaces of those times that still stand beside the port are larger and more efficient than those of Sinai.

Before the construction of a hotel complex and the modern coastal road, the isolated ancient site at 'Ain Sukhna – with its chandleries, its warehouses, its furnaces and all its other facilities – had lain undetected and remarkably intact beneath the windblown sand. Like those of Sinai, the furnaces of 'Ain Sukhna had been set along the sides of a small desert wadi. Here, though, the archaeologists were able to establish the ancient methods of working in such detail that they were able to replicate the processes of smelting, which had first reduced the copper ores, and the secondary processes in which the resulting mix of slag and copper globules had been crushed, sorted and re-heated in little crucibles by gangs of workers using ceramic-tipped blowpipes, a technique so simple yet so efficient that the resulting liquid metal could be cast in small ingots of remarkably pure metal.

Except for water and some copper ore, which may have been mined locally, virtually all the provisions and materials used at 'Ain Sukhna were transported to that desolate location from the region of the lower Nile. This was a considerable undertaking. It has been calculated, for example, that for the reduction and refinement of copper ore four times the weight of the resulting copper would have been required in fuel; analysis of the surviving charcoal from 'Ain Sukhna's desert furnaces shows that the wood which they consumed had been transported from the Nile Valley. The archaeologists also excavated bread ovens, some slaughterhouses and two dismantled sea-going boats still lying in the rock-cut magazines, all neatly stacked with their planks tied up in bundles. Here, too, a large pit was uncovered, whose distinctive shape, along with the numerous post holes set all around it, suggested that pharaoh's ship builders had used it as a form in which dismantled boats brought piecemeal from the Nile-side shipyards could be accurately and easily reassembled. To the modern eye, the sprawling site has what one of its archaeologists, Pierre Tallet, has described as a 'pre-industrial' appearance. 'Ain Sukhna was certainly a vital crossroad in the procurement of some of the materials required to make the monuments of the refounded kingdom. It was an entrepôt of the Itj-towy court that had received fuel and provisions, craftsmen, miners and the dismantled timbers of Byblos boats from the regions of the lower Nile and copper from Sinai, where mining had been resumed at a similar pace to that of the times of the later Memphite kings.

The best part of Sinai's ancient copper mines lie in the zone between the plateau of central Sinai and the wadis which run westwards from that high plain down to the coastal plain of el-Markha where the Memphite court had established a caravanserai and port. It is a much faulted and eroded landscape of jagged hills, mountains and wadis that appears, when seen from space, to resemble the hide of an old rhinoceros.

Sinai's copper ores were formed by the same high-pressured processes that had created the beds of sandstone and granite underlying the limestones of the Nile Valley. And later, the bad lands of south-western Sinai were eroded and shaped by the same diluvial rains as those that cut the valley of the Nile, the crystallization of its rust-red copper ores encouraging the formation of tell-tale streaks of oxides and bright green malachite that would signal to pharaoh's prospectors where the richest deposits were to be found. When the copper of those ores had mixed with other metals, alternatively, gemstones were occasionally created in those same processes, producing in the case of Sinai a characteristic blue-green turquoise, a high-shining stone that had been used by the craftsmen of the lower Nile long before the times of the first pharaohs. In consequence, perhaps, of the appearance of this fine stone in Sinai's dun-red sandstone cliffs, the region of the copper mines was awarded the somewhat misleading pharaonic name of the 'Terraces of Turquoise', the gemstone standing, it appears, as a courtly emblem of pharaonic interest and activity in those desolate mountains. Yet, although turquoise was a royal stone and the ancient miners' tunnels which trace its glittering seams may still be seen in Sinai, the prime target in that region's extensive exploitation by the officials of the pharaonic court was copper ore.

An off-road journey through these mountainous regions is still very hard: in the manner of his times, a scholar of the 1930s remarked that it was 'only possible with a considerable supply of food, camels

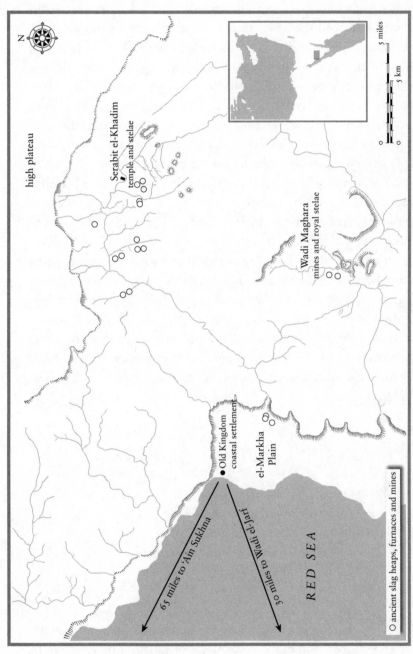

Pharaonic mines in south-western Sinai. Although turquoise was mined in many of these locations, copper was the prime objective. The locations of the main sites are indicated, but there was widespread ancient activity in this region, a further 3,000 mines and smelters having been recorded since the turn of the last century.

and Arabs'. The area is so large and so intractable, so dense with ancient mines, so laced with track ways and the ruins of antique settlements, that almost every new survey of the region uncovered inscriptions, huts and workings that were previously unknown.

The centre of those millennial activities was the Wadi Maghara, the 'valley of caves'. Here it was that the ancient mining expeditions cut the largest number of mine shafts, and, since the times when stone blocks were first used as building materials, millennia of court sculptors had engraved royal cartouches and unique and complex courtly scenes upon the glowering cliffs. Here as well is an extra-ordinarily diverse range of more modest engravings, texts and images recording the names and titles, invocations and images of expedition personnel from viziers to 'scorpion repellers', from miners to court treasurers, many of whose names and titles also appear across the sea, on the rocks of 'Ain Sukhna.

Walls and huts built in the times of the Itj-towy pharaohs run along the bottom of Wadi Maghara, and ancient track ways twist and turn above them to heights of 500 feet and more. Picks, pounders, mauls and grinding stones lay all around the workings and the mining settle-ments. Large numbers of beautiful globular storage jars from the workshops of the Itj-towy potters were buried in the floors of some of these ancient dwellings in the belief, it may be imagined, that the miners would return.

INCENSE – *HIGH SAHARA*

> *Now let them enter and before the gods*
> *Tender their holy prayers. Let the temples*
> *Burn bright with sacred fires, and the altars*
> *In hallowed clouds commend their swelling incense . . .*
> John Fletcher and William Shakespeare, c. 1614

To modern minds, and in comparison to such fundamental materials as stone and copper, the perfumed smoke of burning incense might seem superfluous to the burgeoning needs of a newly refounded state. Yet nowhere is the unflinching determination of the ancient court to obtain the traditional ingredients of court life more dramatically epitomized than at a recently discovered rock inscription in the Western Desert, at a location far beyond all previously recorded evidence of ancient Egyptian penetration of the Sahara, at that lonely point on modern maps where a dotted nexus of colonial cartography marks out the modern borders of Libya, Egypt and the Sudan.

Determined by British Imperial surveyors and confirmed during the infamous Berlin Conference of 1884–5, this remote convergence is marked by the mountainous outcrop of the Gebel Uweinat, a mysterious ring-shaped granite crust some fifteen miles across, with sandstone plateaux running off its eastern slopes that have been cut into deep valleys and are yet watered by desert springs. Other than a handful of border guards, no one now lives in this isolated region. It is so remote, indeed, that its splendid prehistoric rock drawings – memorials, perhaps, of Neolithic transhumance – went unnoticed until the 1920s, and the pharaonic images and texts accompanied by a grand cartouche of Montuhotep II were not discovered until 2008.

Expertly drawn and lightly pecked into the golden surface of a sandstone boulder lying on a rocky slope, this remarkable inscription is set beside a drawing of Montuhotep II enthroned beneath a royal

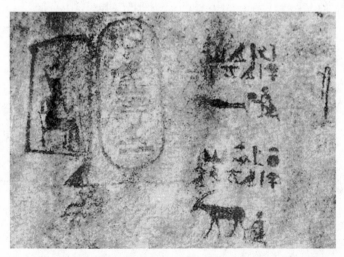

The courtly text of Montuhotep II that was inscribed upon a boulder on the Gebel Uweinat.

canopy. Two groups of fine-made hieroglyphs face this regal image. The upper text tells that the people of 'Yam' are bringing balls of incense to the royal audience; the lower, that the inhabitants of 'Tekhebet', who are announced by a splendid hieroglyph of a desert oryx, are presenting Montuhotep with something whose name has long-since been eroded by the wind. Set between the seated king and those two groups of text, a large cartouche spells out the royal name in somewhat modest hieroglyphs, as if to emphasize that the court scribes of the pharaoh 'Montuhotep, son of Re', for whom the great temple of Deir el-Bahari had been constructed, had also journeyed into distant deserts.

No further evidence of pharaonic caravans has been found upon the Gebel Uweinat, nor in any other such far-flung locations. Four hundred miles to the north and east, however, at Dakhla Oasis, inscriptions made a few generations later record that a certain Mery, a steward of the Itj-towy kings, had set out 'to find the people of the oasis'. These texts appear to stand as signposts to the Abu Ballas Trail, along which the caravans of the Memphite pharaohs had established depots of grain and water pots. So the discovery of Montuhotep's name at Gebel Uweinat, which is a grand extension of the direction of the Abu Ballas Trail, suggests that the enigmatic groups of signs known now as 'water mountains' that were engraved in the times of the Giza kings at two locations close to the Abu Ballas Trail may represent the crags and cascades of the Gebel Uweinat, whose name, indeed, is Arabic for 'the mountain of little springs'.

Perhaps those gallant ancient travellers had met the people of the desert at the Gebel Uweinat. There are, however, literary indications that they may have journeyed even further south across the desert, to

Some of the many 'water mountain' signs that were cut into the rocks beside the ancient caravan routes of the eastern Sahara.

Lake Chad, in epic caravans whose adventures came to serve other somewhat unexpected functions than the provision of courtly raw materials. For the physical realities of such heroic journeys through the Sahara to an enormous desert lake some ten times larger than it is today, with marshy shorelines, trees, rush and pythons, crocodiles and baboons, hippopotami and immeasurable quantities of fish and birds, may have entered the pharaonic consciousness in ways that modern travellers with GPS technologies and four-wheel drives cannot easily imagine. For those same landscapes seem to have formed the perimeters of a world view that was inhabited by both the living and the dead, landscapes that are described in the funerary texts within the Memphite pyramids and also in funerary monuments of the times of the Itj-towy kings. And in later ages, when the court scribes were engrossed in creating detailed literary explorations of the geographies of life and death, memories of those same epic journeys, those same landscapes, were elaborated and enlarged.

In the high desert, amongst the quietness of the rock and sand and the ever-present sense that you are literally standing at the edge of life, those half-recollected visions of the distant reed beds of a sparkling lake appear to have loomed in the pharaonic imagination. And in the times of the reviving kingdom, royal caravans and boats were revisiting the edges of that ancient Memphite universe to obtain the traditional ingredients that enabled the theatres in which the king and his appointed priests could ritually commune with other worlds. And with every trip outside the region of the lower Nile, with each voyage and each caravan, the edges of that ancient universe were revisited and touched again. And, thus confirmed, that ancient universe revived.

THE WONDERFUL THINGS OF PUNT

In the 1830s two pioneering egyptologists, travelling in separate camel caravans through Egypt's mountainous eastern deserts on their way to the Red Sea coast, found two stelae by a remote ancient well. Both were engraved with the courtly images and hieroglyphs of the time of the Itj-towy kings. After offering praise to Amenemhet II, who sat upon the throne of Horus and was beloved of the god of Coptos, the texts of one of these fine works named a ship's captain, Khentywer, whose boats had returned in safety to the Port of Saww after a voyage to the Land of Punt; two locations that in the 1830s were completely unknown.

The text upon the other stela recorded parts of the court career of the son of a provincial governor, one Khnumhotep, who 'grew up in the royal residence under the instruction of the king', who served as 'superintendent of the royal audience chamber' and who ended his long career at court, as other sources tell, as the vizier of Senwosret III. Like Captain Khentywer, Khnumhotep had long connections with places outside the lower valley of the Nile. Even as a young man he had appeared on the walls of his father's splendid tomb chapel in the cliff cemetery known as Beni Hasan in Middle Egypt, in a register that shows him bringing a group of brightly dressed foreigners into his father's presence: this is a much-celebrated scene that nineteenth-century reverends mistook for images of Joseph and his kin coming down to Egypt, but which in reality shows a Levantine caravan carrying bags of kohl, a powder widely used as a pigment of black eye paint which they had brought from the galena mines in the Eastern Desert.

In the 1970s, an Egyptian archaeological expedition returned to the desolate Red Sea coast close to the wadi where the stelae of Khentywer and Khnumhotep were found. There, at the mouth of the Wadi Gawasis, on a low ridge overlooking a modest bay that was rarely visited by Arab dhows, they discovered further traces of the ancient port of Saww. For on that low ridge, a half mile from the sea, Abdel Monem Sayed and his team excavated some forty inscribed potsherds, fragments of the records of the provisions – fish and figs, dates, meat, grain and beer – of an expedition which had been dispatched and supplied from Itj-towy during the reign of Senwosret III. A mission, so the texts described, that had been led by a certain Nebukaure, a court official who had overseen a staff of stewards, scribes and priests that had controlled the expedition.

Two fine stelae were also uncovered on that low ridge, the memorials of another expedition that had been undertaken in the twenty-fourth year of the reign of Senwosret I and had been led by Antefoker, a much-documented vizier of those times. The stelae described two different stages of the expedition. The first, on *terra firma*, concerned its preparation in the Nile Valley and the journey to the Red Sea coast, which had been overseen by an official named Ameny, who also appears in the records of other desert expeditions of the times. The expedition's second leg had consisted of a sea voyage to the Land of Punt that was led by a certain Ankhow. Both stelae were still standing in their original positions facing the sea and both were framed and supported by wedge-shaped blocks of stone which, Sayed suggested, had served as the anchors of Ankhow's boats.

In the absence of any firm archaeological evidence of an ancient port in the vicinity, however, and a pithy academic dispute concerning the true function of the so-called 'anchor stones' stemming from the ambiguous and often fragmentary nature of the hieroglyphic, Sayed's remarkable discoveries failed to convince traditional scholars that he had found the Port of Saww, for they had long since doubted that the ancient Egyptians had been adventurous enough to sail the rough waters of the Rea Sea or that a desert beach that was 150 miles from the Nile could have served as a pharaonic sea port. And in the 1990s that view was bolstered by a coastline survey of the area by a team of divers who failed to find any offshore underwater evidence of an ancient harbour. Nonetheless, the shapes of some of the ancient planks and beams that Sayed and his team had excavated were identified as the timbers of pharaonic boats, and in 2001 a joint expedition from Boston and Naples universities, led by Kathryn Bard and Rodolfo Fattovich, gathered a multinational team of archaeologists, archaeo-geologists, palaeo-biologists and geophysicists to conduct a thorough survey of the area. And they uncovered unequivocable evidence that a Red Sea port had been in operation at the mouth of the Wadi Gawasis in the times of the Itj-towy kings.

The true purpose of those contentious 'anchor stones' was quickly resolved. Similar to others that have been found in harbours by the Red Sea and the Mediterranean, the two distinctive chamfered holes in many of those stones had accommodated sea-going cables: one that had held the rope by which the anchor had been pulled sideways to disengage it from soft sea mud whilst the other had accommodated the rope by which the anchor had been lowered and lifted into the water.

The ancient harbour had been invisible to earlier travellers and archaeologists because it had been first choked and then entirely buried deep in desert sand, which had blown down along the Wadi Gawasis from the Eastern Desert more than a thousand years before. In pharaonic times, the desert ridge where Sayed had found the ostraca and stelae had stood at the mouth of a large lagoon fringed with mangrove swamps. And the ancient harbour had lain within that lost lagoon, half a mile inland from the modern shoreline.

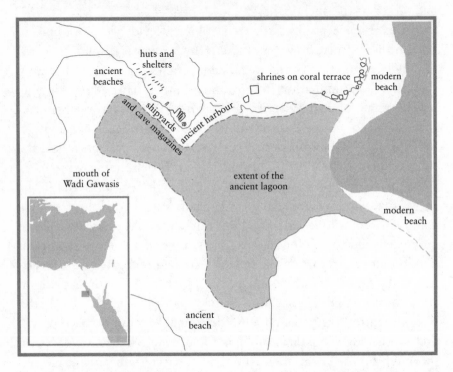

The ancient port at Wadi Gawasis. Hardly any permanent structures were erected at the site, the archaeologists locating and excavating simple shrines, man-made caves and areas of work and habitation.

Though rare fragments of pottery showed that the waterfront had been used in Old Kingdom times, and quantities of shells mixed with prehistoric tools of flint suggested yet earlier indigenous occupations, numerous inscriptions and the vast majority of the surviving ceramics showed that it had been most heavily occupied in the times of the Itj-towy kings.

9. Part of the western half of Anktifi's tomb chapel at Mo'alla. Two column texts appear in the foreground and the remnants of the painting of Ankhtifi's regatta upon the wall behind.

10. A fragment of Ankhtifi's regatta, with two boat crews paddling vigorously along. Prepared with a mix of mud and straw, the wall surface had a rough dun-coloured ground that gave the painted surfaces great vivacity and the draughtsmen's lighter pigments an unusual luminosity.

11. Head of a seated statue of Montuhotep II dressed in festal costume. The climax of a series of similar though smaller sandstone statues that were set around his Deir el-Bahari temple, this colossal work was found in darkness and alone inside a funerary chamber deep underneath the mortuary temple.

12. Montuhotep's temple tomb at Deir el-Bahari following its excavation and restoration during the first decades of the last century. The pits for the temple's grove of plants and trees still mark its courtyard; the hills beyond are grooved by the terraces of some near-contemporary nobles' tombs.

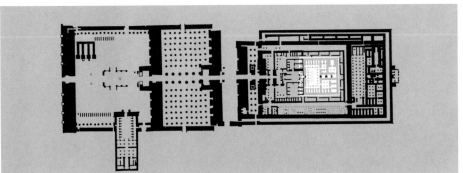

13. Jean Lauffray's excavation of the remains of Middle Kingdom Karnak in the winter of 1977–8.

14. Karnak temple's east–west axis as it stands today. The highlighted area on the plan, an open court some 45 yards square, has been overlaid with a tentative reconstruction of the plan of the lost temple of Senwosret I. The line of three black blocks within that plan are all that remains of the anciently dismantled monument and can be seen in the photograph above.

15. One of the row of colossal limestone statues that had stood along the front of Senwosret I's temple at Karnak and were subsequently re-used and buried in later buildings at the site.

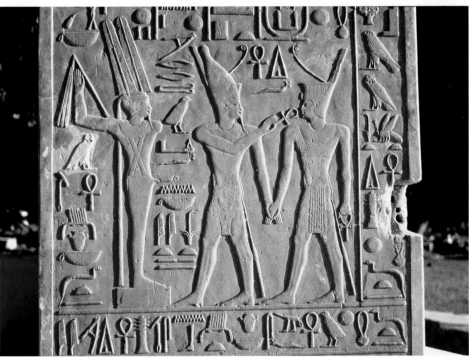

16. A shrine of Senwosret I that may once have housed the bark of Amun during its processions around Thebes. It has been entirely reconstructed from blocks buried within one of the great pylons of the later temple.

17. One of many fine liturgical scenes that cover the surfaces of Senwosret I's reconstructed shrine. It shows the king being led into the presence of the god Amun-Re by another deity, the god Atum, who gives him life in the form of the ankh hieroglyph.

18. A larger than life-sized granite statue of a king robed as a priest, which, on the basis of its similarity to other works bearing the name of Amenemhet III, is often described as a likeness of that king in old age. In both its costume and its use of form, however, this sophisticated work harks back to other and far older sculptures.

19. The subtle surfaces of this six-inch slip of quartzite appear to hold the volumes and textures of human skin. It is generally considered to be a likeness of Senwosret III.

Yet the harbour installations had been transient affairs, the accommodations of expeditions mounted at five- and ten-year intervals by the Itj-towy court. The ancient sailors, the archaeologists discovered, had camped upon a beach that presently lies inland but which in pharaonic times had also held the slipways of their boats. Here they recovered the scant remains of huts and tents and cooking fires and the remains of some of the fish bones, mostly sea bream and colourful Red Sea parrotfish, that the ancient expeditions had caught and cooked. Here too were the bones of donkeys, presumably those of some of the pack animals which had brought the sailors and their supplies through the desert to that lonely place. Above the beach and set up on another coral reef, the archaeologists uncovered traces of similarly light structures that had provided accommodations for some fifty people who, so the fragments of their pottery showed, appeared to have been of Nubian culture. Like some of the inhabitants of Gebelein in Ankhtifi's time, this group may have served the expeditions as guards and a militia, whilst the ostraca found by Sayed's team and the text of Antefoker's stela may also suggest that Nubians had taken part in the sea voyages.

More than thirty small limestone stelae have been recovered in these ongoing excavations. All of them are cut from Nile Valley limestone and some are uninscribed, in anticipation, it appears, of a successful voyage and a subsequent celebratory inscription that would have been engraved within the port. In common with the writings that describe other pharaonic expeditions, the texts on some of the stelae are out of the ordinary, some unique. A few praise the god Min of Coptos, the Nile-side settlement from which the overland stage of some of these expeditions appears to have begun; one holds a unique epithet of the god Amun: 'Amun of the sea'. Most of the Itj-towy pharaohs are named in these seaside texts, and they show that their courts had sent expeditions from the Port of Saww to the Land of Punt throughout successive reigns.

The niches carved for the accommodation of these small stelae show that they had been destined to be set in the lower terraces of coral beside the harbour in the lost lagoon. Others, however, grander monuments like those of Ankhow and Antefoker, had been set up above them on a higher coral terrace. And on the terraces beside the ancient entrance to the lagoon, above the harbour installations,

the sailors had marked the location of their home port on the coastline in the manner of a lighthouse, notching the low flat horizon
with a series of mounds and pavements and shrines, made of local
stone and fossil corals. At least one of those shrines had been roofed
with mangrove branches. Inside, the archaeologists found 700 conch
shells – this, perhaps, either evidence of offerings or an ancient example of a custom of modern-day Red Sea fishermen, who still embed
such shells in the walls of their seaside shelters.

As at the other pharaonic Red Sea ports, the people at the Port of
Saww had quarried a series of long deep cave-like magazines into the
terraces above the ancient beach. One of them yet holds heaps of ship
cables lying in tidy heaps upon the floor: thirty perfectly bundled
coils of thick rope, each one between sixty and a hundred feet long
and made, in the manner of the pyramid builders, from the stems of
Nile papyrus plants.

Desiccated fragments of sycamore figs, garlic, snails and crabs,
bulgur, barley and other grains lay in and around some of the magazines, along with the shells of weevils that had eaten part of those
stores as they lay within the darkness of the caves. Nearby lay the
stone querns on which the imported Nile wheat had been ground into
flour and the ovens and moulds in which the people had baked their
bread. Here, too, were found stacks of evenly sized dishes especially
designed, so it appears, to hold a sailor's ration. And more scribal
ostraca were found within this camp, along with wooden labels and
fragments of the seal impressions of types used by the expeditions'
scribes to seal everything from letters and ceramic storage jars to
warehouses. Some of these stamped impressions named individuals,
others settlements such as Thebes and Itj-towy. A single fine green
seal stamp appeared to have been dropped and lost by its ancient
owner and was found lying where it had fallen on the ancient strand.

The green-glazed scarab seal from Wadi Gawasis.

Four large and simple huts made of mud brick and mangrove poles had been built by the harbour slipways and, as the quantities of shavings, fragments of wood and tools suggest, appear to have served as workshops for the boat makers. Here, then, the timbers of sea-going boats that had been brought piecemeal from the Nile would have been assembled for the voyage. At the same time, shells of shucked barnacles in the area showed that the shipwrights had also repaired working boats and, as the fragments of rotted planks studded with barnacles and riddled with the boreholes of various shipworms vividly testified, they had serviced vessels which had spent long months at sea.

The archaeologists also excavated a considerable assortment of ninety-odd ships' timbers in that same area, which, apart from the occasional use of softer local mangrove wood, had all been cut from imported wood. Some of these were sections of the huge cedar bulks of the long keels that were the spines of pharaonic boats. There was as well an assortment of the distinctive individually shaped planks from the decks and hulls of those same craft; timbers so strong and thick that the vessels for which they had been shaped and fitted had not required supporting ribs or transoms.

Like those found in the other Red Sea chandleries, these timbers had been carried in donkey caravans from the Nile Valley through the mountains of the Eastern Desert to that desolate coast along with the heavy coiled ropes, the ships' sails, the stelae, the pottery, the provisions and equipment of the sailors, carpenters and militia, the scribes, the foremen and the expeditions' leaders.

Some rare fragmentary papyri of the times of the Itj-towy kings tell that at least two state-operated Nile-side boatyards were operating in those times: one at the settlements of Coptos, the other close to Thinis, by Abydos, information that was confirmed by part of the text on the stela of Antefoker:

> His Majesty ordered . . . Antefoker to construct this fleet coming from the boatyards of Coptos, to go to Punt and to return . . . [And] the registrar Ameny, son of Montuhotep, was on the sea coast occupied with constructing these boats together with a large assembly of [people] from the region of Thinis.

Then, as the accompanying stela describes, Ankhow and his brave flotilla, its cargoes, its crews and its militia had sailed from the Port of Saww to the Land of Punt.

Two fourteen-foot-long steering oars found in the deep sand of the ancient harbour suggests that these reassembled boats had been at least sixty-five feet long. With a crew of thirty oarsmen and a square-rigged sail set at the centre of its elegantly shaped hull, a recent reproduction of just such a vessel by a team led by Cheryl Ward has a displacement of thirty tons and a cargo capacity of more than half that weight. This reconstruction further demonstrated that these Byblos boats were thoroughly suited to sea voyages, though, as in so many other aspects of ancient life, its modern sailors had to adapt to methods of sailing that were quite foreign to them. Sea trials conducted during the winter of 2008–9 confirmed that Byblos boats could have comfortably managed the ten-foot swells along the Red Sea coast and, given the right conditions, would have sailed at some nine knots. Where then, exactly, on what seas, had these ancient boats once sailed to arrive at the enigmatic Land of Punt?

Amongst the thousands of ceramic sherds found at Wadi Gawasis – mostly from domestic wares and large storage jars, either roughly made locally or carefully potted from Nile Valley clays – the archae- ologists also recovered fragments of contemporary pottery from Crete and Aden, from Ethiopia and Eritrea, from the Yemen and the Levant. The Port of Saww, therefore, had links with the central trade routes of the ancient Eastern world. Just as pharaoh's Red Sea fleets were mostly built of cedar, oak and pine from the eastern Medi- terranean, so some of the people who had sailed from Saww may have also been Levantines or, as some of the pottery and texts found at Saww might suggest, some of pharaoh's sailors were Nubian or Ethiopian or may, indeed, have hailed from the Land of Punt. Seen in this light, the Port of Saww appears as a node in a far wider and more ancient Bronze Age circuit of travel and exchange: a temporary port established by the Itj-towy court to enable it to re-join more ancient networks in its search for courtly goods.

Pharaonic texts of different ages describe journeys to the Land of Punt by land and sea and even by lengthy voyages up the Nile. Certainly, it had lain to the south of Egypt, for most of the produce of

Punt named in pharaonic texts – aromatic gums and resins such as frankincense and myrrh, ebony, ivory, leopard skins, baboons and monkeys and even, perhaps, people like the pygmy that Harkhuf brought to the court of the young king Pepi I – were typical of tropical Africa.

Although the earliest-known records of pharaonic expeditions to Punt are the voyages whose exotic cargoes are pictured on the walls of the temples of Abusir, the presence of such materials within the valley of the lower Nile is very ancient, and they had been in prominent use at the pharaonic court from its beginnings. Though slight, perhaps, it appears to have been a fairly constant traffic in pharaonic times and, indeed, reciprocal, for portable pharaonic objects of various ages have been excavated at Kassala in east Sudan, in the Barka Valley, at Adulis in Eritrea, and in Somalia and Kenya.

Four carbonized rods of ebony found in one of the port shrines at Wadi Gawasis had probably been burnt in offerings. Along with other African timbers that the carpenters at Saww had occasionally used, ebony, a dark and precious wood used for courtly furnishings and temple fittings, grew right across the tropics. Deepening those botanical connections, a recent DNA analysis of mummified baboons, which had been imported as live animals into pharaonic Egypt from the Land of Punt, suggests that they had either been captured in the upper reaches of the Nile or in the regions to the east of that river. A few of the fragments of pottery found at Saww, moreover, are similar to those made at the port of Adulis in the Gulf of Zula, a thousand miles south along the coast of Africa; was this, perhaps, a port that served as an entrepôt to mythic Punt?

Based on pharaonic texts, various theories have placed the Land of Punt in such specific modern locations as east Sudan, the hinterlands of the Ethiopian and Sudanese lowlands and the Horn of Africa. The presence of ceramics from Aden and Yemen at Wadi Gawasis has also suggested south Arabia – not as the source of Punt's exotic goods but as a place of contact where such African goods had been obtained. Nor, certainly, was the Red Sea the main route of pharaonic interconnection with the south. The deserts of the upper Nile, that most ancient highway, are crisscrossed by ancient tracks connecting the Ethiopian-Eritrean highlands to adjoining regions north and south;

sea shells, for example, are commonly found in ancient graves in east Sudan.

Rather than a single fixed location, therefore, the Land of Punt may have sometimes served as a generic term for the origins of exotic southern produce and may have shifted in its usage in other ways over the millennia, for ancient people did not possess the mindset of modern map makers.

Nonetheless, buried deep within the sand that had obliterated the ancient lagoon of Saww, the archaeologists uncovered forty cream-painted near-identical wooden boxes, laid out in careful lines in front of the rock-cut chandleries. Though similar to a few boxes that have been found in contemporary settlements within the valley of the Nile, at the Port of Saww these well-proportioned chests had not served as household furniture but as storage units on pharaoh's boats. For in one of those rare moments in archaeology where the physical remnants of the past are touched directly by the information held in formal court inscriptions, one of those boxes was found to have a cartouche of Amenemhet IV inked upon its side, along with an accompanying description telling that it had once held 'the wonderful things of Punt'.

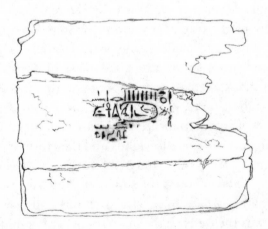

The inscription inked on the side of a whitewashed cargo box, one of many such left by the harbour magazines at Wadi Gawasis, telling that it had once contained 'the wonderful things of Punt'.

Voyages from Saww to Punt were ponderous and complex undertakings. Preliminary trips both on the Nile and on the Mediterranean were required to obtain the ships' timbers. Copper was needed for the tools that shaped them. Fashioned in Nile-side boatyards, those vessels were then transported in sections through the Eastern Mountains along desert wadis to the shore of the Red Sea, considerable journeys that sometimes required the excavation of fresh wells in the desert. Once at the Port of Saww, teams of carpenters from Nile-side shipyards had reassembled the boats by the lagoon. Then the little squadron had set out, sailing south along the coast for what, the boats' timbers tell, had been substantial voyages to meet the peoples whose goods they so prized, before returning, as the prevailing winds and tides still indicate, along the Arabian coast and finally tacking briefly across the rough Red Sea to Saww. There, the ships' cargo boxes would have been emptied and their exotic treasures loaded into donkey panniers for the trek back through the mountains to the gentle river and their eventual distribution to the storerooms of the temples and the royal residence. And at the Port of Saww in that same period of time, the Byblos boats would either have been refitted for further voyages or dismantled and taken in caravan along with the wonderful things of Punt, back into the valley of the Nile for other journeys, perhaps, along the seaboard of the eastern Mediterranean.

Such complicated expeditions would have been as costly in state provisions and materials as the construction of stone monuments; ultimately, they had served the same purpose. Just as the dramas of the daily rites and offerings, the regular contact and communication with deity and the dead, took place in temples and tomb chapels whose construction was a main activity of government, so contact and communication with deity and the dead within those monuments had required goods obtained from distant destinations. Incense, perfumed oils and purifying salts, priestly furs and gold, ebony and ivory were as vital to the tasks of ritual and offering as were the stone and copper needed to construct the theatres in which those interactions took place.

Rather than assuming in the traditional manner that the pharaohs had possessed the modern desire for fine consumer goods and displays of wealth and power, we see the officials of the ancient Memphite culture gripped by the need to obtain the necessary ingredients of court life. As their monuments and texts imply, that same urge had constantly inspired the court of the Intefs, the Montuhoteps and their successors at Itj-towy in their drive to re-unite the ancient kingdom, so that the pharaonic culture of the lower Nile would be set in motion once again, and pharaoh and all his people, both the living and the dead, might regain their place at the centre of an ordered universe, just as the verses of a famed papyrus text still tell:

Remember the building of the shrine, censing with incense and to pour a libation from a vessel at dawn.

Remember to set up flag staffs and to carve out offering tables; the priest purifying the sanctuaries; the temple plastered as white as milk; the perfuming of the sanctuary; presenting offerings of bread!

Remember the upholding of regulations, the correct ordering of the calendar. And to expel someone who enters priestly service with an impure body: For this is to do wrong and is afflicting to the heart!

Remember the day which precedes eternity, the months that are counted and the years that are known!

CARNELIAN, AMETHYST AND SILTSTONE – *THE EGYPTIAN DESERTS*

Egypt's oldest rocks, its so-called 'crystalline basement', lie underneath the Sinai Mountains and the high cliffs of the lower Nile Valley. Partially upended in ages long before the Nile had flowed into the Mediterranean, they are exposed at the Aswan Cataract and in the bad lands of the Upper Egyptian deserts. Some of the most splendid stones in this desert jewel box had been quarried and collected since prehistoric times, and in the days of Khafre and Menkaure the court jewellers had worked gemstones from those rich deposits and the sculptors' workshops had used its glistening rocks for major works of sculpture. It was to be expected, therefore, that the courts of the refounded kingdom of Itj-towy would revisit, re-open and rework those ancient desert quarries.

So, once again, pharaonic caravans had travelled into the deep

Sahara south of Aswan, along the fifty miles of desert track laid down in the times of the Memphite kings that led to the so-called 'Chephren quarries' of the Gebel el-Asr, and set up new huts and storerooms. Just as the earlier pharaonic expeditions to those quarries had been but short term enterprises so the accommodations that the Itj-towy quarry-men built are simple huts whose dry-stone walls are made from fragments of the hard stone that their predecessors had split with fire and wedges and scattered all across the sand as they extracted flaw-less boulders from the wondrous matrix, igneous and metamorphic, that lay beneath their feet.

In one of the largest of these huts, archaeologists recently uncovered long lines of handsome globular storage jars made in the times of the Itj-towy kings. Exactly the same type of vessel has been found in most of the sites at which that court had lived and worked. Each of those vessels could carry a hundred pounds of wheat. Here then, once again, bread was baked in desert ovens, the charcoal brought on donkey-back, the flour ground onsite on local stone and mixed with water taken from nearby wells tapping directly into prehistoric aquifers.

The sprawling stone workings on the Gebel el-Asr do not resemble modern quarries. Loosely covered by windborne sand, the hard-stone strata were easily located and they were quarried in some 600 differ-ent locations over a six-mile area. And so the miners' huts and storerooms, the loading ramps and pavements built to aid the trans-portation of stone, were scattered across that same broad area. Close to the centre of the workings, beside a fine large stela bearing Khafre's name and announcing that the area had been 'a royal hunting ground' – this, presumably, a hunt for stone – the expeditions of the Itj-towy kings set up small offering tables, a few small sculptures and thirty-odd stelae, some of whose folk-art images of gods and kings suggest that they had been engraved by the hands of miners working in imitation of the fine manner of court craftsmanship. And one of these stelae tells us directly that in the time of Amenemhet II an expedition had been sent to that lonely spot expressly 'for the pur-pose of bringing *mentet* stone'.

Unlike the workshops of the Memphite court, those of Itj-towy do not seem to have used the stone from the Gebel el-Asr quarries in any great quantity, for few sculptures, bowls or vases of the period cut from its beautifully veined and speckled gneiss appear to have survived. Near to Khafre's stela, however, their expeditions had mined some of the finely coloured gems that were widely used by the jewellers and seal cutters of the Itj-towy court, laboriously extracting glistening red carnelian from seams of chalcedony.

Since a very long time scholars have wondered from whence came all the beautiful amethyst that the ancient Egyptians used so lavishly in their jewellery, especially during the Middle Kingdom . . .

Now, at last, we have in our hands, a description of the amethyst quarries, and the names of leaders of the expeditions which went there, and we know for certain from whence came all the beautiful amethyst which at one time adorned the necks and arms of the queens and princesses of the Middle Kingdom, some of which was luckily preserved, and is now exhibited in the different museums of the world.

The jewellers of Itj-towy had been fascinated by the qualities of the fine stones that their miners extracted from the desert. And they set them exquisitely in golden mounts, in necklaces, bracelets and diadems and beadwork of a dozen different kinds, in forms and settings that displayed the luminous qualities of crystal and garnet, jasper, feldspar, turquoise, carnelian, chalcedony and, an especial favourite, a distinctive pale amethyst of purplish blue that was only found in the Eastern Desert some twenty miles south of Aswan in the wasteland of the Wadi el-Hudi, where there was a sprawl of mines similar to those at the hard-stone quarries of the Gebel el-Ansr.

Drawn in high courtly style and engraved upon an especially imported stone, a stela found at the amethyst mines of the Wadi el-Hudi describes an expedition to those mines that had been led by the vizier Hor in the time of Senwosret I. Like the journeys to the Port of Saww, these mining expeditions were conducted under the direct auspices of the high officials of the royal court. Another stela, that of an official whose name is only partially preserved, declares that the man 'who sent me to carry away the amethyst' had been none other than the vizier Antefoker, the courtier who was similarly memorialized at the Port of Saww and had overseen a voyage to the Land of Punt.

In the last seventy years, a mass of graffiti and small individual stelae have been found at the amethyst mines – all of them products of courtly expeditions that were sent to the Wadi el-Hudi, reign by reign, at the same rate as other royal missions were being dispatched to the seas and deserts. Two large open mines appear to have been the focus of their activity in the Wadi el-Hudi, the pale violet amethysts being separated from the matrix in the miners' encampments, where great heaps of colourless rock crystal still lie around their huts. The amethyst mines appear to have been worked out by later generations, but the quantities of gemstones that were removed in the time of the Itj-towy kings must have been enormous, for still today, after millennia of plunder, the surviving jewellery of the period holds thousands of fine amethysts, whilst its continued use and re-use throughout the Aegean and other regions of the eastern Mediterranean in centuries long after the mines were no longer in operation shows that there had been a widespread traffic in that distinctive stone.

The surviving inscriptions in the Wadi el-Hudi tell that the mines were already open in the reign of the last Montuhotep, at which time a small settlement of simple huts had been built on a hilltop close to one of the large opencast workings. In later reigns, a square state-planned stone enclosure housing many more storerooms and shelters was erected a mile away from it, beside the second large open mine. And somewhere in that general area, a small shrine was set up with two little obelisks and several offering tables dedicated to the goddess Hathor, a divinity commonly associated with bad lands and desert mines. In the same manner that Mary, mother of Jesus, is variously described in her different shrines around the world so, too, at every site in which a shrine for Hathor, the mother of Horus, was established she is distinguished by a different local epithet.

So the inscription on the stela of a certain Sareru, who describes himself as a 'keeper of the treasure chamber', tells that he had brought aromatic oils and resins like those obtained at Punt, to the little temple of Hathor, Mistress of Amethyst, where he had performed the rituals for that goddess. At the same time he tells us that he brought water to every thirsty man working in the Wadi el-Hudi – perhaps by opening some of the many ancient wells in the vicinity.

Set on an irregular piece of local stone, Sareru's inscription is poorly made and the location where it was originally set up is lost, for like so many of the Wadi el-Hudi inscriptions they were found and moved by desert travellers. It would appear, however, that Sareru's stela had once stood inside Hathor's lost temple, for it holds an image of a statue of Sareru, standing, presumably, in the presence of the goddess. In the times of the Itj-towy kings many individuals set statues of themselves within the sanctuaries of shrines and temples. In such a desolate location, however, Sareru could hardly have found the craftsmen or the stone to make a solid image of himself to stand in Hathor's presence, and so a line drawing of a statue had to do.

We set out from Luxor one morning in November, our caravan consisting in all of twenty-three camels, nine of which were ridden by our four selves, my servant, two guards, the Shékh of the camelmen, and the guide, while fourteen were loaded with the three tents, the baggage, and the water-tanks, and were tended by a dozen camel-men who made the journey mainly on foot . . .

[Four days later] we rode up a valley, which was now tortuous and narrow. This is the Wady Hammamat of the archaeologist, and the Wady Fowakhieh of the natives. Dark, threatening hills towered on either side . . . One's voice echoed amongst the rocks, and the wind carried the sound down the valley and round the bend, adding to it its own quiet whispers. A ride of about half an hour's length brought us to some ruined huts where the ancient quarry-men had lived in the days of the Pharaohs. From this point onwards for perhaps a mile the rocks on either side are dotted with inscriptions, from which a part of the history of the valley may be learnt. The place is full of whispers . . .

The Wadi Hammamat is part of a network of valleys in Egypt's Eastern Desert that connects the modern town of Qift, ancient Coptos, in the valley of the Nile to the Red Sea port of Quseir. And since prehistoric times, miners, quarrymen, caravans of boat transporters, scribes, surveyors, Egyptians, Greeks and Persians, Roman legionaries, Aramaeans, Christian monks and pagan south Arabians have left their various graffiti on its rocks and cliffs.

Amongst these myriad inscriptions is a cartouche of Montuhotep

II accompanied by the same epithet with which he is described at the Gebel Uweinat in the Sahara: 'son of Re'. Not far away, a long inscription describes the progress of an expedition led by Henenu, whose splendid courtyard tomb lies to the north of Montuhotep II's Deir el-Bahari temple and who had also served at the court of that king's shadowy successor. Henenu's text within the Wadi Hammamat, indeed, describes an otherwise unrecorded expedition to Punt from the court of Montuhotep III, of which no trace has been found at the Port of Saww, and which comprises the best part of the historical records of that obscure reign:

> My lord has sent me with great ships to Punt to bring fresh myrrh for him . . . I went forth from Coptos . . . a troop from the south was with me . . . I made twelve wells . . . and then I reached the sea. I made this ship, and I dispatched it with offerings of cattle, bulls and ibexes. After my return . . . I did that which his majesty commanded and brought all the gifts that I had found at Punt for him. I returned through the Wadi Hammamat, I brought for him great blocks for statues for the temple . . .

Whilst serving as a prime pharaonic route to the Red Sea and to numerous gold mines in the surrounding hills, parts of the steep rock walls of Wadi Hammamat were also major quarries. The valley's cut reveals part of the remarkably varied strata of Egypt's geologic underbelly, from granites, greywacke and siltstone to rare high-shining conglomerates of beautifully flecked greens, reds, greys and blacks along with a colourful range of jaspers, cornelians and fluorspars in the nearby hills.

Siltstone, especially, the equitable rock that the pharaonic scribes called *bekhen*, was mined in considerable quantities within the Wadi Hammamat. For though bands of siltstone frequently occur throughout the intractable mountains of the Eastern Desert, large sections of the Wadi Hammamat's high dark cliffs are composed of that distinctive stone, and the smooth-floored wadi provides relatively easy access to the valley of the Nile. And from the first pharaoh to the last, Hammamat's siltstone was continuously used within the royal workshops.

As the track along the bottom of the Wadi Hammamat twists up through the Red Sea Mountains through cliffs of green-grey siltstone

and red gold-bearing granites, sometimes passing through narrow shadowed corridors, sometimes opening into wider sunlight areas, the stone
walls of ancient huts and the traces of the ancient quarrymen lie all
around. Half-finished sarcophagi and the roughed-out forms of abandoned statues that had shivered and cracked as they were being worked
still lie at odd angles amongst heaps of shattered stone at the bottom of
the quarry faces. And many of the cliffs and rocks within that moonlike
landscape still hold the names of kings and quarrymen pecked lightly
with a chip of that same rock onto the smooth grey cliffs and rocks, a
process that embeds a whitish crystalline dust within their surfaces and
serves to emphasize the lines of the inscriptions and the images.

The texts are many and diverse. Some simply record the names of
otherwise anonymous individuals, others, like that of the steward
Henenu, record the exploits of some of those millennial expeditions.
Here, too, great wide rock surfaces have allowed the ancient scribes
space for an unusual loquacity, so they sometimes list the full titularies
of the pharaohs whose courts dispatched those expeditions, their various participants and some of the incidents that had occurred along the
way. And a great deal of this information is laid out in lines of stately
hieroglyphs, in the measured manner of the finest stelae of the court.

Perhaps the most extraordinary of these records is inscribed in four
long texts that describe a mining expedition undertaken during the
reign of the last Montuhotep and led by a vizier named Amenemhet,
a man who many historians have suggested may have succeeded that
king to the throne to become Amenemhet I, in whose reign the royal
residence was moved from Thebes to Itj-towy.

The King of the Lands of the Delta and the Valley, Nebtawyre, son of
Re, Montuhotep [IV],

Year 2, Second Month of the Inundation, day 15.

His Majesty commanded the erection of this stela for his father Min,
lord of the highlands, on this majestic mountain . . . Nebtawyre, may
he live like Re forever, says: 'I sent the . . . vizier, overseer of works,
royal confidant Amenemhet, together with an expedition of ten thousand men from the southern provinces . . . to bring me a precious
block of the pure stone of this mountain whose excellence was made

by Min, for a sarcophagus, as an eternal memorial. . that I may be given life, and live like Re forever.

Then, as an addition:

Day 28. The lid of the sarcophagus was taken down, a block of 4 cubits by 8 cubits by 2 cubits [6 3/4 feet x 13 3/4 feet x 3 1/2 feet] . . . calves were slaughtered, goats were sacrificed, incense was put on the fire and three thousand sailors from the provinces of the Delta delivered it safely to the kingdom.

As is usual with such memorials, the size of the workforce, which is quoted in round numbers and whose participants are described in a large list of professions and court titles, appears enormous. Assuming the ancient lists were composed in the manner of a modern balance sheet, the numbers of participants in a similar later expedition would have totalled almost 19,000 people! Such figures, however, may refer to man days of working rather than the numbers of the expeditions' personnel, for that was a typical accounting method of the age, which enabled the court to estimate the quantities of rations required for a specific task.

Nonetheless, those nice round figures have been taken by generations of scholars as accurate, and thus those desert trips have been transformed into events resembling the Field of the Cloth of Gold, with exaggerated visions of the administrative systems required to manage such vast events. Yet even the largest of stone blocks could not have commanded the attentions of such enormous crowds. Jamming the narrow wadi in their thousands, they would have thwarted the work of mining, emptied the scanty desert wells of water and consumed hundreds of tons of provisions during the months the miners are recorded as working in the desert. Nor, indeed, were such numbers required to pull the quarried blocks back to the valley of the Nile. So whether or not they are a record of man days of working or simply an ancient equivalent of 'squillions', such figures should be taken in similar vein to the temple inscriptions which describe the construction of columns so high that they pierced the sky itself, or the text of another quarrying expedition to the Wadi Hammamat that claims to have filled the deserts with lakes and colonies of settlers.

Hard archaeological evidence from a variety of pharaonic quarries shows that, in common with pyramid building, both quarrying and the transportation of stone blocks had been a piecemeal affair and more inventive and less standardized in its methods than those exaggerated figures of personnel and lengthy lists of accompanying officials might suggest. Recent analysis of the largest of all the anciently recorded stone-quarrying expeditions, for example, has concluded that, for its efficient operation, some 200 to 300 participants would have been required to extract and transport the stone described, and that, working in teams of twenty, such a force covering six to eight miles a day could have hauled the quarried blocks back down the Wadi Hammamat to the valley of the Nile in just ten days.

In all likelihood, therefore, such expeditions were organized erratically whenever the court required more stone for its projects, and they were staffed by considerably less than a thousand people. In that respect, the mining expeditions had resembled the voyages to Punt; Henenu and several other court officials, indeed, are described as controlling both quarrying and voyaging expeditions.

Everything about those quarry texts is enlarged and amplified: the task the scribes described as travelling into the desert, to that zone between life and death, to obtaining the stone of royal statues and sarcophagi so that pharaoh would live forever was, of itself, exaggerated. As the stoneworkers hacked out hard rock in quarries filled with the scent of sacrifice and incense, they had laboured in a zone of marvels, one filled with the powers of gods and kings:

> This wonder happened to his majesty [i.e. to the members of his expedition]. Creatures from the hills came down to him. A pregnant gazelle came down to him, with her face towards the people whilst she rolled her eyes. But she did not turn back until she arrived at this majestic mountain, at the block [intended] for the lid of this sarcophagus.
>
> She dropped her young upon it, while the expedition of the king was watching.
>
> Then her neck was cut, and she was sacrificed on it as a burnt offering.
>
> Now, it was the majesty of the august god [Min], who made the sacrifice to his son Nebtawyre [Montuhotep IV], may he live forever, so

that his heart might be joyful, that he might be alive upon his throne forever . . . leader of what heaven gives, earth creates, and the Nile brings . . . the vizier Amenemhet.

Ten days later they had finally freed the block that would become the lid of the sarcophagus:

And again a wonder happened. A command was issued and the authority of this god [Min] was manifested to the people.

The upland was turned into a lake and water rose over the roughness of the stone. A well was found in the middle of the valley, eighteen feet on every side, filled with water to its brim, kept pure and clean from gazelles and hidden from tribesmen and foreigners. It had been passed by the expeditions and the kings of earlier times as they had travelled up and down. No eye had seen it, the glance of no man had fallen upon it. To his majesty alone it was revealed.

He [the god] had . . . done something new in his mountainous land for his son Nebtawyre [Montuhotep IV], may he live forever!

Most of the Itj-towy kings are named within the Wadi Hammamat, and all of them appear to have sent expeditions to its quarries. Only a few of those texts, however, give more than a bare record of their expeditions. Only those inscriptions made in the first generations of the re-united kingdom record the spectacular dimensions of those journeys to a place apart – the timid approach of a gazelle, the roar of a flash flood, the presence of a god – to that zone where the physical and metaphysical of the pharaonic universe merged into a single landscape.

ALABASTER – *BESIDE THE NILE*

The stone Alabastrites is found about Alabastrum a citie in Egypt . . . white of colour it is, and intermedled with sundry colours.

From Philemon Holland's translation from
Pliny's Natural History, *1601*

Not all the expeditions that the Itj-towy court dispatched entailed sea voyages or desert caravans. Like most of the stone blocks that were used for building pyramids and temples, the pharaohs' fine white alabasters – or 'travertine', as geologists generically define them – were customarily quarried from cliffs close to the valley of the lower Nile.

In pharaoh's hard-stone quarries, blocks were often disengaged with the aid of a carefully directed fire and by working the fire-damaged portions of the rock with stones and wedges so that 'what the flame had wrought was pounded from it', as an inscription in the Wadi Hammamat graphically describes. Alabaster, on the other hand, can be prised and split away from its matrix or simply cut with copper saws and chisels. Relatively soft when first extracted from the living rock, Egyptian alabaster hardens after a while and bleaches to brilliant whiteness on exposure to the sun. In pharaonic times, it held strong connotations of purity and was widely used for courtly bowls and vases, for amulets, for altars and embalming tables, as well as for statuary and shrines. So the famous statues of the king within Khafre's valley temple had stood on gleaming blocks of light-veined alabaster, and the enormous blood-collecting basins in the slaughtering courts of the Memphite sun temples were cut from the same stone.

The largest of Egypt's nine known ancient alabaster quarries lies in the hills of Middle Egypt, some ten miles from the Nile and twelve miles upstream from the modern town of Mallawi. The ancient name of these quarries, Hatnub, literally 'house of gold', was also that of an otherworldly region inhabited by the dead, and the same term was used, too, as a description of similarly ambiguous though entirely earthly locations such as burial crypts and temple shrines, like that which housed the image of Amun-Re within Senwosret I's temple at Karnak.

Hatnub's ancient quarries consist of a series of irregular open cuts and tunnels in a few wide upended veins of alabaster that are exposed on the ridges of the low-sloping limestone hills, some ten miles from the river on its eastern bank. Though Hatnub alabaster was certainly used by earlier pharaonic craftsmen, the first recorded visit of the court to that most generous deposit was in the time of Khufu, when that monarch's name and image, a very rare occurrence for his time, was sculpted high above an ancient quarry track upon a worked quarry face. Subsequently, the names of several other Memphite monarchs and many of their courtiers were also drawn within the quarries.

Following the Old Kingdom's dissolution, local governors had mined Hatnub's alabaster on their own account, as their inked inscriptions in the quarries tell. Then, following the restoration of the court, Montuhotep II's name appears and, quite untypically though in common with the inscriptions of his Saharan expedition, the royal epithet 'the Son of Re' was set inside rather than outside his cartouche. After that royal reappearance, the names of several later kings and many of their courtiers appear within these quarries; an inked hieratic text upon an alabaster ostracon from the quarries records the numbers of a seemingly enormous expedition that had taken place in the reign of Senwosret III.

Taken all together, that rich gathering of inscriptions shows that the oldest pharaonic quarry at Hatnub was a considerable sheer-sided egg-shaped cut, some 50 feet in depth and almost 200 feet across, in which Khufu's name and image had been inscribed. Fresh workings, however, subterranean and open cast, appear to have been initiated in the times of the Montuhoteps. Set a mile to the west of the older quarries, a broad new track was laid down through the hills to join a larger older causeway that ran across a wide flat plain to landings at the riverside and the waiting stone barges.

In the times of the Itj-towy kings, Hatnub's quarries had been controlled by a succession of regional governors whose tombs, a line of chapels with beautifully refined internal architecture, were set in high limestone cliffs near to the modern village of Deir el-Bersha, opposite Mallawi. The governors' tombs stand over the considerable burying grounds of the communities that they had once controlled; the area, indeed, appears to have been heavily inhabited in ancient times and holds extensive remains of ancient alabaster workshops and an as yet unexcavated town site.

It may well be that the alabaster ostracon which describes a huge quarrying enterprise during the reign of Senwosret III records the same ambitious project that is pictured in a unique scene in the tomb chapel of one of those governors, a man named Djehutihotep. Four gangs of men are shown hauling a statue of a seated man lashed to a wooden sledge, which an accompanying inscription describes as 'the transport of a statue of 13 cubits of Hatnub stone', that is, of a statue that had stood some 22 feet high and had weighed around 80 tons.

This long tomb-chapel inscription begins by recounting the hauling of a single enormous stone block out of the quarry; a block that is described as 'squared', that is, a block that has been roughly shaped into the traditional form of a pharaonic seated statue, a labour that would have required the careful attentions of master craftsmen to ensure that the pose and proportions of the finished statue were well contained within the stone. Then, gangs of men recruited from the surrounding farmsteads had hauled that great block along the quarries' purpose-built slipways to loading quays at the riverside.

Djehutihotep's texts describe how 'the work of dragging the large block was difficult for the haulers because the ground was very hard', and that the ancient slipway along which the unfinished statue was hauled had passed 'up and down' on its way through the foot hills. In fact, the designers of the ancient quarry tracks had greatly aided the progress of large blocks by driving a straight track through the stony hills that traversed the lowest natural angles in the landscape and by further levelling the terrain in a series of considerable cuttings and embankments, in the manner of railway engineers.

It has been estimated that the groups of ancient huts alongside one of these ancient tracks were of sufficient size to have accommodated 300 people; about the same number that is recorded in the contemporary inventories of desert caravans. As with the ancient activities of caravanning, of building pyramids and of sculpting colossal statues, a strong cohesion, a sense of fraternity even, was essential between the members of such groups. With each man pulling an estimated dead weight of some 200 pounds, encouraging such great stone blocks to inch gently through the hills down to the riverside and onto barges was a perilous activity, a slow progress marked out along the track ways by a series of small cairns and accompanied by prayers and drumbeats, and probably also by rhythmic group singing, just as similar activities are often undertaken in non-industrial societies today.

A section of the lengthy text from Weni's tomb at Abydos describes the progress of an earlier expedition to Hatnub, in which he had obtained alabaster for a large offering table. It had taken seventeen days, the stela tells, to quarry the stone and slide it to the riverside harbour, where men working under Weni's supervision had built a 100-foot stone barge especially to transport the alabaster blocks to the workshops of the royal residence: 'I moored at the royal pyramid in safety,' Weni's report concludes; 'it happened through my offices and entirely in accordance with the order of the king.'

The skilled and time-consuming processes of sculpting and finishing a colossus such as that of Djehutihotep would certainly have been undertaken in the governor's workshops, close to the craftsmen's homes and close, presumably, to its eventual emplacement sitting within a local temple. So to modern eyes the unique scene in Djehutihotep's tomb chapel would appear to picture the last stages of the statue's journey as it is pulled up from the river landing to its final destination by four teams of rope haulers, each one of which comprises twenty-one pairs of men.

> I had squads of young recruits to make the way along with companies
> of miners and quarrymen, foremen and officials. And the workmen say
> 'We come to bring [Djehutihotep's statue] . . .

Mounted on a sturdy wooden sledge, the finished and painted colossus has been carefully padded with ox skins to protect it from chafing on the massive hauling ropes that have been tightened around the statue with the aid of twisting sticks. A chanting priest stands on the statue's knees, clapping out the rhythms of the haulage gangs in a cry that is recorded in hieroglyphs above his head: 'Djehutihotep, beloved of the king'. A figure at the statue's feet pours water to lubricate the passage of its mighty sledge. A team of water carriers and another carrying sturdy rolling logs further aid the statue's progress, whilst the project's overseers, the master sculptor Neki-ankh and Sepa, his son, walk alongside in attendance. And all the while priests burn clouds of incense to aid the statue's progress from the otherworldly edges of the dry high desert into the living kingdom.

The numbers of men required for these colossal labours are clearly shown, and, as in the Wadi Hammamat, they flatly contradict the figures listed in the ancient texts. Rather than serving as a modern accounting of a workforce's size, those texts were intended to emphasize, like the splendid scene in Djehutihotep's tomb chapel, the magnitude of the task performed and the strength and enthusiasm of its participants:

> And the hearts of those who pulled the great colossus swelled and filled with joy . . . behold this statue, a great block coming from the mountain and larger in value than anything . . . and the courage of the strong men and the weak both rose, their arms grew powerful like the strength of a thousand men.

The hauling of the colossus from the sculptors' workshops to the temple was, in fact, a time of celebration:

> My children . . . all beautifully enrobed, accompanied me and the citizens of my district shouted prayers . . . I arrived at the settlement, its people praised me and it was beautiful to see, above all things . . . my heart was glad and the people of the settlements rejoiced.
>
> This was a procession, a provincial festival which, like the great state occasions of Thebes, had manifested the efficacy and order of the state and its bond with all of the forces, seen and unseen, that inhabited the valley of the lower Nile.

> The Hare District [the ancient administrative region] is in celebration and hearts rejoice. 'The load [i.e. the sculpture] is moved to Cherti [a settlement?] and the ancestors are rejoicing. His fathers are in festival . . . rejoicing in his beautiful monuments . . . The West is in festival, and hearts are glad when they see the monuments of their master, the heir who was in his father's house when he was a child . . .' the elders and the young men are thriving. The children shout joyfully, their hearts in festival when they see that their masters and their master's son are in the favour of the king . . . and the priests of the Hare District say: 'Beloved of Djehuti [i.e. the regional deity Thoth] and Djehutihotep [literally, 'Thoth is satisfied'], beloved of the king, beloved of the people of the settlement and praised by all the gods.'

As for Djehutihotep himself: 'None of the ancestors,' he states, 'nor the local officials, nor the administrators of the settlement had thought of doing what I have done. I have established a chapel and offering altars . . . and this statue for all eternity.' Ironically, there is no trace today of Djehutihotep's alabaster colossus, and only the words and images within his tomb chapel remain.

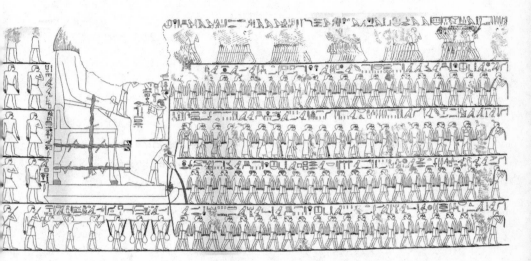

The unique scene of the hauling of a colossus from the quarries of Hatnub in the tomb chapel of the courtier Djehutihotep at Deir el-Bersha. From a drawing made in 1892 by Howard Carter.

25

The Levant and Nubia

TRAVELLERS TO AN ANTIQUE LAND

In front of the west pylon lay a block of granite much defaced. It bears part of a long and finely engraved inscription, which was partly copied with difficulty owing to the battered condition.

W. M. Flinders Petrie, 1909

Dug over and about for centuries, the ruins of ancient Memphis lie at the edge of the cultivation in plain sight of the Saqqara pyramids. This had been the city of palaces and temples that the ancient Greek and Roman travellers celebrated as the archaic ancient capital of pharaoh. Today, it is a scattered sprawl of dusty mud-brick mounds amidst old village houses, clumps of palms, blocks of stone and a pretty, rush-fringed pool which fills the sites of several early digs. No evidence survives of a Memphis of the times of the Itj-towy kings, nor, indeed, of the times when Menes, the legendary first pharaoh, was supposed to have built a mighty dam and fortress at the capital of his newly conquered kingdom, at a place named Memphis.

Archaeologists had been reluctant to excavate those silty ruin fields until 1905, when Flinders Petrie came to search for the plan of the temple of the Memphite deity Ptah, one of several sanctuaries of Memphis that the classical writers had described as being as large as Karnak and far older. What Petrie found, however, were the ruins of a temple erected in the time of Ramesses II, the stones of which had been culled from dozens of earlier tomb chapels and temples. And there it was, amidst the dust of ancient mud brick and a jigsaw of broken stone, that he uncovered an irregular slab of granite bearing a lengthy hieroglyphic text describing some of the offerings and donations that King Amenemhet II had made to temples, to courtiers and to royal mortuary cults.

The Middle Kingdom text uncovered during Petrie's excavation of the temple of Ptah at Memphis.

In the 1990s, further work inside the ruins of Ramesses' temple brought to light a larger fragment of that same granite slab, which had been recycled to serve as part of the base of a colossal statue that had stood beside the temple's doorway. The original location of the complete inscription is unknown. Had it stood in a lost and unknown temple of the Itj-towy kings or had it been taken from one of the temples of Amenemhet II's pyramid, which had stood a few miles to the south? The historical importance of those fragments lies in the fact that the fifty columns of hieroglyphs that they hold between them is one of the largest formal documents to have survived from the period of the Itj-towy kings. So, though the fragments do not share a common edge and their surfaces are partly lost, the damaged text yet holds information about aspects of the history of the Itj-towy kings that are mostly shrouded in uncertainty, whilst the lengthy reign of Amenemhet II, his household, his monuments and any narrative of the history of his reign, is virtually unknown. As one authority has observed, 'Although the king ruled more than thirty years, few monuments are datable to his time. His family relations are unclear. It can be assumed that he was the son of Senwosret I, but this is not precisely stated anywhere.'

The text on those two broken granite slabs holds part of a record of a two-year period in Amenemhet II's reign. Similar in style to the earlier royal annals, though providing greater detail, it appears to have been part of a larger history of the time; a history that the royal court had considered to be of sufficient import to record in well-cut hieroglyphs upon enormous slabs of granite.

Petrie's fragment holds part of a list of traditional funerary endowments that were common to both courtiers and kings: lands are granted to supply the produce for the cult; quantities of bread, beer, grain, cakes, and wild fowl are specified to be delivered to the altars and the priestly communities serving the mortuary cult in the temples of his predecessor, King Senwosret I. And other lists of offerings are granted to state temples: to Amun at Thebes, and to a temple of the god Ptah, the ancient Memphite deity, whose dwelling was given granite stelae and columns of cedar wood inlaid with gems and precious metals.

The text upon the larger second stone, alternatively, contains what Western historians have traditionally considered to be 'real' history, for amidst more lists of donations and endowments to temples at Karnak, Tod and Memphis, Armant and Heliopolis, accounts of the distribution of rewards to certain courtiers and the reception of Nubians and 'desert dwellers' at the Itj-towy court, it describes the progress of a royal expedition from the Nile Delta to some Bronze Age settlements in the northern Levant.

Unfortunately, the history of that journey is difficult to follow. The locations named in the text remain unidentified, and many of the words describing the expedition's personnel are still little understood. Yet the outline of the journey seems clear enough, for it is depicted in terms similar to those used on the stelae that describe voyages from the Red Sea ports and mining expeditions into the Eastern Desert. Here, however, the text does not tell of expeditions to mysterious places in Africa or to the high Sahara, but of a journey along the most ancient land and sea routes of the eastern Mediterranean to other ancient courts.

Pharaonic voyages on the eastern Mediterranean departed from ports within the Nile's delta and crossed the coast of northern Sinai before heading northwards, up along the Levantine seaboard towards Syria and Cilicia, a route that ran parallel to an accompanying ancient land route, the caravan track known as the 'Way of Horus'. The sea voyage the stela's damaged text describes seems to have visited ports and settlements on the Lebanese coast and even, perhaps, the Isle of Cyprus, which would have added only an extra day to a four- or five-day trip, most of which would have consisted of a series of short hops along the Mediterranean coastline. Having arrived in the north Levant, the broken text appears to tell, the crew and a militia on pharaoh's boats had joined with an overland expedition that had previously travelled up along the Way of Horus, and together they had 'hacked down' the walls of two settlements. Both the boats and the overland expedition then appear to have returned to Itj-towy with prisoners and goods, some of which were carried in caravan across Sinai and some shipped back in two boats. All in all, the adventure had taken seven months.

Along with many traditionally minded egyptologists today, Champollion and Maspero would certainly have considered this a record of a ruthless raid, a military campaign in which regiments of infantry and marines had been sent off to plunder foreign cities. Here is a conventional view, as expressed by Donald Redford:

> Suddenly, as it were, the veil is lifted . . . we see a court and government immensely rich, powerful, and efficient, able to work its will not only inside the country but beyond the borders as well. Moreover, one senses the resolve to be ruthless. In a single year paramilitary expeditions of some size are dispatched to tap the resources of Sinai and the Lebanon, two punitive campaigns are mounted . . . The amount of produce, minerals, and manufactures brought back are enormous, and even the number of prisoners is substantial, although the numbers of weapons (which may indicate the number of enemy dead in conflict) appear modest . . .

The problem with such interpretations is that, although the lengthy lists of goods and peoples that are described as being brought from the Levant are remarkably specific, the terms of their acquisition are extremely vague. The story of the expedition is mixed with lines of text that appear to be quite unrelated, and even those parts of the inscription that describe the relationship between its two components, land and sea, are far from clear. And the expedition's disparate personnel have been variously translated as 'groups', 'work gangs' or 'armies', as civilian or military, according to the translator's disposition.

Was this, then, an expedition like those of the southern caravans that had been sent from the Itj-towy court to acquire materials and goods from the Levant as gifts or tribute and had engaged in some kind of small-scale conflict? Or was it a naval and military operation dispatched by the court to plunder goods and people by brute force? One thing seems sure: a reasonable estimate of the expedition's size, based both on the journey's long duration and the logistics of other Itj-towy expeditions, suggests that this Levantine excursion was undertaken by just a few hundred people, for the territories through which it passed had been sparsely inhabited by tribes of semi-pastoralists and could hardly have sustained larger numbers for any length of time.

Clearly, acts of cruelty, sacking and rapine need not be excluded from such adventures, and certainly some form of militia may well have been included to protect the expedition's personnel, provisions and goods. Yet there is no shred of evidence that there were standing armies in Middle Kingdom times, nor is there evidence that the modern distinctions of military, commercial and diplomatic enterprises can be sensibly applied to that most ancient world. So just as there is no evidence of foreign armies threatening the Itj-towy kingdom, there is little possibility that it undertook an extensive military campaign of plundering in the Levant. The traditional visions of pharaonic regiments returning to Itj-towy in triumph after plundering the East are little more than an *orientaliste* fantasia.

At all events, whatever the means by which that expedition had acquired, by barter or by plunder, as tribute, gifting or exchange, the long list of foreign products that are so carefully enumerated on the granite text is another fine example of the Itj-towy court's determination to obtain the materials required for the full maintenance of courtly life: copper and cedar wood, silver, precious stones, lead, malachite, varieties of plants for the temple gardens, abrasive sands for the pharaonic stone workshops and aromatic oils and resins for cosmetics and the embalmers' studios.

Cheryl Ward's reconstructed Byblos boat suggests that each of the two vessels of the Levantine expedition could have returned home to port carrying cargoes of some fifteen tons. The granite text, in fact, tells that their manifests had included more than half a ton of metals, mostly silver, copper and bronze, hundreds of ceramic storage jars of various sizes containing aromatic oils and resins, 200 sacks of spices and timber with which to build ten more similar-sized boats – or, alternatively, a sufficient quantity of darkly aromatic cedar planks, famed for their preservative qualities, to build about a hundred of the massive coffins in which the royal family and their courtiers were laid to rest. All in all, this is a cargo that two Byblos boats could well have accommodated.

In a society without money, in which nothing was counted as explicitly economic or political, the prime purpose of the acquisition of such goods was not to gain prestige or possessions in the modern manner. Like the stones mined in the desert and the wonderful things from Punt, those goods from the Levant were part of the essential ingredients of the state, a fact wonderfully borne out by the discovery in the 1930s of a treasure packed into four sturdy solid copper chests, each bearing the cartouches of Amenemhet II, which French archae-ologists found buried underneath a pavement in the beautiful temple of Tod, a few miles upstream from Thebes.

Cushioned in clean yellow sand, the four chests, each one around a foot and a half long and half as wide, were filled with precious objects: beautifully worked seals made in the workshops of Anatolia and Iran, raw gems, lapis lazuli, amethysts, quartzes and obsidians, ten gold ingots and gold jewellery, 150 silver bowls of rare design and some silver ingots along with large amounts of silver and electrum scrap, the debris of jewellery workshops. The four copper chests alone weighed 280 pounds, and they had held some fifteen pounds of gold and per-haps twice that amount of silver before corrosion took its toll.

Recent analyses have determined that the silver of the bowls, which are of unique design and unknown manufacture, was mined in either Anatolia or the Greek islands, the copper in the Levant or regions further north. Many of Tod's treasures, indeed, are similar to contemporary objects that have been found in ancient settlements throughout the eastern Mediterranean whose workshops had held a commonality of culture. Here, though, they were not found in fragments nor as a solitary treasure as is usually the case in archaeology, but in the fullness of an ancient hoard.

Remarkably, many of the objects found in the copper chests are similar in their materials and forms to those listed and described in the granite text of the time of Amenemhet II as the products of the court's expedition to the north Levant. And the temple of Montu at Tod is specifically listed in that text as the recipient of a royal donation whilst the four caskets bear Amenemhet II's name.

If those expeditions had been a military adventure then this treasure would best be described as booty hidden away, perhaps in time of peril. If, alternatively, those goods had been obtained by other means, then the four chests and their contents would best be described as a royal endowment, but one that was not displayed as booty or church plate nor placed within a treasure chamber but carefully buried underneath the temple's pavement, as in the darkness of a tomb. Those chests, therefore, are best seen as holding goods brought from regions far outside the orbit of the state and buried seed-like in the house of a court god, between the seen and unseen world – an act that had beautifully expressed a concept which is explicitly stated in later texts, that the domain of pharaoh encompasses all earthly things.

A second similarly scanty but yet more informative record of another pharaonic excursion to the Levant by land and sea had been led by the vizier Khnumhotep, who had also supervised a voyage to the land of Punt from the Port of Saww. Undertaken a few decades later, this expedition had consisted of a sea voyage along the coast of the Levant to some of the ports of 'Lebanon' – this being the first-known occurrence of that word.

This text had been engraved on the elaborate limestone façades of Khnumhotep's splendid mastaba that had stood beside the pyramid of Senwosret III at Dahshur. The tomb, however, was demolished by ancient lime burners, and the surviving fragments of its texts, which number in their hundreds and were scattered all around the tomb, were only recently reassembled to reveal what James Allen, their meticulous editor and interpreter, has described as 'one of the more important historical texts of the Middle Kingdom'.

Though only 40 per cent of the original survives, those fragments yet provide a vivid outline of Khnumhotep's account of a voyage of a state flotilla to the seaport of Ullaza in northern Lebanon to obtain cedar wood. Before arriving at Ullaza, however, Khnumhotep's boats had put in at the port of Byblos, whose rulers had long since supplied the pharaonic court with cedar wood and whose ancient temples were stocked with fine pharaonic gifts made in the Memphite workshops. Here, so Khnumhotep's broken texts tell, he had visited the palace of the local ruler, a man the text calls Maliki, which, in the local Semitic language, was simply a term for king. After the appropriate greetings had been observed and offerings made, Maliki asked why Khnumhotep's boats were headed north to Ullaza. This was, apparently, a rather pointed question, for the Itj-towy kings do not seem to have maintained the Memphite pharaohs' millennial connections with Byblos, which was currently in dispute with Ullaza, Maliki having recently dispatched a hundred fighting men to that settlement under the command of his son.

In reply, the broken text reports, Khnumhotep had reminded Maliki of the earlier relationship between pharaoh and the rulers of Byblos, whilst hinting all the while that a pharaonic land force was marching northwards up the Way of Horus to the Lebanon. Whether this was intended as a threat or a proposal of alliance is unclear. At all events, the upshot of the encounter was that pharaoh and Maliki of Byblos exchanged letters renewing their previous relationship of ruler and vassal, and, though the ending of the tale is lost, it seems unlikely that Khnumhotep would have had the text inscribed upon his tomb had he not returned with cedar wood.

A contemporary text upon a funerary stela of a courtier named Khusobek may part confirm Khnumhotep's broken account, for it too tells how the Levant had acceded to the will of Senwosret III. It describes how Khusobek, after having previously 'overthrown' some Nubians in the south, had travelled in the Levant with a squad of men: '. . . and I struck the northern foreigner and had his weapons . . . as Senwosret lives for me'. The text continues, 'I have spoken the truth. And he [Senwosret III] gave me a staff of electrum [an alloy of precious metals] for my hand, and a sheath and dagger worked in electrum.' Though set in a less literary style than the text from the tomb of the vizier Khnumhotep, this would appear to describe an intervention in which a militia had safeguarded pharaonic interests.

Curiously enough, a rock fall that occurred in the 1920s which brought down part of the splendid sea coast overlooking Byblos' ancient harbour had already provided an inadvertent footnote to those two stories. For the collapse of the cliff exposed a cemetery of some of the rulers of Byblos, the oldest of which had governed just a few decades after Khnumhotep's encounter with Maliki, the city's king.

Although the two oldest burials in that seaside cemetery, those of Abi-Shemu and Ipi-Shemu, were no longer named as kings, as 'maliki', the two rulers had been interred as would befit a courtier of pharaoh, in two great pharaonic coffins with traditional pharaonic inlays set into their sides. And though those two great wooden boxes had rotted in the damp air of the coast, one might well guess that they had been made, in the manner of pharaonic burials, of cedar wood. Besides local jars of provisions and a superb Levantine copper sword, those two princes had been buried with fine-made pharaonic objects from Itj-towy. Abi-Shemu's sarcophagus held a beautifully finished vase cut from a rare block of velvet-black obsidian, handsomely framed and lined with bands of yellow gold engraved with Amenemhet III's cartouche, whilst Ipi-Shemu's crypt held a fine small chest of obsidian and gold bearing one of the names of Amenemhet III and a great stone vase engraved with the name of that king's successor, Amenemhet IV. Such donations – and other gold work from the Itj-towy jewellery workshops has also come to light at Byblos – suggest that the city's rulers were supplying cedar to the court of pharaoh once again, and were receiving royal favours in exchange.

Similar hoards of fine pharaonic goods, of gold and Hatnub alabaster and amethyst from Wadi el-Hudi, that point to other Levantine contacts with the Itj-towy court have been found in the great graves of Ebla, an enormous walled city set in the hills to the north of Byblos some seventy miles from the Mediterranean coast. The nature of the traffic between Ebla and the Itj-towy court, however, is otherwise unknown, as are the reasons for similar but less spectacular finds of objects made in Middle Kingdom Egypt that have been excavated throughout the region. None of this tells us if the rulers and the peoples of those cultures, pharaonic and Levantine, had regarded one another in fear or friendship.

The setting of a story, the near-contemporary tale of the adventures of Sinuhe, the longest and most celebrated work of literature from ancient Egypt, which has survived in many and various forms, would, however, appear to hold something of that lost reality, just as aspects of Victorian London make their appearance in the works of Dickens.

Composed in the times of the first Itj-towy kings, the story of Sinuhe tells how he had fled the Nile Valley at the death of pharaoh because, for reasons never clearly stated, he thought himself endangered. Lacking water in his long journey north and thinking that he is dying, Sinuhe hears cattle lowing and is rescued by some herders whose leader recognizes the courtier from his visits to the Nile Valley. Given water and then milk to drink, Sinuhe heads for Byblos. Months go by, however, as he is passed powerlessly from court to court until one of the local rulers, a certain Amunesh, takes him to his home in the northern Levant, where several of Sinuhe's country men were already in residence. 'You will be happy with me,' Amunesh tells the fugitive, 'for you will hear the speech of your own country.' Sinuhe then tells his Levantine host about pharaoh's death, and in reply Amunesh launches into a lengthy panegyric: pharaoh is a peerless and far-striding god, he says, and none can escape his arrow; he is a lord of kindness and sweetness, a king who conquered in the egg, who was born to smite Levantines and sand dwellers! Amunesh then adopts Sinuhe and places him amongst his family, giving him land rich with figs and grapes, honey and barley and cattle without number. And Sinuhe lived at the court of Amunesh, serving him as he would have served a pharaoh.

Scribes copied the story of Sinuhe's adventures for a thousand years and more and used it as an exemplar for their pupils. Though the bulk of the text describes modes of rhetoric and the manners and comportment of pharaonic courtly life rather than a narrative of high adventure, modern interest has mostly been concerned with debates about its use of grammar and the amount of political history it may or may not contain. One truth the story indisputably holds is that the pharaonic scribe describes his Levantine neighbours in terms of kindness and humanity rather than as actors in the bloodthirsty two-dimensional politics that are so often conjured from the surviving texts.

THE SINAI STATION – *A LEVANTINE SYNTHESIS*

I was in Sinai and inspected it . . . I sealed its treasury at the mountain of the domain 'Hathor of the Terraces of Turquoise' . . . I travelled on the order of my lord [the king] and did what he had willed. I have defended the Levantines in their own countries and I returned in peace to the palace and brought to him [the king] the best of foreign lands . . .
From the tomb chapel of Khety at Deir el-Bahari

Though working far from the valley of the lower Nile, the copper miners of Sinai had a pharaonic temple in their midst, a royal foundation established in the times of the Itj-towy kings that housed the goddess Hathor, Lady of Turquoise, her cult, her festivals and offerings and the settlement of her attending priests, their families and assistants.

Set high in the mountains and some thirty miles from the sea at a site known now as Serabit el-Khadim, Hathor's house in Sinai stood like the Theban cliff-top temple of the Montuhoteps at the peak of a high hill. Clusters of its stelae and the stone of its beams and lintels still stand along the skyline like rows of broken teeth. The beginnings of this temple lay in its modest central shrine, a small cave set into the crest of a cliff. Similarly unsophisticated cave shrines are found beside several desert tracks that were used by pharaonic travellers. But only the shrine at Serabit el-Khadim lies outside the valley of the lower Nile, standing utterly alone within its landscape, entirely disconnected to the orientation of a river, star or human settlement, its unique shape simply determined by the angle of the sandstone ridge on which it stood. Yet in the same manner that desert cairns commonly marked out the way ahead on ancient caravan tracks, so Hathor's cliff-top temple stood on a route by which the millennial traffic travelled down to Egypt from the Levant, a route parallel to the Way of Horus that ran down through modern Syria and Jordan and which is known nowadays by the Biblical term 'The Kings Highway'.

Serabit el-Khadim in the 1890s, before its excavation, depredation and restoration.

Serabit el-Khadim was a charmed location. Millennia before a pharaoh's court had been founded, the craftsmen of the lower Nile had already understood the subtle relationship between copper and turquoise, as they made turquoise-coloured glazes using copper ore as a colorant. Brought from unearthly regions at the boundaries of life and death, such materials had been transported into the regions of the lower Nile to stand at the heart of the pharaonic state. The mountain at Serabit el-Khadim held in its living rock glistening veins of turquoise that the ancients had long quarried, whilst major pharaonic copper mines, including those of the Wadi Magara, lay in the valleys to the east and west. And as the extraction of such materials could only be accomplished by employing the resources of the pharaonic court, turquoise held a regal aura and was widely used in courtly jewellery. Thus it was duly celebrated in the shrine of Hathor, Lady of Turquoise, who was, in her turn, the mother of Horus and thus, of pharaoh and of the state itself.

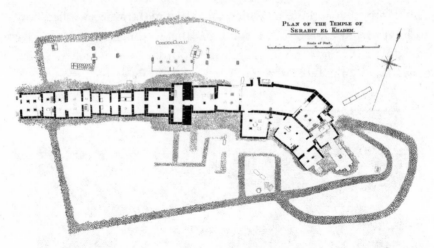

Petrie's plan of the temple of Serabit el-Khadim. Although the names of later pharaohs appear upon its architecture, recent excavation has underlined its Middle Kingdom form in which a series of doorways gives access to two shrines of the period, the largest of which, the so-called 'Cave of Hathor', lies at its eastern end.

The temple at Serabit el-Khadim was successively enlarged throughout the times of the Itj-towy kings so that it came to include a shrine for the royal ancestors and other gods. The workmen enclosed the approach to the little cave in a series of rectangular courtyards, gateways and offering halls and surrounded the whole with dry-stone walls which, in the traditional manner, held the houses of the temple priests along with potteries, bakeries and even furnaces for copper smelting. Numerous texts describe how this remarkable establishment had been provisioned in much the same manner as the copper miners had been, with supplies sent directly from Itj-towy accompanied by some of the court's sculptors, who cut fine-drawn inscriptions into the local stone, and potters, who made courtly tableware onsite from local clay.

Large numbers of stelae, all measured out and cut in high court style, were set up at Serabit el-Khadim in the times of the Itj-towy kings. Well over fifty have been recorded, and many more must have been lost or broken or simply eroded beyond all recognition or, indeed, now stand in far away museums. Nonetheless, those ancient dedications had been so numerous that modern visitors on their way up to the central cave still pass through a small forest of such monoliths.

Most of these stelae show the monarch of the day in the usual fashion, in the presence of the shrine's goddess. Others were inscribed on behalf of the courtiers who oversaw the provisions that were dispatched from Itj-towy to all of its various enterprises, including those in Sinai. And hundreds of graffiti were cut directly onto the surrounding rocks along the ancient pathways to the temple, naming and sometimes picturing the humbler members of those courtly expeditions – their guides and scribes, foremen, the cattle herders, scorpion catchers and quarrymen. Some cut small stone offering altars and little stelae, many of which were made by unskilled hands and dedicated to some of Hathor's companions in that splendid wilderness: the gods of Heliopolis, the Nile Delta and the Eastern Desert.

Just as the rows of standing stelae at Serabit el-Khadim had resembled the obelisks at the Byblos temple and those at other sites in the Levant, so the internal architecture of the temple also bears comparison with Levantine shrines. Serabit el-Khadim, in fact, is a geographic and cultural half way house between those relatively modest structures and contemporary pharaonic temples. To that extent, and like the story of Sinuhe, it demonstrates a communality shared by the Itj-towy court and their northern neighbours. And that was new, for their Memphite predecessors had cut reliefs upon the rocks of Sinai that show pharaoh smiting his northern neighbours with a mace.

Just as Nubians had served in the southern expeditions of the Itj-towy pharaohs, so in those same times some of pharaoh's northern neighbours had worked in the Sinai copper mines. Some of their leaders, too, had paid visits to the site where they were celebrated in pharaonic relief; one man is shown riding a long-eared Syrian donkey and carrying the same distinctive weapons that are pictured in the painting of the young Khnumhotep in his father's tomb chapel at Beni Hasan, which shows him greeting the members of a Levantine caravan. Recent archaeology in the Wadi Arabah has shown that Levantines had been mining and smelting copper in the deserts to the north and east of Sinai for millennia, and the copper workers of the Itj-towy pharaohs may well have employed their expertise. The ancestors of the Levantines shown at Serabit el-Khadim, indeed, might also have mined the ores of Sinai long before the craftsmen of the Memphite pharaohs had cut those apprehensive images of their northern neighbours upon its dark red rocks.

The most remarkable product of these cultural encounters in the high desert was discovered in the course of a pioneering expedition into Sinai in the winter of 1904–5 during which Petrie had located and copied a small number of short, stick-like inscriptions that, although they had first appeared to be but badly formed hieroglyphs, had subsequently proved indecipherable. One of these strange texts had been inscribed on the base of a small locally made statue of a sphinx; others were scratched directly onto crude pharaonic statues. Most, however, had been scored onto rocks around the mouths of mine shafts. Ten years after their discovery and in a work that he would later describe as his single most important contribution to ancient history, the great egyptologist Alan Gardiner published an essay on those same inscriptions entitled 'The Egyptian Origins of the Semitic Alphabet'. Though part-related to pharaonic hieroglyphs, Gardiner asserted, these graffiti had been written in a previously unknown alphabet a few signs of which, he demonstrated, spelled out the name of the goddess, Ba'alat, the goddess of Byblos' largest temple whom the pharaonic inscriptions at that site had identified with Hathor. Considering their age, Gardiner concluded, those brief inscriptions were far and away the earliest-known form of Semitic writing, for Ba'alat's name signifies 'queen' or 'lady' in that wide-spread group of ancient languages – a group which contains many modern languages as well. Millennia later, indeed, and on another continent, those same spare letters would also form the backbone of the Greek and Latin alphabets.

Considerable amounts of research have since been conducted on these so-called 'Proto-Sinaitic' texts, though less than a hundred and fifty of those spare inscriptions have ever been located. A handful have been found in the south Levant, scratched into rocks beside copper mines close to the Kings Highway and a few more have been spotted to the west of Thebes on a rocky outcrop alongside an ancient caravan route. The great majority, however, are at Serabit el-Khadim and a recent analysis suggests that the forms of their letters were derived from hieroglyphs that were visible at that site in the times of the Itj-towy kings. So the lengthy processes by which some of the elements of pharaonic hieroglyphs were transformed into the letters used in this book appear to have had their beginnings far from the centres of ancient culture, in a remarkable ancient synthesis of cultures that took place on a Sinai hilltop.

LEVANTINE SETTLEMENTS – *AMORITES AND TELL EL-DAB'A*

> *A pipe, too, and a drum, and shortly after,*
> *A most unoriental roar of laughter . . .*
>
> *. . . it was the Pyrrhic dance so martial,*
> *To which the Levantines are very partial.*
>
> Lord Byron, *1821*

In the times of the Itj-towy kings the Levant was largely populated by a people of a widespread and disparate culture who would have a remarkable and long-lasting impact on the history of ancient Egypt. This culture has been traditionally described as 'Amorite', a term that should not be confused with that same word in the Old Testament, where it is employed to distinguish one of the tribes of Canaan. In its historical sense, the term 'Amorite' was coined by a group of late eighteenth-century German linguists to describe one of the earliest forms of a major modern language group, which had previously been termed 'Oriental' but which, in another of their Biblical borrowings, those same linguists had re-named as 'Semitic', after Shem, the son of Noah.

The first-known traces of the Amorite language are in Mesopotamian texts of the beginning of the third millennium BC. No texts appear to have been written in Amorite, however, the scribes of Mesopotamia and the Levant always employing the traditional literary languages of Mesopotamia. So the appearance of Amorite in those regions is only witnessed by the growing use of Semitic words and the novel names of people and of deities in texts written in other languages. That rare phenomenon, however, finds powerful archaeological concordance in the simultaneous appearance of a distinctive material culture with a highly specific range of bronze weaponry and walled enclosures. Thus identified, Amorite culture, a synthesis of written and material artefacts, can be seen to have spread throughout the region during the following millennium, a diffusion that led to unsubstantiated theories of an Amorite invasion of the ancient East from central Asia, in much the same manner that the Victorians had described the barbarian invasions at the ending of the Roman Empire.

In the times of the Itj-towy pharaohs, people of Amorite culture had long since taken control of the ancient Mesopotamian city state, whilst previously modest settlements, such as Babylon and Mari on the Euphrates, had been greatly enlarged and girt in fortress walls. In the Levant, where Amorite culture appears to have arisen, some of the larger settlements were similarly building mud-brick fortifications as protection from their fractious neighbours, and texts of the period tell of the formation of confederations of Levantine settlements based at various times at cities such as Byblos and Ashkelon and archaeological sites such as Ebla, Ugarit and Qatna.

Like Homer in a later age, the court scribes of the times sing of their ruler's martial exploits in a vivid, formal prose of cruelty and conflict, so that their texts give the impression that the cities and confederations of both Mesopotamia and the Levant were engaged in continuous bouts of warfare and that their roles in the history of the region had continuously changed. Yet archaeology has shown that those fortified confederations were also engaging in elaborate processes of gifting and bartering and that the high-walled cities were providing security for caravans and enabling the ancient transport networks to operate more fluidly than before, a traffic that, through the levying of tithes on transported goods, was enriching the material culture of the rulers. The very presence of those fortresses, indeed, appears to have signalled a kind of stability in the region rather than an age of interminable small-scale warfare.

At all events, these new Levantine trading networks served to connect a spectrum of ancient cultures and traditions from Persia and Afghanistan to the flood plains of Mesopotamia and the coastal cities of the Levant. Here, then, was their point of contact with the court of Itj-towy, which, as we have seen, took in enormous quantities of Levantine timber, copper, wine and fruit, olive oil and unguents, along with lapis lazuli and ingots of copper, tin and silver from far more distant regions. In return, some of the finest products of the Itj-towy workshops were sent up along those age old highways, to the courts of Byblos, Hazor and Qatna, Mari, Ugarit and Ebla.

So, despite the scribe's bloodthirsty prose, the extent of internecine warfare in the Levant of those times need not be exaggerated. Hostilities, indeed, may well have taken the form of ritual combat between lavishly equipped Bronze Age champions. Certainly, there is no evidence of pitched battles having taken place, and archaeologists have found scant evidence of siege within the hundreds of ancient fortresses in Mesopotamia and the Levant. Outside the cemeteries, only a handful of corpses have ever been recovered from the excavation of the fortresses, and those are more suggestive of a fracas than a massed assault, and the soft ash and burnt brick of fire and destruction has seldom been encountered. At all events, the rise of Amorite culture had not interrupted the underlying rhythms of Middle Eastern Bronze Age society; indeed, it had facilitated the dispersal of technologies and design, a remarkably creative process that was accompanied by an increasing material prosperity.

Levantine workshops, especially, were expert in the ancient arts of casting copper and in mixing it with small quantities of tin, arsenic and lead to aid its flow in casting or to produce a bronze or other alloy that was harder than pure smelted copper. Nothing so exemplifies the reality of this new culture as its so-called 'warrior graves', which are found throughout the Levant and Mesopotamia and also in the Nile Delta – burials of men interred with a range of fine-made weapons, including axes, daggers and spear points, wrought with copper mined in the Levant, in Anatolia, in Cyprus and on the Greek mainland. These were cold-hammered into their final forms, a technique that involved the constant annealing of the copper-alloy blades, which gave those elegant novel arms remarkably hard edges.

The most distinctive element of this sophisticated arsenal is the so-called 'duck bill' axe blade, which with its curving wooden handle is pictured in an enormous range of contemporary images. In the tomb chapel of Khnumhotep's father at Beni Hasan, for example, two such weapons, neatly balanced in their carriers' right hands, appear in the sharply observed painting of a Levantine caravan. Here, alongside their harps and weaving spools, their bows and throw sticks, their tamed ibex and their pack donkeys, the distinctively dressed and coiffured group is identified as 'thirty-seven Aamu from Shu'. Following the Old Testament use of the term, early egyptologists had identified these exotics as 'the Amorites of Shu'. Today, however, they are usually described as 'Asiatics', a word which, whilst it avoids Biblical allusion and thus inadvertent reference to political tensions in the modern Levant, is as nebulous as the term 'Libyans', often employed to describe all the ancient peoples who inhabited the regions to the west of the ancient Nile Valley.

The Aamu family pictured in the tomb chapel of Khnumhotep at Beni Hassan in Middle Egypt. Duck-bill axes are held in the right hands of two men in the leading group of figures.

Pharaonic craftsmen of later ages came to distinguish the various subcultures of their northern neighbours by their tattoos, clothing and hair styling, distinguishing them as precisely as they differentiated species of birds and animals. Yet there is still debate about the origins of the 'Amorites/Asiatics of Shu' in the Beni Hasan tomb chapel, for whilst their dress, their weaponry and comportment clearly show that the pharaonic draughtsmen had identified their material culture as Levantine, they did not distinguish them precisely. Was 'Shu' a region or a place? Were the Aamu people from the north or south Levant, from Palestine, the Lebanon or Syria? Were they nomadic shepherds, the 'sand dwellers' that many pharaonic texts describe, or were they envoys from one of the high-walled settlements in the north Levant?

The question has great resonance in the history of ancient Egypt. For at the same time that the Aamu of Shu were pictured in the tomb chapel at Beni Hasan, a substantial Levantine community was living in the eastern Nile Delta, in dwellings built on the abandoned ruins of a farming settlement established in the times of the Montuhoteps. Generations later, another larger Levantine settlement was built on another, half a mile to the east, and other settlements, with cemeteries and temples, were established in the same area on other turtlebacks, so that by the time of the last Itj-towy kings they had amalgamated to form a conurbation covering some twenty acres. Throughout the following millennium and with the aid of a considerable harbour cut from the banks of one of the many small branches of the Nile Delta, these settlements came to serve as the core of a complex of far larger conglomerations, jigsaw remains that yet lie buried, for the most part, a few feet beneath the straight flat fields of the delta farmers. This is the archaeological sensation that egyptologists collectively named, after one of the local villages, Tell el-Dab'a. It has been extensively excavated since 1966 by a team of Austrian archaeologists led by Manfred Bietak.

Unlike the settlement of the times of the Montuhoteps at Tell el-Dab'a, which in the usual manner of courtly colonies within the Nile Delta had consisted of modular and modest accommodations set in gridded blocks, the Levantines' houses were often large and generous affairs whose exotic symmetries and proportions had travelled through time and space from the settlements of the north Levant, where similar designs had served both as houses and as temples and whose origins yet lay at one remove, in southern Mesopotamia. Further confirmation of this remarkable intercontinental exchange was found in a cemetery beside the oldest-known Levantine settlement at Tell el-Dab'a, some of whose occupants had been buried with duck-bill axes, copper-alloy spear points and all the other accoutrements of so-called Amorite warrior burial. More of those tell-tale axes, indeed, have been excavated at Tell el-Dab'a than at any other site throughout the ancient East.

That the Levantines' settlements within the Nile Delta were not products of aggressive colonization nor even unwelcome immigration was underlined by Bietak's remarkable discovery of the fragments of an over life-sized statue of a seated man. A skilful product of a courtly pharaonic workshop, this considerable sculpture seems to have been intended to receive offerings, for it was set in an annexe close to a tomb. Fashioned from a large block of Nile Valley limestone and seated in pharaonic pose, the statue's pudding-basin haircut, its yellow-painted skin and the remains of stripes and squares drawn on its sculpted robes are all attributes of the images of the Aamu of Shu that are pictured in the Beni Hasan tomb chapel, just as the form of the throw sticks carried by the people in that painting – which is also the form of a hieroglyph that denotes the word for several types of 'foreigner' – had been sculpted sceptre-like across the sculpture's chest. This had been a fine pharaonic statue of an honoured Levantine.

Statues had similarly flanked the doorways of some of the grandest burial crypts in the contemporary cemeteries of the north Levant. The graves the Austrian archaeologists excavated from Tell el-Dab'a's onion fields, however, were of traditional pharaonic design, with a brick-built vault set over the corpse in the manner of the desert cemeteries at Abydos. The burials, too, were accompanied with offerings held in ceramics of pharaonic design, and the great limestone statue appears to have had a standard pharaonic offering formula engraved in hieroglyphs upon its base. Yet some of the dead within that cemetery had also been equipped with the armoury of Levantine warrior burial and were accompanied by pairs of slaughtered donkeys, a custom typical of contemporary interments in the north Levant.

Other burials at Tell el-Dab'a held works from other cultures with which the Levantines had been in contact. So whilst the dead in one small cemetery had been laid in typically pharaonic coffins and were accompanied by masses of pharaonic gemstone beads and tableware imported from the north Levant, one grave had also contained a splendid golden pendant designed and made by Minoan craftsmen, and several more held painted pottery made in that same distant culture. These were hardly the burials of bands of nomads from the Levantine deserts, but the graves of a sophisticated cosmopolitan community that, whilst it retained its own distinct identity, had prospered in the region of the lower Nile and adopted many aspects of pharaonic culture.

The Tell el-Dab'a pendant

In the broader span of history, such eclectic mixes are characteristic of the Nile Delta's archaeology. Despite the pharaohs' ageless title as 'rulers of the lands of the sedge and the bee', the delta's sedgy marshes were a fluid, somewhat liminal zone well outside the narrow prism of the Nile Valley through which high pharaonic culture was always mediated, a region over-inundated during generous Nile floods and subject to penetration by the salt waters of the Mediterranean when the river was running low. Yet the delta served both as bread basket and pasture land for the Memphite and Itj-towy courts, and its ever-shifting streams and mud banks, its luxuriant water meads and pastures, were colonized, exploited and enjoyed throughout millennia by pharaoh and his agents.

So several of the deities housed in the pharaohs' delta shrines had other shrines at Serabit el-Khadim in Sinai and were similarly invoked in stelae made at the Red Sea port of Wadi Gawasis. And as the courtiers of pharaoh had identified the local deity of Byblos – Ba'alat – as Hathor, and those two names appear side by side in different scripts at Serabit el-Khadim, so Horus, Hathor's son, a falcon god, was similarly identified in Nile Delta shrines as the falcon deity Sopdu, 'the sharp one', who is, as well, a god of foreign lands.

The delta too, was pharaoh's door to the Levant. Just as Khusobek's land force had marched out of the delta and north along the Way of Horus, so the vizier Khnumhotep's expedition to the Lebanon would have sailed from a delta port like that at Tell el-Dab'a, the meandering streams of the Nile's dividing branches holding many harbours and access also to the open sea. These would have been the quays from which the Byblos boats had cast off on their voyages to Crete, Cyprus and the Aegean.

And the Levantines at Tell el-Dab'a had probably played a part in these international exchanges. Just as Levantine copper workers may well have lent their skills to pharaoh's workforce since the first days of the kingdom, just as the temple reliefs of the Abusir pharaohs show Levantine sailors at the steering oars of pharaoh's sea-going boats, so the very name of 'Byblos boats' may have spoken of their navigators' origins rather than their port of destination.

Austrian archaeologists have estimated that some two million Levantine amphorae, those splendid sea-going ceramic packing cases, were imported into Tell el-Dab'a. Yet that settlement between pharaoh's narrow valley and the open sea would serve as more than an entry point for imported goods, for woods, metals and precious oils and incense, since with them came a wider vision of the world, its ways of life, its crafts, its patterns, its workmanship, its architecture. And the effect upon pharaonic culture would be profound.

NUBIAN FORTRESSES

In comparison with the Levant, where water came down from the sky and landscape seemed to be an orderless confusion of rivers, hills, and plains, the Nile Valley upstream of Aswan was familiar ground for pharaoh's courtiers, for Nubia was a leaner version of their homeland. And though lonely and remote, the deserts to the east and west of Nubia were similarly familiar, having been long exploited for metals and hard stone, their unforgiving environment having been overcome to the extent that pharaonic mining expeditions carried sufficient skins of water to enable them to wash gold from the mother lode out in the desert.

South of Aswan, the Nile Valley was inhabited by bands of semi-nomadic pastoralists and farmers whose little villages were scattered amongst spare pockets of river silt. Long before the expeditions of the

Memphite courtier Harkhuf, pharaonic voyagers had travelled in relative security throughout all those territories, and when they had ventured further south and west into the Sahara they had also travelled in relative safety. When that courtly traffic was resumed there is no hint of enmity in the inscription of Montuhotep II that his envoys left on a solitary rock at the Gebel Uweinat, which simply states that the people of Yam had brought gifts or goods to pharaoh.

At that same time, however, the situation along the Nubian Nile seems to have been different. A graffito scratched upon a rock close to Aswan records that a river-based expedition from Montuhotep's court, which had travelled 200 miles south of Aswan to the Nile's Second Cataract, had clashed with indigenous communities along the way. So it appears that access to the exotic produce of the 'land of the horizon', was occasionally threatened by the inhabitants of lower Nubia, along with access to the pharaonic gold and copper mines. Reaction to this danger finds immediate expression in some of Montuhotep II's modest temples, where the hapless victims of the classic courtly image of pharaoh smiting the enemies of state no longer display the attributes of Levantines but those of the inhabitants of Nubia; that is, people with curly hair, distinctive clothes and gestures, and a skin colour far darker then the yellow and red ochres which pharaonic craftsmen employed to colour their images of Levantines and, indeed, those of the male inhabitants of pharaoh's kingdom.

Such growing hostility may have encouraged some pharaonic expeditions to avoid the river and take to the caravan tracks in the Western Desert, or even to sail to the south in Byblos boats from the Port of Saww. At all events, the interruptions in court traffic appear to have become more frequent during the following decades, for in the reign of Senwosret I, and 'after twenty years of comings and goings', another somewhat exasperated graffito tells that during one of the vizier Antefoker's many expeditions there had been a violent reaction:

> Antefoker says: 'I am a valiant citizen, a pleasant man from Thebes, a scribe of excellent fingers, one who is humble, who loves his Person [i.e. the king], who [distributes] clothes among his troops . . . I sailed upstream victoriously, slaughtering the Nubians on the riverbanks and I returned downstream pulling up their corn and cutting down

their trees. I set fire to their houses, as one does to those who have rebelled against the king . . .

And written underneath is:

Renika says: 'I made this [graffito] while I was here with the . . . vizier . . . Antefoker, in the [boat named] "Great Oar" . . . The scribe Renika, born of Hekat, who is dead.

Another contemporary response to such southern insecurities, and one of greater consequence, was the initiation of the construction of a line of fortresses that in a century and a half had amounted to some seventeen separate citadels set along a 250-mile-long stretch of the Nubian Nile; a project that the archaeologist William Adams has described as 'a chain of the mightiest fortifications ever erected in the ancient world'.

Some of these impressive mud-brick fortresses were built close to the quarries and the gold mines of the Itj-towy kings and had served as processing plants, as storerooms and protection. The greatest number, however, was clustered in a thirty-mile stretch along the desolate region of the Batn el-Hagar – the 'Belly of Stones' at the river's Second Cataract – a huge mass of white water rushing through the toughest and most desolate of deserts. Set on the river's banks and on several of its multitude of rocky islands, many of these fortresses were in direct line of sight one to the other. When that had not proved possible, contact between them was maintained, as hundreds of graffiti show, by watchtowers and observation posts set up and down the line amongst the rocks and cliffs that rise above the river. In all of its previous ancient history, the pharaonic court had never built anything remotely like it.

Unfortunately, the best part of that extraordinary enterprise now lies beneath Lake Nasser, along with the rest of lower Nubia. The fortresses' massive mud-brick walls are completely liquefied, and the limestone temples that were later built within their courtyards have been dismantled block by block and re-erected nearby or in museums in Egypt and the Sudan. In earlier millennia, however, that imponent procession had dominated the lonely desert valley and had resembled a sequence of Alpine castles.

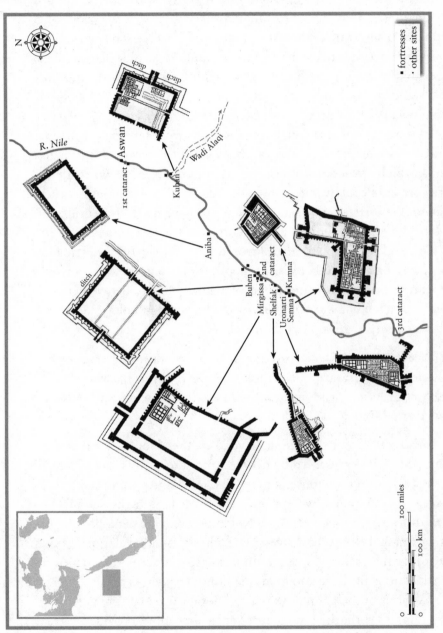

N

R. Nile

Aswan

1st cataract

ditch

ditch

Kuban

Wadi Alaqi

Aniba

Buhen

Mirgissa

Shelfak

Uronarti

Semna

Kumna

2nd cataract

3rd cataract

ditch

100 miles

100 km

Map showing the locations and some of the plans of the Nubian fortresses, most of which were clustered in the rocky region of the Nile's Second Cataract.

Though varying widely in their plans, for they accommodated the rugged Nile-side terrain, all those fortresses had shared the same fundamental design that consisted of an outer wall surrounding a doughty citadel. Typically rectangular and ranging along their longest sides from 200 feet to more than 1,000 feet, each fortress had contained accommodations for three hundred people, large magazines and a small temple. Rising to heights of thirty feet and more and standing over deep dry moats, their outer walls, which were some twenty and thirty feet thick, had accommodated well-planned archers' embrasures, and elaborate bastions were set along their sides and at their corners. Colossal gateways lay at the centre of the longest walls, which opened to both the desert and the riverside, where defensive corridors contrived to enable the garrison's continuous access to water. One fortress, at least, is thought to have had a drawbridge.

In short, those buildings had held most of the elements that Champollion and his contemporaries would have considered fundamental for surviving a considerable siege; appropriate constructions, it would appear, for a line of kings, one of whose names, Senwosret, was awarded to a great warrior pharaoh of classical mythology, Sesostris, whose mighty armies, Herodotus relates,

> made a progress by land across the continent, conquering every people which fell in his way . . . [and] in this way he traversed the whole continent of Asia, whence he passed on into Europe, and made himself master of Scythia and of Thrace . . .

Until their recent drowning, several of these fortresses had been remarkably well preserved by drifted sand, their walls and turrets in better condition than those of many medieval European fortresses. In the 1950s and 1960s, when they were excavated in the scramble to record the archaeology of lower Nubia before it was engulfed by the rising waters behind the Aswan Dam, they were a revelation. And in the years that followed, the photographs, the plans and paper reconstructions of those commanding buildings were used to illustrate the histories of their times, in which quotations from some of the inscriptions that the Itj-towy court set up in Nubia provided a clear literary motive for such an astonishing architectural invasion.

One of these inscriptions, that of a so-called boundary stela, states that it marks 'The southern border, made [so as] to not allow any Nubian to pass', whilst the text of another that was set up at Semna, one of the southernmost of the Itj-towy fortresses, similarly declares it to be:

> The southern boundary made in Year 8 under the majesty of the King of Upper and Lower Egypt, Khakare [Sesostris III] in order to prevent any Nubian from passing it going downstream, either on land or in a boat, or any herds of the Nubians, apart from a Nubian who comes to trade in Iken [a fortress upstream at Mirgissa] or is on an official mission . . .'

The most explicit of these texts was engraved in duplicate upon a pair of stelae, two huge blocks of pink Aswan granite some five and a half feet high, one of which was set up within a little temple in the Semna fortress, the other inside a nearby fortress on a rocky outcrop on Uronarti Island. Quoted below in an amended version of Breasted's 1906 translation, which was a standard text for English-speaking historians throughout the best part of the last century, the unpleasant tone set an easy seal on the interpretation of the ancient fortresses as a grand act of ancient imperialism:

The so-called Second Semna Stela of Senwosret III. The figure shows the first presentation of this celebrated text, in Lepsius' Denkmäler (1849).

Year 16, third month of the Flood [when] his majesty Senwosret III made the southern boundary . . . beyond (that) of his fathers . . .

I am a king who speaks and executes; that which my heart conceives is that which comes to pass . . . [I am] eager to possess . . . attacking him who attacks, silent in a matter, or answering a matter according to that which is in it; since, if one is silent after attack, it strengthens the heart of the enemy.

Valiance is eagerness, cowardice is to slink back; he is truly a craven who is repelled upon his border; since the Negro hearkens to . . . the mouth; it is answering him which drives him back; when one is eager against him, he turns his back; when one slinks back, he begins to be eager. But they are not a people of might, they are poor and broken in heart. My majesty has seen them; it is not an untruth.

I captured their women, I carried off their subjects, I went forth to their wells and smote their bulls; I reaped their grain, and set fire thereto. [I swear] as my father lives for me, I speaking in truth, without a lie coming out of my mouth.

Now, as for every son of mine who shall maintain this boundary which my majesty has made, he is my son, he is born to my majesty . . . Now, as for him who shall relax it, and shall not fight for it; he is not my son, he is not born to me.

Now, behold, my majesty caused a statue of my majesty to be made upon this boundary, which my majesty made; in order that ye might prosper because of it, and in order that ye might fight for it.

Powerful visual precedent for such statements date back to the earliest times of the Memphite kings, when images of pharaoh smiting a cowering Levantine had been engraved upon the rocks of Sinai; in words and images, both demonstrate the consequences of disobedience, of upsetting the harmony and balance of the ordered pharaonic universe.

There is clear precedent, too, for the fortresses' idiosyncratic architecture though no such buildings were erected north of Aswan, and the detail of their architecture is completely alien. In the Levant, however, many contemporary Bronze Age fortresses share their design.

And pharaoh's expeditions, of course, had long since visited those powerful foursquare buildings, and images of them had been engraved and painted on the walls of temples and tomb chapels since the times of the Memphite kings.

The representations of Levantine fortresses that were engraved in some of the temples of Abusir are very badly fragmented. Several of those placed in the courtiers' tomb chapels, however, have survived and show small bands of pharaonic militia storming those foreign citadels. Though lively, seemingly even anecdotal in their detail, the substance of these scenes – the lines of attackers, the poses of the fortresses' inhabitants as they are subjected to a hail of arrows and attacked from scaffolding and ladders – are but standard images of the craftsmen's repertoire, and neither they nor their accompanying texts hold any information as to the fortresses' sizes or locations.

One of the finest surviving examples of the genre was painted in the reign of Montuhotep II on a row of columns in a large saff tomb at Deir el-Bahari. This tomb was made, so its inscriptions tell, for a certain Intef, who had been a royal seal bearer. It stands like a guard beside the great wide causeway leading up to Montuhotep's temple. Beyond its open courtyard, amongst its shadowed colonnade and the usual images of farming and the activities of courtly households, is a scene of Intef and twenty-three armed men aboard three boats. The next column shows the same group attacking a Levantine fortress, whilst a scene below shows Intef apparently supervising the removal of the fortress's inhabitants: five women, a few children and a dozen men. And all those people wear the brightly striped and chequered robes and have the yellow skin colour that the craftsmen of the times employed to distinguish their subjects as Levantines.

Intef's militia, alternatively, are clad in plain white kilts, whose linen will not take brightly coloured natural dyes. His troop includes five dark-skinned Nubian archers. Fighting, and with quivers filled with arrows at their feet, these Nubians are identified by tassels and distinctive headbands, as are some of their predecessors who had worked as militiamen within the valley of the lower Nile and who also appear in Ankhtifi's tomb chapel. As in other scenes of similarly embattled forts, the fortress's attackers are shown using a wooden scaffold to scale its walls, from which several of its defenders are shown tumbling down onto the ground.

In the spring of 1926, Winlock uncovered grisly evidence of the risks of such encounters just a few hundred yards away from Intef's tomb, when his workers opened the corridor of a modest tomb and found it to be piled with sixty desiccated corpses of felled militia men, some of whom still wore their archers' wrist guards and were accompanied by well-strung bows. None of them had been injured, Winlock notes, in hand-to-hand fighting, which is not surprising as there is no evidence of pitched battles being fought in such distant ages. The angle of their wounds, however, was consistent with those that would have been sustained during an attack on the high walls of a fortress. A medical analysis establishing that many of them had been dispatched by blows to the head, the *coup de grâce* inflicted after the victims had been either stunned by heavy objects dropped from on high or shot from above by ebony-tipped arrows, some of which were still stuck in the corpses. A number of those unfortunate combatants had been abandoned for some time, and birds had partly stripped the flesh from their bones. But then the birds had been scared away, and the bodies from those unrecorded encounters had been collected up and an expedition had carried them back to pharaoh's kingdom and the courtly burial grounds of Deir el-Bahari.

Recent estimates suggest that those warriors had been entombed around 1870 BC, during the reign of Senwosret II. By that time, the designers of the Levantine fortresses had elaborated their original plans, so that the simple straight-sided fortress type shown in Intef's tomb had developed complicated systems of defence, including steeply angled bases at the bottom of the fortresses' walls intended, it would appear, as a protection against battering rams. Such angled walls are also shown in the contemporary siege scenes in tomb chapels at Beni Hasan and in the fortresses of Nubia, which demonstrates that their builders were well aware of recent developments in Levantine military architecture.

In fact, that highly distinctive military architecture had a long pedigree, the origins of which lie, as Aaron Burke has recently established, on the plains of northern Mesopotamia in the time of the first recorded traces of the Amorites, when walls and moats were set around far older settlements. By the middle of the third millennium BC, the confederations of the principalities of both Mesopotamia and the Levant had greatly strengthened and elaborated those older systems of defence. And over the following centuries moats, ramparts and square turrets were developed, along with large fortified gateways; monumental structures with three pairs of stone piers supporting a high barrel-vaulted corridor, innovations that had been followed in short order by angled walls, bastions and archers' embrasures.

Major Levantine principalities built clusters of these idiosyncratic structures. Set on ancient trading routes and protecting the leading households of those little states, the largest of them shielded urban centres such as Aleppo, Ashkelon and Qatna, whilst smaller settlements, villages and hamlets situated at strategic locations were similarly provided with substantial fortifications, as outlying elements in integrated systems of defence. So very regular, so coherent and so widespread was this military Levantine architecture that it would appear that the fortresses were all designed by specialized groups of travelling craftsmen.

Now, the Itj-towy fortresses of Nubia display exactly that same architecture, the same regularity, the same details of design, the same unified systems of defence. The similarities are so close, indeed, that, if not Levantine themselves, their designers had perfectly understood how such Levantine fortresses had been designed and built. From the efficient deployment of bastions and archers' embrasures, to the signature three-tiered gateways that gave access to the Nile and the desert, all the foreign elements of Levantine fortress architecture were built according to pharaonic methods of mud-brick construction. All the fortresses in Nubia were made with mud bricks of large and consistent dimensions, and in their laying ancient pharaonic methods of construction had been employed that took account of the fact that, with such enormously thick walls, the fresh-made and still slightly soft mud bricks would shift as they hardened, a process that took many years.

This fascinating cultural exchange is best seen at the fortress of Buhen, whose designers had set the rigorous symmetries of high pharaonic design and craftsmanship within the outlandish architecture of another continent. Presumably, the Itj-towy court had felt

itself faced with a situation in Nubia similar to that which they themselves had witnessed in the Levant, and they had reproduced an
architecture that had projected security and force within an alien
land.

Yet the circumstances of the Nubian fortresses were entirely different from those in which the sturdy originals had been developed.
Whilst Levantine principalities appear to have expended more of
their resources on the construction of their fortresses than on any
other architectural project, the Itj-towy court, the greatest single
entity within the ancient East, was simultaneously erecting pyramids
and temples with great blocks of stone; mud brick, by comparison,
was a ubiquitous commodity whose employment demanded a fraction of the state's resources.

Many of the Levantine fortresses, moreover, were erected on the
mounds of ancient settlements whose surrounding fields had long
supported their inhabitants, who, presumably, had been set to work
building the new fortifications. The pharaonic fortresses of Nubia,
alternatively, were mostly built on virgin ground, beside a river in a
stony desert, where the local populations of farmers and cattle herders were hardly of sufficient size to undertake the construction work.
Nor does it appear remotely possible that those spare populations
were planning to gather in alliance and invade the kingdom to the
north. Nor, certainly, despite the translations of the pharaonic stelae
and graffiti, were the fortresses of Nubia designed and built from a
pharaonic fear of immigration. Just as the Levantines who had settled at Tell el-Dab'a had peacefully and successfully assimilated
pharaonic culture, so many Nubians had long since worked at the
courts of local pharaonic governors and pharaohs; indeed, various
communities of Nubians had lived within the fifty-mile stretch of the
river north of Aswan for several millennia.

It should never be imagined, of course, that life in ancient Egypt
was as secure as that within a modern state. Records from all periods
of pharaonic history tell that both individuals and communities were
subjected to threats of violence. Like most of humankind throughout
its history, the people within pharaoh's domain were vulnerable to all
sorts of dangers, just as were the boats and caravans that carried
incense, gold and copper back to the pharaonic court. Certainly, the

fortresses of Nubia were established in what the modern military would describe as defensive positions; and the adjectives that form parts of their ancient names – 'curbing the deserts', 'repelling the Medjay [i.e. the Nubians]', 'subduing ', 'repressing', 'warding off' – betray similar insecurities.

In reality, however, life on the ground in lower Nubia was rather different. There is not the slightest archaeological evidence that those fortresses were attacked – no arrows lodged in the mud-brick walls and not a single body bearing marks of violence found inside them. The scanty layer of ash that archaeologists have uncovered in many of their rooms was not evidence of sacking but the product of the burning of their roof beams after the pharaonic garrisons had departed and also the product of cooking fires which, as the remaining pottery testifies, were lit during several centuries of later local occupation.

By great good fortune, fragments of some of the written correspondence of the garrisons in the Nubian fortress have been recovered from a tomb at Thebes, in much the same manner as the archives of the farmer Heqanakht. And these texts too show that in the times of the later Itj-towy kings, at least, the era of Senwosret III's bombastic stelae, the reality of life in lower Nubia was rather different:

> . . . The frontier patrol that went out to patrol the desert edge [by] the fortress 'Repeller of the Medjay' in Year 3, third month of the Flood, the last day, has returned to report to me saying, 'We found the track of thirty-two men and three donkeys . . .

> . . . two Medjay-men, three Medjay-women, and two infants (?) came down from the desert hills in Year 3, third month of the Flood, day 27. They said, 'We have come to serve the palace, life prosperity health'. They were questioned about the state of the desert . . . then I, your humble servant, had them dismissed to their desert hills on the same day . . .

> . . . [a number of] Nubians [arrived in Year] 3, fourth month of the Flood, day 7, at evening time in order to do some bartering. What they had brought was bartered . . . They sailed south to the place they had come from after they had been given bread and beer as is customary, in Year 3, fourth month of the second season, day 8, at time of morning.

[in a postscript] Six other Nubians arrived at the fortress . . . in order to do some bartering . . . in the fourth month of the Flood, day 8. What they had brought was bartered. They sailed south on the same day to the place they had come from.

Neither an ancient Egyptian Maginot Line nor products of imperial megalomania, the fortresses' architectural braggadocio had in reality protected grain stores, copper furnaces, some installations that washed grains of gold from crushed ore. But above all else, the fortresses had served as trading outposts and as imposing caravanserai facilitating traffic with the south. Canals were cut beside some of the fortresses so that pharaoh's boats would avoid the dangers of the cataracts in times of inundation. Slipways, too, simple structures of clay and wood that ran for miles through the desert, served the same purpose. Until the Aswan Dam, some of those installations remained intact, and they had held the scored marks of the keels of the pharaonic boats that had been dragged along their water-slippery surfaces.

So this 'chain of the mightiest fortifications ever erected in the ancient world' had not served as Beau Geste outposts of colonial power, as traditional historians assume, but, as with most old and ancient fortresses, as warehouses and to control and facilitate through-traffic.

A unique venture in pharaonic history, the fortresses of Nubia were a novel addition to the older systems of court supply, and from the days of the vizier Antefoker, in the reign of Amenemhet I, to the times of Senwosret III, their construction had continued in an unchanging manner, their creation and their integration in the administrative structures of the Itj-towy court underlined by the unity of the architecture and the information contained within the archive of the garrisons' surviving dispatches. That they had operated directly under the courtiers' control is indicated by the seals of several viziers and other court officials that have been found within the fortresses. Some of these seals also show that the fortresses' personnel were drawn from all regions of the kingdom; one such, for example, describes its owner as an 'overseer of the marshland dwellers', that is, an official from the Nile Delta.

There are indications that this great project was successful. The considerable increase in the numbers of the courtiers' inscriptions and graffiti inscribed upon the granite rocks of the First Cataract suggests a growth in traffic south of Aswan. There was something of a boom at Aswan as well, many new buildings being erected on Elephantine Island along with another cemetery in the nearby cliffs for the local governors, whilst an additional channel was cut beside the Cataract which further increased year-round access to Nubia and its distant chain of fortresses.

Not surprisingly, the operation of those fortresses had significant effects upon the local populations. Nubians who served as militia in the pharaonic state and had established households in the pharaonic manner had long since been designated by the term 'Medjay', that is, as people from a region in the south-eastern desert that bore that same name. By the time of Senwosret III, however, the fortresses' scribes were describing all of Nubia's various inhabitants – the desert dwellers, the cattle herders and the farmers who lived beside the fortresses – as 'Medjay'. And in their turn the various communities of Nubia appear to have embraced something of a common identity under that same word.

The operation of the fortresses also had considerable effect upon pharaonic government. Never before had that age-old structure administered or provisioned such far-flung outposts on such a scale; nor indeed had it engaged in grand construction projects, other than the excavation of canals and the erection of pyramids and temples. In earlier times, both central and local government officials had maintained small bodies of militia, often Medjay, who were controlled by people who are usually entitled, in translation, 'overseers of soldiers'. By the time of Senwosret III, however, the administration and supply of the garrisons in Nubia had led to the development of more formal and more complex structures of control, which are reflected in a new range of titles and epithets within the court, in some of which several historians have detected 'the birth of an ancient Egyptian military'. For, at that time, terms that are now commonly translated as 'regiment', 'officer' and 'commander' were introduced, and all of them, it would appear, were overseen by 'the great commander' at Itj-towy. Thus are great ancient armies born, though, in reality, the combined population of the Nubian garrisons could hardly have amounted to more than a few thousand men.

Telling tokens of real-life conditions in lower Nubia in those times are the two large, traditionally designed courtly mansions that were erected on two rocky islands at the Second Cataract. Set high above the stream at the head of their respective islands, they were placed precisely on the four points of the compass, an orientation which suggests that, like the royal pyramids, they may have been built to house the kings themselves. Certainly, their architecture provides sufficient space for the living quarters of a courtly household and for the ritual theatre of pharaonic daily life. Unlike the nearby fortresses, however, those two great mansions had relatively thin walls and no defences at all.

In common with the rhetoric of the Nubian inscriptions, the Nubian fortresses were sophisticated cultural artefacts. However 'functional' they may appear in reality, their architecture was essentially a façade imported from a quarrelsome region far away that with the traditional use of imagery and architecture had sought to allay a specific set of anxieties. It had been one thing, after all, to voyage to the Land of Punt or travel in desert caravan to the Gebel Uweinat in order to supply the court of Itj-towy, the centre of the universe, with the materials that gave it life and form and full identity, but quite another to permanently control regions outside the ordered world of the pharaonic state.

In the 1960s, before Nubia had been entirely flooded and several of the fortresses were under excavation, archaeologists unearthed some caches of pots, dishes and models with curses scribbled all over them. They belonged to a highly specific and not uncommon class of objects that had been made since the times of the Memphite pharaohs and were intended to be broken into pieces in acts of atropoeic execration, in the same manner that dolls representing feared or hated individuals are stuck with pins.

The greatest cache of these pharaonic nightmares – a genuinely alternative ancient Egypt to the self-confidence its stone monuments displayed – was found buried outside the largest of the Nubian fortresses, in the scattered landscapes of rock and sand that lie around Mirgissa. A large pit had been dug and hundreds of broken pots and dishes, many of them covered in inked texts, had been thrown down into it along with modest models of the things of daily life – animals, birds, boats, bound prisoners, bread moulds, bows and arrows, images of heads, limbs, eyes and even miniature copper-smelting crucibles, all tossed in together before the assembled mass had been covered as if it were an ancient burial. A short distance away, more objects and more models of bound prisoners with badly damaged heads had been buried in a shallow pit; further pits nearby contained accretions of melted red wax – the residue, presumably, of ceremonial – and a flint knife next to a human head, probably that of a Nubian whose decapitated body was found buried in a shallow grave a short distance away.

Groups of similar objects have been found at Thebes and at Aswan. One that is particularly well known for its good condition and its curses holds a lengthy list of undesirables, which appears to include a son of the vizier Antefoker, who are all insulted along with their mothers, before the scribe takes off on a cautionary tour of all regions bordering the lower Nile, ending with the following imprecation:

> . . . upon every rebel who plans to rebel in this entire land:
> all the Medjay . . .
> all the Nubians . . .
> [their] heroes, [their] runners,
> all the people [i.e. ancient Egyptians] who are with them,
> all the Asiatics who are with them,
> all the families [?] of the sedge and the bee who are with them
> . . .
> all the foreigners who are with them
> all the people of all the western hill-countries
> . . .
> their heroes and their runners
> the dead man Antefoker
> born of Satsobek and Antefoker
> [and] Senwosret, born of Imas.

Similar texts curse bad dreams, evil speech, social strife and all of those people, dead and alive, who might think of plotting, fighting or rebelling against pharaoh. The same texts were written on the broken pots and dishes in the caches found next to the Nubian fortresses and also upon the statuettes of bound prisoners which are posed in the manner of a sacrifice, thrust down upon their knees in the age-old way, hands tied behind their backs, their throats exposed.

The order of these weird interments show that they were the residue of lengthy and careful processes, whilst the words and imagery they hold resemble some religious texts of later ages, describing the endless daily journey from death to resurrection. So, in the vast wastes of lower Nubia, a group of scribes and militiamen had commissioned and collected an anciently proscribed set of objects and sat within their fortresses covering them in inky curses. Then they had carried those tangible and concrete images of their fears, along with a bound captive, through the great arched stone-clad gateway into the disturbing landscapes of dark hard rocks and drifted sand. And there, with amulets strung around their necks and the great fortress walls behind them, they had supervised the excavation of a shallow pit in a low rise above the rushing river. Then they smashed the inscribed pottery, burnt the models of their enemies and decapitated their captive with a flint slaughtering knife. And all their fears were thrown down into the pits, and they were covered like a burial, in sand.

PART EIGHT

Middle Kingdom
The Re-made State,
2000–1660 BC

26

The Court at Home

THE ROYAL SETTLEMENT OF ITJ-TOWY

kings of the residence of Itj-towy: eight kings, making 213 years, 1 month, 17 days.

> Turin Canon, VI, 3

One of the greatest mysteries surrounding the kings of Itj-towy is the whereabouts of their royal residence. For Itj-towy has entirely disappeared.

That the court of the Itj-towy kings often followed the manners and customs of the Memphite age, and that the residences of those earlier kings seem to have been situated close to their pyramids, suggests that Itj-towy is to be located in the vicinity of the modern village of Lisht, some forty miles south of Cairo and close to the ruins of the first two Middle Kingdom pyramids, those of Amenemhet I and Senwosret I.

The very name of Lisht, indeed, appears to be a corruption of 'Itj', to which the Arabic indefinite article has been added, so 'el-Itj'. Recent excavations in the desert behind that village, moreover, have uncovered part of a haphazard group of houses that were inhabited in the centuries that followed the era of the Amenemhets and Senwosrets, when a line of fleeting monarchs had held the throne in quick succession. Now, several sources tell that Itj-towy had continued to serve as the royal residence in those times, so that a group of excavated house walls may well represent additions to an older central settlement whose remains still lie beneath the rows of beans and onions and the clumps of bright berseem that grow in the muddy waters of Lisht's kitchen gardens.

Housing complexes built by the pharaonic state were generally designed symmetrically, and certainly the handful of such buildings of the times of the Itj-towy kings that are known today were laid out in patterns of orthogonal orthodoxy. The rectangular hieroglyphic determinative for the term Itj-towy suggests that the royal residence was set inside a high-walled enclosure and may have been built according to those same traditional principles; the walls of that rectangular hieroglyph, indeed, bear a patterning of mud-brick panelling that had already been employed in Memphite palaces for a thousand years.

What that royal rectangle may have contained, however, is difficult to determine. Like all other buildings of the time other than tomb chapels and temples, its accommodations were certainly built of mud brick, with stone doorframes and roofs made of logs of acacia and palm. And their various parts would have corresponded to the standard set of forms employed in state domestic architecture: conical grain stores, courtyards and oblong rooms of harmonic proportions, the largest of which would have held rows of roof-supporting columns. And, as the plans of pharaonic residences of other ages would suggest, those buildings would have been low, wide and somewhat modest structures that had not greatly taxed the state resources.

Contemporary scribes variously name the residence of Itj-towy as the 'royal house' or the 'domain', the 'compound' or the 'palace of the king', or even, 'the temple of the god', which gives the impression that its architectural arrangements had been a synthesis of shrine, store and royal household. For the first time in pharaonic history, various parts of the Itj-towy residence or, perhaps, parts of its bureaucracy that lay outside the residence's rectangular walls, were described in parts of the courtiers' titles. Thus courtiers could be described as the 'sealers' or 'keepers' of various warehouses and strong rooms from which, presumably, court provisions had been dispensed and craftsmen had collected their materials. Like the titles and epithets of earlier times, however, it is difficult to determine what fixed roles, if any, those courtiers performed at court. Which renders equally uncertain both the shape of the Itj-towy bureaucracy and the arrangement of the buildings that had contained it.

On the other hand, the royal cemeteries at Lisht were organized along strict lies of precedence in much the same manner as those of the Memphite and Theban kings. Here, one compound holds the royal pyramid and the minor pyramids and shaft graves of royal women, whilst the tombs of most of the court officials stand at a slight remove outside that central compound. This suggests that the living settlement at Itj-towy had similarly consisted of separated zones, one highly circumscribed area containing the rectangle of the royal residence and other less defined areas holding state warehouses along with the households and offices of the courtiers, craftsmen and scribes and those practically concerned with the state activities of building and the collection and disbursement of state goods. And if the settlement at Giza may stand as precedent, there may also have been a further physical division outside the royal rectangle between the residential zones and the state warehouses, grain stores, stone yards and harbours.

Fundamentally, the rectangle of the royal residence, the house of the living pharaoh, had housed the king, the royal offices and the members of his household, human and divine. Here, the king was called the Horus of the Residence. So along with the central archives of the state and pharaoh's earthly household, its retinue of servants, scribes and musicians, the royal compound had also to accommodate rites like those conducted daily in the temples of the gods but which were centred on the figure of the living king. There was, as well, a hall of royal audience, and in those times when he was not visiting other parts of the kingdom, pharaoh had sat in conclave at the royal residence with senior state officials; those courtiers, that is, who translators entitle 'friends' or 'confidants' and who bore such titles as viziers and treasurers. The royal residence was probably also the location for the preparation and point of departure of a millennial continuity of pharaonic festivals such as the Heb Sed jubilee, which was certainly observed at Itj-towy.

Though the residences of the senior courtiers at Itj-towy may well have been somewhat smaller than that of pharaoh, for they did not require space for the preparation and performance of the daily royal rituals and they do not appear to have accommodated so many women, nevertheless the households of both the king and the courtiers had required similar living accommodation and storage facilities. All those residences, too, had shared several formal architectural elements, most especially a large main entrance gate, some open courtyards with wooden columns and, often, a central rectangular pool, and several enclosed halls with more columns in them and access to rows of smaller rooms. Both the royal residence at Itj-towy and the mansions of senior courtiers had also held halls of audience, where the heads of those households had met their staff and visitors and had issued the orders and commands that the inscriptions record. And such halls, of course, would also have accommodated scribes and the archives of papyrus.

And all those residences would have certainly accommodated potteries, weaving sheds and bakeries, kitchens, breweries and butcheries and, perhaps, craftsmens' workshops, along with accommodations for the main family, with smaller units for families of servants, scribes and musicians. The living air of one such household, indeed, is yet held in the funerary models of vizier Mekhet-re, whilst the ghosts of their reality, their column bases and the thick stubs of their surviving mud-brick walls have been excavated at the site of other court settlements – at Lahun some thirty miles south of Lisht, at Abydos, at several sites within the Nile Delta and on a smaller scale, at the mansions that had stood beside the fortresses of lower Nubia. By pharaonic standards, some of those provincial residences were large and complex structures, with many open courtyards and large storerooms and some seventy rooms of varying sizes, all of which suggests that they may have been built to accommodate both the permanent households of local officials and also the entourage of a visiting monarch, for the Itj-towy kings are known to have travelled widely throughout their kingdom.

We may imagine, therefore, that the rectangle of the royal residence at Itj-towy had lain amidst the similar though somewhat smaller residences of the courtiers. And certainly the peoples of those various households had been in close contact. For many texts tell how the children of senior courtiers had grown up within the royal household, whilst the linens woven in the households of several senior courtiers were buried in the graves of women of the royal household at Deir el-Bahari.

The settlement at Itj-towy had also included satellite households, studios and workshops of scribes and craftsmen along with those of the court sculptors and pyramid builders. Some of those workshops may have been situated within the great houses of the courtiers, others in the compound of the royal residence itself. Just as a Memphite text describes how pharaoh had overseen the inscription of a block of stone within the royal residence, so, too, the professions of royal gold worker, furniture maker, sculptor and other craftsmen stand out amidst a haze of ambiguous courtly epithets. At all events, though other state-supported workshops were situated at sites such as Saqqara and Abydos, the households of most court craftsmen were certainly at Itj-towy. And the artisans and craftsmen of that royal settlement had been so numerous, so well supplied and so closely integrated that a new court style had emerged soon after Itj-towy was established, a style that, from its exquisite reliefs and jewellery down to its domestic pottery, is easily identified as a product of the royal settlement.

With such a gathering of households, the population of Itj-towy, that uniquely literate community of court ritualists, state government and fine craftsmen, the living heart of pharaonic culture, would have numbered in its thousands. And the structures of authority that ran right through it is yet glimpsed in some surviving documents. One royal command, for example, orders an Itj-towy courtier to travel to Abydos to reform Osiris' cult and restore his temple:

> The king's command to the prince, count, royal seal-bearer, sole companion, overseer of the two gold-houses, overseer of the two silver-houses, chief seal-bearer, Ikhernofret . . .

> My majesty commands you to journey upstream to Abydos in the region of Thinis, to make monuments for my father Osiris, foremost of the Westerners, and to adorn his secret image with the fine gold which he has caused my majesty to bring back from Nubia in victory and triumph.

> You will surely do this in the best way for the benefit of my father Osiris . . . for you were brought up as a pupil of my majesty. You have grown up as foster child of my majesty, the sole pupil of my residence. My majesty made you a companion when you were a youth of twenty-six

years. My majesty did this because I saw you as one of excellent conduct, keen of tongue, who had come from the womb as one wise.

Now my majesty sends you to do this, because my majesty knows that
no one could do it but you. Go then and return when you have done
all that my majesty has commanded . . .

The text continues by describing how Ikhernofret restored the
Osiris temple that had been built a century earlier in the reign of Senwosret I; how he had adorned the god's bark and the sacred images
with precious metals, fine woods and gemstones; and how he had
reformed the rituals of the priests, leading them in festivals that had
gladdened the hearts of east and west alike. And all of this the courtier from Itj-towy recorded on three stone stelae, which were drawn
and sculpted by excellent court craftsmen and set into a little
mud-brick chapel built on the wide plain of Abydos.

Clearly, Ikhernofret's texts are those of a royal friend and companion, a senior courtier close to the king, who had led a considerable
team of craftsmen, scribes and ritualists. Another stela from Abydos
shows how a similar order had been passed down through the offices
at Itj-towy, from men like Ikhernofret to members of their staff:

> The scribe of the vizier Seneb's son, Tjati, came to summon me on a
> mission of the vizier. And I went with him, and found the overseer of
> the settlement, the vizier Ankhu in his office. And this official set a
> royal command before me, saying:
>
> 'It is commanded that you purify the temple complex of Abydos.
> Craftsmen are given to you for this purpose, together with the priesthood
> of the temple of that province and the storehouse of god's offerings.'
>
> And then I purified it, its lower and upper buildings, its walls out-
> side and inside, draughtsmen repainting the designs . . .

A ROYAL AUDIENCE

The better part of pharaonic cargoes, the provisions and materials
destined for the state's warehouses and granaries, its builders' yards
and treasuries, were destined for the settlement of Itj-towy. As many

texts describe, the court's suppliers, the caravan leaders, the sailors, the leaders of the mining expeditions and the commanders of the fortresses of Nubia, had audience with pharaoh in the throne room of the royal residence.

Nor was this a mere matter of court procedure or etiquette. Just as some temple builders and the men whom the vizier Antefoker had ordered to deliver supplies of wheat to the royal residence had to shave their heads as if they were officiating priests, so, too, an audience at the royal residence took place in the same perfumed atmosphere as the daily rites enacted around the figure of pharaoh – just as was the issuing of a pharaonic order to build a temple or a fortress, to quarry a block of siltstone for a sarcophagus or, indeed, to send provisions to Itj-towy. Those expedition leaders, those builders, sailors and craftsmen, had been summoned to the centre of their universe, as is described in the story of the prodigal courtier Sinuhe, who had fled to the Levant but who finally returns and meets the king in royal audience.

> When it was dawn, very early, they came to summon me. Ten men coming, ten men going, ushering me to the palace. And I touched my forehead to the ground between the sphinxes as the royal children were standing in the doorway to meet me.

Sinuhe's description of the sphinxes at the doorway of the royal residence echoes the arrangements of the entrance to a royal temple, such as Khafre's valley temple at Giza and the temples of Abusir, all of which had similar leonine images at their entrances. And as at a temple, those Itj-towy sphinxes set before the Great Double Doorway of the royal residence had announced a zone of transition from the profane to the otherworldly.

Both the plans of other courtly residences and the determining hieroglyph denoting the word for 'broad hall' – that is, a chamber of audience – show that an audience with pharaoh at Itj-towy would have been approached through a disorienting series of right-angled turns, a highly asymmetric progress that is quite outside the usual run of both formal pharaonic architecture and the natural landscapes of the Nile Valley, and, indeed, this approach was only shared by the passages that led to royal burial chambers and to some temple shrines.

We may imagine, therefore, that, after passing through those sunlit sphinxes at the entrance gateway, the mixture of the dark confusions of the convoluted entrance corridors and sudden sunlit courtyards, Sinuhe would have arrived at the doorway of the hall of royal audience having lost all sense of direction and, as the story tells, in a state of apprehension. For palaces could be dangerous places, and not only for supplicants like Sinuhe but also for the kings themselves: another story of the time tells how pharaoh had been murdered at night within his palace by people of the royal household 'when weapons intended for my protection were turned against me'.

Like all other domestic buildings of the time, the royal residence would have had small open windows set high on the walls, serving both for illumination and to enable the circulation of air. Of itself, mud brick is a splendid form of natural insulation, and pharaonic builders were skilful manipulators of the prevailing winds, so those cool, shadowed interiors would have provided a dramatic contrast to the dazzling sunlight outside. Shot through with small bright beams of light glistening with golden dust, interiors were closed, gloomy and relatively chill.

Angling from clerestory windows, the illumination from successive beams of light would have led Sinuhe's eye along a dappled line of columns towards a stepped dais at the far end of the audience hall, where the king, a small man in starched white linens gleaming with jewellery, sat on an elaborate golden chair of archaic design. Such pillared halls resembled the interiors of temples and had probably affected unaccustomed visitors like Sinuhe in a similar way. So even though he was accompanied by some of the king's closest courtiers and his name had been announced as he had come into the presence of the king, he had thrown himself upon the ground, the story tells, and was paralysed with fear.

> And I found his majesty on the great throne . . . in the portal of electrum. And his majesty said to one of these friends 'Lift him up and let him speak to me! . . .

Whereupon his majesty, the story goes, had expiated upon Sinuhe's foolishness at abandoning the royal court so many years before. Then women of the royal household came into the audience chamber and the king had said to the queen:

> 'Look, here is Sinuhe, who has returned as a Levantine, as a child of nomads!' She uttered a very great cry, and the royal women shrieked all together and said to his majesty: 'Is it really him, O king, our lord?' And his majesty said: 'It is really him!' And they had brought their necklaces, their rattles and their sistra which they offered to his majesty . . .

Which implies that the royal women had proposed that they should sing a song accompanied by some percussive instruments, including sistra, musical instruments with small cymbal-like disks that rattle like hard dry leaves when they are shaken. And his majesty seems to have agreed to their suggestion, for the tale continues with the words of twenty-odd lines of carefully composed verses. In the conventional manner of court address, the women of the royal household first wish pharaoh good health and long life, then congratulate him on unifying the kingdoms of the sedge and the bee, before concluding by asking pharaoh to show the same compassion for Sinuhe as he naturally displays towards his subjects. A plea to which his majesty must have acceded for the following lines report that:

> His majesty told Sinuhe not to fear, that he will be taken to the robing chamber and appointed as [royal] friend. And when I came from the robing hall, the royal children gave me their hands, and we went though the Great Double Doorway.

Sinuhe, the story seems to tell, had close connections with the women of the royal household who had pled his case before the King. Far from being shut away in an *orientaliste* harem, therefore, the royal household could be a lively and powerful presence in state affairs, and, whilst the royal audience itself appears to have been a highly formalized procedure, the multi-textured rhythms of the royal household echoed around that darkened hall just as they did in the temples of the gods. And this it would appear, had been the usual way of things at Itj-towy, for the beginning of Sinuhe's tale tells that the death of a previous pharaoh had been signalled by an eerie silence and the closing of the Great Double Doorway.

FEEDING PHARAOH – *SUSTAINING ITJ-TOWY*

The Doctrynal Princyplis and Proverbys Yconomie, or Howsolde keepyng

Lambeth Ms. 306, fol. 64

Just one contemporary document has survived that deals directly with the nationwide supply systems that had provisioned the courts of the Amenemhets and Senwosrets, a formal letter concerning a grain shipment to the royal residence that, as its modern editor William Kelley Simpson has surmised, was probably the court at Itj-towy. That its sender was the same vizier Antefoker who organized and undertook expeditions to Punt and Nubia on behalf of Itj-towy's first resident king, Amenemhet I, enables the 'year 17' of its date to be assigned to the reign of that same king.

Year 17, second month of the Flood, day 8.

The overseer of the settlement, vizier, and overseer of the six great law courts, Antefoker, commands the stewards of the palace adminis-tration who are in the region of Thinis [near Abydos]:

See that you ready yourselves and prepare in the manner that I have ordered you to send downstream to the [royal] Residence a hundred and fifty hekat-measures of wheat, a double hekat-measure of malted barley, and ten thousand loaves from each one of you.

I shall reckon them at the Residence. Try to furnish new wheat . . .

Delivered by the dog-keeper Montuhotep's son Montuhotep, and Intef's son Senbef, of the crew of Si-agerteb.

The *hekat* was a measure of volume, which is a convenient way of quantifying stored grain, though, in a manner similar to the litre/kilogramme equivalence employed in European market places to this day, it also served as a unit of weight. Though the modern world encourages standardization of weights and measures, this was hardly the case in previous centuries. Many Western communities for example, dealt simultaneously in inches, ounces, grams, bushels, metres and litres, which may also have varied in their quantities and measurements from community to community. In round terms, however, a *hekat* was close to an imperial gallon, so that the grain that Antefoker ordered to be delivered to the residence would probably have weighed in the order of half a ton.

If copper may be said to have shaped pharaonic Egypt, then its fuel, the enabler of its skills and the root of its prosperity, was grain. Though labour-intensive and a relatively low-yielding crop, it was a hardy and dependable staple and, unlike many foods that must be eaten fresh, it was easily conserved. Hence the enormous numbers of granaries of all shapes and sizes that archaeologists continue to uncover in Egyptian excavations from the settlements of the northern delta to the fortresses of Nubia.

The most common grains of pharaoh's kingdom were emmer and barley. They had complementary qualities. Heqanakht (p. 372 *ff*) was certainly not the first farmer in the valley of the lower Nile to plant those two varieties in different locations according to the height of the annual flood; emmer, the preferred grain for making bread, flourished in well-irrigated soil, whilst barley, which in good years was mostly used for beer and fodder, would grow in drier, salty soil.

Though surviving relics easily give the impression that grain and beef had been the principal foods of Itj-towy, the reliefs and paintings in the tomb chapels and temples of the time along with a range of data gleaned by archaeologists confirm that hunting and fishing were vital parts of the kingdom's day-to-day provisioning, various accounts describing the delivery of fish, pigeon, water fowl and joints of wild meat to the temples' altars, to the households of the court and to gangs of leveed workers. Many larger households, indeed, included families of river fishermen and hunters of desert game; huntsmen had also accompanied state mining and caravanning expeditions.

In reality, therefore, the food of the Itj-towy court, along with that of the wider population of the lower Nile, was derived from both the cultivated and uncultivated spaces of the wider region of the lower Nile. Field crops, horticulture, viniculture and herding mixed with wild foods from the marshes, the river and the surrounding deserts, providing a well-balanced diet which had enabled the maintenance of a general level of consumption well above subsistence level within a rising population, just as the condition of their mummies yet attests. And as the archaeology of several considerable state enterprises confirm, it was a diet which in the times of the Itj-towy kings had been watchfully maintained.

A rare record of the diet of the Itj-towy court over a two-week period is described in a fragmentary papyrus that, like the archive of Heqanakht and the day books of the Nubian fortresses, was found in a Theban tomb; on this occasion, within the burial crypt of a certain Neferhotep. Titled, in translation, an 'accountant of the main enclosure [i.e. Itj-towy?]' the fragment tells us that Neferhotep was given a fine burial and appears to have served the vizier Ankhu, the high court official who had overseen a restoration of the Abydos temple, for another scrap of papyrus from Neferhotep's tomb concerns that vizier's estates.

Neferhotep's accounts detail the consumption of food over a period of thirteen days by a king and members of his court during a visit to Thebes. As ever, the figure of this pharaoh is surrounded in a haze of incense and anonymity; on this occasion, even his name does not appear. Other texts, however, name vizier Ankhu as serving the courts of several of the short-lived monarchs that had followed the Amenemhets and Senwosrets and who had also resided at Itj-towy. Certainly, Neferhotep's papyrus records its unnamed king performing the same role as his predecessors, receiving some provincial courtiers and a delegation of three Medjay leaders and visiting the temple of the god Montu at Medamud near Thebes, whilst it was in festival.

The royal party appears to have travelled to Thebes in flotilla on the river and had been housed, presumably, in the palace built beside the great temple of Amun-Re at Karnak in the times of the king's predecessors. Neferhotep's accounts list the royal entourage as consisting of various overseers and stewards, some scribes, musicians and militiamen along with the vizier Ankhu, numerous members of the king's domestic household, four royal children and a queen who may have been related to the vizier Ankhu. All in all, an interesting mix that would confirm the constitution of the royal audience described in the story of Sinuhe in which female members of the royal household had played an important role.

Neferhotep's papyrus is laid out as neatly as the records of the Abusir temples, but in two columns of accounts. Entitled 'revenue' and 'expenditure', both columns are filled with carefully quantified amounts of food: loaves of bread, jugs of beer, and sacks and bundles of dates and vegetables, which are all added up at the ending of each day, with any residual supplies listed under the heading 'remainder'. Vegetables would have been brought in daily with the other perishables, and, naturally, they are counted swiftly in and out. Other longer-lasting comestibles, alternatively, serve as reserves in the accounting columns and also as supplies that could be augmented as need arose, with food raised by levy and donation in the same manner that the officers of court employed in their travels through the kingdom.

Presumably, this unique record reflects similar processes of supply at Itj-towy itself. Certainly the various tiers of courtiers and their assistants which are listed as receiving rations during the trip to Thebes reflect the same divisions as those that can be reconstructed for the settlement of Itj-towy; one line listing the consumption of the officers of government and leading courtiers, another the extended royal family and the palace staff.

The list of all of those consumers – that is, of the account's 'expenditure' in Neferhotep's accounts – is balanced by a list of court supplies collected under 'revenue'. Apart from the extra provisions that were levied as need arose, the sources of supply are contained in four categories. One of these categories contains loaves of bread that had been supplied directly from the Amun temple and may have been ritually prepared, as were the daily offerings to the gods. Those provisions were probably sourced from the produce of the domains that previous kings had established to support the daily offices of Amun and the families of the god's priests and servants. The other three sources of provision, however, are listed as being under the control of three courtiers, but it is impossible to determine where their supplies had originated. Like many roles within the court the functions of those officials are hardly described in the translations of such titles as 'the head of the south'.

Certainly, there is no evidence from those times of a consistent nationwide system of tithing or collection, although a single surviving papyrus sheet recording a land survey and the declaration of its results to a 'royal treasurer' is sometimes taken as evidence of a state tax on harvests. And, of course, that ancient survey effectively registers an assessment of that land's potential yield. Yet the document could just as well be a record of the measuring of land endowed for the upkeep of a tomb chapel or temple and nowhere does it describe a tax upon the coming harvest destined for the upkeep of the state. Nor, indeed, is there any mention in Heqanakht's careful correspondence and accountings of a state tithe or tax; nor indeed is there even a reference to the king or an officer of state.

In explanation of this gap in the surviving record it has been argued that a pharaonic tithe was levied immediately after the gathering of crops and was not accounted for by Heqanakht, as tax, like death, was simply an enduring fact of life. Yet taxes as a proportion of income are an entirely modern invention; the notion of a statewide system of taxation levied as a regular method of increasing the funds in the pharaonic exchequer is a pure invention. And in the unlikely event that similar pseudo-monetary processes had been in operation in pharaonic Egypt, some record, surely, of such vital components of state resource would have been sanctified along with the rest of the state's activities, and thus some trace of such operations would have survived.

There are, of course, simpler alternative methods of court supply, methods similar to those that operated in the majority of courts before the modern age. Neferhotep's accounting of pharaoh's trip to Thebes, for example, suggests that, when extra supplies were needed by the court to provision expeditions and building projects, they were variously sourced, court officials enlisting fishermen and huntsmen and obtaining grain from farm stocks on an *ad hoc* basis. Listed as gifts and donations, such sources of supply are described in Neferhotep's accounts in the same way that manpower for court projects also appears to have been enlisted from the general population as need arose. And a wide variety of documents and royal edicts specifically exempt temple staff and temple stocks from the depletions of just such erratic tithing.

As for the provisioning of the population of Itj-towy, the court may well have obtained its food from a series of estates, royal domains and colonies both in the delta and in the valley, in the same way that the tithes – the offerings – presented to the dead were raised from estates that had been specifically established for that purpose when the recipients had been alive or the temple estates that had been established by the court and were administered by priests who served the gods. Seen in this light, large building projects such as pyramids and temples may well have required the colonization of new farmlands and new foundations, using labour levees fed from court-held stocks of food.

Such speculations are sometimes described as a search for the 'ancient Egyptian economy'. Yet no one living in Memphis, Thebes or Itj-towy could have recognised those words, for there was no 'economy' in ancient Egypt in the modern sense, no abstract theory governing the elements of daily life, either on the farm or at the court; simply farming of itself, in a lush land and on such a scale that its continuous expansion had fed the wider population and supported the activities of the court along with the activities of offering and building that catered for the gods, the dead and all their living servants.

The unity that binds all the relics of this state – the pyramids, the tombs and temples, the written documents, the settlements, the products of the craftsmens' studios – is not a set of social, religious and political abstractions invented in other times on other continents, but an intricate set of relationships, of obligations between the living and the dead, to the gods and to the office of the king which bestrode them all.

This, then, is a key point at which historians of the pharaonic culture decide to render their subject as either a primitive or aberrant version of modern society – the vision of 'Ancient Egypt' that Hollywood has derived from traditional academia – or, alternatively, to attempt to portray that lost and very ancient kingdom on its own terms, as honestly as the surviving relics and modern sensitivities permit.

FLOODS AND THE FAYUM

It is an obvious though much neglected truth that in states such as that of the Itj-towy kings, those who do not produce food are immediately dependent upon the farmers, fishermen and hunters who do. So, naturally, for the people of Itj-towy the acquisition and storage of supplies of food, the need to keep provisions flowing from the farmers to the court and all of its activities and dependents, was the overriding interest of the pharaonic courtiers. And from the time of the first pharaohs, as the earliest monuments testify, the state administration had driven agricultural production well beyond the limits of subsistence farming and had used those surpluses to enable the construction of pharaonic culture.

Unlike the modern world, the pharaonic state achieved its colossal surpluses without the aid of technological innovations and with the most ancient modes of farming. Ultimately, of course, the demands it made upon its farmers had been met by the cornucopian fertility of the region of the lower Nile, its rich earth, wide river and strong sun. Such was its bounty that farming was lightly regulated, the officers of the state never precisely measuring its harvests, for the fragments of pharaonic accounts that have survived are filled with elementary errors of addition and subtraction. As long as the annual inundation was generous and uncultivated lands were available for further colonization as need arose, the court had functioned easily and so prosperously that it was able to simultaneously accommodate both its lavish building projects and a steady rise in the size of the general population.

The river was the key. Flood levels, it appears, had begun to rise again in the times of the Intefs and Montuhoteps. And in the following generations, as the court moved north to Itj-towy, the three farming settlements of the times that were established to the north of Memphis and have been excavated all employed the usual modular plans of state housing projects and were supplied with plates, bowls, cooking pots, storage jars and bread moulds made in Nile Valley potteries. One of these colonies was founded on an abandoned Memphite settlement at a site now known as Merimda Abu Ghalib, which was situated at the beginning of the river's delta on an oxbow on a meander in a small branch of the Nile as it had begun its lazy passage to the sea. The other two were established on virgin land, on sandy delta turtlebacks, and are the first-known communities to have been built at the site of Tell el-Dab'a in the eastern delta, where Levantine communities would later settle.

The first of the settlements at Tell el-Dab'a consisted of at least 400 tiny homes. Set beside a natural harbour amongst the meanderings of several delta streams it may also have had connection with as yet unexcavated shipyards. But the humble nature of those dwellings suggests that, like the delta settlements of Memphite times, they had been designed to house families of workers who had laboured in centres of food storage and production. And, indeed, the settlements at both Tell el-Dab'a and Abu Ghalib have yielded quantities of small flint blades bearing that rare high shine – the so-called 'sickle sheen' – that is only produced by reaping.

At all events, the relocation of the Theban court to Itj-towy at the southern end of the narrow Memphite plain must have required a considerable reorganization of its sources of supply, which led to the exploitation of the delta in the manner of its Memphite predecessors. Certainly, many more settlements like those at Abu Ghalib and Tell el-Dab'a lie undetected in the delta silt. At Bubastis, for example, in the eastern delta, a great palace, a governor's residence of the times of the Itj-towy kings, has been located, whilst two small temples have been excavated at other sites within the region. Some thirty presently unlocated delta settlements, moreover, are named in contemporary texts, and material from several cemeteries of that age has been found throughout the region.

The court's move from Thebes to Itj-towy had also prompted a renewed interest in the region of the Fayum, a large and somewhat mysterious depression in the Western Desert that lies some sixty miles to the south and west of modern Cairo and just a few miles from Lisht. In the times of the Itj-towy kings, the Fayum was sustained by a tributary of the Nile known now as the Bahr Yusuf. In earlier millennia the tributary had broken through a slim gap in the Nile's western cliffs to empty some of the silty waters of the annual inundation into the Fayum Depression and create an enormous desert lake, a quiet, closed adjunct of the river some forty miles across. Nile silts in the lake's surrounding marshlands had supported farming populations since neolithic times, whilst the Pyramid Texts had described the Fayum's fine fishing and rich pasturage as a place of creation, its fearsome local crocodile god announcing himself as

> Sobek, green of plumage, alert and sparkling . . . I come to my water-
> ways which are the banks of the flood of the great inundation to the
> place of contentment, green of fields, which is in the western horizon.

So with the court's return to the slim strip of northern silt at Memphis and Itj-towy, the means of its food supply had been secured not only by establishing state farms in the delta but also by improving the supply of Nile water to the Fayum, whose narrow passage through the mile-long gap in the Nile-side cliffs may well have silted up in earlier centuries due to insufficient inundations, and may even have been entirely choked by drifting sand during the interregnum.

Such irrigation works were hardly revolutionary. From the begin-nings of the kingdom, a variety of records tell of irrigation schemes and many texts describe extensive preparations for the annual flood. First levees were raised amongst local populations – these, perhaps, the origins of the state workforces that built the pyramids and temples. These levees were then set to work both to renew the ancient man-made channels that ran from the Nile out to the edges of the silt and to rebuild the catchment dykes built up within the farmers' fields. Once freed of silt, the channels could again conduct water across the full width of the flood plain. Then, in time of flood, the re-made catchment dykes would trap the inundation's overflow upon the fields to create a series of shining shallow lakes such as could still be seen throughout the length and breath of Egypt before the building of the two dams at Aswan. Thus trapped, the floodwaters were parcelled out amongst the various farming households of the area throughout the coming months, the supervision of those vital operations being a common claim of the texts in the tomb chapels of many governors and courtiers. Thus, the size of the cultivated land was maximized and the length of the growing season extended. Without recourse to such works in the times of the Itj-towy kings, the state's ability to supply the farmers' surpluses to its monument makers and to provi-sion Itj-towy and all its other enterprises would probably have been impossible.

No writings or inscriptions tell the name of the pharaoh in whose reign the work to improve the Fayum's water supply was initiated. In Medinet el-Fayum, the single modern city in the region, however, an obelisk-like column of pink Aswan granite some forty-two feet high, bears the name of Senwosret I. In common with the granite column of itself, most of the deities pictured on this unique monument – the principle gods of Itj-towy, including Montu and Amun of Thebes, Atum of Heliopolis, Ptah of Memphis – have been imported into the Fayum. It has been suggested that the indentation on the column's top had once held a statue of a hawk. If that were true, it would appear that the column had been placed near the rejuvenated lake as the reed which had grown up on the mound of creation, as the reed on which Horus the hawk had perched in the first days of the world.

Along with some odd granite blocks from long-lost shrines and some statue fragments bearing the name of Senwosret I's predecessor, Amenemhet I, this splendid solitary column is the first evidence of substantial pharaonic building projects in the Fayum. None of these early monuments show evidence of the complex local cults of Fayum deities that, as the numerous fragments of later monuments found in the Fayum suggest, had been developed and monumentalized during those later reigns.

The greatest symbols of the involvement of the Itj-towy court with the Fayum, however, are the placement of two royal pyramids, the first of which was made for Senwosret II, his builders having abandoned the plain of Dahshur where all the pyramids of the later Itj-towy kings were built. Senwosret II's builders, alternatively, had set his tomb exactly at the point in the Bahr Yusuf's progress where it turns sharply westwards through the break in the Nile cliffs to feed the Fayum Lake. Today, the area is known as el-Lahun, which is a corruption of its ancient name meaning 'the mouth of the canal': that once-meandering ancient tributary of the Nile had already been converted into the deep straight-sided waterway known as the Hawara Channel, which still runs deep and fast through that bone-dry desert to feed the lands beside by the lake.

Half a century later, the builders of the long-lived king Amenemhet III erected a second royal pyramid complex beside the Hawara Channel. A work, it would appear, that had been part of a considerable national project for which, as the graffiti on his pyramids still tell, a

large workforce had been drawn from all parts of the ancient kingdom and assembled at the royal residence.

Recent studies of the geology of the region show that renovations
to the flow of water along the Bahr Yusuf and through the Hawara
Channel had returned the Fayum Lake to the vast size it had attained
500 years before, in the era of the Giza kings. Those changes in the
Nile's flow also had considerable effect in the regions of the river
downstream from that re-opened water syphon. At its peak, it has
been estimated that the ancient Hawara Channel had diverted around
one fifth of the Nile's water from the river. And this had served not
only to decrease the height of the river's annual inundation below the
branch of the Bahr Yusuf but also to increase the river's flow in those
same regions in the succeeding months, as the flood waters had
receded and almost half the water that had entered the Fayum had
drained back again into the main stream of the Nile.

The powerful syphon of the Hawara Channel had a considerable
calming effect upon the annual rise and fall of the great wide river
from the Bahr Yusef to the Mediterranean. An immediate result was
that the builders of the Itj-towy kings were able to set the valley
temples of the royal pyramid complexes closer to the river than before
and lower down in the valley, whilst at the same time the burial
chambers within the pyramids were set far lower down, with the
result that some of those crypts now lie underwater and have never
been examined. Another effect of this partial pacification of the Nile
was that the lowest regions of its Delta had been transformed from
marsh to meadow.

In normal years, the Nile's flow had decreased to about a sixth of
its usual volume in the months before the inundation, the full height
of the following flood, as recorded by Itj-towy officials from Nubia
to Memphis, serving as an anticipation of the size of harvest in the
coming year. Yet the flow of the great river, its annual extremes of
high- and low-water levels, were not dependent on a single source, for
it was fed from three separate tributaries. Known nowadays as the
White and Blue Niles and the River Atbara, these sources were ultimately dependent upon the Ethiopian snowmelt and the annual rainfall
in central Sudan, yet the three rivers supplied entirely different volumes of water to the lower Nile in varying times throughout the year.

So if climatic conditions in the different regions through which they flowed had been erratic, the fluctuation between high and low Niles could be dramatic.

That the Nile lost its usual majestic balance in the reign of Amenemhet III is testified by graffiti made by the scribes of the Nubian garrisons, who recorded a series of floods on the cliffs above the river that were some twenty feet higher than normal. In Nubia, some fortresses were damaged and others may have been entirely washed away. Downstream in the kingdom, both canals and dykes would have been devastated, grain stocks soaked, planting delayed, riverbank settlements and dockyards washed away and large parts of the newly reclaimed delta re-submerged. Recording similar disasters, graffiti of later ages describe the papyrus columns of the Theban temples, standing deep in floodwater, as the swamp at the beginning of creation.

It may well be, therefore, that those furious floods in the reign of Amenemhet III, the monarch in whose reign a considerable national workforce had been assembled and whose builders had set a second royal pyramid above the Hawara Channel, had prompted a further enlargement of the Bahr Yusef designed to lessen the effects of such disastrous inundations at Itj-towy, Memphis and the delta. Certainly, the Fayum priests of classical times had worshipped Amenemhet III as a god along with his wife, the goddess Isis, Lady of the Granaries, and they had told the classical historians who visited their temples that the legendary monarch had undertaken enormous projects in the region.

Those ancient tales are given powerful credibility by two seated statues of Amenemhet III that had once stood at the edges of the ancient lake and whose fragments Flinders Petrie had recovered in 1888. One morning, he recalled, as he was walking to his excavations:

> I saw two boys lugging a stone over to show me, and it glittered in the sunshine, the polish was so bright. They laid it down, and I puzzled what it was: could it be the paw of a sphinx, battered about? No, it was the nose of the colossus . . . all but a foot wide; and hence there must have been a statue about eight times life size, or about 36 feet high, seated. And what work! The rough-grained sandstone was polished until after all these ages it still reflected like glass.

Petrie's excavations soon determined that the quartzite statues had been some fifty feet high and that they had both been mounted upon limestone pedestals that had stood to half that height again and were decorated with the images of fecund so-called 'Nile Gods'.

Part of Petrie's visual record of his brief excavations beside the village of Byahmu in the Fayum.

The purpose of this strange arrangement – such high plinths are otherwise unknown in pharaonic architecture – was explained by the height of the rectangular walls which had enclosed each of the colossi in paved temple courts. In times of low Nile, the statues of Amenemhet III had sat side by side at the edges of the ancient lake, the two enormous figures looming over the walls of their enclosures and dominating both the lake and the surrounding land for miles. In time of inundation, however, the waters of the flood had lapped at the statues' feet, entirely filling their enclosures and submerging their pedestals so that they seemed to stand, reflected, upon a vast lake that had extended to cover the entire width of the silty plain behind. As Petrie records, the gaps in the surviving blocks of the colossi's pedestals had been filled with clean alluvial sand and silt deposited by those powerful floods.

At that same time, the natural banks of sand that had built up around the edges of the ancient lake in earlier ages had been greatly strengthened and, on occasion, capped with mud bricks. This, it would appear, was to contain those same high floods. It has also been suggested that a second man-made cutting off the Hawara Channel, which was operated as a sluice in classical times, had originally been opened in the last century of the times of the Itj-towy kings not as an improvement to irrigation, but to syphon more of the Nile's high-rising flood waters into another nearby depression in the desert, to create a secondary overflow basin within the Fayum to contain those disastrous high Niles. At all events, just as Amenemhet III's colossi had dominated the lakeside throughout the following millennia, so, too, the ruins of his pyramid stand at the point in the Hawara Channel where the second cutting had been made.

The settlement of Shehet, the ancient centre of the region of the Fayum, now lies beneath the provincial capital of Medinet el-Fayum. In the times of the Itj-towy kings it held temples part built from blocks of imported stone. At that same time, other temples were established in the Fayum, and new gods such as Osiris of the Fayum were introduced alongside Sobek, the region's ancient crocodile god. A host of splendid statues, some superb images of the Itj-towy kings, have since been found at these little-known monuments, most remarkable of all being a group of near life-sized cast-copper statues of Amenemhet III, some queens, two priests and a crocodile, all of them trimmed with gold and silver and set with lively inlaid eyes. Judging by their beautiful green patina, this unique group had stood for some considerable time within the desert; in the enclosure, perhaps, of Amenemhet III's mortuary temple at his Hawara pyramid, a now largely vanished structure whose inflated size and architectural complexities once earned it the classical title of the Egyptian Labyrinth.

On the north side of the lake, and well beyond the gaze of the two vanished colossi, stands the perfect little temple of Qasr el-Sagha. Made of massive blocks as brown as the surrounding sand, and holding fine-made shrines for seven unnamed deities though not a single text, it is the only temple of the times of the Itj-towy kings to still stand today. Two gridded mud-brick housing settlements were built near to this temple, designed, perhaps, to accommodate its builders and the households of its priests. A landing stage for stone barges lies close by, but nowadays the little group of buildings stand high and dry above the shore of the brackish and shrunken successor of the ancient lake, a white line in the distant haze. When its waters had been high and harvests good, that ancient temple was reflected in the mirror of the lake.

27

Living in the State

WORKING FOR THE STATE – *THE THINIS DOCKYARDS*

In 1904, George Reisner's excavations in the provincial cemeteries at Naga el-Deir, close to Abydos, brought to light an anonymous tomb containing a remarkable set of documents. The expedition's photographs show four frail rolls of papyrus, riddled with insect holes, lying just as a hand had set them down 4,000 years ago, on the dusty top of a box-like cedar coffin, one of three that had been crammed together in a little crypt. In all likelihood, for nothing in the tomb told anything about its occupants, the burials were those of the members of a scribal household whose work had been connected with the provincial operations of the Itj-towy court.

Those 'tattered ledgers', as their editor and interpreter William Kelly Simpson describes them, proved on average to be six feet long, the largest almost twice that length. And written on them all, in swift workman-like hieratic by hands honed on thousands of such documents, several scribes had set down records and accounts in a series of page-like folios, each one a little larger than an A4 sheet of paper, one following another along the scrolls. Though modest in their content, they document some of the daily activities of one of the widespread communities who had supplied the Itj-towy court and built its boats and monuments, but whose lives and daily work are otherwise unknown.

Compiled in the times of the vizier Antefoker in the reign of Senwosret I, the so-called Naga el-Deir papyri record some of the activities at the nearby boatyards of Thinis. At least as old as the early Memphite kings, the Thinis boatyards had been revived by the Itj-towy courts and were serving as a regional centre, as both a transit hub for state traffic on the Nile and as a staging post on the caravan and sea routes to the south; the Thinis dockyards, indeed, had supplied both ships and shipwrights to the Port of Saww during Antefoker's expedition to the Land of Punt.

Three letters of command sent from the offices of the vizier Antefoker are recorded in the Naga el-Deir papyri, which suggests that their recipients at Thinis had operated under his direct control. They also tell that the settlement at the boatyards had access to the produce of local estates, for one of Antefoker's letters orders large stocks of grain to be shipped from the boatyards, downstream to the royal residence. Operating as a dependency and outlier of the Itj-towy residence like the staff of royal temples, its workforce was protected from recruitment in the state corvee, for another of the vizier's letters concerns the improper requisition by another court official of some of the dockyards' craftsmen.

Whilst the third letter deals with the intricacies of finishing and delivering a royal boat, its oars and bailing scoops, its cleats and mallets, by far the better part of the contents of these papyri consist of various accountings. One, for example, records the work of the shipyard's toolmakers, detailing the delivery of copper and its recasting into the boat builders' chisels, adzes, axes and other blades and engraving tools. The brevity of these records, however, along with lacunae produced by insects, time and the scribes' use of many as-yet-untranslated terms, hampers their full translation. Nonetheless, the compilers' minute attention to detail emphasizes once more the essential role of copper, that precious hard-won ingredient, in shaping courtly culture.

No less fascinating are the lengthy lists of the names of sons and daughters from various households in the region of Thinis that were recruited to work on various state projects. Each person is identified by his father's name, followed by his own. Sometimes, three generations of the same family appear to have been called into service at the same time: 'Ankh's son Nakhti', followed by 'Nakhti's son Sobekemhet', being listed as members of the same gang one beneath the other. Grouped in ten, fifty and a hundred people, the gang numbers seem quite small given the tasks that they were set, although the individuals that are named may well have brought other members of their households with them or even sent substitutes for their own presence at the worksite.

At all events, the gangs' tasks ranged from serving as sailors on the voyages of court officials to making mud bricks – the latter task accompanied by a close accounting of the quantities of the chopped straw used for their bonding, which is an expensive commodity in rural Egypt down to this day. The gangs' work also included cutting acacia and sycamore trees that grew down by the riverside, this perhaps to fuel the boatyards' copper furnaces and for use in cooking fires, for some of the records in the papyri seem to record deliveries of fish, pigeons, fowl and joints of meat.

Other sections of the Naga el-Deir papyri appear to deal with the construction of tomb chapels or temples, for they record the dimensions of the chambers of an unnamed building and the thicknesses of its walls, along with estimates of the amounts of work required for their construction, from the shipping and hauling of their stone and the making of mud bricks to shaping and laying their column bases and foundations. That the scribes measured those various tasks in man-days would have enabled speedy calculations of the rations of food that such projects had required, the bread rations of each of the individuals enlisted in corvee being accounted in terms of the days that they had worked. These records, therefore, shed light on how the creation of such buildings had been visualized by the Itj-towy court, for they are estimated in terms of the amount of men and provisions required for their completion.

The longest tours of duty on these corvees are of two and a half months, and several gang members are described as 'fleeing' from a project – this, perhaps to help with the family harvest? By modern standards, however, the workloads that the scribes have calculated for the completion of their tasks seem low and rations generous enough, so life on pharaoh's building sites, it would appear, was not so very hard.

HOUSING BY THE STATE –
THE SETTLEMENT AT EL-LAHUN

*The temple stood on a prominent point of rocky ground,
standing forward just over the Nile plain; while on the north
of it the hill swept round forming a sort of bay about a quarter of a mile across. Here the town for the workmen and the
stores was built . . .*

W. M. Flinders Petrie, 1890

Though the pyramids of the Itj-towy kings have been reduced to
formlessness, a settlement connected to the royal cult and to the construction of pyramids and temples has survived remarkably intact.
Set close to the Hawara Channel and the Fayum at a site that is
known today as el-Lahun, it had housed several thousand people for
well over a century and is the largest of all known courtly settlements
of the times of the Itj-towy kings. It was also one of those uncanny
places in Egypt where the intimate debris of ancient lives lay just a
few feet underneath the modern surface of the desert.

> Having spent some weeks in a town of the XIIth dynasty, having
> examined hundreds of the rooms, and having discovered all the ordin-
> ary objects of daily life just as they were last handled by their owners,
> I seem to have touched and realized much of the civilization of that
> remote age; so that it is hard to believe that over four thousand years
> have glided by since those houses last echoed to the voices of their
> occupants.

The settlement at el-Lahun was excavated in the spring of 1889 by
Petrie, who had previously been digging around the denuded ruin of
the nearby pyramid of Amenemhet II. Nothing if not competitive,
Petrie had got wind that another excavator was planning to work at
el-Lahun, so he put a small team of men to dig unsupervised within
the ancient settlement, before taking personal charge of the excavation during the following winter season. His method was
straightforward enough. As the settlement's houses were laid out in

the manner of all such courtly colonies, in precisely measured rows, he simply dug out one dwelling at a time using the rectangular hole created by that excavation as the dump for the filling dug out of the next house in the line. Thus proceeding, he excavated virtually all of the surviving houses at the site in just two short winter seasons; some 230 dwellings of various sizes whose walls had been preserved to two, four and sometimes five feet off their ancient floors. The dig yielded extraordinary amounts of material, which Petrie, a man who more than any other archaeologist working in Egypt at that time was fascinated by the minutiae of ancient daily life, briefly summarized in the resulting publications. At that time, unfortunately, Petrie was at the beginning of his career in Egypt, and modern archaeological method was quite unknown, so that today his speed of working, his ways of digging and recording, have led modern archaeologists (who in the last decades have regained an interest in such domestic sites) to resurrect the processes of his excavations at el-Lahun from his faded photographs, his plans and scribbled diaries.

Despite later discoveries of some similar courtly settlements, el-Lahun remains unique, not only in its sheer size, in the quantity and the quality of domestic objects that it had held, the detail of its daily life, but also because of the large numbers of fragmentary papyri that were found within its houses. And like the site itself, those documents have also been the subject of renewed interest in recent decades. So, along with the careful modern excavation of other somewhat similar contemporary settlements, the renewed study of the documents from el-Lahun has led to a wider vision of that enormous site.

Founded in all probability in the reign of Amenemhet II, the repetitive internal architecture of the houses at el-Lahun was modified over generations, and most of the objects Petrie recovered were from the households of its later inhabitants, when the courtiers and builders of Senwosret III had been engaged in contructing his pyramid and temples, which stood a mile to the north. Nonetheless, a rare piece of Cypriote pottery that Petrie found lying on a house floor and which had probably been imported through Tell el-Dab'a, had been made in yet later generations. So el-Lahun had remained in use in times after the Kings of Itj-towy, its streets and houses continuing to accommodate a variety of households and occupations.

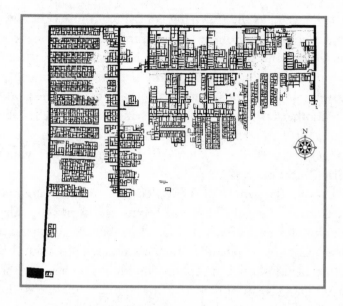

Petrie's plan of the settlement of el-Lahun. It lay almost a mile to the east of the pyramid of Amenemhet II, whose valley temple had abutted the settlement's west wall. The largest dwellings, the so-called 'mansions', lie along the upper section of the plan, each one distinguished from its neighbour by a thick straight wall. The settlement's northern boundary was 400 yards long.

Set within the desert but at the edge of the ancient flood plain, part of el-Lahun has been eroded through the ages, probably as a result of the river's rising inundation levels. Assuming that its original design had been symmetrical and similar to the other courtly settlements of the times, it would originally have been rectangular. Then, it would have held some thirty-two acres of dwellings, the walls of its perimeter entirely filled with 400 tiny houses set on narrow alleys, along with two temples. One of those housed the jackal god Anubis, who was associated with the dead; the other, Sobek, of the nearby Fayum. A third of the entire settlement, however, was taken up with ten spacious dwellings, whilst another larger mansion, often identified as 'the King's House', stood above all the others on a so-called 'Acropolis'. Built along the settlement's northern side on higher ground, those large mansions were similar in plan to others that have been excavated in recent decades at Abydos and Tell el-Dab'a, in Nubia and the delta. And as the surviving contents of those other dwellings serve to underline, each of those eleven mansions had held considerable households and were probably the homes of court officials with connection to the king. Many of the settlement's smaller houses, alternatively, which were set nearer to the silt, contained rakes and sickles and other farming implements, which suggested to Petrie that their occupants had farmed the nearby fields, a supposition borne out by passages from the settlement's fragmentary papyri which deal with agricultural matters.

Placed within the pattern of the settlement's commanding grid, each of the ten great mansions had held rooms and workshops that contained many of the functions that are described and sculpted in such detail in Mekhet-re's Theban funerary models. At el-Lahun, however, rather than being housed in separate buildings as they are shown in Mekhet-re's models, all of those facilities – the animal pens, the granaries, the bakeries, the weaving studios and the like – were packed together side by side into each one of the mansions' half-acre rectangles. And the domestic quarters of all of those great houses had held bathrooms, lavatories and bedrooms, audience halls and gardens, shaded colonnades and shallow pools with rows of trees and flowering plants.

The mansions' most astute observer, the archaeologist Barry Kemp, has calculated that their considerable granaries could have stored sufficient grain to feed the entire settlement for around a year. One might well imagine, therefore, that the inhabitants of the tiny row houses, which were packed in perfect symmetry, alley upon alley, within the lower sections of the settlement, had worked on behalf of those ten great houses, whose inhabitants had probably controlled large estates upon the nearby plains and had gathered their harvests in the mansions' granaries.

Officials and priests working within the nearby pyramid temple of Amenemhet II had also lived at el-Lahun, for some of the settlement's papyri that were drawn up in the times of Senwosret III detail the rotas of the phyles of priests and other staff who had served within that temple. Listing the statues and processions, recording the appearance of Sirius, the rising of the star that announced the coming inundation, parts of those fragmentary archives are somewhat similar in their content to those found within the earlier pyramid temples at Abusir.

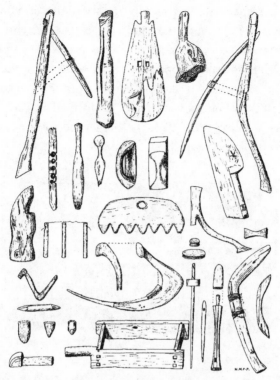

*Some of the wooden tools, toys and farming equipment found in the
houses of el-Lahun: hoes, dibbers and mallets, sickles, fire-making
apparatus, spindles, cleats, ties and tops, plaster floats and brick moulds.*

At el-Lahun, however, some blocks of small row houses close to the
vanished mortuary temple had served, so the papyri tell, to house
both agricultural workers and the phyles of the temple's personnel.
And a dividing wall would have ensured the ritual purity of the members of those phyles whilst they were serving their turn, by isolating
their houses from the rest of the settlement. This mixed usage over
many generations would account for the fact that, of all known settlements set near pyramid temples, el-Lahun was by far the largest and
that its wide range of functions were involved in various court projects, whilst its extensive grain stores may also have helped to support
nearby Itj-towy.

Like the ten great mansions, the row houses of el-Lahun were laid out
in strips of identical size but grouped in rows of eight, line upon line of
them, set back to back and each one entered from a narrow alleyway.

Inside this plan, each dwelling had five or six rooms laid out in modest stripped-down imitations of the mansions up above, with everything down to the dividing streets and alleyways precisely measured out in cubits. Though they do not appear to have had upper stories, for Petrie found no staircases within them, numerous tomb-chapel paintings and models suggest that their roofs may have performed a variety of services, from summer sleeping areas to fuel storage and food processing, and that access to them may have been by ladder.

A contemporary painting of the row houses of el-Lahun, one of a number copied by Petrie from drawings on the walls of some of the settlement's more modest dwellings. It shows a terrace of pretty doorways and, above, some of the furnishings inside an individual unit.

The doorways of these little houses appear to have been arched; Petrie found a painting of a row of them on the wall of one of their rooms. In similar fashion, some of their narrower rooms had been vaulted, their builders simply drawing the outline of an arch on the upper part of a wall and then laying the vault in the manner of modern Nubian bricklayers by working backwards through the open room, placing the dry bricks without any supporting form directly into muddy mortar as they worked along the vault. Larger rooms were roofed by beams and palm leaves, stone and mud, supported as need arose on columns of wood, though most rooms were so small that the modest spans of twisted local woods served on their own. The room's mud-plastered walls had usually been painted with white gypsum over a dark-coloured dado, and, just as Mekhet-re's models have painted bands of colour at the tops of their dados, so those at el-Lahun had been similarly finished in lines of red and black.

Petrie found many wooden doorframes and bolted wooden doors still standing in the settlement. Hinged top and bottom by spikes of wood projecting from the doors and set on stone-block pivots, the wooden spikes had worn down after many years of use, and old sandals had been placed into some of the pivot holes to raise them up again.

Two pharaonic methods of ridding a house of rodents: Petrie's drawing of a rat-trap from Lahun, and a painting of a hunting cat from a contemporary tomb chapel. Much in the modern manner, the trap had a weighted bait within it connected to a sliding door that caught the rat.

Rats had run freely through those little dwellings; Petrie noticed their holes in the mud-brick walls, some of which the householders had stopped up in a vain attempt to block the vermin's progress. He also found a ponderous ceramic rat-trap, though judging from its clean interior it had never been put to use. Many domestic objects – plates, pots, buckets, sickles and hoes – had been perfectly preserved, and Petrie especially remarks that a cache of chisels and a copper pot that had been hidden during a late phase of the settlement's occupation were 'as bright as the days they had been left'. And in white-painted wooden boxes like those the Itj-towy sailors had taken on their boats to Punt, the people of the settlement had stored their mirrors, tweezers and cosmetics. They had also placed dead and stillborn babies in those boxes and buried them beneath the house floors. Sometimes, two or three small corpses had been laid together, with little necklaces and amulets decorated with the names of the Itj-towy kings.

Although the kitchens in the mansions had been set apart, those in the row houses were very small, their simple hearths set directly on the beaten earth against a living room wall. None of those houses, however, were used like modern Western family dwellings. Even the living quarters at the heart of the ten mansions appear cramped and crowded in such comparisons for all of the dwellings at el-Lahun had little room for furniture, some people sleeping in niches set in the walls. Nor were there any open areas within the settlement, no *piazze*, no public space. Other than the audience halls within the mansions and the open courts of temples, there would appear to be no examples of planned public spaces in all of ancient Egyptian architecture. From the ten great mansions above to the tiny row houses below, the accommodations at el-Lahun had housed a tightly closed, face-to-face community.

Nonetheless, all of those accommodations had been most carefully maintained, and at least some of their occupants had greatly appreciated them, for, as a hymn found on one of the settlement's papyri gratefully records, pharaoh had provided them with

> a cool room that allows every man to sleep to daybreak . . . a refuge . . .
> a shelter . . . a sunshade at the inundation, cool in summer . . . a warm
> corner, dry in winter. [From Papyrus University College London 32157]

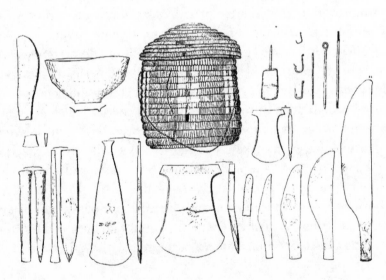

'as bright as the days they had been left': a Lahun basket and its
contents – copper fish hooks, net needles, skewers, axes, knives,
chisels and an awl.

COMMUNITY AND BEING

Amidst the storerooms, the audience halls, the vestibules, the gardens and the workshops, the single central units in most ancient Egyptian houses were the quarters that accommodated extended families. In the smallest houses these had consisted solely of sleeping and living areas, whilst most of the larger dwellings had tiny dressing rooms and bathrooms. Curiously enough, this scheme is hardly represented in the state-designed gridded row houses that are so small that they could only have housed nuclear family units. Later generations, however, had joined together groups of adjacent row houses so that they could accommodate several generations of an extended family, and other people who were outside the family group. At el-Lahun the generations of men who had lived within the row houses had presumably worked together in the fields and in the construction of the nearby royal monuments where, so the papyri tell, they had later served as priests and ritualists. The women of those same households, alternatively, wove cloth, made food and brought up children, a task that, as the numerous bodies of babies that Petrie found beneath the house floors underline, had been a permanent and pressing need.

On a larger scale, the mansions of el-Lahun, like those of other courtly settlements and of the grand provincial households of the time, had been similar to the royal residence at Itj-towy, with satellite households of scribes, factors and craftsmen, farm workers and herdsmen, fishermen, cooks, brewers, gardeners and servants. And in their turn, those smaller households had drawn on pools of skill and labour held in the households of local farmers, whose members could also be enlisted for harvesting the fields of the great estates, for the maintenance of irrigation basins and for conscription *en corvée* for monumental building work.

For the most part, the rations allocated to the smaller satellite households of non-farmers had consisted of goods and provisions that the large households produced on their estates and in their workshops, and these were usually distributed in raw form, requiring further processing: game and fish and joints of meat, grain from the granaries that could be fermented to make beer or baked in household ovens, and wool and flax that had to be spun and woven. On festive occasions, alternatively, and when groups of workers were conscripted to perform work away from home, their rations had included ready-made bread and beer, cakes and clothes, all such provisions being produced by and brought from the manufactories and estates of the great provincial households or from Itj-towy itself.

At first glance, the different house sizes at el-Lahun echo the traditional view of the three-tiered structure of ancient Egyptian society, a view reflected in the decorations of contemporary temples and tomb chapels, from the largest figure of the king or noble to the diminutive images of the craftsmen and the farm workers. Recently, and in much the same manner as Marx had characterized the newly minted rich of the nineteenth century, an emergent 'middle class' has been added to that fundamentally three-tiered vision, conjured from such sources as Heqanakht's archive and the numerous richly furnished but non-noble burials that were set within the cemeteries after the ending of the Memphite monarchy.

Add that picture of Itj-towy society to the common notion that in ancient Egypt the relative sizes of houses and funerary monuments can be measured in the manner of modern consumer goods, as public displays of wealth, and you conjure up the common yet distorted vision of that ancient state with a god-like pharaoh, the kingdom's richest and most powerful individual, with nobles such as Ankhu and Antefoker competing with their contemporaries for power and royal rewards, with squires like Heqanakht, a sort of disassociated rural middle class, operating as 'natural' capitalists, and with the poor old peasants as an unwilling proletariat.

The roots of that travesty lie in Champollion's time and in the following generations, as the order of early modern Christendom broke down and industrial society developed. Subjected to rigorous analyses later in the nineteenth century, the social categories that had been distinguished within those new industrial societies were then imposed upon non-Western cultures, where they served to provide a scientific ring to attitudes of many (middle class!) academics, such as those of the Berlin School, who had instinctively viewed the order of ancient societies as based on power, prestige and wealth. In relation to the realities of ancient Egypt, however, analyses using those criteria are like the reports of Lord Cromer's nineteenth-century government officials which price the labour of illiterate Egyptian village farmers with an eye to paying off the Khedives' international debts.

Pharaoh's Egypt, on the other hand, was a land inhabited by the gods, the living and the ancestors; a land in which stability and prosperity were one and could only be maintained by working in the age-old ways; that is, by building more monuments and continuing to offer to the gods and honouring the contracts between the living and the dead laid down in thousands of offering lists. Although courtly favour could increase individual prestige, the fundamental interrelationships within pharaonic society were fixed along with those of the sun, the seasons and the stars. So it is not surprising that the iconic image of pharaonic culture shows the king performing the act of killing some of the harbingers of disorder, for, in a society where morality, prosperity and social order were all as one, rebellious behaviour – from that shown by frisky animals to that which was apparently displayed by the son of vizier Antefoker – was evil and reviled.

In these terms, 'wealth' was simply the accumulated provisions of a householder, as the text of a stela placed by a certain Montuwoser in the enclosure of Osiris at Abydos neatly defines:

> I am an owner of cattle, with many goats; an owner of donkeys, with many sheep. I am rich in barley and emmer, fine in clothing: there is nothing missing from all my wealth. I am well supplied with boats and rich with vintage.

Such riches served both to physically maintain Montuwoser and his household and to confirm its relationship to the gods, the ancestors and the other living households of pharaonic society.

No Bronze Age culture, of course, had been driven by notions of material progress. It is extremely unlikely, indeed, that the people of those times had held concepts of public and private ownership similar to ours. Despite his worries about the size of harvest and his stocks of grain, Heqanakht was not a capitalist. Rather than working hard to increase his consumption of goods and services within a market-based economy, his overriding objective was simply to maintain his household's well being and its status in the community.

At first glance it seems surprising that in a culture where extreme precision was a hallmark of stone masons and craftsmen, there are dozens of simple accounting errors in Heqanakht's archives, and also in the surviving records of the state. Yet accounting in a modern manner was not their compilers' primary concern. Heqanakht's careful lists of work performed, of his dealings with his neighbours, of lands loaned and goods traded, are not the shoddy records of a tired bookkeeper but the archives of his household's social obligation. No wonder, then, that attempts to establish a 'basic wage' for Middle Kingdom labourers have largely failed, for the records of building work kept by the scribes of Naga el-Deir contain simple errors both in their calculation of man/days worked and in the seemingly over-generous amounts of rations allotted to the workmen. In reality, those 'wages' were simply supplies of provisions of sufficient quantity and quality to keep one or, perhaps, several workmen working well.

This is not to suggest that the Itj-towy state had been an earthly paradise. Doubtless, there were as many cruelties inflicted within the ancient kingdom as there are within our modern world. And, certainly, institutional light-handedness had hardly been a feature of the frenetic age in which the great pyramids were built; like the image of the smiting king, the batons held in the hands of the images of foremen and the courtiers could token painful punishment. Although the demands of the Itj-towy state upon its population had certainly relaxed since the delirium of pyramid building during the reigns of Sneferu and the Giza kings, the kingdom always required manpower of its population. As the Naga el-Deir papyri and some of the texts within the mines and quarries confirm, corvee and conscription was still a part of life in the times of the Itj-towy court, and those caught attempting to flee such work could be harshly punished. And of course there was no liberty in ancient Egypt. For liberty, essentially, is a concept born of slavery – it is, in fact, its opposition – slavery being a product of societies that have reduced human beings to the unitized abstractions of goods for sale in a marketplace.

Nevertheless, in Middle Kingdom Egypt, the state's touch could be light. In all of Heqanakht's surviving correspondence, for example, there is not a single mention of the king nor of the government. And of course, corvee and conscription could never have been more pressing than the need to harvest or to undertake those other seasonal activities which form the universal treadmill of agrarian societies.

There is, as well, a care and kindness in the ancient records, a generosity of vision, which the draughtsmen and designers extended to their images of all living things. Just as the texts of many royal mining expeditions carefully record the safe return of all their personnel and their pack donkeys, so, too, the texts in Djehutihotep's tomb chapel frequently affirm that all the men of the four gangs of conscripts that hauled the alabaster colossus had accomplished that perilous enterprise in safety, without incident or loss. Such activities, therefore, should not be regarded as a public display of power, like those of the North Korean elite, nor certainly as Hollywood tricks out their depiction, with whips and chains. In Djehutihotep's tomb chapel, the arrival of the colossus is described in terms of general rejoicing.

There was, as well, a celebration of the common human need to eat and procreate, the experience of cool rooms on hot days, of a warm dry corner in the winter, of the sensuousness of the human form that the craftsmen rendered so joyfully, of the preciousness of children and the pain suffered at their all too frequent deaths, as the pretty jewellery that Petrie found upon the babies buried at el-Lahun silently testifies. Babies, so the archaeologist reports, that he in turn had quietly re-interred within the nearby desert.

Had those unfortunate children survived they would have lived in a society where solidarity was stronger than that within the cities of the modern West; where people worked together in extraordinary close community; where for millennia the farmers and miners had provided the materials, tools and rations that enabled great monuments to be constructed. Where the work of dozens of anonymous craftsmen had celebrated that extraordinary harmony in jointly creating a vast series of unique images, sculptural and architectural, such as the world would never make again.

Those remarkable abilities had been fostered for millennia in thousands of small face-to-face communities, two long strings of riverside villages with a wide range of extraordinary natural resources at their disposal. When the court was not furiously building a royal pyramid or another major monument, even such settlements as Itj-towy had been small enough for its inhabitants to recognize each other. And all of their various components, the kings, the courtiers, the farmers, held a certain dignity and the fundamental understanding that they were all mutually interdependent.

One of the finest stories to have survived from the times of the Middle Kingdom, in four separate papyri, is known today as the 'The Eloquent Peasant'. Like several other documents of the age, it is set in the previous interregnum, before the court of Itj-towy had been established. And like most of the so-called literary texts to have survived, the greater part of it is an essay upon style and manner.

In this instance, however, the text also reflects on the pharaonic social order and on what is fair and unfair for the population, and the obligation which each part of that culture has towards the other. As in other documents of the time, people of all ranks and professions appear to address each other in a forthright manner and are more plainspoken than is usually the case today, an impression underlined by contemporary sculpture and relief that similarly appears to show pharaonic culture as a canny and direct society.

The story of the so-called Eloquent Peasant tells of the misadventures of a farmer named Khunanup as he travels down into the valley of the lower Nile from a small desert oasis which lies to the west of the river's delta, known today as the Wadi el-Natrun. En route, a minor state official tricks, beats and robs Khunanup, taking both his donkeys and the goods that they were carrying to market.

And so energetically indignant is the farmer in defence of what many would still consider to be the tenets of a just society that, on hearing his impassioned plea, the local governor sends word of Khunanup's eloquence to the king. Sensing entertainment, it would appear, the king then orders the governor to detain Khunanup, that his household should be given rations and that the process of his petitioning should be extended so that a scribe could record his additional orations. So poor Khunanup is constrained to make no less than nine more speeches, each one displaying growing anger and frustration at the injustice he has suffered, and also at bureaucracy's apparent sloth: 'shall I eat your bread and drink your beer forever?' Finally, in exasperation, he threatens suicide, and the dismal process is halted and Khunanup is awarded the goods and holdings of the man who did him wrong, 'his wheat, his barley, his donkeys . . . his pigs, his cattle . . .'

Beneath this literary record of fearless eloquence, there runs a
subtle counterpoint of Kafka-like entanglement, of the loss of freedom and of the cruelties inherent in the order of any structured
state – the same issues, indeed, that modern states still wrestle with
today. The story starts, however, in the heartlands of pharaonic
culture, amidst the warm sweet breezes of the live Egyptian
countryside . . .

> There was once a man whose name was Khunanup. He was a farmer
> in the Wadi Natrun and had a wife named Merit.
>
> And the farmer said to his wife, 'Look here; I am going to the Valley
> to bring provisions for my children. Go and measure the grain that is
> left in the storehouse from last year's barley.' And he measured out six
> rations of grain.
>
> And the farmer said to his wife, 'Look, you have twenty rations of
> grain as provisions for you and your children, now make these six
> rations of grain into bread and beer for me to live on.'
>
> And so the farmer set out for the Valley having loaded his donkeys
> with reeds and herbs, natron, salt, and sticks . . . with staffs from
> Farafra Oasis, leopard skins, jackal hides, and plants and serpentine,
> with pigeons and other birds, with berries and seeds and all the fair
> produce of the Wadi Natrun.
>
> And the man went southwards in the direction of Herakleopolis,
> arriving at the district of Perfefi, north of the region of Mednit . . .

Epilogue
Reflections on a Golden Age

THE POETRY OF CRAFTSMANSHIP –
MIDDLE KINGDOM MATERIAL CULTURE

Some of the most moving images that humanity has ever made were sculpted in Middle Kingdom studios. Much of the painting and sculpted relief of the period is exquisite, the court jewellery unsurpassed. Even the daily products of the Itj-towy potters are very fine.

Clearly, the Itj-towy court had realized the vision of the Intefs and the Montuhoteps in magnificent fashion. During the two centuries of its existence, the Itj-towy court not only re-established high pharaonic culture – its crafts, its architecture and writing – but refined it, bestowing upon it a delicacy and balance that enriched the pharaonic scriptoria and craftsmen's workshops for the next 2,000 years. All in all, it was an intense and thoughtful enterprise.

Today, unfortunately, there is a considerable gap in our understanding of the Middle Kingdom's crafts and architecture. The major enterprises of its court, the beating heart of pharaonic culture, its state monuments and Itj-towy itself, have all but disappeared. Even its colossal statues were recut and re-inscribed by later kings. Set more lightly on the earth than the Memphite monuments and largely obliterated by lime burners and later temple builders, apart from the tomb chapels of the provincial governors all that remains are fragments of a lost and distant age.

At the beginning, however, in the age in which Montuhotep II's Theban temple tomb was built, things seem clear enough. The craftsmen and builders lived in an age bent on regaining the full panoply of pharaonic culture and thus the technical proficiency held in the

Memphite studios. This was a long and somewhat self-conscious process, as some of the passages of a text engraved upon a stela of a certain Irtisen inadvertently underline:

> I know the secret of hieroglyphs, the composition of ceremonial . . . I am a craftsman who excels at his art and is at the forefront of knowledge. I know how to estimate the proportions of figures and how they should sink and rise when they are sculpted in relief. I know the pose of the male figure and the appearance of the female, the poses of birds and cattle, the submission of an isolated prisoner when one eye sees the other, the gesture of a hunter as he harpoons a hippopotamus, the gait of a runner.

Engraved upon a slab of fine white limestone almost four feet high, Irtisen's stela holds fifteen horizontal lines of carefully engraved hieroglyphs and, underneath, a sunken tableau drawn in the traditional manner, showing the craftsman and his wife seated before a bread-laden offering table scattered with game and joints of meat. Despite Irtisen's claims, the relief is dull, naïve, a half memory of the provincial sculpture from the times of the late Saqqara kings. The stela's text, however, is unique; no other pharaonic craftsman ever saw fit to describe his skill with such determination other than through the medium of his craft. To that extent, it outlines the aims and the ambitions of his age, for the courtly crafts and architecture were of supreme importance to pharaonic identity. At the same time, a critical self-consciousness is arising in the studios and workshops, a new space between the craftsmen and their work.

The southern workshops that were maintained by the court of the Intefs and the Montuhoteps had led the way in the revival, and although their craftsmen generally employed provincial, careful, solid, southern forms and compositions, many of their larger royal works are better designed and drawn than Irtisen's stela. Many of them, too, retain some of the engaging and eccentric innovations of the draughtsmen who had worked during the interregnum, such as those who had designed and painted Ankhtifi's pillared tomb chapel at Mo'alla.

The breakthrough, the re-attainment of the gravitas and high skill that had been held within the Memphite court, came after the move to Itj-towy. For there the southern craftsmen seem to have encountered the skill and style held in the rump of the Saqqara workshops, and together they studied the manners of the times of the Giza kings and, reign by reign, created the distinctive synthesis of the mature Middle Kingdom style.

The initial change from older provincial manners to courtly style was accomplished in the first decades following the move to Itj-towy, and so quickly that several of the monuments of the queens and courtiers at Deir el-Bahari show the old and new styles side by side. In similar fashion, the Theban tomb chapel attributed to Senet, vizier Antefoker's mother, offers an extraordinary contrast with the courtly mastaba of her son at Lisht. Set in a thin rock-cut corridor, two of the walls of Senet's tomb chapel are painted in a charming naïf style, and with such spry and lively detail that it is one of the great delights within that vast necropolis. Antefoker's monument, on the other hand, had stood beside the pyramid of Amenemhet I and had taken the form of the mud-brick mastabas and palaces of the times of the first kings, but was sculpted in an eclectic, somewhat etiolated mix of archaism and innovation. And as its surviving fragments – some of which hold the account of his voyage to the Lebanon – show, they already display the elegance of the emerging courtly style.

With the exception of the jewel-like kiosk of Senwosret I at Karnak, which was reassembled in the 1920s from blocks retrieved from the foundations of a later monument, very little remains of the court architecture of those times, although the court craftsmen were building and decorating temples all over the kingdom, from the delta and Heliopolis, to Abydos, Thebes and Aswan. At the same time, however, the craftsmen of the households of the provincial governors were creating splendid tomb chapels with a distinctive use of columns and pillars. Inside the chapels, too, much innovative subject matter was introduced, such as the scene in the tomb chapel of Djehutihotep at Deir el-Bersha which shows the hauling of a colossus, and that of Khnumhotep's father at Beni Hasan, which pictures a group of Amu people. Other scenes, too, in the Beni Hasan tomb chapels hold elaborate images of sieges and desert hunts with monstrous animals, and bouts of wrestling and a range of other entertainments all painted in a fine high style, the like of which had not been seen before.

From Thinis, near Abydos, downstream to Beni Hasan, these governors' tombs are now part of a well-trodden tourist trail – Qaw el-Kebir,

Asyut, Meir, Deir el-Bersha and the rest – and they all display the livelier side of provincial life, observed with a keen eye and often painted in a genuinely innovative style. Some of them hint that their painters copied forms from Crete and other northern cultures, to which such Delta ports as Tell el-Dab'a had given access. The key to this burst of innovation, however, lies with the draughtsman-scribes who sometimes painted lengthy texts – writings in the manner of, and part derived from, the Pyramid Texts – onto the courtier's cedar coffins. Few earlier draughtsman had shown such skill; for the first time, for example, some painters come to terms with changes in the colour of pleated clothes, in bird plumage, and even the glowing ashes of a wood fire, all in exquisite detail. These are some of the surviving masterworks of ancient Egyptian painting, and they emphasize the magnitude of the almost total loss of contemporary courtly monuments.

Hints of what has gone, however – the spare crisp line of fine relief, a novel use of space and design – are preserved on some of the royal stelae of the age and on the few remaining lintels of various temple doorways. Some of the most complex designs that ancient Egyptian craftsmen ever made, such works show an extraordinary and entirely novel sophistication. With the stelae, the draughtsmen sometimes work with but a few scanty motifs to produce hieroglyphic compositions of rare simplicity. On the temple lintels, alternatively, the simple heraldic oppositions of Old Kingdom designers are transformed into elaborate harmonious patterns in which the figures of the king and gods sit within complex, balanced lattices of verticals and horizontals. These, then, show a maturation of the earlier courtly style.

The same rare sense of balance and design is held in the court jewellery of the age. Here, too, is the pharaonic craftsman's ability to change the scale of things, from the colossal to the minuscule, to produce objects in an enormous range of different sizes without any loss of coherent form.

A foretaste of what was to come is seen in the strings of semiprecious stones and silver beads found in the burials of the royal women at Deir el-Bahari and also on the mummy of Mekhet-re's estate manager Wah, who was buried with two splendid silver scarabs and necklaces of faience and silver. Those fine pieces, however, are eclipsed by the famous hoards of domestic jewellery from the burials

A rare balance of design. Strung on a necklace of amethysts and turquoise, bearing the cartouche of Senwosret III and worn by a princess of the royal household, this exquisite pendant is composed of golden cloisons filled with garnets, carnelian and lapis lazuli. The courtly sandstone stela from the region of the Second Cataract bears the brief inscriptions 'Horus, lord of foreign lands' and 'Great God, Lord of Heaven'. It is eighteen inches high.

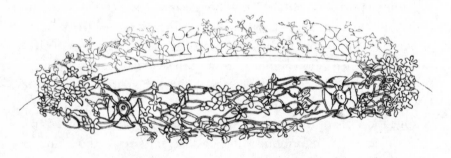

A diadem, a crown of flowers for the Princess Khnumet, daughter of Amenemhet II. Found in a jewellery box in her tomb at Dahshur, it appears to have been worn at court. The flowers and berries are of turquoise, carnelian and lapis lazuli and are individually held in cloisons attached by rings and tubes to a loose mesh of ten interwoven golden wires. They would have shimmered with the Princess's every movement.

of nine royal women and courtiers who were entombed at the royal pyramids of Dahshur and el-Lahun and whose crypts had lain relatively undisturbed throughout the following millennia, deep beneath the rubble and destruction wrought by generations of lime burners and stone thieves in the cemeteries above.

Although the later discovery of the tomb of Tutankhamun has eclipsed those earlier treasures, the jewellery of those royal women holds a restraint not present in the work of later ages – the gentle textures, the soft stone and shining metals, the scale, the harmonious design, the unmatched technical skill, the sheer delight of the Itj-towy craftsmen working in pure gold and purple amethyst, in fine blue faience, turquoise and lapis lazuli, making rings, bracelets, girdles, collars, pectorals and necklaces for the women of the Itj-towy court. And once again, some of the techniques used in the jewellers' workshops had come to Itj-towy from the north, from the Levant and the Aegean.

The simplicity and elegance of the Itj-towy jewellery is encapsulated in its use of seashells. Cowries brought from the Red Sea were drilled to serve as simple beads, or their forms were beautifully sculpted in gold. Strung together on amuletic girdles alongside small dark carnelians shaped and polished to resemble acacia seeds, they would have rattled at the slightest movement, for the golden shells had little pellets in them. Polished oyster shells were strung on necklaces as pendants. Known as 'healthy ones', they were often edged in gold, minutely decorated with filigree, cloisonné and granulation and the cartouche of the reigning king. Men, alternatively, could wear necklaces of a line of tubular faience beads with a pendant oyster shell, whose shining surfaces were lightly engraved with a cartouche drawn in a single delicate line filled with lamp-black pigment.

IMAGES OF KINGS

The most evocative part of the garland that surrounds the central void of Itj-towy's courtly culture are the royal sculptures, because to modern eyes they look like portraits of individual people. Whilst hundreds of these sculptures have survived, most are smashed and broken, and only a handful are intact – notably a hoard of ten life-sized limestone statues of Senwosret I, carefully buried in a pit at Lisht, and some colossal sphinxes that were found in the north-eastern Delta amidst the jumbled blocks of ancient Tanis. Such is the power of the royal sculpture, however, that even the damaged and fragmented works fuse easily together in the mind to create a line of perfect, powerful images of Middle Kingdom royalty.

Once again, the journey to maturity began at Thebes, where Montuhotep II's craftsmen made a series of sculptures of their king to stand in and around his temple tomb. The finest that survives is a near life-sized sculpture that had been wrapped in linen and buried like a human corpse, which was found in one of the burial chambers of that temple tomb (Plate 11). Heavily painted, wide-eyed, full-formed and with tremendous presence, it already shows a complete command of finished sculptural form. Cut from the same distinctive sandstone that is used throughout the temple tomb, it is the epitome of Theban style.

After the move to Itj-towy, the court sculptors started to examine older Memphite works that lay close at hand. So whilst some of the colossi of Senwosret I that had stood along the causeway to his pyramid display the Theban manner, others derive their qualities from some of Sneferu's sculptures made six centuries before. Buried fresh from the craftsmen's studios and never set within a temple, the ten perfect over life-sized seated statues of that king which were found at Lisht show that their sculptors employed a standard Memphite prototype of the sculptures of the Giza kings for their bodies, but placed a series of fresh young faces atop that ideal form to create a tension that, to modern eyes, imparts a curious fragility. Here, the sculptors of Itj-towy are developing manners in which many traditional forms are subtly changed in ways that appear today to be more naturalistic.

Some of the sculptors of the following king, Amenemhet I, used the Great Sphinx of Giza as a model for the royal head, measuring that enormous image and recasting it in a series of large-eared, round-eyed, full-lipped royal faces. Set upon the fifteen-foot-long granite body of a solidly ferocious sphinx, the most celebrated and most perfect of these powerful works was found at Tanis in the nineteenth century and transported to the Louvre. Ageless, enigmatic, highly mannered, that same face would serve as a model for dozens of later sculptures of royal sphinxes and colossi over many centuries.

Occasionally, the court craftsmen looked further back into the past. A commanding, over life-sized granite sculpture of Amenemhet III, for example, wears the elaborate wig, jewellery and animal skins of an archaic priest, whilst the forms of the face owe much to sculptures of those archaic times. (See Plate 18.) On other occasions, the royal craftsmen seem to have re-used forms and poses employed by the sculptors of the Old Kingdom courtiers. Others still employed provincial forms, whilst the idea of a very young pharaonic face was revisited, along with an increasing attention towards a naturalism of proportion. At the other extreme, some royal heads display their kings with care-worn, heavy-lidded faces, though always set upon the perfect Memphite torso first designed in the time of the Giza kings. Young and old, sphinx-like or provincial, these different statue types were sometimes set up side by side. And certainly, those diverse statue types underline the fact that Middle Kingdom style was a carefully cultivated identity rather than some kind of innate ethnic expression, as was long assumed to have been the case.

Changes in the technology of statue making had greatly aided the eclecticism of the Itj-towy sculpture studios. For the first time, it appears, some chisels were made of bronze rather than hardened copper, which allowed jewellery, wigs and beards to be elaborated in far greater detail, or at least with greater ease. Hence, too, the fine sharp edges upon the eyes and mouths, the sphinxes' claws, of hardstone statues, fine lines that had only previously been seen on softer limestone sculptures. By the later Middle Kingdom, the metal workers had gained an increasing command of alloys and inlays, and bronze was being cast in life-sized statues such as those that appear to have been recovered from the enclosure of Amenemhet III's pyramid at Hawara. Such statues employed a technique that precisely reproduced in bronze the forms of a sculpture made from softer substances such as clay, wax or sand. This had provided the royal sculptors with an entirely different way of making form, by addition rather than subtraction, as in traditional stone carving. And the process, it appears, had enlarged the sculptors' sensibilities, for surfaces of granite, serpentine and quartzite started to be treated in new and different ways.

Now, for example, the forms of a royal face could be produced by rubbing the statue with abrasive powder, not in the manner employed in earlier sculptures that gave a high shine to rounded concave surfaces, but so as to reduce the form of the stone and to reproduce the softer convex folds of older male faces. Such is the nature of this work, indeed, that some of those 'old' heads could have been re-worked from statues that had previously shown a young and ideal king. And both types of head still top perfect, ideal Memphite bodies. At all events, those extraordinarily powerful 'old king' images of Sen-wosret III and Amenemhet III, whose combined reigns could have totalled seventy years and more, are some of the finest sculptures ever made, their smashed and broken stones fragmentary evocations of strong, hard-worked, old age (Plate 19).

Many of these different styles of royal sculptures similarly appear in the generations of the nobles' sculpture. These, then, are images of pharaonic courtiers as they had never been shown before. Although the lively, full-bodied sculpture of the Memphite court could also show a male courtier (if not the female statues, which are invariably shown in eternal Memphite youth) in portly, prosperous middle age, which when illuminated and photographed display expressions similar to those of a baroque portrait or the photographs of Yousuf Karsh of Ottawa.

With the notable exception of the now-vanished alabaster colossus of Djehutihotep, the courtiers of Itj-towy are not well represented in hard-stone sculpture. On Elephantine Island, however, at granite-rich Aswan, many hard-stone images of courtiers were preserved in perfect condition, standing in a gathering of shrines set within a unique monument dedicated to the cult of a certain Hekaib. Sole companion, lector priest, overseer of foreigners who instils the fear of Horus in foreign lands, Hekaib had been one of those late Old Kingdom travel-lers to Nubia and the Levant whose tombs stand in the cemeteries in the Aswan cliffs. For reasons yet unknown, generations of later local governors and courtiers had honoured Hekaib as if he were a god, so that today his strange shrine, which was excavated by the Egyptian *Service des Antiquités* under the direction of Labib Habachi, is one of the few places on earth where the Middle Kingdom stands all around you; a geometrically precise environment filled with images of tough-looking determined men, each one in his separate shrine.

Are such images portraits in a modern sense? Certainly, the attrib-utes of individual faces can be detected amongst a range of Middle

Kingdom sculptures emblazoned with royal cartouches and the names of courtiers, and they give easy, characterful identities to individuals that otherwise are largely enigmatic. Many traditional historians, indeed, freely use the careworn portraits of the kings as ancient equivalents of those images of Mussolini burning the midnight oil in the Palazzo Venezia, though here, of course, they work throughout the night to plan the flood defences of the Fayum rather than to drain the Pontine Marshes. From there, of course, it is but a short step to peopling such texts as the stories of Sinuhe and Khunanup, the so-called Eloquent Peasant, with emotions sensed in the statues of the Middle Kingdom courtiers.

Standing in the central courtyard of the shrine of Hekaib, however, under the gaze of a dozen such statues, you are primarily aware that group solidarity was the main ingredient of those courtiers' identities and that, as so many of ancient Egypt's texts and images insist, their notion of personal identity was tied to their behaviour as it affected the order of the state. To modern eyes, therefore, such apparently characterful sculptures call into question the nature of portraiture itself.

The problem is not one of the extent of such sculptures' realism, for the reproduction of the exact forms of an individual human face is not what portraits are about. No human on the planet, for example, has a face with the proportions of the head of the Giza Sphinx, yet we read that ancient face in terms of human personality as easily as we read deep emotion in Rembrandt's portraits.

With Middle Kingdom sculpture we encounter in full measure the astonishing ability of ancient Egyptian craftsmen to endow the forms of their subject matter with the qualities of life. It fills even the fragments of those ancient images, and produces the tension between the ancient stones and modern notions of individual human character. To that extent, perhaps, the works of Middle Kingdom sculptors can be seen as an example of that common trend in the history of artistry and craftsmanship in which the works of earlier ages have seemed to subsequent generations to have rendered their subject matter so completely that the only way to endow new works with authenticity was to repossess the old forms and, by a kind of magical skill, overlay them with fresh observations of living form.

LOOKING BACK, LOOKING FORWARD – SENWOSRET III'S ABYDOS TOMB

Though there is little left today of the Itj-towy pyramids beyond shapeless piles of mud brick, the designers and builders of those once great monuments had looked back to the earlier tradition, so that for half a millennium and more the desert plain that runs from Giza down to Lisht had been studded with a series of high, white, similarly angled, perfectly formed pyramids. The cultural confluence between the courts of Memphis and Itj-towy had run very deep. At Dahshur, sherds of Old Kingdom pottery were mixed into the mud bricks of Middle Kingdom pyramids, for pottery of that earlier period was still strewn across the site. The Itj-towy potters, too, made wares imitating Old Kingdom forms and colourings that were designed to hold the oils and unguents required for purification and for offering within Memphite tomb chapels. In the cemeteries of Lisht, offerings were made that copied those of Old Kingdom burials. Such was the careful replication of earlier ways, indeed, that it has been suggested that the large quantities of such vessels that remain reflect the numbers of offerings which are detailed in the Memphite offering lists.

Underneath the Itj-towy pyramids, however, the court builders constructed an astonishing variety of innovative interior architectures. Reign after reign, increasingly elaborate systems of pits, corridors and chambers, all of them exquisitely built, twist and turn beneath the pyramids' mud-brick vaults, performing a series of architectural tricks that obscure the place of royal burial whilst at the same time performing arpeggios on many of the ancient forms of royal burial. One pharaoh's great, grand granite sarcophagus, for example, imitates the then 700-year-old walls of the first pyramid enclosure, whilst the burial chamber of another is cut from a single block of quartzite weighing more than a hundred tons.

It is usually assumed that those elegant mazes were devised to foil wicked robbers, yet enormous care was taken in their construction, which was hardly necessary for such purposes, and all interested parties, from ancient robbers to modern archaeologists, have well understood that no such monument is impregnable. So those fine interiors had probably held more elevated purposes than mere security. At all events, they certainly exhibit a desire to both embellish and protect pharaonic burial with Itj-towy's finest craftsmanship.

Though none of the Itj-towy pyramids hold any texts at all, the writings in the tombs and tomb chapels of the courtiers of both the Memphite and the Itj-towy kingdoms tell that the rites of funeral and destiny in death were much the same for king and courtier. The essential difference in their funerary arrangements, therefore, had reflected the position of the person in society.

Whereas the courtiers, as the texts and images in their tomb chapels insistently inform us, were distinguished by their role within the organization of the state, pharaoh did not require such validation. Their role placed them above all offices of state, all courts, all provinces, each of their pyramids a universal cosmic model that gave pattern and meaning to the landscape, and life and order to the living kingdom.

So the decision in the reign of Senwosret III to build the king an enormous royal tomb with no pyramid at all and to set it far away from the traditional burial grounds of Memphis represents a revolution in the court's understanding of the nature of kingship itself.

In some ways, however, the transformational tomb that the Itj-towy court made for Senwosret III at Abydos still followed the architectural precedents of the tombs of his royal forebears, with a temple set down near the edge of the cultivated land, the entrance to the tomb itself situated in the desert up above, and those two units, tomb and temple, set upon a single axis which, at Abydos, is almost a third of a mile long.

In place of a pyramid, at Abydos the position of the royal tomb was marked out upon the desert by clearing an area of some five acres of rock and edging it in mud brick, in the T-shaped form of an archaic altar. As at the Itj-towy pyramids, mastabas were built beside this huge enclosure along with a pair of dummy mastabas to hold the debris from the excavation of the royal tomb. For, running steeply down from the surface of the T-shaped enclosure, far into the desert's underlying limestone, is the enormous excavation of the tomb's corridors and chambers that are some 700 feet in length and end beneath the cliffs that fringe the Nile-side desert.

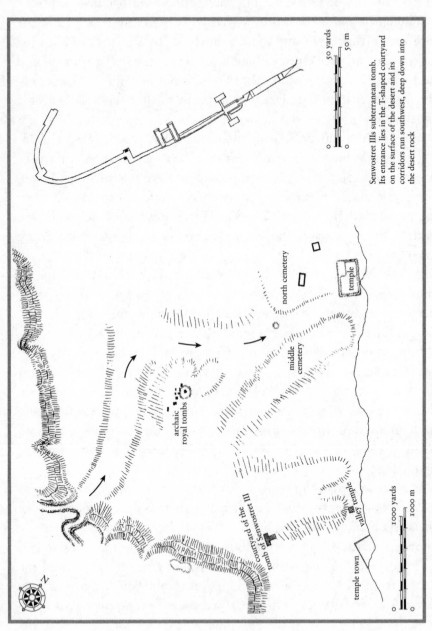

Senwostret IIIs subterranean tomb.
Its entrance lies in the T-shaped courtyard
on the surface of the desert and its
corridors run southwest, deep down into
the desert rock

50 yards

50 m

north cemetery

temple

middle
cemetery

archaic
royal tombs

N

courtyard of the
tomb of Senwostret III

valley temple

temple town

1000 yards

1000 m

*Abydos in the Middle Kingdom, showing the sites of the structures made in the time of
Senwosret III, along with the enormous subterranean royal tomb which was their focus.*

More than three times larger and longer than the corridors and chambers beneath Senwosret III's pyramid at Dahshur, the architecture of his Abydos tomb turns in the same disorientating manner as the interiors of most of the Itj-towy pyramids, a quality they share with the convoluted routes through the palaces that end in the audience chamber or those through some of the temples of the period that led to the shrines of the gods. Here, though, excavating in rock rather than building with rectangular bricks and blocks of stone, a similar asymmetry is achieved by employing a long semi-circular curve rather than a series of right angles.

In the manner of the contemporary pyramids, this huge corridor is beautifully lined with blocks of fine white limestone, though in its lower, curving sections the limestone is sometimes replaced with slabs of tough red quartzite, one of the hardest rocks that ancient Egyptian craftsmen ever worked. Here, as at the Itj-towy pyramids, elaborate architectural tricks were employed to disguise the place of burial; in this instance, the sarcophagus was part-hidden in a small chamber set half way through the excavation. That some of the quartzite blocks of the walls in the lower corridor were torn down, it would appear, in a determined search to locate further hidden rooms and corridors, shows the temporary success of that architectural ploy, although, as in all other royal tombs, the sarcophagus was eventually opened.

Until its recent re-excavation by a team led by Joseph Wenger, this anomalous, somewhat enigmatic monument was considered to be a 'cenotaph', a kind of model tomb and the caprice of a king who must have had some kind of special attachment to Abydos, which, after all, was the most sacred pilgrimage site within the kingdom. And had that king not already had a proper grave, a pyramid built in the manner of his predecessors on the plain of Dahshur?

Yet many earlier kings had two tombs prepared for them, the interminable archaeological debate about which one had actually housed the royal body ignoring the vital role that their construction had played within the living state. In the times of the Memphite kings, for example, a secondary tomb in the form of a small pyramid had been built close to the major monument. Senusret III's successor, alternatively, had two full-sized pyramids built in his name, one on the

Dahshur plain, the other at Hawara by the entrance to the Fayum.
The Abydos tomb, moreover, was certainly planned and built by the
same school of court craftsmen and designers who had planned and
built the pyramids at Lisht, Dahshur and el-Lahun. And at Abydos as
at el-Lahun, they also constructed a gridded courtly settlement beside
Senwosret III's valley temple, to house the court's regional officials
and, presumably, the priests and servants of the royal cult.

Recent excavations at the enclosure that holds Senwosret III's Abydos tomb have determined that some large mud-brick buildings had
stood briefly in the area, and the debris from those structures suggests that rites had been conducted within it on a considerable scale,
though over a short period of time. Such intense short-lived activities
suggest that, whether or not a royal corpse had actually been involved,
elaborate rites of funeral had taken place. What, then, had prompted
the remarkable decision to build a gigantic royal tomb without a
pyramid and to set it far away from the traditional burial grounds of
Memphis?

There is precedent for the shape of Senwosrets III's Abydos tomb
and also for at least one interment to have taken place within it. For
the temple tomb of Montuhotep II at Deir el-Bahari has two tombs
for the royal burial. One is entered by a corridor that runs deep
beneath the Theban cliffs from the temple's second terrace, the other
by a long deep passageway cut down into the middle of the plain in
front of the temple tomb, in a manner very similar to the entrance to
Senwosrets III's Abydos tomb. And in that second tomb, whose
entrance lies within the temple's wide and flat enclosure, the celebrated colossal statue of Montuhotep was laid to rest amidst a
gathering of offerings. The court of Senwosret III, moreover, showed
a direct interest in that Theban monument, emplacing a splendid
series of over life-sized statues of their king upon a terrace there.

There was as well a strong and very ancient precedent for siting
royal tombs at Abydos. For the subterranean cemetery of Egypt's first
kings lies less than two miles away from the enclosure that contains
Senwosret III's tomb. And, once again, the Itj-towy court displayed
direct and powerful involvement with those ancient monuments. For,
in their times, one of those ancient royal tombs was cleared, restored
and re-opened as the tomb of the god Osiris and in the manner of the

arrangements at Senwosret III's Abydos tomb and funerary temple, a considerable temple for Osiris was erected at the edge of the cultivation. The Itj-towy court, therefore, and specifically that of Senwosret III, had returned to the heartland of their state and copied many of its ancient ways. And at the same time they set a precedent for the design of all later royal tombs.

For the courts of later ages did not return to Memphis as the location for the royal tomb, nor did they employ the form of pyramids, but took Senwosret III's Abydos tomb as the model for all royal burials. Situated at the foot of the valley's cliffs at a point where the rock terraces form an enormous natural pyramid, the setting of the Abydos tomb of Senwosret III presages that of the Theban royal tombs in the Valley of the Kings, just as sealings found in the debris of the structures that had stood beside the entrance to that Abydos tomb are the first-known examples of a form typical of many sealings found in the later royal tombs of the Valley of the Kings.

In similar fashion, the plan of Senwosret III's Abydos tomb presages that of the first royal tomb to be cut in the Valley of the Kings. The immediate predecessor of those celebrated tombs, however, is sited to the south of Senwosret III's Abydos monuments, where the funerary complex of Ahmose, the first king of the later Theban dynasties, carefully copies the elaborate forms and structure of Senwosret III's earlier monuments, with a deep subterranean tomb excavated in the desert and a temple and a gridded settlement set down on the plain below. And in careful continuity, King Ahmose's complex was precisely orientated to that of Senwosret III so that together, the axes of their plans, which are a third of a mile apart, form a perfect square upon the desert sand.

This, then, was the Middle Kingdom's enormous, if inadvertent, gift to the future pharaonic state. In abandoning Memphis as the site of royal burial and returning to the archaic heartland of their culture, and by designing a type of royal tomb directly related to the older forms of royal funeral in Upper Egypt, Senwosret III's designers signalled a change both in the role of pharaoh and the destiny of the ancestors. A destiny that in later ages would be expressed in celebrated texts set out upon the walls of the royal tombs of the Valley of the Kings, whose elaborate descriptions of death and resurrection echo the twisting passages and corridors of the Middle Kingdom royal tombs and, above all others, those of Senwosret III at ancient Abydos.

THE MIND'S EYE – *MIDDLE KINGDOM LITERATURE*

The court of the Middle Kingdom pharaohs not only re-established and refined the material culture of the pharaonic state but also simultaneously transformed the form and scope of hieroglyphic writing. For the modern world, this is the so-called 'classical' period of ancient Egyptian texts, the age in which the venerable Memphite tradition was transformed to become the written language that is known today as 'Middle Egyptian'. At that same time, the Itj-towy scribes created a literature whose texts would be copied out as exemplars of good manners and fine prose down to Greco-Roman times – texts that are widely regarded as ancient Egypt's literary masterpieces and which the pharaonic scribes of later ages and modern students of hieroglyphic were and are obliged to study.

It has been estimated that less than 10,000 people could read and write in Itj-towy times; a fact that, if nothing else, re-emphasizes the small, face-to-face nature of that courtly culture. Leaving aside the traditional textual genres which remained a part, if a lively and developing part, of the scribal corpus, less than forty of the novel so-called 'literary texts' are known to have survived from Middle Kingdom times, and most of them, by modern standards, are fairly short.

These are texts that are neither letters nor accountings, nor are they primarily connected with temples or tomb chapels, with offerings or decrees. Written in a distinctive calligraphic script on rolls of leather and papyri, and mostly stored today in European museums, the best part of the original Middle Kingdom versions of these literary texts were brought to light at Thebes in the nineteenth century. Sold on by merchants, they had probably been taken from ancient tombs, though only one of the places where they had been anciently stored is known today, the papyri having been discovered during an early archaeological excavation. Found in a much-used burial vault beneath the storerooms of a later temple, this cache of decayed papyrus scrolls appears to have been part of the private library of a scribe, for a bundle of reed pens had been placed along with the papyri in a little whitewashed box. Amongst several other texts, that box of scrolls had held the Story of Sinuhe and the story of Khunanup, the Eloquent Peasant.

Half of the Middle Kingdom literary texts that have survived were still being copied a thousand years and more after their composition, and that is fortunate indeed, for those later copies include the Papyrus Westcar, which holds the only known version of the tales of Hardjedef and Djedi the soothsayer. Another Middle Kingdom text that only exists in these later copies is the so-called Teaching of Khety, which has survived in some 250 fragmented versions made in many different ages. The name of Khety is given as the author of several other literary texts as well and so a single scribe is sometimes claimed as the creator of ancient Egyptian literature. But, as shown earlier, Khety was a common name of those times, and more modern scholarship generally regards these literary Khetys in much the same manner as Homer or Hardjedef.

Remarkably, the Teaching of Khety, which is also known as the 'Satire on the Trades', extols the virtues of the 'nimble-fingered' scribe above all other professions, whose members are described, along with many other fearful attributes, as swollen-fingered, weary as labourers, bleary-eyed and festering, smelling as vile as fish eggs, and sometimes even covered in excrement! But Khety tells us that good literary manners are a sign of a social distinction, that 'if you know writing all will be well with you!', that his teaching places his pupils on the path of god, and that the proper use of pen and ink can lead to high office at the royal residence. No wonder that he was much used in ancient schoolrooms – and is much quoted by modern academics too.

In common with the visual culture of the times, Middle Egyptian literature developed in an atmosphere of retrospection. On the rocks of the Wadi Hammamat, an Itj-towy scribe scratched the names of three Memphite pharaohs – Khufu, Djedefre, Khafre – side by side, and then erroneously promoted two ancient royal princes to the kingship, namely Hardjedef and Baufre, five cartouches set in a single row. It is a memory of an ancient kingdom founded on the timeless rule of gods and pharaohs which had disappeared, and as a result of this disjunction from that distant past another understanding of the state developed.

With the Memphite pyramids in full view across the desert plain, the court of Itj-towy regarded that earlier age from a distance and with a new awareness of the court's fragility. Now the past was composed of human incident and time, and the future state could either succeed or fail. A preoccupation, perhaps reflected in the faces of the sculptures of the times.

At all events, this was a reflective era, one in which scribes carefully copied the old ways of writing but at the same time transformed them; one in which ancient courtly identity was cultivated with considerable care, down to the use of its very language. So, although the pyramids of the Itj-towy kings were never decorated with Pyramid Texts, some of those texts were placed in the burial chambers of a few Itj-towy courtiers and on many contemporary coffins. And this inherited literary tradition was also used to create new texts filled with the values and attitudes that were considered necessary for the maintenance of the refounded state.

Some of the underlying narratives of those new compositions were borrowed from earlier writings; part of the story of the Eloquent Peasant, for example, resembles part of the ancient story of two gods, Horus and Seth, which is touched upon in the Pyramid Texts. Sometimes, ancient religious imagery provided a new tale with an eerie air, as in the story of the so-called Shipwrecked Sailor, where a man talks to a giant snake. And the structure of the literary texts of Teaching and Instruction was derived from the inscriptions in the Memphite tomb chapels that outline the good works of their owners. In similar fashion, the forms of the biographic inscriptions in the Memphite tomb chapels were enlarged and crossed with the narratives of Memphite expeditions – their departures, their adventures and their climax at the royal court – to contain the Story of Sinuhe. Some texts, however, have scant precedent. The 'Dispute of a Man with his Soul', for example, dispassionately confronts the idea of death as no other pharaonic text had done before, whilst the Admonitions of an Egyptian Scribe, in which the world spins like a potter's wheel, works carefully and imaginatively through the collected misfortunes of society turned upside-down in the way that the writers and visual artists of many later cultures would do.

Yet the spirit of all those literary compositions, their clarity, their straightforwardness, is very different from anything that had been written down before. To some extent, their literary attitude was presaged in a claim found in several funerary texts that earnestly insist their words tell the truth; for that is an attitude to writing which, for the first time, posits a space for reflection between the reader and the text, a space that the Memphite scribes seem never to have imagined.

MURDERED BY EUNUCHS? – *MODERN HISTORY AND ANCIENT LITERATURE*

> *It was after supper, darkness had fallen and I was taking an hour of rest. I was lying on my bed, for I was weary. And as my heart began to follow sleep, weapons intended for my protection were turned against me. I acted like a snake of the desert. I awoke to the fighting, gathered myself together and found it was a skirmish of the palace guard. If I could have quickly taken weapons in my hand, I would have made the cowards retreat in haste. But no one is strong in the night. No one can fight alone. No success can come without help.*
>
> From the Instruction of Amenemhet I, c. 1970 BC

Historians have traditionally used several of the stories in the literary texts to conjure up political histories for the rulers of the Memphite and Itj-towy courts. And who can blame them, for there is little else on which to base such modern narratives.

So the soothsayer Djedi's prophecy that the wife of a provincial priest will give birth to a triplet of kings is used as the basis of a political account of the transition between the Fourth and Fifth of Manetho's dynasties (p. 110). And the so-called 'Prophecy of Neferti', which tells of the emergence of a warrior king of whom 'Asiatics will fall to his sword, Libyans to his flame and rebels to his wrath' is identified as Amenemhet I, who is then murdered by the guards or eunuchs of his palace as per the 'Instruction of Amenemhet I', a plot with which the vizier Antefoker's son is sometimes said to be involved, for is he not cursed in an execration text? The self-same plot, indeed, is also said to have caused such disruption at the court that it had prompted Sinuhe's flight to the Levant!

Lively, if somewhat clichéd, modern story telling, certainly, but hardly ancient history. The arguments against using such sources for constructing political histories are legion. One of the most obvious objections, of course, is that narratives such as those outlined above are entirely dependent upon the rare fragments of texts and papyri that have survived, for there is hardly any external evidence that specifically supports their place within a narrative. There are problems, too, in linking what are often unspecific and contested texts. Only one of the four sources used to create the narrative surrounding the alleged murder of Amenemhet I, for example, names a specific king, and the contents of that text, the Instruction of Amenemhet I, are vigorously disputed by various modern translators who do not agree on the date of its composition or whether the voice of the text's narrator, which is that of the king himself, is alive or dead.

There are also fundamental methodological problems of procedure in determining which texts are suitable for selection. Can historians simply extract those passages that seem to them to be 'real history' from texts that otherwise appear to be ahistorical or fantastic? No one, for example would include in a modern history book the incident in the story of the Shipwrecked Sailor where the unfortunate mariner talks to a giant snake. What then of a god-king murdered in his palace by his eunuchs?

Ultimately, treating such tales as political history is dependent upon the historian's personal vision of the past. The decision to regard the tale of the attack upon Amenemhet I as 'real history', for example, requires the assumption that the pharaohs of Itj-towy had been monarchs in much the same manner as those of Champollion's time. If they are assumed to have been the sole rulers of a society as competitive and dangerous as Champollion's, then Amenemhet I may well have been a seasoned warrior. And if that king had previously been the vizier Amenemhet, who had usurped the throne as many have suggested, then his palace may well have been a perilous place.

But further problems then arise in setting that text in the context of political history. Had its putative author been dead or alive at the time of its composition? Was it written as Amenemhet I's posthumous political testament, or as a guide from an embattled living monarch to his son and successor? If the former, the text could be read as a document that aims to legitimize familial succession after a royal murder. If the latter, it could have been intended as palace propaganda, as an explanation of how those two kings had ruled simultaneously as co-regents, just as many historians believe though others yet deny. And so the processes of historical methodology are ignored, and the words and tenses of the texts are minutely scrutinized to determine whether its narrator is alive or dead.

Now, clearly, it would be foolish to imagine that the terms of the European classical grammar through which most translations of the ancient texts are yet refracted – such notions as the 'first person singular' the 'possessive', and even 'past' and 'present' tenses – can accurately reflect the minds of people who lived within a different universe and with a different sense of time and self. And so traditional historians are themselves swiftly led into the realms of literature, into discussions of motives and emotions of individual ancient characters, discussions that are sometimes even illustrated by the sculptured 'portraits' of those self-same kings. And, of course, questions of modern political attitude start to emerge. Was Amenemhet I, or indeed Richard III, weak or strong, good or bad, Plantagenet or Shakespearian? Do we prefer the nineteenth-century's Thomas Cromwell or that of *Wolf Hall*? And that, inevitably, tells us far more about the modern singers than the ancient song.

In the first days of their translation, Middle Kingdom literary texts had been regarded as folk tales. Erman, for example, had dubbed the tales of the Papyrus Westcar fairy stories. At that time, however, there was widespread academic interest in the relationship of history to folk tales, myth and fairy stories such as those that had been collected by the eminent Göttingen linguists the brothers Grimm. Such texts, it was asserted, held the keys to understanding 'primitive' mentalities, a view that prevailed well into the last century. At the same time, many early classical scholars had believed that classical myths and folk tales held oral histories in the manner of the *Iliad* and the

Odyssey, a notion that was swiftly taken up by Protestant Bible scholars and also by the Berlin School of egyptologists, who conjured a considerable history of the beginnings of the pharaonic state from Greco-Roman accounts of ancient Egyptian myth.

So the renowned historian Eduard Meyer, the unofficial chronologer of the Berlin School, quoted selected passages of Middle Kingdom literature in his influential five-volume history of the ancient world. Folk literature, Meyer maintained, contained a critical source of historical fact, a statement that, at a stroke, effectively extended the insistence of the renowned school of Berlin historians on the use of original source material into the realms of ancient Egyptian literature. And that, it would appear, is the root of much of ancient Egypt's pseudo-history.

For the Middle Kingdom court was neither primitive nor savage nor, certainly, was it a so-called folk culture. Quite the reverse. The composition of its literary texts had been restricted to the few thousand courtly scribes who developed a formal mode of literary composition and the grammar that is known today as Middle Egyptian. And as a steward of Senwosret I makes clear in part of his funerary stela's text, this was an accomplishment of which they were perfectly aware; 'I am one who speaks in the official manner, free from the use of "the" or "this" [i.e. the definite article]' – and this despite the fact that the definite article had long since been recorded in the chatter of workmen given in earlier tomb-chapel texts (p. 165).

Ultimately, therefore, the use of Middle Kingdom literature as history must depend upon the kind of history you value: either the recycling of Western political narratives in *orientaliste* clothing or more tentative histories that deal in different aspects of life within a long lost ancient culture.

> Look, we have reached home!
>   the mallet has been seized, the mooring post driven in and the bowline cast ashore.

> Praises have been offered, god has been thanked, and everyone is embracing his fellow. Our crew has come back safe, with no loss to our expedition . . .

> Look, we have arrived in peace! We've reached our own land!

What is indisputably true about Middle Kingdom literature is that the limits of its imagination, the air in which those stories move, derive from the culture in which they were created. And certainly, they provide vivid and genuine alternative visions of ancient courtly life to the relentless optimisms of the tomb-chapel texts. They tell us something more as well, about how the ancient courtiers had thought. No matter if the literary account of the murder of a king of the Itj-towy court is fact or fantasy; the accommodation of such a deed within the near-contemporary literature not only places it within the realm of ancient possibilities but also, and crucially, further distinguishes the man Amenemhet from the office of pharaoh. And that fact alone offers a rare insight into an age in which hardly a single genuine fact concerning the royal role within the state has been established.

The greater part of the Middle Kingdom's literary texts are not narratives at all but essays on comportment and behaviour; not stories, but instructions, teachings and discourses. Even their much-argued-over narratives are filled with careful descriptions of courtly behaviour, with exemplars of modes of address, of good manners and the proper conduct in audience with pharaoh and when talking to monsters, foreigners and fellow inhabitants of the kingdom.

Obviously, the ancient Egyptian scribes could not have written the hard political narrative that we have today, for the genre did not exist. Just as there were no commodities in the modern sense of that word at the Itj-towy court, so no one valued narratives of news or, indeed, of history. The Middle Kingdom scribes' understanding of the past had grown out of the disjunction between the court of Memphis and that of Itj-towy, and it had led them to a self-conscious awareness of courtly identity as an essential part of their living culture. So whilst the craftsmen and builders of their time re-created and refined the material culture of the Memphite court, the scribes recorded and refined traditional courtly comportment and behaviour down to the very manners of its writing.

The literary texts can provide genuine glimpses into the ancient past, most immediately into its modes of social intercourse and the proper attitudes to pharaoh, the gods and the ancestors, and to all those things which the people of the re-made pharaonic state needed to live in good order, community and well-being. That is why the images and texts of that ancient courtly culture, have a lively beauty, a conviviality of elegance and form.

THE ENDING

The ending of Itj-towy is mysterious. The ancient records seem to signal its demise as they do for the ending of the Old Kingdom, by recording the rule of a female pharaoh, Queen Neferusobek. This time around, however, there is nothing in the archaeological record to suggest that the court's decline was a product of ecological change. Even the destructive Nile floods that had occurred in the reign of Amenemhet III appear to have ceased. Nor is there evidence of plagues or poor harvests that would have denied Itj-towy the manpower and the surpluses required to build grand monuments. There is no evidence, either, of internal revolution or violent invasion, no collapsing house of cards, no trace of Auden's squalid mess of history.

All that the spare surviving records show is that after 1790 BC, in the century and a half that followed the lengthy reign of Amenemhet III – the period that the Greek historian Manetho would name the Thirteenth Dynasty of kings – pharaohs came and went with such rapidity that their very number and the order of their rule is still a matter of dispute.

And in those times, great pyramids were no longer made, and the few small pyramids that were set amidst the earlier grander monuments of south Saqqara and Dahshur were seldom finished. Then, too, there were no more additions to the lines of pretty tomb chapels that had long served the cults of the provincial governors. In Nubia the state retreated, the fortresses were abandoned and families of local people moved into their foursquare mud-brick chambers. At 'Ain Sukhna and the lagoon of the Wadi Gawasis, the court ports were first deserted and then swiftly swallowed by the dunes of the Eastern Desert. And the chatter of graffiti drawn onto the rocks and boulders of the quarries of the Wadi Hammamat by the expeditions of the Itj-towy court first slacken, and then cease. And no more texts were set beside the seams of amethyst in the Wadi el-Hudi, upon the alabaster cliffs of Hatnub or at the copper mines of Sinai and the temple at Serabit el-Khadim.

So the expeditions that the Itj-towy court once sent to obtain fine stone for the state workshops and copper for the craftsmen's tools first slowed then stopped completely, along with the caravans and fleets that it had once dispatched to Nubia, to the Land of Punt and to the Lebanon.

Predicting just such a disaster, a scribe of an earlier generation had admonished his readers to 'Remember the building of the shrine, the censing with incense, the pouring of a libation from a vessel at dawn.' Now, however, the court no longer had the resources to build great pyramids or to maintain temples plastered white as milk or to set offering tables within perfumed sanctuaries to receive bread and game from estates up and down the lower Nile. Remember, the scribe continues, '. . . the upholding of regulations, the correct ordering of the calendar; these are the days that precede eternity, the months that are counted, the years that are known!' But the court's activities, the essential underlying mechanism of tithe and offering that had supported both the living and the dead of the Itj-towy court and was its very core, had slowly slipped away.

Some of the ephemeral pharaohs of the Thirteenth Dynasty had ruled from Itj-towy; the contents of the papyrus found in the tomb of the court scribe Neferhotep, for example, contains the household accounts of one of those transient monarchs during his visit to Thebes. And the royal workshops were maintained, although their output was considerably diminished, for some of the stone work of those small unfinished pyramids is of the highest quality. So, too, are the contemporary royal sculptures, several of which were hidden away inside the grand pyramid enclosures of the earlier Itj-towy kings and found in prime condition by archaeologists. Yet that regiment of little kings seems to have come and gone with such rapidity – more than fifty were listed in the Turin Canon – that it appears as if the office of pharaoh was being determined by a round robin of Itj-towy officialdom, a situation suggestive of a change in the role of pharaoh itself.

Nothing is known of the ending of that court. Just as the household of the kings for whom the first pyramids had been built now seems to have risen out of nowhere, so, too, nine centuries later, the household of the Itj-towy kings fades back into the blank void, as a stream might gently dry in the course of a summer's drought. At the ending there is simply nothing left to say, only to remark once more how very tenuous, how fragile and how fortunate is our continuing connection with those ancient people, how precious the surviving fragments of their lives.

Quietly, however, in that same period of time, on the low silt plains of the river's eastern delta, beside the seaside harbours of the Itj-towy kings whose courts had delighted in the produce of the Levant, of Cyprus and of Anatolia, new settlements were being built, their modest tombs and temples laid out in the manners of Syria and the North Levant. And another history was beginning . . .

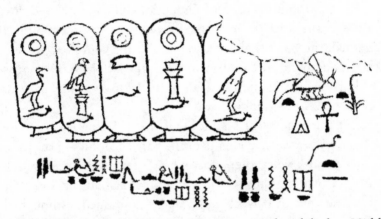

In this graffito from the Wadi Hammamat, a scribe of the late Middle Kingdom prayerfully remembers three Old Kingdom pharaohs – Khufu, Djedefre and Khafre – and sets their cartouches in the order they had ruled. Yet he also places the names of Hardjedef and another member of the royal household in royal cartouches, thus elevating two long dead princes to a position that, by modern lights, they never held.

Chronology

ALL DATES BC

DYNASTY FOUR: 2625–2500 (125 YEARS)

kings:	attested years of rule:	tomb and assumed residence:
Sneferu	24 to 46	Maidum to Dahshur
Khufu	23 to 27	Giza
Djedefre	8 to 11	Abu Roash
Khafre	24 to 26	Giza
Menkaure	5 to 28	Giza
Shepseskaf	5	Saqqara

DYNASTY FIVE: 2500–2350 (150 YEARS)

kings:	attested years of rule:	tomb and assumed residence:
Userkaf	6 to 7	Saqqara
Sahure	12 to 14	Abusir
Neferirkare	10 to 20	Abusir
Shepseskare	7	Abusir
Raneferef	3 to 7	Abusir
Niuserre	24 to 31	Abusir
Menkauhor	7 to 8	?
Isesi	39 to 43	Saqqara
Wenis	15 to 30	Saqqara

DYNASTY SIX: 2350–2200 (150 YEARS)

kings:	attested years of rule:	tomb and assumed residence;
Teti	12 to 26	Saqqara
Userkare	2 to 8	?
Pepi I	34 to 48	Saqqara
Merenre I	9 to 10	Saqqara
Pepi II	63 to 94	Saqqara
Queen Netjerkare Siptah	3 to 17	?

FIRST INTERMEDIATE PERIOD: 2200–2140 (60 YEARS)

Dynasty Seven/Eight	2200–2175?	Memphis?
Dynasties Nine/Ten	2175–2140?	Herakleopolis?

DYNASTY ELEVEN: 2140–2000 (140 YEARS)

kings:	attested years of rule:	tomb and assumed residence:
Montuhotep I	?	Thebes?
Intef I	13	Thebes
Intef II	49	Thebes
Intef III	7 to 8	Thebes
Montuhotep II	50 to 51	Thebes
Montuhotep III	11 to 12	?
Montuhotep IV	7	?

DYNASTY TWELVE: 2000–1780 (220 YEARS)

kings:	attested years of rule:	tomb and assumed residence:
Amenemhat I	29	Thebes to Itj-towy
Senwosret I	45	Itj-towy
Amenemhat II	34 to 35	Itj-towy
Senwosret II	7 to 8	Itj-towy
Senwosret III	18 to 39	Itj-towy
Amenemhat III	45	Itj-towy
Amenemhat IV	8 to 9	Itj-towy
Queen Neferusobek	3 to 4	Itj-towy

DYNASTY THIRTEEN: 1780–1660 (120 YEARS)

kings:	attested years of rule:	tomb and assumed residence:
Wegaf, Amenemhat Sobekhoteps, Khendjer, Neferhotep, Ibiau Wahibre, Sobekhotep, Aya Merneferre, Ini Merhetepre, Swadjtu, Ined, Hori, Dedumose, etc.		Itj-towy

NOTES

Details of the short titles and abbreviations cited below can be found in the Bibliography.

Not wishing to confront the reader with a chronology that has scant reference to those of other histories, I have retained the usual dynastic divisions of the classical historian Manetho. At the same time, however, I have added an extra column – 'tomb and assumed residence' – to enable readers to see the framework of my history, which does not

follow the divisions of that old Greek priest but divides the era of the
Old Kingdom pharaohs into the broad temporal and geographic categories of Giza, Abusir and Saqqara, and that of the Middle Kingdom
at the time of the assumed change of court residence from Thebes to
Itj-towy.

Most previous chronologies covering these periods were constructed around two differing parameters, the so-called 'high' and
'low' systems of fixed dates that diverged at the beginning of this history by some seventy-five years and by a third of that amount a
millennium later, at the Middle Kingdom's ending.

However, the figures recently presented by Michael Dee, 'A
Radiocarbon-based Chronology for the Middle Kingdom', in Shortland and Ramsey (eds.), *Radiocarbon*, consistently affirm a 'high'
chronology and thus serve to underline, as several archaeoastronomers
have recently suggested, that some much disputed dates which are key
to the 'low' chronology and had been calculated from the records of
various astronomical observations should now be discounted – see further on this subject Chapter 10, 'Time Present and Time Past'.

I have, therefore, placed the overall framework of this chronology
within the parameters of 'high' dates.

As with Volume 1, I have resisted the temptation to provide readers
with the spurious reassurance of columns of fixed dates for individual
kings, preferring to list the lengths in years by which their reigns have
been variously assessed – figures that for the most part are derived
from the essays of Verner, Baud, Seidlmayer and Schneider in *AEC*,
and those in Shaw (ed.), *Oxford History*, pp. 480–81. In keeping
with such differences and a range of other uncertainties – the existence, for example, of several ephemeral pharaohs and a plethora of
theories concerning co-regencies during the Middle Kingdom – I have
used multiples of twenty-five years to approximate the lengths of the
Old Kingdom's dynasties and ten years for those of the Middle Kingdom, when more reign dates are anciently attested.

Bibliography

Apart from a short list of general reference works, these bibliographic notes are divided by chapter and set in the order of each chapter's contents. Whenever possible, I have cited authoritative recent works in English. These in turn will cite older texts that are often the intellectual bedrock of the subjects in hand but which, for reasons of length, have not been listed.

Many of the works cited are papers in specialist publications, some of whose titles are given in the form of the abbreviations that are listed below, along with the abbreviations of some frequently cited volumes. After their first listing, all references are given in shortened form.

ABBREVIATIONS

AEC   Erik Hornung, Rolf Krauss and David Warburton (eds.), *Ancient Egyptian Chronology* (Leiden, 2006)

AEL   Miriam Lichtheim, *Ancient Egyptian Literature*, 3 vols. (Berkeley, 1973–80)

AEMT   Paul T. Nicholson and Ian Shaw (eds.), *Ancient Egyptian Materials and Technology* (Cambridge, 2000)

BIFAO   *Bulletin de l'Institut français d'archéologie Orientale*

EAAP   *Egyptian Art in the Age of the Pyramids*, Metropolitan Museum Exhibition Catalogue (New York, 1999)

Haus und Manfred Bietak (ed.), *Haus und Palast im Alten Ägypten*
Palast   (Vienna, 1996)

JARCE   *Journal of the American Research Center in Egypt*

JEA   *Journal of Egyptian Archaeology*

JNES   *Journal of Near Eastern Studies*

LÄ   Wolfgang Helk, Eberhard Otto and Wolfhart Westendorf
          (eds.), *Lexikon des Ägyptologie*, 7 vols. (Wiesbaden,
          1975–92)

LAE   William Kelly Simpson (ed.), *The Literature of Ancient
          Egypt: an anthology of stories, instructions, stele, autobi-
          ographies, and poetry* (3rd edn, New Haven, 2003)

Letters   Edward Wente, *Letters from Ancient Egypt* (Atlanta, 1990)

MDAIK   *Mitteilungen des Deutschen Archäologischen Instituts
          Abteilung Kairo*

SAK   *Studien Zur Altägyptischen Kultur*

Sinuhe   Richard Parkinson, *The Tale of Sinuhe, and Other Ancient
          Egyptian Poems 1940–1640 BC* (Oxford, 1998)

Texts   Nigel Strudwick, *Texts from the Pyramid Age* (Atlanta, 2005)

Voices   Richard Parkinson, *Voices from Ancient Egypt: an anthol-
          ogy of Middle Kingdom writings* (London, 1991)

GENERAL WORKS

Karl Butzer's pioneering work *Early Hydraulic Civilisation in Egypt* (Chicago, 1976) remains fundamental to an understanding of the ancient Egyptian environment; John Baines and Jaromir Malek, *The Atlas of Ancient Egypt* (Oxford, 2002), provides a modern guide to its physical and historical geography; Paul Nicholson and Ian Shaw (eds.), *Ancient Egyptian Materials and Technology* (Cambridge, 2000), contains brief accounts and useful bibliographies of the materials employed within pharaonic culture and the methods of their use. Morris Bierbrier *et al.* (eds.), *Who Was Who in Egyptology* (4th edn, London, 2012), is a fundamental source of information upon the scholars who are described in the text.

'[W]ritten from an avowedly philological point of view', and now somewhat out of date, Sir Alan Gardiner's *Egypt of the Pharaohs* (Oxford, 1961) is a wonderfully consistent court history by a luminary of the Berlin School; Ian Shaw (ed.), *The Oxford History of Ancient Egypt* (Oxford, 2000), is a good modern treatment; Wolfram Grajetzki's *The Middle Kingdom of Ancient Egypt* (London, 2006) served as my first line of reference for the later sections of this volume; Alexander Peden, *The Graffiti of Pharaonic Egypt* (Leiden,

2001), continually offers fresh perspectives; Mark Lehner, *The Complete Pyramids* (London, 1997), gives a succinct overview of its subject and an essential bibliography.

The academic literature on ancient Egyptian texts is vast and yet remains the core of egyptology. Most writings on the subject appear in specialist journals, and the relevant sources have been cited, as necessary, below. For the most part I have employed six volumes of translation: Lichtheim's *AEL*; Wente's *Letters*; Parkinson's *Voices*; Parkinson's *Sinuhe*; Simpson's (ed.) *LAE*; and Strudwick's *Texts*.

PREFACE

For the connection between the European study of linguistics, race and ancient Egyptian language in the eighteenth and nineteenth centuries see Tonio Richter, 'Early Encounters: Egyptian-Coptic studies and comparative linguistics in the century from Schlegel to Finck', in Martin Haspelmath, Eitan Grossman and Tonio Richter (eds.), *Egyptian-Coptic Linguistics in Typological Perspective* (Berlin, 2015), pp. 3–68.

'. . . a great national war' is quoted from Erman's immensely influential *Ägypten und ägyptisches Leben im Altertum* (Tübingen, 1885); an English edition, *Life in Ancient Egypt*, trans. Helen Tirard, appeared in 1893, and both are still in print. Steindorff's *Die Blütezeit des Pharaonenreichs* was first published in Leipzig in 1900; an English edition, *When Egypt Ruled the East*, was translated and edited by Keith Seele (Chicago, 1942) and that, too, is still in print.

For the so-called 'Berlin dictionary', which the on-line *Thesaurus Linguae Aegyptiae* at http://aaew.bbaw.de presently continues, see 'Grammars and Dictionaries' in Chapter 18 (p. 222 *ff*).

Of the generation after Grapow, Walter Wolf was an active Nazi and a leading exponent of the unwarranted notion that 'strong' pharaohs were absolute rulers, warriors and gods. He retired from teaching in 1969; see Thomas Schneider, 'Ägyptologen im Dritten Reich: Biographische Notizen anhand der sogenannten "Steindorff-Liste"', in Thomas Schneider and Peter Raulwing (eds.), *Egyptology from the First World War to the Third Reich* (Leiden, 2012), and also Bernd Schipper (ed.), *Ägyptologie als Wissenschaft: Adolf Erman (1854–1937) in seiner Zeit* (Berlin, 2006), particularly the essay of

Stephan Rebenich, 'Adolf Erman und die Berliner Akademie der Wissenschaften', pp. 340–70.

There is a direct line in the narratives of egyptological histories from the 1890s till today, as Nicolas Grimal asserts in his introduction to *A History of Ancient Egypt* (Oxford, 1992) (trans. Ian Shaw, of Paris, 1988). Two modern course books, one written by an enthusiastic supporter of Nazi policies the other by an active Nazi, are Heinrich Schäfer, *Von ägyptischer Kunst, besonders der Zeichenkunst* (Leipzig, various editions, 1919–1963), trans. John Baines as *The Principles of Egyptian Art* (Oxford, 1974), and Herman Kees, *Das alte Ägypten, eine kleine Landeskunde* (Berlin 1955), trans. T. G. H. James as *Ancient Egypt: a cultural topography* (London, 1961).

For Nietzsche's musings on historians and philologists see, for example, William Arrowsmith's commentaries and translations in *Arion* 2.1, 2.2, 2.4 and *Arion* new series 1.2. Hedda Gabler's protests are quoted from Act II of Ibsen's drama as translated by William Archer and Edmund Gosse; Stephen Dedalus from Joyce's *Ulysses*; parts of *Finnegans Wake* may be read as a wondrously elliptical comment upon the clichés of contemporary academia.

Baines's remark upon ancient intellect is contained in his essay 'The Earliest Egyptian Writing: development, context, purpose', in Stephen Houston (ed.), *The First Writing: script invention as history and process* (Cambridge, 2004), pp. 183; Kemp's comment is in Barry Kemp, *Ancient Egypt: anatomy of a civilisation* (2nd edn, London, 2006), pp. 395–6, n. 31. For Schneider's commentary see 'Ägyptologen im Dritten Reich'.

'entire mythologies are held . . .' is from Ludwig Wittgenstein, *Notes upon Frazer's Golden Bough*, ed. Rush Rees (Oxford, 1979), p. 10e.

For the continuing assertion that a degree of intuition is required for the translation of ancient Egyptian texts see, for example: Maspero's remarks, p. 216 herein; Alan Gardiner, 'The Eloquent Peasant', *JEA*, 9 (1923), p. 6; Raymond Faulkner, *The Ancient Egyptian Pyramid Texts* (Oxford, 1969), p. viii; Parkinson, *Sinuhe*, p. xi.

CHAPTER 1. THE STORY UP TO NOW

The statistics for the construction of the four colossal pyramids are drawn from the appendices in John Romer, *The Great Pyramid: ancient Egypt revisited* (Cambridge, 2007). (The Meidum Pyramid has been excluded from my group of four colossal pyramids as it is somewhat similar in size and construction to earlier pyramids.)

My estimates of population size in pharaonic Egypt are drawn from the figures given in Butzer, *Early Hydraulic Civilisation*, Chapter 7, which are still broadly accepted; see, for example, Kemp, *Ancient Egypt*, p. 49 *ff*, and p. 406, n. 7, and John Baines, *Visual and Written Culture in Ancient Egypt* (Oxford, 2007), pp. 65–6.

CHAPTER 2. WRITING CHANGES EVERYTHING

Ancient attitudes to the past as displayed in pharaonic texts are discussed in Baines *Visual and Written Culture*, Chapter 7 (this being an updated version of the essay 'Third to Second Millennium Evidence' in Robert Layton (ed.) *Who Needs. the Past?* (London, 1989)). A vivid ancient example of such attitudes are the so-called 'Lamentations/ Complaints/Words of Khakheperreseneb'; see the translations of Lichtheim, *AEL*, vol. 1, pp. 145–9, Simpson, *LAE*, pp. 211–13, and Parkinson, *Sinuhe*, pp. 144–50.

For a fascinating re-assessment of Prince Hardjedef's place in history see Harold Hays, 'The Historicity of Papyrus Westcar', *Zeitschrift für Ägyptische Sprache und Altertumskunde*, 129 (2002), pp. 20–130. Hardjedef's appearances in the Book of the Dead are described in Harold Hays, *The Organization of the Pyramid Texts* (Leiden, 2012), pp. 43–4. (For a complete list of Hardjedef's known appearances in pharaonic texts see *LÄ*, vol. 3, cols. 978–9, 'Lehre des Djedefhor' (Georges Posener)). My translation of the Instructions of Hardjedef, of which only the opening section has survived, is derived from Lichtheim, *AEL*, vol. 1, pp. 5–7 and 58–9, and Simpson, *LAE*, pp. 127–8.

For Hardjedef's tomb on the Giza Plateau, numbered G 7210 + 7220, see Peter Jánosi, *Giza in der 4: Dynastie, Die Baugeschichte und Belegung einer Nekropole des Alten Reiches*, vol. 1, *Die Mastabas der*

Kern Friedhöfe und die Felsgräber (Vienna, 2004), pp. 104–6. The excellent archives at www.gizapyramids.org contain Reisner's unpublished manuscript, *Giza Necropolis II*, which contains a description of the graffiti on Hardjedef's tomb; see Appendix B, 'G7210', p. 16. See also William Stevenson Smith, 'Inscriptional Evidence for the History of the Fourth Dynasty', *JNES*, 11, 2 (1952), p. 126 and fig. 5.

'The body was intact . . .' is quoted from Reisner's diary, 23 March 1925, which can be found at www.gizapyramids.org along with the archaeologist's description of the clearance of Hardjedef's tomb and the monuments of Kha that were found beside it. Anna Maria Donadoni Roveri, *I Sarcofagi Egizi Dalle Origini Alla Fine Dell'antico Regno* (Rome, 1969), p. 112 (B10), describes Hardjedef's sarcophagus.

'A man is dead; his corpse is in the ground . . .' is taken from translations of Papyrus Chester Beatty IV; see Lichtheim *AEL*, vol 2, p. 177, and Simpson, *LAE*, p. 1. My quotation of parts of Papyrus Westcar is adapted from Lichtheim, *AEL*, vol. 1, pp. 215–22, Simpson, *LAE*, pp. 13–24, and Parkinson, *Sinuhe*, pp. 102–27.

Edward Said made the observation upon Flaubert's Egyptian diaries; Adolph Erman, Papyrus Westcar's first modern editor, described its narratives as 'fairy stories' – see further, Chapter 18, p. 221.

'an empty noise of argument . . .' is taken from Jørgen Podemann Sørensen's translation of the XVIth Hermetic tractate as quoted in Orly Goldwasser, *From Icon to Metaphor: studies in the semiotics of the hieroglyphs* (Fribourg and Göttingen, 2002), p. 27.

The 'abode of shrines and temples . . .', from Asclepius 24, is quoted from the translation of Arthur Darby Nock in John Cooney (ed.), *Coptic Egypt* (Brooklyn, 1944), p. 21; 'like paleontologists . . .' from James Allen, 'Response to J. Baines, *Research on Egyptian Literature: background, definitions, prospects*', in Zahi Hawass and Lyla Pinch Brock (eds.), *The Proceedings of the Eighth International Congress of Egyptologists*, 3 vols. (Cairo, 2002), vol. 3, p. 27.

CHAPTER 3. REVIVING HARDJEDEF?

'the unfolding excellence of fact' is from George Steiner, *In Bluebeard's Castle: some notes towards the re-definition of culture*

(London, 1971), p. 16; Steiner adds that, nowadays, we look back upon that century's complacent pride 'with bewildered irony'.

Many works still employ Papyrus Westcar as a source of potential historical information; see, for example, Grimal, *History*, Aidan Dodson and Dyan Hilton, *The Complete Royal Families of Ancient Egypt* (London, 2004), and Toby Wilkinson, *The Rise and Fall of Ancient Egypt: the history of a civilisation from 3000 BC to Cleopatra* (London, 2010).

For Brugsch's history see Heinrich Brugsch Bey, *Egypt Under the Pharaohs*, trans. H. D. Seymour (London, 1879); for Gardiner's, *Egypt*.

'what had been made readable . . .' is from Hans Wolfgang Müller's brief biography of Adolf Erman at www.deutsche-biographie.de.

CHAPTER 4. IN THE BEGINNING

Epigraph: from the last paragraph of Jean François Champollion, *Lettre a M. Dacier, relative a l'alphabet des hiéroglyphes phonétique* (Paris, 1822)

'cascade of decipherment' is from Jean Bottero in *Archaeologia*, 52 (1972), and 'voracious chicken' from Erik Iversen, *The Myth of Egypt and its Hieroglyphs in European Tradition* (Copenhagen, 1961) p. 138, quoting Adolf Erman, 'Die Entzifferung der Hieroglyphen', *Sitzungsberichte der Preußischen Akademie der Wissenschaften zu Berlin*, January 1922.

The literature on the Napoleonic expedition is vast and growing. Christopher Herald's *Bonaparte in Egypt* (London, 1962) has provided a standard English-language introduction for generations; Juan Cole, *Napoleon's Egypt: invading the Middle East* (London, 2007), is a more recent account. All modern commentaries, however, should be tempered by such remarkable contemporary records as *Al-Jabarti's Chronicle of the First Seven Months of the French Occupation of Egypt*, trans. Smuel Moreh (Leiden, 1975), Joseph Laporte's *Mon Voyage en Égypte et en Syrie carnet d'un jeune soldat de Bonaparte* (Paris, 2007), and the numerous writings of the *savants* themselves. The material culture of the French expedition and of contemporary Egypt is well illustrated by Fernand Beaucour, Yves Laissus and

Chantal Orgogozo, *The Discovery of Egypt*, trans. Bambi Ballard (Paris, 1990), and the exhibition catalogue *Bonaparte et l'Égypte, feu et lumières*, ed. Jean-Marcel Humbert (Paris, 2008).

Sections of the Napoleonic *Description de l'Égypte, ou recueil des observations et des recherches qui ont été faites en Égypte pendant l'expédition de l'armée française* (Paris, 1809–1828) have been reprinted many times. Charles Gillispie and Michel Dewachter's introductory essays in *Monuments of Egypt: the Napoleonic Edition. The complete archaeological plates from La Description de l'Égypte* (Princeton, 1987), also contains an account of the *Description*'s publishing history.

The literature on Champollion is even larger than that on Napoleon's Egyptian adventure. Beside the extensive publications of Champollion himself, the biography by Hermine Hartleben, *Champollion, Sein Leben und sein Werk*, 2 vols. (Berlin, 1906) and *Lettres de Champollion le jeune*, 2 vols. (Paris, 1909), are the fundamental sources of all later works. Andrew Robinson, *Cracking the Egyptian Code: the revolutionary life of Jean-Francois Champollion* (Oxford, 2012), is a recent addition to the corpus with an up-to-date bibliography.

'the temple of the world' is from Asclepius 24; see Brian Copenhaver (ed.), *Hermetica: the Greek Corpus Hermeticum and the Latin Asclepius in a new English translation* (Cambridge, 1995).

Dupuis is quoted from the English translation of his *Origine de tous les cultes, ou Religion Universelle*, 4 vols. (Paris, 1795); '. . . the torchlight of reason and history' from the preface to that translation, entitled *The Origin of All Religions* (New Orleans, 1872), p. 4.

The calculation of modern dates from pharaonic zodiacs and ancient records of stellar observations has a lengthy history. Some of the errors and inaccuracies inherent in such methods are amusingly recounted by Rolf Krauss, 'Astronomical Chronology', in Juan Antonio Belmonte and Mosalam Shaltout (eds.), *In Search of Cosmic Order: selected essays on Egyptian archaeoastronomy* (Cairo, 2009), Chapter 5.

Fourier's letter is part quoted in another missive by a fellow *savant*, the chemist Claude Louis Berthollet – see *Magasin encyclopédique, ou journal des sciences, des lettres et des arts*, 6 (1801), pp. 115–19.

The events in Champollion's career described in this chapter are recounted in Hartleben, *Lettres*, vol. 1, where p. 12 *ff* outlines the reactions of the *savants* to his discoveries. (Note that as well as describing a type of munition, the French term 'cartouche' is also the name of a common rococo embellishment of a small scroll or panel in which writing is emplaced.)

'immense transmutations of value and perception . . .' is quoted from Steiner, *Bluebeard's Castle*, p. 21.

CHAPTER 5. THE ROAD TO MEMPHIS

Epigraph: from Rifa'a el-Tahtawi, *Takhlis Al-Ibriz fi Talkhis Bariz aw al-Diwan al-Nafis bi-Iwan Baris*, translated and elegantly edited by Daniel Newman as *An Imam in Paris: account of a stay in France by an Egyptian Cleric (1826–1831)* (London, 2004).

'The road to Memphis . . .' is quoted from Hartleben, *Lettres*, vol. 1, p. v, with p. 10 *ff* containing Champollion's account of his experiences in Turin.

Silvio Curto, *Storia del Museo Egizio di Torino* (2nd edn, Turin, 1978) describes the assembly of the Turin collections and the *palazzo* that houses them; Ronald Ridley, *Napoleon's Proconsul in Egypt: the life and times of Bernardino Drovetti* (London, 1998), the origins of the antiquities which Champollion studied and catalogued.

The epigraph to the section 'A Point of View' (p. 32) is from a remark of Stanislavsky's on (European!) 'perfect naturalness', from Oliver Sayler, *Russian Theatre* (New York, 1922), p. 254.

Winckelmann's *Geschichte der Kunst des Altertums* (Dresden, 1764) followed an earlier work from which the famous phrase 'noble simplicity and quiet grandeur' is derived, namely *Gedanken über die Nachahmung der griechischen Werke in der Malerei und Bildhauerkunst* (Dresden, 1755–6), p. 21. Both volumes were published in the major European languages shortly after their first printing. The enduring legend that came to surround the scholar's life is epitomized by Domenico Rossetti's considerable volume *Il Sepolcro di Wincklemann in Trieste* (Venice, 1823), which describes Winckelmann's life, death and entombment. For a fine modern account of the scholar's impact see Suzanne Marchand, *Down from Olympus: archaeology and philhellenism in Germany, 1750–1970* (Princeton, 1996).

Unlike Champollion, Winckelmann did not submit to the enchantments of ancient Egyptian art which, he writes, 'is to be compared to a tree which, though well cultivated, has been checked and arrested in its growth by a worm, or other casualties; for it remained unchanged, precisely the same . . .' (quoted from Winckelmann's *Geschichte*, trans. G. Henry Lodge as *The History of Ancient Art* (Boston, 1874)).

Champollion followed the second century Church father Clement of Alexandria in naming the calligraphic text employed by pharaonic scribes 'hieratic'; see the entry 'Hieratic' in *The Oxford Encyclopedia of Ancient Egypt*, vol. 3, ed. Donald Redford (New York, 2001), pp. 206–10 (Edward Wente), and the remarks of John Baines in 'Last Writing: script obsolescence in Egypt, Mesopotamia, and Mesoamerica', *Comparative Studies in Society and History*, 45, 3 (2003), p. 439 *ff.*

The description of Champollion's study of the Turin papyri is derived from his own passionate accounts published in Hartleben, *Lettres*, vol. 1, p. 79 *ff.* The papyrus that holds the plan of the tomb of Ramesses IV was definitively published in 1917 by Alan Gardiner and Howard Carter, 'The Tomb of Ramesses IV and the Turin Plan of a Royal Tomb', *JEA*, 4 (1917), p. 130–58.

Kim Ryholt, 'The Turin King-List', *Ägypten und Levante*, 14 (2004), pp. 135–55, is a fine up-to-date account of the Turin Canon; Donald Redford, *Pharaonic King-Lists, Annals and Day-Books* (Mississauga, Ontario, 1986), lists and assesses pharaonic registers of kings.

The quotation at the end of the section 'Counting Kings' (p. 39) is from Nigel Strudwick, *The Administration of Egypt in the Old Kingdom* (London, 1985), p. 2: the epigraph to the following section, 'Counting Time' (p. 39), from Jean François Champollion, *Lettres a M. le Duc de Blacas d'Aulps relatives au Musée Royal Égyptien de Turin* (Paris, 1824), p. 92.

'chéri d'Amon' is quoted from Champollion, *Lettres a M. le Duc*, p. 71. For a recent account of the names held within the pharaohs' two cartouches see Ronald Leprohon, *The Great Name: ancient Egyptian royal titulary* (Atlanta, 2013), pp. 17–19, and also see James Allen, *Middle Egyptian* (3rd edn, Cambridge, 2014), p. 64 *ff.*

The 'Robespierre of Grenoble' (Hartleben, *Champollion*, vol. 1, p. 410), was often withering in his judgements, dubbing the man who claimed that hieroglyphs had been invented by the devil as the 'Jupiter Asinarius of Genoa'. As to the Napoleonic *savants*, he considered their drawings to be quite good but that their theories were as 'thin as pudding water' (Léon de la Brière, *Champollion inconnu* (Paris, 1897), p. 67).

The epigraph to the section 'Champollion *Triumphans*' (p. 43) is from Gardiner, *Egypt*, p. 14; the 'accursed Zodiac of Dendera' from Ridley, *Napoleon's Proconsul*, p. 259, quoting a letter of Françoise Artuad found in Silvio Curto and Laura Donatelli (eds.), *Bernardino Drovetti Epistolario (1800–1851)* (Turin, 1983), p. 304 *ff*.

Champollion's working relationship with Rosellini is detailed in Hartleben, *Champollion*, vol. 2, and Hartleben, *Lettres*, vol. 2. For a recent account of the Tuscan's egyptological activities, along with an up-to-date bibliography, see the exhibition catalogue *Lungo il Nilo: Ippolito Rosellini e la spedizione Franco-Toscana in Egitto*, ed. Marilina Betrò (Florence, 2010).

'to give bishops sleepless nights' is from Hartleben, *Champollion*, vol. 1, pp. 427–8; 'the saviour of the biblical chronology', ibid., p. 565.

Hartleben, *Lettres*, vol. 2, holds Champollion's remarkable Egyptian correspondence; *Egyptian Diaries: how one man's passion for codes unveiled the mysteries of the Nile* (London, 2001), is an abridged English translation. Champollion described his visit to the Dendera temple in a letter from Thebes dated 24 November 1828.

The Franco-Tuscan expedition's drawings were published in two sets of folio volumes: *Monuments de L'Égypte et de la Nubie*, 4 vols. (Paris, 1835–45), and *Monumenti Dell Egitto e della Nubia*, 3 vols. (Pisa, 1832–44). A rich commentary on the three Tuscan tomes, which are the most beautiful of all egyptological publications, is Edda Bresciani (ed.), *L'Antico Egitto di Ippolito Rosellini* (Novara, 1993).

'. . . Founder and "Father" of Egyptology . . .' is from Morris Bierbrier *et al.* (eds.), *Who Was Who in Egyptology* (4th edn, London, 2012).

CHAPTER 6. AFTERMATH

'What is your opinion of the *Précis* . . .' is quoted from Francis Bunsen, *The Memoirs of Baron Bunsen*, 2 vols. (London, 1869), vol. 1, p. 153; 'Twenty years have now elapsed . . .' from Christian Carl Josias von Bunsen, *Egypt's Place in Universal History*, 5 vols. (London, 1867), vol. 1, p. vii.

'seventy kings of Memphis who ruled . . .' is from the translation of W. G. Waddell, *Manetho* (London, 1914), p. 57, fragment 23. Most modern histories and chronologies have extended the period of Bunsen's Middle Kingdom: see, for example, Shaw (ed.), *Oxford History* and Andrew Shortland and Christopher Bronk Ramsey (eds.), *Radiocarbon and the Chronologies of Ancient Egypt* (Oxford, 2013) , Chapter 14.

Alan Gardiner, 'A Stela of the Earlier Intermediate Period', *JEA*, 8 (1922), pp. 191–2, appears to have been the first example in print of the use of the term 'intermediate period'. See further, Chapter 21, pp. 285–6.

Kenneth Kitchen's groundbreaking work *The Third Intermediate Period in Egypt (1100–650 BC)* (Warminster, 1973; 4th edn, Oxford, 2009) not only established a firm chronology for the period that followed the ending of the New Kingdom but also christened that dislocated half-millennium as the 'Third Intermediate Period'.

The epigraph to the section 'Denkmäler' (p. 52) is from Thomas Hobbes, *Elementorum philosophiae sectio prima de corpore*, trans. William Molesworth, in *Thomae Hobbes Malmesburiensis*, 5 vols. (London, 1839), vol. 1, p. 13.

The 'urgent need for more material . . .' is from Gardiner, *Egypt*, p. 15.

The *Denkmäler aus Aegypten und Aethiopien* originally comprised twelve volumes (Berlin, 1849–59). In an introduction to a reprint (Geneva, 1972) Robert Hari relates Lepsius' ambition to become the 'German Champollion'.

Lepsius' *Lettre à M. le Professeur Rosellini* . . . was published in Rome in 1837. For a recent description of uniliteral and multiliteral signs see Allen, *Middle Egyptian*, Chapters 2 and 3.

Lepsius first published his *Chronologie der Ägypter* in Berlin in 1849 and issued articles over the following twenty years which refined that earlier work.

Petrie, famously, refused to accept the 'German Chronology', as he termed it; see Margaret Drower, *Flinders Petrie: a life in Archaeology* (London, 1985), p. 313 *ff.*

With one glaring exception, the previously existing gap between traditional and scientific methods of dating has been all but bridged; see Shortland and Ramsey (eds.), *Radiocarbon*.

In the decades between Champollion's publications and the establishment of egyptology in European universities, the study of hieroglyphic was advanced by a small number of European enthusiasts. The era is neatly summarized in Wolfgang Schenkel, 'Bruch und Aufbruch Adolf Erman und die Geschichte der Ägyptologie', in Schipper (ed.), *Ägyptologie als Wissenschaft*, pp. 224–8.

The first use of the term 'egyptologist' recorded in the *Oxford English Dictionary* is that of William Gregory, *Egypt in 1855 and 1856* (London, 1859); five years later, Piazzi Smyth was already complaining about the 'sadly Egyptological Baron Bunsen ...'; see Piazzi Smyth, *Our Inheritance in the Great Pyramid* (London, 1874), p. 418.

The epigraph to the 'Legacy' section (p. 54) is from lines spoken by Pedrillo in Act 1, scene 4, of Mozart's opera *Die Entführung aus dem Serail* (1782), libretto by Christoph Bretzner and Johann Stephanie the Younger.

Champollion wrote a number of plays, poems and satiric pamphlets, notably an oriental farce for the Carnival of Grenoble of 1814, which he entitled *Bejazet* and set in Istanbul. Ten years later, as he worked upon the Turin papyri, he composed a Petition on behalf of the Pharaoh Ozymandias to his majesty Charles Felix, King of Sardinia and Duke of Savoy, in which the pharaoh complains of seasickness during the voyage from Egypt, of the warehouse in which he and his fellow monarchs had been stored – a penance only alleviated by the fine singing of the pharaoh Amenophis – but above all, of the indignity of his rough handling at the museum and, finally, of being set down in the company of the Theban *petite bourgeois* (de la Brière, *Champollion inconnu*, p. 102–69).

The well-known portrait of the members of the Franco-Tuscan expedition that hangs on the staircase of the *Museo Archeologico* in Florence shows them dressed in oriental robes; see, for example, the frontispiece to Bresciani, *L'Antico Egitto*.

Champollion's *Panthéon Égyptien : collection des personnages mythologiques de l'ancienne Égypt* was published in Paris in 1823.

'a mishmash of fallacy and violence' is quoted from Goethe and Schiller's epigram *Zahme Xenien,* number 9; Auden's 'false and boring allegory' from his essays in *Secondary Worlds* (London, 1968), p. 28.

CHAPTER 7. THE ELOQUENCE OF STATUES

Epigraph: from Sir Phillip Sydney, *The Defense of Poesy* (London, 1581).

Christiane Zivie-Coche, *Sphinx! Le Père la Terreur: histoire d'une statue* (Paris, 1997), trans. David Lorton as *Sphinx: history of a monument* (Ithaca, 2002), provides a recent account of the monument. (Rainer Stadelmann's suggestion that it should be dated to the reign of Khufu – see, for example, Rainer Stadelmann, 'Le Grand Sphinx de Giza', in Eugène Warmenbol (ed.), *Sphinx: les gardiens de l'Égypte* (Brussels, 2006) – has not been widely accepted.)

Biri Fay, *The Louvre Sphinx and Royal Sculpture from the Reign of Amenemhat II* (1996, Mainz), perceptively observes the Sphinx's influence on Middle Kingdom sculpture. Freud's little sphinxes are catalogued in Lynn Gamwell and Richard Wells (eds.), *Sigmund Freud and Art: his personal collection of antiquities* (London, 1989), p. 93–5.

The silly notion that the Sphinx is 10,000 years old – one of many such about the Giza monuments – brings to mind the remark of François Bordes when a visitor suggested an outlandish date for the site which he was excavating: 'You tell me Louis XV 'e ride a motorbike. Maybe 'e did, maybe 'e didn't, but me, I do not believe it'; from Glyn Daniel, *Writing for 'Antiquity': an anthology of editorials from 'Antiquity'* (London, 1992), p. 155.

The epigraph to the section 'Khafre and the Golden Hawk' (p. 65) is from Auguste Mariette, *Notice des principaux monuments exposés dans les galeries provisoire du Musée d'antiquités Égyptiennes a Boulaq* (3rd edn, Paris, 1869), p. 203.

The 'Chephren quarries' are described by Ian Shaw, Elizabeth Bloxam, Tom Heldal and Per Storemyr, 'Quarrying and Landscape at Gebel el-Asr in the Old and Middle Kingdoms', in Francesco

Raffaele, Massimiliano Nuzzolo and Ilaria Incordino (eds.), *Recent Discoveries and Latest Researches in Egyptology* (Wiesbaden, 2010), pp. 203–312. The rare qualities of the gneiss from the Chephren quarries are documented in *AEMT*, pp. 32–4 (Barbara Aston, James Harrell and Ian Shaw). Romer, *Great Pyramid*, pp. 176–9, provides a commentary on the difficulties of sculpting granite: gneiss is harder.

The epigraph to the section 'Hard Histories' (p. 69) is from Erman, *Life in Ancient Egypt*, p. 36.

Though many more statues have been discovered since its publication, William Stevenson Smith, *A History of Egyptian Sculpture and Painting in the Old Kingdom* (3nd edn, Oxford, 1949), remains a fundamental study of its subject; for an account of the present corpus see Hourig Sourouzian, 'Old Kingdom Sculpture', in Alan Lloyd (ed.), *A Companion to Ancient Egypt*, 2 vols. (Chichester, 2010), vol. 2, pp. 853–81.

In her catalogue of sphinxes, Fay, *Louvre Sphinx*, pp. 62–9, shows that the well-known quartzite head of Djedefre does not come from a sphinx, as had been widely assumed. Smith, *History of Egyptian Sculpture*, Chapter 3, discusses the sculptures of Khufu's courtiers and, on pp. 28–30, the re-cutting and possible replication of an individual's facial features in sculpture and in tomb relief. See also Jan Assmann, 'Preservation and Presentation of Self in Ancient Egyptian Portraiture', in Peter Der Manuelian (ed.), *Studies in Honor of William Kelly Simpson*, 2 vols. (Boston, 1996), vol. 1, pp. 55–81.

The concept of 'magic' realism to which Assmann and I refer is discussed at length in Georges Charbonnier and Claude Lévi-Strauss, *Conversations with Claude Lévi-Strauss* (London, 1969).

EAAP, cat. 54, pp. 248–9 (Christiane Ziegler) discusses the splendid sculptures of Djedefre from Abu Roash. An overview of recent archaeology at that site is Michel Valloggia, 'Le complexe funéraire de Radjedef à Abu Rawash: bilan et perspectives au terme de dix saisons', in Jean-Claude Goyon and Christine Cardin (eds.), *Proceedings of the Ninth International Congress of Egyptologists*, 2 vols. (Leuven, 2007), vol. 2, pp. 1861–8.

The excavation and the architecture of Khafre's valley temple and the wealth of sculpture that was recovered is described by Uvo Hölscher, *Das Grabdenkmal des Königs Chephren* (Leipzig, 1912); see also Lehner, *Complete Pyramids*, p. 127, and *EAAP*, cats. 56–63, pp. 252–61, for further examples of the remarkable sculptural fragments from that temple.

'remote and divine perfection' is one of dozens of similar examples of the application of early modern notions of European kingship to a pharaonic setting and is quoted from Janet Richards, 'Kingship and Legitimation', in Willeke Wendrich (ed.), *Egyptian Archaeology: from text to context* (Chichester, 2010), p. 63; for another see the introduction to Christiane Ziegler (ed.), *The Pharaohs* (London, 2002).

The assertion that Hérnan Cortés and Captain Cook were considered to have been divinities by the peoples of the non-European cultures which they visited is discussed in Gananath Obeyesekere, *The Apotheosis of Captain Cook* (Princeton, 1992); see also Robert Borofsky, 'Cook, Lono, Obeyesekere, and Sahlins', *Current Anthropology*, 38, 2 (1997), pp. 255–88.

'In some religions . . .' is quoted from Ragnhild Bjerre Finnestad, 'On Transposing *Soul* and *Body* into a Monistic Concept of *Being*: an example from ancient Egypt', *Religion*, 16 (1986), p. 359. The concept of combining some of the qualities of animals with humans is explored in Volume 1 of this history – see, for example p. 130 *ff* – as are the other themes in the remainder of this chapter.

Some fragmentary reliefs from the temples of Sneferu and Khufu are beautifully pictured in *EAAP*, cats. 22, 38, 41; see also Hans Goedicke, *Re-Used Blocks from the Pyramid of Amenemhet I at Lisht* (New York, 1971).

CHAPTER 8. FINDING MENKAURE

Epigraph: from Michael Angelo Titmarsh (William Thackeray), *Notes of a Journey from Cornhill to Grand Cairo* (London, 1846), p. 252.

Much of the information in this chapter is drawn from George Reisner, *Mycerinus: the temples of the Third Pyramid at Giza* (Cambridge, Mass., 1931); see also Lehner, *Complete Pyramids*, pp. 122–37.

The classical fable concerning Menkaure is recounted in Book Two of Herodotus, along with many other splendid tales.

'Under the Majesty of the King . . .' is quoted from Reisner, *Mycerinus*, p. 31. The fragments of the so-called 'Great Alabaster Statue of Mycerinus' are shown *in situ* in Reisner, *Mycerinus*, pls. 7b and 7d, and the restored statue in studio photographs, pls. 12–16.

The epigraph to the section 'Valley Temple' (p. 80) is from Reisner, *Mycerinus*, p. 4; a remarkable series of images of the statues excavated from the Valley temple are given in pls. 36–60 of the same volume. The colour plates and commentaries in *EAAP*, cats. 67–71 (various authors), provide fine modern commentaries on some of Reisner's finds, as does Mark Lehner, 'Shareholders: the Menkaure Valley temple occupation in context', in Peter Der Manuelian and Thomas Schneider (eds.), *Towards a New History for the Egyptian Old Kingdom: perspectives on the Pyramid Age* (Leiden, 2015).

CHAPTER 9. ROYAL HOUSEHOLDS

Epigraph: from Reisner, *Mycerinus*, p. 6; 'In the temples of Mycerinus . . .' is from the first paragraph of Chapter 7 of that volume.

Two contrasting essays on Menkaure's much-studied statues are Wendy Wood, 'A reconstruction of the Triads of King Mycerinus, *JEA*, 60 (1974), pp. 82–93, and Florence Dunn Friedman, 'The Menkaure Dyad(s)', in Stephen Thompson and Peter Der Manuelian (eds.), *Egypt and Beyond: essays presented to Leonard H. Lesko* (Providence, 2008), pp. 109–44.

My account of sculpting siltstone is based on personal experience and has benefited from Mark Warden's online essay 'Recarving the Narmer Palette', in *Nekhen News* 12 (2000). For the unfinished statues found in Menkaure's valley temple see Reisner, *Mycerinus*, pp. 115–18; for the siltstone quarries see Barbara Aston *et al.* in *AEMT*, pp. 57–8.

For the locations of royal residences during the Old Kingdom see Rainer Stadelmann, 'La ville de pyramides à l'Ancien Empire', *Revue d'Égyptologie*, 33 (1981), and also Miroslav Verner, 'Several Considerations Concerning the Old Kingdom Royal Palace (aH)', *Anthropologie*, 48, 2 (2010), pp. 91–6.

Reports of Mark Lehner's considerable ongoing excavations in the area south of the Giza harbour can be found at the website of the Giza Plateau Mapping Project; see also Kemp, *Ancient Egypt*, pp. 184–92, and Mark Lehner and Ana Tavares, 'Walls, Ways and Stratigraphy:

signs of social control in an urban footprint at Giza', in Manfred Bietak, Ernst Czerny and Irene Forstner-Müller (eds.), *Cities and Urbanism in Ancient Egypt* (Vienna, 2010), pp. 171–216.

The epigraph to the section 'Queens and Goddesses' (p. 87) is from Foucault's essay on Velázquez's *Las Meninas,* which is the opening chapter of *Les Mots et les choses: une archéologie des sciences humaines* (Paris, 1966), translated as *The Order of Things: an archaeology of the human sciences* (London, 1970).

The epigraph to the section 'Mortal and Immortal' (p. 88) is from Samuel Rawson Gardiner (ed.), *Reports of Cases in the Courts of Star Chamber and High Commission* (London, 1886), p. 44.

Both Strudwick, *Administration,* pp. 336–46, and Klaus Baer, *Rank and Title in the Old Kingdom* (Chicago, 1960), pp. 296–302, describe shifts in the patterns of Old Kingdom courtly titles during the periods after the Giza kings, a trend that appears to indicate an increasing differentiation between the members of the royal household and the roles of the courtiers.

Hill, *EAAP,* p. 230, and Romer, *Great Pyramid,* pp. 86–90, discuss the confusions stemming from some of the terms which are said to define familial relationships within the royal household. 'Prince' Hemiunu, for example, a near contemporary of Hardjedef, is described as both a 'king's son of his own body' and as the son of another prince within the royal household. (The unwarranted belief that such titularies had affected pharaonic accession has inspired a range of historical fictions founded upon the common protocols of European courts.)

Such translated titles have also been taken as indications of the presence of 'genius' within the royal household. Hemiunu's titles, for example (see Hill, *EAAP,* p. 230, and Romer, *Great Pyramid,* pp. 86–90 and p. 324, fig. 157), appear to describe him as a vizier and a minister, as a priest of four great temples, as the director of musicians, as the overseer of scribes, and also as the supervisor of the royal construction projects which in his day would have included the Great Pyramid!

CHAPTER 10. AFTER GIZA

The key maps of Lehner, *Complete Pyramids*, pp. 10–11, show the span of the Old Kingdom pyramid fields.

Toby Wilkinson, *Royal Annals of Ancient Egypt: the Palermo Stone and its associated fragments* (London, 2000), holds a recent account of that extraordinary stone. I owe the suggestion that it was originally installed at Memphis to the review of Wilkinson's *Royal Annals* by Michel Baud in *Annales. Histoire, Sciences Sociales*, 57, 33 (2002), pp. 683–4.

For the South Saqqara Stone see Michel Baud and Vassil Dobrev, 'De nouvelles annales de l'Ancien Empire égyptien, une "Pierre de Palerme" pour la VIe dynastie', in *BIFAO*, 95 (1995), pp. 23–63. The earlier, smaller archives, which are in tablet form, are discussed and pictured in Volume 1 of this history, pp. 178–91. Papyri accounts bearing resemblance to the formats of the royal annals have been found in the temples of Abusir and at the Red Sea port of Wadi el-Jarf. See further below, Chapters 12, pp. 124–6, and 20, pp. 263–4.

The translation '[King] Sneferu [year 14?] . . .' is based upon the versions given in Strudwick, *Texts*, p. 66, and Foy Scalf, 'Rereading the 7th Count of Snefru in the Palermo Stone', *Göttinger Miszellen*, 220 (2009), pp. 89–93. For an ongoing re-evaluation of the dating of many Old Kingdom texts that will eventually challenge the suggested '[year 14?]' in Sneferu's annals see John Nolan, 'Cattle, Kings and Priests: phyle rotations and Old Kingdom civil dates', in Der Manuelian and Schneider (eds.), *Towards a New History*, pp. 337–65.

Lists of contemporary dated documents for the post-Giza periods of the Old Kingdom – Manetho's Dynasties Five and Six – are provided by Miroslav Verner and Michel Baud in *AEC*, pp. 124–56, where they are also compared to the list of the Turin Canon.

For the 'year 24' inscription of King Khufu see Klaus-Peter Kuhlmann, 'Der "Wasserberg des Djedefre" (Chufu 01/1): ein Lagerplatz mit Expeditionsinschriften der 4. Dynastie im Raum der Oase Dachla', *MDAIK*, 61 (2005), pp. 243–89, and for a re-evaluation of that and similar inscriptions, Friedrich Berger, 'Rock Art West of

Dakhla: "water mountain" symbols', in *Studies in African Archaeology*, vol. 11, (Poznań, 2012) pp. 279–305.

The epigraph to the section 'Time Present and Time Past' (p. 96) is from Hardy's *Return of the Native* (London, 1878), part 2, section 8.

For a summary of the evidence for prehistoric celestial observations in Egypt see Belmonte and Shaltout (eds.), *Cosmic Order*, Chapters 1 (Shaltout and Belmonte) and 2 (Magdi Fekri). Chapters 8 (Belmonte, Shaltout and Fekri) and 9 (César Gonzáles Garcia, Belmonte and Shaltout) of that work document the orientation of hundreds of pharaonic tombs and temples. Despite its somewhat dated treatment of traditional egyptological material, this volume makes many valuable observations upon long-neglected areas of study.

Juan Antonio Belmonte, 'Astronomy on the Horizon and Dating: a tool for ancient Egyptian chronology?', in *AEC*, pp. 380–85, provides a cautionary note on the inherent inaccuracy of anciently recorded astronomical events, which were witnessed with the naked eye. (Other essays in *AEC*, part 3 (Rolf Kraus, Kurt Lochner and Teije de Jong) offer further treatments of related subjects.)

'the only intelligent calendar . . .' is quoted from Otto Neugebauer, *The Exact Sciences in Antiquity* (Providence, RI, 1957), p. 81.

Juan Antonio Belmonte and José Lull, 'The Egyptian Calendar: keeping Ma'at on Earth' in Belmonte and Shaltout (eds.), *Cosmic Order*, Chapter 4, provide an up-to-date discussion of the study of pharaonic calendars; a summary of more traditional views is given by Leo Depuydt, 'From Twice Helix to Double Helix: a comprehensive model for Egyptian calendar history', *Journal of Egyptian History*, 2, 1 (2009), pp. 115–47.

For the adoption of a solar calendar along the lower Nile by the reign of Menkaure see again, *Cosmic Order*, p. 91 *ff*, and for the use of non-funerary pyramids as solar markers pp. 331–5.

The names of the ancient Egyptian months are discussed in Allen, *Middle Egyptian*, p. 118; for pharaoh's traditional undertaking to leave the order of the year unchanged see, for example, Philippe Germond, *Les invocations à la bonne année au temple d'Edfou* (Geneva, 1986).

The epigraph to the section 'Time and History' (p. 100) is from Vincent Alsop, *A Sermon Upon the Wonderful Deliverance by His*

Majesty from Assassination, the Nation from Invasion (London, 1696), p. 13.

For pertinent observations on the parochial character of Western perceptions of post-Renaissance image-making see, for example, the gentle lectures of Laurence Binyon, *The Spirit of Man in Asian Art* (Cambridge, Mass., 1936), especially p. 138 *ff.* A fine example of a pharaonic depiction of a single event is The Epigraphic Survey, *Reliefs and Inscriptions at Luxor Temple: the Festival Procession of Opet in the Colonnade Hall* (Chicago, 1994).

'. . . the whole range of man-made things' is quoted from the opening lines of George Kubler, *The Shape of Time: remarks on the history of things* (New Haven, 1962).

CHAPTER 11. ABUSIR AND SAQQARA

Lehner, *Complete Pyramids*, pp. 142–9, contains an architectural overview of the pyramids at Abusir. See also Ludwig Borchardt's *Das Grabdenkmal des Königs Ne-User-Re* (Leipzig, 1907) and *Das Grabdenkmal des Königs Nefer-Ir-Ke-Re* (Leipzig, 1909). For early photographs of the Abusir excavations see Borchardt's *Das Grabdenkmal Des Königs Sahu-Re*, 2 vols. (Leipzig, 1910), vol. 1, Chapter 1.

The spare surviving monuments of Huni and his predecessors are discussed by Stephen Seidlmayer in *AEC*, pp. 116–23; the mastaba tombs of Shepseskaf and Khent-kawes by Miroslav Verner, *The Pyramids: their archaeology and history* (London, 2002), pp. 254–64; see also Mark Lehner, 'The Monument and the Formerly So-called Valley Temple of Khentkawes I: four observations', in Filip Coppens, Jiří Janák and Hana Vymazalová (eds.), *Royal versus Divine Authority: acquisition, legitimization and renewal of power* (Wiesbaden, 2015).

The debates surrounding 'Queen Khent-kawes' are part-summarized in Hays, 'Historicity', p. 25, n. 51; see also Miroslav Verner, 'Further Thoughts on the Khentkaus Problem', *Discussions in Egyptology*, 38 (1997), pp. 109–17. For a pyramid complex built for a Queen Khent-kawes at Abusir see Miroslav Verner, *The Pyramid Complex of the Royal Mother Khentkawes* (Prague, 1994); another tomb for (another?) Queen Khent-kawes was discovered at Abusir in 2015.

For the pyramid complex of a Queen Khent-kawes at Saqqara see Patrizia Piacentini (ed.), *Victor Loret in Egypt (1881–1899): from the archives of Milan University to the Egyptian Museum in Cairo* (Cairo, 2008), pp. 11–14 and 67, and Audran Labrousse, 'Les Reines de Téti, Khouit et Ipout Ire : recherches architecturales', in Catherine Berger, Gisèle Clerc and Nicholas Grimal (eds.), *Hommages á Jean Leclant, Bibliothèque d'Étude*, 106 (4 vols.), vol. 1, pp. 231–43.

The epigraph to the section 'Dissolution' (p. 112) is from Marcus Cato, *De Agriculture* 30, 1, trans. W. D. Hooper (London, 1934).

Cyriacus of Ancona's letters frequently lament the destruction of ancient marbles, not least those of Rome itself; see, for example, Charles Mitchell, Edward Bodnar and Clive Foss (eds.), *Cyriac of Ancona: life and early travels* (Cambridge, Mass., 2015), p. 93.

James Quibell, *The Monastery of Apa Jeremias* (Cairo, 1912), describes the architectural *bricolage* within the buildings of that monastery; the sarcophagus cut from a Late Period lintel is pictured in pl. LXXXV.

Some of the demons whose presence in the ancient monuments so scared the early Christians are described by John Ray in his essay 'Ancient Egypt', in Michael Loewe and Carmen Blacker (eds.), *Divinations and Oracles* (London, 1981), pp. 175–6.

For the reliefs that Borchardt found at Abusir and which are part restored within his publications see Borchardt, *Ne-User-Re*, and *Sahu-Re*, vol. 2, works that are memorials of period scholarship and draughtsmanship. John Baines, 'Kingship before Literature: the world of the king in the Old Kingdom', in Rolf Grundlach and Christine Raedler (eds.), *Selbstverständnis und Realität* (Wiesbaden, 1997), pp. 143–52, places the results of Borchardt's restorations in the context of similar scenes made in earlier and later periods.

The copying grids placed on other royal monuments at nearby Saqqara appear to have been drawn in the 7th to 6th centuries BC; see Gay Robins, *Proportion and Style in Ancient Egyptian Art* (London, 1994), pp. 169–70.

Jochem Kahl, 'Archaism' (2010), on UCLA's online *Encyclopedia of Egyptology*, ed. Willeke Wendrich, provides an overview of the compositions copied from those in the Abusir reliefs. Chapters 7 and 8 of Yvonne Harpur's *Decoration in Egyptian Tombs of the Old*

Kingdom (London, 1987), a standard treatment of its subject, provide a detailed listing and commentary of the relationship between the scenes drawn in the royal temple reliefs and those in the nobles' tomb chapels. The later formalization of some of the subject matter of the Abusir reliefs is discussed by Baines, 'Kingship before Literature', pp. 149–52.

The growing complexity of the epithets and titularies of courtiers throughout Old Kingdom times is summarized in Strudwick, *Administration*, pp. 337–46, and analysed in Klaus Baer, *Rank and Title in the Old Kingdom* (Chicago, 1960). There is no evidence, however, as is traditionally assumed, that the growing number and diversity of these titles was symptomatic of an increasing loss of central control.

One of the splendid suckling scenes that had stood at the entrances to some of the Abusir temples is described and pictured in *EAAP*, cat. 118, pp. 352–3 (Dorothea Arnold): the plates in that same volume accompanying cats. 111–14, pp. 333–43, show some of the remarkable qualities of the royal reliefs of Abusir.

CHAPTER 12. MEAT, BREAD AND STONE

The epigraph to the section 'Heliopolis' (p. 119) is from W. M. Flinders Petrie and Ernest Mackay, *Heliopolis, Kafr Ammar and Shurafa* (London, 1913), p. 2.

Though various surveys have planned the walls of Heliopolis in outline since the days of the Napoleonic invasion, no systematic archaeological investigation of the enormous site was undertaken between Petrie's brief foray in 1912 and the current project led by Aiman Ashmawy and Dietrich Raue, whose progress is outlined in *Egyptian Archaeology*, 46 (2015), pp. 8–11, and 47 (2015), pp. 13–16, where the accompanying photographs show the scale and intractability of the work. Recent overviews of the history of ancient Heliopolis include Dietrich Raue, *Heliopolis und das Haus des Re* (Berlin, 1999), Stephen Quirke, *The Cult of Re* (London, 2001), Chapter 3, and Anne van Loo and Marie-Cécile Bruwier (eds.), *Heliopolis* (Brussels, 2010).

For a synchronic overview of the qualities of the god Re see the opening chapters of Quirke, *Cult of Re*; various theories concerning the relationship of Re and Heliopolis in the times of the Abusir kings are outlined in Racheli Shalomi-Hen, 'The Dawn of Osiris and the Dusk of the Sun-Temples: religious history at the end of the Fifth Dynasty', in Der Manuelian and Schneider (eds.), *Towards a New History*, pp. 456–69.

The ancient sight-lines linking Heliopolis with the sun temples at Abusir are carefully described in David Jeffreys, 'The Topography of Heliopolis and Memphis: some cognitive aspects', in Heike Guksche and Daniel Polz (eds.) *Stationen: Beiträge zur Kulturgeschichte Ägyptens, Rainer Stadelmann Gewidmet* (Mainz, 1998), pp. 63–71.

Massimiliano Nuzzolo, 'The Sun Temples of the V Dynasty: a re-assessment', *SAK*, 36 (2007), pp. 217–47, and the same author's 'Sun Temples and Kingship in the Ancient Egyptian Kingdom', in Goyon and Cardin (eds.), *Ninth International Congress*, pp. 1402–10, contain lengthy assessments of those remarkable structures; Quirke, *Cult of Re*, p. 128, holds a handy list of their names, and *EAAP*, cats. 119–21, pp. 354–9, an account of some of the fine reliefs that Borchardt's excavations recovered at the site of Niuserre's sun temple.

The first epigraph to the section 'The Abusir Papyri' (p. 124) is from the thesis of Hratch Papazian, *Domain of Pharaoh: the structure and components of the economy of Old Kingdom Egypt* (2005), published online; the second epigraph is from John Strachey *et al.* (eds.), *Rotuli Parliamentorum* (*The Rolls of Parliament*) (London, 1767–77), 1451, v. 219/1.

For an introduction to the papyri archives of Abusir see Paule Posener-Krieger, 'News from Abusir', in Stephen Quirke (ed.), *The Temple in Ancient Egypt: new discoveries and recent research* (London, 1997), pp. 17–23, and Miroslav Verner, *Abusir: realm of Osiris* (Cairo, 2002), Chapter 6.

The list of temple equipment from the Abusir Papyri described in my text is translated and illustrated in Kemp, *Ancient Egypt*, pp. 166–70 and fig. 60.

The epigraph to the section 'Sun Temples and Slaughter Houses' (p. 127) is adapted from Abusir Papyri, University College Sheet A, UC 32769: http://www.digitalegypt.ucl.ac.uk/abughurab/abusirtranslation.html. Papazian, *Domain of Pharaoh*, provides a modern and extensive guide to the contents of this section of my text.

For an overview of current research on the ancient activities at the Abusir temples see Jiří Janák, Hana Vymazalová and Filip Coppens, 'The Fifth Dynasty "Sun Temples" in a Broader Context', in Miroslav Bárta, Filip Coppens and Jaromír Krejčí (eds.), *Abusir and Saqqara in the Year 2010* (Prague, 2011), pp. 430–42.

'the house of the knife' was excavated by the Czech Mission to Abusir – see Miroslav Verner, 'A Slaughterhouse from the Old Kingdom', *MDAIK*, 42 (1986), pp. 181–9; see also Christopher Eyre, *The Cannibal Hymn: a cultural and literary study* (Liverpool, 2002), p. 175 *ff*; and for the ritualization of hunting scenes in royal temples see Baines, 'Kingship before Literature', pp. 146–52.

Two overviews of the domestic agriculture of the period are Marie-Francine Moens and Wilma Wetterstrom, 'The Agricultural Economy of an Old Kingdom Town in Egypt's West Delta: insight from the plant remains', *JNES*, 47, 3 (1988), pp. 159–73, and Wilma Wetterstrom, 'Foraging and Farming in Egypt: the transition from hunting and gathering to horticulture in the Nile Valley', in Thurstan Shaw, Paul Sinclair, Bassey Andah and Alex Okpoko (eds.), *The Archaeology of Africa: food, metals and towns* (London, 1993), pp. 165–226.

For a further discussion of cosmic cannibalism in ancient Egypt and Belle Époque Berlin see Chapter 19.

Papazian, *Domain of Pharaoh*, p. 175 *ff*, contains a fascinating account of the interrelationship between the personnel of the royal palace and those at the temples at Abusir and, also, of their systems of supply.

The epigraph to the section 'The Value and the Worth of Things' (p. 133) is adapted from Strudwick, *Texts*, p. 69.

Subsistence farming and the colonization of wild land within the region of the lower Nile are described in Volume 1 of this history, Chapters 14–15.

The image of progress as a 'storm blowing from paradise' is taken from Walter Benjamin, *Über den Begriff: der Geschichte*, which was first published in English in the collection of essays entitled *Illuminations* (London, 1968), pp. 258–9. My reflections on the term 'economy' follow those in the introduction to Timothy Mitchell, *Rule of Experts: Egypt, techno-politics, modernity* (Berkeley, 2002).

The quotation from Heraclitus is from Robin Waterfield, *The First*

Philosophers: the pre-socratics and the sophists (Oxford, 2000), pp. 42, F38; those from Aristotle are from Nancy Demand, *Urban Relocation in Archaic and Classical Greece: flight and consolidation* (Bristol, 1990); those from Aristophanes from *The Acharnians*, 30–33.

CHAPTER 13. THE LIVING COURT

The few known literary references to the residences of the pyramid-building kings are gathered in Stadelmann, 'La ville de pyramides', and discussed in Verner, 'Old Kingdom Royal Palace', to which can be added the recently discovered papyri from the time of Khufu that were found in the ancient port at Wadi Jarf – see further Chapter 20, 'Deserts, Boats and Donkeys', p. 261 *ff.*

Excavations on the Dahshur Plain have uncovered parts of an impressive complex of mud-brick buildings and gardens from Sneferu's time; see Nicole Alexanian and Felix Arnold, 'The Necropolis of Dahshur Eleventh Excavation Report of the Work in Spring 2014', published online at https://www.dainst.org. Mark Lehner's ongoing excavations in the area to the south of the Giza pyramids are published at the website of the Giza Plateau Mapping Project.

The literary term the 'northern settlement' at Giza is discussed in Juan Carlos Moreno García, 'Administration territoriale et organisation de l'espace en Égypte au troisième millénaire avant J.-C.: grgt et le titre a(n)D-mr grgt, *Zeitschrift*, 123 (1996), pp. 116–38. The archaeologists' own interpretations of the excavated Giza settlements are given in Lehner and Tavares, 'Walls, Ways and Stratigraphy', and also in Mark Lehner and Freya Sadarangani, 'Beds for Bowabs in a Pyramid City', in Zahi Hawass and Janet Richards (eds.), *The Archaeology and Art of Ancient Egypt: essays in honor of David B. O'Connor*, 2 vols. (Cairo, 2007), vol. 2, pp. 59–81. For a nearby cemetery of workmen see Zahi Hawass, 'The Workmen's Community of Giza', in *Haus und Palast* pp. 53–67.

For the funerary monuments of Userkaf and Shepseskaf see Lehner, *Complete Pyramids* pp. 139–41.

The concluding chapters of Baer, *Rank and Title*, and Strudwick, *Administration*, outline the growth in the complexity of court titularies throughout the Old Kingdom. Volume 1 of this history describes the composition of the earlier pharaonic court; Neal Spencer, 'Priests and Temples: pharaonic' in Lloyd (ed.), *Companion to Ancient Egypt*, vol. 1, pp. 255–73, provides an overview of the ancient Egyptian priesthood.

Nuzzolo, 'Sun Temples of the V Dynasty', p. 290 *ff*, and Ann Macy Roth, *Egyptian Phyles in the Old Kingdom* (Chicago, 1991), Chapter 5, describe something of the pace of life within the court of Abusir and the groups of people involved in its maintenance. Papazian, *Domain of Pharaoh*, Chapters 3 and 4, provides a detailed analysis of that court's economy.

The origins of the systems of the pharaonic court outlined in the section 'Modelling the Universe' are described in Volume 1 of this history, Chapters 14 and 30.

CHAPTERS 14. THE LIVING KINGDOM

Estimates of the amounts of copper that were required to fashion the four colossal pyramids are given in Romer, *Great Pyramid*, pp. 168–70 (please note that the vertical scale on fig. 74 has been incorrectly printed and should read 'tons of copper'). The acquisition of copper by expeditions mounted by the pharaonic court is described in Chapter 24 of this volume.

The extensive use of copper in the architecture of an Abusir pyramid complex is described by Borchardt in *Sahu-Re*, vol. 1, pp. 36–8 and 75–83.

Neki-ankh's tomb-chapel reliefs are discussed along with others at that site in Smith, *History of Egyptian Sculpture*, p. 214, who tentatively ascribes them to the reigns of Menkaure. Their inscriptions are set into historical context by Hans Goedicke, 'Cult-Temple and "State" During the Old Kingdom in Egypt', in Edward Lipinski (ed.), *State and Temple Economy in the Ancient Near East* (Leuven, 1979), p. 122 *ff*. The inscriptions within the two tomb chapels in which Neki-ankh is named are translated in Strudwick, *Texts*, pp. 195–9.

The kings' direct involvement in the systems of supply of food and materials for the court and its activities is described later in this chapter. Papazian, *Domain of Pharaoh*, pp. 107–17, documents the founding of new towns during this period.

A brief history of Thomas Cook & Son is given in Donald Reid, *Whose Pharaohs? archaeology, museums, and Egyptian national identity from Napoleon to World War I* (Berkeley, 2002), pp. 88–92.

The statistics and observations in the section 'All Along the Valley' are based upon the figures given in Harpur, *Decoration*, p. 5 *ff.* For the invention of rock-cut cliff tombs see Jánosi, *Giza*, Part 3, and Dows Dunham and William Kelly Simpson, *The Mastaba of Queen Mersyankh III* (Boston, 1974).

The six volumes of Aylwood Blackman and Michael Apted, *The Rock Tombs of Meir* (London, 1914–53), hold lively examples of provincial tomb-chapel decoration; José Galán, 'Bullfight Scenes in Ancient Egyptian Tombs', *JEA*, 80 (1994), pp. 81–96, analyses some distinctively provincial images.

There has been a revolution in the dating of much of the sculpture discussed in this chapter in recent decades. For an overview of the results, a brief description of the various courtly styles, and an account of their spread into the provinces, see Christiane Ziegler, 'Nonroyal Statuary' and Nadine Cherpion, 'The Human Image in Old Kingdom Nonroyal reliefs', in *EAAP*, pp. 57–71 and 103–13.

The text describing the transportation of Senedjemib Inti's sarcophagus is translated in Edward Brovarski, *The Senedjemib Complex*, Part 1 (Boston, 2000), pp. 108–10, inscription D, and also in Strudwick, *Texts*, p. 305.

'the metropolitan states of Western Asia . . .' is quoted from Donald Redford, 'The Ancient Egyptian "City": Figment or Reality?', in Walter Aufrecht (ed.), *Aspects of Urbanism in Antiquity* (Sheffield, 1997), p. 210. Compare that view with, for example, Erman's foundational description of Memphis City in his *Life in Ancient Egypt*, p. 26: 'The old capital of Egypt . . . has entirely disappeared; the mounds overgrown with palms . . . The famous citadel of the town, the "White Wall", as well as the other buildings, have utterly vanished . . .'. For modern estimates of the size of ancient Egypt's elusive 'urban populations' see, for example, Fekri Hassan, 'Town and Village in Ancient Egypt: ecology, society and urbanisation', and David O'Connor, 'Urbanism in Bronze Age Egypt and northeast Africa', both in Shaw *et al.* (eds.), *Archaeology of Africa*, pp. 551–85.

Christopher Eyre, 'The Village Economy in Pharaonic Egypt', in

Alan Bowman and Eugene Rogan (eds.), *Agriculture in Egypt from Pharaonic to Modern Times* (Oxford, 1999), provides a balanced assessment of pharaonic life outside the households of kings and governors within the region of the lower Nile; in that same volume, the introductory essay by Bowman and Rogan makes pertinent observations about modern historical perceptions of 'ancient Egypt'.

For an analysis of patterns of movement within the ancient farming communities of the lower Nile see Sarah Symons and Derek Raine, 'Agent-Based Models of Ancient Egypt', in Nigel Strudwick (ed.), *Information Technology and Egyptology in 2008* (Piscataway, NJ, 2008). For the most part, the information given in Claire Newton and Beatrix Midant-Reynes, 'Environmental Change and Settlement Shifts in Upper Egypt During the Predynastic: charcoal analysis at Adaima', *The Holocene*, 17, 8 (2007), pp. 1109–18, is also relevant for the period of the Old Kingdom.

'Pull hard, my friend!' etc. have been extracted from Brovarski, *Senedjemib Complex*; a selection of similar workaday phrases is in Strudwick, *Texts*, Chapter 19. Christopher Eyre, 'Peasants and "Modern" Leasing Strategies in Ancient Egypt', *Journal of the Economic and Social History of the Orient* 40, 4 (1997), pp. 367–90, provides an overview of ancient agricultural estates.

Much of the content of this chapter's final section is drawn from the images in contemporary tomb chapels and traces of similar activities within the modern landscapes of the region.

For the Gebelein Papyri see Eyre, 'Village Economy', pp. 40–41, and Strudwick, *Texts*, pp. 185–6.

CHAPTER 15. CULT AND KINGDOM

Goedicke, 'Cult-Temple', provides an overview of the activities of the Old Kingdom court outside Memphis as recorded in contemporary texts. The archaeological evidence for the early history of the court's provincial cults is discussed in Volume 1 of this history, pp. 320–27; see also pp. 169–72, above.

Helen Jacquet-Gordon, *Les Noms des Domaines Funéraires sous l'ancien empire Égyptien* (Cairo, 1962), is fundamental to modern understanding of the royal estates throughout the region of the lower Nile.

'A royal decree . . .' is adapted from a lengthy text that is given in full in Strudwick, *Texts*, pp. 119–20.

Kemp, *Ancient Egypt*, pp. 116–34, provides a description and discussion of the early provincial shrines. The controversy surrounding their role within the state is scrutinized by Papazian, *Domain of Pharaoh*, Chapter 1, whose conclusions I have largely adopted.

The 'name of gold' is described, along with the other elements of the pharaonic titulary, in Leprohon, *Great Name*, pp. 7–18, and Allen, *Middle Egyptian*, pp. 64–6.

For a description of the oldest-known 'Horus of the royal residence' see *EAAP*, cat. 9, pp. 177–8 (Christiane Ziegler); and for a recent commentary on that much discussed relief see Stephan Seidlmayer, *AEC*, p. 121.

Dean Hooker's 'science of things divine' is quoted from *Of the Lawes of Ecclesiastical Politie* (London, 1594–7), vol. 3, Chapter 8.

The epigraph to the section 'Seen and Unseen' (p. 175) is from Thomas Hobbes, *Leviathan* (London, 1651), Book 2, p. 191. The following paragraphs are a part recapitulation of themes widely explored in Volume 1 of this history.

CHAPTER 16. PAPYRUS TO STONE

The quotations from the two decrees or letters that the king sent to Senedjemib are adapted from the translations in Wente, *Letters*, pp. 18–19 (3 and 4), and Brovarski, *Senedjemib Complex*, p. 92 (A2) and pp. 96–7 (B2).

For 'with his two fingers' see Brovarski, *Senedjemib Complex*, p. 90, note o (on p. 92). The quotation from the third decree has been adapted from Wente, *Letters*, p. 18 (2), and Brovarski, *Senedjemib Complex*, p. 90 (A1), as has the text 'Year 11, first month of the third . . .'; see Wente, *Letters*, p. 42 (40), and Strudwick, *Texts*, p. 177 (94).

The epigraph to the section 'Words and Writing' (p. 184) is quoted from the 1580 London printing of the so-called 'Laneham Letter', which describes 'the entertainment vntoo the Queenz Maiesty, at Killingwoorth Castl, in Warwik Sheer'.

My observations upon regionality and local accents within the regions of the pharaonic state are based upon those of Alessandro

Roccati, 'Response to J. Baines, *Research on Egyptian Literature: background, definitions, prospects*', *Eighth International Congress*, vol. 3, pp. 38–44, and the same author's review of Strudwick, *Texts*, in *JEA*, 94 (2008), pp. 323–5.

The refinement of the hieroglyphic sign system at the Old Kingdom court is outlined in Antonio Loprieno, *Ancient Egyptian: a linguistic introduction* (Cambridge, 1995), pp. 12 and 20 *ff*. My estimate of the numbers of scribes working during the period of the Old Kingdom is based upon the updated edition of John Baines and Christopher Eyre, 'Four Notes on Literacy', in Robert Layton (ed.), *Visual and Written Culture in Ancient Egypt* (Oxford, 2007), p. 64 *ff*.

The concept of 'decorum' as a specific attribute of pharaonic culture is defined by John Baines in his essay 'Restricted Knowledge, Hierarchy and Decorum: modern perceptions and ancient institutions', *JARCE*, 27 (1990), pp. 1–23.

The epigraph to the section 'Brief Lives' (p. 186) is from Matthew Prior, *Carmen Sæculare for the Year 1700: to the King* (London, 1700), p. 14.

The numerous records of the reliefs and texts in Dehbeni's tomb chapel made by early egyptologists are listed in Bertha Porter and Rosalind Moss, *Topographical Bibliography of Ancient Egyptian Hieroglyphic Texts, Reliefs, and Paintings*, vol. 3, Part 1 (2nd edn, rev. Jaromír Málek, Oxford, 1974), pp. 235–7.

'As for this tomb' is adapted from the translation given in the account of the excavation and conservation of Dehbeni's tomb chapel: Selim Hassan, *Excavations at Giza IV* (Cairo, 1943), pp. 159–84, and their partial translation in Strudwick, *Texts*, pp. 271–2.

Dehbeni's funerary inscriptions are placed into broader contexts in Hays, *Organization*, pp. 88–9, by Baines, 'Kingship before Literature', pp. 136–40, and also by John Baines, 'Forerunners of Narrative Biographies', in Anthony Leahy and John Tait (eds.), *Studies on Ancient Egypt in Honour of H. S. Smith* (London, 1999), pp. 34–7.

'. . . Niankhsekhmet spoke before his majesty' is adapted from the translation in James Henry Breasted, *Ancient Records of Egypt*, 7 vols. (Chicago, 1906), vol. 1, pp. 108–9 (237–40); see also Strudwick, *Texts*, pp. 302–3 (225).

Peter Dorman, 'The Biographical Inscription of Ptahshepses from

Saqqara: a newly identified fragment', *JEA*, 88 (2002), pp. 95–110, assesses the significance of the courtier's inscriptions and part documents the depredation of many of the tomb chapels of those times in the last decades of the nineteenth century.

'it was his eldest son . . .' is adapted from the translations in Breasted, *Ancient Records*, vol. 1, pp. 111–13 (242–9), and Nicholas Picardo, '(Ad)dressing Washptah: illness or injury in the vizier's death, as related in his tomb biography', in Zahi Hawass and Jennifer Houser Wegner (eds.), *Millions of Jubilees: studies in honor of David P. Silverman*, 2 vols. (Cairo, 2010), vol. 2, pp. 93–104. Hans Goedicke, 'A Fragment of a Biographical Inscription of the Old Kingdom', *JEA*, 45 (1959), pp. 8–11, describes and translates a similar, though now anonymous, inscription.

'The King of the Valley and the Delta . . .' is adapted from the translation of Selim Hassan, *Excavations at Giza I* (Cairo, 1932), pp. 1–38, who also provides an account of the tomb chapel's architecture, and that of James Allen, 'Re-wer's Accident', in Alan Lloyd (ed.), *Studies on Pharaonic Religion and Society in Honour of J. Gwyn Griffiths* (London, 1992), pp. 14–20, whose interpretation I have followed.

Something of the high quality of the sculptures from Ra-wer's devastated tomb chapel can be seen in *EAAP*, cat. 131, pp. 377–8 (Christiane Ziegler), and cat. 144, p. 396 (Christiane Ziegler and Sophie Labbé-Toutée).

'practical rationality' as opposed to 'prelogical mentality' – which remains an underlying assumption of many egyptological explanations – is defined and discussed in Obeyesekere, *Apotheosis of Captain Cook*, Part One.

CHAPTER 17. WRITING IN THE PYRAMIDS

The locations and designs of the pyramids described in this and following chapters are outlined in Lehner, *Complete Pyramids*, pp. 10–11, 16–17 and 153–63.

Hays, *Organization*, pp. 1 *ff* and 262–3, and James Allen, *The Ancient Egyptian Pyramid Texts* (2nd edn, Atlanta, 2015), p. 1 *ff*, provide up-to-date overviews on different aspects of their subject.

The epigraph to the section 'Into the Crypt' (p. 199) is from James Henry Breasted, *The Dawn of Conscience* (New York, 1933), p. 19.

Hays, *Organization*, p. 86 *ff*, discusses the relationship of the Pyramid Texts to contemporary texts in the courtiers' burial chambers and tomb chapels. In a broader context see also Mark Smith, 'Democratization of the Afterlife', in UCLA's *Online Encyclopedia of Egyptology*.

For descriptions of the burial arrangements and the funerary texts of Inti and other courtiers see Brovarski, *Senedjemib Complex*, pp. 22 and 79–82 and pls. 53–7, and Naguib Kanawati, 'Decoration of Burial Chambers, Sarcophagi and Coffins in the Old Kingdom', in Khaled Daoud, Shafia Bedier and Sawsan Abd el-Fatah (eds.), *Studies in Honor of Ali Radwan*, 2 vols. (Cairo, 2005), vol. 2, pp. 55–71.

For the terms 'recitation' and 'end of section' see Allen, *Pyramid Texts*, p. 3.

For a full description of Wenis' pyramid complex see Audran Labrousse *et al.*, *Le temple haut du complexe funéraire du roi Ounas* (Cairo, 1977); *Le temple d'accueil du complexe funéraire du roi Ounas* (Cairo, 1996); and *La chaussée du complexe funéraire du roi Ounas* (Cairo, 2002).

The first epigraph to the section 'The Voice inside the Pyramid' (p. 203) has been adapted from the translation of Laurie Rouviere, 'Bata, Seigneur de Saka: dieu bélier ou dieu taureau?', *Égypte Nilotique et Méditerranéenne*, 6 (an online journal) (2013), pp. 139–58. 'Bati' – the unusual deity named in that text – is described by Edward Brovarski, 'Two Old Kingdom Writing Boards from Giza', *Annales du Service des Antiquités de l'Égypte*, 71 (1987), p. 32; see also a brief reference to the 'Herdsman's Song' in John Baines, *Research on Egyptian Literature: background, definitions, prospects*', in Hawass and Brock (eds.), *Eighth International Congress*, vol. 3, p. 19.

The second epigraph to the section 'The Voice inside the Pyramid' has been extracted from the translations of Lichtheim, *AEL*, vol. 1, p. 49, and Allen, *Pyramid Texts*, p. 180.

Hays, *Organization*, Chapter 3, p. 136 *ff*, discusses the Pyramid Texts' various 'voices'.

CHAPTER 18. THE DEAD AND THE QUICK

A large number of works were consulted for this chapter, primarily: Heinrich Brugsch, *Mein Leben und Mein Wandern* (Berlin, 1894); The Earl of Cromer, *Modern Egypt*, 2 vols. (London, 1908); Charles Edwin Wilbour, *Travels in Egypt*, ed. Jean Capart (December 1880 to May 1891) (Brooklyn, 1936); Afaf Lutfi Al-Sayid, *Egypt and Cromer* (London, 1968); Élisabeth David, *Mariette Pacha* (Paris, 1994); Élisabeth David, *Gaston Maspero: le gentleman égyptologue* (Paris, 1999); and Roger Owen, *Lord Cromer: Victorian imperialist, Edwardian proconsul* (Oxford, 2004).

'What will become of the Bulaq Museum . . .' is translated from David, *Maspero*, pp. 78–7; 'Il y a donc, malgré tout . . .' from David, *Mariette*, p. 264.

'The mummy of a young man . . .' is quoted from a communication by the President, Samuel Birch, in *The Proceedings of the Society of Biblical Archaeology*, 11 (1878), p. 112. For a touching glimpse of Mariette during his last months in office dealing patiently with unexpected visitors with the same tact that his successors employ down to this day see John Weisse, *The Obelisk and Freemasonry* (New York, 1880), pp. 20–23.

The phrase 'the Klondike on the Nile . . .' is from David Landes, *Bankers and Pashas: international finance and economic imperialism in Egypt* (Cambridge, Mass., 1958).

For the details of food shortages in Upper Egypt in 1879 see, for example, William Loftie *A Ride in Egypt, from Sioot to Luxor* (London, 1879), especially p. 363 *ff*, 'An Appendix of Letters Relating to the Famine in Upper Egypt'.

'His assistants had gathered at the Museum . . .' is extracted and translated from a letter of Victor Loret given in Patrizia Piacentini and Victor Rondot, '1881, Musée de Boulaq, mort de Mariette', in Mamdouh Eldamaty and Mai Trad (eds.), *Egyptian Museum Collections around the World* (Cairo, 2002), pp. 949–56. Mariette's photographer published a remarkable souvenir of the archaeologist's house, museum and entombment: Alfred Chélu, *Mariette Pacha* (Paris, 1911).

Gabriel Charmes, *L'Égypte archéologie – histoire – littérature*

(Paris, 1891), provides a fine account of the transition of the control of the Egyptian monuments from Mariette to Maspero, as seen through contemporary French eyes. David, *Maspero*, p. 75 *ff*, and Reid, *Whose Pharaohs?*, p. 172 *ff*, describe the institutional changes that came with Maspero's control of Egyptian antiquities.

Wallis Budge, *Cook's Handbook for Egypt and the Egyptian Sudan* (3rd edn, London, 1911), p. 488, states that the opening of Wenis' pyramid was financed by Thomas Cook & Son.

For a recent account of the discovery of the cache of royal mummies found at Thebes in 1881 see Dylan Bickerstaff, 'The History of the Discovery of the Cache', in Erhart Graefe and Galina Belova (eds.), *The Royal Cache 320: a re-examination* (Cairo, 2010), pp. 13–26.

Drower, *Flinders Petrie*, pp. 43–6, describes Petrie's adventures at south Saqqara and the annoyance that they caused. 'full of difficulties' is quoted from Birch, *Proceedings of the Society of Biblical Archaeology*, 11, p. 112.

'as a boy nearing the end of his schooldays . . .' is from Gardiner, *Egypt*, p. iv. Maspero's remark that 'I have a lot of imagination, you know . . .' and the description of the young Gardiner in Paris are both from Alan Gardiner, *My Early Years* (Andreas, IoM, 1986), pp. 9–10.

'The meaning of the large majority . . .' is quoted from Gardiner, 'Eloquent Peasant', p. 6. In similar fashion, James Allen, the doyen of modern Pyramid Texts scholarship, observes that the Pyramid Texts are 'often obscure, even impenetrable': Allen, *Pyramid Texts*, p. 7.

'the conquest of the ancient world . . .' is from Suzanne Marchand, *Down from Olympus: archaeology and philhellenism in Germany, 1750–1970* (Princeton, 1966), p. 17, quoting Ulrich von Wilamowitz-Moellendorff, *Geschichte der Philologie* (Leipzig, 1921). The following paragraphs describing Gardiner's residence in Berlin are largely derived from Gardiner, *My Early Years*, and Alan Gardiner, *My Working Years* (London, 1962).

My account of the beginnings of classical scholarship in Germany is part drawn from Marchand, *Down from Olympus*, Rudolf Pfeiffer, *History of Classical Scholarship 1300–1850* (Oxford, 1976), Hugh Lloyd-Jones, *Blood for the Ghosts: classical influences in the nineteenth and twentieth centuries* (London, 1982), and the notes of

Friedrich Nietzsche, 'We Philologists', trans. Arrowsmith, *Arion*, new series 1.2.

For the phrase 'the science of history' see, for example, Pfeiffer, *History*, p. 176.

Mark Twain's Travel Letters (1891–2) were written for the Chicago *Daily Tribune*, the essay on Berlin appearing on 3 April 1892. They are part collected in Mark Twain, *The Chicago of Europe: and other tales of foreign travel*, ed. Peter Kaminsky (New York, 2009), p. 191 *ff.*

There is a considerable literature concerning Adolf Erman and the Berlin school of egyptology; see, especially, Adolf Erman, *Mein Werden und mein Wirken* (Berlin, 1929), and Schipper (ed.), *Ägyptologie als Wissenschaft*.

For the standing of the study of ancient Egyptian amongst those of other ancient languages as Erman began his studies see Holger Gzella, 'Expansion of the Linguistic Context of the Hebrew Bible/Old Testament: Hebrew among the languages of the ancient Near East', in Magne Sæbø (ed.), *Hebrew Bible/Old Testament*, 3 vols. (Göttingen, 2012), vol. 3, p. 134 *ff.*

'What a pity' and the 'habit of disregarding . . .' are quoted from Gardiner, *My Early Years*, p. 23.

For an account of the establishment of the Berlin dictionary see Stephan Seidlmayer, 'Das Ägyptische Wörterbuch an der Berliner Akademie: Entstehung und Konzept', in Schipper (ed.), *Ägyptologie als Wissenschaft*, pp. 162–92.

'In making comparisons . . .' and the following two quotations are from the English translation of Adolph Erman, *Life in Ancient Egypt*, pp. 13–15.

Breasted's attitudes to Berlin University in the Belle Époque, which were decidedly different from those of his fellow countryman Mark Twain, are vividly recounted in Charles Breasted, *Pioneer to the Past* (New York, 1943), Chapter 2.

Breasted's translation of Erman's *Aegyptische Grammatik* (Leipzig, 1894) was published, with an enthusiastic if somewhat tactless preface noting the deficiencies of the contemporary French and English equivalents, as *Egyptian Grammar* (London, 1894).

Both Breasted's *History of Ancient Egypt* (Chicago, 1906) and his *Ancient Records of Egypt* (Chicago, 1906) are still in print, and the

History is a permanent fixture in Amazon's lists of bestselling books on ancient Egypt.

'the first to present the Egyptian religion . . .' is quoted from Francis Llewellyn Griffith's preface to the English translation of Erman's *Die ägyptische Religion* (Berlin, 1905), *A Handbook of Egyptian Religion* (London, 1907). Breasted's *The Development of Religion and Thought in Ancient Egypt* (New York, 1912) is described as a 'monument and a classic' in John Wilson's introduction to a 1959 reprint. Breasted's second volume upon ancient Egyptian religion was *The Dawn of Conscience* (New York, 1933).

Allen, *Middle Egyptian*, p. 463, offers an appreciation of Alan Gardiner, *Egyptian Grammar* (3rd edn, Oxford, 1957), and lists other grammars that have since appeared.

'as a boy nearing the end of his schooldays . . .' is quoted from Gardiner, *Egypt*, p. iv. By Erman's day, the study of ancient languages was widely regarded as a branch of science: 'The fact that philology is not a mere matter of grammar, but is in the largest sense a master-science, whose duty is to present to us the whole of ancient life . . .' *Athenæum*, 816, 1 (25 June 1892).

CHAPTER 19. INTERPRETING THE PYRAMIDS

Epigraph: from Breasted, *Development of Religion*, p. 131.

The following paragraphs compare Kurt Sethe, *Die altägyptische Pyramidentexte*, 4 vols. (Leipzig, 1908–22), with Gaston Maspero, *Les inscriptions des pyramides de Saqqarah* (Paris, 1894).

Sethe's commentaries upon the pyramid texts are in six volumes, *Übersetzung und Kommentar zu den altägyptischen Pyramidentexten* (2nd edn, Hamburg, 1962). The text in Wenis' pyramid was subsequently published as an independent entity by Alexandre Piankoff, *The Pyramid of Unas* (Princeton, 1968).

Nietzsche's 'We Philologists', a set of 'jottings, insights, memoranda and quotations' first appeared in an incomplete English translation in 1911, the first full text in any language in 1967; Arrowsmith, *Arion*, new series 1.2.

The first half of Nietzsche's published text contains the sentiments that I describe. For 'The better the state is organized . . .' see Arrowsmith

Arion, 5 [178], for 'shallow rationalism' and the following quotations, *Arion*, 5 [59], and for 'morality was not based on religion', *Arion*, 5 [104].

The epigraph to the section 'The Bones of the Hell-Hounds Tremble' (pp. 232–3) has been extracted from Breasted, *Development of Religion*, pp. 127–8. I have retained Breasted's brackets, though I have changed his rendering of the royal name from Unas to Wenis. The difficulties faced by the translators of such texts can be seen by comparing Breasted's version of those verses with that given in Allen, *Pyramid Texts*, p. 57 (273 *ff*) and both of those, again, with that given in Eyre, *Cannibal Hymn*, pp. 7–10, which offers a cultural exploration of the same text.

'grotesque cannibalism . . .' is quoted from Breasted, *Development of Religion*, p. 90.

'the bull of the sky': both the translation and my explanation of its signification are derived from Eyre, *Cannibal Hymn*, pp. 60, 80 and 84–96.

For 'bull of his mother' see Gertie Englund, 'Gods as a Frame of Reference: on thinking and concepts of thought in ancient Egypt', in Gertie Englund (ed.), *The Religion of the Ancient Egyptians: cognitive structures and popular expressions* (Uppsala, 1989), p. 17.

'The only basis . . .' is quoted from Gardiner, 'Eloquent Peasant', p. 6; 'contains an important statement . . .' from Breasted, *Development of Religion*, p. 90; and 'Those to whom the following . . .' from Erman, *Egyptian Religion*, p. 7.

'. . . arisen out of darkness' is quoted from Erman, *Life in Ancient Egypt*, p. 31. Chapters 2 and 3 of that work are a synopsis of Erman's views upon ancient Egyptian race and history. Though the language employed for such observations has changed since Erman's day, his sentiments are essentially those of traditional historians today.

'To many scholars of the time . . .': such attitudes were further elucidated by the contemporary anthropologist Lucien Lévy-Bruhl, who observes that 'primitive mentality avoids and ignores logical thought'. *La mentalité primitive* (Paris, 1922), p. 32.

For 'a hard and monotonous landscape' and what follows see Erman, *Life in Ancient Egypt*, p. 14. Winckelmann's observations are taken from the opening paragraphs of Book II of his *History of Art*, trans. G. Henry Lodge (Boston, 1873); 'as promiscuous as gorillas' is quoted from Charles Darwin, *The Descent of Man* (2nd edn, London, 1882), p. 590 *ff.*

For a history of German egyptology in the 1930s see the essays of Thomas Schneider and Stephan Rebenich and others in Schneider and Raulwing (eds.), *Egyptology from the First World War,* and also Schipper (ed.), *Ägyptologie als Wissenschaft.*

'the agent and event are erased . . .' is quoted from Hays, *Organization*, p. 252, whose subtle observations inspired the following section, 'Reading in the Dark'.

CHAPTER 20. LOOK AT US!

'there has never been middle-class sculpture . . .' is quoted from Smith, *History of Egyptian Sculpture*, p. 56. Mariette's comments on Old Kingdom statuary are recorded in, for example, Édouard Mariette *et al.*, *Mariette Pacha: lettres et souvenirs personnels* (Paris, 1904), p. 165.

For a history of the pose of the 'seated scribe', which is typical of those of other sculptures of the time, see Gerry Scott, *The History and Development of the Ancient Egyptian Scribe Statue*, 4 vols. (Yale/University Microfilms, 1989), vol. 1, Chapter 1; for inlaid eyes see Arthur Lucas, *Ancient Egyptian Materials and Industries* (4th edn, rev. John Harris, London, 1962), Chapter 7.

As is often the case with Old Kingdom statues, there is uncertainty as to the date of the creation of the 'Sheik el-Beled' and even the origin of the story of its rediscovery, although the well-known tale of the workmen's reaction to the statue was certainly related by Mariette; see Claude Vandersleyen, 'La Date du Cheikh el-Beled (Caire CG34), *JEA*, 69 (1983), pp. 61–5, and Christiane Ziegler, 'Nonroyal Statuary', in *EAAP*, pp. 57–71.

Several agreements between the craftsmen who made the Old Kingdom tomb chapels and those who commissioned them are collected in Strudwick, *Texts*, Chapter 15. For a recent discussion of contemporary wooden statues see Julia Harvey, *Wooden Statues of the Old Kingdom* (Leiden, 2001).

The first epigraph to the section 'Ranks and Titles' (p. 244) is from John Rutt (ed.), *The Diary of Thomas Burton, 1656–1659*, 4 vols.

(London, 1828), vol. 2, p. 403; the second is adapted from the translation of Brovarski, *Senedjemib Complex*, p. 133; the third is from *EAAP*, p. 464; the fourth is from the entry for 'yeoman' in the *Oxford English Dictionary*.

'one of the best organized civilizations . . .' is from Gardiner, *Egypt*, p. 106.

The papyrus naming prince Ankh-haf is described later in this chapter, in the section 'Deserts, Boats and Donkeys'.

Court titles in the times of the Abusir kings are described by Massimiliano Nuzzolo, 'The V Dynasty Sun Temples Personnel', *SAK*, 39 (2010), pp. 289–312; see also the perceptive comments of John Baines in 'Restricted Knowledge', p. 17 *ff*.

'Valiant attempts have been made . . .' is from Gardiner, *Egypt*, p. 102.

If a translated title such as 'Overseer of the Treasury' is assumed to have literally described a minister's role within pharaonic government then might we not equally assume that a 'Minister of Defence' is concerned with floods and plagues of locusts? The present (2016) Gentleman Usher of the Black Rod is Lieutenant-General David Leakey.

Strudwick, *Administration*, pp. 172 *ff* and 300–334, describes the deployment of the title 'vizier'. The translated titles 'hereditary prince', 'chiropodist' and 'butler' have been traditionally awarded to courtiers with such lavish tomb chapels as those of Tiy at Saqqara and Ptahshepses at Abusir; see, for example, Chapter 7 of Verner, *Abusir*, entitled 'The Dazzling Career of the Royal Hairdresser'. See also John Baines, 'Modelling the Integration of Elite and Other Social Groups in Old Kingdom Egypt', *Cahiers de Recherches de L'Institut de Papyrologie et d'égyptologie de Lille*, 28 (2010), pp. 117–44.

The epigraph to the section 'Ordering the Kingdom' (p. 249) is from Benedict Anderson, *Imagined Communities: reflections on the origin and spread of nationalism* (rev. edn, London, 1991), pp. 6–7.

For an outline of the statistics of the Great Pyramid's construction see Romer, *Great Pyramid*, Chapter 6 and Parts 3 and 6.

For a fine account of the archaeological sites known now as 'Naga el-Deir' see 'Naga (Nag')-ed-Dêr', in *LÄ*, vol. 4, cols. 296–307 (Edward Brovarski); for 'overseer of herds' see col. 306. See also the commentary of Baines, 'Modelling the Integration'.

Gardiner's remarks upon the virtues listed in the 'Instructions' are quoted from his *Egypt*, p. 106; conquering 'like a crocodile' is from the so-called 'Maxims of Ptahhotep' 7, 5 – Lichtheim, *AEL*, vol. 1, p. 66, and Vincent Tobin, *LAE*, p. 134.

'Pepi is one of that great group . . .' (Pyramid Text 486) is derived from the translations of Lichtheim, *AEL*, vol. 1, p. 47, Faulkner, *Pyramid Texts*, p. 173, and Allen, *Pyramid Texts*, p. 139.

'It is a widow who addresses . . .' is adapted from Wente, *Letters*, pp. 211–12 and Strudwick, *Texts*, pp. 182–3.

For the early history of transportation routes throughout the Middle East see Volume 1 of this history, pp. 99–107 and 229–39. For an overview of pharaonic traffic on these same routes in Old Kingdom times – though omitting the recently discovered sea ports on the Red Sea Coasts – see Karin Sowada, *Egypt in the Eastern Mediterranean during the Old Kingdom: an archaeological perspective* (Göttingen, 2009). See also Lorenzo Nigro, 'The Copper Route and the Egyptian Connection in 3rd Millennium BC Jordan Seen from the Caravan City of Khirbet al-Batrawy', *Vicino Oriente*, 18 (2014), pp. 39–64, and Graeme Barker, David Gilbertson, David Mattingly *et al.*, *Archaeology and Desertification: the Wadi Faynan Landscape Survey* (London, 2008), Chapter 8.

'I was sent to Byblos . . .': this remarkable text was rediscovered, re-united and translated by Michele Marcolin, 'Iny, a Much-Travelled Official of the Sixth Dynasty: unpublished reliefs in Japan', in Miroslav Bárta, Filip Coppens and Jaromír Krejčí (eds.), *Abusir and Saqqara in the Year 2005* (Prague, 2006) pp. 282–310, and also Michele Marcolin and Andrés Diego Espinel, 'The Sixth Dynasty Biographic Inscriptions of Iny: more pieces to the puzzle', in Bárta, Coppens and Krejčí (eds.), *Abusir and Saqqara in the Year 2010*, pp. 570–615.

Pharaonic trade with Byblos during the Old Kingdom is described by Andrew Bevan, *Stone Vessels and Values in the Bronze Age Mediterranean* (Cambridge, 2007); see also Andrés Diego Espinel, 'The Role of the Temple of Ba'alat Gebal as Intermediary Between Egypt and Byblos during the Old Kingdom', *SAK*, 30 (2002), pp. 103–19, which also discusses the chaotic records of that temple's excavation.

The product of an illicit Anatolian excavation, the scandalous so-called 'Dorak Treasure' contained strips of gold bearing the cartouches of the Pharaoh Sahure that appear to have come from a piece of pharaonic furniture. Beyond a preliminary report in the *Illustrated London News*, 29 November 1959, however, they have disappeared.

For early pharaonic mining activity in Sinai see Pierre Tallet, *La zone minière pharaonique du Sud-Sinaï*, 2 vols. (Cairo, 2013, 2015).

Wadi el-Jarf, has been investigated since 2008, and the work of survey and publication is ongoing, For a fine introduction see Pierre Tallet and Gregory Marouard, 'The Harbor of Khufu on the Red Sea Coast at Wadi al-Jarf, Egypt', in *Near Eastern Archaeology 77*, 1 (2014), pp. 4–14.

For the settlement across the Red Sea from Wadi el-Jarf see Gregory Mumford, 'Tell Ras Budran: defining Egypt's Eastern frontier and mining operations in South Sinai during the late Old Kingdom', *Bulletin of the American Schools of Oriental Research*, 342 (2006), pp. 13–67, and the same author's 'Ongoing Investigations at a late Old Kingdom Coastal Fort at Ras Budran in South Sinai', *Journal of Ancient Egyptian Interconnections*, 4, 4 (2012), pp. 20–28.

The logistics of donkey caravanning are described by Frank Förster, Heiko Riemer and Moez Mahir, 'Donkeys to El-Fasher, or how the present informs the past', in Frank Förster and Heiko Riemer (eds.), *Desert Road Archaeology in Ancient Egypt and Beyond* (Cologne, 2013).

For an outline of the discoveries at 'Ain Sukhna see Pierre Tallet, 'A New Pharaonic Harbour in Ayn Sokhna (Gulf of Suez)', in Dionisius Agius *et al.* (eds.), *Navigated Spaces, Connected Places* (London, 2012), and also Pierre Tallet, 'New Inscriptions from Ayn Soukhna, 2002–2009', in Pierre Tallet and El-Sayed Mahfouz (eds.), *The Red Sea in Pharaonic Times: recent discoveries along the Red Sea Coast* (Cairo, 2012), pp. 105–15.

For images of Byblos boats in Sahure's temples see Borchardt, *Das Grabdenkmal Des Königs Sahu-Re* (Leipzig, 1910), pls. 11–15.

The Old Kingdom graffiti at Aswan and up river are described in Peden, *Graffiti*, pp. 10–13. There is a large and growing literature concerning the Oasis in those times; see, for example, Georges Castel *et al.*, *Balat*, vols. 1–13 (Cairo 2001–2013).

The introduction of the camel into the lower valley of the Nile is documented by Martin Heide; for its domestication see Martin Heide, 'The Domestication of the Camel', *Ugarit-Forschungen*, 42 (2011), pp. 331–82.

Frank Förster *et al.*, 'Tracing Linear Structures: remote sensing, landscape classification and the archaeology of desert roads in the Eastern Sahara', in Wilhelm Möhlig, Olaf Bubenzer and Gunter Menz (eds.), *Towards Interdisciplinarity* (Cologne, 2010), pp. 49–75, is a fascinating account of desert track archaeology; see also, Frank Förster, 'With Donkeys, Jars and Water Bags into the Libyan Desert: the Abu Ballas Trail in the late Old Kingdom/First Intermediate Period', *British Museum Studies in Ancient Egypt and Sudan*, 7 (2007), pp. 1–36, and Peter Schonfeld, 'Wegstationen auf dem Abu Ballas-Trail – Dynastische Fundplätze aus der Western Desert', *Ägyptens Archäologische Informationen*, 30, 1 (2007), pp. 133–40.

'King Merenre, my lord, sent me . . .' is adapted from Lichtheim, *AEL*, vol. 1, pp. 25–6, Simpson, *LAE*, pp. 409–10, and Strudwick, *Texts*, pp. 330–31. W. B. K. Shaw of the Long Range Desert group provides a fascinating account of desert caravanning in 'Darb el Arba'in: the Forty Days' Road', *Sudan Notes and Records*, 12, 1 (1929), pp. 63–71.

For 'road of ivory' see Hans Goedicke, 'Harkhuf's Travels', *JNES*, 40, 1 (1981), pp. 1–20. Tallet's study 'New Inscriptions from Ayn Soukhna', p. 11, proposes that Aswan's desert adventurers also travelled through the sea port at 'Ain Sukhna.

The tomb chapel texts of the travelling courtiers are analysed by Elke Blumenthal 'Die Textgattung Expeditionsbericht in Ägypten', in Jan Assmann *et al.* (eds.), *Fragen an die altägyptische Literatur: Studien zum Gedenken an Eberhard Otto* (Wiesbaden, 1977), pp. 85–118.

'sealed by the king personally . . .' is adapted from Wente, *Letters*, pp. 20–21, Simpson, *LAE*, pp. 410–11, and Strudwick, *Texts*, p. 331–3.

The Tomb of Weni was uncovered in 1860 by gangs working under the direction of Mariette and the great stela in its chapel taken for exhibition in Cairo. The tomb was rediscovered in 1999; see Janet Richards, 'Text and Context in late Old Kingdom Egypt: the archaeology and historiography of Weni the Elder', *JARCE*, 39 (2002), pp. 75–102.

'the longest narrative inscription . . .' is from Breasted, *Ancient Records*, vol. 1, p. 134, which presents a description and translation of the text on the following pages.

'the triviality, from the historical point of view . . .' is from Gardiner, *Egypt*, p. 94; the following pages contain a commentary and part translation of the text. See also Christopher Eyre, 'Weni's Career and Old Kingdom Historiography', in Anthony Leahy and Lisa Montagno Leahy (eds.), *The Unbroken Reed: studies in the culture and heritage of ancient Egypt in honour of A. F. Shore* (London, 1994), pp. 107–24, and Naguib Kanawati, 'Weni the Elder and His Royal Background', in Amanda-Alice Maravelia (ed.), *En quête de la lumière: mélanges in honorem Ashraf A. Sadek* (Oxford, 2009), pp. 33–50.

'This army returned safely . . .' and the following quotation is based on the translation of Simpson, *LAE*, pp. 402–7.

CHAPTER 21. SUDDENLY IT STOPS

For a fascinating account of animal droppings in Old Kingdom tombs see Miroslav Bárta and Ales Bezdek, 'Beetles and the Decline of the Old Kingdom: climate change in ancient Egypt', in Hava Vymazalová and Miroslav Bárta (eds.), *Chronology and Archaeology in Ancient Egypt* (Prague, 2008), pp. 214–22.

'the beauty of Pepi abides' is quoted from Henry Fischer, *Egyptian Studies III: Varia Nova* (New York, 1996), p. 75.

Barbara Aston, *Ancient Egyptian Stone Vessels* (Heidelberg, 1974), p. 64, notes that diorite gneiss was no longer used for stone vessels after the ending of the Old Kingdom.

'seventy kings in seventy years' and the following quotations are taken from W. G. Waddell's translations in *Manetho* (London, 1940), p. 57 *ff.*

For the tale of the nocturnal adventures of a late Old Kingdom pharaoh see Parkinson, *Sinuhe*, pp. 288–9.

The epigraph to the section 'Lamentations and Admonitions' (p. 284) is extracted from various translations of verses 3.3–3.10 of the so-called Admonitions of Ipuwer; Parkinson, *Sinuhe*, pp. 166–99 provides a fine commentary and translation, as does Tobin in *LAE* pp. 188–210.

'. . . unless some support in facts . . .' is quoted from the introduction to Alan Gardiner, *The Admonitions of an Egyptian Sage* (Leipzig, 1909), p. 17.

For a thoughtful discussion upon pharaonic Prophecy and Admonition Texts and similar musings from other cultures see Jan Assmann, *The Mind of Egypt* (New York, 2002), pp. 106–14, a translation by Andrew Jenkins of *Ägypten: Eine Sinngeschichte* (Munich, 1996).

Four years later, the lower-case 'intermediate period' employed in Gardiner 'A Stela' was promoted to upper case by Henry Frankfort in his essay 'Egypt and Syria in the First Intermediate Period', *JEA*, 12 (1926), pp. 80–99.

Assmann, *Mind of Egypt*, pp. 84–5, is an example of a strict diachronic arrangement of the variously recorded, often ephemeral, First Intermediate Period pharaohs. Some of the ruined and uncompleted pyramids of those times are described in Lehner, *Complete Pyramids*, pp. 164–5; Stephan Seidlmayer provides a fine introduction to modern thinking about the First Intermediate Period in Shaw (ed.), *Oxford History*, Chapter 6.

Herakleopolis is a largely literary location. Following a suggestion of Labib Habachi, however, Spanish excavators have worked at the site in recent decades; see, for example, Maria Carmen Pérez Die, 'El proyecto de investigación "Heracleópolis Magna" (Ehnasya el-Medina): Trabajos 2008–2009', in Luís Manuel de Araújo and José das Candeias Sales (eds.), *Novos trabalhos de Egiptologia Ibérica: IV Congresso Ibérico de Egiptologia* (Lisbon, 2012).

The suggestion that the rulers of Herakleopolis were buried in a cemetery north of that site is made by Harco Willems, 'Les fouilles archéologiques de la *Katholieke Universiteit Leuven* dans la région de Dayr al-Barshā', in Laurent Bavay *et al.* (eds.), *Ceci n'est pas une pyramide . . . un siècle de recherche archéologique belge en Égypte* (Leuven, 2012), pp. 126–47.

The primary publication of the tombs at Mo'alla is Jacques Vandier, *Mo'alla: la tombe d'Ankhtifi et la tombe de Sébekhotep* (Cairo, 1950). The modern documentation on osirisnet, however, gives something of the air, space and texture of Ankhtifi's tomb chapel.

'strong and highly organized . . .' is quoted from Gardiner, *Egypt*, p. 106, 'It had been a thousand years . . .' from Breasted, *History of*

Ancient Egypt, p. 143, and his later quotation from p. 144 of the same work.

Various reasons have been proposed for the Old Kingdom's dissolution. For the state fossilized see Grimal, *History*, p. 88 *ff*; for the state destroyed by bureaucrats see Baer, *Rank and Title*, Chapter VII; for the state destroyed by moral collapse due to incipient capitalism (and the quotation 'The state had been the guarantor of prosperity . . .') see David Warburton's review of Arlette David, *De l'infériorité à la perturbation: L'oiseau du "mal" et la catégorisation en Égypte ancienne* (Wiesbaden, 2000), *Discussions in Egyptology*, 53 (2002), pp. 135–52; and for the state as a victim of moral collapse following ecological disaster see Fekri Hassan, 'Droughts, Famine and the Collapse of the Old Kingdom: re-reading Ipuwer', in *The Archaeology and Art of Ancient Egypt: essays in honor of David B. O'Connor*, 2 vols. (Cairo, 2007), vol. 1, pp. 357–77.

The last, somewhat Biblical, destiny in that list, however, is refuted by hard data concerning the ecological realities of the age: see Nadine Moeller, 'The First Intermediate Period: a time of famine and climate change?', *Ägypten und Levante*, 15 (2005), pp. 153–67, whilst Corinne Duhig, 'They are Eating People Here!: anthropology and the First Intermediate Period' in Salima Ikram and Aidan Dodson (eds.), *Beyond the Horizon: studies in Egyptian art, archaeology and history in Honour of Barry J. Kemp*, 2 vols. (Cairo, 2009), vol. 1, pp. 45–88, shows that there are no significant physiological changes in the remains of people who died before and after the First Intermediate Period and that, contrary to traditional assertions, 'no one appears to have needed to eat anyone else' (p. 64).

For broader overviews of the physical realities of that age see Karl Butzer, 'Environmental Change in the Near East and Human Impact on the Land', in Jack M. Sasson (ed.), *Civilisations of the Ancient Near East* (New York, 1995), and Pierre de Miroschedji, 'The Socio-political Dynamics of Egyptian–Canaanite Interaction in the Early Bronze Age', in Edwin van den Brink and Thomas Levy (eds.), *Egypt and the Levant: interrelations from the 4th through the early 3rd millennium BCE* (London, 2002), p 39–57.

At Elephantine, genuine ecological change is carefully documented by Stephan Seidlmayer, 'Town and State in the Early Old Kingdom: a view from Elephantine', in Jeffrey Spencer (ed.), *Aspects of Early Egypt* (London, 1996), pp. 108–27. At Abusir, similar changes are reported by Miroslav Bárta, 'In Mud Forgotten: Old Kingdom palaeoecological evidence from Abusir', *Studia Quaternaria*, 30, 2 (2013), pp. 75–82.

Christopher Eyre, 'Feudal Tenure and Absentee Landlords', in Schafik Allam (ed.), *Grund und Boden in Altägypten* (Tübingen, 1994), p. 133, concludes that both the structures of pharaonic government and land exploitation were never monolithic and had adjusted to circumstance.

'. . . King Merenre told me to journey . . .' is extracted from the translations of Simpson, *LAE*, pp. 412–13, and Mahmoud El-Khadragy, 'The Edfu Offering Niche of Qar in the Cairo Museum', *SAK*, 30 (2002), pp. 203–28.

On the Tell of Edfu, evidence of occupation over several centuries from the late Old Kingdom onwards is briefly documented by Nadine Moeller and Gregory Marouard, 'Discussion of Late Middle Kingdom and Early Second Intermediate Period History and Chronology in Relation to the Khayan Sealings from Tell Edfu', *Ägypten und Levante*, 21 (2011), pp. 88–91.

Contemporary government stores on the Isle of Elephantine are reported by Günter Dreyer *et al.*, 'Stadt und Tempel von Elephantine 28./29./30.', *MDAIK*, 58 (2002), pp. 157–225, and discussed by Cornelius von Pilgrim, 'The Practice of Sealing in the Administration of the First Intermediate Period and the Middle Kingdom', in Brigitte Gratien (ed.), *Le sceau et l'administration dans la Vallée du Nil* (Lille, 2001), pp. 161–72. And for a contemporary settlement at Abydos see Matthew Adams, *Community and Society in Egypt in the First Intermediate Period: an archaeological investigation of the Abydos settlement site* (dissertation) (Ann Arbor, 2005). The production of faience has a considerable literature; see, for example, *AEMT*, pp. 177–94.

The governors' mansion in the Dakhla Oasis of that same age is described in Clara Jeuthe, Valérie Le Provost and Georges Soukiassian, 'Ayn Asil, palais des gouverneurs du règne de Pépy II: état des recherches sur la partie sud', *BIFAO*, 113 (2014), pp. 203–38, and a contemporary Delta cemetery in Willem Haarlem, 'The First Intermediate Period Cemetery and Settlement at Tell Ibrahim Awad', in *Des Néferkarê aux Montouhotep: travaux archéologiques en cours sur la fin de la VIe dynastie et la première période intermédiaire* (Paris, 2005), pp. 195–202.

The epigraph to the section 'The Existential Smash–up ' (p. 297) is from a review article by David Warburton, *Journal of the Economic and Social History of the Orient*, 53, 3 (2010), p. 514.

For a recent discussion of 'iwn' and related terms see David Warburton, 'The Egyptian Example and the Macroeconomic Implications', in Massimo Perma (ed.), *Fiscality in Mycenean and Near Eastern Archives* (Paris, 2006), pp. 259 *ff*; a different perspective on economic histories is provided by the first chapter of Mitchell's *Rule of Experts*.

The region around the hill of Mo'alla has been surveyed by a mission of the Yale Institute in Egypt; Colleen Manassa's online report (2006) may be accessed at their website.

The effects of severe rock fissuring in so-called 'slumped' blocks of limestone that have slid down from the high terraces above the valley of the lower Nile may be clearly seen in the plan of Ankhtifi's tomb chapel given in Vandier, *Mo'alla*, pl. 3.

Vandier's first report upon that tomb, 'La tombe d'Ankhtifi à Mo'alla (Haute-Égypte)', *Comptes rendus des séances de l'Académie des Inscriptions & Belles-Lettres*, 91, 2 (1947), pp. 285–93, contains the scanty recorded details of that monument's rediscovery and conservation. Two of the antiquities that some field egyptologists of the 1950s described as probable products of the war-time despoliation of the Mo'alla tombs are published by Hans Goedicke, 'Two Inlaid Inscriptions of the Earliest Middle Kingdom', in Emily Teeter and John Larson (eds.), *Gold of Praise: studies on ancient Egypt in honor of Edward F. Wente* (Chicago, 1999), pp. 149–57.

'. . . it is with my own copper . . .': this and my later adaptions of the texts in Ankhtifi's tomb chapel have been extracted from Lichtheim, *AEL*, vol. 1, pp. 85–6, from Eric Doret, 'Ankhtifi and the Description of his Tomb at Mo'alla', in David Silverman (ed.), *For His Ba: essays offered in memory of Klaus Baer* (Chicago,1994), pp. 79–86, and from John Baines, 'Feuds or Vengeance? Rhetoric and Social Forms', in Teeter and Larson (eds.), *Gold of Praise*, p. 14.

The influence of the texts of Ankhtifi's time upon later writings is evaluated by, for example, Shih-Wei Hsu, 'The Development of Ancient Egyptian Royal Inscriptions', *JEA*, 98 (2012), p. 269–83.

For an example of the confusions surrounding the translations of rank and title of this and subsequent periods see the section 'Administrative Aspects' in Harco Willems, 'Nomarchs and Local Potentates: the provincial administration in the Middle Kingdom', in Juan Carlo Moreno Garcia (ed.), *Ancient Egyptian Administration* (Leiden, 2013), p. 360 *ff.* The same essay lists the cemeteries of the time which may indicate the locations of other substantial settlements along the region of the lower Nile and outlines the arguments concerning the contemporary military situation.

'Nation shall rise against kingdom . . .' is quoted from a pamphlet of James Bowling Mozley, *War: a sermon preached before the University of Oxford* (London, 1915).

'Nahkampftruppen' etc. is quoted from Anthony Spalinger, 'The Organisation of the Pharaonic Army (Old to New Kingdom)', in Garcia (ed.), *Ancient Egyptian Administration*, pp. 460–71.

Traditional renderings of the First Intermediate Period and its conclusion as times of war are found, for example, in Grimal, *History*, Chapter 6 ('The Struggle for Power') and the commentaries of John Coleman Darnell accompanying his ongoing surveys of desert inscriptions – see, for example, *The Theban Desert Road Survey*, vol. 1 (Chicago, 2002), numbers 6–9.

Following an analysis of the column texts from Ankhtifi's tomb chapel, John Baines suggests, alternatively, that his troubles, at least, were civil and small in scale; see Baines 'Feuds or Vengeance?', pp. 11–20.

The reality of the order of the figures in the wooden tomb models of the so-called marching regiments of the 'Soldiers of Asyut' is demonstrated in Förster *et al.*, 'Tracing Linear Structures', fig. 2.3: they are simply groups of men walking along parallel caravan tracks.

Seidlmayer, 'First Intermediate Period', provides a fine overview of the cemeteries of those times.

My statistics for wooden tomb figures of those times are drawn from Julia Harvey 'Continuity or Collapse: wooden statues from the end of the Old Kingdom and the first Intermediate Period', in Miroslav Bárta (ed.), *The Old Kingdom Art and Archaeology* (Prague 2006), pp. 157–66.

CHAPTER 22. SEMA TOWY

The statistics in the opening paragraphs have been gathered from *LÄ*, vol. 4, cols. 395–427.

For the monumental tomb at Dara see Lehner, *Complete Pyramids*, p. 164, and Raymond Weill, *Dara: campagne de 1946–1948* (Cairo, 1958).

The titularies of the Middle Kingdom kings are described and translated in Leprohon, *Great Name*, pp. 54–60. See also Shih Wei Hsu, 'Development of Ancient Egyptian Royal Inscriptions', esp. p. 278 *ff.*

The term 'Amenemhet Itj-towy' is discussed by William Kelley Simpson, 'Studies in the Twelfth Egyptian Dynasty', *JARCE*, 2 (1963), pp. 53–63. For Itj-towy's physical location see Felix Arnold, 'Settlement Remains at Lisht-North', in *Haus und Palast*, pp. 13–21. See also Stephen Quirke, 'The Residence in Relations between Places of Knowledge, Production and Power: Middle Kingdom evidence', in Rolf Gundlach and John Taylor (eds.), *Egyptian Royal Residences* (Wiesbaden, 2009), pp. 111–30.

'TOTAL: kings of the residence . . .' is quoted from Ryholt, 'Turin King-List', p. 141.

The epigraph to the section 'The King, the Palace, and the State' (p. 321) is from Ludwig Wittgenstein, *Philosophical Investigations*, trans. Anthony Kenny (Oxford 1953), Part One, p. 13, paragraph 31.

For a fine discussion of the historical development of the ancient terms that described the pharaonic state see Ogden Goelet, '*Kemet* and Other Egyptian Terms for Their Land', in Robert Chazan, William Hallo and Lawrence Schiffman (eds.), *Ki Baruch Hu: ancient Near Eastern, Biblical, and Judaic studies in honor of Baruch A. Levine* (Winona Lake, Indiana, 1999), pp. 23–42.

The pacific nature of the pharaonic union of the region of the lower Nile is emphasized by Hans Goedicke, 'ZM;-T;WY', in *Mélange Gamal Eddin Mokhtar*, 2 vols. (Cairo, 1985), vol. 1, pp. 307–23.

Grajetzki's *Middle Kingdom*, pp. 10–28, provides a brief account of the building programme of the Intefs and Montuhoteps. Kaiser *et al.*, 'Stadt und Tempel von Elephantine'. *MDAIK*, 31, 1 (1975), pp. 39–58, describe the extent of early Middle Kingdom activity on that island; pls. 15–23 show something of the quality of the stone cutting and inscriptions typical of building projects of the time.

For blocks from Karnak that are virtually identical to those excavated at Elephantine see, for example, Martina Ullman, 'Thebes: origins of a ritual landscape', in Peter Dorman and Betsy Bryan (eds.), *Sacred Space and Sacred Function in Ancient Thebes* (Chicago, 2007), p. 4.

Geneviève Pierrat-Bonnefois, 'L'histoire du temple de Tôd: quelques réponses de l'archéologie', *Kyphi*, 2 (1999), pp. 63–76, provides an overview of similar building activities at Tod; another contemporary shrine has been resurrected by Elisa Fiore Marochetti, *The Reliefs of the Chapel of Nebhepetre Mentuhotep at Gebelein* (Leiden, 2010), who also provides schematic plans of all of those now largely lost constructions, p. 29, figs. 8 and 9.

The epigraph to the section 'At the beginning' (p. 326) is adapted from the translations of Allen, *Pyramid Texts*, pp. 166 and 265.

For the geomorphology of Karnak see Luc Gabolde, 'Les Origines de Karnak et la Genèse de la Théologie d'Amon', *Bulletin de la Société Française d'Égyptologie*, 186–187 (2014), p. 20 *ff*.

Foundation ceremonies at Egyptian temples are described in Corinna Rossi, *Architecture and Mathematics in Ancient Egypt* (Cambridge, 2006), Chapter 4, and also in Belmonte and Shaltout (eds.), *Cosmic Order*, Chapter 7 (Belmonte, Miguel Molinero Polo and Noemi Miranda).

Though no earlier buildings are known to have stood in the vicinity of the Karnak temples, pre-dynastic pottery has been found in the area; I saw fragments of black-topped wares being dug out of the holes excavated in the 1960s for the foundations to the columns that support the Sound and Light pavilion to the east of the Sacred Lake. See also Gabolde, 'Les Origines de Karnak', pp. 13–20.

'[monument for] Amun-Re, lord of heaven . . .' is adapted from Ullman, 'Thebes', p. 6.

Amun/Amun-Re is one of the most widely documented pharaonic deities. For an overview of his history and roles see *LÄ*, vol. 1, cols. 237–48 (Eberhard Otto), and Vincent Tobin, 'Amun and Amun-Re', in Donald Redford (ed.), *The Ancient Gods Speak: a guide to Egyptian religion* (New York, 2002).

'As when a new Particle of Matter . . .' is quoted from John Locke, *An Essay Concerning Human Understanding* (London, 1690), Book Two, Chapter 26.

The epigraph to the section 'Rising like Temples' (p. 330) is adapted from the translations of Charles Francis Nims, *Thebes of the Pharaohs: pattern for every city* (London, 1965), p. 17, and of Wolfgang Schenkel in Dieter Arnold, *Gräber des Alten und Mittleren Reiches in El-Tarif* (Mainz, 1976), pp. 50–56; the latter volume also contains a full account of the Intefs' tombs.

Dieter Arnold, *The Temple of Mentuhotep at Deir el-Bahari* (New York, 1979), provides a sumptuous account of the architecture and excavation of Montuhotep's temple. For the tools and levers used by the temple's work gangs and craftsmen and for plans of the temple's gardens see pls. 34–6, 38–43 and 49.

My identification of the plaster that presently fills parts of the ditch on the south side of the temple's courtyard is based upon the recollections of Mohammed 'the Bob', an elderly Luxor dragoman who had participated in the making of DeMille's *Ten Commandments* (1956). His unusual nickname stemmed from the tale that DeMille had yelled to him to 'bob down' as he had filmed the Exodus at Deir el-Bahari, for Mohammed had forgotten to remove his tarboush.

How a hundred fragments of beautifully carved relief from Montuhotep's temple came to be set into the walls of a country house in County Donegal is described in I. E. S. Edwards, 'Lord Dufferin's Excavations at Deir el-Bahari and the Clandeboye Collection', *JEA*, 51 (1965), pp. 16–28.

Dorothea Arnold, 'Amenemhat I and the Early Twelfth Dynasty at Thebes', *The Metropolitan Museum of Art Journal*, 26 (1991), pp. 5–48 provides an archaeologically determined date for the enigmatic unfinished temple that lies to the south of Deir el-Bahari.

For the pyramids of Amenemhet I and Senwosret I see Lehner, *Complete Pyramids*, pp. 168–73, Dieter Arnold, *The Pyramid of Senwosret I* (New York, 1988), and Dieter Arnold, *The Pyramid Complex of Senwosret I* (New York, 1992).

The epigraph to the section 'Heliopolis and Abydos' (p. 339) is adapted from the translations of Papyrus Berlin 3029 in Quirke, *Cult of Re*, p. 88, and Parkinson, *Voices*, pp. 40–43.

For an early Middle Kingdom temple in the Nile Delta see Kemp, *Ancient Egypt*, pp. 126–8. A selection of fine fragments from various lost buildings of Montuhotep II is contained in Cyril Aldred, *Middle Kingdom Art in Ancient Egypt* (London, 1950), pls. 16–18 (Armant), Gay Robins, *The Art of Ancient Egypt* (London, 1997), pls. 88 (Dendera), 97 and 98 (Tod), and 103 (Qift), and Joseph Wegner, 'A New Temple: the *mahat* of Nebhepetre at Abydos', in *Egyptian Archaeology*, 46 (2015), pp. 3–7.

Osiris' thirteen origins are listed along with a succinct account of that deity's history and roles, in *LÄ*, vol. 4, cols. 623–33 (John Gwyn Griffiths). The causeway statues of Senwosret I at Lisht are described in Arnold, *Pyramid of Senwosret I*, pp. 21–2 and pls. 3–7.

Osiris' Middle Kingdom temple at Abydos is discussed by David O'Connor, *Abydos: Egypt's first pharaohs and the cult of Osiris* (London, 2009), p. 87 *ff.* The statue group of Osiris on his bier which was emplaced in the tomb of King Djet is pictured in O'Connor, *Abydos*, p. 90. Recent work has recovered fragments of that statue group's enclosing shrine and also the alabaster socle on which it had been set; see Ute Effland, Julia Budka and Andreas Effland, 'Studien zum Osiriskult in Umm el-Qaab/Abydos', *MDAIK*, 66 (2010), pp. 30–35. The ceramic corpus given in that same report shows that the Osiris cult had flourished during the Middle Kingdom. For an overview of the myriad installations of that period which were set up at a distance from Osiris' shrine see O'Connor, *Abydos*, pp. 90–96.

'I myself laid the bricks . . .' is from William Kelly Simpson, *The Terrace of the Great God at Abydos: the offering chapels of dynasties 12 and 13* (New Haven, 1974).

For a reconstruction of Senwosret I's Karnak temple see Luc Gabolde, *Le 'Grand Château d'Amon' de Sésostris Ier à Karnak: la décoration du temple d'Amon-Rê au Moyen Empire* (Paris, 1998), and also Jean-François Carlotti, Ernst Czerny and Luc Gabolde, 'Sondage Autour de la Plate-Forme en Grès de la "Cour Du Moyen Empire"', *Cahiers de Karnak*, 13 (2010), pp. 111–93.

Note that Gabolde's scheme has been assessed and expanded by François Larché, 'Nouvelles observations sur les monuments du Moyen et du Nouvel Empire dans la zone centrale du temple d'Amon', *Cahiers de Karnak*, 12 (2006), pp. 407–592, which proposes a different form and axis for Senwosret I's temple. Those proposals, however, do not greatly affect the burden of my text.

For the 'Mansion of Amun-Re' see Gabolde, Le 'Grand Château d'Amon'.

The limestone of Amun's Theban Mansion came from the quarries of Tura, near Memphis, and Dababiya, close to Thebes; see the petrographic analysis of Thierry de Putter and Christina Karlshausen, 'Provenance et caractères distinctifs des calcaires utilisés dans l'architecture du Moyen et du Nouvel Empire à Karnak', Cahiers de Karnak, 11 (2003), pp. 373–83.

Parts of the gridded plan of Karnak's Middle Kingdom town is given in Jean-Françoise Carlotti, 'Considérations architecturales sur l'orientation, la composition et les proportions des structures du temple d'Amon-Rê à Karnak', in Peter Jánosi (ed.), Structure and Significance: thoughts on ancient Egyptian architecture (Vienna, 2005), pl. 1.

For the 'Heliopolis of the South' see Gabolde, Le 'Grand Château d'Amon', pp. 134–7. The early occurrence of Amun's titles on the Theban monuments and their connection to Heliopolis is assessed by Jadwiga Iwaszczuk, 'Jmn xntj jpwt.f from the Middle Kingdom to the mid-Eighteenth Dynasty', Études et Travaux (Institut des Cultures Méditerranéennes et Orientales de l'Académie Polonaise des Sciences), 26 (2013), pp. 303–25.

Luc Gabolde suggests a single date – 7 January 1946 BC – for the establishment of Karnak's East/West axis, a proposal rejected, as he observes, by several archaeoastronomers; see his 'Mise au Point sur l'orientation du Temple d'Amon-Rê à Karnak en Direction du Lever du Soleil au Solstice d'hiver', Cahiers de Karnak, 13 (2010), pp. 243–56.

For the re-founding of the state calendar see Nims, Thebes, p. 203, n. 37.

The temple on Thebes' western horizon is described in Győző Vörös, Temple on the Pyramid of Thebes (Budapest, 1998), and Győző Vörös, 'The Ancient Nest of Horus above Thebes: Hungarian excavations on Thoth Hill at the Temple of King Sankhkare Montuhotep (1995–1998)', Eighth International Congress, vol. 1, pp. 547–56.

'Amun, lord of the two lands' is quoted from Ullman, 'Thebes',

p. 7 *ff.* Claas Bleeker, *Egyptian Festivals: enactments of religious renewal* (Leiden, 1967), is a fundamental study upon the nature of pharaonic festivals.

For the 'Feast of the Valley' and the routes of its processions see Manfred Bietak, 'Das schöne Fest vom Wüstentale: Kult zur Vereinigung mit den Toten in der thebanischen Nekropole', in Georg Danek and Irmtraud Hellerschmid (eds.), *Rituale – Identitätsstiftende Handlungskomplexe* (Vienna, 2002), pp. 23–36.

'The priest Neferabed . . .' (Spiegelberg Graffito 968) is adapted from the translation in Peden, *Graffiti*, p. 31.

The size of the Karnak barks and the numbers of their carriers have been cleverly computed by Elaine Sullivan, 'Visualising the Size and Movement of the Portable Festival Barks at Karnak Temple', *British Museum Studies in Ancient Egypt and Sudan*, 19 (2012), pp. 1–37.

For reconstructions of the later phases of the so-called 'little temple' at Medinet Habu see Uvo Hölscher, 'The Architectural Survey', *Medinet Habu Reports* (OIC 10) (Chicago, 1931), pp. 61–91; the earliest-known temple at that site is outlined in Uvo Hölscher, *The Excavation of Medinet Habu*, vol. 2 (Chicago, 1939), p. 4 *ff.*

The early connection of the processions of Amun to the little temple at Medinet Habu is posited in Ullman, 'Thebes', p. 9 *ff*, who also suggests a further connection to the Luxor temple, a view strengthened by recent discoveries at Karnak (Ullman, 'Thebes', p. 10, n. 37), and the opening of the processional way between Karnak and Luxor; Mansour Boraik, 'Excavations of the Quay and the Embankment in front of Karnak Temples: preliminary report', *Cahiers de Karnak*, 13 (2010), p. 47.

For a bark procession at Itj-towy see Simpson, 'Studies', p. 54(G), though the date of that text has since been questioned by Richard Parkinson, *Poetry and Culture in Middle Kingdom Egypt* (London, 2002), pp. 311–12.

Labib Habachi, a man of many stories, told me that as a young inspector in Luxor in the 1930s he heard a temple guard shout to the three festival barks of Sheik Abu el-Haggag as they passed the temple's pylon, '*Taala henna Ya Amun!*' – 'Come here, O Amun!'

CHAPTER 23. THE COURT OF THEBES

Epigraph: from W. M. Flinders Petrie, *A Season in Egypt* (London, 1887), p. 14, quoting and translating a passage from Auguste Mariette, *Questions relatives aux nouvelles fouilles à faire en Égypte* (Paris, 1879).

For the geology of the changing landscape north of the First Cataract see Muhammad Abu al-Izz, *Landforms of Egypt* (Cairo, 1971), p. 85 *ff.*

The most recent accounts of the reliefs in the Wadi el-Shatt el-Rigal are in *LÄ*, vol. 6, cols. 1119–24 (Ricardo Caminos), and the same author's 'Epigraphy in the Field', in Jan Assmann, Günter Burkard and Vivian Davies (eds.), *Problems and Priorities in Egyptian Archaeology* (London, 1987), pp. 65–6.

Khety the 'seal bearer' and his contemporaries at Montuhotep's court are documented and discussed in James Allen, 'Some Theban Officials of the Early Middle Kingdom', in Der Manuelian (ed.), *Studies in Honor of William Kelly Simpson*, vol. 1, pp. 1–26, and also James Allen, 'The High Officials of the Early Middle Kingdom', in Nigel Strudwick and John Taylor (eds.), *The Theban Necropolis: past, present and future* (London, 2003), pp. 14–29.

The epigraph to the section 'Sandstone and Limestone' (p. 357) is translated from Petrie, *A Season in Egypt*, pl. XV.

For Gebel el-Silsila and its relationship to Wadi el-Shatt el-Rigal see James A. Harrell and Per Storemyr, 'Ancient Egyptian Quarries: an illustrated overview', in Nizam Abu-Jaber *et al.* (eds.), *QuarryScapes: ancient stone quarry landscapes in the Eastern Mediterranean* (Trondheim, 2009), p. 17, fig. 8.

The provenance of the sandstone used by the masons of the Intefs and Montuhoteps is discussed in Carlotti *et al.*, 'Sondage Autour de la Plate-Forme en Grès', p. 113. For the use of limestone from the Dababiya quarries in Montuhotep's temple at Deir el-Bahari see de Putter and Karlshausen, 'Provenance et caractères distinctifs', pp. 373–83.

'what the sky gives . . .' is quoted from Allen, 'The High Officials', p. 18.

Allen, 'The High Officials', provides an analysis of some of the courtly titles of the times; see also Denise Doxey, *Egyptian Non-Royal Epithets in the Middle Kingdom* (Leiden, 1998), Nathalie Favry, 'L'hapax dans le corpus des titres du Moyen Empire', *NeHet* (an online journal), 1 (2014), pp. 71–94, and Wolfram Grajetzki, 'Setting the State Anew: the central administration from the end of the Old Kingdom to the end of the Middle Kingdom', in Garcia (ed.), *Ancient Egyptian Administration*, pp. 215–56.

Allen, 'The High Officals', p. 2 *ff*, has a schematic map of the Middle Kingdom necropolis at Deir el-Bahari and discusses the relationship of the king to the owners of those tombs.

For 'overseer of horn, hoof . . .' and following see Allen, 'The High Officials', where it is listed amongst the various titularies of stewards, viziers and treasurers.

Herbert Eustace Winlock, *Excavations at Deir el Bahri 1911–1931* (New York, 1942), is the classic account of the excavation of these and many other Middle Kingdom monuments in Western Thebes; the note of Catharine Roehrig, 'The Middle Kingdom Tomb of Wah at Thebes', in Strudwick and Taylor (eds.), *Theban Necropolis*, pp. 11–13, describes the subsequent fate of 'estate manager' Wah.

'wrecks of their former beauty' is quoted from Norman de Garis Davies, *Five Theban Tombs* (London, 1913), p. 39.

For 'royal ornament' see Lisa Kuchman Sabbahy, 'The Titulary of the Harem of Nebhepetre Mentuhotep, Once Again', in *JARCE*, 34 (1997), pp. 163–6, who assesses the 'queens' that were buried around the Deir el-Bahari tomb of Montuhotep II. The remarkable tattoos found on two of their mummies are analysed by Louis Keimer, *Remarques sur le tatouage dans L'Égypte ancienne* (Cairo, 1948), who places them in the broader cultural context of the markings upon contemporary dolls and figures in tomb-chapel decorations.

Meket-re's tomb chapel and wooden funerary models are described in Winlock, *Excavations*, p. 17 *ff*, and in fine detail in the same author's *Models of Daily Life in Ancient Egypt from the Tomb of Meket-re at Thebes* (Cambridge, Mass., 1955). See also Arnold, 'Amenemhat I', and Allen, 'The High Officials', p. 19.

'a cranny of a little tomb' is quoted from Winlock, *Excavations*, p. 57.

'Harhotep speaks to Udja'a . . .' is adapted from the translations of T. G. H. James, *The Hekanakhte Papers and Other Early Middle*

Kingdom Documents (New York, 1962), p. 78, and Wente, *Letters*, pp. 63–4.

For an account of the excavation of the tomb chamber in which Winlock found the archive of Heqanakht see James Allen, *The Heqanakht Papyri* (New York, 2002), pp. 3–5; the following description of those documents is mainly based on the sensitive forensic examination by Allen in that same publication. In similar fashion, my quotations and commentary are based on that same source but also utilize the earlier studies of James, *The Hekanakhte Papers*, Hans Goedicke, *Studies in the Hekanakhte Papers* (Baltimore, 1984), Wente, *Letters*, pp. 58–63, and Parkinson, *Voices*, pp. 101–7.

CHAPTER 24. THE MATERIALS OF STATE

For an overview of the copper mines of Sinai and the Levant see Jack Ogden, *AEMT*, p. 149 *ff*; for a recent survey in the Wadi Nasb, Pierre Tallet, Georges Castel and Philippe Fluzin, 'Metallurgical Sites of South Sinai (Egypt) in the Pharaonic Era: new discoveries', *Paléorient*, 37, 2 (2011), pp. 79–89.

The texts at 'Ain Sukhna are published by Mahmoud Abd el-Raziq, Georges Castel, Pierre Tallet and Victor Ghica, *Les inscriptions d'Ayn Soukhna* (Cairo, 2002); see also Tallet, 'New Inscriptions'. The historical implications of a graffito naming Ipy (AS 7) are discussed by Pierre Tallet, 'The Treasurer Ipi, early Twelfth Dynasty', in *Göttinger Miszellen*, 193 (2003), pp. 59–64.

'Year 1, arrival of the king's men . . .' is quoted from Mahmoud Abd el-Raziq, Georges Castel, Pierre Tallet and Gregory Marouard, 'The Pharaonic Site of Ayn Soukhna in the Gulf of Suez: 2001–2009 progress report', in Tallet and Mahfouz (eds.), *Red Sea in Pharaonic Times*, p. 4; see also, Pierre Tallet, 'Ayn Sukhna and Wadi el-Jarf: two newly discovered pharaonic harbours on the Suez Gulf', in *British Museum Studies in Ancient Egypt and Sudan*, 18 (2012), pp. 147–68.

For the remarkable Middle Kingdom copper-smelting installations at 'Ain Sukhna see Mahmoud Abd el-Razik, Georges Castel, Pierre Tallet and Philippe Fluzin, *Ayn Soukhna II: les ateliers métallurgiques du Moyen Empire* (Cairo, 2011). My estimates for the reduction and refinement of copper ore in southern Sinai are derived from Maryvonne Chartier-Raymond, Brigitte Gratien, Claude Trau-necker and Jean-Marc Vinçon, 'Les sites miniers pharaoniques du Sud-Sinaï: quelques notes et observations de terrain', *Cahier de recherches de l'Institut de papyrologie et d'égyptologie de Lille*, 16 (1994), p. 65.

For the geology of Sinai see Abu al-Izz, *Landforms*, pp. 257–74; for the formation of copper ores etc. see Paul Weis, Thomas Driesner and Christoph Heinrich, 'Porphyry-Copper Ore Shells Form at Stable Pressure-Temperature Fronts Within Dynamic Fluid Plumes', *Science*, 338, 6114 (2012), pp. 1613–16.

'Terraces of Turquoise' is quoted from Tallet, 'Ayn Sukhna and Wadi el-Jarf', p. 151; 'only possible with a considerable supply . . .' from Kirsopp Lake's introduction to 'The Serabit Expedition of 1930', *Harvard Theological Review*, 25, 2 (1932), p. 97.

Identically named 'scorpion repellers' and viziers are recorded at 'Ain Sukhna and in Sinai; see Abd el-Raziq *et al.*, 'The Pharaonic Site of Ayn Soukhna', p. 149.

My description of the relics of mining activities in Wadi Maghara is largely derived from the classic account of W. M. Flinders Petrie, *Researches in Sinai* (London, 1906).

The epigraph to the section 'Incense' (p. 384) is from *The Two Noble Kinsmen, presented at the Blackfriars by the King's Maiesties servants with great applause*, Act V (London, 1634).

The solitary early Middle Kingdom hieroglyphic graffito found in the deep Sahara was reported by Joseph Clayton, Aloisa de Trafford and Mark Borda, 'A Hieroglyphic Inscription Found at Jebel Uweinat Mentioning Yam and Tekhebet', *Sahara*, 19 (2008), pp. 129–34. It was subsequently assessed by Andrés Diego Espinel, 'The Tribute from Tekhebeten', *Göttinger Miszellen*, 237 (2013), pp. 15–19, and Julien Cooper, 'Reconsidering the Location of Yam', *JARCE*, 48 (2012), pp. 1–21, who sets it in the context of ancient caravan routes.

'to find the people of the oasis' is quoted from Förster, 'With Donkeys, Jars and Water Bags', p. 9; see also Michel Baud, Frédéric Colin and Pierre Tallet, 'Les gouverneurs de l'oasis de Dakhla au Moyen Empire', *BIFAO*, 99 (1999), p. 2 *ff*.

For an overview of the environment of Lake Chad in ancient history and its possible relationship to later pharaonic texts see Thomas

Schneider, 'The West Beyond the West: the mysterious 'Wernes' of the Egyptian underworld and the Chad Palaeolakes', *Journal of Ancient Egyptian Interconnections*, 2, 4 (2010), pp. 1–14. Hays, *Organization*, p. 211, n. 778, traces the image of the 'Field of Reeds' back to the Old Kingdom.

The egyptological caravans of the 1830s are described, along with a translation of the texts upon the stelae that they recovered, by Alessandra Nibbi, 'Remarks on the Two Stelae from the Wadi Gasus', *JEA*, 62 (1976), pp. 45–56. Nibbi's interpretations, however, have been superseded; see, for example, El-Sayed Mahfouz, 'New Epigraphic material from Wadi Gawasis', in Tallet and Mahfouz (eds.), *Red Sea in Pharaonic Times*, pp. 117–33.

'grew up in the royal residence . . .' is adapted from Nibbi ,'Remarks on the Two Stelae', p. 50, and James Allen, 'The Historical Inscription of Khnumhotep at Dahshur: preliminary report', *Bulletin of the American Schools of Oriental Research*, 352 (2008), pp. 27 and 38, which places Khnumhotep in historical context.

The celebrated tomb chapel long considered to have held images of Joseph and his brothers was published as 'Tomb No. 3' by Percy Newberry, *Beni Hasan*, vol. 1 (London, 1893).

Abdel Monem Sayed announced the discovery of the pharaonic harbour at Wadi Gawasis in a series of papers, including 'The Recently Discovered Port on the Red Sea Shore', *JEA*, 64 (1978), pp. 69–71. The texts his expedition found are published by El-Sayed Mahfouz, 'Les Ostraca Hiératiques Du Ouadi Gaouasis', *Revue d'Égyptologie*, 59 (2008), pp. 275–322; the remarkable structures and the anchor stones of which they were constructed, are reconsidered in Shelley Wachsmann, *Seagoing Ships and Seamanship in the Bronze Age Levant* (College Station, Texas, 1998), pp. 259–62.

For an overview of the complex series of surveys and excavations, analyses and publications of the various sites examined at Wadi Gawasis see Rodolfo Fattovich, 'Egypt's Trade with Punt: new discoveries on the Red Sea coast', *British Museum Studies in Ancient Egypt and Sudan*, 18 (2012), pp. 1–59.

'Amun of the sea' is from Mahfouz, 'New Epigraphic Material', p. 132.

'His Majesty ordered . . .' is adapted from Claude Obsomer, *Sésostris Ier.: étude chronologique et historique du règne* (Brussels,

1995), pp. 711–12, and Dominique Farout, 'La carrière du [ouhemou] Ameny et l'organisation des expéditions au Ouadi Hammamat au Moyen Empire', *BIFAO*, 94 (1994), p. 144 (T1). (For the papyri from the Nile-side dockyard see further Chapter 27 of this volume.)

The ships' ropes found at Wadi Gawasis are described by Ksenija Borojevic and Rebecca Mountain, 'The Ropes of Pharaohs: the source of cordage from 'Rope Cave' at Mersa/Wadi Gawasis re-visited', *JARCE*, 47 (2011), pp. 131–41.

Rodolfo Fattovich and Kathryn Bard (eds.) *Mersa/Wadi Gawasis 2006–2007* (online report) contains a detailed report of the excavation of the centre of that ancient site, this being but one of many reports of the mission's investigations that were issued throughout the decade of its fieldwork.

The construction of a replica boat – a 'floating hypothesis' based on the timbers found at Wadi Gawasis – and an account of its hand-ling under sail in the Red Sea are given in Cheryl Ward, 'Building Pharaoh's Ships: cedar, incense and sailing the Great Green', *British Museum Studies in Ancient Egypt and Sudan*, 18 (2012), pp. 217–32. The exotic pottery found at the port whose origins lie in other Afri-can cultures are described in Andrea Manzo, 'From the Sea to the Deserts and Back: new research in Eastern Sudan', *British Museum Studies in Ancient Egypt and Sudan*, 18 (2012), pp. 75–106; and see also Fattovich, 'Egypt's Trade with Punt'.

'the wonderful things of Punt' is adapted from Mahfouz, 'New Epigraphic Material', p. 131. Kenneth Kitchen's essay 'The Land of Punt' in Shaw *et al.* (eds.), *Archaeology of Africa*, pp. 587–606, is a standard treatment of the pharaonic sources.

DNA testing on two mummified baboons was reported to the 84th Annual Meeting of the American Association of Physical Anthro-pologists in 2015 by Nathaniel Dominy and Salima Ikram.

'Remember the building of the shrine . . .' is adapted from Gardiner, *Admonitions*, p. 13; Lichtheim, *AEL*, vol. 1, p. 159 *ff*, Parkinson, *Sinuhe*, p. 183 *ff*, and Tobin, *LAE*, p. 203 *ff*.

The Middle Kingdom sites at the so-called 'Chephren quarries' were surveyed by Shaw *et al.* (eds.), 'Quarrying and Landscape at Gebel el-Asr', pp. 293–305. See also Ian Shaw, 'Non-textual Marks and the Twelfth Dynasty Dynamics of Centre and Periphery: a case-study of potmarks at the Gebel el-Asr gneiss quarties [*sic*]', *Lingua Aegyptia*, 8 (2009), pp. 69–82.

'for the purpose of bringing *mentet* stone' is quoted from Rex Engelbach, 'The Quarries of the Western Nubian Desert: a preliminary report', *Annales du Service des Antiquités de l'Égypte*, 33 (1933), p. 66.

The changes in the varieties of stone used in the workshops of the Old and Middle Kingdom courts are described by Andrew Bevan, *Stone Vessels and Values in the Bronze Age Mediterranean* (Cambridge, 2007), pp. 100–101.

'Since a very long time . . .' is from the Preface to Ahmed Fakhry, *The Inscriptions of the Amethyst Quarries at Wadi el-Hudi* (Cairo, 1952). The stone is described in *AEMT*, pp. 50–52 (Barbara Aston, James Harrell and Ian Shaw), the quarries by Ian Shaw and Robert Jameson, 'Amethyst Mining in the Eastern Desert: a preliminary survey at Wadi el-Hudi', *JEA*, 79 (1993), pp. 81–97.

'who sent me to carry away the amethyst' is adapted from Obsomer, *Sésostris Ier.*, pp. 711–12.

For the expedition of the vizier Hor to Wadi el-Hudi see Karl-Joachim Seyfried, *Beiträge zu den Expeditionen des Mittleren Reiches in die Ost-Wüste* (Hildesheim, 1981) p. 267. For the wider usage of amethyst from the Wadi el-Hudi see Jacke Phillips, 'Egyptian Amethyst in the Bronze Age Aegean', *Journal of Ancient Egyptian Interconnections*, 1, 2 (2009), pp. 9–25.

Andrés Diego Espinel, 'A Newly Identified Stela from Wadi El-Hudi (Cairo JE 86119)', *JEA*, 91 (2005), pp. 55–70, discusses the possibility of a temple at Wadi el-Hudi and the stela of Sareru.

'We set out from Luxor one morning . . .' is quoted from Arthur Weigall, *Travels in the Upper Egyptian Deserts* (Edinburgh, 1909), p. 29 *ff.*

For the inscriptions and graffiti in the Wadi Hammamat see *LÄ*, vol. 6, cols. 1099–116 (Wolfgang Helk); for an overview of its stone and quarries see *AEMT*, pp. 57–8 (Barbara Aston, James Harrell and Ian Shaw), and Myriam Wissa, 'Jbh3.t in the Autobiographical Inscription of Weni: developments since 1994', *JEA*, 97 (2011), pp. 223–7.

'My lord has sent me with great ships . . .' is adapted from Grajetzki, *Middle Kingdom*, p. 24.

'The King of the Lands of the Delta . . .' and the following quotations in this section are adapted from Breasted, *Ancient Records*, vol. 1, pp. 213 and 216 (441 and 451), Donald Redford, *Egypt, Canaan, and Israel in Ancient Times* (Princeton, 1992), p. 72, Farout, 'La carrière', and the on-line 'St Andrews Corpus' of Mark-Jan Nederhof.

The absurdity of taking the figures given in expedition texts such as those in the Wadi Hammamat as a realistic record of the numbers of people engaged in such pharaonic enterprises is examined by Dieter Mueller, 'Some Remarks on Wage Rates in the Middle Kingdom', *JNES*, 34, 4 (1975), pp. 249–63, who concludes that they are an accounting device concerned with food rations; Farout, 'La carrière', pp. 143–72, offers an alternative solution. Hard archaeological evidence of the logistics of pharaonic quarrying, however, is supplied by, for example, Elizabeth Bloxam, 'Who Were the Pharaohs' Quarrymen?', *Archaeology International*, 9 (2005), pp. 23–7, and various articles in Abu-Jaber *et al.* (eds.), *Quarryscapes*.

The epigraph to the section 'Alabaster' (p. 407) is from a seventeenth-century translation (*The Historie of the World*) of Pliny, *Natural History*, Book XXXVII, Chapter 10.

For pharaonic alabaster, its qualities and quarries see *AEMT*, pp. 59–60 (Barbara Aston, James Harrell and Ian Shaw).

'what the flame had wrought . . .' is from Tom Heldal and Per Storemyr, 'Fire on the Rocks: heat as an agent in ancient Egyptian hard stone quarrying', in Georgio Lollino *et al.* (eds.), *Engineering Geology for Society and Territory*, vol. 5 (Switzerland, 2014), p. 291, quoting Hans Goedicke, 'Some Remarks on Stone Quarrying in the Egyptian Middle Kingdom (2060–1786 BC)', *JARCE*, 3 (1964), pp. 43–50.

'house of gold' is quoted from *LÄ*, vol. 2, 'Hatnub', cols. 1043–5 (William Kelly Simpson). The Hatnub quarries and the logistics of their mining are described by Ian Shaw, 'A Survey at Hatnub', in *Amarna Reports III* (London, 1986), Chapter 10, and also Ian Shaw, ' "We Went Forth to the Desert Land . . .": retracing the routes between the Nile Valley and the Hatnub travertine quarries', in Förster and Riemer (eds.), *Desert Road Archaeology*, pp. 521–32.

Hatnub's earlier history is described by Sydney Aufrère, 'L'origine de l'albâtre à la Ire dynastie d'après les inscriptions des vases provenant des galeries de la pyramide à degrés', *BIFAO*, 103 (2013), pp. 1–15; see also the reports of an ongoing mission, Roland Enmarch, 'Writing in the "Mansion of Gold": texts from the Hatnub quarries', *Egyptian Archaeology*, 47 (2015), pp. 10–12.

For a recent overview of the site of Deir el-Bersha and its relationship to Hatnub see Harco Willems and Wala' Mustafa Muhammad, 'A Note on the Origin of the Toponym al-Barsha', *JEA*, 96 (2010), pp. 232–6.

'the transport of a statue of 13 cubits . . .' and the following quotations are freely adapted from the translations of Percy Newberry, *El Bersheh*, vol. 1 (London, 1894), pp. 17–23, Breasted, *Ancient Records*, vol. 1, pp. 306–12 (668–706), and Mark-Jan Nederhof.

For the alabaster ostracon of the reign of Senwosret III see Hans Goedicke, 'A New Inscription from Hatnub', *Annales du Service des Antiquités de l'Égypte*, 56 (1959), pp. 55–8.

'I moored at the royal pyramid . . .' is quoted from Shaw, ' "We went forth', p. 528.

Harco Willems, Christoph Peeters and Gert Verstraeyten, 'Where did Djehutihotep Erect his Colossal Statue?', *Zeitschrift*, 132 (2005), pp. 173–89, proposes that the alabaster colossus was set up within an unknown temple at Deir el-Bersha.

CHAPTER 25. THE LEVANT AND NUBIA

Epigraph: from W. M. Flinders Petrie, *Memphis 1* (London, 1909), p. 6.

'Although the king ruled more than . . .' is quoted from Grajetzki, *Middle Kingdom*, p. 45.

Ezra Marcus, 'Amenemhet II and the Sea: maritime aspects of the Mit Rahina (Memphis) inscription', *Ägypten und Levante*, 17 (2007), pp. 137–90, provides a full account of previous work upon that important text and discusses the many ambiguities that face its translators.

For the 'Way of Horus' see p. 417, above.

'Suddenly, as it were . . .' is quoted from Redford, *Egypt, Canaan, and Israel*, pp. 79–80.

For reconstructed Byblos boats see p. 394, above. (Given Ward's estimates for the size of the cargoes of such craft, I opted for Marcus' 'cedar planks' rather than 'cedar logs'.)

For an overview of the Tod Treasure see Joan Aruz, Kim Bezel and Jean Evans (eds.), *Beyond Babylon: art, trade and diplomacy in the Second Millennium* BC (New York, 2009), pp. 65–9 (Geneviève Pierrat-Bonnefois and Michèle Casanova). Michel Menu, 'Analyse du trésor de Tôd', *Bulletin de la Société Française d'Égyptologie*, 130 (1994), pp. 29–45, provides the treasure's statistics; Marcus, 'Amenemhet II and the Sea', pp. 158–60, a summary of the theories concerning the treasure's origins and its relationship to the Mit Rahina inscription.

Allen, 'The Historical Inscription', provides a lengthy discussion of Khnumhotep's dealings with the Levant along with a translation of the surviving portions of his text; 'one of the more important historical texts . . .' is quoted from the conclusion to that paper, p. 38.

'. . . and I struck the northern foreigner' is quoted from John Baines, 'The Stela of Khusobek: private and royal military narrative and values', in Jürgen Osing and Günter Dreyer (eds.), *Form und Mass: beitrage zur Literatur, Sprache und Kunst des altern Ägypten* (Wiesbaden, 1987), pp. 43–61.

Some aspects of Byblos' sea-side tombs have been recently re-assessed by Robert Schiestl, 'The Coffin from Tomb I at Byblos', *Ägypten und Levante*, 17 (2007), pp. 265–72, and also by Lorenzo Nigro, 'The Eighteenth Century BC Princes of Byblos and Ebla and the Chronology of the Middle Bronze Age', *Bulletin d'Archéologie et d'Architecture Libanaises*, 6 (2009), pp. 159–75.

The Story of Sinuhe is the most discussed and documented of all pharaonic texts. My account of it follows that of Parkinson, *Sinuhe*, p. 21 *ff*, and my quotations are adapted from Lichtheim, *AEL*, vol. 1, pp. 222–35, Parkinson, *Sinuhe*, pp. 21–43 and Simpson, *LAE*, pp. 54–66.

The epigraph to the section 'The Sinai Station' (p. 424) is adapted from the translations of Alan Gardiner, 'The Tomb of a Much-Travelled Theban Official', *JEA*, 4, 1 (1917), pp.35–6, and Grajetzki, *Middle Kingdom*, p. 25.

Serabit el-Khadim has recently been re-surveyed and re-assessed by Charles Bonnet and Dominique Valbelle, 'The Middle Kingdom Temple of Hathor at Serabit el-Khadim', in Quirke (ed.), *Temple in Ancient Egypt*, pp. 82–9, and also the same authors' 'Le sanctuaire d'Hathor à Sérabit el-Khadim et la topographie urbaine', in Charles Bonnet and Dominique Valbelle (eds.), *Le Sinaï durant l'antiquité et le Moyen-Age* (Paris, 1998), pp. 44–9.

For the use of copper compounds in faience glazes see, for example, Michael Tite *et al.*, 'The Use of Copper and Cobalt Colorants in Vitreous Materials in Ancient Egypt', in Sylvie Colinart and Michel Menu (eds.), *La couleur dans la peinture et l'émaillage de l'Égypte ancienne* (Bari, 1998), pp. 111–20.

For Sinai pottery of the Middle Kingdom see Janine Bourriau, 'Observations on the Pottery from Serabit el-Khadim (Zone Sud)', *Cahiers de Recherches de L'Institut de Papyrologie et d'égyptologie de Lille*, 18 (1996), pp. 19–32. The allocation of supplies to the staff of the Middle Kingdom Serabit el-Khadim temple is discussed by Mueller, 'Some Remarks on Wage Rates', p. 249 *ff.*

Petrie, *Researches in Sinai*, contains a fine selection of photographs of Serabit el-Khadim stelae, along with a mass of other materials related to that temple.

For a recent review of Levantine shrines in the Nile Delta and south Levant see Manfred Bietak, 'Near Eastern Sanctuaries in the Eastern Nile Delta', *Bulletin d'Archéologie et d'Architecture Libanaises*, 6 (2009), pp. 209–26; for a recent overview of some of the extensive ancient mining activities in the south Levant see Nigro, 'Copper Route'.

Petrie, *Researches in Sinai*, pp. 129–33, contains the first report of inscriptions in an unknown script at Serabit el-Khadim; Alan Gardiner, 'The Egyptian Origin of the Semitic Alphabet', in *JEA*, 3, 1 (1916), pp. 1–16, the account of its initial decipherment. Gardiner's description of that research as his single most important work is from Gardiner, *Working Years*, p. 24 *ff.*

The Proto-Sinaitic inscriptions that have been found in locations other than Serabit el-Khadim and their interrelationship to those at the desert temple are reviewed in the groundbreaking article of Orly Goldwasser, 'Canaanites Reading Hieroglyphs: Horus is Hathor? – the invention of the alphabet in Sinai', *Ägypten und Levante*, 16 (2006), pp. 121–60.

The epigraph to the section 'Levantine Settlements' (p. 429) is from the Third Canto of Byron's *Don Juan*, verse 29.

For Biblical Amorites see John van Seters, 'The Terms "Amorite" and "Hittite" in the Old Testament', *Vetus Testamentum*, 22, 1 (1972), pp. 64–81; for a recent somewhat bellicose view of Bronze Age Amorites see Glenn Schwartz, 'An Amorite Global Village: Syrian–Mesopotamian relations in the Second Millennium BC', in Joan Aruz, Sarah Graff and Yelena Rakic (eds.), *From Mesopotamia to the Mediterranean in the Second Millennium BC* (New York, 2013), pp. 2–11.

Levantine metal working is described in Graham Philip *et al.*, 'Copper Metallurgy in the Jordan Valley from the Third to the First Millennia BC: chemical, metallographic and lead isotope analyses of artefacts from Pella', *Levant*, 35 (2003), pp. 71–100; Graham Philip, 'Metalwork and Metalworking Evidence of the Late Middle Kingdom and Second Intermediate Period', *Tell el-Dab'a 15* (Vienna, 2006), pp. 137–67, provides an overview of that distinctive aspect of Levantine – so-called 'Amorite' – culture, with an emphasis on finds from Tell el-Dab'a in the Nile Delta.

Janice Kamrin, 'The Aamu of Shu in the Tomb of Khnumhotep II at Beni Hasan', *Journal of Ancient Egyptian Interconnections*, 1, 3 (2009), pp. 22–36, is a recent re-evaluation of that much celebrated scene.

The ongoing excavations at Tel el-Dab'a have a bibliography of more than a hundred publications, most of which are listed, along with an interactive site guide, at http://www.auaris.at/html/index_en.html. Though outdated, Manfred Bietak, *Avaris: the capital of the Hyksos* (London, 1996), still provides a handy initial guide to that complex site.

For the Tell el-Dab'a limestone sculpture and its archaeological context see Robert Schiestl, 'The Statue of an Asiatic Man from Tell el-Dab'a, Egypt', *Ägypten und Levante*, 16 (2006), pp. 173–85. Robert Schiestl, 'Three Pendants: Tell el-Dab'a, Aigina and a new silver pendant from the Petrie Museum', in J. Lesley Fitton (ed.), *The Aigina Treasure: Aegean Bronze Age jewellery and a mystery revisited* (London, 2009), pp. 51–8, underlines the international nature of the Tell el-Dab'a settlements.

For evidence of pharaonic penetration of Nubia during the early Middle Kingdom see Peden, *Graffiti*, pp. 23–5; for the indigenous contemporary communities south of Aswan see Kate Liska, ' "We

Have Come from the Well of Ibhet": ethnogenesis of the Medjay',
Journal of Egyptian History, 4, 2 (2011), pp. 149–71.

'after twenty years of comings and goings' and the two following
quotations are adapted from Obsomer, *Sésostris Ier.*, Part 2.1, and
Parkinson, *Voices*, pp. 95–6 (31b and 31c).

'a chain of the mightiest fortifications . . .' is quoted from William
Adams, *Nubia: corridor to Africa* (London, 1977), p. 176.

The span of the Nubian fortresses is shown in Baines and Malek,
Atlas of Ancient Egypt, pp. 178–9; Kemp, *Ancient Egypt*, pp. 231–44,
provides an overview of them. Note that although all the Nubian fortresses were assumed to have been drowned in the rising waters of Lake
Nasser, those at Uronarti and Shalfak, being on higher ground, were
recently found to have survived and are presently under re-examination.

'made a progress by land across the continent . . .' is quoted from
Rawlinson's translation of Herodotus, *Histories*, Book II, 102–10
(London, 1858).

'The southern border, made . . .' is quoted from Christopher Eyre,
'The Semna Stelae: quotation, genre and functions of literature', in
Sarah Israelit-Groll (ed.), *Studies in Egyptology Presented to Miriam
Lichtheim*, 2 vols. (Jerusalem, 1990), vol. 1, p. 136.

'The southern boundary made in Year 8 . . .' is adapted from Grajetzki, *Middle Kingdom*, p. 52. Breasted's translation of Senwosret
IIIs great stela is quoted from *Ancient Records*, vol. 1, pp. 295–7.

Aaron Burke, *Walled up to Heaven: the evolution of Middle
Bronze Age fortification strategies in the Levant* (Winona Lake, Indiana, 2008), is a thorough account of the historical development of
Levantine fortresses of the period; pp. 175–6 contain a list of their
common features.

For the siege scenes in the Tomb of Intef see Brigitte Jaros-Deckert,
Das Grab des Jnj-jtj.f: Die Wandmalereien der XI. Dynastie (Mainz,
1984), pp. 28–30 and 37–46. The same scenes are discussed in Burke,
Walled up to Heaven, p. 52.

Winlock's crypt of Middle Kingdom warriors, which he so vividly
describes in *Excavations*, pp. 123–7, has been convincingly re-dated
by Carola Vogel, 'Fallen Heroes?: Winlock's "slain soldiers" reconsidered', *JEA*, 89 (2003), pp. 239–45.

The siege scenes in the Beni Hasan tomb chapels are described by

Franck Monnier, 'Une iconographie égyptienne de l'architecture défensive', *Égypte Nilotique et Méditerranéenne* (an online journal), 7 (2010), pp. 173–219. The same scenes are discussed in Burke, *Walled up to Heaven*, Chapter 3.

Walter Emery, Harry Smith and Anne Millard, *The Fortress of Buhen: the archaeological report* (London, 1979), is a graphic record of the architecture of that considerable structure. In common with other fortresses, Buhen showed no evidence of siege and a gentle process of abandonment; Emery *et al.*, *Fortress of Buen*, p. 90 *ff.*

For the names of the Nubian outposts see Alan Gardiner, 'An Ancient List of the Fortresses of Nubia', *JEA*, 3 (1916), pp. 184–92.

'. . . The frontier patrol . . .' and the following quotations are adapted from the translations given in Parkinson, *Voices*, pp. 93–5, and Wente, *Letters*, pp. 70–73.

For the varied functions of the Nubian fortresses as revealed by their archaeology see Stuart Smith, 'Askut and the Role of the Second Cataract Forts', *JARCE*, 28 (1991), pp. 107–32. The dramatic mile-long desert slipway at the fortress of Mirgissa is described in Jean Vercouter *et al.*, *Mirgissa 1* (Paris, 1970); see also Barry Kemp *AEMT*, p. 93 and fig. 3.8a.

Grajetzki, 'Setting the State Anew', p. 256 *ff*, outlines the rise of military-style titles in the pharaonic administration.

Janet Richards, *Society and Death in Ancient Egypt: mortuary landscapes of the Middle Kingdom* (Cambridge, 2005), p. 4, and Marc Van De Mieroop, *A History of Ancient Egypt* (Oxford, 2011), p. 151, to cite two recent sources, refer to the Middle Kingdom as the period of the rise of militarism in pharaonic Egypt and specifically refer to the Nubian fortresses in that context.

The two unfortified Nubian Middle Kingdom so-called 'mansions' are described by Kemp, *Ancient Egypt*, p. 241 and fig. 89.

The caches buried outside the fortress of Mirgissa are described by André Vila, 'Un dépôt de textes d'envoûtement au Moyen Empire', *Journal des Savants*, 3 (1963), pp. 135–60. They are placed in a contemporary context by Robert Ritner, *The Mechanics of Ancient Egypt Magical Practice* (Chicago, 2008), pp. 136–80.

'. . . upon every rebel who plans to rebel . . .' is adapted from Parkinson, *Voices*, pp. 125–6 (46).

CHAPTER 26. THE COURT AT HOME

Epigraph: from the Turin Canon VI, 3, quoted from Ryholt, 'Turin King-List', p. 141.

For a recent account of the derivation of the word 'Lisht' from Itj(-towy) see Stephen Quirke, 'Residence', p. 114; for the excavation of some late Middle Kingdom houses at Lisht see Arnold, 'Settlement Remains'.

Plans of all known Middle Kingdom palaces are collected and discussed by Giulia Pagliari, *Function and Significance of Ancient Egyptian Royal Palaces from the Middle Kingdom to the Saite Period* (University of Birmingham e-thesis, 2015), Chapter 4. Chapter 1 of that same work presents a lexicographical study of the pharaonic terms for royal palaces and apartments.

Dieter Arnold, *Middle Kingdom Tomb Architecture at Lisht* (New York, 2008), pls. 1 and 115, shows the disposition of the courtiers' tombs around the central compounds that contain the pyramids of Amenemhet I and Senwosret I and some members of their households.

The epithets and titularies of courtiers and officials, craftsmen and musicians with connection to Middle Kingdom palaces are described in Grajetzki, 'Setting the State Anew', p. 220 *ff*.

Large, apparently non-royal palaces and mansions that accommodated the households of a range of Middle Kingdom officials are analysed and discussed in papers by Manfred Bietak, Dieter Eigner and Charles Van Siclen III, in *Haus und Palast*. See also Josef Wegner, 'The Town of Wah-sut at South Abydos', *MDAIK*, 57 (2001), pp. 281–308, and the same author's 'Social and Historical Implications of Sealings of the King's Daughter Reniseneb and other Women at the Town of Wah-Sut', in Manfred Bietak and Ernst Czerny (eds.), *Scarabs of the Second Millennium BC from Egypt, Nubia, Crete, and the Levant: chronological and historical implications* (Vienna, 2004), pp. 221–40.

For the palace workshops see Grajetzki, 'Setting the State Anew', pp. 252–3.

'The king's command to the prince . . .' is adapted from the translations of Breasted, *Ancient Records*, vol. 1, pp. 297–300, and Lichtheim, *AEL*, vol. 1, pp. 123–5.

'The scribe of the vizier Seneb's son ...' is adapted from John Baines, 'The Stelae of Amenisonbe from Abydos and Middle Kingdom Display of Personal Religion', in Janine Bourriau, Diana Magee and Stephen Quirke (eds.), *Sitting Beside Lepsius: studies dedicated to Jaromir Malek at the Griffith Institute* (Leuven, 2009), pp. 7–8.

'When it was dawn, very early ...' is from the story of Sinuhe and has been adapted from the translations of Lichtheim, *AEL*, vol. 1, pp. 222–35, Parkinson, *Sinuhe*, pp. 27–43, and Simpson, *LAE*, pp. 55–66.

Andrea Gnirs, 'In the King's House: audiences and receptions at court', in Gundlach and Taylor (eds.), *Egyptian Royal Residence*, pp. 13–43, provides pertinent observations on an audience in a Middle Kingdom palace. See also Dorothea Arnold, 'The Royal Palace: architecture, decoration and furnishings', in Ziegeler (ed.), *The Pharaohs*, pp. 271–95, which emphasizes the extraordinary continuity of royal palace design.

The epigraph to the section 'Feeding Pharaoh' (p. 464) is the title of a text written *circa* AD 1530, 'sent from Saynt Bernarde, vnto Raymonde, lorde of Ambrose Castelle', and is quoted from Frederick Furnivall (ed.), *Political, Religious and Love Poems* (London, 1866), p. 29.

'Year 17, second month of the Flood ...' is adapted from the translations of William Kelly Simpson, *Papyrus Reisner*, vol. 2: *accounts of the dockyard workshops at This in the reign of Sesostris I* (Boston, 1965), and Wente, *Letters*, p. 43 (42).

The hekat measure has been recently discussed in Hana Vymazalová, 'The Wooden Tablets from Cairo: the use of the grain unit HK3T in ancient Egypt', *Archiv Orientální*, 70, 1 (2002), pp. 27–42. Note that a weight/volume concordance between units of measurement, a common phenomenon in many cultures, has encouraged several flights of fancy in studies on the design of pyramids and grain stores.

For cultivated foods see, for example, *AEMT*, 'Cereal Production and Processing', pp. 505–36 (Mary Anne Murray). Wild foods are less well documented; see, however, Camille Gandonnière, 'Hunters and Groups of Hunters from the Old to the New Kingdom', *NeHet* (an online journal), 1, pp. 47–69, and María Teresa Soria Trastoy, 'Iconographic and Archaeological Analysis of the Fishing Tackle in the Tomb of Niankhkhnum and Khnumhotep', *Oriental Studies*, 1 (2012), pp. 13–56.

Neferhotep's crypt and its contents are resurrected by Gianluca Miniaci and Stephen Quirke, 'Mariette at Dra Abu El-Naga and the Tomb of Neferhotep: a mid 13th Dynasty Rishi coffin (?)', *Egitto e Vicino Oriente*, 31 (2008), pp. 5–25. For Neferhotep's accounts see Stephen Quirke, 'Visible and Invisible: the King in the administrative papyri of the late Middle Kingdom', in Rolf Gundlach and Christine Raedler (eds.), *Das frühe ägyptische Königtum* (Wiesbaden, 1997), pp. 63–71, and also Mahmoud Ezzamel, 'Accounting and Redistribution: the palace and mortuary cult in the Middle Kingdom, ancient Egypt', *Accounting Historians Journal*, 29, 1 (2002), pp. 61–103.

The papyrus record of a land survey is translated by Paul Smither, 'A Tax-Assessor's Journal of the Middle Kingdom', *JEA*, 27 (1941), pp. 74–6. (The following few paragraphs of this section reiterate themes extensively explored in earlier chapters and, also, in Volume I of this history.)

For the settlement at Merimda Abu Ghalib see Tine Bagh, 'Abu Ghalib, an Early Middle Kingdom Town in the Western Nile Delta: renewed work on material excavated in the 1930s', *MDAIK*, 58 (2002), pp. 29–45, and for those at Tell el-Dab'a, Ernst Czerny, *Tell el-Dab'a IX: eine Plansiedlung des frühen Mittleren Reiches* (Vienna, 1999), who notes that the Middle Kingdom settlement was founded on virgin silt.

The palace at Bubastis is described by Charles Van Siclen III, 'Remarks on the Middle Kingdom Palace at Tell Basta', in *Haus und Palast*, pp. 239–46. For a survey of Middle Kingdom delta sites see Grajetzki, *Middle Kingdom*, pp. 129–33.

'Sobek, green of plumage . . .' is quoted from Edda Bresciani, 'Sobek, Lord of the Land of the Lake', in Salima Ikram (ed.), *Divine Creatures: animal mummies in ancient Egypt* (Cairo, 2005), p. 199.

Though some of its historical conclusions have been superseded – see, for example, Butzer, *Early Hydraulic Civilisation*, pp. 16 *ff* (Bahr Yusuf) and 36–7, and Ginter *et al.*, below – John Ball, 'The Physical History of the Faiyûm and its Lake', Chapter 8 of his *Contributions to the Geography of Egypt* (Cairo, 1939), remains a fundamental guide to the ancient history of the Fayum.

The maintenance of levees and flood basins is reviewed by Christopher Eyre, 'Work and the Organisation of Work in the Old Kingdom', in Marvin Powell (ed.), *Labor in the Ancient Near East* (New Haven, 1987), pp. 18–20; the practical planning involved within a single Middle Kingdom province is described by Willems, 'Nomarchs and Local Potentates', pp. 344–52.

The granite column at Medinet el-Fayum was transported to its present location following its collapse in the nineteenth century; see Marco Zecchi, 'The Monument of Abgig', *SAK*, 37 (2008), pp. 373–86.

The two pyramids that stood beside the Hawara Channel are described in Lehner, *Complete Pyramids*, pp. 175–6 and 181–3.

The Arabic term 'the mouth of the canal' is derived from hiero-glyphic and Coptic forms; see the opening paragraph of Zoltán Horváth, 'Temple(s) and Town at El-Lahun: a study of ancient toponyms in the el-Lahun Papyri', in David Silverman, William Kelly Simpson and Josef Wegner (eds.), *Archaism and Innovation: studies in the culture of Middle Kingdom Egypt* (New Haven, 2009), p. 171.

The geographic origins of various Middle Kingdom pyramid-building workforces are analysed in Felix Arnold, *The Control Notes and Team Marks* (New York, 1990), Chapter 2 and fig. 1.

For the dates of high- and low-water levels around the ancient Lake Fayum and their relationship to the Middle Kingdom settlement and temple in that region see Ginter *et al.*, 'Excavations in the Region of Qasr el-Sagha, 1979: contributions to the Holocene geology, the Pre-Dynastic and Dynastic settlement in the Northern Fayum Desert', *MDAIK*, 36 (1980), pp. 105–69.

It is amusing and instructive to discover that in the 1900s, and following directly in the footsteps of their Ptolemaic predecessors, other colonialists were proposing that a second lake should be created in the Fayum Depression for use in irrigation in the Nile Valley and in the same area, the Wadi Rayan, that Ball (*Contributions*, p. 288) and Ahmed Fakhry ('Wadi el-Rayyan', *Annales du Service des Antiquités de l'Égypte*, 46 (1947), pp. 1–19) considered to have held an ancient lake in times of high Nile flood; see William Willcocks, *The Assuân Reservoir and Lake Mœris* (London, 1904).

The records of Middle Kingdom flood levels are carefully collated by Barbara Bell 'Climate and the History of Egypt: the Middle Kingdom', *American Journal of Archaeology*, 79, 3 (1975), pp. 223–69.

Though the historical commentary of the latter part of Bell's essay has dated, the documentary evidence is still widely used and has been employed in several sections of this history.

'I saw two boys lugging a stone . . .' is from a letter of Petrie's; see Drower, *Flinders Petrie*, p. 132. W. M. Flinders Petrie, *Hawara, Biahmu and Arsinoe* (London, 1889), pp. 53–6, contains the record of his ten-day survey and excavation at the site of the two colossi.

For the unique hoard of life-sized Middle Kingdom copper statues that appears to have left Egypt around the middle of the last century see Ziegler (ed.), *The Pharaohs*, cat. 12, pp. 388–9 (George Ortiz).

Marco Zecchi, *Geografia religiose del Fayyum* (Imola, 2001), provides an overview of the activities of the Middle Kingdom court in the Fayum.

For the temple at Qasr el-Sagha see Dieter Arnold and Dorothea Arnold, *Der Tempel Qasr el-Sagha* (Mainz, 1979), and for the Middle Kingdom settlements nearby, Joachim Sliwa, 'Die Siedlung des Mittleren Reiches bei Qasr el-Sagha', *MDAIK*, 42 (1942), pp. 167–79.

CHAPTER 27. LIVING IN THE STATE

The 'tattered ledgers' from Naga el-Deir are published by William Kelley Simpson, *Papyrus Reisner*, 4 vols. (Boston, 1963–86), from which much of what follows is derived.

For Thinis and its dockyards see *LÄ*, vol. 6, 'Thinis', cols. 475–86 (Edward Brovarski).

Antefoker's letters are placed in historical context in Simpson, *Papyrus Reisner*, vol. 2, Chapter 2 ('Administrative Orders'), and also, briefly, in the reviews of that volume by John Wilson, *Journal of the American Oriental Society*, 87, 1 (1967), pp. 68–9, and Edward Wente, *JNES*, 26, 1 (1967), pp. 63–4.

'Ankh's son Nakhti' etc. is quoted from Simpson, *Papyrus Reisner*, vol. 4, Section C (117–18), and 'fleeing' from Section B (1).

The epigraph to the section 'Housing by the State' (p. 481) is from W. M. Flinders Petrie, *Kahun, Gurob, and Hawara* (London 1890), p. 23, and 'Having spent some weeks . . .' from p. 21 (34).

My description of the uncovering of el-Lahun is based upon Carla

Gallorini, 'A Reconstruction of Petrie's Excavation at the Middle Kingdom Settlement of Kahun', in Stephen Quirke (ed.), *Lahun Studies* (Reigate, 1998), pp. 42–59; and also Petrie, various accounts, including *Kahun, Gurob, and Hawara*; *Illahun, Kahun, and Gurob, 1889–90* (London, 1891); and (with Guy Brunton and M. A. Murray) *Lahun 2* (London, 1923).

The papyri from el-Lahun hold poems to pharaoh, fragments of the records of a census, scraps of stories about gods, wills, remedies both gynaecological and veterinary, and memoranda of inheritance disputes – a similar range of material, indeed, to that one might expect to find in a European nineteenth-century country cottage. For a selection of them in translation see Parkinson, *Voices*, numbers 7, 20, 29b, 36–8 and 42.

For a fascinating account of the Cypriote sherd that Petrie uncovered see Carla Gallorini, 'A Cypriote Sherd from Kahun in Context', in David Aston *et al.* (eds.), *Under the Potter's Tree: studies on ancient Egypt presented to Janine Bourriau* (Leuven, 2011), pp. 397–416.

Petrie's plan of the settlement, which is the only one, is published in his *Illahun, Kahun and Gurob*, pl. 14, where its various units, the 'Acropolis' and so on, were given their common modern names. For a recent interpretation of Petrie's discoveries see Kemp, *Ancient Egypt*, pp. 211–21, and also Manfred Bietak, 'Zum Raumprogramm ägyptischer Wohnhäuser des Mittleren und des Neuen Reiches', in *Haus und Palast*, pp. 25–43.

'as bright as the days . . .' is from Gallorini, 'Reconstruction', p. 48, quoting Petrie's Excavation Journal for April 1889.

'a cool room . . .' is extracted from the third of a series of five poems addressed to Senwosret III. It is translated in Lichtheim, *AEL*, vol. 1, p. 199–200, Parkinson, *Voices*, pp. 46–7 (7), and Simpson, *LAE*, p. 304.

'I am an owner of cattle . . .' is quoted from the Stela of Montuwoser (MMA 12.184) as translated by James Allen, in Allen, *Heqanakht Papyri*, p. 164.

The burial of babies at el-Lahun is reported in Petrie, *Kahun, Gurob, and Hawara*.

'The Eloquent Peasant' is translated by Lichtheim *AEL*, vol. 1, pp. 169–84, by Parkinson, *Sinuhe*, pp. 54–88, and by Tobin, *LAE*, pp. 25–44. My quotations have been adapted from all three sources.

EPILOGUE

'I know the secret of hieroglyphs . . .' is from the Stela of Irtisen, Louvre Museum, C 14; the translation is adapted from various sources.

The diversity of craftsmen's styles gathered at the early Middle Kingdom court are described by Janine Bourriau, *Pharaohs and Mortals: Egyptian art in the Middle Kingdom* (Cambridge, 1988), and Robins, *Art of Ancient Egypt*, Chapters 5–7.

For an overview of the links between the Middle Kingdom and Bronze Age Aegean see the opening pages of Peter Warren, 'Minoan Crete and Pharaonic Egypt', in Vivian Davies and Louise Schofield (eds.), *Egypt, the Aegean and the Levant: interconnections in the second millennium BC* (London, 1995), p. 1 *ff*.

Edward Terrace, *Egyptian Paintings of the Middle Kingdom* (London, 1968), contains an elegant survey of Middle Kingdom painting and is beautifully illustrated.

Most of the surviving pieces of Middle Kingdom court jewellery that have survived are set in historical context by Alix Wilkinson, *Ancient Egyptian Jewellery* (London, 1971); taking a synchronic approach, Cyril Aldred, *Jewels of the Pharaohs* (London, 1971), contains much Middle Kingdom material.

For fine examples of oyster-shell jewellery see Herbert Winlock, 'Pearl Shells of Sen-wosret I', in Stephen Glanville (ed.), *Studies Presented to F. Ll. Griffith* (London, 1932), pp. 388–92.

Rita Freed, 'The Sculpture of the Middle Kingdom', in Lloyd (ed.), *Companion to Ancient Egypt*, vol. 2, pp. 882–912, is a useful overview of Middle Kingdom sculpture and relief. Davis Lorand, 'The "Four Schools of Art" of Senwosret I: is it time for a revision?', in Katalin Kóthay (ed.), *Art and Society: ancient and modern contexts of Egyptian art* (Budapest, 2012), pp. 47–55, exposes the perils of creating ancient schools of art from the evidence of differing sculptural styles.

Joseph-Étienne Gautier and Gustave Jéquier, *Mémoire sur les Fouilles de Licht* (Cairo, 1902), pp. 30–38 and pls. IX–XIII, describes the rare cache of ten complete statues of Senwosret I. Photographs of later royal Middle Kingdom sculpture can be found in many works already cited, along with those in Fay, *Louvre Sphinx*, and Kurt Lange, *Sesostris* (Munich, 1954).

The change in the technology available to Middle Kingdom sculpture workshops is described by Judith Devaux, 'Nature du métal employé pour les outils des sculpteurs égyptiens', *Revue d'égyptologie*, 50 (1999), pp. 275–7. See also Jacques Aubert and Liliane Aubert, *Bronzes et or égyptiens* (Paris, 2001).

The use of abrasives in finishing statues is seldom mentioned in the literature; see, however, Denys Stocks, 'Sticks and Stones of Egyptian Technology', *Popular Archaeology*, 7, 3 (1986), pp. 24–9, and Romer, *Great Pyramid*, p. 177.

For the shrine of Hekaib and its remarkable sanctuaries and sculptures see Labib Habachi *et al.*, *The Sanctuary of Heqaib*, 2 vols. (Mainz, 1985).

The vexed question of the relationship of pharaonic sculpture to human physiognomy frequently invites unsophisticated comparisons between ancient sculpture and traditional Western notions of portraiture. A rare exception is Assmann, 'Preservation and Presentation', pp. 55–81; see also, Binyon, *Spirit of Man*, especially p. 138 *ff.*

Dieter Arnold, *The Pyramid Complex of Senwosret III at Dahshur* (New York, 2002), pp. 26 and 29–31, estimates that the Middle Kingdom pyramids stood intact for at least five centuries. The same volume, pp. 121–2, has a list of features which that pyramid's designers had adopted from far older monuments. For a further fascinating dimension to such careful continuities see Susan Allen, 'Funerary Pottery in the Middle Kingdom: archaism or revival?', in Simpson and Wegner (eds.), *Archaism and Innovation*, pp. 319–39.

Lehner, *Complete Pyramids*, p. 174 *ff*, shows the increasing complexity of the internal architecture of the later Middle Kingdom royal pyramids.

Antonio Morales, *The Transmission of the Pyramid Texts into the Middle Kingdom* (University of Pennsylvania e-thesis, 2013), evaluates the re-use of Pyramid Texts in the funerary arrangements of some Middle Kingdom nobles.

The recent re-investigations of the monuments of Senwosret III at

Abydos are a revelation. Josef Wegner, 'The Tomb of Senwosret III at Abydos: considerations on the origins and development of the Royal Amduat-Tomb', in Simpson and Wegner (eds.), *Archaism and Innovation*, pp. 103–68, lists the earlier literature on the subject and provides a fresh view of its design and function.

The comparison of Senwosret III's funerary complex at Abydos with that of Montuhotep's burial arrangements at Deir el-Bahari is enabled by the plans of Wegner, 'Tomb of Senwosret III', and those in Arnold, *Temple of Mentuhotep*; see also Chapter 22, pp. 335–6, above. (The architecture of the archaic royal tombs and their role in the formation of the pharaonic state is described in Volume 1 of this history, Chapters 17 and 20.)

For the historical and academic contexts of 'Middle Egyptian' see Loprieno, *Ancient Egyptian*, Chapter 1, and Stephen Quirke, 'Archive', in Antonio Loprieno (ed.), *Ancient Egyptian Literature: history and forms* (Leiden, 1996), pp. 379–401, which describes the copying of non-funerary pharaonic writings from the Middle Kingdom down to Roman times.

Baines and Eyre, 'Four Notes on Literacy', and Parkinson, *Voices*, p. 18, provide similar estimates of the numbers of literate people during the Middle Kingdom.

Quirke, 'Archive', lists less than thirty literary texts that have survived from Middle Kingdom times; Parkinson, *Sinuhe*, p. 3, alternatively, *circa* forty. (To distinguish these so-called 'literary' texts from other written sources, scholars employ a range of modern analytical techniques.)

James Quibell, *The Ramesseum* (London, 1898), Chapter 2, pp. 3–4, describes the discovery of a Middle Kingdom crypt beneath that famous temple containing the box which held the so-called 'Ramesseum (literary) Papyri'; Ritner, *Magical Practice*, pp. 222–33, details the context of the box in terms of 'magic'.

'if you know writing . . .' is quoted from 'The Teaching of Khety'; see Lichtheim, *AEL*, vol. 1, pp. 184–92, Parkinson, *Sinuhe*, pp. 273–83, and Simpson, *LAE*, pp. 431–7. A necessary note of caution in understanding such texts is provided by John Foster, 'Some Comments on Khety's Instruction for Little Pepi on his Way to School (Satire on the Trades)', in Teeter and Larson (eds.), *Gold of Praise*, pp. 121–9.

Redford, *Pharaonic King-Lists*, p. 25, succinctly assesses the Wadi Hammamat graffito of a line of Old Kingdom cartouches.

For the structural resemblance between the contending of Horus and Seth and the tale of the Eloquent Peasant see Schafik Allam, 'Social and Legal Aspects Regarding the Trader from the Oasis', in Andrea Gnirs (ed.), *Reading the Eloquent Peasant* (Göttingen, 2000), pp. 83–92; for the derivation of some of the forms of the Middle Kingdom literary compositions from texts in Old Kingdom tomb chapels see Elke Blumenthal, 'Die Textgattung Expeditionsbericht in Ägypten', in Jan Assmann, Erika Feucht and Reinhard Grieshammer (eds.), *Fragen an die altägyptische Literatur: Studien zum Gedenken an Eberhard Otto* (Wiesbaden, 1977), pp. 85–118. An inscription from the amethyst mining region of Wadi el-Hudi has provoked discussion on the origins of another Middle Kingdom literary genre; see, for example, José Galán, 'The Stela of Hor in Context', *SAK*, 21 (1994), pp. 65–79.

'Dispute of a Man with his Soul' is translated by Lichtheim, *AEL*, vol. 1, pp. 163–9, by Parkinson, *Sinuhe*, pp. 151–65, and by Tobin, *LAE*, pp. 178–87; the 'Admonitions of Ipuwer' by Lichtheim, *AEL*, vol. 1, pp. 149–63, by Parkinson, *Sinuhe*, pp. 166–99 and by Tobin, *LAE*, pp. 188–210.

For the slowly opening space between writer and reader that followed the dissolution of the Old Kingdom court see Laurent Coulon, 'Véracité et rhétorique dans les autobiographies égyptiennes de la Première Période Intermédiaire', *BIFAO*, 97 (1997), pp. 109–38.

The epigraph to the section 'Murdered by Eunuchs?' (p. 515) has been adapted from the translations of Lichtheim, *AEL*, vol. 1, p. 137, by Parkinson, *Sinuhe*, p. 207, and by Tobin, *LAE*, pp. 168–9. (Palace eunuchs made appearance in earlier translations of the Instruction of Amenemhet I.)

'Asiatics will fall to his sword . . .' is quoted from Lichtheim, *AEL*, vol. 1, p. 143.

Lichtheim, *AEL*, vol. 1, pp. 211–15, Parkinson, *Sinuhe*, pp. 89–101, and Simpson, *LAE*, pp. 45–53, provide modern translations of the story of the Shipwrecked Sailor.

For a post Second World War description of so-called 'primitive' or 'folk' cultures see, for example, Robert Redfield, 'The Folk Society',

American Journal of Sociology, 52, 4 (1947), pp. 293–308. Earlier in the century and mirroring the story of the conflict between Horus, Osiris and Seth, Kurt Sethe, *Urgeschichte und älteste Religion der Ägypter* (Leipzig, 1930), presented Osiris as an authentic archaic pharaoh who was born in the Delta and, after fighting a series of wars that led to the unification of the pharaonic state, had been buried at Abydos.

For Eduard Meyer's assertion that folk tales, fairy stories and miracles can contain historical truths see *Geschichte des Altertums* (3rd edn, Berlin, 1913), vol. 1.2, p. 25 [157], as Hays, 'Historicity', p. 20, observes. The error, it appears, which was common in those times, was to claim the apparently authentic settings of ancient stories as validation of their historical veracity.

'I am one who speaks in the official manner . . .' is quoted from Antonio Loprieno, 'Linguistic Variety and Egyptian Literature', in Loprieno (ed.), *Ancient Egyptian Literature*, p. 519.

'Look, we have reached home! . . .' is extracted from the translations of Lichtheim *AEL*, vol. 1, p. 212, Parkinson, *Sinuhe*, p. 92, and Simpson, *LAE*, p. 47.

Bell, 'Climate and the History of Egypt', p. 260 *ff*, finds no evidence of radical ecological change that correlates with the period after the reign of Senwosret III. For the diminishing quantities of graffiti left in the pharaonic mines and quarries and, indeed, in Nubia after the late Twelfth Dynasty see Peden, *Graffiti*, pp. 49–51; for an overview of the abandonment of the Nubian fortresses see Daphna Ben-Tor, Susan Allen and James Allen, 'Seals and Kings', *Bulletin of the American Schools of Oriental Research*, 315 (1999), pp. 55–8.

'Remember the building of the shrine . . .' etc. has been adapted from Gardiner, *Admonitions*, p. 13, Lichtheim, *AEL*, vol. 1, p. 159 *ff*, Parkinson, *Sinuhe*, p. 183 *ff*, and Tobin, *LAE*, p. 203 *ff*.

List of Maps and Figures

Whenever practicable, the excavator's original plans and drawings have been reproduced. Many of these figures, therefore, are historical documents in their own right.

The maps are based upon modern physical geography, the ancient geography of the lower Nile being insufficiently established in most instances to allow accurate reconstructions. Recent researches, however, have shown that the Delta appears to have been smaller in ancient times and that the river had tended to shift erratically within its valley, and generally towards the east.

As in the Bibliography, references have been kept to a minimum and after their first citation they are given in a shorter form. A key to the abbreviations employed may be found at the head of the Bibliography.

List of Plates

These plates have been chosen to illustrate specific aspects of the text. No attempt has been made to illustrate the best part of the objects discussed in this book, most of which are copiously illustrated in popular books and TV documentaries. One of the aims of my text, indeed, is to provide a genuine context for many of those things which are often portrayed as if they were items in a fancy sales brochure.

Nothing can replace the genuine first-hand impact of the objects I describe, their true size, colour and texture, especially when they are seen in the shimmering sunlight of the Nile Valley.

Unless otherwise indicated, the photographs are by John and Elizabeth Romer and, as they have been made over the past fifty years, they sometimes show objects and environments that are now greatly changed.

6 Borchardt's excavators engaged in reassembling parts of Sahure's valley temple, after Ludwig Borchardt *Das Grabdenkmal Des Königs Sahu-Re* (2 vols.)(Leipzig, 1910) (vol. 1), fig 10.

7 Sahure's valley temple during its excavation, after Borchardt, 1910, (vol. 1) fig 2.

8 The 'Louvre Scribe', E 3023, photographed before its recent restoration. Removed in the 1860s by Mariette from an unnamed Sakkara tomb chapel whose ownership has subsequently been attributed to a courtier named Kai.

9 The tomb chapel of Ankhtifi at Mo'alla.

10 A fragment of Ankhtifi's regatta, photographed in 1974.

11 A colossal seated statue of Montuhotep II. Cairo Museum, Journal d'Entrée 36195.

12 Montuhotep's temple at Deir el-Bahari.

13 Karnak. The Middle Kingdom temple area, after Jean Lauffrey, 'Les Travaux du Centre Franco-Égyptien d'Étude des Temples de Karnak, de 1972–1977', *Cahiers de Karnak* 6 (1980), p. 24–35 and Pl. VIa. (photo. CRNS 15637).

14 Plan of the main east–west axis of Karnak temple showing a plan of the dismantled temple of Senwosret I, after Jean-François Carlotti, Ernst Czerny and Luc Gabolde, 'Sondage Autour de la Plate-Forme en Grès de la "Cour Du Moyen Empire"', *Cahiers de Karnak* 13 (2010), pp. 111–93, fig. 23.

15 A colossal statue of Senwosret I. Luxor Museum, J. 174.

16 Bark station of Senwosret I. Open Air Museum, Karnak temple.

17 A relief on a column of Senwosret I's bark station. Open Air Museum, Karnak temple.

18 A granite statue of a unnamed king, generally regarded as a portrait of Amenemhet III. From the Fayum. Cairo Museum, Catalogue général 395.

19 Fragment of a royal Middle Kingdom sculpture of unknown provenance, usually identified as a portrait of Senwosret III. Metropolitan Museum, New York, 26-7-1394, and formally in the MacGregor and Carnarvon collections.

Acknowledgements

I would like to thank Alex Peden of Edinburgh and Attilio Brilli of Arezzo for books, photocopies and advice, and Alex Peden and Andrew Wright of Sydney for critical readings of the text. The remaining faults within this volume are mine alone, of course, as are the attitudes and opinions expressed.

At Penguin, Laura Stickney, Shoaib Rokadiya and Richard Duguid and the excellent in-house designers have been extraordinarily encouraging, Laura especially, with her calmness and considerable tact.

But when all is said and done, without Beth, without my wife Elizabeth Romer, this book along with all my other works over the past half century would never have been completed.

John Romer, Arezzo, autumn 2016.

Index

973883270